MACROECONOMICS: THEORY AND POLICY

MACROECONOMICS: THEORY AND POLICY

Gardner Ackley

THE UNIVERSITY OF MICHIGAN

Macmillan Publishing Co., Inc.
NEW YORK

Collier Macmillan Publishers
LONDON

Printed in the United States of America

A portion of this material has been adapted from
Macroeconomic Theory, © 1961 by Gardner Ackley

Macmillan Publishing Co., Inc.
866 Third Avenue, New York, New York 10022

Collier Macmillan Canada, Ltd.

Library of Congress Cataloging in Publication Data

Ackley, Gardner.
  Macroeconomics: theory and policy.

  Includes bibliographies and index.
  1. Macroeconomics. I. Title.
HB171.5.A28 1978   339   77-5343
ISBN 0-02-300290-5

Printing: 1 2 3 4 5 6 7 8   Year: 8 9 0 1 2 3 4

To Bonnie

PREFACE

Macroeconomics; Theory and Policy replaces *Macroeconomic Theory* (Macmillan, 1961), but it is not a revised edition of the earlier work. In a few chapters—particularly those dealing with the "classical model"—I have relied heavily on the previous book and have reproduced a number of pages with only minor revision. Almost all of the remainder, however, has been written from scratch. Much of it deals with topics unknown at the time of the previous writing or then not considered suitable for an intermediate text. (This accounts for the fact that, although several topics have been omitted, this text is considerably longer than the previous book.)

Macroeconomic Theory was considered by many to be the first full-scale textbook in this subject. As such, it was successful far beyond any expectation. It has been widely used both in the United States and abroad (in the original edition, in two "student editions" in English sold abroad, and in a number of translations). One of my greatest pleasures in recent years has been to meet or to hear from people in many countries who "already know you from your book." I hope that *Macroeconomics: Theory and Policy* may sustain our contact and perhaps make new friends.

Following publication of *Macroeconomic Theory*, I was on leave from my academic appointment for eight years and, during most of that time, unable to follow the current literature in macroeconomics. Since returning to the University of Michigan in September 1969, I have been trying to assimilate, understand, organize, and evaluate as much as I can of the large body of theoretical and empirical literature in macroeconomics that has accumulated in the now almost twenty years since the bulk of writing on the previous book was finished. In the meantime, some new and quite different practical macroeconomic problems have engaged economists'—and the public's—attention, problems that cry out for solution, amelioration, or, at least, understanding. (Inflation is, of course, the most notable, and the most difficult.)

Much of the new literature, including what has been written about the new problems, I find to be important and enlightening and to require substantial revisions in economists' previous understanding of our economy and in their views about appropriate economic policies. On the other hand, I find other portions of it puzzling, irrelevant, or misleading. It has thus seemed to me appropriate to attempt a full reassessment and restatement of what I think economists know—and what they still do not know—in macroeconomics. Many users of *Macroeconomic Theory* have encouraged me in this endeavor. Although a number of other new text-books attempt a new, comprehensive appraisal, none of them fully meets my own view of what is right and important.

In this book, therefore, I try to do considerably more than digest and explain current ideas in macroeconomics. I also indicate and explain my agreement or disagreement with many particular ideas and points of view. Probably I misunderstand my colleagues on some points and am unfairly critical or unduly impressed on others. In any case, I have tried, above all, to put across a basic point of view that I find missing in much recent work, that I am convinced is correct, and that I feel strongly is important. This point of view relates both to the nature of our economy and to the scope and approach of macroeconomics as a discipline.

First, it seems to me fundamental to recognize that—at least in their macro aspects—modern, western-style industrial economies are inherently highly unstable and prone to continuous, considerable, and often painful fluctuation. In my view, much of this disturbance is probably associated with what we call economic growth—one of the most pervasive charac-teristics of these economies. In much recent work, I find instead the assumption, sometimes explicit but more often tacit, that the modern macroeconomy is inherently stable, subject to only moderate inherent disturbance, and equipped with powerful automatic stabilizers. Most of the time it is in, or near, some kind of macroequilibrium state. In most treat-ments growth is explicitly assumed absent, so it cannot possibly be a factor of disturbance. Even when the need to analyze and explain growth is recognized, it is seldom suggested as a source of major fluctuations.

Thus what appears to be disturbance and instability is held, either explicitly or implicitly, to reflect the effects of government intervention, past or present. Eliminate such intervention, it is suggested or implied, and the economy would be free from major macroeconomic disturbance. A symptom of this point of view is the fact that for a full generation we have lacked any new—or even a wide acceptance of any older—theory of the business cycle, or, indeed, very much discussion of the cycle in economics. Yet the phenomenon has surely persisted. Now we have finally had pro-posed a *new* business cycle theory, that of the "political business cycle." This theory, of course, contains more than a germ of truth—but dreadfully exaggerated.

Almost never does one still read in respectable theoretical literature about Schumpeter's creative–destructive technological innovation and its destabilizing consequences; about Keynes' animal spirits, contests to choose the queen judged by other contestants to be the most beautiful, or expeditions to the South Pole; nor, even in the new world of floating exchange rates, about destabilizing speculation. Inventory cycles and cobwebs have gone out of fashion—in textbooks but perhaps not in the economy.

There are two principal groups of dissenters from what has become almost the orthodoxy of inherent stability: the Clower–Leijonhufvud axis and the Robinson–Kaldor school. I will be seen to have considerable sympathy particularly with the first of these, although I use a somewhat different vocabulary and may put a somewhat greater emphasis on factors associated with economic growth as elements of disturbance.

A second major aspect of the point of view that pervades this book relates to the nature of economic knowledge (or to the nature of economic theory—I refuse to distinguish the two). To my mind, the business of economics is the accumulation of tested empirical generalizations about relationships that prevail *in the current "real-world" economy*. These generalizations are the more interesting and the more useful the greater their specificity. If all we knew about the major relationships were the probable signs of partial derivatives (based on *a priori* knowledge or casual observation), this would still be better than no knowledge at all. But numerical estimates of fundamental macroeconomic relationships, statistically derived from reliable measurements, and estimates of their temporal stability provide far more important and useful information. Long chains of mathematical reasoning based solely on *a priori* postulates are fun. But they may badly serve the needs of our society.

The last sentence suggests the third element of the point of view I wish to mention here. It is that knowledge is to be applied—brought to bear in the solution of problems that affect people. A textbook in fundamentals is not the place to do very much of this, but some illustrations are necessary to remind the reader what the whole thing is about.

Thus the reader will find here—along with hypotheses derived from *a priori* postulates and the development of their implications—considerable discussion of what statistical testing appears to tell us about the specific shapes and degree of stability of major macroeconomic relationships (for the United States economy), along with occasional discussion of data sources and problems, and of what this knowledge may imply for policy. Ideally the results of macroeconomic study should find their ultimate expression in full-scale macroeconometric models, but the place for such expression is not an intermediate textbook.

To put the matter in another way, it seems to me that it is a proper function of a textbook to warn its readers against widely accepted propositions that appear to be empirically incorrect or insufficiently established—especially those applied in discussion of public policy problems. For example, it seems to me important to point out that, despite the fact that both the classical economists and Keynes (in effect) hypothesized an aggregate production function subject to diminishing returns, most empirical evidence fails to confirm this view. Thus we must not assume (as many economists still seem to do) that employment can normally increase only if real wages decline (or decline relative to trend).

One of the most difficult problems in writing a textbook is to determine which specific topics should be included and the sequence of their discussion. Although a good deal of thought has gone into the selection and order of the topics for this book, instructors inevitably will disagree with my choices. After all, interests and emphases differ, and the selection and sequence of topics will also be affected by the other readings or supplementary materials the instructor may wish to introduce. The book is organized to permit considerable flexibility in selection of topics, and some changes in their order are possible without major discontinuity.

Among topics that can easily be postponed (but I hope not *omitted*) are those considered in either or both halves of Chapter 7 (fiscal policy and Keynesian dynamics), in either or both halves of Chapter 8 (investment and multiplier-accelerator growth models), and in the final sections of Chapter 9 (supply and demand for bonds and the interest rate) and of Chapter 11 (IS-LM dynamics). If one prefers not to wait as long as I have waited to introduce the subject of inflation, the first two sections of Chapter 13 can easily be moved ahead. And if it is desired to introduce money creation by banks and an endogenous money supply considerably earlier than this book does, the first section of Chapter 21 can be assigned at almost any point. Indeed, all of Chapters 20 and 21, dealing with money and finance, can easily be assigned either prior to Chapter 13 or to Chapter 16. Chapters 14, 17, 19, 20, and 21 contain some of the most advanced or specialized materials and can be entirely or partially omitted. The several chapter appendixes are clearly optional.

On the other hand, there are several sections that may seem unnecessary, or even extraneous where they first appear, but are there to set the stage for later discussion. They can, of course, be postponed, but they probably should not be omitted. Examples are several of the topics in Chapter 1, the discussion of wealth accounting in Chapter 2 (now that wealth is widely used as a variable, we need to understand how various concepts of it are related and how they can be measured), discussion of the production-input relationship in Chapters 3 and 4, the treatment of the bond market in Chapter 5, and the brief discussion of expectations in Chapter 7.

Despite its length, the book has two large and glaring omissions, as the reader is warned in Chapter 1—omissions regretted but deliberate. The first is international repercussions; the second, formal growth models more elaborate than simple Harrod–Domar sequences. Less regretted omissions include the variety of "money multipliers" and examples of empirical wage and price determination functions.

I am very conscious of several sections that, despite much rewriting, still do not come off as well as I had wanted, of several points at which I may have let my feelings show a little too much, and of an incompletely disciplined tendency to write sentences that are too long. I could easily spend another year rewriting, pruning, rounding out, depersonalizing, and otherwise improving the manuscript. However I have already spent much too long on this book, and my editor is (or should be) losing his patience. So the manuscript now goes to the publisher and soon to my colleagues. All that is left is to list some of my obligations.

First and foremost, my gratitude goes to the University of Michigan for wanting to bring me back into its stimulating academic environment after each of my several long absences and for providing the relative leisure from routine duties that has permitted me to write this book as well as to engage in other scholarly and public service activities. To recent department chairmen—the late Warren Smith, Harvey Brazer, Peter Steiner, and Harold Shapiro—I owe special thanks.

Under these favorable auspices, writing has proceeded in Ann Arbor from early 1972 through summer of 1976 with a steadily increasing tempo of application. But it took a sabbatical leave spent in Italy in the fall term of 1976 to get the book to this stopping place. In Italy the wonderful hospitality of the Rockefeller Foundation's study center at Bellagio and of the Banco di Roma's offices in Rome have provided the setting for the intensive work that produced most of Chapters 1 and 15 through 21, along with extensive rewriting of the remaining chapters.

Several assistants have been employed from time to time in this effort. I thank them all, but I must express special gratitude to Ronald Anderson, John Gardner, and Bo Kang. A number of secretaries have toiled willingly with me, among whom I particularly wish to recognize Jacqueline Parsons and Rodney Eatman.

Readers recruited by Macmillan have made a large number of extremely helpful suggestions that have greatly improved the final product, and I deeply appreciate their help. They are Professors Richard M. Friedman of California State University, Northridge; Richard J. Froyen of the University of North Carolina; and Rodney L. Jacobs of the University of California, Los Angeles. My colleague Professor Robert S. Holbrook kindly read Chapters 20 and 21, making a number of helpful suggestions. All of these readers also found mistakes that have been corrected; I alone am responsible for those that remain. Editor Anthony English of Macmillan has been at all points supportive, patient, and helpful. His gentle blend of prodding, shame, encouragement, and understanding has been ideally suited to keeping me at work.

I am grateful to the editors and publishers of the *Review of Economic Statistics*, *The Weekly Toyo Kezai* and *The Oriental Economist* for permission to use excerpts from my articles that first appeared in these journals. I also appreciate the willingness of the Atlantic Institute for International Affairs to permit me to adapt for use here some portions of my "Stemming

World Inflation", which the Institute published in 1971 as an *Atlantic Paper*, and of the Federal Reserve Bank of Boston to adapt portions of my discussion in *Consumer Spending and Monetary Policy: The Linkages*, 1971.

This preface is written in Taormina, Sicily, where my window looks out on the ever-changing and always breathtaking beauty of Mount Etna. The scene reminds me to mention that much of the text of *Macroeconomic Theory* was also written in Italy in 1956–1957, as has been some of the best of my other work. Personally, I owe much to this beautiful and tormented land where I have now spent four considerable periods of work and residence. But my greatest debt is to my wife Bonnie, whose patience with me and my work surpasses belief and to whom I have dedicated this book.

G. A.

CONTENTS

Part **I**   Concepts and Measurement

1   Basic Concepts   3
2   National Income, Product, Wealth, and the Price Level   26
3   Employment, Unemployment, and Output in a Growing Economy   60

Part **II**   Classical Macroeconomics

4   Classical Monetary and Employment Theory   83
5   The Classical Theory of Saving, Investment, and the Interest Rate   124

Part **III**   The Simple Keynesian Model

6   The Consumption Function and the Simple Keynesian Model   157
7   Extensions of the Keynesian Model: Fiscal Policy and Keynesian Dynamics   191
8   Extensions of the Keynesian Model: Investment and Economic Growth   243

Part **IV**   The Keynesian-Classical Synthesis

9   The Keynesian Theory of Interest   283
10   A Keynesian Version of the Synthesis   322
11   The "IS–LM" Form of the Model   358
12   More-Classical Versions of the Synthesis   384

Part **V** Inflation

13	Elements of a Theory of Inflation	425
14	Recent Developments in Inflation Theory	459
15	Empirical and Policy Aspects of Inflation	498

Part **VI** Consumer Spending

| 16 | The Theory of Aggregate Consumption | 533 |
| 17 | The Empirical Study of Consumption | 574 |

Part **VII** Investment

| 18 | Classical and Neoclassical Theories of Investment | 607 |
| 19 | A Broader View of Investment | 640 |

Part **VIII** Financial Assets, Interest Rates, and Monetary Policy

| 20 | Financial Assets and Intermediaries | 671 |
| 21 | Money, Interest Rates, and Monetary Policy | 697 |

| | Index | 733 |

PART I

CONCEPTS AND MEASUREMENT

Chapter 1

Basic Concepts

The Nature of Macroeconomic Analysis
The substantive content of macroeconomics
The nature of economic theory
Macroeconomic models
Stock and flow variables
Equilibrium, statics, and dynamics

Macroeconomics and Microeconomics
The problem of aggregation
The microeconomic assumptions of
    macroeconomic theory

Some Limitations of this Analysis

This book is about macroeconomics. By now, nearly everyone knows that macroeconomics deals with the economy "in the large," or "as a whole"—in contrast with microeconomics, which is mainly concerned with the individual components that make up the aggregate economy: consumers, firms, industries, markets.

THE NATURE OF MACROECONOMIC ANALYSIS

We can define macroeconomic analysis as the study of the forces or factors that determine the levels of aggregate production, employment, and prices in an economy, and their rates of change over time. Thus, macroeconomics deals with such overall economic problems as recession, boom, depression, unemployment, inflation, instability, stagnation. Its variables are such global quantities as national income, gross national product, national wealth, aggregate employment, and unemployment; the "general level" of wage rates, prices, and interest rates; and rates of growth or change of the preceding variables.

Macroeconomics deals, too, with the structures or components of some of these big aggregates or averages—but only when this seems necessary to help understand the determination of their level or their change. Thus, national income may need to be broken down between labor and property incomes; gross national product among consumer goods, capital goods, and government goods; wealth into money, other financial assets, and physical wealth; the price level between that of consumer goods and capital goods; interest rates between those on private and on public debts, or on short term and long term, and so on. But the breakdowns are made only when and because we find them crucial to understanding the levels of the aggregates or averages, or the effects of these components on the levels of other important aggregates or averages. In principle, macroeconomics "disaggregates" to the minimum extent necessary for understanding the aggregates and not because it is concerned with understanding the subaggregates or the individual units.

The purpose of studying macroeconomics, like that of microeconomics, is gaining knowledge—understanding: partly for its own sake, because we like to know, but also to use in guiding public or private action. Economics is mainly useful, of course, for guiding public action rather than private. We use it mainly as citizens and voters or as public officials, rather than as workers, consumers, businessmen, or investors. However, as is the case with microeconomics, the knowledge that macroeconomics provides is sometimes important for sensible private decisions, as well.

The Substantive Content of Macroeconomics

All instruction in economics attempts to provide a "tool kit" of questions, methods, concepts, and perspectives for analyzing specific problems. But, far more than is the case for microeconomics, macroeconomics has an extensive substantive as well as methodological content. Macroeconomics is more than a scientific *method of analysis*; it is also a body of *empirical economic knowledge*. Here, we are principally concerned with empirical knowledge of the current United States economy, although some, perhaps much, of this knowledge is applicable as well to other large, advanced, mainly free-enterprise, market economics like that of the United States. (There are, of course, macroeconomics for other types of economies—for example, for large nonmarket, planned economies or for small developing economies—but much of the content is quite different.)

Microeconomics perforce seeks maximum generality and applicability to a wide range of situations, problems, products, markets, and forms of organization that exist in vast and bewildering variety. Thus, microeconomics must and does emphasize concepts and methodology rather than specific substantive content. It is primarily an elegant method of problem solving. In contrast, macroeconomics seeks practical understanding of a particular economy (or type of economy), of which there are relatively few, and solutions to the specific, known macroeconomic problems of such an economy, also relatively few in number.

Macroeconomists therefore are concerned about the particular shape of relevant functional relationships. They want to know the approximate quantitative magnitudes of various slopes or elasticities and are concerned with the length (and the relative length) of particular time lags. They are usually not content merely with the probable sign of partial derivatives, but want to know whether they are quantitatively large or trivial. In short, macroeconomists seek to acquire as much and as specific understanding as is possible about the way a particular type of economy behaves in its overall aspects. As much specific, substantive understanding as is possible is, of course, exactly what microeconomists seek, too, when they begin to *apply* their tool kits to a specific area. This, however, is not what textbooks in microeconomic analysis are concerned with.

To be sure, this difference between micro- and macroeconomics is a difference of degree not of kind, but the degree is so great as to approach a difference of kind. Moreover, students of macroeconomics differ in the extent to which they pursue empirical specificity. Some macroeconomists seek the greater abstraction and thus greater generality that is typical of microeconomics. Their macrotexts contain very little discussion of the apparent size of the marginal propensity to consume and the stability of the consumption function or of the discontinuities provided by "floors" or "ceilings"; not much mention at all is made of time lags nor any reference to "problems of aggregation"; and there is little discussion of specific events or problems. This text does discuss these matters, some will say too much. It is, nevertheless, a book about economic theory.

The Nature of Economic Theory

Economic theory is surely not to be contrasted—as it often wrongly is—with empirical knowledge. Theory *is* empirical knowledge, knowledge that is significant and useful because it is sufficiently organized and simplified that it can be grasped by the human mind and used to find answers to new questions. Theory rests upon measurement but is more than measurement. That which cannot be at least approximately measured cannot be known. But a book or computer data bank crammed with measurements and descriptions is not knowledge and is not directly useful for anything. Data become useful knowledge only as the bits and pieces are distilled, abstracted, organized, generalized, and stated not as unrelated facts but as empirical relationships among facts.

Actually, most of the facts that macroeconomics deals with are already **synthetic facts**, distilled from individual pieces of information: the price level of producers goods, the seasonally adjusted annual rate of disposable personal income, real per capita consumer purchases of durable goods, and the money supply. The particular definition and compilation of these synthetic facts reflects some previous theorizing which had suggested the relevant definitions; further theoretical developments may require new synthetic facts or revisions of previous definitions.

The relationships *among* facts (or synthetic facts) that theory seeks and uses are relationhips either (a) of definition or (b), in some sense, of causation. A definitional relationship is one that has to be true: usually a statement that one variable is the sum of others, or their product, quotient, difference, derivative, and so on. It *defines* one synthetic fact as a relationship among other facts or synthetic facts. When one discovers that, in data relating to the real world, this relationship does exist, it is no discovery at all; it had to be that way. In contrast, the statement of a postulated "causal," or, better, "functional" relationship among two or more facts does not have to be true; and, actually, it probably cannot be wholly true. It reflects some regularity of behavior that is, at best, approximate, and that has been "discovered" rather than "defined."

Two or more variables may be functionally related because—in some regular and describable way—one "causes" or "determines" or "affects" the other; because they mutually affect each other; or because they are each affected by some other variable or variables.

Such a relationship of "cause," "determination," or "affect" may reflect a technological or engineering relationship based on physical, chemical, electrical, or other properties of things; a "behavioral" relationship that reflects physiological, habitual, cultural, or psychological behavior of persons; contractual relationships fixed by agreement; a relationship established by law; or some other source of regular interdependence.

Such functional relationships may be discovered by accident, found by some systematic search process (trial and error), or may be suggested by or deduced from some other body of theory. Knowledge accrues in various ways, and as it accrues, its internal consistency must be constantly tested as new facts emerge and other relationships are proposed.

In economics, the discovery and testing of theoretical relationships occurs mainly in two ways (experiment being largely ruled out): one is statistical investigation (**econometrics**), the other is logical deduction. The former basically involves methods of confronting a hypothesis with the facts, testing the extent to which it is consistent with the facts, and estimating the most probable form and quantitative parameters of the presumed functional relationship. The latter, logical deduction, concludes that if and because relationships (a), (b), and (c) all exist, then this necessarily implies that relationship (d) exists as well. This process of logical deduction is greatly extended by the use of mathematics. Given the premises, the conclusion follows (so long as the premises are correct).

Some of these derived or deduced relationships are based in part on premises that are believed to be true but cannot be (or at least so far have not been) directly confronted with facts, perhaps because measurements are extremely difficult or impossible. These premises, however, do command substantial agreement among informed observers. One such premise is that firms always and effectively attempt to maximize profits. This, in turn, may rest upon other, psychological premises, and/or upon the observation that some firms do behave in this way. Such a premise is *a priori* knowledge that is, and will continue to be, accepted so long as conclusions derived from it (by deduction) seem consistent with the facts. Many of the major controversies in macroeconomics trace back to arguments about the correctness of such *a priori* knowledge—at least its correctness for the purposes to which macroeconomics applies it.

Macroeconomic Models

One of the principal ways in which macroeconomics (like micro) seeks to obtain useful knowledge about an economy is through the construction and use of **models**, which are deliberately simplified representations of the real world—deliberately simplified both in the sense that they omit or suppress much of the detail of reality and in the sense that they deliberately falsify reality in a number of respects. For example, a model may assume an economy without government and without international economic relations; having an unchanging technology and labor force; with perfect information, mobility of resources, and flexibility of prices and wages; having only two financial assets, money and a standard bond; and so on. (The choice of what detail to suppress and what major facts to falsify must in part be an artistic judgment.)

Instead of attempting to represent a real economy, the model describes an economy that has some of the aspects of a real one—presumably, those believed to be quantitatively the most important or those most relevant to the kinds of questions the model will be used to study. Instead of trying (which is impossible) to analyze or calculate everything that would happen in the real world if some event occurred or some government policy were introduced or altered, we analyze and calculate what would happen in the model. This has the additional advantage—if the model is sufficiently simple—that we can understand how and why these results, rather than others, should occur. We trust that the model is enough like the real world, in its essential elements, to help us understand how a real economy functions.

The simplest models even permit graphic representation, which assists many to grasp more easily the nature of the interdependence among variables. Somewhat more complex models consist of a limited number of equations that can be solved simultaneously; in fact, the graphic representation implies such a set of equations and solves them simultaneously by graphic manipulation rather than algebraic techniques. Obviously, to permit simultaneous solution, graphic or algebraic, there must be as many relationships among variables (that is, equations) as there are variables to be solved for (that is, unknowns). In these simple models it is still possible, and extremely important, for the user not merely to find the solutions but to attempt to grasp the individual adjustments and the overall pattern of their movement, which are occurring in the model—just as one can learn simultaneously to hear the parts played by a number of instruments while also hearing the orchestra as a whole.

Macroeconomic models sufficiently large and detailed to be really useful for forecasting or policy simulations unfortunately lose to some extent their ability to be understood. Such models can contain few deliberately false assumptions, and they must contain so many equations in so many unknowns that they can only be solved by complex computer routines. These models take on the character of the **black box**, into which one feeds a series of alternative inputs and discovers the response. Unfortunately, it is sometimes difficult fully to grasp everything that is happening in the box, why the results are what they are, or precisely why they differ from the results of simpler models.

In this book, we shall use only very simple models, but we shall try to indicate in what respects some of the results would be altered with more complex and realistic models. We shall also consider rather more fully the more complex and realistic formulations of some of the major relationships that can be and are used in the large-scale econometric models.

Stock and Flow Variables

There are several elementary concepts commonly used in both macro- and microeconomics that are often the source of confusion but about which it is necessary to be fairly precise. The first of these is the distinction between two types of variables that enter into economic relationships and are used in economic models: **stock variables** and **flow variables**. A stock variable has no time dimension; a flow variable necessarily does.

For instance, a firm's inventory of materials or products is a stock variable, whether measured in physical units or in money value; however, its production, sales, use of materials, and so on, are all flow variables. Thus, the value of its inventory may be $3,500,000—no time dimension used or needed; but its production is valued at $400,000 *a day*—without the time dimension the number alone is meaningless ($400,000 a minute, or a year, would be quite a different matter).

Obviously, both inventory and production need to be given a date in time, for either one can and does change over time. The inventory on June 30, 1977, was $3,500,000 (on May 31 it had been $3,200,000); production in June 1977 was at the rate of $400,000 a day (in July it fell to $380,000 a day).

All this seems very obvious but almost no other single source of confusion is more dangerous in economic theory, and not merely for beginners in the field. Money is a stock, expenditures or transactions in money are a flow; wealth is a stock, income a flow; savings a stock, saving a flow; government debt a stock, government deficit a flow; bank loans outstanding a stock, bank lending a flow. It is meaningless to say that my money transactions, or my income, or my saving is $3,000—a month? a year? a day? It *is* meaningful to say that the government debt is $500 billion, the national wealth $6 trillion, or my money balance $183.20.

Is **price** a stock or a flow variable? Price does not need a time dimension, but it obviously is not a stock magnitude. Actually it can be thought of as a ratio between two (actual or potential) flows—a flow of cash and a flow of goods. In the ratio, the time unit appears both in numerator and denominator and hence cancels out.

Other ratio variables appear in economics. Such ratios may express relationships between stocks, between flows, or between stocks and flows. An example of the first is the concept of "liquidity," as measured, for instance, by the percentage of liquid assets to total assets of a person or firm. An example of a flow ratio is the ratio of saving to income. Examples of ratios between a stock and a flow are the various "velocity" concepts, ratios between a flow of money transactions or income and a stock of money. Since the time dimension does not cancel out, velocity must be expressed in terms of a time dimension: the money stock "turns over" twelve times a year (which can also be expressed as once per month or three times per quarter-year).

Upon encountering any variable, the reader should spend a moment determining for himself whether it is a stock, a flow, or a ratio concept, and, if the latter, whether a ratio between stocks, flows, or a stock and a flow. Much confusion will be saved by this exercise.

We have seen that flows must be expressed in terms of a time unit. What unit we choose is obviously immaterial, although the 1-year unit is often a natural one in income analysis. But whether we express income as per year, per month, per day, or per second, we must have in mind that the flow is either an instantaneous rate at some point of time or is an average of such instantaneous rates over a period of time. We can say that as of 10:03 A.M. on Monday, May 26, 1977, consumer disposable income was at the rate of $1,271 billion per annum (although we have no such data). If we say that, for the year 1976, consumer disposable income was at the rate of $1,181.7 billion a year, we really mean that this was the average rate of income flow during that year. A car can be traveling at the rate of 60 miles per hour at some particular instant, or it can travel 60 miles per hour for an 8-hour day—meaning not that the speedometer was at 60 every moment in that day but that it traveled 480 miles in 8 hours at an average speed of 60 miles per hour. Since most economic flows cannot be read from speedometers or similar measuring devices, in practice we must measure them over a period of time. John Doe received $731 in income payments during March 1976. His March income was thus at the rate of $731 per month, or $8,772 per annum. Conceptually, however, we speak of rates of flow as of any instant of time, expressing that flow in terms of any convenient time unit.[1]

Several crucial problems in economic theory involve relationships between flows and stocks. Except through revaluations, stocks change only through flows. The stock of capital goods increases through an excess of new construction and manufacture over wearing out. Wealth accumulates

---

[1] A convenient simplification often used in economic theory is that of **period analysis**. In period analysis, we assume that flows (such as income) are not capable of continuous change, but rather change only at certain intervals (the ends or beginnings of "periods"). Thus, income (like other flow variables) changes only in stairstep fashion. We say: "Income moves as follows: 100, 90, 85, 82.5 . . . ." If we think of these magnitudes each as the cumulation of income payments over the duration of the period, then the flow takes on the same dimension as a stock, and we (seem to) avoid stock-flow difficulties. Some authors work almost invariably in period analysis terms (whether explicitly or not). We shall not use this concept except at specific points in our analysis, clearly calling attention to the fact that we are doing so. It is the author's conviction that analytical results which depend on the very special assumptions of period analysis have often been quite illegitimately generalized.

through the act of saving (or decreases through dissaving).[2] However, it makes a great difference whether the stock changes rapidly or slowly; the ultimate effect on the stock is the same, but, because the flows involve current transactions, they thus affect other current rates of flow. Some of the trickiest problems in (dynamic) macroeconomic analysis involve just this point (for example, the "acceleration" theory of investment, the relationship of stock and flow theories of the rate of interest, and many problems involving the slippery concept of "hoarding"). We shall have something to say about this matter at later points.

Equilibrium, Statics, and Dynamics

The concept of **equilibrium** is familiar in a general way to all beginning students of economics. A system can be said to be in equilibrium when all of its significant variables show no change and when there are no pressures or forces for change that will produce subsequent change in the values of significant variables. (Perhaps it is better to say that the forces for change are in balance, rather than that they are absent.)

States of equilibrium need never be realized in the economy for equilibrium analysis to be a useful tool of thinking. Corresponding to any given set of external circumstances, there may be some pattern of economic variables which, if once achieved, would show no further tendency to change. Assuming for the moment that there are forces in an economy (or in a particular market) that push it toward equilibrium when it is not in that state, a description of the equilibrium position is a description of the directions in which economic variables are headed. Of course, the external circumstances that determine the equilibrium may always be changing so that equilibrium is never attained. Nevertheless, it remains useful to know the directions in which variables are headed at any given time, whether they are expected ever to reach their equilibrium values or not.

There are circumstances in which disequilibrium produces only a tendency for further change, which may not be in the direction of equilibrium. Even in this circumstance, however, it is useful to be able to identify the equilibrium that, if it could be obtained, would lead to cessation of further change.

States of equilibrium may be of several sorts. Since economic variables are of both stock and flow varieties, full equilibrium would be one in which all stocks as well as flows were stable. This would necessarily mean that the

---

[2] If we represent (net) saving by S and wealth ("savings") by W,

$$S = \dot{W}$$

where the dot above the variable is used to indicate its instantaneous time rate of change, $\partial W/\partial t$. For example, saving \$10 (a day, week, or year) means that wealth increases at \$10 (a day, week, or year).

net flows that add to the stocks would, at equilibrium, be zero. (This does not mean that all flows would be zero. The stockpile of iron ore at a blast furnace may be constant even though the furnace is operating at full speed; it is only necessary that new ore be delivered as fast as it is used.) Such a concept of full equilibrium for the economy as a whole is that of the classical "stationary state," in which the community's stock of capital is just maintained with zero net saving and investment. Such a state of full or "stationary" equilibrium has questionable relevance to our economic society. Nevertheless, it is important to recognize that this is the only full equilibrium, and that, so long as saving and investment are nonzero, changes are occurring in the economy's stock of capital and in consumers' wealth that will surely ultimately affect the rates of current flows.

A more immediately applicable concept of maroeconomic equilibrium is that of short-run or flow equilibrium in which flows (but not stocks) are stable and have no tendency (at least in the short run) to further change.[3] Of course, if this flow equilibrium involves positive or negative net change in stocks, full stock plus flow equilibrium is not achieved and the growth or shrinkage of stocks may contain the seeds of later change in flows. But, because annual accretions of most stocks are relatively small (compared with the total size of such stocks), we may frequently find it useful, in short-run analysis, to ignore the changes in stocks whose effects will show up only over a considerable period of time.[4]

A third possible variety of equilibrium is one sometimes used in analyzing economic growth. This is the moving equilibrium in which stocks grow, but only in the same proportion with the growth of the current flows. Thus, all relevant stock-flow ratios are constant, and the accretion of stocks has no tendency, even ultimately, to affect the rates of current flows.

The branch of economic analysis that confines its attention to equilibrium positions is called **statics**. The most useful variety of statics is **comparative statics**, which compares equilibrium positions corresponding to two or more sets of external circumstances. Static analysis, whether simple or comparative, concentrates only on equilibrium positions. It does not concern itself with the time it takes for an equilibrium position to be achieved nor with the path by which variables approach their equilibrium states. This is *one* concern of dynamic analysis.

Dynamics is concerned essentially with states of disequilibrium and with change. Whether the disequilibrium involves the absence of short-run (flow) equilibrium or the condition and movement of an economy not in long-run (stock plus flow) equilibrium, study of movement and change is

---

[3] If asset markets are perfect, stock equilibrium may be maintained in the short run, as prices of existing assets adjust to keep holders of such assets statisfied with their holding of them. But if the flows which add to stocks are nonzero, full stock equilibrium is not achieved.

[4] Although this assumption *may* be appropriate with respect to the stock of plant and equipment, it obviously is not with respect to inventories. Business cycle analysis cannot possibly ignore changes in inventory stocks.

the province of dynamic analysis. This is sometimes oversimplified by describing dynamics as the study of the movement of economic variables toward equilibrium, or from one equilibrium position to another. Although such study is an important and useful exercise in dynamic analysis, it retains the tie to the equilibrium concept. A broader and more significant dynamics includes as well the movements of a system that is never in equilibrium—because no equilibrium exists, or because the movements of the system are not in the direction of equilibrium, or because of continuous changes in external circumstances, such as productive techniques, population, consumer tastes, government actions, to name the more outstanding ones. Study of the "business cycle" may fall in this broadest category of dynamics. Whether the study of the moving equilibrium of proportional growth should be called statics or dynamics is a matter of taste.

A more formal and sophisticated definition makes the essence of **dynamics** to be that it studies systems or models involving *relationships that hold over time*—that is, relationships in which the value that obtains *now* for a variable may depend not only on the simultaneous values of other variables but also, or instead, on *previous* values of other variables (or even previous values of the same variable).[5] Examples are behavior patterns involving **lags** (the investment expenditures that I make today depend on yesterday's value of the interest rate); or **habituation** (my consumption expenditures today depend, among other things, on my yesterday's level of consumption); or **cumulants** (my savings today are the cumulative total of all my past saving and dissaving). A system that involves one or more such relationships is a dynamic system.

Of course, one special state of any dynamic system may be that of no change, or equilibrium—which occurs when the previous values that determine today's values produce results exactly the same as those of the day before. Thus today's values will produce again the same results tomorrow, and so on. A dynamic analysis of an equilibrium situation is therefore not only possible, but is, indeed, the most fruitful way of considering it.

The preceding definition of dynamics as involving relationships that hold over time would seem, in contrast, to leave as the province of statics only the analysis of systems in which all causal relationships are simultaneous. However, this unnecessarily restricts the scope of statics. If equilibrium is a state of no change over time, then, so long as equilibrium prevails, the time dimensions of a relationship can be ignored. For example, if the interest rate is constant, it makes no difference whether we recognize that investment depends on yesterday's interest rate as opposed to today's, for both yesterday's and today's interest rates are the same. We can simply say that investment (undated) depends on the interest rate

---

[5] A moment's reflection will show that this definition is equivalent to the previous one. For, if all relationships among variables, including the "causal" ones, were simultaneous relationships—that is, involved only variables having the same date—the system would always be in equilibrium.

(undated). Habituation, likewise, has no independent role when there is no change, and habituation can be ignored. Thus, in an analysis that restricts itself to equilibrium positions, the time aspect drops out. To use statics, we do not have to deny that some of our relationships hold over time; this fact simply makes no difference, so long as we confine our attention to equilibrium positions. But the existence of relationships that hold over time obviously cannot be ignored when we deal with disequilibrium and change—which brings us back to our initial identification of dynamics with disequilibrium and change.

However, the more complete view of equilibrium as a special state of a dynamic system leads us to the discovery that not all dynamic systems are capable of achieving equilibrium. This is true even though there may *exist* an equilibrium for such a system. There may be some pattern of variables which, if once achieved, would repeat itself endlessly in the absence of new disturbance. Yet, if the system starts with some pattern other than the equilibrium one, it may show no tendency to approach equilibrium but only to generate endless change. Such an equilibrium is, therefore, not very meaningful. It is called an **unstable** equilibrium. A **stable** equilibrium, on the contrary, is one that the system's movements tend to approach or reach. If a stable equilibrium is disturbed, it will be reestablished. Not so an unstable one.

Now if we confine our analysis only to equilibrium positions, we are obviously unable to distinguish between stable and unstable equilibria. If it were not for this, we could defend statics as a good approximation—saying that we are not interested in, or can afford to ignore, what happens "on the way" but are only interested in final destinations. However, because we find it easy to construct plausible economic models that are unstable, or systems that are only barely stable (take a long time to settle down when disturbed), and because we seem to observe in the real world some movements that resemble the results of these models, we now think that the method of statics is not merely incomplete but potentially misleading.

Nevertheless, because statics is simpler and because it provides a convenient, even necessary, starting point for dynamics, the primary method of this book is statics. Still, dynamic analysis will not be entirely neglected.

MACROECONOMICS AND MICROECONOMICS

Most, but not all, of the content of traditional economic theory, until the last 35 or 40 years, consisted of microeconomics. Price and value theory, the theory of the household, the firm, and the industry, and most production and welfare theories are of the microeconomic variety. However, monetary theory and business-cycle theory also have a long history, and these are clearly macroeconomic.

Actually, the line between macroeconomic and microeconomic theory cannot be precisely drawn. A truly "general" theory of the economy would clearly embrace both. It would explain individual behavior, individual outputs, incomes, and prices, and the sums or averages of the individual results would constitute the aggregates with which macroeconomics is concerned. Such a general theory exists, but its very generality leaves it with little substantive content. Rather, to reach meaningful results, we find that we must approach macroeconomic problems at a macro level and microeconomic problems at a micro level.

One may immediately wonder how a meaningful macroeconomics is possible. It is, after all, true that total output (for example) is the sum of individual outputs. How then can we explain the total except as we simultaneously explain the individual parts? The answer to this question raises some points that are far from elementary and to which we shall frequently have to return in the course of this study. Nevertheless, it is appropriate to comment briefly on this question early in our discussion.

One part of the answer lies in the fact that macroeconomic reasoning can take account of many limitations and relationships that are not applicable to individual parts. For example, for any individual or group of individuals, income and expenditure on currently produced output obviously can and usually will be different magnitudes; however, for a whole society, income and expenditure (properly defined) can be shown always to be equal. Any individual can save without investing or invest without having previously or currently saved; however, carefully defined, saving and investment must be identical for the whole economy. One country's imports may well exceed its exports, but for all countries combined, total imports and exports must obviously be equal. One individual can reduce his stock of cash by paying out in excess of his receipts, but, unless the community's total money stock is changed, society cannot. One firm or industry can almost always increase its output and employment by bidding workers and materials away from other industries; when there is full employment, industry as a whole may be unable to increase total output.

Another part of the answer is that many variables which are extremely important for explaining individual behavior tend to "cancel out" when we deal with aggregates. This can be illustrated by reference to the consumption–income relationship that plays a major role in macroeconomics. Consumption behavior of the individual family depends not only on income but very importantly on many other things—for example, age of the family head; size of the family; the age of its automobile and other durable goods; whether it owns or rents its dwelling; the incidence of sickness, births, weddings, college-age children; and so on. To "explain" individual or small-group consumer expenditures, we would need to include these variables and many more. But, for the explanation of aggregate consumption behavior, many of these variables cancel out, at least in the short run.

The age structure of the total population changes only very slowly, as does the percentage owning homes. Births, deaths, and sickness will this year alter the expenditure patterns of many families, but the incidence of these in the total population is quite predictable and stable; some families have obsolescent cars and furniture, but others have new, and so on. These variables cannot be totally overlooked in dealing with aggregate behavior, particularly when we deal with longer periods; but their importance at one time is slight, and they can frequently be safely ignored. This is one of the most significant of all of the advantages of macroeconomics. Economic behavior is invariably complex and multivariate; even in macroeconomics we shall find it necessary to include a number of variables, but we can usually deal safely with systems involving fewer variables than are relevant for microeconomic theory.

In particular, much of microeconomics has to do with relative prices of different goods and services. Higher prices for one good both attract resources to its production and cause buyers to transfer their purchases in other directions. It is the fluctuation of these price relationships that mold and alter the structure of resource use. But it is always *relative* prices that are the concern—price of good A relative to prices of goods B, C, D, and so on; the wage rate in firm or industry A relative to that paid elsewhere; the price of the services of a factor of production (affecting factor income) relative to the prices which the income recipient must pay for particular consumer goods or consumer goods in general; and so on. But, again, the effects of relative prices may largely cancel out in dealing with the economy as a whole. If one price rises relative to others, other prices have fallen relative to the first. If one industry or product has gained or lost customers or resources in response to a change in relative prices, another has lost or gained in a way that may leave the aggregate magnitudes largely unaffected. Yet it is these internal changes that are of basic concern in microeconomics.

This is not to say that relative prices do not have relevance in macro-economics, although most macroeconomic theory has up to now largely neglected them. But, at least as a first approximation, the neglect of relative prices—which are the cornerstone of microeconomic analysis—can be justified. Since any price is relative not only to prices in general but often significantly to many other individual prices, neglect of relative prices at one stroke reduces tremendously the number of variables with which macroeconomics must deal.[6]

The Problem of Aggregation

Although these are reasons that in part support the assumption that a meaningful macroeconomics is possible, they do not deal specifically with

[6] In Chapter 16, we will explore briefly the relevance of relative prices for aggregate consumer spending.

the relationship that must exist between microeconomic theories of behavior and the corresponding macrotheories. Consideration of this question has not received as much attention from economists as it deserves; but it has received enough to indicate that formidable problems exist in trying to translate microtheories into propositions testable at the aggregate level, as it also does in trying to derive microtheories from empirical regularities observed at the macro level.

Microeconomic theory has developed on a largely *a priori* basis, resting upon a concept of maximization or optimization of position, together with some presumed physiological or technological relationships of inputs and outputs. Although we may sometimes "test" or measure these relationships on a purely microeconomic basis, by studying individual firms or consumers, most of our data relate to some combinations of units. Thus, aggregation problems arise even with respect to the testing of conventional so-called "microeconomic" theories of price and income distribution. Intuitively, we suppose that these problems are the more serious the broader is our aggregation over families, firms, or products.

Aggregation problems are of several orders. One order of problems is statistical in the narrow technical sense. It arises essentially from the fact that there is a certain element of "randomness" or "indeterminacy" in individual behavior and/or a certain inaccuracy in any *measurement* of individual behavior. Our statistical method must make certain (and preferably explicit) assumptions regarding this random element. Although these statistical problems are important, we shall neglect them here, in effect assuming that all measurement is perfect and that there is no random element in individual behavior. Apart from such statistical questions, there are conceptual problems that we can ignore only with peril.[7]

To take a simple example, suppose that our micro theory tells us that investment by a firm is a function (*inter alia*) of its profits. Suppose, however, that we find no relationship between aggregate investment of a group of firms and the total profits of the group. Does this disprove the hypothesis? It may not.

Assume that the separate investment functions are as follows:

$$Case\ A$$
$$I_A = 100 + 0.1R_A$$
$$I_B = -20 + 0.8R_B$$
$$I_C = R_C$$

where I_i and R_i are, respectively, the investment and profits of firm i. For

---

[7] For a more general and more sophisticated treatment of aggregation problems than this (including statistical problems), see H. Theil: *Linear Aggregation of Economic Relations* (Amsterdam: North-Holland, 1954). For a review, largely based on Theil's work, see R. G. D. Allen: *Mathematical Economics* (London: Macmillan, 1959), pp. 694–724.

each firm, investment is linearly related to profits, with a positive slope. Suppose that, at two different times, profits are as follows:

Time 1	*Time 2*
$R_A = 100$	$R_A = 300$
$R_B = 100$	$R_B = 200$
$R_C = 200$	$R_C = 0$
$\Sigma R = 400$	$\Sigma R = 500$

Investment will then be

Time 1	*Time 2*
$I_A = 110$	$I_A = 130$
$I_B = 60$	$I_B = 140$
$I_C = 200$	$I_C = 0$
$\Sigma I = 370$	$\Sigma I = 270$

$$\frac{\Delta \Sigma I}{\Delta \Sigma R} = \frac{-100}{100} = -1$$

Although aggregate profits have increased, aggregate investment has fallen. Yet it remains true that, for each firm, investment is positively related to profits. The reason, of course, is that the distribution of aggregate profits has radically changed.

One might conclude from this example that, if the distribution of the aggregate "independent" variables shifts widely and erratically, we can derive no stable or meaningful macro functions; and, conversely, using aggregative data, we cannot "discover" the "true" micro relationship. This apparent conclusion is, however, subject to several reservations. We obtained the result we did in the previous example partly because the distribution of aggregate profits among firms changed sharply, and partly because the individual micro relationships that we used had widely different slopes. In fact, had the micro slopes been identical, the changing distribution of profits would have made no difference whatsoever. This can be seen by considering the following example.

Case B

$$I_A = 60 + 0.5R_A$$
$$I_B = 10 + 0.5R_B$$
$$I_C = 100 + 0.5R_C$$

(These functions have been chosen to produce the same distribution and same total of investment as in case *A* with the initial distribution of profits.)

Our comparison now shows:

	Time 1			*Time 2*	
$R_A = 100$		$I_A = 110$	$R_A = 300$		$I_A = 210$
$R_B = 100$		$I_B = 60$	$R_B = 200$		$I_B = 110$
$R_C = 200$		$I_C = 200$	$R_C = 0$		$I_C = 100$
$\Sigma R = 400$		$\Sigma I = 370$	$\Sigma R = 500$		$\Sigma I = 420$

$$\frac{\Delta \Sigma I}{\Delta \Sigma R} = \frac{50}{100} = 0.5$$

It will be noted that a change of total profits of 100 produced a change of investment of 50, exactly the marginal relationship that held for each of the three firms. We would get this result for any possible combination of profits having a different sum than at time 1. It should be obvious that even if the slopes of the relationships were not identical for all firms but were, instead, all close together—ranging, say, between 0.45 and 0.55—an increase in aggregate profits would tend to produce an increase in aggregate investment of *roughly* half of the increase of profits, almost no matter how the profits were distributed. Of course, even in this case, the slope of the aggregative relationship could easily fall outside of the 0.45 to 0.55 range, and, in an extreme case, could even be negative, or in excess of 1.0.

For example, assume:

Case C

$$I_A = 200 + 0.45R_A$$
$$I_B = -40 + 0.5R_B$$
$$I_C = -20 + 0.55R_C$$

	Time 1			*Time 2*	
$R_A = -200$		$I_A = 110$	$R_A = -100$		$I_A = 155$
$R_B = 200$		$I_B = 60$	$R_B = 250$		$I_B = 85$
$R_C = 400$		$I_C = 200$	$R_C = 350$		$I_C = 172.5$
$\Sigma R = 400$		$\Sigma I = 370$	$\Sigma R = 500$		$\Sigma I = 412.5$

	Time 3	
$R_A = 500$		$I_A = 425$
$R_B = 100$		$I_B = 10$
$R_C = -100$		$I_C = -75$
$\Sigma R = 500$		$\Sigma I = 360$

As between times 1 and 2, the aggregate marginal propensity to invest is 0.425; but as between times 1 and 3, it is −0.1.

Our first conclusion is, then, that aggregation is a legitimate procedure when the behavior of the individual units subject to aggregation is basically similar and when the distribution of the independent variable does not vary in an excessively violent manner. This suggests, therefore, that it is important, in aggregation, to group together units whose responses can be assumed to be roughly the same, and that aggregations covering widely dissimilar forms of individual behavior may be dangerous, unless we can be sure that the independent variables change in roughly the same way for all units. The latter condition is, of course, often satisfied. If the independent variable is a particular price (or price level) or an interest rate, all firms or consumers may be assumed to experience roughly the same change at any given time. Where the independent variable is an income, we can be less sure. When aggregate disposable income (or profits) rises or falls, the individual recipients may have experiences quite different from the average or aggregate. If this is combined with a considerable variety in the individual responses ("micro slopes"), there may be trouble.

Where we deal with large numbers of units, a wide variety of individual income experience may still not be serious, provided that this variety of experience is random—that is, that there is no systematic tendency for individuals experiencing one particular kind of income movement to have response rates (micro slopes) substantially different from the average for other groups. The fact that individual profit experience varies widely is not serious for our presumed investment function unless the firms whose profits (say) fall when aggregate profits rise can be assumed to have significantly different investment responses than other firms.

Suppose, however, that we have reason to believe that changes in the distribution of the independent variable are not merely random, but instead that different subcategories experience changes that are systematically different from the total (or average) movement. For example, if one group of firms should have very stable profits, and another group (which might be concentrated in certain industries, or be typically of a different size than the others) had highly volatile profits, so that changes in aggregate profits were primarily the result of changes in the profits of the latter group, the slope of the macro function would reflect primarily the (possibly untypical) response rates of this group.[8]

This last point can be illuminated by considering in more general fashion the case in which the distribution of the independent variable depends systematically upon its aggregate size. Consider a simple case in which we have three micro relationships for three individual units, as follows:

$$y_a = a_0 + a_1 x_a$$
$$y_b = b_0 + b_1 x_b$$
$$y_c = c_0 + c_1 x_0$$

---

[8] Thus Thiel (see footnote 6), pages 24–26, argues that, because high incomes are more volatile than low incomes, the aggregate marginal propensity to consume will reflect primarily the presumably lower individual marginal propensity to consume of the high-income families.

Assume, further, the following "distribution functions"—that is, relationships between the movements of the individual independent micro variables (x_a, x_b, and x_c), and the aggregate x, which is the sum of the micro variables:

$$x_a = A_0 + A_1 x$$
$$x_b = B_0 + B_1 x$$
$$x_c = C_0 + C_1 x$$

where $A_0 + B_0 + C_0 = 0$, and $A_1 + B_1 + C_1 = 1$. We are interested in the relationship between the aggregate dependent variable, y (equal to $y_a + y_b + y_c$) and the aggregate independent variable, x.

By simple substitution, we derive the following expression for the dependence of y on x:

$$y = (a_0 + b_0 + c_0) + (a_1 A_0 + b_1 B_0 + c_1 C_0) + (a_1 A_1 + b_1 B_1 + c_1 C_1)x$$

Examination of this equation shows that, in the general case, the intercept (constant term) of the macro relationship equals the sum of the corresponding micro intercepts (first parentheses), *plus* a weighted sum of the intercepts of the distribution functions, each weighted by the appropriate micro slope (second parentheses). The macro slope (third parentheses) is a weighted average of the individual micro slopes, each weighted by the slope of the appropriate distribution function. (We call it a weighted average rather than a weighted sum, because the sum of the weights— $A_1 + B_1 + C_1$—should equal unity.) Thus the macro function depends, in a fairly complicated way (far more complicated, if the number of the independent variables exceeds one) on both the individual corresponding micro functions and upon the form of the distribution functions.

We can also see that (in this simple case) the macro intercept will equal the sum of the micro intercepts only if the constants in the distribution function are all zero (as would be the case if the percentage distribution of the independent variable were constant). We can further see that the macro slope is a weighted average of the micro slopes, in which the systematically more volatile units have the greatest weight. We can also note that, if the micro slopes are identical ($a_1 = b_1 = c_1$), the weights (that is, the distribution of the independent variable) make no difference. Essentially similar results hold for the case in which either y or x is a fixed-weight index number rather than an aggregate of the corresponding macrovariables.

The general conclusion, that the shape of the macrorelationships reflects both (a) the shapes of the corresponding microrelations and (b) the systematic elements in the distribution of the independent variables is of considerable importance for macroeconomics. It means that, even where we find a reasonably stable macrorelationship, its future stability may depend upon the continuation of one or more distribution relationships. If changes in population distribution, consumer tastes, business structure, or government policy should alter the distribution relationships, our macrorelation may be altered, even though the corresponding micro-relations (that is, the behavior patterns of the individual units) are unchanged. Since most macroeconomic models do not explicitly include distribution functions, changes in the latter can upset predictions based on an assumed stability of the macrofunctions.

The aggregation problem becomes considerably more difficult if the underlying micro relationship is presumed to be distinctly nonlinear, as, for example, in the case of the production functions of individual firms. Only if every total output is always distributed in constant proportions among a fixed number of firms does the problem of nonlinearity become remotely manageable. Actually, however, under most circumstances, changes in total output imply distinct changes in its distribution among industries and firms. Moreover, we must not assume that the number of firms is fixed as total output expands or contracts. As will be shown in more detail in Chapter 4, the blithe assumption by many macroeconomists that an aggregate production function exists for the economy, the shape of which is like that postulated for the firm, is quite unjustified. This is particularly serious when policy advice is given—as it has sometimes been—based on an analytical result which reflects this clearly erroneous presumption.

Aggregation problems can be extremely troublesome in macro-economics. Although we shall pay some attention to them from time to time, in other contexts we shall often slide over them—usually because macroeconomists have so far not worked on them and there is nothing to report.

The Microeconomic Assumptions of Macroeconomic Theory

The macroeconomic theories presented and discussed in this book—whether simple "classical" models or modern "post-Keynesian" models—are expressed in terms of macroeconomic variables and involve functional and definitional relationships among these variables. Nevertheless, what is summarized in these macroeconomic relationships is not the behavior of some aggregate decision makers or the constraints imposed by some giant productive machine but the behavior of and the constraints on individual microeconomic units such as households and firms. Obviously, some assumptions, explicit or implicit, must be made about that behavior. Usually, in macroeconomics, these assumptions have been implicit, but it has become increasingly clear that it is necessary to be as explicit as possible about these microeconomic assumptions.

Since we are dealing with an economy like that of the United States, we are obviously assuming that most productive activity takes place in private firms and most consumption in private households; moreover, that the goods and services produced in firms reach households through a system of decentralized markets, and the productive services of households reach firms through similar markets.

Partly from tradition and partly from convenience most macroeconomic theories employ the assumptions about the behavior of households and firms and about the markets that join them that have traditionally been used in microeconomic analysis. The first assumption typically made in this micro analysis is that the buyers and sellers in each market are so numerous and independent that each is a **price taker**, not setting a price but taking one set by the market interaction of buyers and sellers. Since this is obviously not true of many markets of modern economies, we will need to evaluate how the results of macro theory are affected by introducing monopolistic, oligopolistic, or other "imperfectly competitive" market structures in which prices are set and maintained for periods of more than trivial duration.

A second, more subtle assumption is that all markets are always in equilibrium; that is, prices are always such that no economic agent is dissatisfied with the exchanges that take place. To see what is involved in this assumption consider the familiar analysis of a single competitive market. A supply function for such a market makes the planned or desired (flow of) goods or services to the market a direct function of the market price; and a demand function makes the amount of planned or desired purchases an inverse function of the market price. There is some equilibrium price, at which planned or desired sales and purchases are equal. Exchanges at this price will leave no buyer or seller with an unrealized sales or purchase plan or desire. This equilibrium price changes over time, of course, as supply or demand functions shift.

Usually we *assume* that all exchanges take place at the equilibrium price and in the equilibrium quantity. A moment's reflection will show, however, that it is not a correct assumption. It implies that there is some force in the market that instantaneously steers the price to the equilibrium, even when supply or demand conditions change rapidly. Given the assumption of price-taking behavior by sellers and buyers, this cannot be assured without introducing some additional device. One such device might be the presence of an auctioneer. This person is imagined to call a price and to find the amounts desired to be supplied and demanded at that price. If there is either excess supply or excess demand at that price, he will call another price and check again for excess demand or supply. The process of trial and error ("tâtonnement" or "groping" was Walras' term for it) continues until the equilibrium is obtained; only then are exchanges made. Given certain reasonable assumptions, it can be readily demonstrated that such a process would necessarily yield the equilibrium price and quantity.

We may also find a *tendency* of price and quantity to move *toward* equilibrium under other, more realistic, forms of market organization, including those involving price setting and quantity taking. However, under these alternative forms, trading does occur even when the market is not in equilibrium (that is, there is trading at nonequilibrium prices), and the process of moving toward equilibrium takes time. Clearly, therefore, the usual theory provides a somewhat inaccurate description of the market.

A third, and related, assumption of conventional market theories is that all buyers and sellers know the prices of the goods in the particular market in which they operate, as well as the prices of all other goods that are related to buyers' and sellers' behavior in the particular market. It is as though all prices were instantaneously posted at every location where decisions are made, so that all the information useful in making purchase and sales decisions is available to all participants. This assumption is loosely referred to as the agents having **perfect information**. In reality, buyers and sellers do not have such information. Instead, decisions are made in the face of some degree of error or uncertainty about the price. This kind of uncertainty about price is important because it means that exchanges may take place simultaneously in the market at more than one price, or at a price which at least some sellers or buyers did not expect to receive or pay when they decided to sell or purchase. (We could also consider the effects of uncertainty with respect to many other aspects of the market.)

A fourth and more specialized assumption of simpler microeconomic theories is that of unitary price expectations (price expectations of unit elasticity). This means that, although expected future prices may not be the same as current prices, any change in current prices causes an equal percentage change (in the same direction) in all participants' expectations of future prices. This is not necessarily the case; often some quite different pattern prevails.

These (and other) limitations of the assumptions traditionally made in microeconomic analysis may or may not be of major importance for microeconomic purposes, depending on the type of problem considered. On the other hand, as we shall see later, they may be quite crucial for macroeconomic analysis (at least when this is applied to many typical macro problems). For if some or all of the assumptions noted previously inaccurately describe typical microeconomic markets, the absence of the assumed condition may eliminate or greatly weaken any tendency for average price levels and aggregate quantities (of output, employment, and so on) to approach a "true" or "full" macroeconomic equilibrium, and cause them instead to approach or to rest at some "false" equilibrium—or even to move progressively away from the true equilibrium. Such results are almost inconceivable in the individual markets considered in microeconomic analysis.

If this is the case, the reader may question the usefulness of even discussing macroeconomic theories that rely on such highly simplified microeconomic foundations. One reason is merely that of convenience. Relaxing the four preceding assumptions greatly increases the difficulty of analysis, requiring more complicated verbal descriptions and mathematical models, and perhaps introducing large elements of indeterminacy. Thus, it is useful at least to *start* with the simplest underlying micro structure. The macroeconomic theories using these assumptions present difficulties enough! Later, we begin to allow for more complicated micro theories as we try to capture some essential aspects of real economic problems.

In any case, the ancestor macroeconomic theories that we shall examine first (in Chapters 4 and 5)—Say's Law and the Quantity Theory of Money—did rest on these simple micro assumptions. Unfortunately, so has too large a part of all subsequent development of macroeconomic theory.

SOME LIMITATIONS OF THIS ANALYSIS

We have already mentioned that this book deals in only a limited way with dynamic analysis. Other, equally important limitations of its treatment need to be called to the reader's attention.

One is the absence of any formal analysis of economic growth. The subject is not absent; there is probably more reference to it here than in most intermediate macroeconomics texts. However, the only formal theory that seemed at all a candidate for inclusion was the so-called "Neoclassical Growth Theory." To this writer, this seems so sterile and inadequate a treatment for so dominant a characteristic of a modern macroeconomy that it could not successfully compete with other important topics for inclusion in a treatment such as this. Discussion here of growth is thus informal and unsystematic—but seldom absent for long.

The third exclusion is both the most complete and probably the most important: no significant reference to international macrorelationships appears anywhere in this book. The subject is simply too big to fit into such a book; to handle it adequately seems to require too much of the substance of a course in international economics. We can only warn the reader that, at a great many points, the analysis is incomplete because we have failed to admit international influences and repercussions. Thus, the serious student of macroeconomics must be advised to study international economics as well.

However, the reverse is also true: there is a great deal of material here that is vital to the study of international economics. Since no intermediate text in that field can expect to include much of this material, the parallel advice should be given to one seeking to learn that subject: study also macroeconomic analysis.

REVIEW QUESTIONS

1. How does the analysis of comparative statics differ from dynamics?

2. (1) What are the differences among the concepts of stock variable, flow variable, and ratio variable?

(2) Classify each of the following variables into stock, flow, or ratio variable:

a. income	i. velocity
b. savings	j. price
c. money	k. government debt
d. wage	l. inventory of product
e. interest rate	m. bank lending
f. government deficit	n. percentage of income saved
g. sales of product	o. imports
h. wealth	p. investment

3. N firms produce a product by a micro theory production function,

$$Y_i = \frac{K_i}{a_i} \quad (i = 1, 2, \ldots, n)$$

where Y_i is each firms' output, K_i is the capital of each firm, and a_i is the capital-output ratio of the individual firm. Show how a macro relation

$$Y = \frac{K}{a}$$

can be obtained, where

$$Y = \sum_{i=1}^{n} Y_i \quad \text{and} \quad K = \sum_{i=1}^{n} K_i$$

What alternative assumptions are necessary for the macro relation to be unambiguous?

4. It is sometimes said that equilibrium analysis corresponds to taking snapshots of the economy, dynamics—a motion picture. But this is wrong. Why?

SELECTED REFERENCES

A. Marshall, *Principles of Economics*, (Macmillan, 8th ed., 1920), pp. 1–48. (How the great British expositor and synthesizer of economic ideas described the nature of economic inquiry.)

H. Theil, *Linear Aggregation of Economic Relations*, (North-Holland, 1954). (An introduction to the technical problems of aggregating economic relationships.)

E. R. Weintraub, "The Microfoundations of Macroeconomics: A Critical Survey," *Journal of Economic Literature*, 15 (March 1977), 1–23. (A sophisticated guide to the literature—often rather esoteric—on this important subject.)

Chapter 2

National Income, Product, Wealth, and the Price Level

The Concept of National Income

The Concept of National Product
Capital goods
Inventory changes
Exports and imports

National Income and Product in a Simplified Economy
The "circular flow" of production and incomes
Algebraic statement of accounting relationships

Real National Product and the Price level

National Wealth
National wealth as a collection of physical assets
National wealth as the aggregate net worth of persons
The relationship between wealth as physical assets and as personal net worth

As noted in Chapter 1, macroeconomics deals with aggregate magnitudes, more particularly with aggregates that relate to the entire economy, along with certain breakdowns of these totals into major subaggregates. This chapter and the next introduce some of the major aggregate (and subaggregate) concepts commonly used in macroeconomic analysis, and suggest—at least in principle—how they may be measured. Certain simplified relationships among some of these magnitudes are also developed—some definitional (that is, accounting) relationships, plus a few of the many "functional" relationships among them. In later chapters, as we need to discuss empirical findings, expressed as relationships among aggregative variables as measured in a country's national income and product, wealth, and employment statistics, we will occasionally need to amplify the elementary treatment of this chapter.

The concepts described in these chapters—indeed the entire treatment of this book—are intended to apply basically to an economy (like that of the United States) in which the greater part of productive activity is organized in private business firms, and the greater part of consumption activity in private households. However, right from the beginning we will introduce government, which engages in some production itself, purchases a substantial part of the economy's output, levies taxes, and makes transfer payments to households. Although some, or even much, of what is developed in these chapters (and subsequent ones) would also be relevant to a highly socialized or collectivist society, in which the role of government is dominant, we shall not consider the substantial modifications that are necessary in measuring economic activity in such a society.

THE CONCEPT OF NATIONAL INCOME

We may define an *individual's* income as the money value of his earnings from the productive services currently rendered by him or by his property. The macroeconomic concept of **national income** is nothing more than the sum of all individual incomes so defined. Income is obviously a flow concept, measured, in practice, by recording and summing the individual income payments or attributions occurring during a period of finite length.

Defining income as *earnings* distinguishes it from income *receipts*. Some of the income earned during a period may not be received by any individual—either because it is taxed away before receipt or is somewhere retained (for example, the retained profits of a corporation), possibly to be paid (and received) at a later date. On the other hand, income receipts may exceed earnings either through delayed payment of past earnings in excess of current retentions, or through **transfer payments** which do not represent earnings from productive services, past or present. (Welfare payments, social security benefits, and veterans' benefits are examples of "government transfer payments"; bad debts of consumers to businesses, or business contributions to charity are types of "business transfer payments"; gifts or income sharing among individuals are "interpersonal transfers.")

Income must be clearly distinguished from mere asset transformations. If I sell a house, a bond, or a patent right, the proceeds of that sale are obviously not income. Or, if a debt is repaid, the amount of the repayment is not income. All that has happened is that one form of wealth (house, bond, patent right, debt claim) has been transferred into another form—usually cash. On the other hand, the current flow of services from the house, interest from the bond or other debt claim, and royalties from the patent are income.

A special problem is presented by capital gains, arising from an increase in the money value of an asset, whether "realized" by sale of the asset, or "unrealized." The gain represents neither an asset transfer nor true income, except perhaps to the person who is in the business of buying and selling assets and whose ability to buy for less than he sells is the source of his livelihood. In theory, as well as in practice, the borderline between this case and the true capital gain (which is of the nature of a windfall) is hard to draw, but we need not become entangled here in this problem. The ordinary capital gain—for example, from the appreciation of share prices or real estate—does not represent earnings from current productive services; hence, it is not income.

Theoretically, we should deduct from gross earnings all costs that the individual must incur in order to permit the earning of his income. For the worker, this might include the costs of tools, which he must himself supply, union dues, travel to work; for the property owner, brokerage fees, bank charges, safe-deposit box rentals (to the extent that the box is used to keep securities rather than the family jewels). In practice few of these are deducted. One reason is that the borderline is impossible to draw clearly between outlays made in order to permit the earning of income, and outlays that represent merely the use or enjoyment of income. For example, in order to earn, one must eat and be clothed; but we cannot really say how much food and clothing constitute a cost rather than the enjoyment of income. Thus, we deduct nothing for these.

When we come to income earned from ownership of a business enterprise, however, outlays made in order to earn income are all-important, are fairly easily defined, and must obviously be deducted. Business income is, of course, only one species of individual income—corporate profits are, in principle, the earnings of the individual stockholders. However, it is obvious that the gross receipts of a business are not the same thing as the income of its owners. Unlike most consumer expenditures, most business outlays are incurred in order to earn income. (Even here there are some minor ambiguities—for example, in connection with operation of the family farm, often described as a "way of life" as much as a means of livelihood.) Thus, all national income accounting (like private accounting) recognizes that business expenses must be deducted in order to arrive at that national income which represents the earnings (profits) from ownership of an enterprise.

Some of the specific problems connected with this calculation of profit-type incomes will be indicated later; for now, it is enough to recognize that **national income** (NI) is the sum of (a) wages, salaries, commissions, bonuses, and other forms of employee earnings (before deduction of any taxes or social security contributions); (b) net income from rentals and royalties; (c) interest income; and (d) profits, whether of a corporation, partnership, or proprietorship, whether paid out to owners or retained in the business, and before deduction of taxes based on income.

We can also subdivide national income by the sector in which it is earned: wages and salaries and supplements thereto, for instance, are paid by business firms; by governments; by private nonprofit organizations; by households; by foreign or international firms or organizations. Each of these sectors could be further subdivided in any convenient way, for example, the business sector by industry.

An alternative income concept is that of **disposable personal income** (DI). This is, first, a *receipts* rather than an earnings concept, and it is computed after taxes and social security contributions. Thus, to go from national income to disposable income we must add receipts that are not payments for current productive services (government and business transfer payments), and we must deduct all earnings not currently received and all taxes (social security contributions of employees and employers, corporate profits taxes and retained corporate earnings, and personal taxes). It is this figure that consumers can "dispose of"—spend as they choose or save.

An intermediate income concept is also used in the United States accounts, namely **personal income**. This is disposable income plus personal taxes; or current personal income receipts after deducting social security contributions but before deduction of personal taxes. The main reason for this concept is the practical one that it can be computed *monthly*, and is available fairly promptly after the end of the month, providing a reasonable approximation of current changes in national and disposable income and other aggregates.

THE CONCEPT OF NATIONAL PRODUCT

National product is a measure of the value of the economy's aggregate current output of goods and services. In the type of economy with which this book is concerned, most national product is produced in the private business sector; thus each good and service so produced can be valued at the market price it commands (including whatever sales taxes—or other "indirect" taxes—enter into the price at which it is sold). National product is also a flow concept, measured in practice by accumulating sales or other transactions or attributions over a period of time. National product measures the volume of productive activity currently occurring; it is not intended to measure—nor does it more than approximate—consumer welfare. Nor (especially in the case of *gross* national product) does it fully reflect changes in the economy's ability to sustain or increase production and welfare in the future.

The main conceptual difficulties in defining national product relate to the avoidance of double counting. We should not count as output the value of bread, the flour that went into the bread, the wheat that produced the flour, and the fertilizer that helped grow the wheat. Despite all the steps in the process, we end up only with the bread—bread is the product, not bread plus flour plus wheat plus fertilizer. In other words, we want to count only "final products," excluding "intermediate products." Final products might be limited to consumer goods and goods produced for government (collective consumption). In practice, however, we also include in final output the production of new capital goods, and any increase in inventories of intermediate or final products. The problems raised by these inclusions need further consideration.

Capital Goods

It is clear that new capital goods are not final products in the same sense as are goods produced for the use of consumers or governments. They are certainly not wanted for their own sake but only to produce (directly or indirectly) other final products. The services of plant and machinery that contribute to the production of bread are essentially like the services of the flour. Machine methods are often more productive than hand methods; therefore, machinery is produced and used. But sooner or later this production of machines means that more bread will be produced than otherwise. Having counted the value of the bread produced, why should we also count the value of the machinery produced?

One reason is that machines are unlike flour in that the machines render their services over a period of years. What is produced this year in the form of a new machine is an instrument which will contribute to production of bread for many years to come. But does this really make much difference? The value of the machine (and of the resources that went into the production of the machine) will sooner or later be included in the value of the output of bread; why should it be counted in addition to counting the bread? In fact, the value of the machine—and of the resources that produced it—is *derived from* the value of the bread, in just the same sense as is the value of the flour.

The argument that we should not include capital goods in national product would be particularly convincing if (a) all production of capital goods merely went to replace other capital goods as they wore out, and if (b) this wearing out occurred smoothly over time. Suppose, for example, that ten machines are used in bread making, each machine lasting ten years, with one wearing out and being replaced each year. Here we can clearly see that the value of the bread includes the value of the machines in exactly the same way as it does the flour, and we should probably not even be tempted to count both bread and machines as final product. It would be clear that to do so would be double counting of the same nature as adding bread and flour.

Of course, we rarely have so even a correspondence of wearing out and replacement. Suppose all ten machines wear out and must be replaced in a single year; then none for the next nine. If we count only bread as a final product, we will fail to recognize that in the tenth year, either the total production of the economy is in a real sense greater than in the other nine (if bread output is maintained constant, while machine production also occurs), *or* that any dip in bread output in the tenth year (if resources are diverted from bread making to machinery making) does not represent a real decline in production. Output only of consumer and government goods is thus not an adequate measure of the value of *current production* (from which current incomes are earned).

Thus, even if all production of machinery were merely for replacement, we get a more accurate picture of the year to year movements of production if we add together the production of bread and the production of plant and machinery. We call this a **gross national product** (GNP), however, in order to recognize the element of double counting. **Net national product** (NNP) deducts, each year, an allowance—called **depreciation**, or **capital consumption**—for the using up of plant and machine services. In our simple and extreme example in which all machines wore

TABLE 2-1
Hypothetical Gross and Net Products, Totals and by Years

Year	Bread Output	Machinery Output	Gross Product	Depreciation	Net Product
1	$200	—	$200	$40	$160
2	200	—	200	40	160
3	200	—	200	40	160
4	200	—	200	40	160
5	200	—	200	40	160
6	200	—	200	40	160
7	200	—	200	40	160
8	200	—	200	40	160
9	200	—	200	40	160
10	200	400	600	40	560
Ten-year total	$2000	$400	$2400	$400	$2000

out and were replaced in one year, the calculations would be as in Table 2-1 (we assume bread output continues unchanged in the year of machine replacement).

It is clear that either the gross or net product column gives a better picture of the year to year movement of productive activity in the economy than does the measurement of bread output alone. It must, however, also be recognized that, taking the ten-year period as a whole, the sum of the bread output column is the same as the sum of the net product column. Sooner or later, in this case, counting the bread also counts the value of the machines.

However, in addition to reflecting any unevenness of replacement investment, both gross and net product also reflect any net growth, over time, in the value of the total stock of capital goods, through new production of plant and equipment in excess of replacement. One could still argue that any such enlargment of the stock of capital goods will, sooner or later, contribute to an enlarged output of "true" final products and that it is enough to count these final products if and when they emerge. But, if net investment is usually positive (new production exceeds replacement), we are continually late in recognizing this if we wait for the final output to increase. More important, the well-known volatility in investment activity—and in the use of productive services in creating new capital—would not be reflected.

Thus it proves useful to measure a gross product, which consists of the output of "true" final goods, plus the production of new capital goods; and a net product, which is the output of consumer and government goods, plus the net increase in the stock of capital goods—new production of capital goods in excess of replacement.

However, it must be recognized that in practice we have no true measure of the capital goods that wear out or become obsolete in any given year and are replaced from the current production of new machines. The best we can do is to subtract from gross national product some computed "allowance" for **capital consumption** or **depreciation**, in order to give us an approximation of net national product. Until 1976, this subtraction was represented by the particular form of depreciation allowance that private accountants were allowed to treat as a current cost for the purpose of computing the profits on which income taxes are based. Since these tax rules changed from time to time, this made the net national product for any particular year an especially arbitrary figure. To be sure, these private accounting allowances had the useful property that the total of all depreciation allowances taken with respect to any capital good over its life span exactly equalled its original cost. Thus, at some time (although not necessarily at precisely the right time) the net national product account would reflect deductions that recognized that the value of total net "final output" would not include any value for machines other than, or in addition to, the value of the final products of the machines. Note, however, that if the price of the machine had changed over its life span, the sum of the depreciation over its life would not equal its replacement cost.

Beginning in 1976, however, the treatment of depreciation in the U.S. accounts has been radically revised and has become both more economically meaningful and rather more complicated. In the first place, the national income accounts now use an estimate of aggregate depreciation, which is made by national income statisticians rather than by individual tax accountants, and which—although still arbitrary—perhaps better reflects the real "using up" in any particular year of the productive services embodied in existing capital goods. Further, in recognition of the much more rapid inflation of recent years, the tie between the total depreciation taken on any asset over its lifetime and the *original cost* of that asset is now broken; instead, the estimated "physical" depreciation in any particular year is valued in terms of the price level of that year. Since depreciation is a current cost of production, the resulting profits as measured by firms, their owners, and the government tax collectors now no longer correspond to the national income accountants' new definition of profits based on the new estimates of depreciation. However, at this point we shall not discuss these problems, for they are not relevant to the immediate uses we shall make of national income concepts.

Inventory Changes

Problems closely related to those just discussed arise with respect to inventory changes. Suppose that in some year the nation produces more wheat than is used in the production of flour (which is then used for bread). Our output that year can be said to include not only the final product, bread, but also the unused wheat. Again, we could refuse to count this extra wheat as part of this year's national product, reasoning that it would, another year, permit more bread to be made. Instead, we count as this year's product the true final output (which incorporates the value of the wheat used to make this year's bread), plus the increase in inventories of intermediate goods (or less any inventory decrease: if we use up some of our first-of-year stock of wheat in producing bread, we choose to say that our output this year is the output of bread, less the decrease in wheat inventories). Again, we do this in order better to measure the timing of productive activity.

Since there can also be changes in inventories of *final* goods (if we sell more than we produce, or vice versa) which clearly need to be reflected in our measurement of output, we can define national product as the current *sales* (or, the same thing, *purchases*) of consumer, government, and capital goods, plus the value of any increase in inventories, whether it is of final or of intermediate goods. In fact, this is always the way we go about measuring national product: national product equals purchases of final goods plus inventory increase. The change of inventories may be valued in any of several ways, and each creates problems for national income accounting. For now we merely assume that the change is somehow valued in money terms.

Even in a predominantly business economy considerable production occurs as well in households, in private nonprofit organizations, and—very importantly—in government. It should be clear both that this needs to be included in GNP, and that its measurement involves special problems. Inasmuch as we are about to assume—for the purpose of this book—that all production occurs in the business sector, we will skip any discussion of the measurement of nonbusiness production.

Exports and Imports

One further adjustment remains to be noted. Any national economy exports some part of each year's output (both of final and of intermediate goods). This output is obviously part of domestic national product, and should be added to domestic final sales plus inventory increase. Imported products on the other hand obviously are not part of domestic output and should not be counted. However, when we choose to measure domestic output in terms of the total *purchases* by final buyers (consumers, government, and businesses insofar as they purchase new capital goods and add to their inventories), we do not (for good reasons which we need not discuss) limit these purchases to those made from *domestic* producers. Thus, for example, an imported machine is included as part of business gross investment or a vacation trip abroad as part of consumer purchases. Moreover, when we value output sold by domestic producers of final goods at market prices, we overstate the value of domestic production to the extent that these goods incorporate imported *materials*. A $200 suit of clothes made domestically, but using British woolens, does not represent $200 worth of United States production. The $50 worth of cloth—which is surely part of the value of the suit—represents part of the British national product, not of ours.

We handle both of these problems very simply: we add to the total purchases by domestic final buyers (plus inventory increase) not our total exports but our *net exports*. That is, we include as a separate category of United States GNP the value of goods and services exported less the value of goods and services imported, whether these are final or intermediate goods. This clearly gives the correct total value of United States production; but it does not provide a separate measurement of consumer, government, or business purchases of United States domestic output.

NATIONAL INCOME AND PRODUCT IN A SIMPLIFIED ECONOMY

The concepts of national income and national product—and, particularly, an understanding of the relationships among the several measures—are very much simplified if we make two major assumptions, as follows:

1. All production occurs in business firms; government, households, and nonprofit institutions are only purchasers—not producers—of final goods and services; they own no capital goods, hire no workers, and buy no intermediate products. This also implies that all residential housing is owned by businesses, with only the services of the houses sold to households, whose rental payments measure the correct current production of housing services. It is also easiest if we assume that all land and natural resources are owned by households, which sell the productive services of the land or other resources to businesses, for use in production.
2. The economy has no international economic relations—it is a "closed economy."

These assumptions will be maintained essentially throughout this book.[1]

Given the assumption that production occurs only in business firms, all national income (NI) is earned in the business sector; it consists of wages and salaries and other forms of employee compensation (before taxes),

---

[1] In addition, several other less drastic and less important assumptions are made for most of the discussion: for example, that businesses and governments borrow only from (and pay interest to) households; that households do not borrow or pay interest at all; and that businesses do not own other businesses—rather, all businesses are owned directly by households.

paid by businesses for the services of workers; all contractual payments of interest, rents, and royalties for the services of property; plus the profits (before taxes) earned by businesses (for their owners).

Gross national product (GNP) also originates entirely in the business sector. It consists of the value of goods and services produced for and sold to consumers and governments, plus the value of capital goods produced for and sold to other businesses, plus the value of any increase in inventories—that is, the value of goods produced (or purchased) but neither used in production nor sold during the period for which GNP is measured. Looking at these as categories of purchases or expenditures rather than of production or sales, GNP can be said to consist of consumers' and governments' purchases of goods and services, plus businesses' purchases from other businesses of capital goods, plus goods produced or purchased by businesses but not used in other production nor sold. Net national product equals gross national product less capital consumption allowances.

What now must be the relationship between the size of the national income and of the gross and net national products?

The "Circular Flow" of Production and Incomes

We can answer this question in any of several ways. We shall do it first in a visual presentation, based on an elaboration of the "circular-flow" diagram that occurs in an early chapter of a great many introductory economic textbooks. This circular-flow diagram usually shows two entities, one called "business," the other "households." Households purchase the entire product of business, giving to business in payment a flow of money receipts precisely equal to the flow of money payments that business makes to households for the productive services which their members render to businesses. Thus, payments go around a "circle" from business to households to business, and so on. Flowing in the opposite direction from these money payments are flows of goods and services: business products flow from business to households, and productive services flow from households to business. Although this diagram conveys an important understanding of the way in which incomes are earned and used in a business-organized society, it neglects many important qualifications, among others, sales among businesses, the existence and economic role of government, and the existence of saving and investment.

Figure 2-1 provides a rather more elaborate visualization of the circular flow, although still highly oversimplified (by the assumptions listed earlier) from the flows of the "real world." This figure considers *three* entities among which flow money payments, productive services, and produced goods and services: businesses (at the top), governments (in the middle), and households (at the bottom). The *width* of all flows here represents their magnitude measured in dollars. Money payments flow *out* from businesses to the right—to other businesses (for intermediate goods)

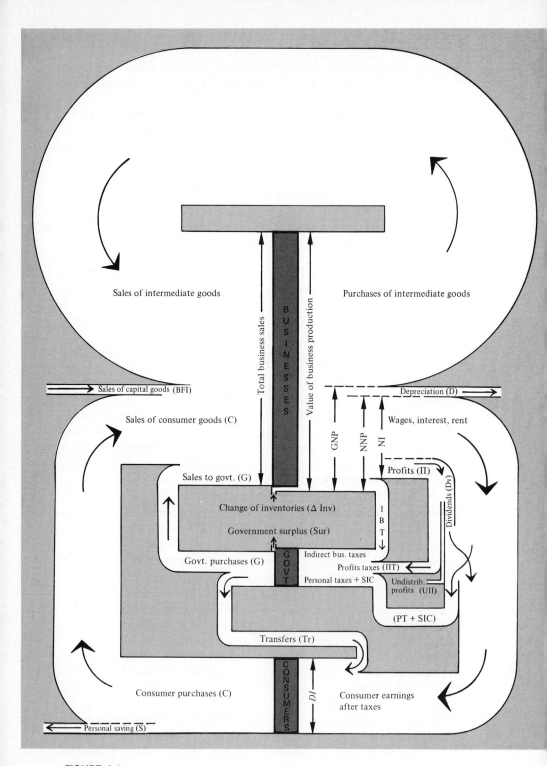

FIGURE 2-1

around the upper "loop," and to the other two sectors below; payments received by business, in the form of sales revenues, flow *in* from the left. Receipts enter households and governments from the right, and their payments flow out to the left. Corresponding to most of the payments flows are opposite and equal flows of goods and services (although not labeled as such): produced goods and services flowing out from businesses to the left; flows of productive services from households and of business intermediate products flowing into business at the right.

We may conveniently start in the middle of the figure with a measurement (just left of center) of the revenue flow labeled, "Total business sales." The sales revenue of each firm, and thus the aggregate of these sales revenues, are classified by type of buyer: produced goods and services are sold to other businesses, to households, and to governments. Given the exclusion of export sales, this exhausts all the possible types of customers. Sales to other businesses, moreover, are divided into two sub-categories, on the basis not of any characteristic of the selling or purchasing firm, but of the purpose (and thus the accounting treatment) of the *purchase*; in particular, whether the purchase is of (that is, is accounted for by the purchaser as) a capital good, the cost of which will be considered as applicable to several years' outputs, or whether it is (that is, is accounted for as) a current input into the production of other goods, and is thus an intermediate good.

This division of business sales appears in the figure just at the left of center: from top to bottom, sales to other businesses of intermediate goods, sales of capital goods to other businesses (**business fixed investment, BFI**), sales to consumers (C), and sales to governments (G). In a complex economy, with much division of labor, sales of intermediate goods among business firms are probably several times as large as sales of final output (including, for example, the sale of most consumer goods from manufac-turers to wholesalers, and from wholesalers to retailers, prior to their sale to consumers). Thus, even the fat "loop" shown at the top of the diagram does not provide a quantitatively realistic representation of the volume of intermediate relative to final sales.

Total business sales fall short of the total value of business production (that is measured just right of center) by the amount of any accumulation of inventories—goods purchased or produced by business but not used in production or sold. If we now deduct from the value of total business production the volume of intermediate sales (as is done by the measure-ment a bit further to the right), we find that we have measured the economy's **gross national product** (GNP). This can be broken down, of course, into the three categories of sales shown left of center: sales to government, or **government purchases of goods and services** (G); sales of consumer goods, or **personal consumption expenditures** (C); sales of capi-tal goods or **business fixed investment** (BFI); plus the value of **change of inventories** (ΔInv).

This same total value of business production can also be identified as the sum of all business costs and profits. The identity of these two quantities stems from the definition of profits as a residual: profits are *defined* (for the firm, and therefore for the economy) as the total value of goods produced, less all costs of producing them. The breakdown of these costs and profits is shown (on the right) as consisting of business purchases of intermediate goods—the noncapital goods that businesses purchase from other businesses; wages, interest, rent—the incomes which employers agree to pay to workers and suppliers of property services; depreciation (D)—the bookkeeping allowance which is made for the current loss of value of business capital goods; indirect business taxes (IBT)—taxes not based on income, payrolls, or profits, such as sales or property taxes; and, finally, profits before taxes (Π)—the residual obtained by subtracting all of the costs from the value of the production. Note that the amount of the profits thus depends on the way in which depreciation is calculated, and on the values attributed to additions to inventories. Profits thus depend not only on transactions, but also on accounting conventions. Here we assume that depreciation and the valuation of inventories are measured in exactly the same way by the firms and by the national-income statisticians.

Further to the right of the diagram, the total earnings of persons from business operations are measured as **national income** (NI). This differs from GNP by the amount of **depreciation** (D), and by the amount of **indirect business taxes** (IBT)—neither constitute any person's earnings. That is, the prices at which goods are sold must (by the definition of profits) cover all costs and profits which are persons' earnings, as well as all depreciation charges and taxes levied on their sale, which are not earnings. **Net national product** (NNP) thus differs from **national income** (NI) only by the **indirect taxes**, and from **gross national product** (GNP) only by **depreciation** (D).

At the bottom of the figure, the net receipts of consumers are measured as **disposable income** (DI). This differs from national income by the *subtraction* from the latter of that part of profits not received by households—that is, **profits taxes** (ΠT) and **undistributed profits** (UΠ)—as well as by the subtraction of **personal taxes** (PT) and **social insurance contributions** (SIC); it also differs by the *addition* of **government transfer payments** and **government interest** (Tr). At the lower left corner, disposable income is shown as divided between **personal saving** (S) and **personal consumption expenditures** (C).

Thus, the lower half of the figure illustrates a clockwise *circular flow* of consumers' incomes—which arise in the production of the GNP, and much of which are spent by consumers in the purchase of the largest part of that production. However, some part of the value of the GNP "leaks out" of the circular flow as depreciation and indirect taxes without entering consumers' earnings. A larger part leaks out to government (*after* measurement as earnings) in the form of taxes imposed on earnings: profit taxes

(IIT), personal taxes (PT), and social insurance contributions (SIC); and another part of earnings leaks out into undistributed profits. What remains of consumers' earnings, augmented by government transfers and interest (Tr), and after a further leakage into personal savings (S), returns to business in the purchase of final output (C).

The tax leakages into government are seen to return to the circular flow by way of **government purchases** (G) or **transfers** and **interest** (Tr). However, there may still be a net leakage if there is a **government surplus** (Sur), or an "injection" into the flow if there is a **deficit** (−Sur). A further injection comes in the form of business purchases of capital goods and inventory accumulation. The diagram does not (although it could) trace the flow of **gross business saving** (undistributed profits plus depreciation), plus the transfer from persons to business of personal savings (through all of which business investment in capital goods and inventories may be financed). However, a little later we will see algebraically what the relationship between these particular leakages and injections must be.

It should be clear from the figure that we can ignore entirely the circular flow of intermediate product, produced by businesses and sold to other businesses, even though these constitute the entire or principal part of many firms' output, and their purchase the major cost of production for most firms. These cancel out completely in terms of their effects on measurement either of "final" output or incomes.

Algebraic Statement of Accounting Relationships

We can, of course, summarize algebraically the relationships pictured in Figure 2-1. We start with the definitions:

$$(1) \qquad GNP \equiv C + G + BFI + \Delta Inv$$

or gross national product equals purchases (sales) of consumer goods, government goods, and business capital goods, plus inventory increase; and

$$(2) \qquad NI \equiv GNP - IBT - D$$

or, national income equals gross national product less indirect business taxes and depreciation. Substituting from (1) into (2) gives

$$(3) \qquad NI \equiv C + G + BFI + \Delta Inv - IBT - D$$

We also derive another relationship involving incomes and outputs. Start by defining

$$(4) \qquad DI \equiv NI - \Pi T - PT - SIC - U\Pi + Tr$$

or disposable income equals national income less direct taxes ($\Pi T, PT, SIC$), less undistributed profits and plus transfer payments; and

$$(5) \qquad S \equiv DI - C$$

or personal saving equals disposable income less consumption spending. Substituting (4) into (5) and rearranging, we have

(6) $$NI \equiv C + S + \Pi T + U\Pi + PT + SIC - Tr$$

From (3) and (6), we can now derive:

(7) $$G + BFI + \Delta Inv - IBT - D \equiv S + \Pi T + U\Pi + PT + SIC - Tr$$

Many of the items appearing in (7) are either government expenditures (G and Tr) or are government revenues ($IBT, PT, SIC, \Pi T$). Indeed, all of the items which would appear in a (simplified) government account (except one—the net balance) appear in equation (7). Rearrange (7) to put these government items all on one side:

(7a) $$IBT + \Pi T + PT + SIC - G - Tr \equiv BFI + \Delta Inv - D - U\Pi - S$$

The expression on the left can easily be seen to equal the government surplus (Sur)—the excess of revenues over expenditures. Thus, we can substitute this new symbol into (7a) to obtain, with rearrangement:

(8) $$GI \equiv BFI + \Delta Inv \equiv D + U\Pi + S + Sur$$

or **gross investment,** GI (defined as business fixed investment plus inventory increase), equals **gross business saving** (depreciation plus undistributed profits), plus personal saving, plus government saving. If we prefer to treat investment on a net basis,

(9) $$I \equiv U\Pi + S + Sur$$

where I (**net investment**)$\equiv GI - D$. If the surplus is negative—that is, is a **deficit** (Def)—we can write this as

(10) $$I + Def \equiv S + U\Pi$$

Net investment plus deficit equals personal saving plus "*net* business saving."

Although this accounting system ignores many minor categories of production, income, and expenditures—and applies only to a closed economy—it is quite adequate for all the simpler formations we shall make of macroeconomic theory.

Indeed a good deal of macroeconomic theory uses or implies a set of social accounts even less complicated than that set forth above. For example, Keyne's *General Theory of Employment, Interest, and Money* used a system of accounts which ignored all government transactions, and so does a good deal of current purely theoretical literature. Inventory changes and profit retentions are also often ignored. The reason for using accounts which omit government is perhaps understandable. Economic theory traditionally deals with private economic behavior—the actions of households in earning and spending their incomes, and of businessmen in hiring factors of production, producing, and selling goods and services. All of these activities are oriented to the market and are affected mainly by the market. Government actions—in taxing, borrowing, and spending—are not market determined but are decided instead by a political process.

To be sure, government action is increasingly taken in order to offset or prevent market results that fail to conform to certain social standards. But to know what government action is called for in order to achieve desired social ends, one may wish to understand how market forces would operate in the absence of government. Hence, the pure theory often assumes an economy with no government. Such an economy has very simple national accounts: national product (net) equals national income. If we further assume no corporations (or else the automatic payout of all corporate profits) national income and product also equal disposable income.

However, even the business sector of an economy with a government cannot possibly operate in the same way as in its absence; moreover, purposeful government intervention must now be taken for granted. Thus—even for theoretical purposes—we need to use accounts which, at the very least, include government, as the system developed above does. The system remains, of course, dreadfully unrealistic by ruling out all international transactions and any government or household production (as well as a host of other complex—although fortunately minor—details).

For any detailed empirical analysis of any particular national economy—we need to use a complete national accounting system, and must understand its finer points. Presenting and explaining such a system is a task not undertaken in this book.[2]

REAL NATIONAL PRODUCT AND THE PRICE LEVEL

National product, net or gross, can be thought of as comprising a flow of real goods and services, not a flow of money payments. The particular goods and services included are those we choose to identify as "final products"—those going to consumers, government, or abroad, plus any goods that are added to business inventories or provide a gross or net addition to productive capacity in the form of structures and equipment. We can measure the current output of each of these individual goods and services in terms of any or a number of its physical characteristics: its weight (ounces, pounds, or tons), its surface dimensions, its energy equivalent, its productive capability, and so on. But we cannot meaningfully measure total output by summing these physical measurements.

[2] The most recent statistical and conceptual revision of the United States national income and product accounting system was presented and discussed in *Survey of Current Business*, January 1976, Parts I and II (Vol. 56, No. 1). For a summary using the new definitions see Table A, Part I, pp. 4–5; for definitions of all of the entries, see Part I, pp. 34–38.

Obviously, for example, the total "quantity" even of all goods whose individual quantities are adequately described by weight—soft coal, diamonds, prime beef steak, and so on—cannot meaningfully be described by their combined weight. Instead, in summarizing the economic quantity of any collection of diverse goods and services—so that we may *compare* its "size" at one time or place with that at another—we express the output of each good in terms of its money value, add these values, and call the total the national product. Only in this way can we recognize the differing economic importance of the various multitudinous goods and services.

We are all aware, however, that two or more such totals of money value can differ because of differences in the physical quantities of the goods represented, or in the prices at which some or all of the goods are valued, or both. Thus we seek some method of separating that part of any difference in the money value of national products that is due to difference in prices from that which is the "real" or "physical" difference. Various methods exist for identifying these two elements of difference in totals, and the results of the several methods will agree precisely only under very unusual circumstance—for example, that physical quantities of all goods (*or* their prices) differ in some fixed proportion as among the several collections being compared: not a very common case.

One method of computing *real* quantities of GNP's, (or of any other collection of disparate goods) is to value all the goods in each collection at an identical constant set of prices—for example, the prices that prevailed in some base period. This is the method used in the United States GNP accounts: United States GNP in constant prices is obtained (in principle) by multiplying the physical quantity of each good produced in each year or calendar quarter times its unit price in year 1972, then summing the total value of all goods for each year or quarter. The movement of this total can be said to be entirely due to quantity changes, since all prices were held constant. Table 2-2 shows that United States GNP in 1976 is estimated at $1,706.5 billion in "current" (that is, 1976) prices. But, measured in 1972 prices, United States GNP in 1976 is instead $1,274.7 billion. These 1976 values compare with a 1972 GNP in current prices of $1,171.1 billion [which was of course also the 1972 GNP in constant (1972) prices]. Thus, in current prices, GNP rose 46 percent from 1972 to 1976; in constant (1972) prices, GNP advanced by the much smaller 9 percent. We can also use the constant price data for comparisons which do not include the base year. For example, in 1975, GNP in 1972 prices was 98.7 percent of its value in 1974—that is, it fell by 1.3 percent between the two years. In contrast, in current prices, GNP in 1975 was 108.2 percent of its 1974 level—that is, it advanced by 8.2 percent.

We can now use the first two columns of Table 2-2 to compute a third. If we divide 1974 GNP in current prices by 1974 GNP in constant prices, then multiply by 100, we get 116.02. We call this result an **implicit deflator**, and

TABLE 2-2
U.S. GNP in Current and in Constant (1972) Prices, and GNP Implicit Deflator

Year	GNP in current prices (billions of dollars)	GNP in constant (1972) prices (billions of dollars)	Implicit Deflator
1970	982.4	1,075.3	91.36
1971	1,063.4	1,107.5	96.02
1972	1,171.1	1,171.1	100.00
1973	1,306.6	1,235.0	105.80
1974	1,412.9	1,217.8	116.02
1975	1,528.8	1,202.1	127.18
1976	1,706.5	1,274.7	133.88

interpret it to mean that, on the average, prices of goods and services comprising GNP advanced by 16.02 percent between 1972 and 1974. The similar implicit deflator for 1975 in turn is 127.18, meaning that the total price advance over the three years was 27.18 percent. We can now find the movement of prices from 1974 to 1975 by dividing the latter by the former to find that the average of prices of goods and services comprising GNP rose by 9.6 percent.

An alternative procedure for separating changes in the money value of GNP into two elements—one "physical" the other in "price levels"—would be to construct an "explicit" rather than an "implicit" price index. One way to do this would be to hold the physical quantities of each good and service constant at some level—for example, the level of 1972, or of any other year—and then calculate what the money value of this constant physical collection would be at the actual prices that prevailed in each year or quarter. The movement in this total could be thought of as due only to price change, since the physical quantities were the same. If we took this total value as equal to 100.0 in some particular base year—for example, 1972—we could then divide each other such figure by the base-year's GNP in current prices, and call the resulting series a **GNP price index**. Its level and movement would closely resemble—but by no means coincide with—the implicit deflator column shown in Table 2-2.

We could then use this GNP price index to compute a "real GNP" for each period by dividing ("deflating") the value of GNP at current prices by the GNP price index for that period, then multiplying by 100. This would produce a series that would closely resemble in its movements the second column in Table 2-2—but by no means coincide with it. On this procedure, the real GNP data would be "implicit," whereas the price index was "explicit"—just the opposite of the procedure used in Table 2-2.

If we now were to repeat *either* procedure *using some other year as base period*, we would get price and "real" quantity series whose *relative* movements would again resemble those shown in Table 2-2—but would not coincide with it—or with each other.

We are not going to consider the complex theoretical and practical questions of which basic procedure—the explicit calculation of real quantities and the implicit calculation of average prices, or the reverse—is superior or for what purpose it may be preferable, nor will we evaluate the merits of the use of a constant base period in the past versus the use always of the current year as the base period. (It should be noted that the latter procedure would require recalculating, each year or quarter, all past values—thus producing a slighly different view now of what happened to prices and quantities in the past than the view we had of that same past last year or the year before—which would be both inconvenient and a bit unsettling.) We will only note that the United States, and many other national income accounts, use the method of explicit measurement of real GNP, and therefore, of implicit deflators. We also note that a fixed base period is ordinarily used to evaluate real output and average prices over a consecutive period of a few years; the base is then shifted forward to a later year, and the subsequent results "chained" to the previous ones.[3]

It should be noted that exactly the same procedures as described previously are possible, and are used, for the various subaggregates of GNP, in order to separate their changes, as well, into two components, one real and one of prices. Thus, the United States national income and product accounts show personal consumption expenditures (PCE) in 1972 prices and an implicit deflator for PCE. The same procedure is followed for government purchases of goods and services, for private gross domestic investment, and for net exports. These, in turn, can be broken down into sub-subaggregates in whatever detail is desired, each measured not only in current but also in constant prices and with its own implicit deflator. It should be noted that on this method of calculation, the subaggregates in constant prices will necessarily add up to the total calculated in constant prices. The implicit deflator for GNP will be a weighted average of the deflators for the sectors, the weights being the relative shares of the sectors in GNP. Since these shares change each year, so would the relative weights.

There are also, of course, other price indexes not derived from or directly related to national income and product accounts, particularly the *consumer price index* and the *wholesale price index*. These are both *explicit* measures of price change. Because we will make essentially no use of them

[3] For example, when (in January 1976), the base period for GNP was last shifted forward—from 1958 to 1972—all real GNPs previously calculated for years prior to 1972 were multiplied by the ratio of 1972 GNP in 1972 prices to 1972 GNP in 1958 prices. This did not alter *relative* movements of real GNP (nor of prices) as previously calculated through 1972. However, the relative movements of real GNP and prices for years 1972 through 1975, as previously calculated on the base of 1958, were modestly altered through use of the new base. (However, other conceptual changes and statistical corrections which were introduced at the same time *did* alter slightly the relative moments prior to 1972.)

in this book, we will not take the space to explain their construction. In fact, other than because they long precede in time the development of national product data and because people are used to hearing about them and using them, there is really little reason for them to exist. In almost any respect, the implicit GNP deflator of personal consumption expenditures is a superior measure of the change in prices consumers pay (to the limited extent that the two indexes diverge). The wholesale price index measures the average movement of a miscellaneous collection of goods the content of which has no intelligible justification. To be sure, almost all of the basic data used in the construction of the GNP deflators has been obtained for the purpose of constructing these two indexes; but this in itself does not require or justify their continued calculation.

NATIONAL WEALTH

Recent economic theory has increasingly stressed the importance of national wealth as a macroeconomic variable. It is therefore important to explore this concept and to understand how it might be measured.

We defined an individual's income as the amount of his earnings from the productive services currently rendered by him *or* by his property, and national income as the sum of all individual incomes. We can correspondingly define an individual's wealth as the value of his property, and the national wealth as the sum of all individual wealths. An obvious difference between the *coverage* of the concepts of national income and national wealth thus lies in the exclusion from wealth of any consideration relating to services rendered by persons, as opposed to those rendered by their property. The reason for this is that (in our society) the current money value of one's ability to render current and future labor services is not ordinarily measured as such. Certainly, it does not have a "market value," for persons are not allowed to buy or sell an enforceable claim on their own or another person's future services. To be sure, economists sometimes find it very illuminating to use the concept of "human wealth," in contrast to "nonhuman wealth," that is, property. And the value of this human wealth can even be estimated by "capitalizing" the estimated value of future labor services using some interest rate. However, at the individual level, the concept of human wealth has no quantitative real-world analog—except in a slave society.

National income, of course, is a flow variable. In contrast, national wealth is a stock variable. Like national income, national wealth is measured at some point in time (or as an average over some period of time), but it is not expressed as a rate per unit of time, for that has no meaning in the case of a stock variable. National wealth on the last day of December 1975 may have been $4.8 trillion. (But it was not $4.8 trillion per year, nor per month, nor per day.)

For the current discussion of wealth accounting, we continue to assume an economy without international economic relationships of any kind. And as it simplifies national income accounts if we assume no government production, it simplifies wealth accounting to assume that government neither produces national product nor engages in lending to the private sector.

National Wealth as a Collection of Physical Assets

Just as we have the several closely related aggregate flow concepts, such as national product, national income, and personal and disposable income, each of which represents a somewhat different way of looking at or attempting to measure the value of current productive activity, so we have several alternative ways of looking at or attempting to measure national wealth. Perhaps the simplest way of thinking about aggregate wealth is—like that of national product—as a "physical" concept. The national wealth is a collection of certain tangible and valuable objects. Thinking in this way, the broadest measure of national wealth would be the aggregate value of a country's land and other natural resources, land improvements, machinery and equipment, buildings and other structures, and inventories, including the inventories of consumers. Or, at least, it would be the value of those goods that are owned by someone, and are capable of being bought and sold and thus of having a market value. (Just as we do not include the current value of sunshine or rain in national income, we do not include the value of rivers, lakes, seas, air, or climate in our wealth. To the considerable extent that sunshine contributes to production, its contribution to output and income is of course measured in the value of that output and income. In a similar way, rivers contribute to the value of dams and generators, which are measured as wealth; but the rivers themselves are not.)

However, we may prefer (depending on our purpose) also to exclude certain further categories of physical assets. First of all, we may wish to exclude all nonproductive assets (for example, battleships or cathedrals)—assets not used for the production of goods or services included in the national product. Second, we may wish to exclude the value of all assets owned by government, thus further restricting the concept of national wealth to those objects directly or indirectly owned by "private" entities. (This is not an important exclusion if governments do not engage in substantial production.) These inclusions or exclusions obviously produce different totals. For the present we will deal only with the narrowest of these concepts of wealth, private, productive assets—often otherwise described as the **private capital stock**. (We shall refer later to the use of this concept as a measure of the aggregate capital input into production.) This stock of private productive assets can be subdivided into "man-made" wealth and land.

So far as possible, the individual items that make up this stock of physical wealth should be valued at market prices that reflect their relative scarcity and productivity. However, most items in the stock are not newly produced. Indeed, they may be of a type no longer produced, and there is often no effective secondhand market for the exchange of many of them. It is thus often difficult even to *estimate* a current market or replacement value for many specific items of wealth. We are forced to use an "adjusted book value" for much of it. This is usually based upon an earlier market price, at the time it was purchased by its present owner, adjusted in some arbitrary way for "depreciation," and also perhaps adjusted for the subsequent change in the price level of newly produced items of that class since the date of its production of purchase. As in the case of national product, we can measure this aggregate value "in current prices" (book or replacement) prevailing at the point in time for which wealth is measured, as well as in the constant prices of some base period. Changes in the latter would measure changes in "real" wealth.

The "physical" concept of private, productive, man-made wealth bears an obvious close relationship to the concept of private *net* domestic investment, in that the *current net production* of these kinds of assets is very close to what is measured as net investment. If private productive capital on December 31, 1976, was $4,000 billion, and on December 31, 1977, was $4,020 billion, net investment of $20 billion must have occurred between the two dates, adding $20 billions worth of plant, equipment, and inventories. However, consumers' stocks of durable goods, as well as their inventories of nondurables—shirts, canned goods, stationery—are also clearly part of national productive wealth, but the national income accounts ordinarily do not measure additions or subtractions to stocks of these assets as investment. In effect, these goods are treated as "consumed" at the moment of purchase. Thus, if we wanted our concept of wealth to include these stocks, and wished full consistency with the national income accounts, the concept of gross national product should be correspondingly changed to treat the net increase in consumer stocks as investment. Rather than their purchase being measured as their consumption, the value of the "current services" rendered in the using up of this stock would be estimated instead. (As will be seen in Chapter 16, some private estimates have in fact done this, at least for consumer durable goods. And for some purposes this makes a significant difference.) Fortunately, residential construction (and depreciation) are already treated as part of gross (and net) private investment in national income accounting, and only the value of current housing services is included in consumer purchases (although we have not here explained exactly how this is done in the case of owner-occupied houses). Treating houses as part of national wealth—indeed constituting a very substantial part of it—is quite consistent with their treatment in national income accounting. The physical quantity of land of course does not change; but neither are purchases of land treated as part of net investment (nor is "depletion" treated as part of capital consumption) in national income and product accounting. That is, land is part of wealth, but not of any change in (real) wealth.

The "physical" concept of wealth is thus conceptually relatively simple, and the relationhip of its change over time to national income accounting concepts is easy to grasp. To be sure, when we seek to measure either real wealth or real investment as prices change and technology alters, extremely complex problems arise in maintaining consistent treatment of stocks and flows. However, we have ducked these problems in our discussion of national income and product accounting. (For example, we have not explained the "inventory valuation adjustment" nor the "capital consumption adjustment" in national income.) We shall similarly avoid for now the equally difficult parallel problems in national wealth accounting.

National Wealth as the Aggregate Net Worth of Persons

There is, however, a second and very different concept of national wealth, which is framed not in terms of a collection of physical assets but as the aggregate of the net worth of all individuals in the society. **Net worth** is the difference between the aggregate value of all the assets which an individual or family owns (whether "financial" or physical) and the value of its debts (the "financial claims" which others have against it). For each individual or family, net worth is a relatively simple concept and the aggregation of these amounts for all families presents no special problems. To be sure, it raises tricky questions of how to value financial assets which either (a) cannot be traded and thus have no market value, for example, the pension claims the family owns, or (b) the market prices of which change over time, for example, stocks, bonds, and almost all other marketable financial assets other than money and deposits. (Again, we will duck the more difficult problems raised by price changes.)

Just as the physical assets which constitute the national wealth in the first concept are the cumulative product of all past net investment, so the national wealth, thought of as the aggregate net worth of individuals, is clearly the cumulative product of all past net personal saving. A person saves only by acquiring some kind of an asset—physical, financial, or monetary—or by repaying some debt, in either case enlarging his net worth. When a person dissaves, he either loses an asset or aquires a debt—in either case reducing his net worth. One can, of course, sell one kind of asset and acquire another, without saving or dissaving, and one can also borrow to acquire assets in excess of his saving; but neither of these increases net worth, individual or national. We saw that private productive national wealth (other than land) is the value of the stock created by the flow of net investment. Similarly, we now see that personal net worth is the value of the stock created by the flow of personal saving. Sometimes calling it **savings**, we shall refer to this concept whenever we refer to the wealth of consumers. We are now ready to investigate the relationship between the size of these two stocks.

To do this, we need to look in more detail at the components of personal net worth. Any individual's assets include some that are physical assets of the kind we have already considered—for example, house, car, household goods, and (in case of owners of unincorporated businesses) land, plant, equipment, and inventories. Aside from houses, however, the overwhelming bulk of individual assets consists of financial claims. These are of four general kinds. First, a relatively small number of individuals own **primary securities**: the stocks representing ownership claims against incorporated businesses, and the bonds, notes, commercial paper, bills, mortgages, and so on, representing the indebtedness of businesses, governments, or other individuals to the owners of these claims. Second, almost all individuals own varying amounts of **claims against** (or liabilities of) **financial intermediaries**: deposits or other accounts in banks or savings and loan associations, policies issued by insurance companies, shares in mutual funds, claims against pension funds, and the like. These usually constitute the bulk of households' assets. Third, a small number also own a personal **equity** in some **nonincorporated business**. Finally, all individuals own some of a fourth class of assets: the noninterest-bearing debts of government that are called **currency**.

Selected physical assets, primary securities, claims against financial intermediaries, equity in unincorporated businesses, and currency constitute the classes of assets that individuals or families own. Many or most also owe debts either to other persons, to nonfinancial businesses, or to financial intermediaries. The difference between the totals of assets and debts is personal net worth, and the aggregate of these net worths constitutes the second concept of national wealth.

We often show this total net worth of consumers in an arrangement called a "balance sheet." A **balance sheet** is a simple summary statement showing the values of the assets, the liabilities, and the net worth of a unit, arranged with assets in one column and liabilities and net worth in a second. Since net worth is defined as assets minus liabilities, it is clear that the *sums* of the entries in the two columns must be identical. This must be true of every individual balance sheet because of the way net worth is defined. It must therefore be true as well for the aggregate balance sheet of the household sector. Such an arrangement appears on page 50.

The Relationship Between Wealth as Physical Assets and as Personal Net Worth

What, now, is the relationship between national wealth viewed as a collection of productive physical assets, and national wealth viewed as the aggregate net worth of individuals? We can approach the answer by providing aggregate balance sheets for each of three other sectors of the

Balance Sheet

All Households

Land, residences, and consumer goods	Private debts owed
Primary securities owned	Personal net worth
Corporate stocks	
Private debts	
Government debts	
Claims on intermediaries owned	
Equity in unincorporated businesses	
Government money owned	
Total assets	Total liabilities and net worth

private economy. These are (1) nonfinancial corporations; (2) unincorporated nonfinancial businesses (including most professional practices, farms, and so on); and (3) financial intermediaries. Together with households, these three sectors comprise the entire private economy. We begin with the balance sheet for all nonfinancial corporations.

Balance Sheet

All Nonfinancial Corporations

Land, plant, equipment, inventories owned	Private debts owed
Primary securities owned	Corporate net worth
Corporate stocks	Corporate stock
Private debts	Surplus
Government debts	
Claims on intermediaries owned	
Government money owned	
Total assets	Total liabilities and net worth

Look first at the assets. At the top appear the physical assets: land, plant, equipment, and inventories. For nonfinancial corporations, these constitute the primary assets owned. In the case of plant and equipment, these assets should, in principle, be valued at approximate current market prices, recognizing whatever depreciation has occurred through use. In practice, they are instead likely to be valued at some kind of "original cost" less "book depreciation." Inventories, too, should be valued at current replacement prices, but may not be. Obviously, whatever valuation basis is used for the physical assets will be reflected in the size of corporate net worth. The remaining assets are financial, and their ownership is essentially incidental to the operations of nonfinancial firms. They consist of any stocks that corporations may own in other corporations—including their subsidiaries (these stocks are probably valued at acquisition cost, but, in principle, could and should all be adjusted to current market values); the debts owed by private entities (other than financial intermediaries) that corporations may own—including the substantial amounts of "trade credit" they may have extended to their customers; any bonds or other private debt securities which they are holding as an interest-bearing reserve for planned future capital expenditures or as protection against emergencies; any government debt held for the same purposes. In addition, corporations hold claims on financial intermediaries, including their demand and time deposits, and, finally, they all have a certain amount of currency in their tills. The total of these financial assets is, however, relatively small for most nonfinancial corporations—and the same is true for the aggregate of all such corporations.

In the right-hand column are shown all the corporations' debts, regardless of ownership of these claims—whether held, that is, by other nonfinancial businesses (including those which have extended "trade credit" to them), by banks or other financial intermediaries, or by households. These debts may take the form of bonds, mortgages, bank loans, commercial paper, unpaid bills, and so on. (Since we have assumed no government lending, there are no debts to government.) The remaining item is the net worth of the corporations. It will be divided between some nominal value for the stock certificates outstanding (representing the proceeds from the original sale of the stock) plus a "surplus"—which is simply the value of total assets less the financial liabilities and less the nominal value of the stock.[4] In principle, assuming all assets and liabilities are properly valued, the total net worth is what the business is worth and what its stockholders own—regardless of how it is subdivided and labeled.

The balance sheet for unincorporated nonfinancial businesses is essentially the same. As it appears below, the left-hand column is identical with that for corporations. And, on the right, the only difference is that we have called net worth "Personal equity of owners." This is the owners' investment in their businesses.

Balance Sheet
All Unincorporated Nonfinancial Businesses

Land, equipment, inventories owned	Private debts owed
Primary securities owned	Personal equity of owners
Corporate stocks	
Private debts	
Government debts	
Claims on intermediaries owned	
Government money owned	
Total assets	Total liabilities and equity

[4] Some parts of the surplus may be labelled as "undivided profits," or as "reserves"—for bad debts, contingencies, and so on—but that does not change their character.

Nor does the account for financial intermediaries ("institutions") appear to be very different, although the relative magnitudes of the various classes of assets are very different than for nonfinancial businesses. What do we mean by financial intermediaries, and what differentiates them from other businesses? First of all, their physical assets (building and equipment) are incidental to their operations and usually constitute a tiny fraction of their total assets. Instead, the financial assets they own dominate the asset side of their balance sheets. Intermediaries are the principal owners of primary securities—that is, of the financial claims against all entities other than intermediaries. These include corporate stocks (owned mainly by mutual funds, trusts, and pension funds); private and government bonds, notes, and bills (owned by all kinds of intermediaries, including banks); bank loans outstanding (the debts of borrowers to banks); and the mortgages owned (principally by banks, savings and loan institutions, and insurance companies). In addition all financial intermediaries own some claims against other intermediaries, including, particularly, bank deposits. They also have cash in their vaults and tills.

On the right side of the account are the liabilities of financial intermediaries: bank deposits of all kinds, insurance and pension fund claims, obligations to beneficiaries of trust funds, obligations to the share owners of mutual funds, and so on. After subtracting these liabilities (which dominate this side of the balance sheet), there remains the corporate net worth of incorporated financial institutions, or the personal equity of the owners of unincorporated or mutual financial institutions.

Balance Sheet
All Financial Institutions

Land, buildings, and equipment owned	Liabilities of (claims against) financial intermediaries
Primary securities owned	Corporate net worth (of incorporated institutions)
Corporate stocks	
Private debts	Personal equity of owners (of unincorporated institutions)
Government debts	
Claims on intermediaries owned	
Government money owned	
Total assets	Total liabilities and net worth

The nature of the intermediaries' business is thus mainly that of (a) owning, and receiving a return on, those kinds of financial assets—namely, "primary securities"—which many or most individuals or other (nonfinancial) businesses may not wish to or are unable to own directly; and (b) issuing (that is, "owing"), and usually paying a return on, kinds of financial claims which many or most consumers and businesses do wish to or need to own. In general, these claims against intermediaries are (as compared with primary securities) less risky, more liquid, more easily divisible into smaller amounts, or more convenient; or they may provide ancillary benefits such as insurance; or they provide transaction services which facilitate consumption or production, for example, checking accounts. These various desirable attributes constitute the reasons why they are preferred by their holders over primary securities. Claims against intermediaries, however, either pay no current or future monetary return to their owners (in the case of demand deposits), or pay only a future return (insurance or pensions), or pay a lower return than the primary securities which the intermediaries own. That difference in yields between financial assets owned and owed pays the costs of the intermediaries' services and permits them a profit. They would not otherwise exist.

In a very meaningful sense, of course, the owners of claims against financial intermediaries are really the *indirect* owners of the primary securities which the intermediaries own. The difference between the total value of the two sets of claims (those owned and those owed by intermediaries) of course consists of the value of the equity of the owners of the intermediaries. (In the case of "mutual" financial institutions, these "owners" are also the claimant depositors, policy-owners, or whatever.)

(Many of the liabilities of, or the claims against, financial intermediaries are, of course, called "money." Certainly, demand deposits always are so considered, and sometimes time and savings deposits, or even savings and loan shares as well. To these, we can add the government money that exists—that is, currency—and call the total the **money supply**. However, for the present, we need not be concerned with this total.)

Now it should be clear that if we added together all of the left-hand (asset) columns of these four sector accounts—the three kinds of businesses plus households—we would have included everything that we earlier counted as national wealth in the form of physical productive assets: land, plant, equipment, inventories, and residences. But the total of *all* the assets of the four sectors would be far greater than the national wealth, for it would include many financial assets as well. Similarly, if we added all the right-hand column entries for all four sectors, we would include the national wealth measured as the aggregate net worth of all households, but also a great deal more.

The reason why both totals are so much larger than the corresponding concepts of national wealth is that with a few exceptions every private financial asset is also a private financial liability; thus, all financial assets appear *twice* in these balance sheets: once on the asset side of one sector's balance sheet, then on the liability and net worth side of another. A financial asset which adds to the net worth of a business or individual who owns it is a subtraction from the net worth of another business or individual. For the nation as a whole, these financial assets or claims are, on balance, neither asset nor liability.

Clearly, for instance, the sum of the intermediary claims *owned*, which appear on the left (asset) side of each sector balance sheet, must exactly equal the aggregate of claims against financial intermediaries appearing as a liability on the right side of that sector's balance sheet.[5] Suppose we cross out these duplicating claims wherever they appear. We can do the same with all other private debts: bonds, bank loans, mortgages, or whatever. Their total looked at as ownership must equal their total looked at as liability. Cross them all out. Cross out, as well, personal equity of owners in unincorporated businesses, which appears on the asset side of the personal account and on the right in the unincorporated business and financial institutions accounts.

Finally, and at least tentatively, we can identify the corporate stock owned—which appears on the left side of each of the four balance sheets—with corporate net worth, which appears on the right in the nonfinancial corporations and financial institutions accounts. Since corporate net worth is, clearly, the property of the stockholders, it should be equivalent to the value of the corporate stocks owned. We will return to this question shortly. Meanwhile, and tentatively, cross out all of these entries for corporate stocks and net worth.

Having made all of these cancellations (and the reader should, in fact, make them) what we are left with as the total assets of all sectors combined (the aggregate of all left-hand columns) now consists only of (a) physical wealth, consisting of land, plant, equipment, inventories, and residences, plus two kinds of government obligations, (b) government debt (interest-bearing), and (c) government money (noninterest-bearing debt). What is left on the right-hand side is only the aggregate of personal net worth.

Thus, the national wealth when measured as private, productive, physical assets—*the cumulative total of all past net investment* (plus land)—is almost, but not quite, the same as the national wealth as measured by the aggregate of all personal net worth—*the cumulative total of all past net personal saving*. The two measurements of wealth differ by exactly the amount of government bonds and government money (in each case, the amount held outside the government itself—that is, held by the private sector). This difference can be identified as *the cumulative total of all past net government deficits*. For any and every government past deficit (excess of payment over receipts) had to be financed either by borrowing or issuing new money; every surplus either reduced money outstanding or paid off debt.

The preceding relationship should not be surprising. Earlier, in equation (10), we demonstrated that for any year or other period the sum of the flow variables in the national income accounts of net private investment (including inventory accumulation) plus government deficit must exactly

[5] Ignore the fact that governments may own a certain amount of bank deposits.

equal the sum of private saving plus net corporate saving:

$$(10) \qquad\qquad I + Def \equiv S + U\Pi$$

We can think of the capital stock—national wealth in terms of real goods—as the cumulative total, over all past time, of I. We can think of total individual net worth as the cumulative total over all past time of S—personal saving in the national-accounts sense—plus the cumulative increment of the value of corporate stocks which reflects the investment of undistributed profits.[6] These two cumulative totals can then differ only by the cumulative deficit of the government.[7]

Although we shall, immediately following, have to qualify this conclusion in various ways, it is nevertheless a fundamental relationship of profound meaning and usefulness in understanding the economics of nonstationary societies—those whose income and wealth are growing (which is the case for nearly all modern Western economies and has been true for most of them for centuries). Let us repeat this conclusion for emphasis: The level (as well as the growth) of the stock of private productive physical capital plus the level (as well as the growth) of the stock of private claims against government also measures the level (and the growth) of the net worth of all individual members of the society. Obviously, if government budgets are exactly balanced—on the average over any period of years—the growth in the value of the private capital stock just equals the growth in the wealth of the consumers. And this is true even though very little of the stock of private capital assets (other than houses) is directly owned by consumers, who instead mostly own deposits, insurance policies, trust and pension claims, plus some part of the equity and debts of the nonfinancial business which in turn own most of the nation's physical assets.

---

[6] Recall that, on the left side of all balance sheets, corporate stocks were to be valued at market prices, while on the right side of corporate accounts, corporate stock is valued at original issue price. In principle, the difference in valuation might represent the cumulative investment of undistributed profits.

[7] In the above, we have purposely ignored all government-owned assets, and private nonproductive (or noncommercial) assets—e.g., "cathedrals." For some purposes, it may be desirable to include some or all of these in an accounting of wealth. If we do, this can affect the relationship between the total value (as well as the *change* in the total value) of physical assets and aggregate personal net worth. Although we may wish for some purposes to list new *government-owned* assets as additions to national wealth, we should recognize that no *individual* is clearly the richer because the government has acquired another nuclear-powered carrier, 1,000 more miles of interstate highway, or 100 new elementary schools; nor, probably, does anyone even "feel" more affluent in any meaningful sense as a result of this additional collective wealth. Similarly, no one's economic or psychic net worth increases because his diocese acquires a new cathedral (in the medieval world it may have been different!). It is possible, of course, that the cost of the extra carrier was just matched by an equivalent increase in the national debt (government bonds held by the public), which would add to personal net worth; however, that would be pure accident: deficits can occur with no acquisition of tangible assets; and tangible government assets may be acquired in periods when governments run surpluses not deficits.

We must now begin to qualify this conclusion insofar as it is relevant to the perceptions on which economic behavior is based. When we looked at the corporate sector's balance sheet, we noted that the physical assets were usually not valued at current (indeed, not at any single consistent) market value but at book values that represent original purchase prices and arbitrary allowances for depreciation. The stocks and bonds among the corporate assets are also likely to be valued at an original purchase price. This makes it unlikely that the *book value* of corporate net worth equals the "true" current net worth of the corporations, based on current economic values of all assets and liabilities.[8] Moreover, there is no good reason to suppose that the *market values* of corporate stocks at any given time reflect *either* the book value of corporate net worth *or* its "true" economic value (in the preceding sense). Surely, fluctuations in share prices considerably exaggerate changes in the current replacement values of corporations' assets less liabilities. In 1976, the Council of Economic Advisers constructed estimates of the aggregate market value of nonfinancial corporations, as measured by the current values of their outstanding stocks and bonds, and compared these with estimates of the aggregate replacement value of corporate net assets. Figure 2-2 shows the ratio of these two magnitudes over the period 1960–1976, which ranged from a peak of 1.361 in 1965 to a low of 0.745 in 1975.[9] Clearly, current market values of corporate securities do not accurately reflect, in the short run, the economic value of firms' assets.

Moreover, we noted that some financial assets (of which pension claims are the best and most important example) do not have even a book value—at least one that is known to the ultimate holders of the claims (to say nothing of a market value). Many consumers, moreover, do not consider as the value of their insurance policies their current "cash-surrender value." Even if they did, this would not, except by chance, correctly reflect the "true" value of the underlying financial assets owned by the insurance companies. Thus, wealth *as perceived* by its ultimate owners—individuals and families—is some hazy blend of obsolete and arbitrary book values, adjusted (to the extent corporate stocks and bonds are owned *directly*, and by individuals who follow their current prices) by some perception of fluctuating security prices.

These problems, however, are primarily relevant whenever the short-run role of wealth changes is under discussion. For purposes of long-run growth analysis—which is where wealth variables become truly important—these problems tend to wash out. Over any period of a decade or more, the net accumulation of physical assets, however valued, plus the

---

[8] By "current economic values" we might mean, for physical assets, replacement costs, for financial assets and liabilities, current market prices.

[9] Figure 2-2 is reproduced from the *Annual Report of the Council of Economic Advisers, 1977*, contained in *Economic Report of the President*, transmitted to the Congress January 1977. U.S. Government Printing Office, 1977, p. 30.

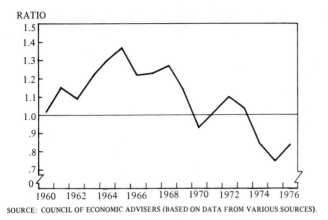

RATIO

SOURCE: COUNCIL OF ECONOMIC ADVISERS (BASED ON DATA FROM VARIOUS SOURCES).

FIGURE 2-2 Ratio of Market Value of Nonfinancial Corporations to Replacement Cost of Net assets.

cumulative growth of government debt and money will be essentially reflected in the perceptions of individuals about the value of their accumulated savings.[10]

REVIEW QUESTIONS

1.

(a) Gross national product (GNP) and national income (NI) are both measurements of the results of current productive activity. Why then are they numerically different, and of what principal specific items does this difference consist?

(b) NI and disposable income (DI) are alternative measurements of people's current income. Why then are they different, and of what specific items does the difference consist?

(c) Using your answers to (a) and (b), explain which factors are relevant, and why, in determining *by how much DI will change when GNP changes.*

---

[10] Some economic theorists insist that individuals recognize that the government debt will some time have to be repaid, by additional taxes. The present value to them of their pro rata shares of these added taxes is thus felt as a liability, and needs to be subtracted from personal net worth as a measure of national wealth. Whether or not government debt will need to be, will be, or should be repaid are matters that can well be argued. However, the real question— whether this debt is felt as a current burden by members of society, each visualizing his pro rata share of future taxes to repay it—is quite another matter. In the absence of in-depth psychological surveys of public attitudes and conceptions of this matter, anyone is entitled to hold (and the writer does hold) the opinion that government debt is not so regarded.

2. The table below contains some approximate data for the United States economy in 1976. Compute the values of GNP, NNP, NI, DI, and PI.

	Billions of dollars
Capital consumption allowances	180
Personal income taxes	195
Indirect business taxes	160
Government transfer payments	244
Gross private domestic investment	240
Net exports of goods and services	7
Corporate retained earnings	45
Corporate profits after taxes	90
Personal consumption expenditures	1080
Government purchases of goods and services	365
Social insurance contributions	123
Corporate profits	150

3. Below are some fourth-quarter data from U.S. National Income and Product Accounts. Data are seasonally adjusted annual rates in billions of dollars.

	1973 IV	1974 IV	1975 IV
GNP: In current prices	1353	1449	1588
In 1972 prices	1241	1192	1219
NI in current prices	1107	1156	1264
DI in current prices	940	1016	1120

(a) Compute the GNP implicit deflator for each year. How is the implicit deflator estimated?

(b) Distinguish between an implicit deflator and an explicit deflator. How would an explicit deflator be estimated?

(c) NI and DI are expressed only in current prices, in the table. How would you, in principle, estimate the NI and DI in constant prices? Given the data that you have, what procedure would you propose to estimate the NI and DI in constant prices? Using this method, estimate them.

(d) The change in DI in current prices over this period exceeded the change in GNP in current prices. Is this the "normal" relationship between these changes? What is "normal"? What are the major *possible* explanations for this result? Which would you suspect as the main explanation or explanations?

(e) The following statement relates to the period between 1973 IV and 1974 IV: "Although GNP in 1972 prices has declined, this does not imply that people are worse off, for all other figures show a moderate, if not substantial, increase." Comment.

(f) What does "seasonally adjusted annual rate" mean?

4. List several alternative concepts of national wealth, and explain the differences among them.

SELECTED REFERENCES

United States Department of Commerce, *The National Income and Product Accounts of the United States, 1929–74* (A *Survey of Current Business* Supplement), 1976.

(Presents the latest revision of the official United States concepts, and revised data. For current estimates of national income and product, and their components, see the latest monthly issue of the *Survey of Current Business*. The July issue each year presents a full set of tables containing latest revisions.)

M. Bailey, *National Income and the Price Level* (McGraw-Hill, 2nd ed., 1971), Chapters 2 and 3. (A good, short discussion of theoretical issues involved in national income accounting.)

E. F. Denison, "Welfare Measurement and the GNP," *Survey of Current Business*, 51 (January 1971), 13–16. (What the GNP does and does not measure.)

R. Goldsmith, *The National Wealth of the United States in the Postwar Period*, National Bureau of Economic Research (Columbia University Press, 1962). (The basic work by the principal U.S. expert on wealth measurement.)

Measuring the Nation's Wealth, volume 29 of *Studies in Income and Wealth*, National Bureau of Economic Research, 1964. (A report on a study recommending regular and improved measurements of national wealth in the United States.)

N. Ruggles and R. Ruggles, *The Design of Economic Accounts* (National Bureau of Economic Research, 1970). (The standard work on conceptual and empirical issues in national accounting.)

J. M. Keynes, *The General Theory of Employment, Interest, and Money* (Harcourt Brace, 1936), Chapter 4. (Explaining how J. M. Keynes proposed to deal with the problems of measuring "real" national income.)

Chapter 3

Employment, Unemployment, and Output in a Growing Economy

Employment, Unemployment, and Labor Force
The goal of full employment
Frictional and structural unemployment
Unemployment from inadequate demand
The full-employment target and potential output
Total labor time

Employment and Output
Factors affecting output per hour
Production and employment with economic growth
The growth of potential and the growth of actual output

In this chapter we continue the development of basic macroeconomic concepts and their methods of measurement, particularly those involving the employment (and unemployment) of labor, and then consider the relationship between changes in employment or unemployment and national product.

EMPLOYMENT, UNEMPLOYMENT, AND LABOR FORCE

Of equal importance to the measurement of real output and wealth is the measurement of employment and its correlate—unemployment. These magnitudes are of obvious interest as purely economic concepts. Labor is in many ways our most fundamental productive resource, and the income earned from labor services is the largest part of the national income. Beyond that, employment and unemployment—and changes therein—also have obvious social and even political significance. In the United States, the most comprehensive labor force data are obtained through a monthly survey of a scientifically selected sample of households representing the noninstitutional population. Each household member over 16 years old in the sample is identified as having been, in a prescribed week, either employed (including the "self-employed" and those working without pay in a family business), unemployed, or not in the labor force. To be counted as unemployed—if not working in the particular week—it must be established that he was "involuntarily" unemployed—that is, either

1. available for and actively looking for work
2. waiting to be recalled from temporary layoff
3. waiting to report to a new job scheduled to start within 30 days

Those neither employed nor unemployed are classified as not in the labor force. In other words, the labor force equals the number of those working plus the number of those seeking or awaiting work. The principal weakness of the measurement of unemployment and thus of the labor force is that there is no objective way of determining whether one who is actively seeking work is seeking with a realistic or unrealistic concept of the kind of work for which he is qualified and the remuneration he is likely to be able to attain.

Data from the sample are "blown up" to provide estimates for the entire population, using Census employment and population data as "benchmarks." Data are also obtained on the number of hours worked in the given week by each employed person in the sample, which are used to make estimates of total manhours worked each month in the entire economy. Data on both employment and hours are also available from other sources (for example, social insurance records and monthly surveys of samples of employers), and these can be used to supplement or refine data from the monthly surveys and the population censuses.

Note that these data are all "stock" data. They are measurements, at a point in time, of absolute numbers, not rates per unit of time. Just as the stock of physical capital provides (a flow of) productive services which contribute to the flows of national product and income, so the stock of employed labor provides productive services which contribute to the flows of product and income. Changes in the size of the labor stock, of course, reflect the difference between the net *flow* of entries and departures. Changes in the stock of *employed* labor occur through the net flows of hires, layoffs, and quits.

The seasonally adjusted monthly unemployment rate (the number of those unemployed as a percentage of the civilian labor force) is perhaps the single monthly figure most widely used—by economists and public officials, as well as by the general public—to assess the current state of the economy. To be sure, concentration on the overall unemployment rate can sometimes be rather misleading. It conceals wide variation in the unemployment rates of various subdivisions of the labor force—by age, sex, color, occupation, region, and so on—which for some purposes may be as important as the overall rate. Moreover, changes in the unemployment rate are affected not only by changes in employment but sometimes even more by changes in the size of the labor force.

Changes in the labor force are of several types. The first is the slow and relatively steady long-term expansion of the labor force, which reflects an excess of young persons coming to working age over deaths and retirements, as modified by the rather steady long-term upward trend in the rate of participation in the labor force by women, and only partly offset by trends toward earlier retirement, and toward later entry (reflecting longer years of schooling). This "normal growth" of the labor force can be projected fairly accurately for up to 10 years ahead. Quite important short-term changes in participation rates—and thus in the labor force—are closely related to changes in job availability. As jobs become less plentiful, many women, young people, and older men simply drop out of the labor force (cease actively seeking work). As employment picks up, they return to the labor force. These are the so-called "hidden unemployed," or the "discouraged workers." Perhaps they conclude that, when jobs become scarce and jobseekers are many, they have no chance of finding a job, so they stop trying. Or, perhaps, they are close to the borderline of indifference whether they work or not, and need the fairly obvious availability of work, or even the offer of a job, to make them interested in working. In any case, their number is significant, and variations in it need to be taken into account in any analysis of employment conditions and prospects.[1]

Despite many necessary qualifications, the overall unemployment rate nevertheless remains one of the key measures of an economy's performance. The economic policy of every country is focused on keeping this rate as low as possible as much of the time as possible. How low is "as low as possible" for the United States economy, how steadily the actual rate can be mantained at that target level, and by what means, are questions to which we shall frequently return.

The Goal of "Full" Employment

Public economic policy in almost every country is thus centered on the attainment of a high level of employment, with involuntary unemployment regarded as an evil to be avoided or minimized even at considerable cost. When there are persons who seek work and the income from work but are unable to find it for considerable periods, the consequence is not only personal disappointment and damage to individual morale, but often, as well, personal or family hardship, suffering, even tragedy. The leaders of any government, radical or conservative, recognize that substantial unemployment generates social unrest and political instability. Moreover, it represents the waste of a valuable national economic resource, which could have been used to advance individual welfare and national goals. It is not surprising that nearly all governments now give high priority to "full" or maximum employment.

The "Employment Act of 1946"—which represents the basic charter of U.S. Federal Government economic policy—puts high employment as the primary goal of government action in these words:

"The Congress hereby declares that it is the continuing policy and responsibility of the Federal Government to use all practicable

---

[1] To be sure, when a principal "breadwinner" is unemployed, other members of his family, not normally in the labor force, may begin to seek employment, somewhat offsetting the decline in participation rates due to "discouragement."

means . . . to promote maximum employment, production, and purchasing power."[2]

Nevertheless, whether the goal of policy is expressed as "maximum employment" or "full employment," it does not and cannot mean zero unemployment. Some degree of unemployment is inevitable and even desirable.

Frictional and Structural Unemployment

In the first place, there must always be, in a free and dynamic society and economy, a certain amount of unemployment that can be called "frictional." Hundreds of thousands of workers are always entering and leaving the labor force—some, especially women, often for the second or third or tenth time in their lives. Many students enter and leave the labor force once or even several times a year. Some persons work only during the Christmas season or during an agricultural processing season. Unless new entrants find a job the instant they start to look for it, they have (by United States definitions) entered the labor force before finding a job and are unemployed for a period which may average several weeks.[3] Moreover, in a changing economy, individual employers often are forced to lay off workers temporarily, or separate them permanently, even while other employers are actively seeking to add similar persons to their working forces.

Those on temporary layoff are not likely to seek other employment; and it may take some time for the permanently separated to find a new employer or for the employer with vacancies to find the worker seeking a

---

[2] The words omitted from the above passage are more numerous than those quoted, and constitute a series of qualifications and explanations that formed an integral part of the political compromise necessary to the passage of the Act, but which most reasonable persons would probably take for granted. The substitution of "maximum" for "full" employment was also an essential part of the compromise, even though most people would be hard pressed to explain the difference. The full declaration of purpose, including the words quoted above, reads as follows:

"The Congress hereby declares that it is the continuing policy and responsibility of the Federal Government to use all practicable means consistent with its needs and obligations and other essential considerations of national policy, with the assistance and cooperation of industry, agriculture, labor, and State and local governments, to coordinate and utilize all its plans, functions, and resources for the purpose of creating and maintaining, in a manner calculated to foster and promote free competitive enterprise and the general welfare, conditions under which there will be afforded useful employment opportunities, including self-employment, for those able, willing, and seeking to work, and to promote maximum employment, production, and purchasing power."

[3] Some foreign definitions exclude "school leavers"—that is, persons seeking their first job—from among the unemployed.

job. Even when the number of new jobs opened up by incessant changes in the production rates of particular firms and industries equals or exceeds the number of workers displaced by the same kinds of changes, some workers are inevitably unemployed for a time as they move between jobs. Further, large numbers of workers voluntarily quit their jobs every month, not in order to leave the labor force but to seek a different, and possibly better, job. While they are seeking the other job, they are unemployed. In a reasonably free yet progressive and dynamic economy, these kinds of **frictional unemployment** can easily amount to two percent or more of the labor force. How long the average worker who is so unemployed takes to find a job depends at least partly on the effectiveness of information flows in the job market, on the existence of aids or barriers to occupational and geographical mobility, and other institutional and structural factors, including, of course, the terms and availability of unemployment insurance or "relief" payments, which may permit or encourage the unemployed to take their time in seeking or accepting new jobs.

Structural unemployment differs from frictional more in degree than in kind. Frictional unemployment reflects the absence of perfect information and perfect mobility and the necessity, therefore, for search and choice on the part of workers, employers, or both. The term "structural unemployment" usually refers to the more serious and enduring limitations on worker mobility—using the term mobility in its broadest sense to include mobility as among geographical locations, as among employers and industries, and as among skills and occupations. Even though new job opportunities may equal the number of job displacements plus the net entry of workers into the labor force, the movement of the unemployed over geographical space, or between occupations, skills, or industries often may take considerable time, and may incur appreciable costs to employers, workers, or both. Frequently, it requires training or at least experience before the new or displaced worker can meet the employer's standards. Yet most such barriers to employment or reemployment are ultimately surmounted.

Some barriers to mobility are rather more formidable than mere distance, or the lack of specific training for or experience in the new job. If all of the vacancies are for professional engineers but all of the unemployed are high school dropouts, if there is a large supply of female high school graduates trained as stenographers but the demand is only for truck drivers or longshoremen, structural unemployment may appear to be capable of elimination, if at all, only through a complicated redesign of production processes, or through substantial changes in educational systems. Actually, the adjustments to the hypothetical cases mentioned may not be as impossible as they sound at first. There are many and continuous gradations of workers (and jobs) between professional engineers and high school dropouts, or between stenographers and roustabouts. Even though most of the workers "in between" are already employed, there can occur long chains of marginal shifts in the nature of the work individuals do, through which the vacancies get filled and the unemployed get absorbed. There are also market mechanisms that tend to bring about these substitutions, but they often take much time. While they are occurring, other instances of structural unemployment are created by the ceaseless change of technology, of public needs, of consumer tastes, by the discovery or exhaustion of natural resources, and so on. Moreover, some of those displaced by structural change—especially older workers—are unlikely ever to be reemployed. And some poorly trained and poorly motivated young entrants to the labor force have little prospect of steady employment.

Unemployment from Inadequate Demand

Of those persons unemployed at any given time, it is usually quite impossible to determine which *particular* ones are frictionally or structurally unemployed, and which (if any) are without jobs simply because there is an inadequate aggregate demand for the products which labor can produce. A particular undereducated, unskilled, and inexperienced youth may appear to be structurally unemployed; yet even in a relatively slack period there may be millions of others just like him who are at work. When the aggregate demand for labor picks up, he may very well be hired. No one can say which specific workers at any given time are frictionally or structurally unemployed and which are unemployed because of inadequate demand, but we know that there are always some of each. We may even make rough estimates of how many.

However the estimates are only rough. An increase in the demand for labor tends to shrink the amount of frictional and structural unemployment even as it absorbs those who were unemployed purely as the result of a lack of sufficient demand for final products and services. In a period of rapidly rising employment, new entrants, reentrants, and those who have voluntarily quit or were discharged from other jobs find that it takes less time than before to find a job. Thus, frictional unemployment shrinks, along with unemployment due to inadequate demand. Many of those handicapped by inadequate education or training do find jobs in such periods, even though their employers would have preferred more qualified workers. When local labor shortages begin to limit the expansion of output in favored localities, firms in previously "depressed areas," where unemployment had been unusually heavy, often find the demand for their output growing rapidly. Then what had appeared to be "hard core" unemployment in these areas begins to melt away. Thus, structural unemployment, too, responds to an increased demand for workers. Although it might seem reasonable to set our employment target at a level which just accounted for frictional plus structural unemployment but made no allowance for unemployment due to inadequate demand, such a prescription is simply nonoperational.

As unemployment—of whatever type—is progressively reduced, beyond some point, increased labor costs per unit of output are almost sure to be incurred. Costs of recruitment and training rise, reflecting the increasing relative importance of the frictions and the structural maladjustments. The workers last to be hired may, on the average, be less productive even after training. Many workers are probably less diligent when jobs are easy to find. Workers also quit more freely under those circumstances, so that turnover costs rise. Most important, as we will analyze in more detail at a later point, wage rates are very likely to begin to rise more rapidly at such times, and employers may also begin to seek wider profit margins above their rising unit costs. This is not so say that the only explanation for a general rise in the price level is "overfull" employment; there may well be others. It is to say that, in any case, lower levels of unemployment are almost sure to generate "inflationary pressures," whether other forces do or not. And, if other forces are generating inflation, overfull employment will magnify their impact.

The Full-Employment Target and Potential Output

In the longer run many of the difficulties encountered in further expanding employment when employment is already high might be mitigated or eliminated through more effective public and private manpower policies, better information, and other measures, as we shall discuss in a later chapter. At any given time, however, and with any given institutional and economic structure, a reduction of unemployment after some point inevitably begins to be associated with some degree of inflation (or of additional inflation), and further reductions in unemployment with progressively higher rates of inflation. As a result, the target rate of unemployment set for a nation's economy—the effective definition of "full" employment—must always represent some uneasy compromise between what are seen to be the social and economic costs of inflation and the clear social and economic advantages of high employment. In the United States during the 1960s, that compromise was expressed in an officially defined "interim target" rate of unemployment of 4 percent (although from 1966 through 1968 the rate averaged 3.7 percent, and in some months reached 3.3 percent).

More recently, changes in the composition of the labor force and the experience of the substantial inflation of the 1970s have led many economists, as well as public officials and public opinion generally, to conclude that a target rate of 4 percent unemployment is now too low and that what corresponded to a 4 percent rate in the 1960s may in the 1970s be 5 percent, or even $5\frac{1}{2}$ percent. However, at least as of 1977, there had not yet emerged any new, even semiofficial definition of a target rate corresponding to "full employment."[4] In Chapters 13–15, we will further explore the reasons why, and the extent to which, low unemployment rates may be associated with inflation, and what more detailed considerations might appropriately be used in choosing a target for public policy. For the present, however, we will simply assume that some socially determined definition of "full employment" exists, and will, for the present, mainly confine our attention to changes in employment and unemployment within the range up to full employment.

Corresponding to the concept of full employment is its important correlate, **potential output**—defined as the level of real GNP which would be produced at full employment of the labor force. It is, therefore, that level of total national output which is the highest that might be produced, without itself generating an unacceptable inflation (or an unacceptable increase in inflation). It is a concept which first came into use in the early 1960s, and one which we will use extensively in our subsequent discussion. In practical terms, U.S. potential output (measured in billions of dollars in 1972 prices) is a number now widely used both in economic analysis and in policy discussions.

To be sure, this strict identification of potential output with a target level of "full" employment is not the only possible way in which this term might be defined. Some would argue that the effective noninflationary limit on aggregate output may relate as much or more to available capital facilities and/or natural resources as to available labor, and that the concept of potential output—as a level presumed to be itself noninflationary—should be defined at least partly independently of the degree of employment.

While one could then get the same relationship between the concepts of potential output and full employment by working backward—that is, defining full employment as the number of jobs which would be required to produce the potential output—that is, the highest presumed noninflationary output—something more than different words is involved in the two approaches. For this second approach might produce a "full employment" level that did not imply any particular unemployment target. For example, it might imply 4 percent unemployment one year, 6 percent another year, $3\frac{1}{2}$ percent another.

However, it is implicit in the standard United States definition of the concept that, in "normal circumstances," the effective limit on

---

[4] The closest thing to a new "official target" appears in the *Report of the Council of Economic Advisers, 1977*, where it is estimated that "the full-employment unemployment rate equivalent to 4.0 percent in 1955 is now 4.9 percent." See *Economic Report of the President*, transmitted to the Congress January 1977 (United States Government Printing Office, 1977), p. 51. George Perry reaches the same 4.9 percent figure, although by somewhat different methods, in his "Potential Output and Productivity," in *Brookings Papers on Economic Activity*, 1: 1971, pp. 11–47, The Brookings Institution, 1971.

nonflationary output is, in fact, determined by pressures which come into focus *in the labor market.* Given structural changes in the labor force or labor market organization, the precise numerical unemployment percentage that represents the presumed noninflationary limit may well change. Ordinarily, however, it is labor supply—not plant capacity nor natural resources—that limits total production.

We will return to this question shortly, after first recognizing that full employment not only can be, but should be, converted to a concept measured in hours, not persons.

Total Labor Time

Total employment, as well as the target or "full employment" level of that variable, has, in the foregoing, been defined in terms of numbers of persons. The concept thus makes no distinction between workers highly skilled or possessing specialized abilities and unskilled or marginal workers; it is a simple count of bodies at work. For some purposes, especially as a measure of productive input, some economists have developed concepts of **weighted employment** in which workers more strategic for production count as a larger "quantity" of employment than workers less strategic. (One simple method is to weight workers by their hourly pay rates; if one worker is paid twice what another is, his contribution to production is taken as twice as great.) This may be a useful, if debatable, refinement. However, there is a more obvious shortcoming of a simple "body count," and one more easily corrected: it takes no account of the number of hours each employed person works. Inasmuch as the average number of hours per worker can and does vary considerably, a measure of employment in terms of total hours worked is clearly a better measure of the amount of employment than a mere count of persons. It relates more closely than does the latter to the amount of income earned from employment, to the aggregate costs of production, and to the amount of real output produced.

Although most individual workers have little effective choice of how many hours they will work—they work whatever number of hours their employer schedules for them—employers do have considerable flexibility, varying the number of hours per day, days per week, and weeks per year, at least up to some "standard" work schedule which is fixed by custom, agreement with their workers, or even, in many cases, by law. They can, of course, exceed the standard, requiring extra working hours on regular work days, extra work days per week (weekends and holidays), even shortening standard vacation periods. However, hours in excess of standard usually carry extra costs—time-and-one-half rates for overtime, and, perhaps, double- or even triple-time for weekends and holidays. Almost as important in raising costs are the reduced efficiency and increased absenteeism that go along with overtime work.

As total employment in the economy, measured in persons, rises and falls, the average number of hours worked per week tends to move in the same direction. Thus, the percentage variation in total hours of employment is considerably larger than the variation in numbers employed. Moreover, the relative movements of the two elements of the total exhibit a fairly stable and predictable relationship. At a time when the unemployment rate falls toward the target or "full employment" level, hours per week are usually approaching "standard" in most firms and industries, with, of course, always some below standard and others working limited amounts of overtime. But as numbers of employed reach—and surpass— the full employment target, increasing numbers of firms and industries are found to be resorting to overtime. Both the further reduction in unemployment (for reasons referred to earlier) and the further increase in average hours per worker are becoming increasingly costly and thus tend to be associated with unacceptable inflation.

Thus, we can, with little difficulty, translate our definition of "full employment" in terms of persons—as an "uneasy compromise between the costs of inflation and the advantages of high employment"—into a definition of "full employment" in terms of total hours worked. And, as noted earlier, at least through Part IV of this book, we will be mainly considering variations in employment—measured either in persons or total hours—up to but not beyond this full employment level.

EMPLOYMENT AND OUTPUT

We have now considered several broad measures of the current performance of a whole economy: national income, national product, and total employment, in persons or in hours. We have also considered the simple, accounting-type relationship that exists between the output and income measures. We now wish to examine the relationships between the income and output measures and total employment.

Obviously, if each hour of total employment is multiplied by what it earns, we would get the total of "wages, salaries, and supplements" that constitutes by far the largest element of national income. (Since self-employed persons are included in employment, their earnings may in fact appear in the national income as a species of business "profit," rather than wages—but that is a minor detail.) We also can (and national income statisticians do) compute a global **average compensation per manhour** that reconciles the aggregate national-income-account figure for wages, salaries, and supplements with the independent estimate of manhours employed. Not surprisingly, this global compensation figure moves closely with other, more conventional measures of average wage rates, although, in some respects and for some purposes, it is superior to them. However, the more interesting relationship—which we now wish to discuss—is that between real national product and total labor time worked. This is obviously not an "accounting-type" relationship.

Gross or net national product in constant prices is a measure of the physical volume of aggregate output in the economy. Total labor time, in hours, can be thought of as a measure—also in "physical" terms—of the amount of labor used to produce that national product. It is tempting to think of national product as analogous to the output of a firm and total labor time as analogous to the firm's "input" of labor, and to relate the two aggregate magnitudes as in the "production function" of the firm—which plays so crucial a role in microeconomic theory. Indeed, many economic theorists do not merely assume the existence of an **aggregate production function** linking total hours of employment and real GNP, but seem very confident that its shape must correspond to that usually postulated (and occasionally observed empirically) for the production function of a "typical" firm.

The *micro*economic theorist postulates, and believes that he observes, that, *ceteris paribus*, the output of the firm varies directly with labor input; but that output increases less than proportionally to input. (*Ceteris paribus* here means "with given production techniques and fixed inputs of other factors of production.") That is, production is subject to diminishing marginal returns as one input increases, with others held constant. The *macro*economic theorist seems unable to resist the temptation to take for granted that the same is true for the relationship between real GNP and total hours worked. That is, he expects average productivity—aggregate real output per hour of employment—to decline as employment increases.[5] However, economists who have tried empirically to approximate the observed aggregate, short-run production function have typically been unable to establish the existence of diminishing marginal returns to labor input in the aggregate relationship. Either they find the relationship to be roughly linear (constant returns) or, more frequently, to show *increasing* marginal returns. Because of the important role given to this relationship in many

---

[5] For example, one class of production functions which meets these specifications is the so-called "Cobb–Douglas" function, which can be written algebraically as

$$Y = aN^b K^{1-b}$$

where $Y \equiv$ real national product, $N \equiv$ hours of employment, $K \equiv$ real capital stock, $a > 0$, and $0 < b < 1$. The average product of labor then is

$$\frac{Y}{N} = aN^{b-1} K^{1-b}$$

and the derivative of Y/N with respect to N is

$$\frac{\partial Y/N}{\partial N} = a(b - 1)N^{b-2} K^{1-b}$$

Since $(b - 1) < 0$, this derivative is negative, that is, the average product of labor (output per man hour) declines as N increases.

theoretical macroeconomic models, we need to consider this problem somewhat further.

Factors Affecting Aggregate Output Per Hour

As is always the case, in trying to establish an empirical approximation of a theoretical concept, it is difficult to separate the relationship being studied from all the other influences affecting the variables in question. In this case, we are trying to isolate the impact of changes in hours of employment on aggregate output, holding constant all the other factors that are simultaneously affecting total output. In particular, improving technology, changes in the average quality (as opposed to the quantity) of labor, and changes in organizational and managerial skills, among others, have been tending steadily to raise output per hour in the private economy, regardless of the number of hours worked. Since it is difficult separately to quantify variables such as the average level of technology, average labor quality, managerial effectiveness, or even the quantity of capital employed—particularly so at the level of the total economy—it is almost impossible to "allow for" or to "control for" variation in all of these other factors. However, it is probably adequate to express the effect of these other variables on output per hour in the form of a steady trend. To be sure, revolutionary technological changes do occur discontinuously (for example, the invention of the railroad, the electric generator, the computer); but because even discontinuous changes spread only gradually through the economy, it is probable that we can adequately allow for these factors by fitting a "medium term" trend to data for output per hour, and then consider the relationship between changes in hours worked and deviations of actual output per hour from the trend.

One other higher important further influence on output per hour is clearly the stock of private productive capital, which has increased rapidly in most modern economies most of the time. On the average over any considerable period of years the capital stock has increased considerably faster than the input of worker hours. Clearly, there is no reason why the effects of the growth of the capital stock should be accurately represented by a trend factor. Growth of capital is the cumulative result of the flow of net investment, and the flow of net investment is highly variable over time. Still, net investment is rarely negative (apart from periods of major war or deepest depression) and thus the capital stock almost always is growing. Often, however, it does not grow as fast (for example, during the early stage of recoveries from recessions) as does the number of hours employed; yet it may continue to expand even when hours of employment stabilize or decline.

Thus, we might still expect to observe diminishing marginal returns to labor in the form of deviations of actual output from the general trend of output per manhour. Yet, as indicated earlier, almost no economist has been able to discover evidence of this in aggregative data. Why not? Perhaps some or all of the following factors explain it.

1. Even if there should exist a determinate relationship (at any given time) between the real output of *every* firm and the number of hours of labor time it employs—one which showed diminishing marginal returns to labor—it does not follow that there would exist an equally determinate relationship between the aggregate national product and total hours of employment, except under extremely simple and artificial assumptions. For this relationship involves, among other things, "the aggregation problem," which was briefly discussed in Chapter 1 of this book. As pointed out in that discussion, the aggregation of nonlinear functional relationships is fraught with many difficulties. Moreover, it makes a great deal of difference whether we are able to assume the number of firms constant, or the number variable as output increases. If the number is variable and increases in proportion to output, we should not necessarily expect diminishing returns, whatever the shape of the individual functions.

One dimension of the aggregation problem appears when we recognize that the value of output per hour of employment varies extremely widely among the various firms and industries that make up the total economy—e.g., as between the manufacture of electronic computing equipment, the manufacture of furniture, and the supplying of beauty and barber services, with the output per hour in the last perhaps one-eleventh that of the first of these. To be sure, if the *proportions* of output, among products and services with different output-to-employment ratios, always remained fixed as total output varied, one might expect to find a fairly precise relationship between aggregate output and employment. If the proportions among outputs were not fixed (which they obviously are not) but did vary in some reasonably systematic way as total national product varied (something which we might choose to assume, and might even find ways to describe), there might again be some reasonably systematic relationship between real national product and employment; but it would not necessarily resemble the microeconomic production relationship which existed for any individual firm or industry. It might well show output per hour rising as employment increases, even though this were not the case for any firm.

2. Moreover, so far as the individual firm is concerned, the actual "real-world" relationship between changes in labor hours and changes in output may not exhibit diminishing returns for the simple reason that all other productive inputs may, in practice, vary at least in the same proportion as the labor input—they are not held constant at all. For example, if a plant is designed in such a way that each of its machines can only be operated by a fixed labor crew, then, as workers are laid off, machines are also shut down. There is no reason at all why this should raise output per hour on the remaining machines. Nor does the fact that the factory space is less fully utilized than before raise output per hour.

3. A considerable fraction of the worker input into production is of what may be called **overhead labor**. For example, the employment of most office, sales, research, and managerial personnel, as well as of many fore-men, maintenance workers, and inspectors is quite insensitive to variations in output. In the longer run, the employment of such workers may be adjusted more or less in line with the growth of the firm's or the economy's output; but, in the short run, speedups and slowdowns in the growth of output have little effect on the employment of overhead labor. For exam-ple, the operation of a movie theater takes about the same number of employees (ticket seller, ushers, popcorn seller, projectionist, janitor) whether the theater is typically one-quarter or three-quarters filled. As movie going expands (or contracts) in the longer run, the number of theaters, each with its standard complement of workers, may increase or decrease. But, in the short run, changes in real "output" measured (for example, by seats occupied) has little impact on employment, and large impact on output per worker or per hour, such that output per worker rises rapidly with employment.

4. There is the phenomenon of "labor hoarding" as applied even to production workers. One might assume that employment (in terms of hours)—at least of *production workers*—would expand or contract roughly proportionally with production. But there are costs of hiring and discharge. A trained worker laid off during a slack period may take another job; when output again expands the employer may have to find, hire, and train a new man. Often, it is more sensible to keep him on the payroll, at least for a while, in the hope or expectation that he will soon be needed again. Again, productivity will decline and rise with output. A rather extreme case of this phenomenon occurs where there are legal or customary inhibitions against layoff of workers. In Japan, for example, with its tradition of "lifetime employment" for "regular workers," the number of workers employed declines hardly at all even during severe recessions and even hours worked decline only moderately. Thus (the rate of growth of) output per hour fluctuates violently between booms and recessions.

5. At any given time, the layout, design, organization, and technology of existing productive plants and equipment have been designed for a particular level of operations. When output falls short of that level, many inefficiencies in addition to those already described may develop that disappear as output returns toward the level for which operations were designed. In the longer run, the design of productive facilities can be adjusted to another scale of operations; but, in the short run, inflexibilities are inevitable, and operation at another scale will tend to involve less efficient use of labor.

None of these factors is necessarily inconsistent with the expectation that diminishing returns might be observed given (a) a constant com-position of aggregate output as among products and sectors with different output per hour, (b) constant levels of technology and of the average quality of labor and management, (c) a constant capital input, and (d) a long enough time for full adjustment of the nature of the capital equipment used, the size and number of plants and firms, and the size and composition of work crews. If we compared two equilibrium situations in which the *only* difference was the number of hours worked, we might very well find that output per hour declined with an increase in employment. But the "real world" produces no such comparisons for us to observe. The *actual* fluctuations of aggregate employment and hours worked—those associated with recessions and booms—do not relate to any sequence of alternative equilibrium positions, either for firms or for the economy. Yet they are the circumstances to which macroeconomic analyses relate, and for which macroeconomic policies are prescribed. Moreover, we do find reasonably dependable empirical regularities in the relationship between aggregate employment (in persons or in hours) and levels of real output, even if they are not the regularities which the microtheorist finds familiar.

For the simple theoretical models of Parts II, III, and IV of this book, we will need to specify something about the relationship between aggregate employment and aggregate output. What we shall normally assume is a simple proportionality between output and employment (in hours), occasionally pointing out what difference it would make if we assumed something else. The implications of these assumptions for employment theory will first be considered in the next chapter.

Production and Employment with Economic Growth

The previous sections of this chapter have developed most of the concepts necessary for the "supply side" of the simple, static, "short-run" Keynesian and classical macroeconomic models which are the staple diet of every introductory treatment of macroeconomic theory. We could, therefore, end the chapter at this point. We choose not to do so because of the conviction that *economic growth* is of such fundamental importance to macroeconomics that even the simplest models must be prepared to incorporate it, albeit often in an oversimplified and stylized way. The fundamental character of economic growth in the modern world involves a number of types of progressive changes, to many of which we have already referred and which can be recapitulated as follows:

1. In most advanced countries, a relatively steady increase has occurred and continues to be experienced in available full-employment labor hours, as the result of population growth, and/or a steady increase in the labor-force participation rate of some categories of potential workers (especially women). Although standard hours have almost universally trended downward, still, in many countries, and for long periods, the aggregate of full-employment labor hours has nevertheless steadily increased, and

still does, at a rate which currently (late-1970s) is about $1\frac{1}{2}$ percent a year in the United States.

2. The stock of capital (private productive wealth) has steadily increased—through positive net investment—at a rate which ordinary has (proportionally) will exceeded the growth of available labor input.[6]

3. The aggregate wealth of individuals (personal net worth) has steadily risen, reflecting the growth both of the capital stock and of government liabilities.

4. New productive knowledge and improved human productive capabilities as the result of better health and education (including "learning by doing") have steadily accrued, resulting in relatively steady increases in potential output per labor hour and in potential output per combined unit of capital-plus-labor input.

5. The combination of items 1, 2, and 4 of course implies that potential output has increased steadily over time. Most estimates have placed its trend rate of growth in the United States at around 4 percent a year since the mid-1950s.[7]

Growth in the capital stock and improvements in knowledge are listed separately. Yet, in fact, the two are inextricably intertwined. For one thing, much new knowledge is incorporated into production precisely through its embodiment in capital goods of new kinds. Although this embodiment can occur even with zero net investment—through replacement of old capital goods as they wear out (or by junking them) without growth of the net capital stock—embodiment of new technology can come much faster if net investment is substantially positive and the capital stock therefore is steadily growing. In this circumstance, a considerably larger fraction of the capital stock can embody the newest and best technologies. Thus, the higher the level of investment, the faster the embodiment of technological progress.

Moreover, it is almost impossible to imagine a growth of capital per worker hour—that is, a faster growth of capital than of labor input—which does not also involve changes in *methods* of production. If a worker

[6] In the United States, the capital stock has increased in every year since 1944, after declining substantially from 1929 to that year (as the result first of depression and then war). Since 1950, the average rate of growth of the stock of real business plant and equipment has been very close to 4 percent a year. Although growth has been slower since 1973, it is not yet clear whether this represents other than a temporary response to the unusual conditions since that year.

[7] See, however, the discussion in pages 45–58 of the 1977 *Report of the Council of Economic Advisers*. This revises downward past estimates of both the recent level of potential output and its rate of growth, placing the latter at 3.6 percent a year, projected to be "about $3\frac{1}{2}$ percent per year in the near future." George Perry, however, *op. cit.* (see footnote 4) estimates the growth of potential output, 1976–1981, as 3.9 percent annually in one version and 4.1 percent in an alternative one.

equipped with a single shovel is given a second shovel just like his first, he will be able to dig no faster; only if he is given a *better* shovel (which probably costs more to make, thus embodying more capital), or some substitute for a shovel, such as a front-end loader or a ditch-digging machine, will his output per hour increase. In other words, for there to be increased capital per worker there needs also to be a change in the technology of production; using more capital-intensive methods of production normally implies using a *technologically different* method of production. This means that any steady increase in capital employed per hour worked implies a steady increase in *knowledge* about alternative methods of production. In practice, in modern economies, knowledge has surely so expanded.

Indeed, as we all know, the advance of knowledge concerning possible methods of production has usually involved considerably more than the mere acquisition of knowledge about alternative production methods which increase output per hour of employment by the use of more capital per employment hour. Rather, the progress of technology often can and has raised output per labor hour considerably more than in proportion to the increase of capital per hour—indeed, many specific innovations have raised output per labor hour while using *less capital* per labor hour. A worker may be given a new and *more efficient* shovel, which also *costs less* (that is, embodies less capital) than the old one, yet increases his output. Or he may be given a shovel or digging machine that costs more but increases his output more than in proportion to the increased cost. That is, the new method may be more capital-intensive than the old one, and at the same time may increase output per unit both of capital and of labor. In the aggregate, this is typically what has happened. Capital employed in production has increased considerably faster than labor input, and total real output has increased about as fast or faster than capital.[8]

It is a complex task to separate, either analytically or empirically, the many elements involved in the growth in modern economies of output per employment hour. It is, however, a task to which economists have devoted much attention in recent years. We will have a bit more to say about that in a later chapter.

Here, however, we can content ourselves with the fortunate fact that, whatever these many elements may be and whatever their separate contributions, the growth of output per employment hour can reasonably be taken—at least for periods of several years or even up to a decade—as a process adequately described by a simple trend. For the United States, for example, growth of output per employment hour in the private economy

---

[8] It may also be noted that a significant part both of the increase in capital per hour, and of the relevant technological change, has been "embodied" not merely in physical capital goods but in workers or organizations—in the improvement of human knowledge and productive skills or in improvements in the division of labor.

averaged 3.3 percent a year between 1948 and 1966. Perhaps for special reasons, between 1966 and 1973 it slowed to 2.1 percent.[9] Although productivity growth in the private sector is likely to be less than 3.3 percent a year over the next decade, it is difficult to be confident what its new trend may be, which leads to some corresponding uncertainty about the rate of growth of potential output. Because (for reasons we need not review) national product in government is conventionally measured in a way which assumes constant output per employment hour, a 3 percent a year increase in private output per private employment hour translates into about a $2\frac{1}{2}$ percent increase a year in total (public plus private) output per total employment hour. Given a $1\frac{1}{2}$ percent a year rise in available employment hours, this would add up to a 4 percent a year rise in potential output.

The Growth of Potential and the Growth of Actual Output

Although gaps between actual and potential output have been, unfortunately, all too common in almost every country, still the growth rates of actual and of potential output usually have not been materially different when averaged over periods of a decade or more. Presumably, this parallel growth of actual and potential output is the joint result of (a) various feedbacks from an independently determined growth of potential output to the growth of actual output which will be explained in subsequent chapters (for example, through the effects of growing consumer wealth on their demand for output, or through certain automatic changes in absolute and relative prices, which tend to speed up the growth of actual output whenever actual falls below potential); (b) public policies that have operated to maintain the growth rate of actual output reasonably close to an independently determined growth of potential; and (c) feedbacks from the growth of actual to the growth of potential (for example, depressed rates of growth of actual output reducing the growth rate of net investment and thus ultimately of potential).

To be sure, many of the questions regarding the relationships between actual and potential output can be analyzed in terms of a stationary economy—one in which potential output is approximately constant, and only actual output varies. This is, indeed, the way most simple macroeconomic analysis is conducted—explicitly or implicitly assuming no growth in potential. However, the character of an economy in which growth occurs is entirely different from one without growth. There is little resemblance between the actual economies of today and the stationary economy characterized by net investment averaging to zero, static technology, a constant labor force, and no change in the aggregate wealth of consumers.

[9] For possible reasons and prognosis, see Council of Economic Advisers (reference in footnote 7 in this chapter) and, for a somewhat different view, George Perry (reference in footnote 4).

Thus, even though the analysis of the sources of growth and of fluctuations in its rate is exceedingly complex, wherever it can be done we will analyze economic processes in the context of a growing economy. We will treat the stationary-economy case only as a first approximation, one often necessary in order to simplify an argument but never of great interest in its own right.

REVIEW QUESTIONS

1. "The employment target should be set at a level which would allow for frictional and structural unemployment, but not unemployment due to inadequate demand."

(a) What is meant precisely by "unemployment," at least in the United States concept? How in practice is the unemployment rate measured in the United States?

(b) Distinguish the concepts of "frictional" and "structural" unemployment in terms of their causes. What might be appropriate measures to reduce each type of unemployment?

(c) Do you agree with the proposition quoted above? Why or why not?

2.

(a) Describe the concept of "potential output" as commonly measured and used.

(b) What is the approximate current growth rate of potential output, and what are the principal changes that contribute to this growth?

3. Conventional macro models that will be studied in later chapters include an aggregate production function subject to diminishing returns. What does this mean, and what is the basis for assuming it? Unfortunately (for such models) there is little, if any, empirical evidence of diminishing returns in a modern economy such as that of the United States. How might this be explained?

4. Over long periods, actual output has grown more or less in line with potential output. What kinds of forces could account for this?

SELECTED REFERENCES

J. E. Bregger, "Unemployment Statistics and What They Mean," in *Monthly Labor Review Reader*, Bulletin 1868 of U.S. Department of Labor, Bureau of Labor Statistics, 1975, pp. 6–13. (A short account of how United States unemployment data are collected and what they reveal; for further details, see other articles in the same volume.)

A. M. Okun, "Potential GNP: Its Measurement and Significance," in A. M. Okun, *The Political Economy of Prosperity* (Norton, 1970) pp. 132–145, reprinted in W. L. Smith and R. L. Teigen (eds.), *Readings in Money, National Income and Stabilization Policy* (R. D. Irwin, 3rd ed., 1974) pp. 285–292. (Reporting and explaining the first estimates of this concept.)

Monthly Labor Review Reader, Bulletin 1868, 1975, Chapter V, pp. 236–281. (Seven reports on the factors determining and the problems of measuring labor productivity.)

Annual Report of the Council of Economic Advisers (in *Economic Report of the President,* Transmitted to the U.S. Congress, January 1977), pp. 45–58. (Presents and explains revised empirical estimates of potential output in the United States.)

G. L. Perry, "Potential Output and Productivity," *Brookings Papers on Economic Activity,* 1:1977 (The Brookings Institution, 1977). (A detailed study of past and future trends in the components of potential output, reaching conclusions somewhat at variance with the previous item.)

PART II

CLASSICAL
MACROECONOMICS

Chapter 4

Classical Monetary and Employment Theory

Say's Law

The Quantity Theory of Money
Velocity and the demand for money
Some determinants of velocity
Exceptions to the quantity theory

Wages, Prices, Employment, and Production
Aggregate supply of labor
Aggregate demand for labor and labor market
  equilibrium
The relation of money wages to the price level
Graphical and algebraic representation:
  I. Traditional classical assumptions
  II. Some nontraditional assumptions
A pricing function instead of a demand-for-labor
  function

Rigid Wages and Monetary Policy in the
Classical Model

Modern macroeconomic analysis constitutes a marriage of two quite diverse approaches: one commonly called **Keynesian**, the other **classical**: the former the product of the 1930s, the latter an accumulation and refinement of ideas developed during the previous century and a half. Actually, J. M. Keynes' own ideas, as set forth in his revolutionary *General Theory of Employment, Interest and Money* (1935), incorporated many ideas borrowed directly from classical theory, as well as modifications of classical ideas which he developed to replace the originals. Keynes recognized the need to integrate that which was new and original in his vision of the world with the theoretical ideas that he had inherited.

Subsequent analysis and reflection have shown that Keynes may have exaggerated the conflict between his own approach and those that preceded it. It is now rather more clear than it was at first that Keynes' ideas relate to a special case of a more general theory, which also embraces much of the classical ideas (although the Keynesian special case might be precisely that which closely corresponds to the economic world of today!). In any case, the conflict between Keynesian and classical elements is now seen as less clear-cut than it was once regarded. The macroeconomic theories now most widely accepted among economists and taught to their students constitute a marriage of Keynesian and classical elements—sometimes described as a **Keynesian–classical synthesis**.

Nevertheless, for purposes of presentation of this synthesis, it has seemed to the writer (as to many others) useful to present separately, and in their starkest form, the basic elements of (a somewhat modernized version of) the classical theory without any Keynesian admixtures. Then this is contrasted with a simple, purely Keynesian model, which includes only the uniquely Keynesian contributions. Only thereafter we see how the two sets of elements can be fitted together. The alternative—to attempt to develop the synthesis right from the beginning—is judged, at least by most writers of textbooks, to be less productive of understanding than the procedure followed here of doing first one, then the other, followed by their attempted merger.

This procedure also permits us to consider one by one, and in a more leisurely and thorough fashion, a number of theoretical and analytical problems that arise with respect to both the Keynesian and classical systems, as well as in any synthesis of their elements. Almost all important building blocks of any eclectic or synthetic macroeconomic model are here expounded as they first come up in developing either the pure classical or the simple Keynesian model. For this reason the reader (and his instructor) are warned not to skip blithely over the treatment of either model on the way to the synthesis. To do so would leave a considerable number of puzzles unexplained.

There is an important reason, besides expository convenience, for presenting the classical and Keynesian elements separately. We have called modern macroeconomics a "marriage" of two diverse approaches; however, the marriage is not always perfectly happy. There clearly remain elements of incompatibility between the partners, and these are exacerbated by friends on each side who still have not fully accepted the union and continue to disparage the other partner. The reader will have a better background for understanding many of the recurring controversies in macroeconomic theory (and policy), if he sees clearly each of the approaches as a coherent whole.

Gradually, perhaps, as some quarrels have been resolved, and the remaining disagreements brought into better perspective, the classical–Keynesian marriage begins to seem more stable. Still, the main thing that holds the partners together has been, and remains, the fact that neither can really survive alone. The simple Keynesian theory lacks any theory of wages, prices, money, and interest rates, and a significant part of what the classical writers said about these is still regarded as largely correct and relevant. The classical theory, as it stood even in 1930, almost completely lacks an explicit theory of "aggregate demand," which Keynes surely supplied.

By the *classical economics* we here mean the basically English tradition as it existed (and developed) between the principal works of Adam Smith (*The Wealth of Nations*, 1776) and Alfred Marshall (*Principles of Economics*, 1890). (Others prefer to extend the term to include the mainstream of Anglo-American economics through 1930. No matter.) Particularly if one considers English economics as it existed in 1890, one can well conclude that no macroeconomics really existed yet—classical or otherwise. And, although macroeconomic questions received increasing attention between 1890 and 1930, the birth of a full-fledged macro-economics clearly came only with Keynes. Nevertheless, a fairly coherent macroeconomics is at least *implicit* in the classical tradition, and it occasionally even reached the surface. However, making this classical macroeconomics complete and explicit has been mainly the work of post-Keynesian writers.

The main body of classical economics was microeconomic in character. It dealt with the determination of (relative) prices for and quantities of individual goods and services, the determination of (relative) incomes to individual factors of production, and the determination of (relative) prices of classes of assets, real and financial. Its principal *explicit* macroeconomic subject was the determination of the money price level, which, however, was believed to have essentially no significance for relative prices and incomes.

In understanding the reconstructed classical macroeconomics it is important to remember that it emerged from the study of microeconomic questions and to recall the assumptions that lay behind the microeconomic analysis. As we proceed we shall attempt to make those classical assumptions explicit. For what may have been and still are perfectly reasonable and useful assumptions to simplify a microeconomic analysis could well turn out to be responsible for misleading conclusions when carried over to the macroeconomic sphere. Indeed, we shall later so argue.

SAY'S LAW

One of the few explicitly macroeconomic propositions of classical theory was **Say's Law of Markets** (named after J. B. Say, the French economist, 1767–1832). This theory sprang from the controversy of the early nineteenth century over the question: can there exist a general "over-production" or "glut" in a market system of production and exchange? Say's law held that there cannot. Much of macroeconomic theory to date examines the conditions under which this principle will or will not hold true.

Say's Law is usually summarized as *supply creates its own demand.* If goods are produced, there will automatically be a market for them. This can easily be seen to be true in a barter economy, although its application was not supposed to be limited to that circumstance. More fully set forth, what Say appears to have had in mind can be expressed in this way: People work not for its own sake (indeed, work is unpleasant) but only to obtain goods and services that yield satisfactions. In an economy that practices division of labor and exchange, one does not obtain most of these goods and services directly (as did Robinson Crusoe) by his own efforts. Rather one produces goods in which one's efficiency is relatively the greatest and exchanges the surplus above one's own use for the products of others. The very act of production therefore constitutes the demand for other goods, a demand equivalent to the value of the surplus goods each man produces. How then can there ever be a general overproduction of goods? Each man's production (supply) constitutes his demand for other goods; hence, the aggregate demand must in some sense equal the aggregate supply. Total output may be limited by the fact that, at some point, for each individual, the satisfactions of a little more leisure will outweigh the sacrifice of a little more of goods that might have been obtained, but such "unemployment" will be "voluntary," not "involuntary."[1]

It is necessary clearly to distinguish this theory from the definitional identity among national product, national income and total expenditure. The identity exists at any level of income, output, or spending. What Say's Law implies is that any increment of output will generate an equivalent increase in income and in *spending*. Thus income and product can always be at a "full-employment" level. If they should be at a lower level, with some resources unwillingly idle, additional production will generate an equivalent amount of additional income, *which will all be expended in the purchase of the added product.* And since no one will be content at less than "full employment," additional production *will take place* until the *full-employment* level is reached.

To be sure, Say's Law admitted that individuals might not correctly direct their production in accordance with one another's wants. The man producing shoe laces might produce more than people want to buy at the price (in terms of other goods) he had assumed would exist before he brought his product to market. As a result, the surplus shoe laces buy fewer potatoes and less beer than he had anticipated. There is a demand for his shoe laces, all right, from the producers of potatoes and beer, who brought their surpluses to market to trade for shoe laces. But it is not the demand he had expected—in that sense, there was a glut of shoe laces. This, however, is merely the temporary maladjustment of relative outputs and barter ratios, to which producers can easily adjust. The shoe-lace producer's adjustment will involve either a decision in favor of more leisure or a decision to produce some other product, more in demand.

When Say's Law is framed in terms of a barter economy, it seems self-evident. But does it also hold true for an economy *using money*? In the case of barter, it is literally true that one can supply a commodity or service to the market only as a demand for another commodity or service. It is not so obvious when goods are sold for money. Can we be sure that the money received will be inevitably and promptly and fully spent against other goods? As we shall see in the second part of this chapter, the monetary theory contemporary with Say's Law did explain in some detail how and

---

[1] For an excellent treatment of Say's Law, see J. A. Schumpeter, *History of Economic Analysis* (Oxford University Press, 1954), 615–625.

why money's role was solely that of a "veil," behind which everything operated in fundamentally the same way as if all exchanges took the form of barter. But this result depends on a chain of reasoning and on specific assumptions about behavior, the correctness of which might be subject to challenge, and, in any case, is surely not obvious.

The elementary form of Say's Law was also framed in terms of one-person or family firms, each producing final products. These producing and consuming units owned their own land and capital and used it, along with their own (rather than hired) labor, to produce final goods and services. These in turn were sold to other one-person or family units that directly consumed them. But is it necessarily true that Say's Law holds as well for an economy where production is organized by entrepreneurs, who hire workers for a wage, perhaps buy from other firms some or the larger part of the services of capital and land used by the firm, and sell their products and services not only to ultimate consumers, but to other firms to use in producing still other products?

The price, wage, and employment theory contemporary with Say's Law was believed to explain how and why the existence of separate markets for labor, for intermediate products and materials, and for the services of capital and land operated to assure the full employment of all factors of production, so long as all such markets were free and competitive. This was why the supply of goods and services—which created its equivalent demand—must always be the maximum supply which was permitted (given the existing technology) by the full use of all the labor, capital, and land services that their owners wished to provide. But, once again, we can challenge either the assumptions or the reasoning of this argument. And the result is surely not obvious.

The elementary and self-evident formulation of Say's Law also paid no attention to the phenomena of saving and investment. The market in which Say's producer–consumers bartered with each other was presumably a market for consumer goods only, and each participant was presumably spending his entire real income for consumer goods. At least there was no discussion of the possibilities either that some might wish to save, or that others might desire to add to the capital facilities with which they produced. To be sure, classical economics also developed a theory about saving and investment (to be taken up in the next chapter) which seemed consistent with Say's Law; but, again, its conclusions are not obvious.

Thus, to understand the entire basis for Say's Law in a real-world economy—which uses money, not barter; in which most people sell labor services, not final products; and in which people save and invest—we need to look at a whole range of classical ideas, each of which turns out to be fairly complex. In most cases, the formulations we will present long postdate J. B. Say; indeed, some postdate J. M. Keynes. The first of these basic Classical ideas is the "quantity theory of money."

THE QUANTITY THEORY OF MONEY

The quantity theory asserts that money determines only the price level, not real output. The root idea of the quantity theory is that no rational person holds money idle, for it produces nothing and yields no satisfactions. Rather, people promptly use all the cash they receive from the sale of their goods or services to buy other goods and services. How promptly that occurs depends on how production is organized, how frequently incomes are paid, and other structural or institutional factors that were judged to be quite independent of the quantity of money or the level of prices. Given these assumptions, the theory showed how the quantity of money determines the level of money prices, and in a way which is without impact on the demand or supply of any individual product, and thus cannot affect relative prices nor the absolute quantities of products produced and sold. Thus it cannot affect aggregate production, either.

Formally, we can state the quantity theory in any of several ways. We start with two, closely related formulations of the theory:[2] the **transactions** form

(1)
$$MV = P_t T$$

and the **income** form

(2)
$$MC = P_O Y$$

The symbols have the following meanings, each of which is further explained in the paragraphs that follow:

M = quantity of money in circulation

V = "transactions velocity" of money

P_T = average price level of all transactions

T = physical volume of transactions

C = "income velocity" (or "circular velocity") of money

Y = real national product

P_O = average price level of national product

M is to be measured as the total number of monetary units (for example, dollars) "in private circulation." Although other meanings are possible, for now, M can be thought of as including only "cash" (bills and coin), plus bank deposits subject to check. Since all cash and deposits are owned by some business or individual (we do not include in the supply

---

[2] These equations are to be understood as equilibrium conditions, not as identities. That is, V is determined independently of M, P_t, and T. If V were defined (measured) as $(P_t T)/M$ (or C as $P_O Y/M$), then the equations are true by definition and therefore devoid of predictive or explanatory value. As theories, these equations assert propositions that are capable of being found untrue, whereas as definitional identities they cannot be.

those amounts held by banks or governments), M is the sum of all of the individual "balances" of cash and deposits held at any given moment by businesses and individuals. As money is "used" in transactions, each particular balance rises or falls; but so long as all transactions are among businesses and individuals, the *total of all balances* does not change through money's use. Its total amount can, however, be changed in other ways, now mainly by means of transactions between businesses or individuals and banks (including central banks) or governments, the nature of which we do not need to specify or describe at this time.

Originally, when economists first developed the quantity theory, M referred to the amount of metallic money in the economy—then the only kind. Thus, increases in the money supply occurred, for example, through the mining of gold, or its importation from abroad. Decreases occurred through conversion of gold into jewelry, or its export. Later, the quantity theory was reinterpreted to apply to an economy which used paper or bank money (first, bank notes, later on, checking accounts). This made an important difference. For the supply of paper or bank money can be controlled with relative ease by government policy. Thus, in modern economies, where the medium of exchange (money supply) consists essentially of government currency and demand deposits, the quantity theory may say something useful about the consequences of the government's "monetary policy"—the policy which determines changes in the money supply.

V is expressed as the average number of times per year (or other period) that units of money are used in any purchase-sale transaction. Individual units of money may turn over more slowly or rapidly, but, on the average, a unit of money changes hands V times per year.

P_T is some price index, which reflects changes in the average of prices at which transactions occur, appropriately weighted. (If it is an "explicit" index, it will be used to deflate the money value of all transactions to get their real volume, T, or, if T should be measured otherwise, P_T will be an "implicit deflator," obtained by dividing the money value of transactions by T.)

T is the real or physical total volume of money-using transactions—either the total of all payments or of all receipts, corrected for changes in P_T—which occur during a year (or other period: obviously, the same period as for V).

C, like V, is expressed as the average number of times per year (or other period) that units of money are used: but not in just *any* purchase-sale transaction, rather, only in a purchase-sale of final products.[3] C is

---

[3] An alternative version expresses C as the average number of times that units of money are used not in purchasing final goods, but in paying incomes; that is, it counts only purchase-sale transactions of productive services. However, in a simple economy, with only consumption output and no government, income and product are equal. This alternative version does, however, imply P_O as a price index of factor services, rather than of goods.

obviously less than V in that it ignores all turnovers of money in the purchase-sale of intermediate goods or productive services.

Y is real national product, expressed per year (or other period—same period as for C), while P_O is the national product deflator. $P_O Y$ is obviously the money value of the national product (and it is a matter of indifference whether P_O is an explicit or implicit index).

Consider, now, equation (1). Why must $MV = P_T T$? Simply because the product on each side of the equals sign is the same; it is the money value of total transactions during some specified period. On the left, this is measured by multiplying the number of units of money times the average number of times per period each unit is used in a transaction; on the right, it is measured by multiplying the physical quantity of transactions by the price level.

We assume that V is always constant at its maximum feasible level, since no one ever holds an idle balance—that is, never holds a single unit of money longer than he needs to. This *maximum* level for V (reflecting the *minimum* period for which units of money must be held) depends on structural and institutional factors unrelated to T, P_T, or M, which we shall analyze shortly. Given a constant V, MV is, of course, proportional to M. Look now at the other side of the equation. Assuming that prices are perfectly flexible, T can always be at the maximum level permitted by the technology and the willingness to work of the community. At any given time this maximum level of T can be taken as constant. Hence P_T must be proportional to M: increase M by 10 percent and P_T must rise by 10 percent.

One reason why the "transactions" form of the quantity theory (equation 1) has fallen out of use is that there exists no acceptable measurement of the physical volume of transactions (which is indeed a conceptually fuzzy variable) nor of the price level of total transactions. On the other hand, Y can clearly be identified as real GNP, and P_O as the GNP deflator. Thus we turn to equation (2) (dropping the subscript O as no longer necessary to distinguish an index of final output prices from one of transaction prices).

Why does $MC = PY$? Again, because both are alternate expressions for the money value of the national product during a given period. On the left, this is measured by multiplying the number of units of money by the average number of times per period each unit is used to buy final output (or pay incomes); on the right, it is measured by multiplying the physical quantity of final output by its price level. Reasons that make V constant at its maximum level make C constant as well, if we add the plausible assumption that, at any particular time, the volume of transactions in final output is some constant fraction of the volume of total transactions. Thus, if money stays in all balances only the necessary minimum period of time, and if the number of intermediate balances the average dollar must pass through in making a complete circuit from one purchase of final product to another is fixed, C will be a constant—of course smaller than V. Again, assuming competition and flexible prices, Y can be taken always to be at its maximum level, and P therefore proportional to M.

One root idea of either equation (1) or (2) is clearly the notion that no one—consumer or business—holds "idle" money. He holds some (slowing down what would otherwise be an infinite velocity of circulation), but only because there is imperfect coincidence between his discrete lumps of inpayment and his discrete lumps of outpayment. People hold money by necessity, but they hold as little, and for as short a time, as they can.

A second root idea of either equation (1) or (2) is also clearly that of flexible, competitive prices. Additional money bids up prices—rather than increasing the physical volume of output or transactions—because output or transactions were already at their maximum amount. How do we know that they were? Because if they had not been, someone, unable to sell all that he wished, would have offered his supply at a lower price, and prices would have fallen—output expanding—until output had reached its maximum. (We shall see, in the third part of this chapter, that the idea just summarized needs to be expanded, and somewhat qualified, in a society in which people sell their services to a business which in turn sells goods.)

Velocity and the Demand for Money

The versions of the quantity theory that we have just discussed (equations 1 or 2) use the concept of velocity—the average frequency with which units of money are used. However, the theory can be—and usually is—reformulated in a somewhat different terminology. Ignoring the "transactions" formulation as nonoperational, we replace the "income (or circular) velocity" formulation by

$$M_d = mPY$$

where M_d is the **demand for money**, and m is that (constant) fraction of PY which, in the aggregate, members of the community (businesses as well as consumers) desire to hold in the form of money balances; and

$$M = M_d$$

or

(3) $$M = mPY$$

where M is (as before) the supply of money. Equation (3) says that all the money that exists must be in someone's balance, and, in equilibrium, it must be willingly held. It should be obvious that $m = 1/C$. It is therefore clear that whatever factors determined the size of C must also determine the size of m. However, whereas the formulation in terms of C directed attention toward the institutional and structural factors which influence the *frequency of money payments*—which operate as *constraints* on behavior—the formulation in terms of m directs attention to the *factors or attitudes* which influence people to *hold* money. Both sets of factors are obviously important in thinking about the basic phenomenon involved.

Formulation (3) explicitly differentiates between the demand for money balances by members of the community and the supply of the balances which in the aggregate they actually hold. Thereby, perhaps, it makes it easier to understand that the quantity theory equation expresses an equilibrium condition. Any absence of equality between the balances people in fact hold and those that they want to hold would mean that the system was in disequilibrium. People would then be attempting to reduce or increase the money they held by buying more or selling less than usual, or the reverse. This action could not change the amount of money they actually held, nor could it change the production of goods and services. But it would tend to bring the system into equilibrium through altering the net demand–supply balance for goods, and thus the price level. Suppose that, at some level of PY, people find themselves holding more money than they desire to hold. They immediately try to get rid of the excess, by buying more goods. Because Y is at its maximum, they cannot really buy more; but they can bid up the price level of what is available, and will continue to do so until PY is high enough to make them willing to hold the money that they in fact have.

A parallel expression of the equilibrium condition in the previous (velocity) formulation (equation 2) implies differentiating between an actual value of C and an equilibrium value of C—say C_E—and stating $MC_E = P_0 Y$ as the equilibrium condition. In that case, while C_E might be constant, actual C could vary over time, indicating absence of equilibrium. Actually, as we shall later see, still more sophisticated versions of the quantity theory treat m (or C_E) as an economic *variable*, so that variation of M (or C_E) does not, in itself, *necessarily* signify disequilibrium.

The strict quantity theory, either in formulation (2) or (3), however, makes m or C_E a constant, and it is important to understand the basis for this view. It is, essentially, that no rational person wishes to hold any more money, or hold it any longer, than he absolutely needs to. And what he needs to hold at any given time depends on the time pattern of his (expected) receipts and payments in money, given that he wishes and expects his money balance to be zero as often as possible during his cycles of payments and receipts. A recurring minimum cash balance of zero means that money is merely a medium of exchange, not wanted for its own sake. It means that the demand for money is strictly proportional to money income at the lowest possible proportion, or that velocity is constant at its highest possible rate. To see what determines this lowest possible proportional or highest possible rate requires some elaboration of the determinants of velocity.

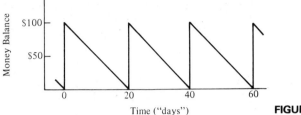

Time ("days")   **FIGURE 4-1**

Some Determinants of Velocity

Consider the behavior over time of the money balance of an individual member of a money-using economy. His balance might look somewhat like the diagram in Figure 4-1. At time point 0, this individual receives money in the amount of $100, presumably in payment for productive services. Just prior to this receipt, his balance had been zero. Now it becomes $100. His next receipt of $100 will come 20 time units ("days") later. The particular balance pattern assumed in this diagram has our individual spending one twentieth of this money each day, reducing his balance to zero just before his next pay period. We could equally well assume some other balance pattern—say, one that is concave upward—without altering the essential principle described.

We can say that our individual holds a balance that varies from $100 to 0. On the average, he holds $50 (in the straight-line case). This average balance ($50) is equal to one half his income ($100), if we state his income as per pay period. If we state his income as a "yearly" rate, and there are four pay periods in a "year," his average balance is one eighth of his income. (Since income is a flow, and money balance a stock concept, the size of any ratio between them must depend on the time unit used to express the income flow. This unit is obviously a matter of indifference, except for the convenience and custom of the annual unit for reckoning.)

This individual holds no money for its own sake. His only reason for holding it at all is to bridge a gap in time between receipts and outpayments of funds. Yet we find him, in fact, holding money, and doing so quite "rationally" and "willingly". He can be described as having a "demand for money" equal to one eighth his "annual" income. (If the descending phase of his balance were concave upward, his average balance would be less, and his demand for money a smaller fraction of his income.) We call this demand a **transaction demand**, indicating that he holds money only to make necessary transactions.

There is a second way in which we can describe our man's money-holding behavior. It is to say that the average dollar he receives is held for 10 days. Some dollars are held for 1, 2, 3, 18, 19, and 20 days. But the average dollar is held 10 days. (If we had assumed a curvilinear time path of his balance, the average period would be less.) Alternatively we can say that the average dollar he receives is passed along (turns over) in 10 days. Since 10 days is half his income period, and there are four such periods per year, we can say that the average dollar he receives is turned over at a rate equivalent to eight times per year. This is its (partial) **velocity**.

It should be obvious that to describe his demand for money as equal to one eighth his annual income or to describe the velocity of his money receipts as eight times per year are merely alternate ways of expressing a single phenomenon. Likewise, it should be clear that we can use another time period and get different numerical results. (For example, it is sometimes convenient to think of the payment period as our time unit. If so, his demand for money is half his income, and the velocity of his money is two.)

To complete the picture on this matter of money use (or money holding) in society we need to expand our example. Suppose that Figure 4-1 represents the total balance position of *all* income recipients in our economy. Let us suppose that all wages, salaries, interests, and profits are paid out to individuals on the same day. They receive, in the aggregate, $100 of income on days 0, 20, 40, and so on. Where does the money come from, and where does it go when they release it? Assume all business is organized in one giant firm (and that there is no government). The pattern of the business balance is obviously a mirror image of that of income recipients. Figure 4-2 shows this relationship between the balance of business and that of consumers. As the figure is drawn, business balances are reduced to zero as incomes are paid out on day 0. Thereafter, as consumer balances shrink, business balances grow. By day 20, when consumers are out of money, business has accumulated, through sales to consumers, exactly enough to pay the incomes then due, and the sequence is repeated thereafter.

Now our business also has a money balance, the average size of which is also $50. This balance also turns over eight times per year. The total of

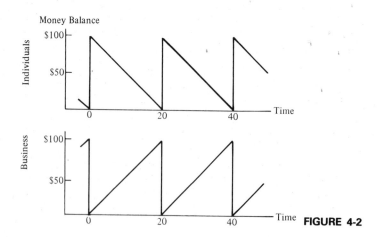

FIGURE 4-2

money in circulation is clearly $100. Every dollar of this sum is always either in the balance of business or of consumers. It bounces back and forth between them mediating sales of productive services from individuals to business, and sales of goods from business to individuals.

The total "demand for money" on the part of business plus consumers is obviously $100. This is all a "transactions demand." Since the annual total income in this economy is $400, the demand for money can be described as one fourth of a year's income or product. The total transactions in this economy are $800 per year, so the demand for money can also be described as equal to one eighth of a year's total transactions. Another way of describing these relationships is to say that the **transactions velocity** of this money is eight times per year. Or we can say that the **income velocity** of this money is four times per year: the average dollar makes four circuits per year from an income recipient, through business, and back to an income recipient again.

It should also be noted that had the shrinkage of consumers' balances followed a path which was *concave* upward, business balances would have grown by a path which was *convex* upward. The smaller average demand for money by consumers would have been precisely offset by a larger average demand by business; the faster turnover by consumers offset by a slower turnover by business. In either circumstance, however, there is no idle money. *Minimum* balances are zero both for business and consumers.

We can adapt this picture to reflect more closely real economies. All income payment dates do not coincide. The period for income payment is not the same for all types of incomes. Business is not organized in one giant firm, but in separate firms having intermediate transactions among themselves, each one holding necessary transactions balances. All of these complications can be incorporated without alteration of principle. Even the fact that people save and lend, and deal in existing assets, and that business gets money not only from sale but from borrowing can also be brought in. (Other problems, however, cannot be so easily handled: particularly, perhaps, the assumption not only of stationary conditions, but of *certainty* regarding the timing and amount of future payments. More of these things later, however.)

We turn now to brief consideration of some of the factors that determine the amount of money balances necessary to accommodate any particular level of transactions or income. One of these factors is, clearly, the **payment habits** of the community. Suppose that, in our previous example, the pay period were cut to 10 days. Suppose $50 of income were paid out each 10 days instead of $100 each 20 days as in Figure 4-3. Exactly the same level of annual income payments and volume of business sales could now be accomplished with half the previous stock of money. The demand for money would now be only one sixteenth of a year's transactions, only one eighth of a year's income. The income velocity of money would now be 8, its transactions velocity 16.

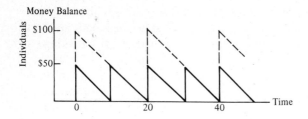

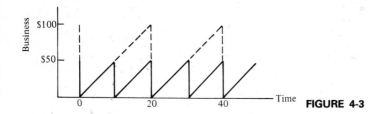

FIGURE 4-3

The payment habits that are relevant here are not only those relating to frequency of income payment, but also those relating to frequency of settlement of bills for goods. Suppose, for example, we introduce charge accounts, which need to be settled only once per year. This obviously reduces substantially the need for money. "Trade credit" among firms in the business sector operates similarly to reduce the need for money by business.

A related determinant of velocity is the degree of business integration. If business is vertically integrated, less money is needed than if business is vertically disintegrated, each "layer" holding a necessary balance. For discussion of these points the student should consult the section on "determinants of velocity" in any standard money and banking text.[4]

Given the payment habits and the industrial structure of the community, the amount of money *needed* for transactions obviously depends only on the money volume of these transactions. If our highly simplified economy considered earlier doubled in size—twice as much production and real income—twice as much money would be required to mediate the enlarged volume of transactions, assuming the price level remained the same. Aggregate income would double to $200 per period and sales of goods to $200, meaning that a money supply of $200 would be needed to make the necessary payments, with average balances of business and consumers each now $100 instead of $50 as before. But if the money

---

[4] A further significant determinant, less often discussed, is the degree of "overlapping" of payment dates. See Howard S. Ellis, "Some Fundamentals in the Theory of Velocity," *Quarterly Journal of Economics*, May 1938, LII, 431–72; reprinted in *Readings in Monetary Theory* (Philadelphia, Pa.: 1951), pp. 89–128.

supply remained at $100, it would be impossible to make $200 worth of payments per period. Half of the goods could not be sold; half of the incomes could not be paid. However, because prices were flexible, prices would instead fall by 50 percent, and the doubled volume of goods could then be sold and the doubled real incomes could then be paid with the same $100 money stock.

Similarly, if changes in payment habits or in the degree of business integration doubled the volume of transactions required for the same volume of final output, this would reduce income velocity, C, by one half. Either M must double or prices fall by 50 percent. But *given these institutionally determined patterns of payment frequency, business integration, and so on,* C or m was constant because rational individuals would never hold idle balances. Minimum balances during the payment cycle would always be zero.

Exceptions to the Quantity Theory

To be sure, not all classical writers ruled out the possibility of changes in C or m as the result of irrational waves of "hoarding" or "dishoarding." Suppose that for some reason—for example, severe uncertainty about possible future political developments—people generally wished to increase by 10 percent their average stock of money balances, by returning to the spending stream in some period only 90 percent of the money they had received, acquiring minimum balances equal to 10 percent of their (previous) money incomes per period. The previous real output could, of course, still be sold—but only at a price level now 10 percent lower than before—even though M had not changed. Assuming perfect flexibility of all prices, the price of every good would fall by 10 percent, and—so long as no further desire to add to balances appeared—the economy would continue to function at the new 10 percent-lower price level, with each participant receiving a money income which was 10 percent less, but which would buy the same quantities of goods as before. As it was spent, it would provide others with money receipts adequate to purchase the (now 10 percent lower priced) goods or services which he supplies. With 10 percent of the money supply immobilized in idle balances, it was just as if that money had disappeared.

If, at some later time, members of the economy should desire to get rid of the idle money previously laid by (again assume all at once, for simplicity), all prices must rise by 11 percent, reflecting the excess of money demand over supply at the lower price level. General hoarding and dishoarding were not, however, assumed to occur in ordinary circumstances. Rational men had no use for idle money. Therefore, they did not hoard it, and, having not previously hoarded, they could not dishoard. Thus the source of price level fluctuations was not ordinarily to be found here.

Another aberration sometimes recognized as an exception to the quantity theory was the possibility that wages and prices might be temporarily rigid—especially in the downward direction. It is easy to see that, if there occurred a drop in M and velocity remained constant, then although the money value of the national product would necessarily fall in proportion to the decline in M, it would be Y, not P, that would decline. Real output would fall short of the full-employment level. Likewise, this might occur if growth in the level of full-employment output were not accompanied by a proportional rise in M. Then, if, for some reason, P failed to decline, Y would have to.

In either of these circumstances, a subsequent increase in M would then be more likely to raise real output than the price level. And since, in the real world, prices are not as flexible as the quantity theory assumed, it is not surprising that there were times when classical economists actually advocated deliberate increases in the quantity of money as a means of increasing real output and employment. To be sure, this would not be necessary if only wages and prices had been fully flexible; but they may not always be that flexible. And if unemployment had arisen from a previous *fall* in M, or from a rise in Y as the result of greater productivity or a larger labor force, it would not even be "inflationary" to increase M—at least if "inflation" were defined as an increase in P.

Irrational hoarding–dishoarding and irrational price rigidity[5] were nevertheless the exceptions that proved the rule. Generally speaking, changes in the price level were only the result of changes in M. Thus, the classical economists saw the mining or importation of gold as *mainly* responsible for changes in the price level. Their successors today, often described as "monetarists," explain changes in the price level as *mainly* determined by the "money creation" of central banks (in the United States, the Federal Reserve System.)

Subsequent developments in monetary theory—which will be explained fully later—have considerably modified this analysis, with significant consequences both for Say's Law and the quantity theory. First, they have added other sources of a demand for money in addition to the "transactions demand" contemplated by the quantity theory's assumption that money is used merely as a medium of exchange. (Existence of these additional sources of demand for money can be described as providing a "rational" explanation for systematic hoarding and dishoarding.) In addition, they have recognized that even the transactions demand for money is not simply a parameter that is given by the structure of society, but, instead, that it is an economic variable that needs explanation in a more adequate theory. As will be seen, this view holds that the pattern of

---

[5] Price rigidity would be irrational because it must have arisen from a deliberate choice to accept unemployment of labor or capital rather than a wage or price reduction—which might not have been even a reduction in *real* wage or *relative* price.

payments is not uniquely determined by institutions but rather reflects a choice—based on their relative costs—among many possible payment patterns. Changing relative costs may thus give rise to different patterns of payments, and a different transactions demand for money. One factor, in particular, which determines these relative costs is the rate of interest. Thus, it will be argued, the velocity of circulation, or the demand for money, is a function, in part, of the rate of interest.

All this will be elaborated below. Here we need merely to be aware that, in assuming a fixed velocity of circulation, we are making the simplification which the classical economists made.

WAGES, PRICES, EMPLOYMENT, AND PRODUCTION

We saw in the previous part that classical macroeconomics maintained that the value of the national product, PY, is determined by the money supply, M. With a given stock of money, aggregate price times quantity is a constant. More can be sold only at proportionately lower prices. If prices are flexible, they will fall whenever there are idle resources; this fall in prices somehow automatically promotes or accompanies the absorption of these idle resources and an expansion of the physical volume of output. In this part, we examine more specifically *how* price flexibility promotes full employment in an economy in which people work for wages, rather than supply final goods directly to the market.

We simplify this analysis very greatly (as did the classical writers) by assuming that perfect competition prevails in all industries and that each industry is vertically integrated. It hires only labor and produces final output (using a given stock of capital goods and natural resources); there are no intermediate goods. We further assume that sellers attempt always to maximize short-run profits.

So far as employment and wages are concerned, we can make the further assumption that there exists a single, national labor market, in which all workers provide and all employers seek to hire a single, undifferentiated type and quality of labor service, and that the competition of workers for jobs and of employers for workers thus produces a single, uniform wage rate. This implies the absence of effective labor unions (or employer's associations) that restrict competition. It also implies sufficient mobility of labor among firms, industries, and localities, and complete information freely and instantly available to all workers and firms, so that all employers must pay the going (uniform) wage in order to hire or retain any workers; yet none needs pay more because each can hire all he needs at that wage.

A more complete and realistic but still classical theory can recognize the existence of partially separate markets for a wide variety of specialized types and qualities of labor, with only limited mobility of workers among the various markets as well as among the various localities. Such a theory can then explain the existence of both temporary and permanent wage differentials, as well as changes in these differentials which reflect altered relative supplies and demands for particular types of workers and at particular places. However, so long as effective competition is assumed among the workers and employers involved in the supply and the demand for each and every particular quality of labor and in each and every local labor market, as well as adequate information within each such market, we can still make sense of the concepts of an aggregate supply of labor of all kinds, and an aggregate demand for all labor. These factors together determine the *average* wage level, from which all differentials can be measured. Each particular wage rate would always flexibly adjust to "clear" each and every particular labor market, while any *net* change in *aggregate supply* or *aggregate demand* for labor would alter the average wage. For the present, however, we assume the single, undifferentiated labor quality, and the single, competitively determined wage rate.

It should be obvious that actual labor markets of the "real world" bear little resemblance to the above assumptions.

Aggregate Supply of Labor

The total supply of labor hours was (at any given time) assumed by classical economists to vary directly with the real hourly wage that potential workers found they could earn—that is, more workers would seek jobs (or offer to work longer hours) the higher the available real wage. (However, at least at relatively high real wages, the supply might be argued to depend *inversely* on the real wage—even on classical assumptions. For already well-paid workers might wish to take some part of the higher real incomes made possible by a still higher real wage in the form of more leisure.)

In today's world it seems more reasonable to assume that the supply is essentially independent of the real wage, reflecting mainly the size of the population and the social and institutional factors that determine who seeks to work and for how many hours. This view would stress the fairly rigid conventional or legal definitions of the length of "standard" work day and work week; the traditional or legal limits on the ages at which workers enter into and exit from the labor force; and institutionalized concepts of the work roles of women, youth, and older workers in society. It would also stress the fact that most workers have little effective option as to the number of hours per day or week that they work. In any case, since most people in the active labor force must work in order to live, any impact on the total labor supply of modest changes in the real wage must be relatively slight in percentage terms. Thus, graphically, the supply curve of labor might slope very slightly upward to the right, slightly upward to the left, slightly upward to the right at lower real wages and then to the left at higher ones, but it must be very close to vertical in the relevant range.

Denoting the aggregate supply L as a function of the real wage W/P—the ratio of the money wage W to the price level P—we have

(4)
$$L = L\left(\frac{W}{P}\right)$$

where the sign of the first derivative of this function is unknown:

$$\frac{dL}{d(W/P)} \gtrless 0$$

that is, the supply of labor may increase as the real wage increases, may be independent of the real wage, or may decrease as the real wage increases. It is simplest to assume that it is independent of the real wage, as we shall often do. (In that case, L is no longer a function, but simply a given quantity.)

Aggregate Demand for Labor and Labor Market Equilibrium

Traditional microeconomic theory assumes perfect competition in all product markets as well as in the labor market. Under these circumstances, the demand for labor—like the demand for any other input—by each profit-maximizing firm depends on (a) the price of the input—that is, the wage rate that it must pay; (b) the marginal contribution in physical terms of each unit of input to the firm's total output; and (c) the price at which that output can be sold. Formally, we assume that the physical output, Y_{ij}, of the ith firm in the jth industry ($i = 1 \cdots n, j = 1 \cdots m$) is a function of its "variable" inputs of labor (N_{ij}), its "fixed" inputs of services of capital and land (K_{ij}), and its variable inputs purchased from other firms (M_{ij}):

(5)
$$Y_{ij} = f^{ij}(N_{ij}, K_{ij}, M_{ij})$$

This "production function" is assumed to involve diminishing marginal returns to each input. That is, the marginal product of labor is positive but declines as N_{ij} increases. Designating the first partial derivative of this function with respect to N_{ij} as $\partial f^{ij}/\partial N_{ij}$, and its second partial derivative as $\partial^2 f^{ij}/\partial N_{ij}^2$, we state these conditions formally as

$$\frac{\partial f^{ij}}{\partial N_{ij}} > 0$$

that is, labor's marginal product is positive in each firm; and

$$\frac{\partial^2 f^{ij}}{\partial N_{ij}^2} < 0$$

that is, this marginal product declines as the firm's labor input is increased. If we assume (for simplicity) that, in the short run, each firm's inputs of capital and land services are fixed, and that each firm is fully integrated so that $M_{ij} = 0$, we can define the firm's profits

(6) $$\Pi_{ij} = P_j Y_{ij} - W N_{ij} - F_{ij}$$

where $P_j Y_{ij}$ is the value of its sales, $W N_{ij}$ is its wage bill, and F_{ij} are all its capital and other costs (assumed fixed). Profits are maximized when employment is determined such that

$$\frac{\partial \Pi_{ij}}{\partial N_{ij}} = P_j \frac{\partial f^{ij}}{\partial N_{ij}} - W = 0$$

This condition for maximum profit can be arranged in any of three ways:

(7) $$W = P_j \frac{\partial f^{ij}}{\partial N_{ij}}$$

(8) $$P_j = \frac{W}{\partial f^{ij}/\partial N_{ij}}$$

or

(9) $$\frac{W}{P_j} = \frac{\partial f^{ij}}{\partial N_{ij}}$$

The first arrangement (equation 7) says that the profit-maximizing competitive firm carries its output and employment to the point where the market value of its workers' (declining) marginal product equals the market wage which has to be paid; the second (equation 8) says that at this profit-maximizing output and employment, the industry price equals each firm's (rising) marginal cost; and the third (equation 9) says that at this output and employment, its "real wage," W/P_j, equals each firm's (declining) marginal product of labor. (Note that "real wage" is here measured in terms of the product price of the firm's own industry—*not* in terms of the general price level.) P_j, of course, which is taken as given by each firm in industry j, is itself determined by the total demand for that product and the aggregate supply response of all of the firms producing that product.

As either the economy-wide money wage, W, or the industry-wide price, P_j, or both, vary, altering the real wage, individual firms will necessarily adjust their employment in response to that variation. In short,

(10) $$N_{ij} = \theta_{ij}\left(\frac{W}{P_j}\right)$$

The firm's demand for labor depends on the real wage it must pay, a function derived from the firm's production function. It carries its employment to the point where its own workers' marginal product equals the real wage; since this marginal product declines with additional employment, the demand curve is downward sloping.[6]

So far the analysis has been based on observations at the microeconomic level. For the purposes of classical macroeconomics, however, it was deemed necessary to establish the total demand for labor by all firms as a function of the economy-wide real wage, that is, of W/P where P is some average of all of the individual P_j. The usual way in which this is done is to treat the entire economy analogously with a single firm. Thus we might suppose that there exists an aggregate production function,

$$(11) \qquad\qquad Y = F(N, K)$$

where Y is total output, N is total employment, and K is the aggregate stock of capital. Then, with capital fixed, we consider the change of output as total employment varies, asserting the condition

$$(12) \qquad\qquad \frac{\partial F}{\partial N} = \frac{W}{P}$$

corresponding to the condition of maximum profit for the firm. It says that the *aggregate* "marginal product" should equal the economy-wide real wage.

This system is completed by the prescription that equilibrium requires full employment:

$$(13) \qquad\qquad L = N$$

The preceding procedure seems incorrect or, at least, highly unsatisfactory in a number of respects. In the first place, the concept of an aggregate production function raises severe difficulties. There was mention in Chapter 1 of the difficulties of aggregating nonlinear functions and considerable discussion in Chapter 3 (in the section entitled "Employment and Output") of the problems involved in specifying an aggregate production function, even if the production functions of the individual firms were all well defined. Moreover, it was shown that, if one postulates the existence of such an aggregate function and attempts to quantify it using aggregate data, he fails to discover any evidence of diminishing returns. But even if we might wish to ignore these difficulties and to assume that

---

[6] A simple production function in labor alone which meets the classical specification of diminishing returns is $Y_{ij} = aN_{ij} - bN_{ij}^2$. The derivative of this function—the marginal product of labor—is

$$\frac{dY_{ij}}{dN_{ij}} = a - 2bN_{ij}$$

Setting $dY_{ij}/dN_{ij} = W/P_j$, and rearranging produces the firm's demand for labor function:

$$N_{ij} = \frac{a}{2b} - \frac{1}{2b}\left(\frac{W}{P_j}\right)$$

a downward sloping function of W/P_j.

there exists a single-valued, continuous, and differentiable aggregate production function displaying diminishing returns, it is unclear what the condition (12) is supposed to represent. Its single-firm counterpart is a condition for maximum profit. But what profit does it here refer to: the aggregate of all firms' profits? There seems little point in defining such an aggregate profit, since no individual or government decision is based on it. Certainly there is no decision to maximize it.

A preferred alternate procedure is, however, available, which avoids some of these difficulties by dispensing with any aggregate production function and by working directly with the demand-for-labor functions (θ_{ij}) of individual firms, where each firm's demand for labor is derived from its own production function (f_{ij}). Thus, we define an economy-wide aggregate demand-for-labor schedule:

$$(14) \qquad N = \theta[W, P_j \, (j = 1, 2, \ldots, m)]$$

where N is the sum of the employment in each firm: that is, where $N = \Sigma_j \Sigma_i N_{ij}$. We can still specify that $\partial\theta/\partial W < 0$; that is, that a rise in the economy-wide wage rate, all prices constant, will reduce the total demand for labor (since it will reduce it in every firm). And, of course, $\partial\theta/\partial P_j > 0$ for all commodities j: that is, a rise in any one price, all other prices and the wage rate constant, will increase the total demand for labor. Assumptions sufficient (but not necessary) for such a function to exist are that all firms are fully integrated and that all commodities are so defined that there are no complementary or substitute relationships among them *in production*. Under these conditions

$$(12a) \qquad N = \theta[W, P_j \, (j = 1, 2, \ldots, m)] = \sum_j \sum_i \theta_{ij}\left(\frac{W}{P_j}\right)$$

and one can easily verify that $(\partial\theta/\partial W) < 0$ and $(\partial\theta/\partial P_j) > 0$ for all j. But we are still faced with a problem, for a demand-for-labor function which depends on the price of every product is hardly useful in a highly aggregative macroeconomic model!

In an attempt to avoid such a function we could define an overall price index, P, which is some weighted average of all product prices; that is,

$$(15) \qquad P = \sum_j w_j P_j$$

where the weights (the w_j) are normalized to sum to 1. We would like to be able to specify appropriate weights so that we could write

$$(14a) \qquad N = \Phi(W, P)$$

such that

$$\frac{\partial\Phi}{\partial W} < 0 \qquad \text{and} \qquad \frac{\partial\Phi}{\partial P} > 0$$

But it seems unlikely that a weighting scheme can be found which would make possible a rigorous derivation of (14a) from (14) and (15). Even if the individual firms' demand-for-labor functions are independent of each other, as assumed for (14), there is no unique relationship between the price index, P, and the value of the function, Φ. Moreover, one can be certain that a change in the value of W determines a unique change in the value of Φ at a given P, only if P is constant because each P_j is constant.[7]

It seems necessary to compromise somewhat between what is analytically rigorous and what is theoretically useful. We can note that for changes in W or in P *that do not involve "substantial" changes in relative prices or in the relative composition of aggregate demand* we would expect to observe a loose, *empirical* relationship between N, W, and P. We can employ as a shorthand for this loose empirical relationship the notation

(14b)
$$N \simeq \Phi(W, P)$$

where changes in N are positively related to changes in P and negatively related to changes in W, that is,

$$\frac{\Delta\Phi}{\Delta P} > 0 \quad \text{and} \quad \frac{\Delta\Phi}{\Delta W} < 0$$

---

[7] For example, using the form of θ specified in (14), compare changes in P arising from changes in two individual product prices (P_k and P_l). Let

$$\frac{\partial\theta_{ij}}{\partial(w/P_j)} = \theta'_{ij}$$

In one case

$$\Delta P = w_k \, \Delta P_k \quad \text{and} \quad \Delta N \simeq -\sum_i \theta'_{ik}\frac{W}{P_k^2}\Delta P_k$$

(One could calculate ΔN exactly by using a Taylor series expansion of each θ_{ij}. Since the thrust of the argument does not depend on the approximate representation of ΔN, we avoid that unnecessary complication.) In the other case,

$$\Delta P = w_l\Delta P_l \quad \text{and} \quad \Delta N \simeq -\sum_i \theta'_{il}\frac{W}{P_l^2}\Delta P_l$$

If ΔP is the same in both cases, $\Delta P_l = (w_k/w_l)\,\Delta P_k$. The same change in unemployment will occur only if

$$\sum_i \theta'_{ik}\frac{W}{P_k^2}\Delta P_k = \sum_i \theta'_{il}\frac{W}{P_l^2}\Delta P_l$$

or

$$\sum_i \frac{\theta'_{ik}}{P_k^2} = \frac{w_k}{w_l}\sum_i \frac{\theta'_{il}}{P_l^2}$$

For such a relationship to hold always, the weights in P must be in a particular ratio. But since that ratio depends on the individual product prices, it is impossible to construct a set of weights that is appropriate for all changes in P. Similarly, one could show that if two individual prices change in such a way that P remains constant ($w_k \, \Delta P_k = -w_l \, \Delta P_l$), N may change even if W remains fixed.

as long as it is clearly understood that this relationship holds only approximately and only as long as there are no substantial changes in the composition of aggregate demand or in relative prices.[8] While in most cases we would expect the inequalities in (14b) to describe the directions of influence in Φ (and will assume throughout the rest of this chapter that they do), we are not constrained by theory from making different assumptions if they appear to be plausible in a particular case. We regard this flexibility as a strength of this approach which more than offsets any weakness in its theoretical underpinnings.

We can now combine this approximate aggregate demand for labor function (14b) with the aggregate supply of labor (equation 4) to describe the overall labor market. The labor market will be in equilibrium only if the total supply of labor equals the total demand for labor. Thus the equilibrium condition is

$$(13) \qquad\qquad L = N$$

Assuming there is some real wage at which equation (13) holds,[9] this condition implies the equilibrium real wage. And, at real wage rates above this equilibrium, supply would exceed demand, and at lower real wages, demand would exceed supply. If we assume perfect competition in the

---

[8] It is difficult to be very specific about what a "substantial" change is in this context. For instance if P changes because all the individual P_j which change move in the same direction (though not necessarily in the same proportion), then N will surely change in that same direction, and we will observe that $\Delta N/\Delta P > 0$. But the reasoning in footnote 7 above suggests that if two individual prices move in opposite directions, the ratio of price index weights may be such that ΔN and ΔP have opposite signs. In the language of the text, such a pattern of price changes would indicate a "substantial" change in relative prices (possibly because of or in conjunction with a change in the composition of aggregate demand), and (14b) would not accurately describe the macroeconomic result of such a change.

Then what do we do when changes in W or P are accompanied by substantial changes in relative prices? We must simply acknowledge a truth too often forgotten by those decrying recent "failures of modern economic analysis": a model that is useful for analyzing one set of problems may not be appropriate for studying a different set. A highly aggregative macroeconomic model is not the best framework for analyzing problems involving significant disturbance of normal microeconomic relationships.

[9] This does not have to be the case. We can imagine that in an overpopulated country with very little capital, or in a situation in which a large part of a country's capital has been destroyed, the two curves might look like this:

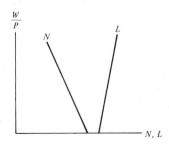

labor market and complete flexibility for the money wage rate, an excess of supply of labor over demand will cause the money wage to fall without limit, and an excess of demand will cause it to rise without limit.

In Chapter 3, we argued that the money wage tends to rise not at "full employment" in the literal sense—that is, zero unemployment—but rather at some low positive level of unemployment, reflecting the inability of every unemployed person desiring work to be able to find a job immediately, even when vacant jobs existed. Although the unemployment level at which wage rates begin to rise appreciably cannot be known precisely, we perhaps can and often do represent it by some "convention-al" positive rate of unemployment, which is used as a target or goal for policy. Although the classical analysis ignored this problem, we make approximate allowance for it by interpreting the phrases "an excess of supply of labor over demand" and "an excess of demand (for labor over supply)" in the last sentence of the preceding paragraph to refer to the situation in which the unemployment rate falls below this conventional representation of "full employment." We return to the real problem involved only in Chapter 13.

In any case, whether a rise or fall in the money wage—consequent upon an excess or deficiency of labor demand—will also mean a rise or fall of the real wage is a question to which we will shortly turn. For, unless it does, disequilibrium in the labor market would not be corrected: excess demand would continually raise money wages, excess supply continually depress them—without limit.

First, however, return to equation (11), the hypothesized aggregate production function. Although we have denied that any such function exists, or that—even if it did—the aggregate demand for labor could properly be derived from it, there can be no question that some approximate empirical relationship does exist between aggregate employment and aggregate production, even though it should not be thought of as a production function. That is, we shall specify an approximate, empirical output–employment relationship[10]

(11a) $$Y \simeq F(N, K)$$

Unless there is some such relationship, our macro model cannot be completed. For it is necessary to know what the level of employment determined by equations (4), (13), and (14b) imply about Y, and (in the classical model) about the demand for money associated with each level of Y. Earlier, in the section of Chapter 3 entitled "Employment and Output,"[11] we explained that this empirical relationship need not have, and in fact

---

[10] The same kind of qualification applies to the F relationship as was cited for the relationship in (12d), namely, that no "substantial" shifts occur in the relative composition of aggregate output.

[11] The reader is urged to review that section.

does not appear to have and should not be expected to have, the general shape assumed to exist for individual firm production functions—namely, that $\partial^2 F/\partial N^2 < 0$. All that we assume is that $F(N_1) > F(N_0)$ if N_1 significantly exceeds N_0. That is, any significant increase in employment raises real output. However, we do not specify that this increase in real output is necessarily less than (or more than) in proportion to the increase in N. Moreover, while this empirical aggregate production–employment function must bear some indirect relationship to our empirical aggregate-labor-demand function, it is clear that there is no simple or precise relationship between them. It is clear, though, that a significant shift in the production–employment function must also shift the aggregate demand-for-labor function, in the same direction as the traditional treatment requires.

The Relation of Money Wage Rates to the Price Level

Although the *aggregate* supply of labor was described as a function of the economy-wide real wage, and the aggregate demand for labor as at least an approximate function of that real wage, individual competitive employers, as well as their workers or prospective workers, obviously take the price level—both of that employer's product and of products generally—as entirely independent of the money wage paid or offered by the particular employer. Thus, so far as individual employers and workers are concerned, variation in the money wage necessarily constitutes an equivalent variation in the real wage: both the real wage expressed in terms of the individual product price, which is relevant to the employer's offer; and the real wage expressed in terms of the general price level (and thus the "cost of living"), which is relevant to the worker's acceptance.

However, when we move from the microeconomic level of individual hiring and employment decisions to the macroeconomic level of the entire economy, we must recognize, first, that not only wages—but also individual prices and the average price level—are variables, not fixed quantities; and, second, that the level of the economy-wide wage rate and the average level of prices are not independent. That is, we must not assume that a reduction of the money wage necessarily produces a reduction of the real wage. Suppose, for example, that at the existing money wage rate and average level of prices, employers in the aggregate find it profitable to employ fewer workers than wish to work at the implied real wage. If there is full and free competition, we have assumed that the unemployed workers will offer their services at lower money wage rates, rather than remain idle; that is, W will rapidly decline. However, we cannot conclude that this automatically increases the demand for labor. For whether and to what extent this results in additional employment and output depends on what happens to product prices. If prices should not fall at all, or should fall in smaller proportion than did wages, employers would find it profitable to increase output, absorbing some of the unemployed. But if all prices, or the average of prices, should fall in the same proportion as the money wage, there would be no incentive for employers to increase employment and output. What happens to the real wage when money wages fall depends on the response of prices to a change in the money wage.

In his *General Theory of Employment, Interest and Money*, John Maynard Keynes pointed out that classical employment theory provided no satisfactory explanation why the level of selling prices would not, in the face of a general wage reduction, fall in exactly the same proportion as wages.[12] On the assumption that, in the short run, labor is the only variable factor of production, marginal costs are proportional to wage rates, and—if prices equal marginal costs—they should fall in proportion to wages. If some classical writers appeared, either explicitly or implicitly, to assume that the price level would remain constant when money wages fell, that was simply an illegitimate extension to the entire economy of an assumption possibly appropriate for a single employer. If there were general unemployment and flexible wages, Keynes argued that classical theory should have assumed an equal deflation of *both wages and prices*, which would continue indefinitely, since there would be no reduction in the real wage and thus no increase in employment, and the unemployed would thus continually bid the money wage level downward, accompanied always by a proportional reduction in the price level.

However, this result ignores another significant strand of the classical analysis—which we have already considered—the quantity theory. For if prices were to fall as fast as wages, with no increase in employment and output, idle balances would automatically be created in the hands of business or consumers or both. Since rational people are not willing to accumulate idle balances, this could not happen. A fall in the demand for money with no change in the supply would violate the quantity theory.

Explicitly adding the quantity theory (or some substitute) to the model is indeed necessary to make it determinate. So far, we have represented the "traditional version" of the classical system by equations (4), (11), (12), and (13), as follows:

(4) $$L = L\left(\frac{W}{P}\right) \qquad \frac{dL}{dW/P} \gtreqless 0$$

(11) $$Y = F(N, K) \qquad \frac{\partial F}{\partial N} > 0 \qquad \frac{\partial^2 F}{\partial N^2} < 0$$

(12) $$\frac{\partial F}{\partial N} = \frac{W}{P}$$

(13) $$L = N$$

[12] See Chapter 2, "The Postulates of the Classical Economics."

We have also introduced a preferred, alternative version of the classical model which does not depend on the questionable existence of an aggregate production function with an aggregate marginal product of labor that declines with increasing employment. This substitutes, for (11) and (12),

(11a) $$Y \simeq F(N, K)$$

where $F(N_1) > F(N_0)$, when N_1 is significantly $> N_0$

(14b) $$N \simeq \Phi(W, P)$$

with $\Delta\Phi/\Delta W < 0$, $\Delta\Phi/\Delta P > 0$ for significant changes in W or P.

However, either system involves five macroeconomic variables: Y, P, W, N, and L, but only four equations. To make the system determinate we need one more equation in these variables. It can be supplied by the quantity theory:

(3) $$M = mPY$$

where m is taken as constant, or institutionally determined, and M is (at any given time) fixed.

The quantity theory thus provides a classical answer to the question what happens to the general price level as wages fall in the presence of unemployment. So long as $L > N$, W falls without limit. Now, however, there is a *lower limit to the fall of P*; it is the point at which $M = mPY_P$, where Y_P is the level of "potential" output. This is the level of output found from the aggregate production-employment relationship (equation 11 or 11a), and corresponds to the N at which $N = L$.[13] Given the real wage, W/P, which is necessary for $N = L$, and given the P that satisfies the quantity theory when $Y = Y_P$, the necessary W can be determined. If W falls without limit so long as $L > N$, this equilibrium will be established and maintained.

Graphic and Algebraic Representation: I. Traditional Classical Formulation

We can now summarize and illustrate the equilibrium system which we have constructed in the preceding pages. This section will do so using the traditional formulation with an aggregate production function and an aggregate demand for labor derived directly from that function, and a supply of labor which increases with the real wage. The section that follows will use the less traditional model, which employs an empirical demand for labor function and an empirical production–employment relationship not necessarily subject to diminishing returns, and, again, a forward sloping supply of labor schedule. In each case, we shall first present a graphic summary of the model, then some numerical algebraic examples.

[13] Where L represents total labor force less minimum (conventionally defined) unemployment.

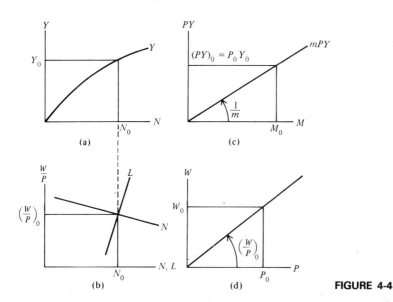

FIGURE 4-4

A graphical representation of this model is shown in Figure 4-4. Part (a) shows the aggregate production–employment relationship, or aggregate "production function," subject to diminishing returns. For each level of labor input there is a corresponding total output. Part (b) shows the intersection of supply and demand curves for labor. The demand for labor, N, is here taken as precisely reflecting the "marginal product" of labor from the aggregate employment–output function of part (a). The curve N represents, of course, the slope of the production function, which declines as employment increases because production is subject to diminishing returns. Corresponding to each production function there is one and only one aggregate marginal product curve. A change in the height of the production function, with no change in its slope at any level of employment, would leave the marginal product curve unchanged. (This would represent a rise in the *average* productivity but not the *marginal* productivity of labor.) But any change in slope of the production function curve will alter the marginal product, that is, the labor-demand curve.

The intersection of the two curves in part (b) defines the point of full employment, N_0, and the real wage, $(W/P)_0$, which corresponds to full employment.[14] If the real wage were somehow maintained higher than that which corresponds to the intersection of the two curves, there would be an excess of supply over demand for labor. If the real wage were lower than that which corresponds to the intersection, the result would be a labor shortage. Assuming perfect labor market competition, the former condition results in a rapid decline in the money wage; the latter in a rapid rise in the money wage. Stability of the money wage is obviously a condition of

[14] Recall that the point of "full employment" involves some positive level of unemployment.

equilibrium of the system. Therefore, equilibrium requires stable money wage and a stable price level which produce a real wage of $(W/P)_0$.

We find the equilibrium price level in part (c) of the figure. Here the straight line through the origin, mPY (whose slope is $1/m$) shows the amount of money required for each level of money income, or, read in the other direction, the level of money income which each possible quantity of money can support. If the actual stock of money is that shown by the vertical line marked M_0, then money income must equal $(PY)_0$. Since we know the equilibrium income Y_0 (from part a), we can immediately compute the equilibrium price level P_0.

Part (d) permits us to find the necessary level of the money wage. In part (d) we plot as a diagonal line the equilibrium real wage found in part (b). Any real wage is a *ratio* of price to money wage. Therefore, corresponding to each real wage are numerous possible combinations of P and W, all of which fall on a straight line through the origin whose slope measures the real wage. Given the equilibrium real wage and the equilibrium price level, there is only one money wage consistent with both of these. This is read off in part (d) as the vertical coordinate of the intersection of equilibrium price, P_0, and the equilibrium real-wage angle.

A better understanding of the model and of the diagram will come from analyzing the effects on the equilibrium values of the several variables of various changes in parameters. For example, we may consider the effects of an increase in M; a shift in the production function; or a shift in the supply schedule of labor.

An increase in the quantity of money permits an increase in the product of P and Y as shown in part (c) of Figure 4-5. The previous output,

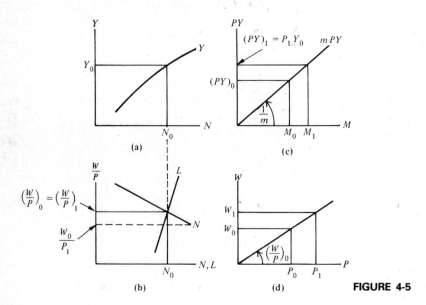

(a)

(b)

(c)

(d)

FIGURE 4-5

Y_0, could now sell at a higher price, P_1. If money wages did not rise, real wages would fall. This would induce employers to try to increase output, bidding against each other for workers. Since no more workers are to be had (indeed, fewer if prices rise without a proportional rise in wages), the money wage must rise far enough to eliminate the excess demand. (The gap between demand and supply at the new price and old wage is shown in part (b) of Figure 4-5.)

The result of an increase in money, then, is to raise wages and prices in equal proportion, leaving output, real wages, and employment unaffected. The results of a decrease in M can easily be worked out.

The next shift we shall consider is a change in the production function. The change shown in Figure 4-6 involves an increase in both the average and in the marginal products of labor.

The new production function in Figure 4-6, Y', gives a new marginal product curve, or demand-for-labor curve, N'. The equilibrium real wage

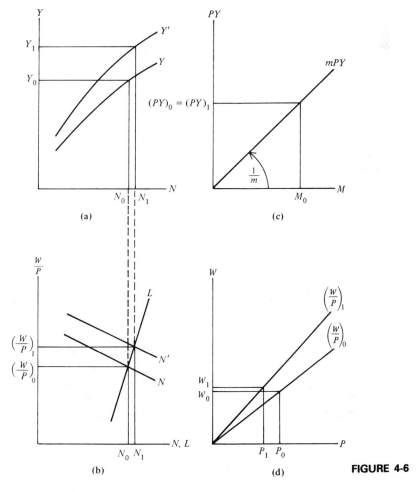

FIGURE 4-6

is increased from $(W/P)_0$ to $(W/P)_1$, as is the equilibrium volume of employment, from N_0 to N_1. Output is enlarged to Y_1, both because of the higher production function and because of the larger employment. If M and m are unchanged, the larger output can be sold only at a lower price level, P_1. Despite the drop in prices, the money wage (in this example) can nevertheless rise to W_1. (Depending on the slopes of the various functions, the new money wage might be lower rather than higher; however, the real wage will certainly be higher—prices will fall more than wages.)

The interested reader can readily derive graphically the effects of an increase in the supply of labor. They are: a lower real wage, a larger employment, a larger output, a lower price level, and a lower money wage.

It will again be noted that we can divide this analysis into two parts—a "real" and a monetary. The real wage and the levels of employment and output are determined by "real" factors alone: the marginal productivity of labor and the marginal disutility (or other "real" factors underlying the supply) of labor. Money wages and prices are determined solely by monetary factors. Changes on the "real" side can affect prices and wages, but changes on the monetary side have no effect on the "real" magnitudes. This presumably justifies the classical tradition of developing the theory of output and employment entirely in real terms (Say's Law), leaving the theory of absolute prices to a chapter at the end of the book, or to a separate treatise on monetary theory.

Since any line on a graph corresponds to some particular numerical equation, we can also illustrate the use of this model by the simultaneous solution of numerical equations. We start with an assumed supply of labor,

(i)
$$L = 20 + 5\frac{W}{P}$$

embodying the usual classical assumption of a positive slope. Next, the assumed demand for labor,

(ii)
$$N = 80 - 10\frac{W}{P}$$

is consistent with the assumed aggregate production-employment relationship which exhibits classical diminishing returns,[15]

(iii)
$$Y = 8N - 0.05N^2$$

---

[15] If we take the first derivative of this "production function," the **aggregate marginal product,**
$$\frac{dY}{dN} = 8 - 0.1N$$
and if we now assume that employment is carried to the point at which marginal product equals real wage,
$$\frac{dY}{dN} = \frac{W}{P}$$
we can substitute W/P for dY/dN in the preceding expression, and rearrange terms to produce our demand-for-labor equation (ii).

Then we add the equilibrium condition,

(iv) $$L = N$$

and the quantity theory equation, assuming $M = 100$ and $m = 0.5$:

(v) $$M = 100 = 0.5PY$$

The reader should now perform the calculations summarized in the following paragraphs, and verify the results shown.

Substituting (i) and (ii) into (iv), we find the equilibrium real wage:

$$\frac{W}{P} = 4$$

substituting this real wage into either (i) or (ii) yields

$$N = 40$$

substituting this level of employment into (iii) yields

$$Y = 240$$

substituting this total output into (v) yields

$$P = 0.833$$

and substituting this price level into the real wage yields

$$W = 3.333$$

The effect of now increasing the supply of money to, say, 150, would be to increase P to 125 and W to 5 (both increases of 50 percent); if M fell to 70, P would become 0.58333, and W would be 2.333 (both decreases of 30 percent). But no other values—that is, no "real" magnitudes—would be affected.

If, on the other hand (with $M = 100$), the supply of labor increased to

(ia) $$L = 25 + 5\frac{W}{P}$$

all values would be changed, as follows (the reader should calculate to be sure):

$$\frac{W}{P} = 3.667$$
$$N = 43.333$$
$$Y = 252.778$$
$$P = 0.79121$$
$$W = 2.901$$

It will be noted that both prices and wages have declined, but wages more than prices (the real wage now being lower). N increases, although by less than the shift of 5 in the supply of labor schedule, because the lower real wage discourages some workers from working; Y rises, but less than in proportion to N, because of diminishing returns.

Finally, if improved technology shifts the production function upward to

(iiia) $$Y = 8.8N - 0.05N^2$$

causing the demand for labor to rise to

(iia) $$N = 88 - 10\frac{W}{P}$$

and the supply of labor and quantity of money are unchanged from the original assumptions, the new equilibrium values will be:

$$\frac{W}{P} = 4.5333$$
$$N = 42.667$$
$$Y = 250.311$$
$$P = 0.799$$
$$W = 3.622$$

Note that, as compared with the original situation, prices have fallen, but wages—and the real wage—have risen[16]; output and employment are higher. Despite the substantial increase in labor demand, the rise of employment is modest, because labor supply is relatively inelastic.

Illustrative Case II: Some Nontraditional Assumptions

We next take a less traditional classical case, involving proportionality between output and employment, and a demand for labor not strictly consistent with the production–employment relationship. This time we first use algebra and then show the equivalent graphs. The hypothetical equations are

(i) $$L = 20 + 5\frac{W}{P}$$

(iib) $$N = 120 - 25\frac{W}{P}$$

(iiib) $$Y = 6N$$

(iv) $$L = N$$

(v) $$M = 100 = 0.5PY$$

[16] The rise in the money wage rate is not an absolute requirement; it merely reflects our particular numerical assumptions.

Some comment is appropriate regarding equation (iib). It was shown earlier that, while there must be "some relationship" between the approximate aggregate empirical production function and the approximate aggregate empirical demand for labor, the one could not be strictly derived from the other, as classical theory had supposed. The derivative of production function (iiib) is simply 6. Setting this equal to the real wage would produce $W/P = 6$. We can think of this as a demand for labor function infinitely elastic at a real wage of 6, and the system could as well be solved using instead equation (iic):

(iic)
$$\frac{W}{P} = 6$$

Moreover, referring back to the discussion of equations (14a) and (14b), it is clear that the demand for labor not only does not need to be mathematically derived from the production–employment relationship, but also that it need not be symmetrical with respect to changes in W and in P. For example, still another demand for labor function might have been (iid):

(iid)
$$N = 120 - 25W + 15P$$

Using (iia), we solve, as before (and the reader should do the arithmetic, too), to find[17]

$$\frac{W}{P} = 3.333$$
$$N = L = 36.667$$
$$Y = 220$$
$$P = 0.909$$
$$W = 3.030$$

Once again, an increase in M changes only absolute levels of wages and prices, but nothing else. If $M = 150$

$$P = 1.364$$
$$W = 4.545$$

Moreover, an increase in the supply of labor to $L = 25 + 5W/P$ once again reduces the real wage (at least slightly) and alters the absolute levels

---

[17] Using (iic), the results are

$$\frac{W}{P} = 6$$
$$N = L = 50$$
$$Y = 300$$
$$P = 0.667$$
$$W = 4$$

of P (down) and Y (up); N increases by somewhat less than the shift in the supply function. But Y rises in the same proportion as N:

$$\frac{W}{P} = 3.167$$

$$N = L = 40.833$$

$$Y = 245$$

$$P = 0.816$$

$$W = 2.585$$

Finally, an increase in the production–employment relationship to

$$Y = 6.5N$$

with a more or less corresponding increase in the demand for labor function

$$N = 130 - 25\frac{W}{P}$$

with all else unchanged, produces the new values

$$\frac{W}{P} = 3.667$$

$$N = 38.333$$

$$Y = 249.167$$

$$P = 0.803$$

$$W = 2.943$$

As before, the real wage is increased, employment and output rise, prices fall and (this time) the wage rate falls as well. (This is not an absolute requirement—it reflects the particular numerical assumptions.)

Graphically, the model would be represented as in Figure 4-7. The reader can experiment with the graphic treatment of further variants, such as an infinitely elastic demand-for-labor function (a constant real wage), or a vertical or backward sloping supply-of-labor schedule. The combination of vertical supply and horizontal demand curve (each of which may be reasonably realistic) produces a degenerate form of the classical model which, nevertheless, still produces the fundamental classical results: (a) the money supply affects only prices and wages, but nothing else; while (b) if money wages are flexible, the only equilibrium is at full employment.

A Pricing Function Instead of a Demand-for-Labor Function?

In this degenerate case, it becomes more sensible to think of the demand for labor as simply a function of the demand for total output (and proportional to such output). What we have, up to now, been calling the "de-

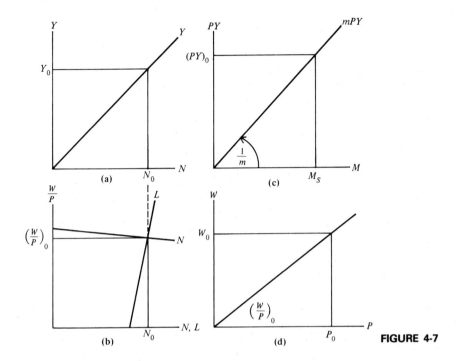

FIGURE 4-7

mand-for-labor function" can then be relabelled a **price determination function**—a relationship between the price level and the wage level.

However, it is not only in this case that it may be equally enlightening to conceive of what we have termed a demand-for-labor function as, instead, a price function. If, for example, we take the demand for labor function used in our first numerical illustration,

$$N = 80 - 10\frac{W}{P}$$

and rearrange it as

$$P = \frac{1}{8 - 0.1N} W$$

we have an expression which says that prices depend on the money wage level, in such a way that prices increase (slightly) relative to wages as N (and Y) increases.

Although such a price-determination function (in approximate form—because of aggregation problems) could easily be derived from the classical equality of prices and marginal costs—which should rise as N and Y increase—it can also be derived from substantially nonclassical descriptions of pricing behavior. One frequently used hypothesis, not substantially inconsistent with empirical observations, holds that prices are based on markups over unit labor costs, with markups that may either be essentially constant, or on the average, expand slightly as total output rises toward full employment. Much of contemporary inflation theory uses essentially this kind of a price determination function, as we shall see.

Thus, we can be as nonclassical as we wish with respect to many of the elements of the "classical model" and still derive its fundamental conclusions, so long as we assume perfect wage flexibility, and money demanded only as a medium of exchange.[18] But what if wage rates are *not* perfectly flexible? We consider that question briefly in the final section of the chapter; then, more fully, in Chapter 11.

RIGID WAGES AND MONETARY POLICY IN THE CLASSICAL MODEL

We consider now the effects of an absence of perfect labor market competition—that is, a limitation on or absence of any tendency for money wages to fall so long as men are unemployed. This might result from an organization of workers which refuses to accept a reduction of money wages when unemployment develops, or which actually forces the money wage upward when there is no excess of demand over the supply of labor. Or it might result simply from custom, legislation, a government wage policy (e.g., President Herbert Hoover's exhortation to employers not to cut wages in 1930 and 1931), or to (misplaced?) social sympathy on the part of employers. Any of these can create unemployment if the money wage is held or raised too high.

Consider the situation shown in Figure 4-8, with strictly classical assumptions in all respects other than money wage flexibility. Here there is an equilibrium money wage, W_0, consistent with full employment. But suppose that the wage is instead fixed at W_1 (in part D). To simplify exposition, suppose that the money wage was originally W_0, but was pushed up to W_1. What will be the new levels of P, N, Y, and W/P?

In the first place, we can easily see that prices must rise, at least somewhat. For if prices did not rise, the real wage would be higher than before, and employers would produce less; and a smaller output with no increase in price would be inconsistent with a constant M and m. Prices must rise. Second, we can see that prices could not rise as much as did wages. For if prices rose in the same proportion, the real wage would be unchanged; employers would want to produce as much as before. However, for them to sell the same quantity, at a higher price, is also

[18] This makes it clear that the conclusions of the classical model do not rest on the existence of an aggregate production function, a diminishing marginal product of labor, profit maximization, nor (though we have not specifically dealt with the question) the existence of perfect competition in all product markets.

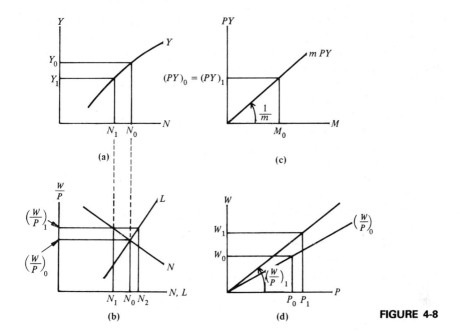

FIGURE 4-8

inconsistent with a constant M and m. The new PY must be the same as before; therefore, P must rise and Y must fall.

The diagram is not well adapted to finding directly the new equilibrium levels of the other variables, although this can be done by a process of successive approximation. However, the new equilibrium must, we have shown, involve both a higher price and a higher real wage than before; therefore it necessarily involves less employment and output. It can be seen that the solution shown in Figure 4-8 is consistent with all of the requirements of the classical model, except the requirement that equilibrium can only be at the intersection of N and L because this is the only solution consistent with a stable wage.

The results of an arbitrary increase in the money wage (from W_0 to W_1) thus are higher prices, a higher real wage, smaller employment and output, and a volume of unemployment equal to N_1N_2. (Note that the sum of new employment plus unemployment is greater than the previous employment.) Those workers still employed are clearly better off.

Clearly, monetary policy could be used to offset the effects of too high a money wage. If employment drops off because the money wage fails to *decline* in response (say) to an increase in the average productivity of labor (upward shift in the production function), monetary expansion could permit the full employment level to be restored. It should be clear that in this particular case an expansion of M need not in any meaningful sense be inflationary. Prices would merely have to be prevented from falling in response to larger output. However, if money wages were too high because they had been artificially pushed, the monetary authority would have the difficult choice of either "ratifying inflation" or permitting unemployment to develop. Since it could be supposed that the inflationary solution might tempt workers to try again, whereas the "discipline" of unemployment might teach them better manners, the choice might be difficult.

We shall pursue none of these questions in the present context; for, as we shall see, these classical analytical tools have weaknesses which make them not fully suitable for application to public policy. Of their logical completeness and consistency, however, there can be no doubt. This reconstructed "classical theory" cannot be attacked except by attacking the behavioral or technical assumptions on which it is based. Keynes was surely wrong in sometimes attacking it as logically incomplete or inconsistent. However, there is still another aspect of the matter which needs to be explored, and which was explored in the classical literature, namely, the problem of saving and investment in relation to employment, output, and the price level. This is the subject of Chapter 5.

REVIEW QUESTIONS

1. "An increase in labor productivity would have the same effect on output, employment, real wage, price level, and money wage as an increase in the supply of labor under the traditional classical formulation."
Do you agree? Why or why not?

2. Given the traditional classical assumptions, what are the implications for output, employment, real wage, price level, and money wage of an increase in the amount of money needed to be used for each dollar's worth of production or income? You may answer verbally, graphically, or algebraically.

3. Derive the condition under which an increase in labor productivity would raise money wage rates under traditional classical assumptions. (This condition would verify the comment in footnote 16.)

4. The traditional classical formulation led to a dichotomized analysis of the economy, with real variables determined by real factors, and monetary variables by monetary factors. Relaxing some assumption (or assumptions) would destroy this dichotomy. An example was given in the text. What is it, and how does it destroy the dichotomy? Can you identify another classical assumption (or assumptions) the absence of which also would impair the dichotomy?

5. "The effectiveness of monetary policy depends crucially upon the assumptions made about the labor market." Comment.

6.

(a) Define "full employment" in the sense in which that term might be used in the classical macroeconomic model.

(b) In the real world, the classical definition of "full employment" is clearly not meaningful. What, if any, significant meaning can then be given to that term in the real world?

(c) How does the U.S. Bureau of Labor Statistics define and measure unemployment?

SELECTED REFERENCES

I. Fisher, *The Purchasing Power of Money*, 2nd ed. (Macmillan, 1922) (Reprinted A. M. Kelley, 1971).

(A classic statement of the quantity theory of money.)

J. M. Keynes, *The General Theory of Employment, Interest, and Money* (Harcourt, Brace, 1936), Chapter 2.

(Keynes' version of the classical economics.)

J. A. Schumpeter, *History of Economic Analysis* (Oxford University Press, 1954), pp. 615–625.

(An excellent introduction to the origins and evolution of Say's Law.)

A. S. Skinner, "Say's Law: Origins and Content," *Economica*, 34 (May 1967), 153–166.

(A modern review of Say's Law.)

H. S. Ellis, "Some Fundamentals in the Theory of Velocity," *Quarterly Journal of Economics*, 52 (May 1938), 431–472; reprinted in *Readings in Monetary Theory*, selected by a committee of the American Economic Assn. (Blakiston, 1951), pp. 89–128.

(An article which carried the conventional discussion of velocity about as far as it could go.)

Chapter 5

The Classical Theory of Saving, Investment and the Interest Rate

Saving and Investment
The supply and demand for bonds
Removing some restrictive assumptions
Interest rate and bond price
Supply and demand for bonds with a resale market

Saving and Investment in Relation to the Quantity Theory
Wicksell's elaboration of the quantity theory
Saving and hoarding

Money and the Interest Rate: Equilibrium and Disequilibrium

Saving, Investment, and Employment

Classical Macroeconomics: Its Applications and Limitations
Applications of the classical model
Monetary and fiscal policy in the classical economics
Limitations of the classical analysis

At the beginning of Chapter 4, Say's Law was stated in its simplest form—applied to an economy in which individuals produce final products, and barter the surplus above their own consumption for the corresponding surpluses of others. For such an economy, the correctness of Say's Law is self-evident. Since then, we have been considering whether and how Say's Law is affected by assuming more realistic forms of economic organization. First we asked what difference it made that people used money for the exchange of goods instead of barter. The classical answer was that, since money was merely a medium of exchange that rational individuals had no desire to hold for its own sake, money made no difference. It was merely a "veil" behind which transactions occurred, with results no different than under barter. To be sure, the quantity of money determined the average price level (given the full-employment output and the institutional determinants of velocity).

The second potential challenge to Say's Law was the existence of employment for hire. What difference did it make that most people do not supply final products to the market but rather labor services, which a relatively small number of entrepreneurs purchase in order to produce goods for sale in the market? The answer was that, so long as wages and prices—and their ratio, the real wage—were fully flexible, Say's Law still held, the only equilibrium being at full employment. The quantity of money determines the price level at which the full-employment output can be sold. The demand for and the supply of labor determine the real wage necessary for full employment. A competitive labor market determines the money wage at the level which will yield the full-employment real wage, given the full-employment price level.

We now must consider a third possible challenge to Say's Law. Suppose that some—indeed, most—income recipients save some part of their incomes. Their incomes derive from the value of final output, but the part which they save clearly does not directly constitute any demand for final output. Does the supply of goods still create its own demand? The fact that people save clearly poses the most significant challenge to the correctness of Say's Law. How classical macroeconomics met that challenge is the main subject of this chapter. Along the way, however, we will also make a brief excursion into the arithmetic of bond prices and interest rates that will be needed later on.

SAVING AND INVESTMENT

The fact that most people save some part of their incomes means that they do not, as a rule, automatically spend on consumer goods and services whatever they have available to spend as rapidly as they can. Unless people are misers, however, they do not accumulate money simply because they save. Other forms of saving, that yield a return, are clearly preferable— securities of various kinds, savings deposits, savings and loan association shares, or life insurance. Saving in the form of repaying mortgage or other debts also yields a return in the elimination of interest payments. However, even if people save in these other noncash forms, can we be sure that the flow of spending on goods is not interrupted? We may buy a security with our saving; but the security is not output, and it probably is not even a *new* security, the sale of which by a business firm would provide funds to be used for the purchase of newly produced capital goods. Rather, we frequently buy an existing share of stock or a bond from some other security holder. (Of the total of securities bought and sold in any given week or year, a very small proportion consists of new securities.) Moreover, we may not even buy a security, we may merely repay an outstanding debt (thus extinguishing an old security).

In the face of all this, can we still be sure that, even if people do not willingly hold idle cash, aggregate spending on newly produced output is nevertheless a fixed multiple of the quantity of money? And can we be sure that all the income earned from producing current output is respent on current output? Still another part of classical theory implies an answer of "yes" to these questions.

The Supply and Demand for Bonds

We can simplify, to begin with, by making four assumptions, which will later be relaxed, at least in part. First, we assume that only one kind of security is sold by businesses and held by savers—a perpetual bond. There are no shares sold—entrepreneurs either borrow all of the funds needed by their enterprises, through sale of the standard bonds, or, if they supply any funds themselves, it is through direct investment in the physical properties of their enterprises. Second, we ignore the existence of a market for old securities. We assume that a person buying a security is "married" to it, and there exists no market for its resale. Correspondingly, the security which any saver purchases must therefore be a newly issued one. Third, we assume that intermediate financial institutions (other than commercial banks) do not exist: no life insurance companies, savings banks, savings and loan associations, pension funds, investment trusts, and so on. All securities must therefore be sold directly to individual savers or to commercial banks. Fourth, there are, for the moment, no commercial banks, or at least, none with fractional reserves.

A saver, then, has three things he can do with the margin between his income and his consumption expenditure. He may add to his cash balance, he may—if he is an entrepreneur—purchase capital goods directly, or he may buy a bond newly issued by an entrepreneur. Our assumption is that the rational saver will not do the first of these. The reason is that wealth accumulated in the form of cash is barren—it yields no return. Bonds have a positive yield, and are therefore preferred. Those relatively few savers who are entrepreneurs do the second (although they account for a fair fraction of total saving); most savers do the third.

We shall have much to say later about the assumed unqualified preference for earning assets over cash. However, this is an essential element in any version of a classical model. Note that the assumption here is not necessarily that people save only in order to obtain a return on their savings, nor that they save more or less if the rate of return is higher or lower. The assumption is rather merely that, given some amount of saving, so long as a return is available, it will be preferred to no return. It is also true that most classical writers thought of saving as an increasing function of the interest rate, but that is a separate matter.

The issuers of the bonds which savers may buy are, of course, the entrepreneurs who wish to acquire capital goods at a rate in excess of that possible from their own saving. They are willing to incur an obligation to pay interest because they see an opportunity—through use of the capital goods—to earn a margin over all of their costs, including the interest payments which they contract to make.

The bond market therefore provides a means whereby the nonspending of income by savers who are not entrepreneurs is translated into investment spending by entrepreneurs. What classical theory had to say about this market was that—barring certain interferences—it worked quite like any other market, bringing about an equality between lending or bond purchase, which can be assumed to equal saving, and borrowing or bond sale, which can be assumed to equal investment. (We can ignore that part of

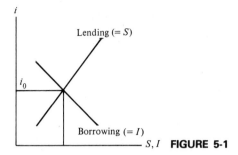

FIGURE 5-1

entrepreneurs' saving which they invest themselves, since, by definition, that saving and that investment are equal.) The equality of saving and lending arose from the rational consumer's preference for a positive return over no return; the equality of borrowing and investing from the reasonable proposition that entrepreneurs will not incur an interest obligation unless they have some productive use for the funds borrowed—they will not pay interest for the privilege of holding idle cash. The equality of lending and borrowing was maintained through fluctuations in the market rate of interest.

For the market rate of interest (i) to succeed in equating lending and borrowing—and therefore saving (S) and investment (I)—it is necessary (a) that either savers will save more at higher rates of interest than at lower rates, and/or that investors will desire to borrow more at lower than at higher rates, and (b) that there exists some rate greater than zero at which the amount saved equals the amount invested.[1] Economists generally assumed that both saving (lending) and investment (borrowing) were at least somewhat interest-elastic, and the possibility that condition (b) might not be fulfilled never entered their minds. Their usual picture of the bond market looked like Figure 5-1. Although individual economists may have emphasized the interest elasticity of either one or the other of these curves, and even have suggested that the other was completely interest-inelastic (that is, in the figure, a vertical line), there were excellent reasons advanced why both schedules were interest-elastic. If *either* of them should be sufficiently interest-elastic, condition (b) (an intersection at i_0 in the positive quadrant) is assured. It should be clear that the concepts of "lending" and "borrowing"—like those of saving and investment—are defined as *flows*.

According to the classical theory, borrowing occurs in order to purchase capital goods which will add to total production in the future. Just as increased employment of labor results in a positive but diminishing marginal product, it was assumed that the marginal product of capital also

---

[1] The market rate of interest could equate saving and investment even if the saving schedule sloped the "wrong" way, so long as its negative slope was less than that of the investment schedule.

diminished the greater the cumulative investment. In that case, the entre-
preneuer will borrow only to the extent that the productivity of the
increased capital warrants the payment of interest at the going market rate.
If the rate of interest falls, a greater investment is justified. Thus the
borrowing (investment) schedule is a declining function of the interest
rate.[2]

With regard to the lending (saving) schedule, it was argued that people
value consumption in the present more highly than consumption in the
future—they have a positive **time preference**. Thus they will forego some
amount of present consumption—that is, save—only if that will allow them
to increase *future* consumption by more than that amount, as will be
possible if they receive a positive return on saving. Furthermore, they will
increase the amount of present consumption denied themselves—that is,
increase their saving—only when they find they are able to lend at a higher
interest rate (to balance the increased current utility foregone). This means
that the lending schedule is an upward sloping function of the rate of
interest.[3]

Later we will have occasion to review the reasoning of the last two
paragraphs in a critical light. However, accepting these descriptions of
these forces on the supply and demand sides of the market for saving (and
the fact of an intersection), it seems clear how the interest rate—if free to
fluctuate—would necessarily settle at a point where saving and investment
were equal. For, if the rate were higher than this, saving and lending would
exceed borrowing and investment. Some savers, unable to find a borrower
and preferring a lower return to none at all, would bid the rate down. If the
rate were below the equilibrium level, investors would seek more funds than
savers would provide. Competition among borrowers would force the rate
up.

The level of the equilibrium rate would depend on the slopes and
relative positions of the saving and investment schedules. Other things
equal, the more thrifty the population, the lower the rate; and, the greater
the marginal productivity of capital, the higher the rate. In equilibrium the
rate of interest would equal both the marginal productivity of capital and,
as well, the "marginal rate of time preference."

If the interest rate fluctuates freely, settling at whatever level equates
saving and investment, then the act of saving does not require any
qualification of the classical model presented in the previous chapter. All
income earned in production is spent. Its recipients may not *themselves*
spend it all (to the extent that they are savers). However, because the saver
wishes to hold his savings in a form that produces a positive yield, he will
not hold idle cash. Thus, the quantity theory assumption of zero minimum

---

[2] The theory of investment implied here will be developed more fully in Chapters 8, 18, and
19.
[3] The theory of saving implied here is developed in further detail in Chapter 16.

balances remains valid. And because the rate of interest will adjust to the point where someone else (an investor) will want to spend precisely the amount that the saver did not choose to spend, all of the income earned from the production of any output is completely respent on current output: supply still creates its own demand.

In Chapter 4, we saw that the existence of employment for hire—instead of self-employment—need not invalidate Say's Law, so long as prices and wages are fully flexible. Now we see that neither does the existence of saving and investment, so long as interest rates are fully flexible. The former condition permits the full-employment output to be produced; the latter condition permits it to be purchased, either as consumer goods or capital goods.

Removing Some Restrictive Assumptions

Now this argument has been conducted under highly simplified assumptions. It would be useful to know if the same results held under more realistic assumptions. First, we may recognize that different borrowers might have to pay different rates of interest at any given time because of different degrees of risk of default on their interest contracts.[4] We might call the "pure" rate of interest the rate which would have to be paid by a completely riskless enterprise. (There might or might not be any such enterprise.) The actual rate paid by any given enterprise is then the pure rate plus a risk premium designed to compensate the lender for the particular risk of default which he assumes. The actual rates paid, and their dispersion and average, might fluctuate with changing lender judgments concerning risk premiums. But given the risks of default, the whole family of market rates would move up or down together, reflecting changes in the "pure" rate, due to changed conditions of thrift or productivity.

We would also greatly increase the realism by permitting variations in rate based upon differing maturities of the loan. However, this change of assumptions is postponed until Chapter 21, where it is seen to play a central role in modern monetary economics. Also, we shall continue (until Chapter 19) to assume away all financial intermediaries other than commercial banks—there are no savings banks, savings and loan associations, mutual funds, insurance companies, pension funds, and so on. Only then will we also relax the assumption of a single type of security—a perpetual bond. We can immediately, however, introduce greater realism by providing a resale market in which not only newly issued but existing bonds are bought and sold. Thus, we remove the rather ridiculous assumption that savers are "married" to the bonds they purchase. Then, in the next major

---

[4] Since we still assume perpetual borrowing, there is no problem as to risk of default on the principal.

section of this chapter, we begin to introduce the role of commercial banks, which will be developed much more fully in Chapters 20 and 21.

Interest Rate and Bond Price

To facilitate this discussion, it is helpful if we consider somewhat more fully the nature of a bond market, and recognize that what we have described until now as interest-rate variations can equally well (and for some purposes, better) be described as changes in the average level of bond prices. To understand this, it is necessary to be clear about what a bond is. Essentially, a bond is a negotiable (that is, salable) promise to pay its holder a certain fixed amount of money at regular intervals in the future (these are called **coupon payments**) and, eventually, at some fixed future time, a larger amount of money (the **principal**). After that, the obligation expires. The perpetual bond is a special case, in that it promises regular coupon payments in perpetuity—but it promises no repayment of principal.

If we assume that equal coupon payments in amount Q are promised to be paid annually for t years, ending with payment of the principal R, then we can compute from the price V at which a bond trades what percentage rate of return ("yield") on its purchase price—over its remaining term—would be secured by its purchase. This rate i can be found by solving the equation below (for i), given V, Q, R, and t.

$$V \equiv \frac{Q}{1 + i} + \frac{Q}{(1 + i)^2} + \frac{Q}{(1 + i)^3} + \cdots \frac{Q + R}{(1 + i)^t}$$

If $t = 1$—that is, the bond matures in one year—this calculation is relatively simple:

$$V \equiv \frac{Q + R}{1 + i}$$

or

$$i \equiv \frac{Q + R}{V} - 1$$

For $t > 1$, the arithmetic gets rather complicated. However, published "bond tables" allow anyone to find the approximate i implied by any given combination of V, Q, R, and t, or alternatively, what should be the market price V given any particular i, Q, R, and t.

There is one other case in which the arithmetic of interest yield and bond price is also very simple—namely, the perpetual bond, for which the earlier definition of V simplifies to[5]

$$V \equiv \frac{Q}{i}$$

or

$$i \equiv \frac{Q}{V}$$

In this case, if a bond carrying a perpetual coupon of $50 sells for $1000, the yield is exactly 5 percent. (This simplicity is the primary reason why most textbook descriptions of the bond market and the interest rate like to assume perpetual bonds!)

Now coupon rates on existing bonds vary widely. But if all bonds were riskless (or if we abstract from risk), it is clear that, at any given time, all V's, on bonds of whatever coupon and principal, should tend to reflect a single uniform i. For otherwise, it would pay smart traders to sell those bonds whose prices reflect lower i's, and buy those reflecting higher i's. This **arbitrage** would depress the price of the former (raising their i's), and raise the price of the latter (lowering their i's) until all V's reflected a single i which we of course call "the" market rate of interest. Obviously, any seller of a *new bond* cannot expect to borrow at a rate of interest lower than this market i, nor need he pay more (adjusted for his particular default risk). The usual practice is for him to set his coupon rate at a level such that the bond will initially sell at or close to its principal value. That is, he makes Q/P approximately equal to the current i.

This practice is the reason why coupon rates—and thus prices—of existing, old bonds vary so widely—they reflect the different i's that prevailed when they were originally sold.

---

[5] This can be easily demonstrated. For the consol,

$$V \equiv \frac{Q}{1+i} + \frac{Q}{(1+i)^2} + \cdots + \frac{Q}{(1+i)^t} + \cdots$$

Multiplying both sides by $1/(1+i)$, we get

$$\frac{1}{1+i}V = \frac{Q}{(1+i)^2} + \frac{Q}{(1+i)^3} + \cdots + \frac{Q}{(1+i)^{t+1}} + \cdots$$

Subtracting this from the previous expression for V, and simplifying both sides gives

$$\left(1 - \frac{1}{1+i}\right)V \equiv \frac{Q}{1+i} + \frac{Q}{(1+i)^\infty}$$

Since $Q/(1+i)^\infty$ becomes zero, this further simplifies to

$$V \equiv \frac{Q}{i}$$

The reader should study the tables of bond prices and yields published daily in the *Wall Street Journal* or *New York Times* in order to make sure that he understands the arithmetic of prices and yields, and can explain at least *some* of the reasons why different bonds sell at such widely different prices—and even at somewhat different yields.[6] (However, we have not yet tried to explain why bonds of different *maturity* might sell at different yields.)

From the preceding discussion, it should be clear that the level of bond prices and the market rate of interest on bonds are not two separate phenomena. Rather, *the level of bond prices and of the market rate are two ways of describing one and the same set of facts.* In many contexts it is simpler to formulate a theory of the interest rate in terms of changes in bond prices than in terms of changes in interest rates; but it should be clear that any formulation in terms of the one may always be translated into the terms of the other. Thus, the classical theory of interest says that the *price level of bonds* is determined by the schedule of the demand for bonds by savers, which is a *decreasing* function of bond price (an *increasing* function of the interest rate), by the schedule of the supply of bonds by investors, which is an increasing function of bond price (a *decreasing* function of the interest rate), and by the clearing of the bond market—that is, the equality of desired sales and purchases, or saving and investment.

Supply and Demand for Bonds with a Resale Market

When we recognize the existence of sales and purchases of old as well as of newly issued securities, we must reformulate this theory of the interest rate by saying that the level of bond prices is determined by the *total* supply and *total* demand for bonds, including in supply the old bonds offered for sale by previous owners as well as new bonds offered for sale to finance new investments; and including in the demand for bonds not only that by current savers, but by others as well. On classical assumptions this reformulation makes no difference. Let us see why.

The current supply of bonds is made up of the newly issued bonds, sold to finance investment, together with sales of previously issued bonds by their existing holders. These sellers from existing holdings may be consumers, who sell securities that they own, in order to finance dissaving. (Unless they actually dissave, they can merely buy fewer bonds per period, but need sell none.) Their sale of securities absorbs current saving by other consumers who buy these securities. If there should be a net increase in the amount of dissaving, its effect will be to depress bond prices (raise interest rates)—as more old securities are dumped on the market—in just the same way as would a reduction in positive saving. But the fact of dissaving, or a

[6] One reason which is not mentioned in the text is the tax law, which treats differently income from state and local and federal bonds, and treats capital gains from appreciation of bond prices (when realized by sale) differently from interest.

change in the amount of dissaving, does not interfere with the market equality of saving and investment. Net saving (positive saving less dissaving) is kept equal to investment through variation in the interest rate.

Other sellers of old securities may be businesses, which have been holding them as an income-yielding financial reserve but now need funds to expand inventories, meet growing payrolls, or replace worn out equipment. These sales finance investment (in inventories of finished goods, raw materials, or work in process, or in plant and equipment) just as do sales of new securities. A net increase in sales from business reserve portfolios depresses bond prices (raises interest rates) in just the same way as any other method of financing additional investment. We should recognize, of course, that just as some businesses may need to call upon their reserve funds by selling securities, other businesses may be purchasing securities, not out of current saving but in connection with a temporary disinvestment in inventories or in capital goods (depreciation allowances in excess of replacement expenditures). It is not only saving which should be considered net (positive saving less dissaving) but investment, too. Again, there is no reason why fluctuating bond prices (interest rates) should not preserve equality between net saving and net investment.

Another very large volume of "second-hand" sales and purchases will be by individuals (or businesses) whose opinions regarding risk premiums on individual issues differ from the market's opinion. If I hold a security that the market values highly (high price equals low risk premium) but I believe it more risky than another, cheaper issue, I will sell mine and buy the other. A large volume of such transactions may take place as individual security holders move from those issues that they believe the market overvalues to those they believe the market undervalues. But it is clear that this type of transaction cannot influence the general level of bond prices (although it will influence the structure of bond prices). For to say that the "market" overvalues a security I own is to say that someone else is willing to pay a higher price than I think correct. I sell to him. Suppose he is a saver; I have diverted his saving from investment. I then buy another issue that I think is undervalued. This may be a new issue, in which case the diverted savings are rechannelled into investment. If it, too, is an old issue, the seller, who apparently thought that issue *over*valued, has funds to invest in a new issue, or to put in the hands of some other security holder who in turn can buy a new issue, and so on. In short, *so long as no one who has been a security holder desires to shift to idle cash instead*, total spending will be maintained. Since we assume that no rational wealth holder would prefer idle cash to a positive return, second-hand sales create no problem—that is, the supply of such bonds creates its own demand! This is so even though the volume of second-hand sales may dwarf the volume of new issues. New saving and investment might even both be zero, yet a substantial reshuffling of existing securities might proceed, with a substantial volume of current bond transactions.

We could consider still other private sources of bond demand or supply, but all with the same effect. So long as cash is never preferred to income-yielding wealth, the existence of a market in old securities, just as the fact of saving itself, appears to require no qualification of either the quantity theory or of Say's Law. The money that is in circulation all moves, and at a predictable rate, in the purchase of goods. The money value of total output equals money stock times velocity; and the physical volume of output stays at the full-employment level.[7]

Should the thriftiness of the population increase, that is, its desire to spend income on current output weaken, the rise in the price of bonds, that is, reduction of the interest rate, that this automatically brings about will both dampen the desire to save and attract extra investment. The rate will fall until the previous volume of demand is restored. Should the incentive to spend on investment in new facilities weaken, the resulting drop in the rate of issuance of new securities will lower interest rates until the potential drop in spending has been offset. At least, these results seem to follow if we assume no willingness anywhere to accumulate idle cash.

SAVING AND INVESTMENT IN RELATION TO THE QUANTITY THEORY

From this we see that the existence of saving and investment, and even of a securities market which deals both in new and in previously existing securities does not alter the nature of macroeconomic equilibrium, nor change the conclusions of a comparative statics analysis (so long as no one desires to hold idle balances). Nevertheless, the conception of *how* equilibrium is maintained, and *how* the economy moves from one position of equilibrium to another may now be considerably altered. Consider, for example, what happens when the quantity of money increases. If the demand for money is a constant fraction of money income—that is, if income velocity is constant—there can be no equilibrium until aggregate price-times-quantity, PY, has increased in the same proportion as the money supply, presumably through an increase in prices, assuming flexible money wages and a previous full-employment equilibrium. (The increase of PY will, of course, be entirely the

---

[7] To be sure, an increase in the volume of second-hand security dealings may reqire somewhat larger cash balances in the hands of the traders. That is, some extra money gets tied up in mediating purely financial transactions, thus raising interest rates and reducing investment relative to saving. This problem attracted great attention of monetary theorists in the late 1920s and early 1930s. However, it was pointed out that the organization of financial markets permitted tremendous volumes of security transactions to be handled with very small balances—that the "velocity of the financial circulation" was exceedingly high. Thus the security markets "absorbed" very little in the way of funds. Even if some funds were absorbed in this way, it would still cause no problem if prices of goods and services were fully flexible (downward).

result of higher P, with no change in Y, and P and W will have risen in the same proportion.) However, this new version of the quantity theory sees changes in M having their primary impact on prices *by way of the capital market* and interest rates, rather than through the direct spending on goods and services of the new balances by whoever owns them.

Wicksell's Elaboration of the Quantity Theory

In developing this approach, we will find it useful to refer to the discussion of the Swedish economist, Knut Wicksell[8]—one of the first economists to introduce the modern concept of the aggregate demand for goods and services, and, in the process, to convert the quantity theory into a more useful and understandable doctrine. Wicksell emphasized that economists accept an explanation for individual prices—in microeconomic theory— that runs in terms of supply and demand. Thus, he argued, if economists wish to use the quantity of money to explain the general price level (which is only the average of all individual prices), then they must somehow show how changes in M enter into the determination either of the supply or the demand for goods. His own analysis did show how changes in M affected the demand for goods. And while he left the *conclusions* of the quantity theory unchanged, his analysis marked a considerable advance toward that of Keynes and subsequent macroeconomists.

Wicksell asked how, precisely, changes in the money supply come about. One important way is through changes in the volume of commercial bank lending to business. Assume that commercial banks do not need to maintain reserves equal to their deposits, and thus can create "new money" to lend to business firms. If business not only borrows (to finance investment) all of the funds provided by savers but also new money, then there will be an aggregate demand for goods (and for resources to produce goods) in excess of supply. All resources were previously fully employed in producing consumer goods and capital goods. If new investment demand is added which is not matched by any added saving (that is, any reduction in consumer demand), total demand for goods and productive factors will exceed supply. This will bid up prices. This is why and how an increase in M leads to an increase in P. This is how Wicksell connected a change in M to a change in the demand for goods and services and thus in the prices of goods and services.

A simplified version of Wicksell's analysis is illustrated in Figure 5-2. In this figure S is the supply curve of saving, and I the original investment schedule. At i_0, amounts saved and invested are equal. If, now, the investment schedule shifts to I', the equilibrium rate (Wicksell called it the

---

[8] See K. Wicksell, *Lectures on Political Economy*, L. Robbins, trans. (London: Routledge and Kegan Paul, 1934), Vol. II, esp. pp. 159–208. (Original publication in Swedish in 1901–06.)

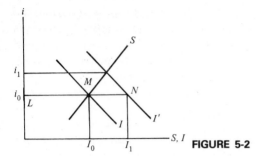

FIGURE 5-2

"natural rate") rises to i_1. Suppose however, that banks meet the additional demand for funds at the old market rate, i_0, or at only a slightly higher rate. This is very likely to happen, for the banks—and particularly individual banks in a system—have no way of knowing what the "natural rate" is. As a consequence of their lending, the quantity of money rises at the rate MN.[9] The increase in investment demand (as the borrowers spend the new money) represents a net increment of total demand for goods, for there has been no equivalent reduction in consumer demand (increase in saving). The excess of demand over supply bids up prices of goods and services.

How far and how long will prices rise? As long as the market rate stays below the natural rate there will continue to be an excess of aggregate demand for goods over supply and prices will rise. Only when bank lending and money creation cease (perhaps because each bank has now created all the "new money" it believes it is safe to create) will the inflation cease. For then the market rate must move up to equal the natural rate, and investment will again just be offset by saving (partly through some expansion in saving, if saving responds to the interest rate, and the rest through some trimming back of the rate of investment).

How far will prices have risen? They must have risen in the same proportion as the money supply, for otherwise there would be idle balances, which would not willingly be held but instead would be depressing the rate of interest below the natural rate, and thus forcing a continuance of inflation.

Money wages must, of course, have risen in exactly this same proportion, too. So long as wages lagged behind the rise of prices, employers would have incentive to increase employment. Since no additional workers are to be had, the excess demand for labor must sooner or later bid up money wages in the same proportion as prices. At this point, all

[9] If we hold to our assumption of only one kind of security, the banks will buy bonds at the rate MN, in addition to purchases by savers at the previous rate LM. If the banks did not buy, the increased supply of bonds would depress bond prices (raise interest rates) to the equivalent of i_1. It must be noted that S and I are flows. MN, the increase in money supply, is also necessarily expressed as a flow.

prices and wages will have risen in the same proportion as the supply of money. (The reader should be sure that he can trace through fully the effects of a drop in the investment schedule.)

In the above example, the initiative for inflation did not come from the banks; rather it was the natural rate that rose, reflecting, perhaps, technological innovations or some other source of a higher marginal productivity of capital. The banks merely reacted passively. It was Wicksell's view that this was the normal situation. However, we can also see how the banks might take the initiative. Assume the market rate and natural rate are equal and that no change occurs in either the investment or saving schedule. Banks, however, acquire new resources (perhaps as a result—in Wicksell's day—of new deposits of domestically produced or imported gold; in a later day, deposits from abroad of foreign currency or of domestic currencies previously held abroad). Suppose that the banks then enter the bond market as buyers, adding their demand to that of savers. So long as they remain in the market, bond prices will be "artificially" raised above the equilibrium level (that is, the market rate of interest depressed below the unchanged natural rate). During this time, aggregate demand for goods and services will exceed supply, and wages and prices will be bid up. When the banks cease to add to the demand for bonds—and to the supply of funds to finance inflationary investment spending—prices will stop rising, and the rate of interest will return to its equilibrium level.

It is interesting to note that Wicksell saw clearly what many even today continue to confuse, namely, that if prices of goods and services are bid up by excess demand, the rise in price does not of itself eliminate the excess demand. If, starting from a full employment equilibrium, entrepreneurs armed with new money come into the market seeking to invest in plant and equipment, they can do so only by bidding goods (or resources to produce goods) away from other uses, through offering higher prices. If we make certain plausible assumptions as to lags, the investors are *able to bid resources* away from consumers, because consumers at first cannot and will not pay the higher prices, since their money incomes are, *for the moment,* unchanged. Thus, prices rise to clear the market by diverting goods and resources from consumption into investment. This process is called **forced saving**. Consumers are forced, by higher prices without increase in money incomes, to consume less. But Wicksell saw clearly that this was only a temporary diversion. For the sale of goods and resources at higher prices automatically creates extra money income in just the amount of the price rise. Consumers now come back into the market with money incomes which have, in the aggregate, risen by the same amount as prices. Their real income position is unchanged; whatever they previously wanted to consume they still want to consume, and the rise in their money incomes permits them to pay the higher prices. Thus the initial rise in prices did not eliminate the excess demand, except during the lag between the paying of higher prices and the consequent realization of higher money incomes.

Unless the source of excess demand is eliminated (for example, by a rise in the interest rate to its natural level, which will reduce both consumption and investment demand), the rise in prices can cumulate indefinitely. (This notion of an inflationary "spiral" that provides its own fuel in the form of higher money incomes is an important element of the modern analysis of inflation.)

Wicksell also saw the reverse—that if a deficiency of aggregate demand develops as a result of a drop in investment relative to saving, that is not corrected by a drop in the interest rate, the resulting fall in wages and prices will not correct the deficiency of demand, except temporarily, for money incomes and goods prices, and wage costs, will all have fallen in proportion. The deficiency of demand will still exist until either real consumption or investment demand increases. This requires (given the saving and investment schedules) that the banks stop absorbing funds—that is, stop maintaining the market rate above the natural level.

Thus we must understand the saving and investment schedules in the Wicksellian diagram as being defined in real terms. In Figure 5-2 the shift of the investment schedule from I to I' produces (at i_0, or at any interest rate below i_1) an "inflationary gap" in the market for goods. The resulting rise in prices does not eliminate the gap because it leaves the S and I schedules unchanged. If the added investment, $I_1 - I_0$, occurs, through a bidding away of goods or resources, actual saving (which has to equal investment) will of course rise, too. (This is the "forced saving," or sacrificed consumption, referred to above.) But desired or attempted saving stays as shown by the schedule.

Here we have another example of the difference between accounting identities and conditions of equilibrium. We know from Chapter 2 that actual saving and investment must at all times be equal. For the purpose of this identity, saving is defined simply as income less consumption. But if we speak of desired or intended saving, which we think of here as a function of the interest rate, we can imagine this differing from investment. However, when it does, actual saving will differ from desired saving, and savers will attempt to eliminate this difference. Only when actual and desired saving are equal is the situation one of equilibrium. Under Wicksell's assumptions, this occurred only when the market and natural rates were equal— that is, when the banks were neither creating nor retiring money.

Saving and Hoarding

Integrating the analysis of saving, investment, and the interest rate with the analysis of money and the price level also throws new light on the question of hoarding, briefly referred to in Chapter 4. In the simpler quantity-theory context, hoarding was seen as a direct withdrawal of demand for goods and services; now it can be seen as a shift in the preference of wealth holders regarding the composition of their savings.

Suppose that wealth holders should develop a desire (however irrational this may seem) to hold cash instead of bonds, that is, to **hoard**. Not only can they fail to buy new bonds with their current saving, but they can, as well, dump on the bond market all or some part of their existing security holdings, the fruit of earlier saving. This act not only reduces the current market demand for bonds (new saving no longer flows into the bond market) but also increases the market supply of bonds. Bond prices fall, and *i* rises, *reducing investment relative to saving* (in the sense of desired investment and saving). The drop in aggregate demand for goods threatens unemployment, which leads to a deflation of money wages and prices. The deflation will continue so long as the hoarding does. When hoarding stops, prices must have fallen in the same proportion as velocity has fallen. Prices will then, of course, remain at their lower level, to which money incomes are also adjusted.

If some equally irrational reason should now lead to dishoarding, the process would be reversed. Demand for bonds would now consist not only of saving but of the idle cash balances which their holders now wish to convert into interest-yielding form. The market rate of interest would be depressed below the natural rate, and while this was the case, an excess of aggregate demand would bid up wages and prices. When the dishoarding stopped, the rate of interest would return to its "natural" level and prices would stop rising, remaining, however, at their higher level. Again, it is via the capital market and the rate of interest that hoarding or dishoarding affect the price level.

Although this concept of the role and mechanism of hoarding and dishoarding provides no explanation of why these should occur, this setting of the problem is one that invites possible explanations—including some which we shall describe in a later chapter.

The simple quantity theory had pictured individuals choosing between spending their incomes as they are received and accumulating cash (and, of course, because they were rational, never choosing the latter). Wicksell's more sophisticated version permits us to sort out two separate decisions: (1) how much shall I spend and save? and (2) in what form—cash or securities—shall I hold my accumulated savings (both that saving which I am currently making and the accumulation of all of my past saving decisions)? These two decisions are, of course, not completely unrelated, nor are the acts by which they are carried out completely unrelated. If I dissave by spending an accumulated idle cash balance, I am dishoarding as well. Further, changes in some factors (for example, my increased fear or uncertainty about the economic future) might simultaneously affect both decisions (for example, that I should save more and that I should convert my present and past savings from bonds into cash). Likewise, it may be that one whose savings are held in cash form will be under greater temptation to dissave; he avoids the time, effort, and possible embarrassment of first cashing a security. Nevertheless, there is no necessary connection between saving and hoarding. I can save without hoarding, hoard without saving, or even save and dishoard, hoard and dissave. Therefore it is a most useful step to sort out for separate analysis the saving and the hoarding decisions. The more sophisticated quantity theory permits us to do exactly this.

Wicksell's analysis not only contributed to this separation, but it also gave us, as has been stressed, a rudimentary theory of aggregate demand for goods. This demand consists of two main divisions: consumer demand and investment demand. Each of these demands was conceived to be interest-elastic: the lower the interest rate, the greater the investment demand; and the greater consumer demand, too (the latter idea is, of course, merely a restatement of the idea that saving depends negatively on the interest rate). Separate forces influence the volume of investment and consumer spending decisions—in the one case, the host of factors summarized in the concept of the marginal productivity of capital, in the other case, the social and institutional factors determining the thriftiness of the population. But a single rein would keep these two forces pulling in balance, and prevent them from either running away or slowing down. This rein was a freely fluctuating rate of interest. If there were an increase in either of the two components of demand, the resulting rise in the rate of interest could prevent any increase in aggregate demand through cutting back on both elements of demand and, in the process, shifting some resources from the satisfaction of the demand that had not increased to the demand that had. If either type of demand declined, the resulting fall in the rate of interest would stimulate them both, and shift resources to the one which had not declined.

If, however, for any reason (particularly expansion or contraction of the money supply by the banks) the rate of interest were prevented from performing this regulatory function, aggregate demand, consumption plus investment, would be altered, producing inflation or deflation in the process.

MONEY AND THE INTEREST RATE: EQUILIBRIUM AND DISEQUILIBRIUM

The classical theory of interest presented early in this chapter was represented by the following three equations:

(1) $$S = S(i)$$

(2) $$I = I(i)$$

(3) $$S = I$$

Equation (1) is the savings function, (2) is the investment function, and (3) is the equilibrium condition in the capital market. In this account, equilibrium in the capital market, through variation of i, assured that the flow of saving would necessarily equal the flow of investment. However, this formulation neglects Wicksell's contribution, which lay in showing the *interrelations* among saving and investment, money, the choice between holding money and holding bonds, the rate of interest, and the price level. We can incorporate Wicksell's insights if we replace equilibrium condition (3) with Wicksell's interest rate theory, as in equation (3a):

$$(3a) \qquad\qquad S + DH + \Delta M = I$$

where ΔM is the rate of addition to the money supply, and DH represents "dishoarding"—the rate of use of cash balances to buy securities. (If ΔM is negative, it represents a decrease in the money stock; if DH is negative, it signifies "hoarding," an increase in cash balances.) The meaning of equation (3a) is as follows: The supply of funds to the capital market (or the demand for bonds) consists of three parts, current saving S, dishoarding DH, and any increase in the supply of money ΔM. The sum of these three sources of funds (demand for bonds) must equal I, the demand for funds (supply of bonds). The rate of interest must adjust to clear the market— that is, we assume that bond prices adjust freely to find the level at which supply equals demand. Since S and I are expressed as (say) annual rates, ΔM and DH must also be current flows, expressed as annual rates.

The quantity theory asserts that people will not willingly hold *idle* balances—balances in excess of transaction needs. Thus "dishoarding" occurs only when people find themselves with actual cash balances M greater than current transactions demand mPY. It is assumed that:

$$(4) \qquad\qquad DH = h(M - mPY) \qquad h > 0$$

The quantity within the parenthesis on the right side of equation (4) is, of course, a difference between two stock magnitudes, the actual and the desired, or needed, stock of money. The constant h merely converts this stock into a time dimension.[10] The interpretation of equation (4) when "hoarding" occurs is that if transactions requirements (mPY) *exceed* actual cash holdings, people will become demanders of funds on the capital market—they will borrow, but not for investment purposes, or they will sell their existing holdings of old securities, or they will retain in cash (fail to lend) some part of their current saving. All of these acts, of course, depress bond prices—raise interest rates.

Equations (1), (2), (3a), and (4) [or some variant of (4)], constitute what is often called a "loanable funds" theory of the interest rate. The loanable funds approach to the interest rate, and its contrast with other

---

[10] That is, if the excess of actual over desired money holding at some point in time is $1 billion, there is an extra demand for bonds of h billion per time unit (the same time unit in which other current flows are expressed). Thus, if flows of saving, investment, and money creation are expressed on a daily basis, a value of 0.05 for h would mean that 1/20 of the excess, or $50 million, would flow into the bond market in a day, bidding up the price of bonds. If both M and mPY were unchanged, this would continue indefinitely.

approaches, have long been the source of much confusion both in economic theory and in public understanding. This confusion is unnecessary, although it is easy enough to understand how it has developed. One important part of the difficulty originates in the failure to be clear about stocks and flows (a failure which mars many discussions of the problem); the other important part is the failure to distinguish between equilibrium and disequilibrium conditions.

The revised model, equations (1), (2), (3a), and (4), contains eight variables: S, I, i, DH, P, Y, M, and ΔM. If we assume that Y (along with W/P, and N) is already determined by the supply of and demand for labor, and that both M and ΔM are policy-determined parameters, the number of variables is reduced to five. But the system is indeterminate; there are five unknown variables and only four equations.

We can also observe that this system is not an equilibrium system. Equation (3a) permits S to be unequal to I. But if S is unequal to I, some savers or some investors or both must be unsatisfied, or surprised. For we know that actual saving and investment must be equal, and if desired or intended saving and investment diverge, some desires or intentions are frustrated. In Wicksell's description of the process, for example, so long as I exceeds S, "forced saving" is occurring; consumers will be trying to raise their consumption, leading to further changes, without limit.

To make the system determinate, one can restore the equilibrium character of the model by adding an equation which defines equilibrium. This could be equation (3):

$$S = I$$

The combination of (3a) and (3) would thus imply that, in equilibrium, $\Delta M + DH = 0$. That is, any money creation is exactly balanced by (willing, intended) hoarding. But it is also clear that equilibrium further requires that DH and ΔM each be zero. Substituting ΔM for DH in equation (4) and rearranging gives

$$M + \Delta M = mPY$$

In equilibrium, the right hand side is constant over time; therefore, so must be the left—which means ΔM must be zero in equilibrium. Equation (4) therefore collapses into

(4a) $$M = mPY$$

the equation for the quantity theory.

This result should not surprise us. For Wicksell's analysis differed from the simple quantity theory only in the *process* by which its results were achieved, not in its results. *In equilibrium*, for Wicksell, prices are proportional to the money supply, and both are constant in time. *In equilibrium*, neither do idle balances flow into the capital market nor are additions to cash balances needed in order to finance a growing money volume of transactions.

However, this solution—to make our formal system a static or equilibrium system—loses the whole benefit of Wicksell's notable insights. The only way to incorporate these insights is to construct an explicitly dynamic model. However, it cannot only be a dynamic model of interest rate determination; it must be a dynamic model of the entire economy at the macro level. To do this requires a number of further assumptions about the disequilibrium behavior of savers (that is, consumers), investors, producers, and workers. To reduce these to a set of equations is not simple. If it can be done, we have a dynamic model which tells us not only the ultimate effect of a displacement of equilibrium but also shows us what happens along the way: how long it takes, and what time patterns the several variables follow in the meantime. Moreover, it should be observed that there are many such dynamic models possible, all with the same equilibrium solution but with different patterns and time sequences. Each model corresponds to some particular set of assumptions about lags and about the disequilibrium behavior of workers, employers, consumers, and banks. The particular dynamic model implicit in Wicksell's own description of the inflationary or deflationary process is actually a rather complicated one. A dynamic equation system embodying it can, however, be constructed, although it will not be attempted here.[11]

SAVING, INVESTMENT, AND EMPLOYMENT

In Chapter 4, we saw that if wages were inflexible, they could be set at a level too high for full employment, given the quantity of money. In that case, the quantity theory became not a theory of prices, but a theory of output. A reduction in the supply of money would create unemployment and lower output; an increase in the supply of money when there was unemployment would lead to larger output rather than only to higher prices.

Introducing inflexible wages into the Wicksellian scheme converts it from a saving-investment theory of prices to a saving-investment theory of output. Starting from a full-employment equilibrium, suppose investment opportunities deteriorate. If the market rate of interest would immediately drop (that is, bond prices rise) to the new, lower natural rate, aggregate demand would be maintained. Saving would decrease (that is, consumption increase), and the lower rate would also stimulate investment. But if the banks should prevent bond prices from rising by selling bonds from their portfolios (and thus reducing the money supply), at only slightly higher prices than before (not high enough to reflect the new "natural rate"),

---

[11] Several explicitly dynamic models of interest-rate determination exist. Most of them, however, include additional elements beyond those so far considered here. As an example, see W. L. Smith, "Monetary Theories of the Rate of Interest: A Dynamic Analysis," *Review of Economics and Statistics*, Feb. 1958, XL, 15–21.

investment would drop with no offsetting increase of consumption. The total of consumption plus investment spending would decline.

Nevertheless, because Wicksell assumed completely flexible wages and prices, no unemployment except of a very temporary sort occurred in his analysis. Prices fell as fast as did the supply of money and the demand for total output in money terms. The decline in investment was balanced by what we should call, by analogy, "forced consumption," as the decline in prices occurred in advance of the decline in money incomes. Actual consumption, in real terms, increased as much as investment declined. But because the schedule of intended or desired saving did not shift to the left, the excess of saving over investment remained, and the deflationary pressures did not disappear (until the interest rate fell to its new, lower "natural" level).

If wages and prices should *not* decline, with the interest rate maintained too high, the drop of aggregate money demand would become a drop in aggregate real demand, too. Workers would become unemployed, and real as well as money income would be cut. Do we then have a continuing downward spiral, this time of output and employment instead of prices? Are Wicksellian price spirals converted by sticky wages into employment and real income spirals?

Wicksell and the other classical writers did not try to answer this question. They may not have believed that wages and prices really were completely flexible. But they did not try to analyze very specifically or clearly what would happen if wages did not decline. Had they done so in the spirit of Wicksell's aggregate demand analysis, they would surely have made some interesting discoveries, one of the first of which probably would have been the "Keynesian" "consumption function." And with the consumption function would have come the theory that aggregate demand determines not (or not only) the price level but real output instead (or as well).

CLASSICAL MACROECONOMICS: ITS APPLICATIONS AND LIMITATIONS

This and the preceding chapter have described a classical theory of employment, output, and prices. It may be useful to bring the strands of that theory together in a single, summary statement.

The basic elements of this classical theory can be condensed into the following eight equations:

(5) $$Y = F(N)$$

(6) $$N = N\left(\frac{W}{P}\right)$$

(7) $$L = L\left(\frac{W}{P}\right)$$

(8) $$N = L$$

(4a) $$M = mPy$$

(1) $$S = S(i)$$

(2) $$I = I(i)$$

(3) $$S = I$$

Equation (5), usually described as the **aggregate production function**, is probably better thought of as merely an approximately empirical statement of an observed positive relationship between aggregate output and employment. Since employment is the only argument of the production function, this seems to imply that the capital stock and other productive inputs are fixed, which would restrict the model's application either to the short run—in which capital can be taken as essentially given—or to a stationary economy in which net investment and saving average out to zero. However, this limitation need not prevent our using a model such as this for certain kinds of longer run analyses, so long as we assume an upward shift in the production function over time in order to represent the combined effects of capital accumulation and technological change. Equation (6) describes the demand for labor as a function of the real wage; however, it is better thought of as an approximate empirical statement of an observed relationship. Although the classical economists assumed the demand for labor to be inversely associated with the money wage and directly associated with the price level, we have seen that there is no compelling theoretical presumption that this must be the case. Equation (7) describes the supply of labor as also a function of the real wage, although of uncertain slope. Equation (8) is the condition for equilibrium in the labor market; and it is assumed that an equilibrium is achieved—that is, that the real wage level rises or falls to whatever extent is necessary to achieve it. Equation (4a) describes equilibrium in money holdings: the money supply equals the amount of money demanded for transactions purposes. This is the quantity theory of money. Given M and m, and the Y (determined by equations (5) through (8)), equation (4a) determines the price level. Equation (1) describes desired or intended saving as a function (assumed increasing) of the rate of interest. Equation (2) describes desired or intended investment as a function (assumed decreasing) of the rate of interest. Equation (3) states the equilibrium condition in the capital market: intended saving equals intended investment. Assuming such an equilibrium exists, it determines the rate of interest, and the amounts saved and invested.

This classical model is a system of eight equations in eight unknowns (Y, W, P, N, L, S, I, and i). It contains three equilibrium conditions—(8), (4a), and (3)—involving three "prices": W, P, and i. Under the assumptions made by classical economists, these equilibrium conditions can all be met simultaneously: it is an equilibrium system. Unemployment is not a problem within this system. In equilibrium all unemployment is voluntary. So long as the system reaches equilibrium without delay, unemployment is a temporary maladjustment.

Applications of the Classical Model

If this classical model is a reasonably accurate description of the economy, we can use it to predict the effect of possible changes or to explain the effect of actual changes in specific elements of the system. We proceed by assuming an initial equilibrium, disturb the equilibrium by a single hypothetical change, find the new equilibrium, and evaluate the net change in the other variables of the system. This is the method of comparative statics. Some important comparative static results for the classical system have been discussed in this and the preceding chapter, and may be summarized as follows. (Here we assume the traditional versions of equations (5) and (6).)

Given an initial equilibrium in the model, suppose the money supply increases. Equation (4a) no longer holds. There are unwanted money balances. This leads to increased demand for output, and, in turn, for labor services. Prices and money wages both rise. Eventually the increased price level restores equilibrium in equation (4a), and a proportionate rise in the money wage maintains equality between the supply and demand for labor— at the initial real wage, employment, and output. Only money wages and prices will have changed—both in the same proportion as the change in the supply of money. This prediction is clearly broadly consistent with the experience of actual economies over many centuries—ranging from the "price revolution" that occurred in Europe in the sixteenth century, when the gold of the New World flowed back to the old, to any of Milton Friedman's numerous "demonstrations" that United States inflation in the 1970s neatly "fits" the quantity theory explanation.

Suppose that the supply of labor increases. Excess supply of labor causes the money wage to fall. Employment, and, hence, output increase (equations (2) and (1)). The larger output can be sold only at lower prices—equation (4a). At the eventual new equilibrium, money wages will have fallen by more than prices, so that the real wage is lower, a necessary condition for the higher output and employment. Saving, investment, and the interest rate will be unchanged.

Or, suppose that growth occurs through an upward shift of the production function in a way that yields a larger demand for labor at every value of W/P. In equilibrium, the real wage will have increased, and so will employment if labor supply is an increasing function of the real wage, otherwise not. Output will, however, normally increase; thus prices will fall. Whether money wages rise, fall, or remain the same depends on the elasticities of the production function and labor supply, and the value of *m*. But if they fall, it will be less than the fall in prices; that is, the real wage necessarily will increase.[12]

If both the supply of labor and its productivity increase together (as consistently occurs in a growing economy) output grows for both reasons. Whether the real wage increases or decreases depends on whether labor supply grows faster or less rapidly than labor productivity. But in either case, the price level must fall. This tendency for prices to sag in a growing economy (unless the money supply grows suitably) has been frequently confirmed in many economies. The impact of deflation from this source on debtors has sometimes been described as the source of "populist" political movements in the American West during the nineteenth century.

Suppose that the marginal productivity of investment increases, thus raising the investment function. The equilibrium of equation (3) then requires a higher interest rate, along with higher investment and saving. However, all other variables—in particular, output and employment—are unchanged, although the composition of output must have shifted somewhat from consumption goods to capital goods. Economists have frequently used one or another form of this aspect of classical analysis to explain, for example, cyclical fluctuations in interest rates, or long-period trends, or international differences in interest rate levels.

It is clear that an essential requirement of the model is the flexibility of money wages and their tendency to fall without limit whenever there is unemployment (or to rise without limit whenever labor demand exceeds supply). Without this condition the results of the system are very different. In particular—as already noted—without flexible wages, unemployment is possible. The levels of real output and employment then depend, in part, on the supply of money.

Price rigidities elsewhere in the system might also seem to alter the results. For example, assume that output prices are inflexible downward. Starting from an initial equilibrium, an increase in output and employment to reflect an enlarged labor supply or an increase in labor's productivity would then be impossible, because the transactions balances needed for the handling of more output at the old price level would exceed the existing stock of money. However, if wage rates were flexible downward in response to unemployment, it is difficult to imagine how prices could remain rigid very long in this situation.

Similarly a rigid interest rate might prevent equilibrium in the capital market. If the interest rate were raised or held too high, for example, as the

---

[12] If the supply of labor is sufficiently backward sloping, output might actually decline. In that case, prices would rise, not fall, but the real wage would still rise.

result of "hoarding" or of a contraction of the money supply by the banking system, saving would exceed investment demand and wages and prices would fall without limit—so long as the interest rate were maintained above its equilibrium. By falling sufficiently rapidly, flexible wages could, however, prevent this disequilibrium in the capital market from causing unemployment. To be sure, so long as the interest rate remained too high, the system as a whole would not not be in equilibrium, for wages and prices would have to continue falling. It is only if wages were rigid—or even "sticky," so that they could not fall fast enough—that full employment would not be maintained.

Monetary and Fiscal Policy in Classical Economics

Thus it is proper to say that wage rigidity is the cause of unemployment, and the only cause, recognized in the classical system. Whether the *need* for wage reductions to maintain employment arises from growth of the labor force or technological change, or from some unfortunate event in the monetary sphere (hoarding or money contraction), or whether its original source lies in an increase in saving or a decrease in the desire to invest which generates an entirely passive response from the banking system (for example, see Wicksell), the flexibility of money wages could apparently always provide a complete and automatic corrective for unemployment.

However, many economists in the classical tradition recognized that it was undesirable as a practical matter to throw all burdens of adjustment on the level of money wages, certainly after Britain's experience in the 1920s, or the United States' experience following 1929. The need for upward or downward adjustment of wages and prices could be greatly reduced by a monetary policy which prevented the banking system from interfering with the saving-investment process by either creating or destroying money, whether in response to changes in saving or investment propensities, or independently thereof. Reforms in banking systems, including the creation of central banks under government control, had this important objective. *Keeping M stable* would prevent the banks or the gold supply from causing trouble, or shifts in saving propensities or investment prospects from requiring wage and price changes in either the inflationary or deflationary direction. *Controlled variations in M* would be necessary, however, to stabilize wages and prices against the effects of shifts in the supply of labor, or its productivity, or against changes in the public's demand for money resulting either from changes in the institutional determinants of velocity or from irrational hoarding or subsequent dishoarding. A government monetary policy could assure such changes as needed. Monetary policy, in short, was seen as a useful instrument for avoiding the necessity for price and wage fluctuations—for maintaining stability of the price level against inflation or deflation.

However, it was not only that either inflation or deflation was itself objectionable. The need for deflation was quite likely also to involve unemployment, because of the admitted difficulty and slowness of downward wage adjustments. This outcome could be avoided by an intelligent monetary policy that avoided any need for deflation (or too rapid a deflation). And if unemployment had developed, because wage rates were too high, an increase in M could always cure it. Thus it is not surprising that many economists in the classical tradition began to see monetary policy as an important and powerful tool of government intervention for the maintenance of both reasonably stable prices *and* full employment. On the other hand, the original classical economists saw no useful role for fiscal policy in dealing with either unemployment or inflation, nor do their present intellectual descendents.

The typical instrument of monetary policy (in the United States) is the central bank's open-market sale or purchase of securities. When the central bank buys securities on the open market, it either buys them from the nonbank public, thus directly increasing the public's holdings of money, or it buys from a bank, in which case the bank's reserves are increased and it is enabled to (and, it is hoped, will) either expand its loans to business or buy open-market securities, thereby increasing the public's holdings of money. If the central bank sells bonds on the open market, it either sells to the public, absorbing some of the public's supply of money, or it sells to a commercial bank, absorbing bank reserves, requiring or inducing the bank to reduce its other loans and investments, and thus the public's holdings of money. Through this and other means, a central bank can control within fairly narrow limits the quantity of money in circulation.

Fiscal policy, in contrast, involves alterations in government expenditures for goods and services or changes in the level of tax rates. Unlike monetary policy, these measures either involve changes in the *government's* own direct demand for goods and services (in the case of expenditures) or a direct impact on the *private* demand for goods and services (in the case of taxes). Monetary policy operates less directly, affecting in the first instance only the net supply and demand for loans or securities. Yet, despite its greater directness, fiscal policy was seen by classical economists to have no place in the arsenal of stabilization measures, except as it might incidentally and indirectly serve as an instrument of monetary policy.

To illustrate, suppose that there should be unemployment as a result of an increased labor force and a rigidity of wages which prevented the appropriate decline of prices. Proposals might be made for increased government spending to create jobs for the unemployed. Classical economists argued that this would either be futile or redundant. Were this new spending to be financed by higher taxes, the private spending of taxpayers would be reduced by as much as government spending increased (it was assumed). Were it to be financed by selling bonds to the public, it was argued that this could only raise interest rates and thus cut back private investment spending (and/or increase private saving) by as much as government spending increased. The government bonds would have to compete with the bonds issued by private investors for the available supply of saving, thus driving down bond prices (raising interest rates) to choke off any net increase in demand. Only if the increased government spending were financed by new money creation (operating the printing press or selling new government bonds to the central bank or to private banks with excess reserves) would there be a net increase in demand for goods and for labor. But this would be using government finances—awkwardly and unnecessarily—*as an instrument of monetary policy*, a means for increasing the supply of money. Exactly the same effect could be secured by central bank open market purchases of bonds—the conventional instrument of monetary policy. By this means the supply of money can be increased, but without any diversion of resources from public to private use.

Said economist R. G. Hawtrey in 1925, commenting on proposals for public works expenditures to relieve unemployment in England:

"Here, then, is the real virtue of the proposal. If the new [public] works are financed by the creation of bank credits, they will give additional employment.... But then the same reasoning shows that a creation of credit unaccompanied by any expenditure on public works could be equally effective in giving employment. The public works are merely a piece of ritual, convenient to people who want to be able to say that they are doing something, but otherwise irrelevant. To stimulate an expansion of credit is usually only too easy. To resort for the purpose to the construction of expensive public works is to burn down the house for the sake of the roast pig."[13]

One of the most striking changes made by modern macroeconomic thought is to alter considerably the previously conceived roles of monetary and fiscal policy. Today, monetary effects are recognized and monetary policy is still seen to be important, but equal or greater emphasis is placed on fiscal measures in securing economic stabilization (or, if badly used, in creating instability). This is the case even where fiscal measures are used in a way which has no effect, direct or indirect, on the quantity of money.

Limitations of the Classical Analysis

There can be no doubt that the classical model captures reasonably well a number of broad aspects of the macroeconomic performance of actual economies and makes some relevant prescriptions for public policies. On the other hand, it is easy to give many examples of predictions from the model that are quite imperfect; for example, that unemployment is, at most, a temporary phenomenon of adjustment from one equilibrium to another. Or that fiscal policy (for example, wartime deficit spending) has no effect on employment or the price level unless it incidentally alters M. To

---

[13] "Public Expenditure and the Demand for Labour," *Economica*, 5 (March 1925), 43–44.

be sure, a defender of classical macroeconomics may argue that even what are called predictive failures of the classical system are fully consistent with it in the sense that they must reflect the absence of appropriately flexible wages, prices, and/or interest rates. Moreover, the predictions of the classical system would be fulfilled if only the many "artificial" obstacles to free competition, such as trade unions, minimum wage legislation, industrial monopoly, and so on, were removed. However, the fact is that the world in which we live is full of such "artificial" obstacles, many of which represent highly durable characteristics of real economies and some of which are believed to perform important social functions—or, in any case, have strong political support. For better or worse, most of them will continue to exist, and one can argue that we need an economic theory that more accurately describes how actual economies operate, and that suggests the various ways in which some of the unfortunate consequences that often occur (for whatever reason) in these economies can be avoided or mitigated.

But the shortcomings of the classical theory may actually be considerably more serious than its assumption that no "artificial" obstacles interfere with full flexibility of all prices, wages, and interest rates. For it may well be that there exist other, highly important, and quite unavoidable aspects of every real economy which would prevent realization of the classical results, even in the complete absence of "artificial" restraints on competition and price flexibility. These aspects may inhere in such important characteristics of actual economies as continuous change in technology, tastes, labor supply, and so on; uncertainty; imperfect information (and the costs of obtaining less imperfect information); costs of and limitations on the free mobility of productive factors; or the fact that people learn and remember and therefore develop expectations. Even many of the "institutional" features of actual economies, which are sometimes described as imposing "artificial" obstacles to full competition and freely flexible prices, may in fact be in some sense a "natural" response to the existence of change, uncertainty, imperfect information, or the costs of mobility. The very existence of governments, as well as some almost unavoidable aspects of their performance, also invalidate certain results of classical theory. We need a macroeconomic theory which embodies all of these elements of the "real world".

The modifications in classical macroeconomics needed to take account of its limitations require many refinements and alterations of the particular elements and relationships already contained in the classical model presented previously. Actually, they require more than this. Once we dispense with some of the assumptions that gave the model its unique classical properties, completely new and different relationships become important for an understanding of the functioning of real-world economies. One clear example is that of the "consumption function." So long as we conclude that output and income are always and necessarily at full-employment levels, it is of little interest and no practical importance to know what consumption expenditures (and saving) would have been at less-than-full-employment levels of output and income. But once the inevitability of full employment is removed, the relationship of consumer spending to income must and does become a fundamental building block of macroeconomic theory.

One way of describing the many modifications and expansions of the classical model which are necessary to make it useful is to say that the classical model remains basically correct in its description of a macroeconomic system *in full (short-run) equilibrium*;[14] but that many actual features of real-world economies (both those that are "artificial" and those that are "inherent") operate to make the adjustments to full equilibrium exceedingly slow. Thus we need a macroeconomics of "disequilibrium" or "partial equilibrium." It is true that many of the modifications or expansions of the classical model which we shall discuss might about equally well be described as the disequilibrium behavior of a simple classical model, or as the (equilibrium) behavior of an expanded or modified—and thus non-classical—system. We shall, however, introduce these new elements without serious attention to this important but rather esoteric distinction, returning to the question only when most of the elements of the larger model are in place.

REVIEW QUESTIONS

1. Does the existence of saving and investment invalidate Say's Law? Why or why not?

2. Explain briefly but carefully each of the following pairs of concepts:
(a) natural rate of interest versus market rate of interest
(b) forced saving versus desired saving
(c) saving versus hoarding

3. The classical macroeconomic model attempts to demonstrate that the economy tends always to maintain an equilibrium consistent with full employment of all productive resources. In particular:

---

[14] The qualification "short-run" is inserted here to remind us of the fact that, so long as equilibrium involves $S = I > 0$ (and there is nothing in the specification of the model which prevents this) capital accumulation will be occurring, causing, among other things, shifts in production functions and increments of consumer wealth, the consequences of which will almost surely progressively alter the future *short-run* equilibrium of the system. However, since this accumulation is insignificant over any moderately short period of time, we can reasonably ignore its effects, and make our analysis on the assumption that production functions and wealth are given and unchanging. This does not prevent our comparing short-run equilibria over longer periods of time, over which production functions and wealth differ, as the result—among other things—of $S = I > 0$, as we have, in fact, done. We have, however, treated these longer period changes as exogenous, whereas, at least in part, they are endogenous.

(a) "A reduction of consumer demand, arising from an increased desire to save, should not create any problem of inadequate aggregate demand." Explain carefully why, and what would be the effects of an increased desire to save on the equilibrium value of each major macroeconomic variable.

(b) "An increase in the supply of labor will not engender any permanent unemployment." Explain carefully why, and what the effect of an increased supply of labor would be on the equilibrium value of each macroeconomic variable.

(c) "A decrease in the money supply will not produce unemployment." Explain carefully why, and what would be the effect of such a decrease in M on the equilibrium value of each macroeconomic variable.

(d) In case (c), suppose that the money wage rate were rigid. What would then be the effect of such a decrease in the money supply on the equilibrium value of each macroeconomic variable?

(In answering (a) through (d), you will probably find it helpful to use diagrams. If you do, be sure to label them carefully.)

4. Explain why an economist in the classical tradition might believe that monetary policy is an important and powerful tool of stabilization, while fiscal policy is an ineffective tool (except as an instrument of monetary policy)? What, do you think, are the weaknesses of this view?

5. In the "classical model," an increase in (potential) supply creates its own demand.

(a) Use carefully labeled diagrams to depict the classical macroequilibrium of total employment, output, real wage, money wage, price level, saving, investment, and the interest rate.

(b) List in tabular form the direction of the effect (indicated by $+$, $-$, or 0) on each of the eight variables listed above of the following changes, each occurring separately (all other conditions unchanged):

(1) an increase in the supply of labor
(2) a doubling of the money supply
(3) an improvement in technology
(4) the accumulation of capital

SELECTED REFERENCES

K. Wicksell, *Lectures on Political Economy* (translation by L. Robbins) (Routledge and Kegan Paul, 1934), Vol. II, esp. pp. 159–208.
(Wicksell's integration of quantity theory with saving, investment, and the interest rate.)

W. L. Smith, "Monetary Theories of the Rate of Interest: A Dynamic Analysis," *Review of Economics and Statistics*, 40 (February 1958), 15–21.
(An example of a dynamic theory of interest retaining the tie to the classical formulation.)

J. M. Keynes, *The General Theory of Employment, Interest, and Money* (Harcourt, Brace, 1936), Chapter 14.
(Keynes' interpretation and critique of classical interest theory.)

PART III

THE SIMPLE
KEYNESIAN MODEL

Chapter 6

The Consumption Function and the Simple Keynesian Model

Supply of and Demand for Total Output

Consumer Expenditures
Simple consumption functions
Consumption functions by statistical regression
Consumption, saving, and the propensity to consume
Statistical saving functions
Validity of the simple consumption function

The Keynesian Model without Government
Unemployment, business cycles, and economic growth

The Keynesian Model with Government
Government purchases
Other government expenditures affecting aggregate demand
Taxes, and the government balance
The "net-tax" system and disposable income
The size and meaning of the multiplier
Graphical representation of the model
Other leakages from the circular flow

Appendix: Does the Consumption Function Reflect Only Reverse Causation?

We are now ready to consider the Keynesian theory of the determination of the volume of national output, the associated levels of national income and employment, and the level of prices. Even before considering any of the details, it will be helpful to sketch the general nature of the approach that was pioneered by Keynes and now is largely accepted by economists of almost every doctrinal persuasion.

SUPPLY OF AND DEMAND FOR TOTAL OUTPUT

In brief, economists today regard *changes in the volume of total real output as essentially determined*, certainly in the short run, *by changes in "aggregate demand"*—the aggregate purchases of real "final output," which consumers, businesses, governments, and the rest of the world desire to make. This proposition needs, of course, to be qualified by adding the condition: "within limits set by existing supplies of labor and capital, and by the productive technologies presently embodied in plants, organizations, and the working methods and skills of individuals." *Within these limits,* as more output is demanded, it is produced, and the services of workers and of capital facilities are employed to produce it. Thus, in a real and important sense, the direction of causation is exactly the reverse of Say's Law: the demand for output creates its own supply. And because aggregate demand determines output, it in turn determines the levels of employment and (given the size of the labor force) unemployment and (given the stock of capital in place) the rate of utilization of plant and equipment.

The previous paragraph refers to limits on total output set by supply constraints in physical terms. Such limits surely exist. With the labor supply, the capital equipment, and the technology and skills that existed 100 years ago, or even 25 years ago, it would surely be physically impossible to produce today's real GNP, whatever the volume of aggregate demand might be. But exactly where these physical limits to aggregate output lie at any given time is not and cannot be known with precision. Only rarely are these limits even closely approached. At such times, either the effects of the resulting rapid inflation will have indirectly restrained aggregate demand, and/or public policies will have been adjusted, one way or another, to do so. We can never be entirely sure whether, in the end, output was restrained by physical limitations on supply or by the absence of any further expansion of aggregate demand.

At least for the present, we neither wish nor need to explore the response of supply to demand when aggregate demand is closely pressing against the ultimate physical limits on aggregate output. Thus we confine attention for now only to variations of output at or below the socially determined "full-employment" level of utilization of the labor force and thus within the limits of the corresponding "potential output," defined in Chapter 3. Our working proposition thus becomes: aggregate demand creates its own supply, within the limits set by potential output.

In this chapter, we will begin to explore the determination of total output and employment with the help first of very simple, and subsequently of slightly more complex, models of the determination of aggregate demand. We will consider how certain "exogenous" events affect aggregate demand and thus output, and we give particular attention to the ways in which government policies affect demand and output and how they may be used to maintain or restore approximately full employment.

Although potential ouptut is, at any given time, fixed, we know that, over time, it grows. Thus, even if aggregate demand at one time is adequate to achieve full employment, the growth of potential may itself create unemployment, with no change in aggregate demand. On the other hand, although this growth of aggregate capacity does not *automatically* produce a corresponding growth of aggregate demand, if the existence of a gap between actual and potential output should have repercussions on aggregate demand which would cause it to increase, the growth of potential output *may* indirectly lead to a growth of actual output. Moreover, if potential output more or less continuously exceeds aggregate demand, the resulting deficiency may also gradually tend to reduce the growth rate of potential—in this way, also, perhaps tending to restore full employment. All of these interrelationships between aggregate supply and aggregate demand can be incorporated in progressively more complex models of the aggregate economy.

Of course, since potential output is not a physical limit, aggregate demand can exceed potential and sometimes does. Assuming that "full employment" (and thus "potential output") have been correctly defined, this implies an unacceptable inflation. (To be sure, an unacceptable inflation may also occur even with output below potential, but it will have a somewhat different explanation.) As we consider the nature and consequences of inflation, we shall also consider whether, or under what circumstances, the inflation that arises from demand at or in excess of potential ultimately "burns itself out" by automatically reducing aggregate real demand.

Thus, our theory employs two global magnitudes, which, in the short run, are more or less—but not completely—independent of one another: **potential output,** which can be thought of as summarizing the impact of the many factors on the "supply side" of the economy, which *permit* aggregate output to be produced; and **aggregate demand**, which reflects the strength of all the forces which lead to the purchase of aggregate output and thus *cause* it to be produced. Although conceptually separate, the two magnitudes have many and complex interconnections that we shall from time to time pursue. Yet it remains vitally important to keep these concepts separate, and to recognize that most factors which directly affect either one of them may leave the other unaffected, certainly in the first instance.

This way of looking at the aggregate economy is perhaps the most fundamental product of the "Keynesian revolution" (although as already noted, there were hints of it in Wicksell and perhaps a few other pre-Keynesian economists).

The preceding discussion has referred to aggregate demand as though it were all one big lump. In one fundamental sense it is, in that decisions to purchase final output have essentially similar short-run effects on production and employment regardless of who made the purchase decision, what was bought, or for what purpose. But in attempting to understand why aggregate demand is what it is, and what may cause it to change, economists immediately begin to break the big "lump" of aggregate demand down into its major components. And when they seek further to refine and improve their understanding of the sources and variation of any one of these major components, they are apt further to break it down into subcomponents.

These breakdowns of GNP could, in principle, be made on any of a number of bases—by geographical area, by industry, by the extent of use of capital versus labor, or in many other ways. But the distinction that best advances our analysis and understanding is believed to be a breakdown by class of buyer: as among consumers, businesses for investment purposes, governments, and the rest of the world. It is thus no accident that national income accountants use exactly these major breakdowns of data on actual GNP or NNP; it is the natural result of this way of thinking about aggregate demand.

Just as, conceptually, we see changes in aggregate demand occurring independently of any change in the factors affecting potential output (or vice versa)—even though there exist indirect relations between them—so do we regard any one category of aggregate demand as capable of varying independently of another, although, again, we shall find repercussions of changes in one upon the others. We begin, in this chapter, to provide an explanation of the largest single component of aggregate demand: consumer purchases or **personal consumption expenditures**. We then use this explanation to develop a first and very simple model, but one which already begins to provide important insights into the working of the aggregate economy.

CONSUMER EXPENDITURES

Personal consumption expenditures in recent years have constituted between about 62 percent and 65 percent of the United States gross national product. Thus, once we understand what determines consumer purchases, we will have "explained" the largest part of GNP. Economists probably have a better understanding of the determinants of consumer expenditures than of any other element of GNP. Indeed, not many years ago, many economists were confident that they knew nearly all that was needed to be known about what determines aggregate consumption. Unfortunately, as they have learned still more, they have become considerably less satisfied with their explanations. It is now obvious that there is a great deal about consumer spending that is not fully understood. Chapters 16 and 17 will take up in considerable detail some of the more important theoretical and empirical findings of recent years about consumer spending and focus attention on the major puzzles that still remain. Nevertheless, these puzzles are surely fewer than in the case of investment expenditures.

Simple Consumption Functions

Perhaps the single most important contribution of Keynes to modern macroeconomics was his invention of the **consumption function**. Aggregate consumer purchases of goods and services, he said, were a stable function of aggregate consumer income. It is clear from his context that, by "income," he meant what subsequently came to be defined as **disposable**

income. Representing aggregate consumption by C, and aggregate income by Y, he postulated that

$$C = C(Y)$$

where dC/dY (the "marginal propensity to consume") is positive but less than 1. Indeed, he called this "a fundamental psychological law." It is clear that he "discovered" this law not by careful statistical analysis of data (there were no time series of national income and product data at the time he wrote) but simply by casual observation and introspection. And, although it is possible to derive something like Keynes' law from economists' standard theory of the behavior of rational consumers, Keynes appears to have made no effort to do so. The act by which an economist asserts a fundamental psychological law on the basis of meditation in his easy chair may offend psychologists as an act of interdisciplinary imperialism. Yet when national income and product data shortly afterward began to become available, they seemed fully to support Keynes' arrogant claim.

The simplest possible form of a consumption function that would meet Keynes' specification would be one which made aggregate consumer purchases a roughly constant fraction (less than one) of aggregate disposable personal income. During the 30 years, 1946 through 1975, the share of United States disposable income which was consumed averaged 93.35 percent, and fell within plus-or-minus 2.0 percentage points of that average in 27 of those years.[1] Indeed, the share fell within 1.0 percentage point of the average in 15 years.

Expressing this finding in the form of an equation, we have the simple descriptive **consumption function**:

$$C \simeq 0.9335\, DI$$

where C is aggregate consumption[2] and DI aggregate disposable personal income. The fact that C in every year was not precisely equal to $0.9335\, DI$ might be interpreted to mean either that there are errors in the measurement of C and DI, and/or that there are factors other than DI alone that influence C. Still another possibility would be that $0.9335\, DI$ represents the "equilibrium value" of consumer expenditures, once consumers have had full opportunity to adjust their expenditures to the (changing) value of DI, but that in some (or all) years, they were not entirely in equilibrium with respect to (that is, not fully satisfied with) their expenditures, given what their incomes turned out to be. However, the errors, other influences,

---

[1] The values outside the range of 91.35 percent through 95.35 percent were 97.1 in 1947, 96.4 in 1949, 91.7 in 1975.

[2] Actually, here we have used the concept of "personal outlays" in the United States national income accounts, which is the sum of "personal consumption expenditures," "interest paid by consumers," and "personal transfer payments to foreigners." "Personal consumption expenditures" however make up approximately 98 percent of "personal outlays."

or absences of equilibrium were apparently approximately "random" in their effects. The algebraic sum or average of the percentage deviations of consumption from the basic relationship was about zero, and the deviations appear to have been more or less "normally" distributed around the average.

That consumption should depend at least mainly on disposable income, and should "use up" by far the largest part of it, is not surprising. Indeed, many families spend just about every dollar they get their hands on. And most individuals and families find that as their resources expand, their wants and needs keep pace. If they get more, they spend more. Indeed, we all know at least a few families who, regardless of changes in income, are constantly in debt, sometimes to the maximum extent which their creditors will permit. Many families, if they save any part of their disposable incomes, save only when more or less "compelled" to do so by a contractual commitment to make payments on a mortgage, insurance policy, or installment debt, or through payroll deductions for savings bonds or for contributions to a private retirement system (deductions for Social Security are already subtracted in computing disposable income). These forms of contractual saving constitute a substantial fraction of all personal saving.

The irresistible pressure and indefinite expansibility of human wants, however, explain too much. For the fact is that most families do save something, and some middle and higher incomes families save substantial fractions of their disposable incomes. Moreover, they save year after year, at least during their years of peak earning power. Saving, obviously, is also a "good" that competes with other goods and services, winning at least a small share of most incomes and of most increments of income. We need to understand how the competition between consumption and saving for the income dollar is decided. However, we postpone any serious attention to the theory of individual saving until a later chapter.

Consumption Functions by Statistical Regression

Figure 6-1 shows, for each year, 1929–1975, aggregate United States consumption (personal outlays) in 1972 prices (measured vertically), and aggregate disposable income in 1972 prices (measured horizontally). Consumption (personal outlays), C, and disposable income, DI, are as recorded in the United States national income and product accounts. The price level, P, is measured by the deflator for personal consumption expenditures (PCE), 1972 = 100. Also shown in the figure are two consumption functions. Function C_1 shows real consumption at every level of income as equal to 0.9335 times real disposable income:

$$(1) \qquad \frac{C}{P} = 0.9335 \frac{DI}{P}$$

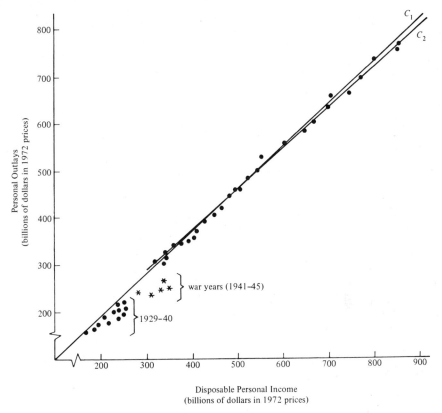

FIGURE 6-1   Personal Outlays and Disposable Personal Income, 1929–75.

(Since, on the average, C was 93.35 percent of DI during the years 1946–1975, C/P was the same percentage of DI/P.)

Function C_2 is, instead, a statistical regression "fitted" to data for the 30 years 1946 through 1975. The statistical procedure used assumes that C/P is a linear function of DI/P and discovers that linear function—of all possible ones—for which the sum of the squared differences between each year's recorded C/P and a hypothetical C/P computed according to that function, is minimized. The resulting equation is

$$(2) \qquad \frac{C}{P} = 12.25 + 0.9130 \frac{DI}{P} \qquad (R^2 = 0.99885)^3$$

[3] The **coefficient of determination** (R^2) for the function is a measure of its "goodness of fit." If the correlation between consumption and disposable income were perfect (every dot in Figure 6-1 fell precisely on line C_2) R^2 would have the value of 1.0. The value, 0.99885, of the coefficient in this case can be shown to mean that the fitted relationship "explains" 99.885% of the total (squared) deviations of the individual C's from the mean C for all years combined. The remaining 0.115 percent must reflect some combination of measurement errors, random fluctuations, temporary disequilibria, and/or the net influence of other factors that also systematically influence the volume of consumption.

This equation "predicts" that aggregate consumer expenditures in any year, expressed in 1972 prices, will be $12.25 billion plus 91.3 percent of that year's aggregate disposable income in 1972 prices. Obviously, the difference between functions (1) and (2) is very slight, and either function seems to "explain" annual consumer expenditures very well. The statistical regression is, of course, a procedure much to be preferred.

Most economists agree that it is preferable to relate *real* consumer expenditures to *real* disposable income, as does equation (2)—rather than to relate the corresponding dollar aggregates. Consumers, they hypothesize, will normally not change their real expenditures if both money incomes and prices rise (or fall) in the same percentage; but they will change them if money incomes change by more or less than prices change. Moreover, most agree, it is better still to relate these magnitudes on a per capita basis, on the ground that any variation in aggregate income that merely reflects population growth may affect aggregate consumption differently from that which reflects changing income per capita. The consumption function fitted to real, per capita data for the years 1950–1975 is

$$(3) \qquad \frac{C}{Pop \times P} = 112.01 + 0.8983 \frac{DI}{Pop \times P} \qquad (R^2 = 0.99695)$$

where *Pop* means population, and *P* is again the PCE deflator. The equation predicts that consumer expenditures per capita, in 1972 prices, will be $112 plus 89.83 percent of disposable income per capita in 1972 prices. If we multiply both sides of equation (3) by *Pop*, we again get an expression in aggregate terms:

$$(3a) \qquad \frac{C}{P} = 112.01 \, Pop + 0.8983 \frac{DI}{P}$$

The form of equation (3a) differs from that of equation (2) only in that the first term on the right is no longer a constant but rather changes with population. It will be seen that the coefficient of aggregate real disposable income is somewhat lower than in equation (2) because some of the growth of *C* is now "explained" by population growth and, therefore, somewhat less of it by rising income. However, it will be noted that (judging by the R^2) the fit of equation (3) is no better (indeed, a bit poorer) than of equation (2). Moreover, levels of aggregate consumption predicted by equation (3a), are, for most years, insignificantly different from those predicted by equation (2), or, for that matter, equation (1). This is the case because the constant term in equation (3), as in (2), is not far from zero. That is, real consumption per capita is almost proportional to real income per capita. Thus, the numerical value of the term 112.01 *Pop* in any year is small relative to the numerical value of *C* (about $22.5 billion with a population of 200 million) and aggregate consumption in constant prices is thus approximately proportional to aggregate consumer disposable income. If the constants in equation (2) or the coefficient of *Pop* in equation (3) had turned out to be substantial, the predictions given by the two equations would differ significantly. Then we could really test the correctness of the assumption that consumer behavior is best described in per capita terms by comparing the R^2 (and other statistical properties) of equations (2) and (3).[4]

Consumption, Saving, and the Propensity to Consume

Existence of a simple linear relationship between consumption and disposable income implies as well a simple linear relationship between personal saving and disposable income, and, further, one between consumption and personal saving. For personal saving is simply the difference between disposable income and consumption:

$$(4) \qquad\qquad S \equiv DI - C$$

Thus, if we postulate the generalized linear functional relationship,

$$(5) \qquad\qquad C = c_0 + c_1 DI$$

between consumption and disposable income, substituting (5) into (4) and rearranging terms gives us

$$(6) \qquad\qquad S = -c_0 + (1 - c_1)DI$$

which we may describe as a **saving function**, corresponding to consumption function (5). Likewise, by substitution between the same two equations, we can eliminate *DI*, giving us a *CS* **function**:

$$(7) \qquad\qquad C = \frac{c_0}{1 - c_1} + \frac{c_1}{1 - c_1} S$$

The graphic relationship among the three functions can be seen from Figure 6-2. The 45° diagonal line through the origin of the $C : DI$ quadrant permits *DI* to be measured vertically as well as horizontally. Thus, the vertical distance between the diagonal line and the consumption line measures the amount of saving. This amount is shown in the $S : DI$ diagram directly below. The third relationship simply plots in a $C : S$ quadrant the associated values of C and S from the other two quadrants. If $c_0 > 0$, and

[4] As noted earlier (footnote 2), interest paid by consumers (other than mortgage interest) and personal transfer payments to foreigners are not included in personal consumption expenditures. If we exclude these items, and represent the concept of consumption by "personal consumption expenditures" alone, we can recompute equations (2) and (3) as follows:

$$(2a) \qquad \frac{C}{P} = 18.638 + 0.88050 \frac{DI}{P} \qquad (R^2 = 0.99806)$$

$$(3b) \qquad \frac{C}{P} = 171.89 + 0.85771 \frac{DI}{P \times Pop} \qquad (R^2 = 0.99719)$$

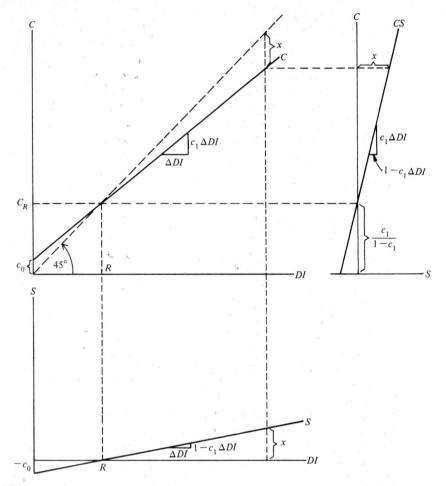

FIGURE 6-2

$c_1 < 1$ (as drawn) saving will be negative for all levels of disposable income less than R, and the saving and CS functions will both slope upward to the right. All evidence supports the assumption that $c_1 < 1$, although, other than in the very short run, it appears that c_0 is close to zero. If $c_0 = 0$, all three functions in Figure 6-2 will pass through the origin, their equations being:

$$C = c_1 DI \qquad S = (I - c_1)DI \qquad C = \frac{c_1}{1 - c_1} S$$

It should be clear that any one of these functional relationships implies the other two. For various purposes we may find it convenient to work with any one of them, either in assessing the empirical evidence about consumer spending and the problems posed by that evidence, or in building macro-economic models.

Before proceeding further, we need to introduce some frequently used terminology concerning these functions. The slope, c_1, of the consumption function is frequently referred to as the **marginal propensity to consume** (MPC), and its complement $(1 - c_1)$ as the **marginal propensity to save** (MPS). By definition, their sum is necessarily 1, and we believe that each is normally positive but less than 1. The related concept of **average propensity to consume** (APC) is, of course, simply the percentage of income consumed, or C/DI; the **average propensity to save** (APS) is S/DI. If the consumption function is linear, the two marginal propensities, c_1 and $(1 - c_1)$, are constant. However, the average propensities are not necessarily constant; they are, respectively,

$$\text{APC} = \frac{C}{DI} = \frac{c_0 + c_1 DI}{DI} = \frac{c_0}{DI} + c_1$$

and

$$\text{APS} = \frac{S}{DI} = \frac{-c_0 + (1 - c_1)DI}{DI} = \frac{-c_0}{DI} + (1 - c_1)$$

If c_0 is positive, APC can be seen from the above to be always positive and greater than the MPC, falling toward MPC as DI increases. (APC will be greater than 1 at low levels of income—that is, as DI approaches zero.) Similarly, APS can be seen from the above to be less than MPS but rising toward it as DI increases. (APS is less than zero at low levels of DI.) If $c_0 = 0$, both average propensities equal their corresponding marginal propensities, and both are of course constant, always positive, and less than 1.

We can easily conceive of nonlinear consumption functions. For example, MPC might be less than 1, but declining as income increases, with APC less than 1, and falling. (J. M. Keynes, inventor of the consumption function, believed that it had these particular properties.) Or MPC might be less than 1 but rising as income increases, remaining less than 1, as would also APC. As an exercise, the reader should draw the functions just described; moreover, he should describe verbally the marginal and average propensities to consume for each of the possible consumption functions shown in Figure 6-3, and draw the corresponding saving functions and describe their marginal and average propensities. He should also identify which (if any) of these consumption functions is consistent with Keynes' hypotheses about its shape.

Statistical Saving Functions

Given that there exists a saving function corresponding to any consumption function, we can, of course, investigate the nature of the empirical relationship among DI, C, and S equally well by using data on S and DI (or even C and S without DI). Figure 6-4 plots data for the years 1946–1975

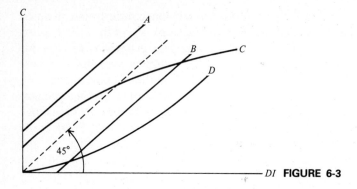

DI **FIGURE 6-3**

on S/P and DI/P (where S is personal saving and P is the GNP deflator for personal consumption expenditures, $1972 = 100$).

Fitting a linear regression to the data plotted in Figure 6-4 produces the saving function:

$$(8) \qquad \frac{S}{P} = -12.25 + 0.0870 \frac{DI}{P} \qquad (R^2 = 0.88772)$$

Since, if C depends on DI, we have seen that the corresponding equation for S should be

$$(6) \qquad S = -c_0 + (1 - c_1)DI$$

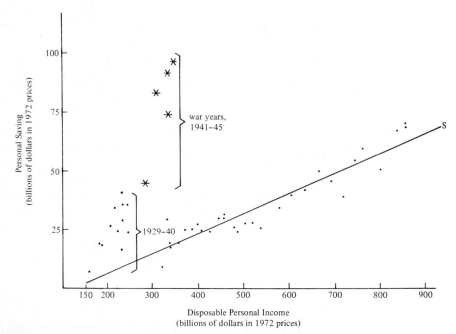

FIGURE 6-4 Personal Saving and Disposable Personal Income, 1929–1975.

we can use the numerical values from equation (8) to derive an indirect statistical estimate of the consumption function, as

(9)
$$\frac{C}{P} = 12.25 + 0.9130 \frac{DI}{P}$$

It will be seen that this indirect estimate is identical with the direct estimate derived earlier (equation 2).

On a *per capita* basis, the statistical saving function is

(10)
$$\frac{S}{Pop \times P} = -112.01 + 0.1017 \frac{DI}{Pop \times P} \qquad (R^2 = 0.80760)$$

This provides the following indirect estimate of a consumption function:

(11)
$$\frac{C}{Pop \times P} = 112.01 + 0.8983 \frac{DI}{Pop \times P}$$

which can be seen to be identical with equation (3).

There is, of course, a considerable difference between the "goodness of fit" of any pair of corresponding consumption and saving functions, as is evident by comparing Figures 6-1 and 6-4 or the coefficients of determination (R^2) for equations (2) and (8) or (3) and (10). This difference merely reflects the fact that a given error or disturbance affecting C relative to DI becomes an error or disturbance of equal amount (but opposite sign) in S. But since S is roughly one tenth as large as C, the *relative* error or disturbance is about 10 times as great.

There could well be argument which R^2 should be used to characterize the goodness of fit of the statistical consumption (saving) relationship. However, even the lower coefficient—that for the saving function—is high enough to confirm that there is some clear relationship between the two variables. Of course, merely finding a statistical correlation between C and DI (or any other pair of variables) does not prove anything about "causation." In this case, the direction of causation might be the reverse of that postulated, that is, C might determine DI; or causation might run both ways; or both C and DI might be determined by some other variable or combination of variables, but are not themselves "causally" related. All that we can ever conclude from a study of data is that the "facts" are or are not consistent with a proposed explanation. They might be equally consistent, or even more consistent, with an alternate explanation.[5]

---

[5] In this case there is an alternate explanation implied in the simple model which we will consider in the next chapter. This alternate explanation is that C is a major determinant of DI, one stage removed. An appendix to this chapter considers whether this reverse causation might fully explain the statistical relationships we have just measured (and finds that it cannot).

Validity of the Simple Consumption Function

In the preceding pages, we have presented evidence which suggests that variation in disposable income seems to account for most of the observed variation in consumer purchases. The purpose of this demonstration is not to support the conclusion that this is *all* we need to know in order to understand what role consumer spending plays in determining GNP. It is intended only (a) as the starting point for a later, far more detailed and critical analysis of the determinants of aggregate consumption, and (b) to provide one ingredient for the simple static macroeconomic models that are described in Parts III and IV of this book. These models typically assume that consumption essentially depends on disposable income and on nothing else.

We have tried to suggest, on the one hand, that a reasonable empirical basis does exist for the assumption used in the simple models; it seems broadly consistent with available data. However, we have also tried to suggest that there may be a great deal more—both known, and still to be learned—about the determinants of consumption. We have noted that the simple function used was not derived from economists' standard theory of consumer behavior, implying that the latter body of theory may specify some rather different relationship between consumption and disposable income. We have reminded ourselves that statistical findings in any case do not prove causation. We have also hinted that this (or some other) relationship may hold only when the economy is in full equilibrium (which it never is) and that a different, or at least more complex, explanation is needed for the actual movements of real-world consumer purchases. Finally we have suggested that a number of variables other than disposable income may be required for a full explanation of consumer spending.

The simple consumption function is an adequate "working tool," not inconsistent with available data; for the present, that is all that we contend for it. Given that conclusion, we proceed to incorporate it in some exceedingly simple, yet, from a heuristic standpoint, exceedingly useful models, providing a means for organizing our thinking about some major forces at work in our economy. They are called Keynesian models because their main ingredient is Keynes' consumption function.

THE KEYNESIAN MODEL WITHOUT GOVERNMENT

We start with the simplest model of all. It relates to an imaginary world with no government (thus no purchases, transfers, or taxes). We also assume no retentions of earnings in businesses and no international transactions of any kind. In this world the national accounts are even more simplified than the system developed in Chapter 2: net national product, national income, and disposable income are all identical; all can thus be represented by a single variable Y, which stands indifferently for each of these. Thought of as net national product, Y is the sum of consumption and net investment (the latter taken, until further notice, as exogenous):[6]

(12) $$Y = C + I$$

We simplify our notation by defining these magnitudes in constant prices (so that their money values now would need to be written as PY, PC, etc.).

We can now add a consumption function

(13) $$C = c_0 + c_1 Y$$

where the Y now also represents real disposable income. We specify that the marginal propensity to consume (c_1) is positive and less than 1; the constant (c_0) may be positive, negative, or zero. We also specify that we are dealing with levels of Y up to and including some fixed level of potential output.

Substituting (13) into (12) gives

$$Y = c_0 + c_1 Y + I$$

or

(14) $$Y = \frac{1}{1 - c_1} (c_0 + I)$$

Corresponding to every possible exogenous value of I, there is thus some corresponding value of Y.

If, for example, $c_0 \equiv 12$ and $c_1 \equiv 0.75$, equation (14) becomes

$$Y = \frac{1}{0.25} (12 + I)$$

or

$$Y = 48 + 4I$$

Thus, if $I = 12$, $Y = 96$; if $I = 20$, $Y = 128$; if $I = 37.829$, $Y = 199.316$.

The upper panel of Figure 6-5 represents this model graphically. In the figure, Y is measured horizontally, C and I vertically. We are concerned only with levels of Y up to and including Y_P, the potential output. (Recall that potential output is not the physical limit on output which corresponds to 100 percent employment, but some institutional policy target.) The consumption function is the straight line labeled C, the vertical intercept of which is, of course, c_0 and the slope c_1. It shows what consumers will spend (measured vertically) for every income level (measured horizontally). The lines $C + I_0$, and $C + I_1$, above and parallel to it, show

[6] We can think of equation (12) as not merely a definition of Y, but as an equilibrium condition, once C is defined as the "desired" or "planned" consumption, as it is in equation (13), and if we assume, further, that producers will continue to produce any output only if it is exactly the amount which their purchasers desire to buy.

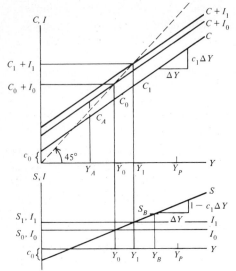

FIGURE 6-5

the total expenditures that would be forthcoming at each level of income, given each of two possible levels of investment—I_0 and I_1. The vertical distances between these lines and the C function, of course, equal the (exogenous) investment, which is the same regardless of income. We can think of the $C + I$ lines as representing aggregate demand.

The "solution" to the model is obviously found where $C + I$ (measured vertically) equals Y (measured horizontally). Graphically, this can be located with the aid of a 45° diagonal line through the origin, which connects all points in the quadrant at which vertical and horizontal measurements are equal. The solution, or "equilibrium"—given this consumption function and the particular investment level I_0—is found at $Y = Y_0$ and $C = C_0$. Y can be at no other level because, if it were, aggregate demand ($C + I$) would either exceed or fall short of output. For example, if Y were somehow established at Y_A, aggregate demand ($C_A + I_0$) would exceed production; the resulting increase of production, and thus of disposable income, would further raise the consumption component of aggregate demand but, of course, by less than the rise in income. Still, aggregate demand would necessarily exceed production until output (income) reached the equilibrium level, Y_0.

If I now should rise to I_1, the aggregate demand function would shift upward as shown, and the equilibrium income (output) would rise to Y_1.

An alternative formulation of this model, in terms of saving and investment, differs only superficially. If we define saving, S, as disposable income minus consumption,

$$(15) \qquad\qquad S \equiv Y - C$$

and our consumption function is, as before,

$$C = c_0 + c_1 Y$$

we can substitute this into equation (15) to get

(16) $$S = -c_0 + (1 - c_1)Y$$

We can express the equilibrium requirement as

(17) $$S = I$$

which implies that businesses wish to purchase exactly that part of any output that consumers do not wish to purchase. Substituting (16) into (17) and rearranging, we again obtain

(14) $$Y = \frac{1}{1 - c_1}(c_0 + I)$$

Graphically, the model in this form appears as in the lower panel of Figure 6-5, where S is the saving function (corresponding to the C function in the upper panel), and I_0 and I_1 two different levels of autonomous investment (the same levels used in the upper panel). Given I_0, S and I are equal only at Y_0; given I_1, S and I are equal only at Y_1. Thus, Y_0 and Y_1 are the equilibrium values for Y, given I_0 and I_1 respectively. If, with $I = I_0$, output were somehow established at Y_B, saving (S_B) would exceed investment (I_0). The sum of consumption spending ($Y_B - S_B$) together with investment spending (I_0) would thus fall short of output (Y_B). (Unfortunately, this is not easily seen graphically, although it appears clearly if Y_B is extended to the upper panel of Figure 6-5.) Such a deficiency of aggregate demand would necessarily lead to a drop of production, which could only terminate when Y reached Y_0 where total purchases would equal production. (A fuller description of the "disequilibrium behavior" of the model is postponed to a later point.)

Equation (14) tells us that any change in I will lead to a change in Y equal to the change in I times $1/(1 - c_1)$. With $c_1 < 1$, this fraction is necessarily greater than 1; thus its common name **the multiplier**, implying that an increase in I has a "multiplied" effect on the economy. Since $(1 - c_1)$ is the marginal propensity to save, we can say that, in this simplest of models, the multiplier is the reciprocal of the marginal propensity to save. We shall have more to say about the multiplier after we have developed a slightly more complicated model which introduces a government which levies taxes and grants transfers.

Unemployment, Business Cycles, and Economic Growth

In this model, it is clear that unemployment in excess of society's target, and output short of potential output (Y_P) will result when and if investment falls short of the amount that consumers wish to save at the target "full-employment" level of output. Put otherwise, unemployment in excess of target will result if the amount of consumption at Y_P plus the amount of investment falls short of Y_P. We can define some level of investment (I_P) necessary for full employment, equal to the saving that would occur at potential output. Whether, or under what circumstances, this amount of investment will be forthcoming is a subject to be investigated later, using somewhat more elaborate and, we hope, more realistic versions of this model. Here, however, we merely note that, whatever determines the rate of investment, if, for any reason, it fluctuates below I_P, for example, in cyclical fashion, output and incomes will also fluctuate below Y_P. If c_0 (the constant in the consumption function) is approximately zero—as seems probable—the fluctuations in Y will be essentially proportional to those in I, although larger in absolute amount, that is, larger in the proportion given by the multiplier. If peaks in the investment cycle approach or surpass I_P, this will carry the economy to, or close to, full employment during booms. If investment peaks below I_P, it will leave a varying margin of unemployment, even in booms.

If we now recognize that, over time, potential output grows—as the result of growth in available employment hours and/or in output per hour (because of more capital per worker or technological progress)—the level of investment necessary to maintain full employment (I_P) will grow in essentially the same proportion as the growth of potential. If investment fails to grow at this rate, the gap between potential and actual output will steadily rise. (Later, we will investigate some simple models in which such a steady growth of investment might seem plausible.) If investment were to grow at a trend rate equal to the growth rate of potential, but with cyclical fluctuations around that trend, the unemployment rate would rise and fall; however, the growth of output would on the average parallel that of potential, and no trend would appear in the unemployment rate.

It should be clear that, without some further theory that explains why investment (or the consumption function) moves upward over time, or without some automatic mechanism that causes investment to increase as the result of any rise in unemployment, the simple Keynesian model has nothing to contribute to the explanation of economic growth. A rise in potential output in the simple model produces only a larger gap between actual and potential output.

THE KEYNESIAN MODEL WITH GOVERNMENT

A second major component of the aggregate demand for national product, namely, government purchases of goods and services—can now be incorporated into the model along with consumer purchases. In most Western countries, government purchases now constitute a substantial share of GNP; in the United States, government purchases of goods and services are close to one third as large as consumer expenditures.

Government Purchases

In 1929, United States government purchases of goods and services were 8.2 percent of GNP; in 1976, they were 21.6 percent. Most of this increase had already occurred by the early 1950s. Since then the percentage has varied between a low of 20.4 percent of GNP in 1964 to a high of 22.4 percent in 1975. The variations have mainly reflected changes in defense spending. Indeed, during World War II, government purchases reached (in 1944) an astonishing 45.9 percent of GNP, falling precipitously after 1945 to a low of 13.3 percent in 1950 (just before the outbreak of the Korean War and then the "Cold War").

Since the early 1950s, *federal* purchases have trended down as a percentage of GNP, from about 13 percent in 1954 to 7.9 percent in 1976, whereas state and local government purchases have steadily risen (from 6.8 percent of GNP in 1953 to 13.7 percent in 1976). State and local now exceed federal purchases by more than 70 percent. As these figures suggest, swings in the size of government purchases have been substantial—especially those swings associated with changing military activity; but, relatively speaking, aggregate purchases are considerably less volatile than business investment, although perhaps somewhat more volatile than consumer purchases.

Changes in government purchases are the result of a political process; thus we can take them as essentially an autonomous or exogeneous element of aggregate demand. To be sure, the volume of government purchases, at least by the federal government, is often adjusted for reasons associated with the state of the economy. But any relationship leading from changes in macroeconomic variables to changes in government purchases is far too irregular and unpredictable to be incorporated in a macroeconomic model—at least in a "descriptive" model. ("Normative" models, dealing with possible *optimal* patterns of variation in government spending, and in other elements of the government budget, are of some interest and, conceivably, of some future practical relevance.)

Other Government Expenditures Affecting Aggregate Demand

Purchases of goods and services—which constitute a direct demand for national output—are by no means the whole of government expenditures. And, although they are the only government expenditures that constitute a direct component of GNP, they by no means exhaust government's impact on aggregate demand. Transfer payments are a large and rapidly growing element of total expenditures, and a large and growing element in disposable income—thus affecting consumer purchases. In the United States, federal transfers have risen from roughly a fifth as large as federal purchases in 1953 to 1.3 times the amount of such purchases in 1976. Transfer payments of state and local governments have also risen, but considerably less rapidly than their purchases, and are now only roughly 10 percent of the latter. Another large and rapidly increasing element of federal expenditures, not part of GNP, consists of grants-in-aid to state and local governments. However, when we consolidate the accounts of all governments, these cancel out; thus, a macroeconomic analysis can largely ignore them. The remaining substantial element of expenditures, in the case of the federal government, is interest paid. Since it shares many characteristics of transfer payments, we will need to consider essentially only two elements of government expenditure: purchases and transfers (including interest).

Although we indicated that it was not useful to think of government purchases other than as an exogenous element in aggregate demand, it is useful, and important, to recognize that the volume of transfer payments does depend, at least in significant part, on macroeconomic variables. In a simple model, we can assume that, in the short run, transfer payments are linearly and inversely related to GNP: for every \$1 billion *rise or fall* in GNP (also in NNP), there occurs an automatic \$$X$ billion *fall or rise* in transfers. In the United States today, the X might be taken at roughly 0.035 billion. (Actually, the relationship is far better taken between transfer payments and the movement of GNP relative to potential output. But in order to keep the models simple, we use the cruder version.) However, the automatic relationship of transfers to GNP holds for only so long as the legislation governing transfer payments remains unchanged. Repeated legislative changes boosting transfer payments have (in the United States) far more than countered the tendency of transfers to fall as GNP rises. Moreover, there have often also been legislative changes during recessions specifically intended to increase transfer payments temporarily by even more than the amount of their "automatic" or "built-in" inverse variation. These legislated elements of variation in transfer payments we will treat as exogenous.

Taxes, and the Government Balance

Taxes are obviously not a category of aggregate demand. But they affect GNP in at least two ways. All taxes reduce aggregate disposable income relative to GNP and thereby directly affect consumer purchases. In addition, the fact that taxes reduce the disposable income of individuals means that they may also affect incentives—to work, to save, and to invest—and thus indirectly affect consumer and investment demand. One may admit the existence of incentive effects without believing that they are significant; in contrast, the direct effects of taxes on consumer demand are strong and unmistakable.

In the United States, the major taxes are direct—that is, levied on income—rather than indirect—that is, levied on goods and services or on property. Personal income taxes account for about 30 percent of total government revenues, corporate profits taxes around 15 percent, and payroll taxes nearly 20 percent; the remainder are indirect taxes: general sales taxes, various excises, and property taxes.

Like transfer payments, tax receipts can appropriately be treated as endogenous at any given time, since their amount varies automatically with the state of the economy—but in the opposite direction from transfers. In a simple treatment, it is legitimate to regard the aggregate amount of tax collections as dependent on GNP, although more detailed models can do considerably better. As is the case with transfers, there is an exogenous variation as well—every time the tax law is altered. In principle, such alterations may change not only the level, but also the slope of the aggregate tax function, although it may seem surprising that most recent revisions of tax schedules appear to have had only modest effect on the slope, which can now be taken for the United States as roughly 0.3; that is, each $1 billion increase or decrease in GNP alters tax collections by roughly $300 million.

Thus, as noted earlier (in Chapter 2), our simple models employ an equally simple structure of consolidated government accounts, which recognize only the following elements:

> Government purchase of goods and services (G)
> Government transfer payments (Tr)
> Government expenditures ($G + Tr$)
> Taxes (Tx)
> Government deficit (Def) = ($G + Tr - Tx$)

With government, algebraic (and graphical) representation of the model become a bit more complicated. Now, the definition[7] of national product is

(18)
$$Y \equiv C + I + G$$

where Y is NNP and G is government purchases of goods and services, all in constant prices. Moreover, NI and DI now differ from NNP, and we cannot use Y for all of them. We therefore let Y continue to represent NNP, and (ignoring NI) represent disposable income as DI. Of course,

(19)
$$DI \equiv Y - Tx + Tr$$

We will assume that these tax and transfer payment systems are flexible, that is, that the amounts of taxes and transfers are each responsive to changes in Y. If we make these linear, we have, for taxes,

$$Tx = m + nY$$

The constant m, in this tax function, is (for the United States, at least)

---

[7] If, however, we define C, I, and G as the planned or desired quantities of purchases, and recognize that any Y will continue to be produced only if it is exactly the amount which buyers wish to purchase, we can describe equation (1) not merely as a definition, but also as an equilibrium condition.

surely negative; the slope n is some positive "marginal tax rate"—less than 1 because, as Y rises, taxes do not take the whole of the increment of income.

We also assume, for transfers,

$$Tr = q + rY$$

The constant in this equation, q, is positive; the slope, r, is some small *negative* number, which reflects the marginal rate at which transfers fall as Y rises—obviously numerically less than 1 because, as Y rises, transfers do not fall enough to keep earnings plus transfers constant (or, as Y falls, transfers do not rise enough to replace all, or even any very large part, of the income loss). We will assume, for simplicity, that the constants in these equations, m and q, are changed by legislation which, however, leaves unchanged the slopes, n and r, of the two functions.

Of course, legislative changes in tax and transfer systems obviously could affect both the levels *and* the slopes of the tax or transfer functions. However, the mathematics of dealing with shifts in slopes quickly becomes rather complex. Moreover, (as noted earlier) it appears to be true that recent changes in federal tax and transfer legislation have affected level far more than slope.

The "Net-Tax" System and Disposable Income

Although it is quite feasible to work with separate tax and transfer equations, it is somewhat simpler to combine them into a single, flexible "net-tax" system represented by the definition

$$T \equiv Tx - Tr$$

or

$$T = m + nY - q - rY$$

or

$$(20) \qquad T = t_0 + t_1 Y$$

where $t_0 = (m - q)$, and $t_1 = (n - r)$. For an economy like that of the United States, with m negative and q positive, t_0 would in practice be substantially negative. By previous definition of n and r, t_1 is necessarily positive, and, in practice, less than 1. For reasons already noted, we shall think of any legislative change that either raises taxes or cuts transfers as (algebraically) increasing t_0; for simplicity, we assume t_1 constant, even with changes in t_0.

Incidentally, the idea of combining taxes and transfers into a single net-tax function is not merely an analytical convenience. It is often quite illuminating in other contexts to think of transfers merely as negative taxes—or taxes as negative transfers; indeed, proposals to substitute a "negative income tax" for some of our transfer systems very much suggest this connection. Both taxes and transfers share the characteristic that they are transactions between government and individuals that do not involve any explicit *quid pro quo*. They do, of course, differ in the fact that the transfer from citizen to government (the tax) is compulsory, whereas one may refuse (or simply not apply to receive) social security or welfare or veterans' benefits. However, the government is compelled to pay them to eligible beneficiaries on request.

The upper panel of Figure 6-6 shows, graphically, separate tax and transfer equations as well as the "net-tax" function T, which represents $Tx - Tr$.

Inasmuch as

(19) $$DI = Y - Tx + Tr$$

or

$$DI = Y - T$$

we can substitute from (19) to obtain

(21) $$DI = -t_0 + (1 - t_1)Y$$

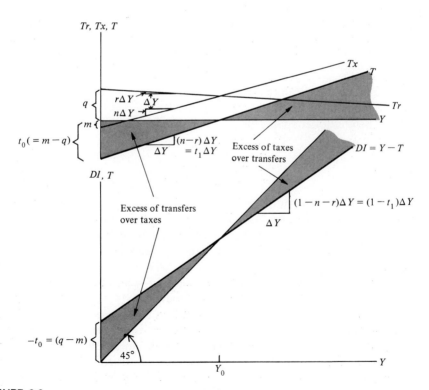

FIGURE 6-6

The lower panel of Figure 6-6 shows DI as a function of Y, reflecting the net impact of the tax and transfer systems. The 45° diagonal line in the figure shows *what DI would be* at each level of Y, *if there were no taxes and transfers*. The line $DI = Y - T$ shows what DI is after the subtraction of taxes and the addition of transfers. The shaded area (in both panels) represents—at the left, an excess of transfers over taxes; at the right, an excess of taxes over transfers. Up to Y_0, where taxes and transfers are equal, DI exceeds Y; thereafter DI falls short of Y. Note that, because t_1 is positive and less than one, DI rises when Y rises, but by appreciably *less than Y* in absolute amount; moreover, because the constant in the net tax function is negative, DI also rises considerably *less than in proportion to Y*.

The Size and Meaning of the Multiplier

If we now substitute equation (21) into our consumption function, we obtain

$$C = c_0 - c_1 t_0 + c_1(1 - t_1)Y$$

substituting this into equation (18) we get

$$Y = c_0 - c_1 t_0 + c_1(1 - t_1)Y + I + G$$

which reduces to the equilibrium income,

(22) $$Y = \frac{1}{1 - c_1(1 - t_1)}(c_0 - c_1 t_0 + I + G)$$

(Once again, we recall that we are concerned only with levels of $Y < Y_P$—that is, within the limits of potential output.)

The multiplier applicable to any change in I can be seen from (22) to be the fraction

$$\frac{1}{1 - c_1(1 - t_1)}$$

that is, any increase or decrease in I (which appears within the parenthesis on the right of equation (22)) would give rise to an increase in Y that was $1/[1 - c_1(1 - t)]$ as large. This is a smaller multiplier than the one calculated earlier in the absence of a government with flexible taxes and transfer payments. For example, if c_1 were 0.75 and there were no government, we have seen that the multiplier would be 4. With a government and a t_1 of, say, 0.2, the multiplier is $1/[1 - 0.75(0.8)] = 2.5$. Whereas without government an increase in investment of 10 would raise output and income by 40, with government it raises it only by 25. In order to explain this difference, we need to consider more fully the meaning and nature of the multiplier. *Why* is it, *how* is it, that \$10 of extra investment purchases can result in \$40 (or \$25) more in extra production and purchases? Can we describe, verbally, the "logic" of the multiplier?

Actually, we should probably never speak of "*the* multiplier," because we will shortly be computing other multipliers—for example, a "tax-cut multiplier"—with different values. The particular multiplier just derived should instead be described as a **private investment multiplier**, since it applies to changes in private investment purchases. However, inspection of equation (22) shows that a **government purchase multiplier** would have exactly the same value. These are more descriptive terms. However, since both multipliers reflect a response of consumption spending to changes in other variables, they are sometimes called **consumption multipliers**, and this adds to the confusion. Actually, it would probably be just as well not to give fractions like this a name; indeed, one can fairly conclude that attention to the multiplier concept as such is not only unnecessary but has often created about as much confusion as enlightenment. Nevertheless, the notion of "multiplied" effects of changes in certain variables has considerable didactic value. It dramatizes certain relationships; it makes people ask questions that help them understand how the economy works.[8]

To explain in words how multiplication is possible almost requires a "disequilibrium" as opposed to an "equilibrium" analysis, something to the following effect. If, when the economy has idle resources, businesses increase their purchase of plants and equipment, or if government buys more output, extra production is needed to satisfy the new demands. Extra workers will be hired to produce both these goods and the materials that this production in turn requires; they will earn extra wages, and the sellers will make extra profits. Most of these extra earnings immediately become extra disposable income, although some are drawn off as extra taxes. Recipients of this extra income in turn will wish to, and now can and do, buy more consumer goods. However, this puts still more men to work and earns still more extra wages and profits. Recipients of these extra incomes (after their extra taxes) in turn raise their consumption, creating further production and income gains in an endless but rapidly diminishing chain. When the whole process has worked itself out, the total gain in production will substantially exceed the original spending which started the process: it will indeed be a multiple of that.

How large this multiple will be depends, the formula says, on c_1 and t_1. The larger the former and the smaller the latter, the larger will be the multiplier. The slope c_1 of the consumption function tells what fraction of

---

[8] The author's favorite anecdote about President John F. Kennedy is appropriate here. In early 1963 President Kennedy was trying to persuade the Congress and the country to make a major tax cut in order to expand GNP and reduce unemployment. One day the author, then a member of the Council of Economic Advisers, received a call from President Kennedy's secretary, saying that, in the absence of Council Chairman Walter Heller, the President wanted to see him. When he arrived at the President's office, he was asked, "Gardner, explain to me again about the multiplier. I understood it once but I have forgotten." Thereafter, the President never forgot how $10 billion of tax cut could produce perhaps $20 billion more of GNP, and delighted in explaining it to businessmen and Members of Congress.

any rise in disposable income is spent. The higher this fraction, the bigger, clearly, will be each round of "secondary" spending just described. The slope t_1 of the net tax relationship shows the extent to which extra earnings, generated by extra production, are drained off by the government before reaching consumers. The smaller the proportion (t_1) of each "round" of extra spending (and thus of extra earned income) that is so drained off, the larger will be the proportion $(1 - t_1)$ that becomes available to be respent and, thus, the bigger the chain of "secondary" spending. The product $c_1(1 - t_1)$ thus gives the rate at which consumption increases as GNP increases; the larger either term of this product, the greater the ultimate expansion of income and output through the chain of respending. This product might be called the "marginal propensity to consume national product," showing how consumption increases with increases in Y. The quantity $1 - c_1(1 - t_1)$ is thus the marginal propensity *not* to demand additional national product, sometimes referred to as the marginal "leakages" from the income stream (into saving, higher taxes, and reduced transfers). The less the amount of these "leakages," that is, the smaller is $1 - c_1(1 - t_1)$, the greater the multiplier.

Before developing further the fiscal policy implications of this model, we can pause to note that the constant, c_0, of the consumption function also appears within the parentheses of equation (27). What this means is that any *shift of the level* of the consumption function also changes Y, and by a multiple of the amount of that shift. Although we normally assume that the consumption function is reasonably stable, nevertheless we can imagine exogenous events that would cause it to shift—either up, representing the desire, on the average, now to spend more (and save less) than before at each level of income; or down, representing a desire now to consume less (and save more) at each income level. Given stable levels of I, G, t_0, and so on, the former shift would cause income, consumption, and employment each to rise to a higher equilibrium level, leaving actual saving unchanged—even though what caused the shift was a desire to save less. The downward shift would cause income, consumption, and employment all to fall to lower equilibrium levels, again leaving actual saving unchanged—even though what caused the shift was a desire to save more. The algebra of these shifts can be easily worked out using the model just developed.

Graphical Representation of the Model

Figure 6-7 attempts a graphic representation of the model we have been dealing with. It is, unfortunately, rather complicated, which is why algebraic treatment is almost necessary. The figure can be understood only by first going back to Figure 6-6, to review how DI was derived from the (net-tax) T-function. Figure 6-7 starts with the DI function of the lower panel of Figure 6-5, and the darkly-shaded area has the same meaning in both figures, namely, indicating an excess of transfers over taxes or vice

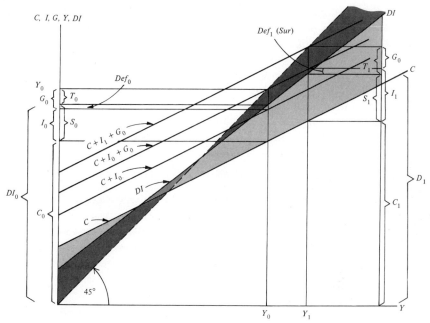

FIGURE 6-7

versa. Since C depends on DI, and equals DI plus dissaving (at low incomes) or DI minus saving (at higher incomes), we can plot the C function by subtracting its complement (the saving function) from DI. Thus, the vertical distance between the DI and C lines represents dissaving (on the left) and saving (on the right), each shaded light gray. In the area where dark and light gray shadings overlap, DI exceeds Y—that is, the net-tax system is on balance adding to income—but C falls short of DI—that is, saving is positive.

I_0 is an initial amount of (autonomous) investment, constant regardless of income; I_1 is a larger amount, at another time; G_0 is the amount of government purchases.

Consider first the case of $I = I_0$. Aggregate demand is shown by the line $C + I_0 + G_0$ (parallel with the C function). Income and output equilibrium is found where this line crosses the 45° line; that is, where $C + I + G = Y$. This occurs at Y_0. The corresponding levels of C_0, I_0, and G_0 can be read on the vertical axis (at the left). Also on the left, we can read off the level of DI at Y_0, and find the corresponding amount of saving, S_0 (shown by the light gray shading). We can also read off the level of net taxes (shown by the dark gray area), and the deficit (the excess, $G_0 - T_0$).

A second equilibrium, corresponding to I_1, is also shown. This involves higher levels not only of I and Y, but also of DI, C, S, T; and also a smaller Def (which has now become a surplus). It is also easy to represent in this diagram a shift of *G*, with *I* constant, or a shift of the *C* function, with *I* and *G* constant. However, although it is in principle possible to show a shift in the *T* function, it becomes in practice exceedingly difficult to trace comparative results graphically. Likewise, changes in the *slope* of the *C* function or *T* function become exceedingly complicated in graphic representation. (Alternative graphic representations using *S*, *I*, *T*, and *G* seem either to have fatal defects of conception or to become equally confusing if any substantial manipulation is attempted.) In short, for this model, the algebra is simpler than the graphics.

Other Leakages from the Circular Flow

In the model we have just been using, the only possible difference between *Y* and *DI* consists of taxes and transfers. But in any real economy, there are many other items, besides taxes and transfers, that cause *DI* to differ from *Y*. By far the largest of these differences arises from the existence of corporations, the profits of which (after taxes) are not immediately and automatically paid out as dividends thus to become disposable income of consumers.

For reasons that we need not stop to consider, it is an important fact that, as NNP (or GNP) varies relative to potential output, corporate profits tend to vary far more than in proportion to changes in NNP. The relationship is not entirely regular, but, at least in certain situations, as much as a quarter or a third (possibly even more) of any short-run variation in NNP is reflected in an increase in corporate profits before taxes. The resulting variation in profits taxes is, of course, already fully built into our model. Because (at least in the United States) both the marginal impact of NNP changes on profits, and the marginal corporate-profits tax rate are rather high (the latter around 40 percent), changes in profits tax collections account for an appreciable part of the leakage into taxes as NNP increases. However, to repeat, account is already taken (in principle) of all the tax leakage in our *T* function. What has not been taken account of, to this point, is the fact that the remaining after-tax portion of profits is not automatically paid out to stockholders (in the form of dividends), thus to become part of disposable income. Most simply summarized, the *marginal* share of dividends in United States corporate after-tax profits is typically very low—perhaps (at least in the short run) no more than 0.1 or 0.2. Thus when, with a rise in GNP, there occurs a large bulge in corporate profits, both before and after taxes, only a small part of this is reflected in *DI*. Instead, there is a substantial further "leakage" out of the circular flow into "undistributed profits." This leakage might, of course, have some *positive* effects on investment (which we are not ready to consider), but it clearly has a substantial *negative* effect on consumer purchases. By substantially reducing fluctuations in *DI* relative to *Y*, it therefore reduces the size of effective multipliers.

It is, of course, a possible—and, in many contexts, useful—simplification to combine the fiscal and the nonfiscal leakages between NNP and *DI* into a single "leakages-function" (*L* function), incorporating and replacing the *T* function used up to now. This summarizes the tax, transfer payment, and undistributed profits (and other miscellaneous) leakages considered up to this point.

We can define

$$L = Tx - Tr + U$$

where *U* represents undistributed profits (and other miscellaneous leakages.) Then, if we assume the linear functions,

$$Tx = m + nY$$

$$Tr = q + rY$$

and[9]

$$U = w + uY$$

then,

$$L = (m - q + w) + (n - r + u)Y$$

which can be simplified to

$$L = t_0 + t_1 Y$$

where, now, $t_0 = m - q + w$, and $t_1 = n - r + u$. Since *w* (the constant in the *U* function) and *m* are, in practice (for the United States at least), negative, and *q* is positive, the constant, t_0, of the *L* function is clearly a negative number; the slope t_1 is equally clearly positive, and (in practice) less than 1. Then if

$$DI = Y - L$$

as before,

(21) $$DI = -t_0 + (1 - t_1)Y$$

If

(18) $$Y = C + I + G$$

then, as before,

(22) $$Y = \frac{1}{1 - c_1(1 - t_1)}(C_0 - c_1 t_0 + I + G)$$

---

[9] Since profits turn negative even while GNP still is positive, the constant, *w*, must be negative.

The only difference from the earlier equations is that the meanings of t_0 and t_1 have now been broadened *to include nonfiscal leakages* between Y and *DI*.

In order to convey some sense of the relative importance of the various leakages, we may refer to a study by Arthur Okun (designed to measure the economic impact of the 1964 tax cut), in which Okun developed some simple empirical estimates of the relationship, as of the mid-1960s, between GNP and *DI*.[10] Okun's estimates (here further simplified) implied a marginal tax "leakage" equal to about 0.302, a transfer leakage of 0.035, and a leakage into undistributed profits of about 0.15 of any change in GNP, for a total leakage of 0.487 of any such change. Thus, a rise of $1 billion in GNP (or in NNP) implied total added leakages of about $0.487 billion, or a rise in *DI* of about $(1 - 0.487) = \$0.513$ billion. If these estimates are correct, only roughly one half of any increase in spending on final output returns to consumers as additional disposable income, prompting a further rise in spending—that is, personal consumption expenditure. Okun's estimate of the marginal propensity to consume was 0.95. Combining these values produces an investment (or government purchases) multiplier:

$$\frac{1}{1 - c_1(1 - t_1)} = \frac{1}{1 - 0.95(0.487)} = 1.95$$

[10] See Arthur M. Okun, "Measuring the Impact of the 1964 Tax Reduction," in W. W. Heller, ed., *Perspectives on Economic Growth* (Random House, 1968); reprinted in W. L. Smith and R. L. Teigen, *Readings in Money, National Income, and Stabilization Policy* (R. D. Irwin) 3rd ed., 1970, pp. 314–323.

A simplified, static version of Okun's model of the United States economy in the mid-1960s can be represented as follows:

$$Y = C + I + G$$

$$DI = Y - Tx + Tr - U - X$$

$$Tx = -43 + 0.302Y$$

$$Tr = 35 - 0.035Y$$

$$U = -75 + 0.15Y$$

$$X = 31$$

$$C = 4 + 0.95Y$$

where Y = gross national product; Tx = taxes; Tr = transfers; U = undistributed profits; X = other items (including depreciation), the magnitudes of which are independent of Y and which must be subtracted from Y to obtain *DI*.

"Somewhere around 2.0" is thus a good estimate of the U.S. multiplier applicable to G or I.[11]

APPENDIX:
DOES THE CONSUMPTION FUNCTION REFLECT ONLY REVERSE CAUSATION?

In the text of Chapter 6, we noted that "merely finding a statistical correlation between C and DI (or any other pair of variables) does not, of course, prove anything about 'causation.' In this case the direction of causation might be the reverse of that usually postulated—C might determine DI; or causation might run both ways; or both C and DI might be determined by some other variable or combination of variables, but are not themselves 'causally' related. All that we can ever conclude from a study of data is that the 'facts' are or are not consistent with a proposed explanation. They might be equally consistent, or even more consistent, with an alternate explanation."

If we had only the evidence of correlation between consumption and disposable income, this would surely not prove anything about causation. Indeed, since C constitutes by far the largest part of DI, it would appear that there almost has to be a strong correlation between C and DI, even if C were a purely random variable.[12] Alternatively, the observed correlation

---

[11] In the foregoing we have ignored one further significant leakage—that into imports. The reason for this is that we have assumed throughout a closed economy. In fact, of course, no economy is completely closed to international trade (or capital movements), and for some economies the import leakage is very substantial. The nature of this leakage is easy to grasp. When income rises or falls, with consequent changes in consumer spending, not all of this increment of spending is directed toward domestic products; some consumer purchases are made directly from abroad (very few, other than vacation travel); but increased consumer purchases from businesses include the purchase of products wholly made abroad (for example, purchases at retail of foreign-made products), while other consumer products are manufactured in whole or in part from imported materials. If a dollar's worth of extra consumer disposable income results in (ultimately) 90 cents' worth of extra purchases, but only 80 cents' worth of extra *domestic* production, the *effective* MPC is not 0.9 but 0.8. However, having once noted this point, we shall continue to ignore it.

[12] D. B. Suits (extending a line of argument that appeared in pp. 233ff. of this writer's *Macroeconomic Theory* (Macmillan, 1961)) has argued that, simply as a result of the definition that $DI = C + S$, the correlation between C and DI "should be around 0.9 even if consumption and saving were random variables." ("The Determinants of Consumer Expenditure: A Review of Present Knowledge," Research Study One in *Impacts of Monetary Policy* (a series of research studies prepared for the Commission on Money and Credit), Englewood Cliffs, N.J.: Prentice-Hall, 1963, p. 24; reprinted in W. L. Johnson and D. R. Kamerschen (eds.), *Macroeconomics: Selected Readings* (Boston, Mass.: Houghton Mifflin Co., 1970), pp. 59–92.) But this is misleading. C and S could not *both* be random variables. A family's (or a nation's) DI is not determined as the sum of independent decisions about C and S. Rather each spending unit's DI is determined (largely) externally to it; then, once *either* C or S is determined—randomly or otherwise—so is the other. We can imagine that C, or S, or C/DI might be randomly determined but not both C and S. The more nearly correct version of this argument is, the writer believes, that which follows.

between C and DI may reflect a line of causation running not from DI to C but from C to DI. Such a line of causation is indeed implied in the simple models that are presented in the second and third major sections of Chapter 6.

Take, for example, these equations from the model with government:

(i) $$DI = Y - T$$

(ii) $$T = t_0 + t_1 Y$$

(iii) $$Y = C + A$$

where A ("autonomous spending") replaces $I + G$. Substituting, we can derive

(iv) $$DI = (1 - t_1)(C + A) - t_0$$

which suggests a clear positive association between C and DI, *quite independent of any association based on C being influenced by DI.* (Note that we have not used the consumption function at all.)

It would thus be possible to argue that the observed correlation between C and DI might be largely or entirely the result of a causal chain just the reverse of that postulated in the usual consumption function. As the largest part of Y, C largely determines Y, which, in turn, largely determines DI. C and DI would be closely correlated even if C were determined entirely independently of DI.

Assume, for example, that C were simply a large random number[13]— meaning by "large" about twice as large on the average as the average value of A. From equation (iv), we have, then, that the amount of DI would then be a fixed proportion $(1 - t_1)$ of the sum of A and a large random number C, plus a small constant $-t_0$. We might conclude that DI determined C, when, in fact, it was entirely the other way around; C was completely random, but C determined DI.

However, there is an easy way to prove that this is not the only or even the main source of the correlation between C and DI. For, by substituting the definitional relationship $C + S \equiv DI$, into equation (iv) we get

$$C + S = (1 - t_1)C + (1 - t_1)A - t_0$$

or

(v) $$C = \frac{1 - t_1}{t_1} A - \frac{1}{t_1} S - \frac{t_0}{t_1}$$

Since t_1 is clearly positive, Equation (v) asserts that, if indeed the *only* relationship between C and DI were the indirect one whereby C helps to

---

[13] This is an extreme assumption. Alternately, C could depend on other factors: for example, consumer wealth, consumer attitudes, or a time trend, or some combination of these and other factors.

determine *DI*, we would expect to find a *negative* relationship between *C* and *S*. Instead, we know that the empirical relationship between *C* and *S* is clearly positive. Thus, we can conclude that the evidence up to this point is quite consistent with the proposition that *DI* determines *C* (and *S*), even though we now see that there also exists a second (indirect) relationship between *C* and *DI* which runs in the opposite direction. For the basic hypothesis lying behind the consumption function implies much more than that *C* and *DI* are correlated. Rather, it implies that an increment of *DI* will be divided in some consistent way between *C* and *S*: in short, that *C* and *S* are positively correlated. In a fundamental sense, the "*CS* function" (presented earlier) embodies the basic relationship hypothesized in the consumption function. And the data we have presented so far are quite consistent with that hypothesis.

REVIEW QUESTIONS

1. Graph consumption functions that conform to each of the following different sets of specifications; then draw the corresponding saving functions and describe verbally their marginal and average propensities to save.

(a) constant average propensity to consume (APC) and constant marginal propensity to consume (MPC)

(b) APC < 1, MPC increasing as income increases

(c) APC < 1, MPC = 1

(d) APC = MPC

(e) both APC and MPC less than 1 and falling as income increases.

Which of the above functions are consistent with Keynes' hypothesis about the shape of consumption function?

2.

(a) What is meant by a "multiplier"?

(b) Derive algebraically the formula for the multiplier applicable to private investment in a simple model in which consumption depends linearly on disposable income, disposable income equals net national product minus taxes, and taxes depend on net national product.

(c) If one takes account of typical corporate behavior with respect to the "payout" of profits to shareholders, and the response of government transfer payments to changes in employment, the multiplier applicable to investment is further modified. Explain verbally whether each of these modifications increases or decreases the size of the multiplier, and why.

3. It was argued in this chapter that if the world were correctly described by the simplest Keynesian model, an increased or reduced collective desire to save would be frustrated.

(a) Present the simplest Keynesian model without government.

(b) Determine the equilibrium level of income using *either* graph *or* algebra.

(c) Show, using *both* graph *and* algebra, that a desire to save less will leave actual saving unchanged.

SELECTED REFERENCES

J. M. Keynes, *The General Theory of Employment, Interest, and Money* (Harcourt, Brace, 1936), Chapters 8–10.
(Keynes' original presentation of the consumption function hypothesis.)

P. A. Samuelson, "The Simple Mathematics of Income Determination," in *Income, Employment, and Public Policy* (W. W. Norton, 1948), reprinted in W. L. Johnson and D. R. Kamerschen (eds.), *Macroeconomics: Selected Readings* (Houghton Mifflin, 1970), pp. 39–49.
(One of the first and best algebraic statements of the simple Keynesian model.)

J. S. Duesenberry, "Income and Consumption Relations and their Implications," in *Income, Employment and Public Policy* (W. W. Norton, 1948), reprinted in M. G. Mueller (ed.), *Readings in Macroeconomics* (Holt, Rinehart, and Winston, 2nd ed., 1971), pp. 61–76.
(An early "second look" at the empirical support for the Keynesian hypothesis.)

D. B. Suits, "The Determinants of Consumer Expenditure: A Review of Present Knowledge," Research Study 1 in *Impacts of Monetary Policy* (A series of research studies prepared for the Commission on Money and Credit) (Prentice-Hall, 1963), reprinted in W. L. Johnson and D. R. Kamerschen (eds.), *Macroeconomics: Selected Readings* (Houghton Mifflin, 1970), pp. 59–92.
(A detailed review of more recent evidence.)

Chapter 7

Extensions of the Keynesian Model: Fiscal Policy and Keynesian Dynamics

The Simple Theory of Fiscal Policy
The tax-cut multiplier
The endogenous budget deficit
The balanced-budget multiplier
Numerical examples of fiscal operations
Built-in stabilization
A digression on flexibility versus progressivity (and the aggregation problem)
A cyclically stabilizing fiscal policy
Fiscal policy in a growing economy
Measuring the impact of the budget

Elementary Dynamics of the Keynesian Model
A dynamic multiplier model: consumption lag
Dynamic multiplier model: production lag
The role of inventories
Dynamics and the stability of equilibrium
Expectations and equilibrium

Appendix: Stability Conditions

This chapter, and the one that follows, extend the simple Keynesian model in four ways: first, they develop a theory of macroeconomic effects of government fiscal policy; second, they present some "dynamic" versions of the Keynesian model set forth in Chapter 6 and discuss the "stability properties" of these versions of the model; third, both the static and dynamic models are extended by the incorporation of several alternative simple theories of aggregate investment; and fourth, the models, as extended, are used to consider certain aspects of the process of economic growth. The results undoubtedly have some interest in themselves as possible representations of certain important forces at work in an actual economy. They also serve, however, as a vehicle for introducing and illustrating some methodological and analytical ideas which will subsequently have larger application.

One thing which these four types of extension of the Keynesian model have in common is that the theories of consumption and investment used are "real" theories; they (appropriately) involve relationships among physical or deflated variables. This of course does not mean that, if prices vary and money values thus change, this makes no difference. However, so long as we consider only output variations which occur within the range of less than full employment, no substantial change in price levels should result from output changes, *per se*. And we continue to assume only output variations below full employment.

Clearly, however, all of these "extended" Keynesian models will need reconsideration when, in later chapters, we begin to deal with price level variations and with possible impacts of such variation on real aggregate demand. However, when we do, it will be useful to have already developed a number of building blocks for such more complete and realistic models through the present treatment.

THE SIMPLE THEORY OF FISCAL POLICY

The simple model of income determination developed in Chapter 6 is surely far from an adequate representation of any real-world economy. Nevertheless, even in the simple form now developed, it also serves as the basis for a theory of fiscal policy that has been and continues to be widely applied. This theory constitutes the subject for this part of Chapter 7. In order to simplify our algebraic treatment, and to focus attention on fiscal problems alone, we will, in this part, revert to the assumption that taxes and transfers constitute the *only* difference between Y and DI.

One fiscal policy application of the model has already been noted: namely, that changes in government purchases—exactly as do changes in investment—have a multiplied effect on national product. Such purchases constitute a part of the aggregate demand for output; a rise in the level of such expenditures thus increases, at every level of output, the demand for output. In a time of recession, or whenever unemployment exceeds the target level, government could thus (according to this model) reduce or eliminate the excess unemployment, bringing actual output up to potential output, through an appropriate increase in its own purchases. Likewise, if aggregate demand threatens to or does exceed potential output, an appropriate *decrease* in purchases could eliminate the excess. How much of a change in government purchases would be required can be computed by dividing the deficiency of aggregate demand (or the excess) by the multiplier $1/[1 - c_1(1 - t_1)]$. If the "gap" between actual and potential output is $60 billion, and the multiplier is 3, purchases must be increased by $20 billion to reach the target; if the multiplier is 2, they must be increased by $30 billion, if $1\frac{1}{2}$, they must be increased by $40 billion.

The Tax-Cut Multiplier

There is another means, moreover, by which fiscal policy could raise (or curb) GNP. It would be to cut (or raise) net taxes. A reduction in taxes means that, at any and every level of NNP, disposable income will be larger than before the cut; so, therefore, will be consumer purchases.

Equation (22) in Chapter 6

$$Y = \frac{1}{1 - c_1(1 - t_1)} (c_0 - c_1 t_0 + I + G)$$

permits us to calculate how large a net tax cut (or increase) is needed to achieve any desired change in NNP—that is, to derive a multiplier applicable to any shift in the net-tax schedule. Mathematically, we do this by differentiating the equilibrium level of Y, equation (22), with respect to t_0. (The multipliers previously calculated for I, and G, are simply the derivatives, dY/dI and dG/dI, of that equation with respect to I and G.) The tax-*increase* multiplier obviously is

(1)
$$\frac{dY}{dt_0} = \frac{-c_1}{1 - c_1(1 - t_1)}$$

Inasmuch as a tax *cut* is represented by a decrease in t_0, the tax-*cut* multiplier is positive:

(1a)
$$\frac{dY}{-dt_0} = \frac{c_1}{1 - c_1(1 - t_1)}$$

The tax-cut multiplier differs from that for an increase in G in that it equals the latter multiplied by c_1, and since $c_1 < 1$, the tax-cut multiplier is smaller than the multiplier for G. Thus, if c_1 were (for example) 0.8, $\$X$ billion of legislated tax-cut or transfer increase would produce only 0.8 as large a rise in Y as would $\$X$ billion of increase in purchases. Assuming t_1 were 0.3, the purchase increase multiplier would be 2.27, but the tax-cut multiplier only 1.82. Thus, if there existed a $60 billion gap between actual and potential output, it could be eliminated either by a roughly $26.4 billion expenditure increase or a $33 billion tax cut. If t_1 were instead 0.35, the two multipliers would be 2.08 and 1.67, respectively, and the necessary increases in purchases would be $28.8 billion or the tax-cut $36 billion.

It is not difficult to explain verbally why the tax-cut multiplier is smaller than the government-purchases multiplier, and smaller in the proportion c_1. Any $10 billion increase in G constitutes a direct demand for $10 billion more of output, which will be produced, setting off a further chain of extra spending. But a $10 billion tax cut does not produce an initial rise of aggregate demand in this amount. Consumers receive $10 billion more of DI, but they *increase spending* only by the smaller amount $c_1 DI$. This *smaller* amount *is* an increase in aggregate demand, causes increased production, and is then expanded by the further chain of re-spending.

We have noted the need to be careful in referring to the size of a "tax cut" (or increase), because tax collections are at least partly endogenous. If a tax increase or tax cut affects income, it will thus also have further effect on tax collections. The *full* effect of a tax cut on tax collections can be shown by substituting the expression for equilibrium income—equation (22), Chapter 6—into the net-tax function—equation (20), Chapter 6—producing the equation for equilibrium taxes:

(2)
$$T = t_0 + \frac{t_1}{1 - c_1(1 - t_1)}(c_0 - c_1 t_0 + I + G)$$

A reduction in taxes—that is, a reduction in t_0 obviously has *two* effects on equilibrium tax collections, for t_0 appears twice in (2) with opposite signs. The first or direct effect is to reduce T by the amount of the tax cut $(-\Delta t_0)$; however, to the extent that the tax cut raises income, there is a second and indirect effect that causes T to increase in an amount equal to t_1 (the marginal effective tax rate) times the amount of the rise in income (equation 1): $-c_1/[1 - c_1(1 - t_1)] \cdot \Delta t_0$. The total effect on tax collections of a tax cut is, of course, its direct effect plus its indirect effect. Differentiating (2) we obtain the complete effect of a tax cut on tax collections:

$$(3) \qquad \frac{dT}{-dt_0} = -1 + \frac{c_1 t_1}{1 - c_1(1 - t_1)}$$

The effect on collections is negative but by less than the initial amount of the cut; for a tax increase, the effect on tax collections is positive but by less than the amount of the increase at the original income level.

Henceforth, in referring to the amount of a tax cut, we will specify whether we refer to its amount at the initial equilibrium level of income or to its ultimate (smaller) amount, after income has fully adjusted to its new and higher equilibrium level.

The Endogenous Budget Deficit

Now we proceed to consider the effect of fiscal changes on the outcome of the budget. We define deficit as government expenditure less government revenues, or

$$Def \equiv G + Tr - Tx$$

(The deficit, of course, can have either sign; if negative, it is a surplus.) Substituting net tax, T, for $Tx - Tr$ we get

$$Def \equiv G - T$$

(This substitution is not possible if the nonfiscal leakages are also included along with taxes and transfers in a single portmanteau "leakage function.") If the expression for T obtained in equation (2) now replaces the T in the definition of deficit, we derive

$$(4) \qquad Def = G - t_0 - \frac{t_1}{1 - c_1(1 - t_1)}(c_0 - c_1 t_0 + I + G)$$

Perhaps the first thing we should note from equation (4) is that the outcome of the government budget does not depend only on political decisions about purchases (G) and about the level (t_0) and slope (t_1) of the net-tax system but also on the position of the consumption function (the coefficients c_0 and c_1) and on the amount of private investment, I. Thus, the drop in I that occurs in every "business-cycle recession" shifts the government budget sharply in the direction of deficit. This happens even if nothing is done, politically, to change tax rates or government purchases;

conversely, prosperity generates a strong shift toward budget surplus. Likewise, it may be noted that shifts of the consumption function also affect net-tax collections and the deficit.

However, levels of government purchases and of the net tax function obviously also affect the deficit. Take the latter first. The effect of a tax change on the deficit clearly equals its effect on tax collections (equation 3); or

(5)
$$\frac{dDef}{dt_0} = 1 - \frac{t_1 c_1}{1 - c_1(1 - t_1)}$$

which is clearly less than 1, since the fraction on the right is positive and less than 1. That is, a dollar of tax reduction produces less than a dollar of added deficit. We can also see that an increase in government purchases raises the deficit by less than the amount of such increase, for the term G appears twice in equation (4). The first and direct effect of an increase in G is to raise the deficit dollar-for-dollar; but there is a second, indirect effect that is negative. The total effect is

(6)
$$\frac{dDef}{dG} = 1 - \frac{t_1}{1 - c_1(1 - t_1)}$$

The second term reflects the effect of higher government purchases, in raising equilibrium income by the multiplier $1/1 - c_1(1 - t_1)$, and the impact of this on tax collections, in an amount equal to the marginal tax rate, t_1, times the change in equilibrium Y.

The Balanced-Budget Multiplier

We have considered above the effects of changes both in tax rates and in government expenditures, considered separately. There is also interest in the effects of simultaneous changes of various simple kinds in both tax rates and expenditures. To analyze these, we can differentiate the equation for equilibrium Y (equation 22 of Chapter 6), with respect to simultaneous changes in both t_0 and G,

(7)
$$dY = \frac{1}{1 - c_1(1 - t_1)}(-c_1 \, dt_0 + dG)$$

where we assume that $dc_0 = dI = 0$—that is, we assume a fixed consumption function and a given amount of investment. We can consider two kinds of simple simultaneous changes.

CASE I: Assume that $dt_0 = dG$, implying that purchases and taxes are raised simultaneously by the same amount *at the initial income level*. Would equilibrium income change at all? Substituting dG for dt_0 in equation (7), the answer is clearly, yes, and by the amount

(8)
$$dY = \frac{1 - c_1}{1 - c_1(1 - t_1)} dG$$

This multiplier is clearly positive, the stimulative effect of the expenditure increase more than offsetting the restrictive effect of the tax increase; but it is not very large. For instance, with $c_1 = 0.75$, $t_1 = 0.2$, it amounts to $0.25/0.4 = 0.625$. However, its small size is not surprising when we recognize that —at the new equilibrium—the rise in tax collections would clearly exceed the rise in G. The increase in tax collections is $dT = dt_0 + t_1 \, dY$, or

(9)
$$dT = dG + \frac{t_1(1 - c_1)}{1 - c_1(1 - t_1)} dG$$

which clearly exceeds dG; thus the budget would have moved toward surplus. What really seems surprising is that, although the budget moves toward surplus, Y nevertheless rises. Clearly, we cannot identify a "stimulative" fiscal policy exclusively with a shift of the budget toward deficit!

CASE II: What would happen, now, if the dt_0 were so selected that the resulting increase in taxes *at the new equilibrium Y* would just equal the increment of G, that is, would just leave the deficit *unchanged*? That is, we define a tax rate increase, such that, in equilibrium, the increase in tax collections, dT, just equals the simultaneous increase in purchases, dG. From the tax function, we know that the increase in collections is

$$dT = dt_0 + t_1 \, dY$$

Substituting $dT = dG$ and rearranging, this defines the necessary shift in t_0

(10)
$$dt_0 = dG - t_1 \, dY$$

Substituting (10) into (7) leads to

$$dY = \frac{1}{1 - c_1(1 - t_1)} [-c_1(dG - t_1 dY) + dG]$$

Collecting terms and simplifying easily yields

(11)
$$dY = dG$$

This is the (flexible-tax) version of the famous **balanced budget multiplier principle**: "an equal increase in government purchases and (realized) tax collections will raise output and income by the amount of the increase; the balanced-budget multiplier is precisely equal to 1." This means that there is still another way, in addition to tax cuts and expenditure increases, to close a gap between actual and potential output. It is one which does not involve a deficit (or an increased deficit). If there is a $60 billion gap, raise government spending by $60 billion while adjusting tax rates so that collections will also rise by $60 billion.

We can also use equation (10) and (11) to find the necessary amount of the tax rate increase:

(12) $$dt_0 = (1 - t_1)\, dG$$

That is, for the budget to remain balanced, the government must change the level of the tax function by a multiple $(1 - t_1)$ of the change in purchases.

Numerical Examples of Fiscal Operations

Using this simple algebraic model, we can now insert particular numerical assumptions as to the position of functional relationships and as to the amounts of each exogenous item in order to illustrate the concepts developed in the preceding sections. In what follows, our numerical assumptions are that the consumption, tax, transfer, net tax, and disposable income functions have these initial values:

$$C = 10 + 0.8DI$$
$$Tr = 50 - 0.05Y$$
$$Tx = 10 + 0.2Y$$
$$T = Tx - Tr = -40 + 0.25Y$$
$$DI = Y - T = Y + 40 - 0.25Y$$
$$DI = 0.75Y + 40$$

We also assume that Y_P (potential output) is 280, and that initial (exogenous) values of I and G are 35 and 15, respectively. Given these, we can calculate the equilibrium value of Y and the amount of the Y "gap," as follows:

$$Y = C + I + G,$$
$$= 10 + 0.8(0.75Y + 40) + 35 + 15$$
$$= 92 + 0.6Y$$

then

$$0.4Y = 92 \quad \text{and} \quad Y = 230$$

so that

$$Y_P - Y = 50$$

By substitution of $Y = 230$ in our net tax equation, we find

$$T = -40 + 0.25(230) = 17.5$$

and therefore

$$DI = 230 - 17.5 = 212.5$$
$$C = 10 + 0.8(212.5) = 180$$
$$C + I + G = 180 + 35 + 15 = 230$$

(which checks with the earlier result for Y). We can also calculate the deficit

$$Def = G - T = 15 - 17.5 = -2.5$$

that is, a surplus of 2.5.

We now wish to explore the implications of each of three different policies to raise Y to 280 ($= Y_P$):

1. Raise government purchases leaving tax schedules unchanged
2. Cut taxes, leaving purchases unchanged
3. Raise both taxes and purchases in such a way as to leave the deficit unchanged.

1. *Raise G*

First we compute the multiplier for G. It is

$$\frac{dY}{dG} = \frac{1}{1 - c_1(1 - t_1)} = \frac{1}{1 - 0.8(1 - 0.25)} = 2.5$$

Thus, every \$1 billion ΔG raises Y by \$2.5 billion. To raise Y by \$50 billion thus requires $\Delta G = 20$, or G must rise to 35. Solving for Y, with $G = 35$, we get

$$Y = 10 + 0.8(0.75Y + 40) + 35 + 35$$
$$= 80 + 0.6Y + 32$$
$$0.4Y = 112$$
$$Y = 280$$

Substituting this value of Y into tax, disposable income, consumption, and deficit equations, we compute the following "full-employment" values.

$$T = -40 + 0.25(280) = 30$$
$$DI = 280 - 30 = 250$$
$$C = 10 + 0.8(250) = 210$$
$$Def = 35 - 30 = 5$$

2. *Cut T*

We first need the multiplier applicable to the constant in the tax function. It is

$$\frac{dY}{dt_0} = \frac{-c_1}{1 - c_1(1 - t_1)} = \frac{-0.8}{1 - 0.8(1 - 0.75)} = -2$$

Thus, to raise Y by 50, we need to cut taxes (at the initial level of Y_1) by 25; thus the tax function becomes

$$T = -65 + 0.25Y$$

and therefore

$$DI = Y + 65 - 0.25Y = 65 + 0.75Y$$
$$C = 10 + 0.8(65) + 0.8(0.75Y)$$
$$= 62 + 0.6Y$$
$$Y = 62 + 0.6Y + 35 + 15$$
$$0.4Y = 112$$
$$Y = 280$$

Substituting this value for Y, we compute numerical values at the new equilibrium, as

$$T = -65 + 0.25(280) = 5$$
$$DI = 280 - 5 = 275$$
$$C = 10 + 0.8(275) = 230$$
$$Def = 15 - 5 = 10$$

3. *Raise both G and T, keeping Def = −2.5*
   The multiplier applicable to this policy is 1; thus

$$G = 15 + 50 = 65$$

For *Def* to equal −2.5, T must $= 67.5$; therefore, we must shift the tax function by an amount which we can find as follows:

$$T = 67.5 = X + 0.25(280)$$

where X is the constant necessary to produce $T = 67.5$ at $Y = 280$. Solving, we get

$$67.5 = X + 70$$
$$X = -2.5$$
$$T = -2.5 + 0.25Y$$
$$DI = Y + 2.5 - 0.25Y = 2.5 + 0.75Y$$
$$C = 10 + 0.8(2.5) + 0.8(0.75Y) = 12 + 0.6Y$$
$$Y = 12 + 0.6Y + 35 + 65$$
$$0.4Y = 112$$
$$Y = 280$$

Substituting, we get

$$T = -2.5 + 0.25(280) = -2.5 + 70 = 67.5$$
$$DI = 280 - 67.5 = 212.5$$
$$C = 10 + 0.8(212.5) = 180$$
$$Def = 65 - 67.5 = -2.5$$

4. *Comparison of results*

The table that follows compares values of all variables at the initial, less-than-potential-output equilibrium, and after application of each policy has brought output up to potential.

	Initial equilibrium	New Equilibrium		
		Policy 1	Policy 2	Policy 3
Y	230	280	280	280
C	180	210	230	180
I	35	35	35	35
G	15	35	15	65
T	17.5	30	5	67.5
Def	−2.5	5	10	−2.5

All three policies increase output by 50, but the use of this extra output is very different in the three models. Increased government expenditures, policy (1), directs 60 percent of the extra output to consumers and 40 percent to public use; tax-cut policy (2) directs 100 percent of the extra output to additional private consumption; whereas balanced-budget policy (3) directs 100 percent of the extra output to public use. Thus, important questions of social priorities—as between public and private use of resources—are involved in deciding which policy to use to raise output to potential. Correspondingly, if the problem were of restraining aggregate demand in order to prevent an excess of output over potential, the three policy options of (1) cutting government purchases; (2) raising taxes; and (3) cutting purchases and taxes equally involve the same questions of social priorities.

Clearly, various combinations of these policies can be used to achieve whatever distribution of the extra output existing social priorities may require. For example, it would not be difficult to compute what would have to be done to *taxes* to raise Y to Y_P if it is predetermined *on other grounds* that G should go to 25 and C to 220 (assuming I remains at 35). The reader may wish to test his understanding of the model and the algebra by computing the necessary tax function.

There are clearly other possible considerations in the choice of policies. Higher or lower taxes may have effects on incentives to invest or to save (that is, to consume), or both. We need to be aware that these effects exist, whether or not we attempt to adjust explicitly for them. (The effectiveness of our forecasts and policies will, of course, reflect the accuracy of our knowledge of these further effects.) Also, changes in the level of the aggregate net-tax function may also require changes in the *distribution* of after-tax (and transfer) income. For example, if tax schedules applicable to high incomes already take 60 percent of pretax income of high-income tax payers, and this is regarded as a feasible maximum, a large rise in tax collections must inevitably raise significantly the share of total taxes paid by lower income groups.)

The model remains, of course, dreadfully simple for many reasons. Not the least of these is its assumption that investment expenditures will remain unchanged even in the face of large changes in fiscal policy. The counterpart of this assumption is that policy tools can only affect the amount of private consumption, not investment. Some later models attempt to repair this deficiency, although we may not be able to place great confidence in the effectiveness of policies designed to influence the investment component of aggregate demand, given our relative ignorance about the determinants of investment.

The theory and numerical examples set forth previously also lack any time dimension. They seem either to assume that all fiscal policy decisions can be made instantly, are instantly carried out, and their full effects instantly achieved, or else that everything else remains unchanged while fiscal policy changes work themselves out. Although we are not yet prepared to move to an elementary dynamic analysis, we can introduce a bit more realism by considering some types of progressive changes in the external economic environment in which fiscal policy operates. First, we deal with business cycles, then with an economy experiencing growth in potential output.

Built-In Stabilization

One simple extension of the preceding model is to a world in which, for whatever reasons, there occur broad swings in private investment expenditures, for example, of the sort associated with so-called business cycles. For the present, assume that no use whatsover is made of the kind of deliberate or "discretionary" fiscal policy moves just discussed; instead, we first note some implications of the mere *existence* of a partly endogenous fiscal system.

It is frequently asserted that a system of partly endogenous taxes and transfer payments exerts a degree of "built-in stabilization" on the way in which the economy responds to changes in investment. We need to be clear what this means and what determines the extent of any stabilizing effect. The term "stabilization" necessarily implies some standard of comparison: endogenous taxes and transfers stabilize the economy *relative to what*? One standard for comparison, sometimes used or implied, is with an economy without government. The proposition thus is that the existence of government (with its taxes and transfers) means that variations in private investment will have *less effect on Y* than they would have had in the absence of a government. The extent or degree of this stabilization might then be measured by the relative size of the investment multipliers derived previously for an economy with government: $1/(1 - c_1(1 - t_1))$; and for one with no government: $1/(1 - c_1)$. The ratio between these is

$$\frac{1}{1 - c_1(1 - t_1)} \div \frac{1}{1 - c_1} = \frac{1 - c_1}{1 - c_1(1 - t_1)}$$

This ratio measures the extent of the stabilization built into the economy by the tax system. For example, if c_1 were 0.8, a change of 10 in investment would produce a change in Y of only 50, without government. But, with government, and $t_1 = 0.25$, a change of 10 in investment would produce a change in Y of only 25—only one half as large: $(1 - 0.8)/(1 - 0.8(1 - 0.25)) = 0.5$. If investment moves in cycles of some given amplitude, the amplitude of the resulting cycles in income and consumption would be only half as great in the economy with government as in the one without.

Actually, this comparison is sometime held even to *understate* the higher degree of stability in the economy with government, simply because private investment might seem to be bound to be a higher percentage of Y in an economy without government than in one with it. For example, compare two economies, with the same national products, but one (economy A) without and the other (economy B) with government, as follows:

	Economy A	Economy B
Y	500	500
C	400	280
I	100	70
G	0	150

In each case, private output is divided in the same proportion (4 to 1) between C and I. I is obviously a smaller proportion of Y in economy B; the same *relative* fluctuation in I in the two economies would thus necessarily have less effect in economy B, even if the multipliers were the same. For example, assume a 50 percent decrease in I—to 50 in economy A and to 35 in economy B. If the appropriate multipliers are 5 in economy A and 2.5 in economy B, output falls by $50 \times 5 - 250 = 50$ percent in economy A; it falls by $35 \times 2.5 = 87.5 = 17.5$ percent in economy B. The ratio here is not 0.5, but only $87.5/250 = 0.35$ as much instability with government as without.

However, further consideration suggests that an economy without government is an unrealistic standard for comparison. After all, an economy without government would have to be different in a great many other ways from one with government. The only "behavioral" element used in our model is the consumption function; it is inconceivable that, in an economy without government, the consumption function would be the same as in one with government. (For example, consider the effects on the motives for personal saving of the absence of a social security system.) Moreover, we probably cannot assume that the division of private output between consumption and investment would be the same in the absence of government. (For example, capital goods are probably needed to produce government goods as well as consumption goods.)

An alternative standard for comparison, sometimes suggested, is with an economy which has a government of about the same size, but in which all taxes and transfers are of the "lump-sum" variety—their amounts are independent of production and income. There may be changes in their amounts, but only through legislative action. However, such an economy has never existed, is difficult to imagine, and we cannot really be sure how private spending would behave in these circumstances.

Thus, the best way to make sense of the built-in stabilization proposition is perhaps to compare it with a world in which a government of the same size and type uses taxes and transfers of the same character but follows a policy of taking legislative (or administrative) action whenever and to whatever extent is necessary to maintain a balanced budget (or some constant surplus or deficit). This could be done, for example, by making equal changes in G whenever revenues change; alternatively, it could be done through altering tax or transfer payment systems sufficiently to keep net taxes equal to a constant G. In either way, the effects of any tendency for tax collections to grow or shrink or of transfers to expand or contract would be fully offset, and the "cushioning" effect of net-tax variation on disposable income would disappear. Every variation in Y would produce an equal variation in DI.

This is perhaps an unrealistic comparison, too, for such a policy has never been fully carried out. But the comparison is, at least, with a policy that, *in principle*, was long accepted as the only appropriate standard for fiscal policy—and is, indeed, still advocated today by many conservatives. If we accept this as our standard for comparison, we can speak meaningfully of the stabilizing effect of a policy of *allowing the built-in fiscal stabilizers to work* versus one of attempting to *cancel out their effects* by maintaining a balanced budget. (If this is our context, however, perhaps we should really refer, not to the "stabilizing" effects of a flexible tax-transfer system but to the *de*stabilizing" effects of a balanced budget policy!)[1]

How much stabilization, then, is imparted by flexible tax and transfer systems as compared with a policy of cancelling out their effects through "balanced-budget" adjustments? That depends on whether the maintenance of budget balance is assumed to be achieved by expenditure variation as revenues rise and fall, or by tax level changes to keep revenues

---

[1] Using the balanced-budget policy in an otherwise identical economy as the standard of comparison, of course, has the advantage of avoiding problems related to the relative size of variations in private investment in economies with and without government.

equal to fixed expenditures, or by some combination. However, with $c_1 = 0.8$ and $t_1 = 0.25$, and assuming variation only in *purchases* (cutting the budget to match falling revenues in a recession, spending every extra dollar of growing revenues in a boom), the appropriate investment multiplier is 6.67 compared with 2.5 if the fiscal stabilizers are allowed to work. If, instead, it is the level of the *tax system* that is adjusted (rates raised in a recession, cut in a boom, with expenditures constant), the multiplier is 5.0 rather than 2.5 if the built-in stabilization is allowed. That is, "built-in stabilization" cuts the variation in Y resulting from fluctuations in I more than in half (if the alternative "balanced-budget policy" were to spend whatever revenues might be); it cuts the variation in half (if the alternative policy were to keep net taxes equal to constant expenditures). (*Warning:* These values apply only to the hypothetical economies described and are purely illustrative.)[2]

Although, for simplicity, we are conducting the analysis of fiscal policy on the assumption that taxes and transfers constitute the *only* difference between Y and DI, we recall that, in the real world, the other leakages do exist, the most important of which is the leakage into undistributed profits. Thus, it should be remembered that, in addition to the "built-in" fiscal stabilizers, there are also very important "built-in" *nonfiscal stabilizers*. That is, the investment multiplier is considerably lower than it would have been if there were no nonfiscal leakages. However, the question "Stabilization (from nonfiscal stabilizers) relative to what?" recurs, and the comparison implied is not easy to specify. Perhaps we should answer: "Relative to an economy in which corporations were required by law (or induced by taxation) to pay out all profits in dividends and prohibited from paying dividends except out of profits." The unrealism of this implied

---

[2] Multipliers for the balanced budget policy can be derived, more generally, as follows.

Case A. Spending is varied to exhaust revenues. Here we assume, in effect, that policy keeps $dG = t_1 \, dY$. From equation (22), Chapter 6,

$$Y = \frac{1}{1 - c_1(1 - t_1)} (c_0 - c_1 t_0 + I + G)$$

we derive, by differentiation with respect both to I and G, with $dG = t_1 \, dY$:

$$\frac{dY}{dI} = \frac{1}{1 - c_1(1 - t_1)} + \frac{t_1}{1 - c_1(1 - t_1)} \frac{dY}{dI}$$

$$= \frac{1}{1 - c_1(1 - t_1) - t_1}$$

Case B. Tax rates are adjusted to keep collections equal to a constant G. Thus, we assume that $-dt_0 = t_1 dY$. From (22) we therefore derive

$$dY = \frac{1}{1 - c_1(1 - t_1)} dI + \frac{c_1 t_1}{1 - c_1(1 - t_1)} dY$$

$$\frac{dY}{dI} = \frac{1}{1 - c_1}$$

comparison, however, becomes most evident when we add the necessary further requirement: "and in which stockholders must reimburse the corporation with negative dividends whenever losses are incurred"!

Whether or not we have succeeded in providing a convincing comparative context for this well known concept of "built-in stabilization," at least we should now be fully aware that the fiscal system (and the existence of undistributed profits) do play an important role in determining how the economy responds to changes in investment (or other changes in private demand). And, unless the stabilizing effect of the government budget's endogenous response is fully offset by discretionary budget adjustments, the movements of output and income will be considerably less than in proportion to fluctuations in I. This can be seen simply by examining the solution for equilibrium Y:

$$Y = \frac{1}{1 - c_1(1 - t_1)}(c_0 - c_1 t_0 + I + G)$$

With $(-c_1 t_0)$ a substantial positive number, and $G > 0$, fluctuations in Y will be considerably less than proportional to any that occur in I.

A Digression on Flexibility Versus Progressivity and the Aggregation Problem

Inasmuch as the built-in stabilization of the fiscal system has important consequences for economic performance, it is unfortunate that some economists have carelessly and mistakenly described the essential source of this stabilizing effect. The behavior of tax collections obviously accounts for a substantial part of the difference between movements in GNP and in *DI*, and the frequent mistake is to identify the degree to which tax collections respond disproportionately to changes in GNP with the degree to which the tax system is "progressive" rather than "regressive." The fact that this error illustrates more general problems in moving from microeconomic concepts to macroeconomic ones may provide additional justification for this digression.

The "progressivity" of a tax, or of a tax system, ordinarily means the extent to which the tax or the tax system requires persons with higher incomes to pay, on the average, a higher proportion of their incomes to the government than do persons with lower incomes. A system with such a requirement is called progressive; one that collects roughly the same percentage from people at all income levels is called proportional; one that collects a higher proportion from those with lower incomes is called regressive. The degree of progressivity *in this sense* may be *one* determinant of the degree to which taxes respond to GNP changes, but probably a relatively minor one. In any case, it is the sensitivity of aggregate tax collections to aggregate income, not the progressivity of the tax structure, that imparts built-in stabilizing effects.

For example, we can imagine a highly progressive tax system under which tax collections show very little response to changes in GNP. Suppose that the taxes due in a given year were based on a 10-year average of income, and with a high degree of progressivity in the tax schedule, so that marginal tax rates approached 99 percent in the top bracket and zero at the median income. Collections under this tax system will be quite insensitive to short-run changes in GNP, despite the high progressivity of the tax. The fact, for example, that (as economist Henry Aaron has recently argued) the property tax is quite progressive, in the ordinary sense of the term, does not make its collections respond at all sensitively to GNP fluctuations. In short, unless the *base* of the tax is *current income*, tax collections will be insensitive to aggregate income, even though the taxes paid *by different individuals* are highly sensitive to their income differences.

Moreover, even if a tax is based on current income, the response of collections from that tax to changes in aggregate income (or GNP) cannot be derived from the income tax schedule in any simple way. Suppose that a 10 percent rise in aggregate income comes about not through *any individual* receiving a higher income, but entirely through an increase in the number earning some income. The tax schedule may not be progressive, yet the increase in tax collections may be more than in proportion to the rise in aggregate income. (In fact, rises and falls in *aggregate* income associated with business fluctuations normally include both additions and reductions to the *number* of taxpayers as well as rises or declines in the incomes of former taxpayers.)

This may be illustrated by the case of the United States payroll tax, which is proportional up to a ceiling. (As of 1976, no worker, regardless of income, paid the 5.85 percent tax on earnings beyond $15,300.) Altogether, the tax is highly regressive. Nevertheless, payroll tax collections are highly sensitive to fluctuations in GNP. As employment expands, many who were paying nothing (while unemployed) again become taxpayers. In addition, of course, many workers receive higher incomes and some bump into the ceiling and pay no more even if their incomes rise beyond it. However, the significance of the ceiling for the sensitivity of collections is reduced by the fact that both employment and average hours fluctuate less among the overceiling workers than among the far larger number below the ceiling.

Another example is the corporate profits tax, which is basically proportional, not progressive. Except for the very smallest corporations, the tax rate is essentially the same for moderately small corporations as for giants such as Exxon and GM. Yet because the tax rate on corporate profits is higher than the average rate on other forms of income, and especially because changes in GNP give rise to exaggerated changes in corporate profits, collections under this tax are the most sensitive of all to fluctuations in aggregate employment and GNP.

Thus, the *flexibility* of a tax system—defined as the responsiveness of its collections to changes in aggregate income—has very little to do with the *progressivity* of the tax system. More generally, systematic differences in the ways in which a cross section of individuals with *different incomes* (or with differences in other characteristics) behave often tell us very little about how their aggregate behavior changes with changes in aggregate income (or changes in some aggregate or average measure of the other characteristics). In short, *there are aggregation problems*, to be neglected at peril.

A Cyclically Stabilizing Fiscal Policy

The built-in stabilizers (if allowed to work) will substantially reduce what would otherwise be the amplitude of any regular or irregular cycles in Y resulting from cyclical movements in I, but they will not eliminate such cycles. However, discretionary adjustments of G and or of the level of the T-function could, in principle, completely eliminate cyclical fluctuations in Y, even in the face of pronounced cyclical fluctuations in I.

(Whether, given such a stabilizing fiscal policy, pronounced cycles in I could or would continue is a question we are not ready to attack, even less to answer. However, if cycles in I were thereby reduced or eliminated, the need for discretionary fiscal adjustments would of course also be reduced or eliminated. For the sake of argument we will here assume that cycles in I, or at least some sort of fluctuations, are unavoidable.)

If there were no lags either in taking fiscal action or in its effects, the requirements of the stabilizing fiscal policy would be simple: Compute for each point in time (for example, each calendar quarter) what the level of Y would be in the absence of discretionary adjustment, given the level of I in that quarter; compare it with Y_P; divide the difference by the multiplier appropriate to the policy tool to be used; and make the appropriate discretionary adjustment. Full employment would then be maintained at all times. This policy obviously implies that the government's surplus or deficit would vary continuously—unless all adjustments involved equal increases in G and in tax collections. If swings in investment were at all substantial it would seem rather unlikely that this method, which we recall requires extremely large adjustments to achieve much impact, would be chosen. Indeed, in a context merely of cyclical fluctuation it might be assumed appropriate to use mainly tax-schedule adjustments for stabilization purposes, holding G at whatever level seemed appropriate on grounds other than those of stabilization policy. However, whatever combination of expenditure and tax adjustment was used, the budget outcome would vary over the cycle, and this variation in surplus or deficit would be entirely "discretionary," not built-in. By keeping Y constant, the policy would eliminate any built-in changes in Tx or Tr; that is, it would eliminate all changes that merely responded to changes in Y.

What the average outcome of the budget would be over the cycle would depend on the choice of fiscal policy and on the average level about which I fluctuated. If I were, on the average, fairly weak, though fluctuating, periods of deficit would be likely to prevail over surpluses; if I were, on the average, strong, periods of surplus might prevail. Whether there are longer run impacts from a policy that requires surpluses or deficits on the average over the cycle is another question that we can address only considerably later.

Fiscal Policy in a Growing Economy

In Chapter 6, considering an economy without government, we concluded that, if there is growth of potential output (through growth of available labor hours and/or their productivity) I would also need to grow—and at the same rate as Y_P—if the growing potential were to be utilized. This conclusion needs now to be reevaluated for an economy with a fiscal system.

Clearly, growth of I at the same rate as potential is no longer an absolute requirement. In the *absence* of any growth (or of sufficient growth of) I, a steadily growing potential could nevertheless be consistently fully utilized through a more than proportionate growth either in consumption or government purchases or some combination thereof. And, with a fiscal system, the tools are available to achieve such more than proportionate growth of C or G. It should be obvious, however, that whatever the combination of progressive reductions in tax schedules (or increases in transfer systems) used to expand consumption, and/or of growth of government purchases, a rather steadily growing deficit would be required. Again, the consequences, if any, of this are a topic that we are not ready to consider.

Take, however, the more favorable case in which growth of potential output is accompanied by a tendency for I to increase at a rate equal to (or close to) the growth of potential. Although no substantial progressive increases in fiscal stimulus would be necessary, this does not mean that there would be no requirement for fiscal adjustment.

To see what this requirement is, assume that I grows at exactly the same percentage rate as Y_P but that no adjustment is made in fiscal policy; that is, G is not changed nor is the net-tax function adjusted. Growth of I would still produce growth of Y; but with a given net-tax system, this would generate a "built-in" expansion of net-tax collections; with no change in G, the budget would shift toward surplus, C would grow less than in proportion to I, and a gap would develop between Y_P and Y.

Put otherwise, with a given fiscal system, we know that

$$Y = \frac{1}{1 - c_1(1 - t_1)}(c_0 - c_1 t_0 + I + G)$$

With rising I, the multiplicand (the quantity in the parentheses) expands, and Y grows in proportion to that expansion. However, if I alone expands, the expansion of the multiplicand and thus of Y is less than in proportion to the growth of I. Thus, even if I grows in the same proportion as Y_P, Y will not. This is the phenomenon which has come to be known as **fiscal drag.**[3]

The solution to fiscal drag is, in principle, simple: either G must grow to *offset* the fiscal drag of rising net taxes, or the net-tax schedule must be progressively reduced to *eliminate* the drag, or some combination. In an economy with a growth in labor force and/or in living standards (GNP per capita), it would not be surprising if social priorities should dictate that some part of the growing national product be devoted to public purposes. (It might even be a proportionately larger share of the growing output.) In any case, the optimal policy would seem to be to let the growth of G be determined by social priorities, on the assumption that Y grows along its potential path and then use net-tax function adjustments to assure the proper expansion of aggregate demand. Again, this course is simple in principle: calculate Y_P for each period; then figure what Y would be, given the expanding I, the desired level of G, and the existing tax-transfer system; subtract this Y from Y_P, divide the resulting positive or negative gap by the tax-change multiplier, and adjust the net-tax function by this amount.

As we shall begin to see in the next chapter, although "in principle" such adjustments are simple, there are some practical difficulties.

We should note, however, that if (1) I could be counted on to grow on the average, in proportion to Y_P; (2) G were always to grow in proportion to Y, that is, government purchases remained a constant fraction of national product; and (3) c_0 were zero, that is, consumption were proportional to disposable income (as seems to be the case); then avoiding "fiscal drag" would only require preventing tax revenues from growing faster than Y—and therefore faster than G. That is, it would only be necessary to adjust taxes to prevent the emergence of a proportionally increasing government surplus. If investment grows in proportion to potential, maintaining full employment in a growing economy through fiscal policy probably does not require ever-increasing government deficits.

Measuring the Impact of the Budget

Earlier we characterized the budget deficit as "endogenous," noting that its size depends not merely on "fiscal policy" (government decisions which set or alter expenditures, tax rates, and transfer payment arrangements) but also on the state of private aggregate demand, that is, the position of

---

[3] This seems to be the most *appropriate* use of the term. However, it has also sometimes been used to describe the impact of a *cyclical* rise in I, that is, as synonymous with the concept of "built-in stabilization" effects.

investment and consumption functions. This endogeneity of the deficit deprives the observer, however knowledgeable, of any direct measure of the posture of fiscal policy, that is, of any simple way of judging the appropriateness of past fiscal-policy performance or of evaluating proposals for future fiscal policy. The fact, for example, that budget deficits greatly increased during each of the recessions which occurred while Dwight Eisenhower was President does not itself prove that his administration was actively using fiscal policy to minimize recession. (In fact, he mainly was not; the deficits were simply the byproduct of the recessions.) Nor does the large surplus which accrued in the Federal budget in 1966–1968 mean that President Lyndon Johnson was using a restrictive fiscal policy to counter the inflation resulting from Vietnam War expenditures. (In fact, he was not; the surplus was simply the result of overfull employment and inflation.)

Several possible measures of the *direction* and the *extent* of fiscal-policy stimulus or restraint have been proposed. None is more than a rough measure; and each involves a somewhat different implicit definition of stimulus–restraint. However, all represent a substantial improvement over the mere historical record (or forecast) of actual budget deficit or surplus. We shall refer only to the two such measures most widely used.

The simplest direct measure of the amount of fiscal stimulus or restraint—or, at least, of *change* of fiscal stimulus or restraint from one year to the next—can be constructed simply by adding together (a) the *increase in government purchases* from the previous year, plus (b) the nonendogenous or policy-determined part of any *increase in transfer payments*, plus (c) the nonendogenous or policy-determined part of any *decrease in taxes*. (The nonendogenous parts are those that result not from changes in income and employment but those that stem from deliberate changes in tax rates, transfer payment rates, and eligibility rules.) These nonendogenous changes are normally estimated on the basis of the actual income and employment levels of (say) the previous year. In order to permit meaningful comparisons of these totals of stimulus–restraint over appreciable periods of time, each year's amount can be expressed as a percentage of the (previous) year's GNP. If this percentage is positive, the budget is stimulative; if negative, restrictive. And the extent of the stimulus or restraint is judged by the size of the percentage. Note that this method measures as net stimulus (or restraint) any fiscal-policy action (or the net balance of several fiscal actions) which, *ceteris paribus*, would tend to raise (or lower) GNP from one year to the next. It does not, however, deal directly with the further question whether such stimulus-restraint was or will be appropriate given the level of potential output for that year.

The **full-employment surplus** (FES) concept attempts this more ambitious measurement. The FES is defined as **full-employment expenditures** (FEE) less **full-employment receipts** (FER). FEE is the total of actual or planned expenditures in any given year, with the amount of its endogenous elements—usually confined to transfer payments—estimated on the basis of a full-employment economy in that year (as conventionally defined). FER is the total of hypothetical revenues in any given year, with the amount from each revenue source estimated on the basis of the actual or proposed tax rates for that year, and assuming a full-employment economy.

These calculations are complicated, but reasonably noncontroversial, given a definition of full employment. FER requires estimates, based on statistical regressions, of the amounts of the various types of incomes subject to taxation (and of the size of the base for other taxes) at full employment, to which a set of tax rates can be applied. FEE requires estimates of the volume of insured unemployment, number of persons eligible for Social Security, welfare, food stamps, etc., at the GNP corresponding to full employment in each year, to which actual or proposed schedules of benefits may be applied. In a growing economy, all of these amounts would steadily grow (or shrink) from each year to the next, given any particular set of tax laws and transfer arrangements. But FER, FEE, and FES are entirely independent of *actual* (or predicted) income and employment in any year.

The FES of any year could have been changed (or, for a future year, can be changed) only by the deliberate alteration of government purchases and/or a deliberate change in tax or transfer-payment laws and regulations. Thus, its estimated size reflects only the potential output of that year and the fiscal policy in effect that year (or proposed for a future year). In fact, of course, actual receipts and actual expenditures in any given year— and thus the actual surplus or deficit—will differ from these hypothetical figures. But they will differ from the FER, FEE, and FES only because and to the extent that actual income and employment levels diverged or will diverge from the full-employment levels. If actual output is below potential, the endogenous elements of expenditures will tend to make actual expenditures larger than FEE, and the endogenous character of most taxes will make actual receipts less than FER; both will cause the actual budget to have larger deficit (smaller surplus) than that in the full-employment budget.

Table 7-1 presents official estimates of the Federal Government's *actual* receipts, expenditures, surplus or deficit (and the change therein), for the years 1972–1976, as well as of its *full-employment* receipts, expenditures, surplus or deficit (and the change therein) for the same years. (These are based on the Council of Economic Advisers' new estimates of potential output and full-employment unemployment rates, referred to in Chapter 2.)

The table shows, for instance, that, in 1972, and especially in 1973, actual and full-employment receipts, expenditures, and surplus are nearly the same. This reflects the fact that actual unemployment in those years was very close to (only slightly higher than) the full-employment unem-

TABLE 7-1
Actual and Full-Employment Federal Receipts and Expenditures, National Income and Product Accounts Basis, Calendar Years 1972–1976

Year	Receipts	Expenditures	Surplus or deficit (−)	
			Amount	Change from Previous Year
		(billions of dollars)		
Actual				
1972	227.5	244.7	−17.3	4.7
1973	258.3	265.0	−6.7	10.6
1974	288.2	299.7	−11.5	−4.8
1975	286.5	357.8	−71.2	−59.7
1976*	330.6	388.9	−58.3	12.9
Full-employment				
1972	222.1	243.6	−21.5	−12.3
1973	257.5	265.4	−7.9	13.6
1974	311.8	297.7	14.1	22.0
1975	337.6	350.1	−12.5	−26.5
1976*	371.6	381.9	−10.3	2.2

* Preliminary.
Note: Detail may not add to totals because of rounding.
Sources: Department of Commerce (Bureau of Economic Analysis), Office of Management and Budget, and Council of Economic Advisers. (Adapted from Table 18, page 76, *Annual Report of the Council of Economic Advisers* in *Economic Report of the President* Transmitted to the Congress January 1977.)

ployment rate, and actual output very close to (only slightly below) potential output. The last column shows that the actual surplus for 1972 (−$17.3 billion) represented a change of $4.7 billion from 1971's actual surplus. The full-employment surplus in 1972 (−$21.5 billion), however, represented a change of −$12.3 billion from 1971. This large increase in full employment deficit clearly says that fiscal policy was shifted rather sharply toward stimulus between 1971 and 1972 (something which often happens in election years). In 1973, the economy was even closer to full employment, helping to make the actual deficit considerably lower than in 1972. But fiscal policy also contributed to the lower actual deficit in 1973; the FES increased by $13.6 billion. Essentially, the extra stimulus supplied in 1972 was pulled back in 1973.

Unfortunately for the policy makers, actual GNP in 1973, although very close to potential, essentially ceased to grow after the first quarter; by the end of the year a recession (GNP decline) began that lasted for six quarters. It was the most serious recession since 1929. The sharp increase in restrictiveness of the budget in 1973 surely contributed to turning the economy down. But the fiscal policy posture shown for 1974 was even more restrictive, and contributed both to the length and depth of the recession. The table shows a further shift toward surplus in the FES of $22.0 billion. Only in 1975, as the economy started to move from recession to recovery was there a massive $26.5 billion shift toward stimulus. (The quarter-by-quarter timing shows that most of this shift came after the lower turning point had already been reached; thus fiscal policy did not contribute to the turn but it did strengthen the early stages of recovery.) A small part of that stimulus, however, was withdrawn in 1976, as the FES shifted $2.2 billion toward surplus.

Most observers pay more attention to the *change* in the full-employment surplus, rather than to its level, it not being entirely clear how its absolute level should be interpreted. However, its level is important in the sense that a small move toward full-employment surplus (as in 1976) may still represent a quite stimulative budget if the previous year's budget was already highly stimulative as a result of previous moves toward full-employment deficit. Moreover, it is quite meaningful to note that, even in the worst year of our worst modern recession (1975), the full-employment deficit was only $12.5 billion—far below the $21.5 billion full-employment deficit of the rather prosperous year, 1972! And in 1974, the year of the sharpest decline, there was full-employment surplus of $14.1 billion: the Federal expenditures, and tax and transfer laws then in force would have produced a surplus of $14.1 billion had the economy been at full employment! Clearly fiscal policy was highly perverse during this period— destabilizing rather than stabilizing. (To be sure, inflation was exceedingly severe in 1973–1975. But the table makes it clear that policy makers sought to fight this inflation by a deliberate policy of creating massive unemployment—or else they didn't believe their economic advisers, who must have known at least the rough dimensions of the fiscal restraint being imposed.)

It is clear that the *change in FES* differs from the simpler measure of stimulus-restraint described first in only two respects. Whereas that measure evaluated taxes and transfers at the previous year's level of income and output, the FES always evaluates them at the current full-employment level. A theoretical case can be made for preferring either basis. Second, instead of setting as "par for the course"—defining as neither stimulus nor restraint—a budget which offers fiscal push neither toward expansion nor toward decline of GNP, the FES defines as "par" enough fiscal push to overcome the normal "fiscal drag" along the economy's growth path. This is the main sense in which the two measures "answer different questions" about a budget policy.

Both measures are obviously crude and imperfect. By adding together (or subtracting) revenue changes and expenditure changes, both measures imply that the multipliers applicable to tax, expenditure, and transfer payment changes are the same. But we know that they are not. Both measures implicitly treat the "balanced-budget multiplier" as zero rather than unity. And the most severe problem with both measures is their inability to separate changes due to inflation from those related to real expansion or contraction.[4]

ELEMENTARY DYNAMICS OF THE KEYNESIAN MODEL

The first part of this chapter employed the Keynesian model as the basis for a simple theory of fiscal policy. For that purpose, it was necessary to treat taxes and transfers (either considered alone, or combined in the concept of "net taxes") separately from other factors (that is, leakages) that cause DI to differ from Y. However, now that fiscal policy is no longer our principal concern, we can more simply treat DI as a function of Y:

$$DI = d_0 + d_1 Y$$

where d_0 is some positive constant (which can change to reflect alterations of tax rates, transfer systems, and other factors), and d_1 is a slope, positive but considerably less than 1, reflecting the fact that, as Y rises, tax collections systematically expand, transfers are systematically reduced, and undistributed profits systematically increase. (These three are, of course, the major leakages between Y and DI whose size depends on Y.) Representing, for the moment, all expenditures other than consumption by A, we have

$$Y = C + A$$

Adding the consumption function,

$$C = c_0 + c_1 DI$$

we find the equilibrium level, by successive substitution, to be

$$Y = \frac{1}{1 - c_1 d_1} (c_0 + c_1 d_0 + A)$$

The expression $1 - c_1 d_1$ in the denominator of the fraction reflects the combined effects of all of the systematic leakages between Y and DI together with the leakage of DI into personal saving. Since both c_1 and d_1 are positive and less than 1, their product $c_1 d_1$ must also be positive and less than 1, and the investment or government expenditures multiplier is therefore positive, finite, and greater than 1.

In Chapter 6 we noted that verbal explanations of how the multiplier "works," inevitably slip into a dynamic, that is, a nonequilibrium, framework. This framework refers to successive "rounds" of spending and responding of increments of income, each smaller than the previous one, with the cumulative amount of these increments approaching the

[4] Readers interested in exploring some of these issues can consult A. M. Okun and N. H. Teeters, "The Full Employment Surplus Revisited," in *Brookings Papers on Economic Activity*, 1:1970, pp. 77–116.

equilibrium result given by the static multiplier times the amount of whatever exogenous change set off the process of income change (for example, an increase or decrease in I or G, a cut or boost in taxes or transfers, or a shift in the level of the consumption function).

The reason why verbal explanations necessarily slip into a dynamic framework is, simply, that it is impossible to imagine the multiplier process condensed into an instantaneous change. For example, consumers cannot easily be imagined to respond to an increase in disposable income before they know about it—indeed, not even simultaneously with its receipt, unless they have expected the increase. Similarly, producers cannot be imagined to alter production rates simultaneously with changes in demand for their products, unless these changes were expected. Yet, for the multiplier to work instantaneously, this is what would be required: All consumers would need to know what the ultimate increase in their incomes would be—including that resulting from current and future changes in their own spending—and instantly begin consuming on that basis. Producers would need to know what the ultimate increase in the demand for their products would be and instantly adjust production and income payments to that level. But there would be no market signals, either to consumers or producers, that would tell them what those ultimate, full multiplier effects would be.

Lacking sure knowledge of where the economy is ultimately going—to say nothing of what this implies for their own individual situations—households and firms must (at least in part) adjust to current changes as they occur. To the extent that they do so adjust, each household or firm thereby transmits to others (through its purchases of goods and services, including productive services) some reflection of changes that have recently occurred in the demand for the products or services it supplies. During this process of change, households and firms take actions which may well differ from those which they would have taken had they known for sure what either the near-term or the ultimate changes in their situations would be. In the process, each is affecting what others do, just as each is affected by the recent and current actions of all others; yet none knows the full dimensions of the changes underway.

What the economist seeks to discover and to be able to describe is how this process of interactive individual decisions, based on partial knowledge, leads to cumulative changes in the national aggregates of production, incomes, and jobs; what factors determine the ultimate outcome of major changes in the general economic environment or in governmental economic policy; how long this takes; and what path it follows.

For many purposes, the economist is content only to know what would be the ultimate result of any single individual major external or policy change, taken alone. For this he uses the concept of equilibrium—meaning (usually) a state of no change—and a method of analysis called "comparative equilibrium" or "comparative statics." This method asks only what will be the ultimate results of some once-and-for-all external change, occurring in an economy in which all previous such changes had been fully digested and with no subsequent external change occurring at least until after the one he is interested in has been fully completed. This is the type of question to which the multiplier is addressed. Nevertheless, as we will see, the economist may not be able fully to answer such a question about the ultimate outcome without understanding quite a bit about the process of change: about the individual reactions, and their interactions, during the period when the change is occurring. Even if he were only interested in, and would be content only to know, the "comparative-statics" answer, he may be unable to achieve that knowledge without learning something about the far more difficult and complex "dynamics" of the system he is studying.

In the following sections we will introduce three very simple formal dynamic models of the multiplier process which, until now, we have been summarizing entirely in comparative statics terms. Having examined these three models, we will then use them to illustrate some important relationships between dynamic and static theory.

A Dynamic Multiplier Model: Consumption Lag

It is a relatively simple matter to make the "multiplier model" formally dynamic by introducing lags explicitly into the process of income and output change. Such lags might exist in the dependence of C upon DI; of Y upon C, I, and G; of DI upon Y; or any combination of these. A lag of C behind DI might reflect any or all of several phenomena: the necessity that a change in DI be received before consumers' spending is adjusted; the need for some time to elapse before consumers are able to sort out a "genuine" change in DI from mere erratic fluctuation; the existence of contractual arrangements governing some consumption spending (if, for example, incomes rise, some people may wish to consume more housing space by moving into larger apartments, but only when existing leases expire); the durability of many consumer goods (for example, if disposable incomes rise, some people may wish to move up to larger refrigerators, faster motor cars, and so on, but those with relatively new existing models may wait for the older ones to wear out or depreciate a bit more); and so on.

If one thinks of Y as production and C, I, and G as sales, changes in production might lag behind changes in sales for a number of reasons: producers may need some time to separate a "genuine" rise in sales (for which they will need to make an adjustment in production) from a mere erratic variation in sales; a change in sales (at least of most consumer goods) occurs in the first instance at retail, and it may take a while before a changed volume of orders is received by producers and a change in production is planned; and changed production plans then may take time to be realized (extra workers hired, more materials ordered and received).

A lag of DI behind Y may reflect the fact that most wages and salaries are paid weekly, biweekly, or monthly, not daily or hourly—thus a change of employment alters wage incomes only a bit later. For that portion of income that consists of profits, the recognition that profits have indeed changed may require the end of a conventional accounting period. And, in the case of corporations, a change in profits may be translated into dividends (and thus influence disposable income) only with a further lag.

Simple dynamic equations for consumption, production, and disposable income could be written as follows (assuming unitary rather than "distributed" lags):[5]

$$C_t = c_0 + c_1 DI_{t-w}$$
$$DI_t = d_0 + d_1 Y_{t-x}$$
$$Y_t = C_{t-y} + A_{t-z}$$

where the subscript t represents the value of the variable at a particular point in time, and where w, x, y, and z represent the length (in days, weeks, or months) of the lags between changes in DI and in C, changes in Y and in DI, changes in C and in Y, and changes in A and in Y, respectively. Each of these lags may exist, and all may be of different duration.

However, we assume, for illustrative purposes, that only one lag exists—of C behind DI—all other changes occurring instantaneously.[6] Define a unit of time as equal to the length of this lag. For example, suppose that it takes 14 days before a change of income produces a change in spending. If we represent by DI_t and C_t the values of these variables in some 14-day period, then DI_{t-1} and C_{t-1} become their values in the previous 14 days, DI_{t+1}, C_{t+1} their values in the following 14 days, and so on. Our dynamic model (with only the single lag) can then be written as

(13) $$C_t = c_0 + c_1 DI_{t-1}$$
(14) $$DI_t = d_0 + d_1 Y_t$$
(15) $$Y_t = C_t + A_t$$

Substituting, from (14) into (13), gives

(16) $$C_t = c_0 + c_1 d_0 + c_1 d_1 Y_{t-1}$$

from (16) into (15) gives the dynamic income equation

(17) $$Y_t = c_0 + c_1 d_0 + c_1 d_1 Y_{t-1} + A_t$$

---

[5] Unitary lags assume that no effect occurs until a certain time has elapsed, then the total effect occurs all at once. A distributed lag is one in which different parts of the total effect occur over time rather than all at once.

[6] One can of course, develop a model involving lags in any two, or in all three, relationships, although (for the mathematics to be manageable) one must assume that the length of the various lags has some common denominator, and must express all lags in terms of integral multiples of that common-denominator period.

Equation (17) says that the value of Y in any 14-day period depends on the value of A in that same period, on the value of Y in the previous period, and on the parameters c_0, c_1, d_0, and d_1. Obviously, it is not necessary that $Y_t = Y_{t-1}$; that is, that Y should be constant over time. Indeed, that is only a very *special case*.

However, this "special case" is the one we can define as *equilibrium Y*, or Y_E; that is, when $Y_{t-2} = Y_{t-1} = Y_t = Y_{t+1} = Y_{t+2}$, and so on, then $Y_t \equiv Y_E$. For such an equilibrium to exist, it seems obvious that A must be constant over time, that is, that $A_t = A_{t-1} = A_{t+1} = A$, as well as that all functional relationships are stable over time, that is, c_0, c_1, d_0, and d_1 do not change. In this special state of affairs, where $Y_{t-1} = Y_t = Y_E$, equation (12) reduces to

$$Y_E = c_0 + c_1 d_0 + c_1 d_1 Y_E + A$$

which collapses into our previous expression for equilibrium Y:

(18) $$Y_E = \frac{1}{1 - c_1 d_1}(c_0 + c_1 d_0 + A)$$

Using equations (17) and (18) we can now illustrate numerically both equilibrium values of Y, and its path of adjustment—that is, both the static (or comparative-static) and the dynamic properties of this model. Assume that $c_1 = 0.9$, $d_1 = 0.5$; and add the assumptions that $c_0 = 0$, $d_0 = 20$, and A is (at first) steady at 37. Then

$$Y_E = \frac{1}{1 - 0.9(0.5)}[0 + 0.9(20) + 37] = \frac{1}{0.55}(55) = 100$$

At this value of Y,

$$DI = 20 + 0.5(100) = 70$$
$$C = 0 + 0.9(70) = 63$$

and

$$Y = 63 + 37 = 100$$

This is the static, or equilibrium solution corresponding to $A = 37$.

It is an equilibrium because, if Y once achieves this value, Y will remain at this level. To prove this, substitute $Y_{t-1} = 100$ into the dynamic income equation (17). If we do, we find that

$$Y_t = 0 + 0.9(20) + 0.45(100) + 37$$
$$Y_t = 100$$

and, so long as A remains at 37, equation (17) will continue to generate $Y = 100$ for all subsequent periods.

We can now illustrate the "dynamic," as well as the "comparative statics," properties of this model by assuming that the economy is in the initial equilibrium corresponding to $A = 37$, $Y = 100$, and $C = 63$; then that this equilibrium is disturbed by a "*once-and-for-all*" *change* of A in period t to $A' = 43$: that is,

$$A = A_{t-3} = A_{t-2} = A_{t-1} = 37$$
$$A' = A_t = A_{t+1} = A_{t+2} = \cdots = 43$$

To solve for Y and C in period t we substitute into equation (17) and obtain

$$Y_{t-1} = Y_E = 100$$
$$Y_t = 0 + 0.9(20) + 0.45(100) + 43 = 106$$

For the next period, substituting again into (17)

$$Y_{t+1} = 0 + 0.9(20) + 0.45(106) + 43 = 108.7$$

thereafter,

$$Y_{t+2} = 0 + 18 + 0.45(108.7) + 43 = 109.92$$
$$Y_{t+3} = 0 + 18 + 0.45(109.92) + 43 = 110.46$$
$$Y_{t+4} = 0 + 18 + 0.45(110.46) + 43 = 110.71$$

If this series were carried forward for an indefinite number of periods, Y would approach, by ever smaller increments, some new equilibrium Y. Rather than carry the series further, we can find the new ("comparative statics") equilibrium merely by substituting $A = 43$ into the equilibrium income equation (18):

$$Y'_E = \frac{1}{0.55}(18 + 43) = 110.91$$

We can prove that this is the new equilibrium by substituting ⊦10.91 for Y_{t-1} into equation (17) and calculating the next period's Y. It is

$$Y_t = 0 + 0.9(20) + 0.45(110.91) + 43 = 110.91$$

That is, if Y ever reached 110.91, it would stay there. That is not true of any other value of Y.

It will be noted that the *change* in GNP between the two equilibrium positions is $110.91 - 100 = 10.91$. This equals the change in the multiplicand (that is, in A) of $43 - 37 = 6$ times the (static) multiplier of $1/0.55 = 1.82$, or $1.82(6) = 10.91$. We may also note that this new equilibrium is approached by successively smaller increments above the preceding period's Y: $+6, +2.7, +1.22, +0.55, +0.25$, and so on—each increment 0.45 times the previous one. [A mathematical proof is available that the cumulation of a series of such increments approaches, as a limit, $6 \times 1/(1 - 0.45) = 10.91$.]

If we suppose, instead, that A had risen in period t from $A_{t-3} = A_{t-2} = A_{t-1} = 37$ to $A_t = 43$, and *then immediately dropped back* to

$A_{t+1} = A_{t+2} = A_{t+3} = \cdots = 37$, the calculations using equation (17) would be

$$Y_{t-1} = Y_E = 100$$
$$Y_t = 0 + 0.9(20) + 0.45(100) + 43 = 106$$
$$Y_{t+1} = 0 + 0.9(20) + 0.45(106) + 37 = 102.7$$
$$Y_{t+2} = 0 + 18 + 0.45(102.7) + 37 = 101.22$$
$$Y_{t+3} = 0 + 18 + 0.45(101.22) + 37 = 100.55$$
$$Y_{t+4} = 0 + 18 + 0.45(100.55) + 37 = 100.25$$

Continued indefinitely, Y would, of course, approach as a limit the initial equilibrium value of 100. [The meaning of the multiplier in this case of *"one-shot" change* is that the sum of all of the individual periods' increments of Y above 100—that is, $6 + 2.7 + 1.22 + 0.55 + 0.25 + \cdots$, also equals $6 \times 1/(1 - 0.45)$.]

This exercise demonstrates how the "equilibrium value" of a dynamic model system can summarize the tendency, over time, for such a system, when disturbed by some exogenous shock or change of structure, ultimately to approach a situation of rest, at least until it is subject to some new disturbance. (At rest, the dynamic model continues to generate each successive period's values on the basis of past values, but these are all the same values.)

However, we do not need to assume that equilibrium is ever attained in order for the dynamic model to describe the behavior of the system. For example, suppose that, in this simple model, values of A change each period, as shown in the second column of Table 7-2. The dynamic version

TABLE 7-2

Period	A	Y	DI	C	"C Desired"
t (equil.)	37 → 100	→ 70	63	63
t + 1	39 → 102	→ 71	63	63.9
t + 2	43.5 → 107.4	→ 73.70	63.9	66.33
t + 3	44 → 110.33	→ 75.17	66.33	67.65
t + 4	40 → 111.65	→ 75.83	67.65	68.24
t + 5	42 → 110.24	→ 75.12	68.24	67.61
t + 6	45 → 112.61	→ 76.31	67.61	68.68

of the model will, of course, still trace out the path of movement of Y, using equation (17). Using equations (14) and (13) we can also find concurrent values of DI and C.

We have assumed (although that is not necessary) that in period t, the system was in equilibrium at values corresponding to $A = 37$. The consequences of subsequent continued changes in A (shown in the second column) for Y, DI, and C appear in the third, fourth, and fifth columns. The sixth column, "C *Desired*," shows what consumers *would have wanted to spend* at the DI level shown for the period (notice the arrow from each number in the DI column to the entry in the "C *Desired*" column for that same period), had they known in advance that their income level would be what in fact it turned out to be. They actually spend this amount (and this amount is produced) in the next period, as shown by the arrows from C *Desired$_t$* to C_{t+1}. The other arrows show the simultaneous (*non*lagged) determination of Y_t by A_t and C_t, and DI_t by Y_t. Consumers are here continually not "in equilibrium"—in the sense that they are doing something they would not have done had they known earlier what they learn later—namely, what their incomes would be each period. (In the case of "once-and-for-all" or of "one-shot" changes examined earlier, consumers were satisfied with what they were doing when the economy was in equilibrium but not at other times.)

It will be noted that, in this sequence, A was assumed to rise, reach a peak (in $t + 3$), decline, then rise again. But Y continues to increase for at least one period after A has turned down (peaking in $t + 4$), and C turns down still one period later (with a peak in $t + 5$). No simple multiplier relationship exists between any period's change in Y and the simultaneous change in A. Rather, any particular period's change in Y depends on the whole past time pattern of A's.

Of course, there exists at all times an equilibrium value of Y—a different one for each successive value of A. But the system never has a chance to reach any of such incomes. And, since equilibrium is never attained, we never observe the results of the multiplier nor can we measure its size historically. However, if we can capture, that is, measure accurately, the *dynamic structure* of the system, we can always compute the implied multiplier. Moreover, even if the multiplier is never directly observable, the "multiplier process" at work in this situation is the same process and operates to the same extent and in the same manner as in the simpler cases of "once-and-for-all" change or "one-shot" change that we examined earlier.

Dynamic Multiplier Model: Production Lag

Suppose, now, that instead of a consumption lag, we had instead assumed a production lag (but that all other responses were instantaneous: consumers fully adjusted their consumption within each period to the incomes they earned in that period, and earned income immediately became disposable income). One possible formulation for the production lag would be the assumption that producers each period make their best guess of what they will sell, and that, in the case of consumer goods, their best guess as to their sales is what they sold yesterday. This does not mean that sellers necessarily believe that they *will* sell what they sold yesterday; merely that, given past experience, this is the best guess they can make in planning their production. (Investment and government goods are assumed to be ordered in advance so that production plans do not need to depend on past sales.) The dynamic model would now appear as follows:

(13a) $$C_t = c_0 + c_1 DI_t$$

(14) $$DI_t = d_0 + d_1 Y_t$$

(15a) $$Y_t = C_{t-1} + A_t$$

Substituting, as before, from (14) into (13a), and then from (16a) into (15a) gives

(16a) $$C_t = c_0 + c_1 d_0 + c_1 d_1 Y_t$$

(17) $$Y_t = c_0 + c_1 d_0 + c_1 d_1 Y_{t-1} + A_t$$

It will be noted that this is identical with the dynamic income equation of the previous model. Thus, the responses of Y to changes in A are identical to those just worked out for the cases of once-and-for-all change, one-shot change, and continuous change in the presence of a consumption lag. But the economic meaning of the model is very different, and the implied use of each period's output is also somewhat different. Table 7-3, for instance, illustrates the case of continuous change using the same assumptions as Table 7-2. (The reader should also work out numerical examples of the cases of one-shot, and one-and-for-all changes.) The first five columns are identical with the previous table. We no longer have a column "C desired"—which differs from actual C—because consumers are here assumed to be able to adjust their consumption to actual disposable income within the same period. (They are thus never "out of equilibrium.") Rather, we have a column "C Production." which is based on what was sold the previous period. As the arrows indicate, it is this "C Production" (not actual consumption) which, along with A, determines current total production Y and disposable income DI; the latter in turn determines consumption C.

We have also added a seventh column, ΔInv, which equals "C Production" minus C—the change in inventories that occurs as the result of the wrong forecast that sellers make when they base expected sales on actual previous sales. This change of inventories was both unplanned and

TABLE 7-3

Period	A	Y	DI	C	"C Production"	ΔInv.
t (equil.)	37 → 100	→ 70	→ 63		63	0
t+1	39 → 102	→ 71	→ 63.9		63	−0.9
t+2	43.5 → 107.4	→ 73.70	→ 66.33		63.9	−2.43
t+3	44 → 110.33	→ 75.17	→ 67.65		66.33	−1.32
t+4	40 → 111.65	→ 75.83	→ 68.24		67.65	−0.59
t+5	42 → 110.24	→ 75.12	→ 67.61		68.24	+0.63
t+6	45 → 112.61	→ 76.31	→ 68.68		67.61	−1.07

undesired. It created a disequilibrium situation for producers, and they attempt to remedy this in the subsequent period by adjusting production. Note that the change of Y from one period to the next equals the change in A (which is known in advance) plus the previous period's ΔInv, with sign reversed. Sellers are attempting to avoid inventory changes, yet they keep experiencing them. Only in the "once-and-for-all" or "one-shot" cases do unexpected inventory changes ultimately disappear, as the system approaches equilibrium. Then the rule, "produce today what you sold yesterday," involves no change in inventories. If the economy stays much of the time in (or close to) a stable equilibrium, this behavioral rule thus makes perfectly good sense and never produces important surprises or disappointments.

The Role of Inventories

It will be noted that the mechanism of the previous model depended on the existence of sellers' inventories, which could absorb an increase in demand while production was being adjusted. Had there been no inventories, sales of consumer goods could not have increased in advance of an increase in production. The unavoidable occurrence of some production lag is, of course, one of the main reasons why sellers do maintain inventories. Unable to be certain in advance what their sales will be (except for goods made only to order) and recognizing that production cannot be instantaneously adjusted (and, indeed, that excessively rapid production adjustments are very costly), stocks are held in order to absorb the impact of an increase of demand and to give time for an efficient adjustment of production. Moreover, when demand drops, inventories are allowed to increase while production is being efficiently cut back.[7]

However, once we recognize that inventories exist and that they permit producers to adjust production without excessive haste to changes in their sales—whether these changes are mere erratic fluctuations or new and unforeseen trends in the movement of sales—it is clear that the notion that each period's production is simply passively adjusted to equal the previous period's sales is not the only, nor even the most reasonable, form of production planning. For example, if, for several successive periods, sales have been trending in a single direction while sellers have been planning their production on the assumption of no change in sales, cumulative changes will have occurred in the size of their inventories. If sales were rising, inventories would be consistently depleted; if sales were falling, inventories would be consistently piling up. If inventories get too low, or run out altogether, sales may be lost; if inventories get larger than necessary, they represent an unnecessary and perhaps avoidable cost. Thus, sellers will probably wish to adjust production not merely to their best estimate of sales, but, as well, in order to permit a rebuilding of depleted inventories or a reduction of unnecessary past accumulations. Moreover, if sales have been steadily trending in one direction, it may not be sensible to continue to assume that the best forecast of tomorrow's sales is today's sales.

Economist Lloyd Metzler was the first to investigate the consequences of an effort by sellers to maintain a desired stock of inventories, through appropriate correction of production plans, as well as the consequences of sellers' projections of future sales on the basis of past sales.[8] His simplest model assumes that sellers produce this period what they sold last period *plus* such additional amount as may be necessary to restore last period's unintended decline of inventories or *minus* such amount as may be necessary to remove last period's unintended accumulation of inventories.

That is, he assumes that sellers have some constant desired level of inventories, the aggregate of which we can designate as X. *Production* of consumer goods in any period, $\bar{C}_t$, is thus:

$$(20) \qquad\qquad \bar{C}_t = C_{t-1} + (X - N_{t-1})$$

where C_{t-1} represents last period's *sales*, and N_{t-1} is last period's actual

---

[7] The crucial importance of the existence of inventories in permitting output expansion is often neglected. Two treatments that develop and stress this importance are G. Ackley, "The Multiplier Time Period: Money, Inventories, and Flexibility," *American Economic Review*, 41 (1951), p. 70–73 (reprinted in *Readings in Money, National Income, and Stabilization Policy*, 3rd ed., W. L. Smith and R. L. Teigen, eds. (R. D. Irwin, 1974) pp. 104–14; and J. R. Hicks, *The Crisis in Keynesian Economics* (Basic Books, 1974) pp. 1–30.

[8] See L. Metzler, "The Nature and Stability of Inventory Cycles," and "Factors Governing the Length of Inventory Cycles," *Review of Economic Statistics*, XXIII (August 1941), 113–29, and XXIX (February 1947), 1–5.

ending stock of inventories. We add the definition:

(21) $$N_t = N_{t-1} + \bar{C}_t - C_t$$

that is, ending stock equals beginning stock plus production minus sales. Our consumption and disposable income functions are, as before:

(13a) $$C_t = c_0 + c_1 DI_t$$
(14) $$DI_t = d_0 + d_1 Y_t$$

that is, without lags. And the definition of income is

(22) $$Y_t = \bar{C}_t + A_t$$

where $A_t = I_t + G_t$.

We substitute as follows from (20) into (22):

(23) $$Y_t = C_{t-1} + X - N_{t-1} + A_t$$

from (21) into (23):

(24) $$Y_t = 2C_{t-1} + X - N_{t-2} - \bar{C}_{t-1} + A_t$$

from (20) into (24)

$$Y_t = 2C_{t-1} + X - N_{t-2} - C_{t-2} - X + N_{t-2} + C_{t-1} + A_t$$

which reduces to

(25) $$Y_t = 2C_{t-1} - C_{t-2} + A_t$$

and from (14) into (13a) and then into (25) giving

(26) $$Y_t = c_0 + c_1 d_0 + 2c_1 d_1 Y_{t-1} - c_1 d_1 Y_{t-2} + A_t$$

This dynamic equation says that any period's production and income depends in a particular way on incomes in the past two periods as well as on the current level of investment and government spending. It has, however, the usual static multiplier solution. If we substitute into (26) the definition of equilibrium,

$$Y_E = Y_t = Y_{t-1} = Y_{t-2}$$

with A constant we find the familiar

(18) $$Y_E = \frac{1}{1 - c_1 d_1} (c_0 + c_1 d_0 + A)$$

But if, from an initial equilibrium of constant production and sales, and of actual inventories equal to desired inventories, there is some disturbance in the form, say, of a once-and-for-all rise in A, and we trace out the successive pattern of adjustments through the dynamic model we have just postulated, we find that the result is not a simple monotonic adjustment to the new equilibrium. Rather, production will rise to a level above the new equilibrium, then decline to a level below the new equilibrium, and continue to move in a cyclical pattern around that equilibrium level.

We can easily illustrate this numerically for one particular assumed set of values of our parameters. Suppose, for example, we assume

$$c_0 = 5$$
$$c_1 = 0.9$$
$$d_0 = 100$$
$$d_1 = 0.6$$
$$A_{t-3} = A_{t-2} = A_{t-1} = 89$$
$$A_t = A_{t+1} = A_{t+2} = \cdots = 100.5$$

Substituting these values into the expression for equilibrium income, we find that the initial equilibrium income is

$$Y_E = \frac{1}{1 - 0.54}(5 + 90 + 89) = 400$$

and the new equilibrium income is

$$Y_E' = \frac{1}{1 - 0.54}(5 + 90 + 100.5) = 425$$

The pattern of movement is as follows, as found through successive substitutions of previous values into equation (26):

$$Y_t = c_0 + c_1 d_0 + c_1 d_1 Y_{t-1} - c_1 d_1 Y_{t-2} + A_t$$
$$= 5 + 90 + 1.08(400) - 0.54(400) + 100.5 = 411.5$$
$$Y_{t+1} = 95 + 1.08(411.5) - 0.54(400) + 100.5 = 423.92$$
$$Y_{t+2} = 95 + 1.08(423.92) - 0.54(411.5) + 100.5 = 431.1236$$
$$Y_{t+3} = 95 + 1.08(431.1236) - 0.54(423.92) + 100.5 = 432.1967$$
$$Y_{t+4} = 95 + 1.08(432.1967) - 0.54(431.1236) + 100.5 = 429.6568$$
$$Y_{t+5} = 95 + 1.08(429.6568) - 0.54(432.1967) + 100.5 = 425.9367$$
$$Y_{t+6} = 95 + 1.08(425.9367) - 0.54(429.6568) + 100.5 = 423.5002$$
$$\vdots$$

Although a new equilibrium exists (at $Y = 425$), within three periods Y overshoots this, then declines below it. If we carry the calculations through further successive periods, we would find that the decline is reversed, followed by a rise of Y to a level *above* 425, a subsequent decline below it, and so on. The amplitude of these cycles would, however, gradually diminish, and Y would ultimately approach the new equilibrium level.

The common sense of all this is not too difficult to disentangle (once it has been demonstrated arithmetically). With an unexpected increase in sales (which occurs when increased investment raises consumer incomes), producers of consumer goods—not anticipating the rise of sales and not able therefore to prepare for it—find their inventories depleted. They respond not only by raising their production to meet the new higher level of sales, but above this level in an attempt to restore their depleted inventories. This effort to restore inventories is, however, only partly successful, because the higher incomes resulting from enlarged production cause a further (again, unexpected) increase in sales, which prevents the restoration of desired inventories, leading to further expansion of production, income, and sales. However, this cannot go on forever. Income soon rises above the level that the multiplier (given the new higher level of investment) could support, *except as it is maintained above this level by extra production to restore previously depleted inventories*. The rise in incomes and sales thus slows down, and, at some point, inventories *are* restored to normal. When this happens, there is no longer extra production in order to add to inventories, and income consequently drops toward the equilibrium level. But this drop in income leads to a drop in *sales*, and inventories start to pile up. This leads to a further reduction of production, as producers try to use up their excess stocks instead of producing all that they expect to sell. This attempt is also self-defeating because it reduces income and thus further reduces sales. Again, however, there is a limit, and excess inventories are finally worked off; but this occurs only after income has fallen below its equilibrium level, which causes it to rise towards equilibrium again.

By some fairly complicated mathematics, which we have no need to reproduce, it can be proved that equilibrium in this model is "stable," in the sense that the amplitude of the resulting cycles will diminish toward zero. And this is true for any values of the dynamic model's parameters, so long as $c_1 d_1$ (the product of the marginal propensity to consume and the marginal share of disposable income) is less than 1. (We normally assume, of course, that each of these, and thus their product, is less than 1.)

Metzler, however, complicates the model further (in the direction of greater realism) by introducing two further assumptions, each eminently reasonable. One is to make the desired stock of inventories not constant but proportional to current sales. The other is for producers to assume that, when sales have been rising they will continue to rise, and vice versa. Instead of producing the amount that they actually sold last period (plus an inventory correction) they will extrapolate rising (or falling) sales into the future, and produce on that basis. Metzler shows that *either* amendment of the simpler model (or the two in combination) can produce nondiminishing (or ever expanding) cycles (as well as several more complex types of movement), *even with* $c_1 d_1 < 1$. That is, there may *exist* an equilibrium that is consistent with the higher value of A_t but will not be attained because of the assumed pattern of dynamic response.

Dynamics and the Stability of Equilibrium

Metzler's inventory cycle model, just reviewed, is, for all its apparent complexity, an extreme simplification of "real-world" business behavior with respect to inventories. Nevertheless, the model may capture some part of the explanation for the observed facts (a) that inventory investment is the most volatile of all major components of GNP, and (b) that the recession and early recovery stages of most "business cycles" are dominated by changes in inventory investment.

However, the purpose of introducing the Metzler model at this point was not as a contribution to an understanding of the business cycle, but rather, simply as an illustration of still another dynamic theory whose comparative-statics counterpart is the simple multiplier model. That is, all of the forms or elaborations of the Metzler model have an equilibrium solution indistinguishable from the simple static Keynesian model; also indistinguishable, therefore, from the equilibrium solution of the simpler dynamic multiplier versions involving either one-period consumption or production lags.

We have thus tried to illustrate through these three dynamic models several methodological points of some importance. Summarizing them, they are:

1. Any static or equilibrium model is only a simplified, "special state" of some dynamic model, that special state in which time is allowed for all consequences, direct and indirect, of any change fully to work themselves out, until every relevant economic process has achieved a steady state.

2. One static model may have a number of dynamic counterparts, or, put the opposite way, a number of dynamic models may have the same equilibrium solution.

3. Depending on their stucture, some dynamic models may have equilibrium solutions that are unattainable. If the variables all had their equilibrium values, the dynamic model would generate indefinite repetition of those same stable values. Thus an equilibrium exists; but, if the system is ever out of equilibrium, that same dynamic structure will generate only continuous change. Obviously, the equilibrium solution of *such* a model is not meaningful. If ever disturbed, it would not be reestablished nor would any other steady state emerge.

4. Whether an equilibrium is attainable, and thus meaningful, cannot be discovered by analyzing merely the static counterpart of the dynamic model but only through analyzing the dynamic model itself. Through such an analysis, we can define the specific conditions or requirements for the "stability" of a model's equilibrium—that is, the range of values of a

model's parameters that may be consistent with an attainable equilibrium (and, as well, the ranges of values that will produce other specified kinds of movements—for example, cycles or sawtooth patterns of various kinds).

We can illustrate the meaning of "stability conditions" by reference to the simplest of all static Keynesian models, that without government:

$$C = c_0 + c_1 Y$$
$$Y = C + I$$

which has the equilibrium solution

$$Y = \frac{1}{1 - c_1}(c_0 + I)$$

Before getting to stability conditions, there are other conditions that we may first wish to evaluate—for example, the circumstances in which equilibrium values of the variables would be nonnegative (since negative values of many economic variables are meaningless). From the above value of equilibrium Y we can see that a positive value of Y requires either

$$c_1 < 1 \quad \text{if} \quad c_0 + I > 0$$
$$c_1 > 1 \quad \text{if} \quad c_0 + I < 0$$

These conditions define a nonnegative equilibrium, but are not sufficient to define a *stable* equilibrium. For example, suppose we have

$$c_0 = -20$$
$$c_1 = 1.2$$
$$I = 10$$

We solve for equilibrium Y as

$$Y = \frac{1}{-0.2}(-20 + 10)$$
$$= 50$$

at which

$$C = -20 + 1.2(50) = 40$$

Equilibrium Y is thus nonnegative. However, the model displays the strange property that a drop of investment will raise equilibrium income, and vice versa. For example, if

$$I' = 5$$
$$Y' = \frac{1}{-0.2}(-20 + 5) = 75$$
$$C' = -20 + 1.2(75) = 70$$

This strange property seems consistent with the value of the (static) multiplier, which we could calculate as

$$\frac{1}{1 - 1.2} = -5$$

In our example, a change of investment of -5 produced a change of equilibrium Y of $-5\,(-5) = 25$. Question: Is this model stable; that is, is the equilibrium attainable?

Suppose we assume that the corresponding dynamic model—of which the equilibrium model is a special, steady-state case—is one involving a consumption lag. The model thus is

$$C_t = -20 + 1.2\,Y_{t-1}$$
$$Y_t = C_t + I_t$$

or

$$Y_t = -20 + 1.2\,Y_{t-1} + I_t$$

and its equilibrium solution with $I = 10$ is $Y = 50$. That this is a true equilibrium can be seen by inserting the equilibrium value for Y into the dynamic equation. With $I_t = 10$ and $Y_{t-1} = 50$,

$$Y_t = -20 + 1.2(50) + 10 = 50$$
$$Y_{t+1} = -20 + 1.2(50) + 10 = 50$$
$$\vdots$$

that is, an equilibrium exists, and, if the model were in equilibrium, it would remain there. However, we can also easily see that this is an unattainable, or "unstable" equilibrium. Continuing the previous series, suppose that, in Y_{t+2}, I falls to 5 (consistent with a new equilibrium of 75). Then

$$Y_{t+2} = -20 + 1.2(50) + 5 = 45$$
$$Y_{t+3} = -20 + 1.2(45) + 5 = 39$$
$$Y_{t+4} = -20 + 1.2(39) + 5 = 31.8$$
$$Y_{t+5} = -20 + 1.2(31.8) + 5 = 23.16$$
$$Y_{t+6} = -20 + 1.2(23.16) + 5 = 12.792$$
$$Y_{t+7} = -20 + 1.2(12.792) + 5 = 0.3504$$

In other words, instead of approaching the new equilibrium value of 75, Y plummets to zero. To be sure, there does exist an equilibrium level of $Y = 75$, which, if achieved, would be continually reproduced. If

$$Y_{t+n-1} = 75$$
$$Y_{t+n} = -20 + 1.2(75) + 5 = 75$$
$$Y_{t+n+1} = -20 + 1.2(75) + 5 = 75$$

If only income could somehow get to 75, it would stay there; but it cannot. This new equilibrium value—like the initial one—is unstable.

The stability condition for this simple model therefore is that $c_1 < 1$. Exactly the same stability condition exists, by the way, for a dynamic model in which there is a production lag instead of a consumption lag. It is also the stability condition for the *simplest* Metzler model. It is *possible*, however, that there is some other plausible dynamic counterpart of the simple static model that would be stable, even with $c_1 > 1$; but, if so, it is not familiar.[9]

One could establish, by trial and error, that the stability condition for all *three* of these dynamic versions of the process of income change is that the MPC (that is, c_1) is less than 1. However, rather complicated mathematical methods are available to discover the stability conditions for any dynamic model more directly than by trial and error.[10] Part A of the appendix to this chapter provides a relatively simple mathematical demonstration that $c_1 < 1$ is the stability requirement for the simple model we have just considered, with the consumption lag; and part B of that appendix lists the equations and stability conditions for the most complex of the Metzler inventory-cycle models. In what follows, we introduce several strands of economists' general discussion of expectations in a macroeconomic context.

Expectations and Equilibrium[11]

It can be seen from the previous discussion that expectations, and the effects of their realization or disappointment, are crucial to the concept of equilibrium. The economy can hardly be in meaningful equilibrium if economic agents have acted on the basis of a set of expectations which, on balance, turned out to be incorrect. Either their expectations or their actions—probably both—will be revised, and this will alter the economic situation on the basis of which others will make economic decisions. Although some economic analyses, which deal only with equilibrium positions, can pay no attention to expectations, most economists recognize the crucial importance of expectations, and a lot has been written about them. Unfortunately, there is little uniformity in economists' treatment of expectations.

[9] More elaborate models—for example, with investment depending on the interest rate—may, however, be stable even with $c_1 > 1$.

[10] The mathematical methods involved in the "difference equations" used to describe these models are treated relatively simply in Alpha C. Chiang, *Fundamental Methods of Mathematical Economics*, 2nd ed. (McGraw-Hill, 1974), Chaps. 16–17. For additional detail and further references the reader can consult William J. Baumol, *Economic Dynamics*, 3rd ed. (Macmillan, 1970), Chaps. 9–13, 15, 16.

[11] Since this section was written, an important paper has appeared on the subject: William Poole, "Rational Expectations and the Macro Model," in *Brookings Papers on Economic Activity*, 2: 1976, pp. 463–505 (followed by "Comments and Discussion," pp. 506–514). Preliminary study of Poole's article indicates both considerable agreement and some disagreement with the substance of the positions taken in this section and throughout this book.

Among the first to emphasize the existence and importance of expectations for macroeconomics were members of the "Stockholm School," whose work first became widely available to English-speaking economists in the 1930s.[12] The economists of this school pointed out that macroeconomic variables can be identified or defined as **ex ante** or **ex post** (looked at "from before" or "from after"). These terms remain in wide use even though the fairly rigid Stockholm analytical framework (using these concepts) was never widely accepted and is now largely forgotten.

The ex post concept is, for all practical purposes, that used in national income accounting—the amounts actually realized and recorded. The ex ante concept is less sharply defined; it is today used to mean, variously, "planned," "desired," or "expected" magnitudes. However, the original Stockholm concept was considerably more rigorous. The framework in which it was used visualized economic agents as possessing, at all times, rather definitely formulated **expectations** about the future, at least with respect to many significant variables. These expectations related both to variables not under one's own control, and, made consistent with these, to variables within one's control (the latter we can call **plans**). Thus, a producer might have an expectation of his sales and plans for his production and inventory change; a consumer might have an expectation regarding his income and a plan for his consumption and saving.

We also can suppose, as the Swedes did, that some kinds or parts of each subject's plans are always carried out as planned. However, all plans cannot always be carried out because these plans may be mutually inconsistent. For example, if the amount which consumers plan to, and do, spend, and the amount which investors plan to, and do, spend add up to more than the incomes consumers expected, then consumers' saving plans cannot possibly be carried out. That is, ex post saving will exceed ex ante saving. Since ex post saving must, by definition, equal ex post investment; and, since, by the assumption that investors' plans were carried out, ex ante and ex post investment were equal, then we could say that ex ante *investment* exceeded ex ante *saving*, and that this excess "caused" income to be greater than expected—i.e., caused income ex post to exceed income ex ante.

We could complicate matters by assuming that investors' plans for capital expenditure are always carried out but that their plans for inventory investment need not be. That is to say, we can visualize producers having sales expectations, and plans for production and inventory change (assume planned inventory change zero for simplicity). If, now, we assume that production plans are always carried out, and, as well, that capital investment and consumption spending plans are carried out, the producers'

---

[12] See B. Ohlin, "Some Notes on the Stockholm Theory of Saving and Investment," *Economic Journal*, 1937, reprinted in American Economics Association, *Readings in Business Cycle Theory*, Blakiston, 1944, pp. 87–130.

inventory plans cannot also be carried out unless the expected sales of producers exactly equal planned consumption plus planned capital investment. If not, then ex post investment (which includes all inventory change) will diverge from ex ante investment.

Thus, we see that ex ante saving can diverge from ex post saving, which must equal ex post investment, which in turn can diverge from ex ante investment. All four will be equal only if all expectations are consistent with all plans; then expected incomes will equal actual incomes and expected sales equal actual sales. One can call this an "equilibrium." However, it is such only in a very special sense, for it is clearly possible that—if plans and expectations should change together in a perfectly consistent way—incomes and sales could be continuously changing yet always in equilibrium.

It should be noted that none of this says very much about the really crucial questions: (1) How are expectations framed? And (2) given the values of expectations, how are plans made? We could, for example, answer question (1) by assuming that consumers always expect that future incomes will be the same as the present ones, and that producers always expect that tomorrow's sales will be the same as today's. We could then assume, to answer question (2), that consumer spending plans derive from a consumption function, in which *expected* income determines planned (and actual) future spending. We could further assume that producers' plans are always to produce just what they expect to sell. (Some of these elements are included in the Keynes and Metzler models discussed in the last few pages.) But these are not the only results which can be fitted into the Stockholm framework. For the Stockholm definitions would be compatible with many other theories regarding how expectations and plans are formulated, giving entirely different results. Thus, it seems preferable to regard the ex ante, ex post concepts as simply a broad framework for analysis, into which any of a number of substantive theories can be fitted. The only common feature of these would be the view that expectations and plans are of crucial importance in economic life and are therefore crucial variables to be isolated in economic analysis.

Subsequent macroeconomic analysis has used a great variety of specific assumptions about the formulation and revision of expectations and plans. Much of the analysis of the remainder of this book, which reviews some leading strands of recent macroeconomic literature, thus either explicitly or, much more often, implicitly deals with expectations in particular contexts. However, as noted, there is no standard, widely accepted general theory about expectations—which perhaps simply means that there is little that is *regular* or *systematic* about expectations relevant to the macroeconomic world. But this does not mean that expectations are unimportant or can be neglected.

Broadly speaking, however, we can distinguish perhaps three main strands in economists' treatment of expectations. One is the view that many (most?) expectations are of the **adaptive** variety. That is, expectations adapt to events, but not all at once—perhaps even quite slowly.[13] For example, an economist may argue that expected income is primarily generated by some long-term moving average or trend of past incomes; or he may hypothesize that the expected future interest rate is generated from observing the central tendency of interest rates over a considerable period of time; or he may suggest that the expected rate of inflation equals the recent or current rate of inflation. Our several explanations of the dynamic multiplier in the last subsection all incorporated adaptive expectations.[14]

A second general kind of treatment of expectations is the theory of **rational expectations.**[15] This holds that economic agents observe events over time, and absorb all available economic information, to produce, with or without the help of any formal economic theory, a conscious or intuitive calculation about how the future will differ from the present and past. And they act directly on that calculation. A trader in the wheat market, for instance, or the foreign exchange or bond market, has to act (if he is rational and if he is to stay in business) on the basis of some fairly explicit view of future wheat prices, or exchange rates, or bond interest rates. These expectations are being constantly tested by events. Somehow, the trader learns that way of arriving at a view of the future price (or exchange or interest rate) (1) which "efficiently" uses all of the available (relevant) information; (2) which gives forecasts not systematically biased in either direction; and (3) which predicts better than any other method he can find. And he acts on the expectations so generated.

Assuming the existence of such expectations, and such actions, can produce rather startling results. If expectations are rational in this sense (and if all or a number of traders in a market are more or less rational), an equilibrium that would take considerable time to emerge if expectations were adaptive can be realized almost at once. For example, if monetary policy is altered in some familiar way, its expected (equilibrium) effects on interest rates, output, and prices induce immediate purchases and sales of assets, and current production and purchase of goods and services, which cause the expected outcome to be approximated almost at once. The existence of rational expectations would imply that actual values are always very close to equilibrium values, no matter how rapidly or widely the equilibrium values change.

There is some evidence that rational expectations may be present in some specific markets. For example, elaborate statistical tests which sug-

---

[13] Sometimes these are termed "extrapolative" expectations, especially if only the most recent experience is "extrapolated" into the future.

[14] Although Keynes' *General Theory* often treated expectations implicitly rather than explicitly, his treatment most often is thought to imply adaptive expectations.

[15] The concept of rational expectations was launched in an article by J. F. Muth, "Rational Expectations and the Theory of Price Movements," *Econometrica*, vol. 29 (July 1961), 315–335.

gest that stock prices follow a "random walk" are interpreted as evidence confirming this theory, as are some reactions to changes in monetary policy. However, not all the evidence studied is consistent with this hypothesis, even for the most perfect markets, dominated by highly specialized traders.[16] And even if one accepts some role for rational expectations in these particular kinds of markets, one cannot easily generalize to the entire macroeconomy—to all the decisions of consumers, investors, and workers, relating not only to prices of existing assets, but to prices and quantities produced, purchased, and sold of consumer and capital goods and services of persons and property.

All of these decisions do require at least implicit expectations about the future (sometimes extending 25 or more years into the future, in the case of capital investment), even if no more than the view that the best guess, and not a very good one, is that tomorrow will be much like today. But are all these expectations "rational" in the special sense used here? And do they have, can they have, the effects of bringing about almost at once the short-run or long-run equilibrium consistent with those expectations?

For example, to revert to our lagged multiplier examples of the last subsection above, rational expectations would imply that when consumers and producers learn of a change in business investment, or an alteration of government fiscal policy, they will, in effect, calculate its ultimate effect on their incomes or the demand for their products, and all begin consuming and producing on the basis of that expectation, which, of course, at once confirms its correctness.

To some extent, this may in fact be the case. For example, our economy is one which exhibits a succession of "business cycles", of roughly similar duration and amplitude, repeating a pattern of several years of expansion, followed by a (usually somewhat shorter) period of recession. At least when once these movements are underway, businessmen may not need to wait for their own orders to expand or to contract before beginning to adjust their production and sales plans; those workers most exposed to cyclical unemployment may not wait for their jobs to disappear (or to reappear) before making some partial adjustments of their spending.

Even though there may be a long chain of processing and distribution between the manufacture, say, of rayon fiber and the retail sale of a blouse (spinner, weaver, converter, finisher, wholesaler, manufacturer, distributor, retailer), an examination of the timing of business cycles in each of these activities suggests that often, perhaps even typically, the turning points in prices and production at levels nearest to and at those most remote from the consumer may occur nearly simultaneously. This surely

---

[16] For example, an unpublished paper by M. Dooley and J. Shafer, "Analysis of Short-Run Exchange Rate Behavior, March 1973 to September 1975," suggests that exchange rates do not follow a "random walk."

suggests some degree of "rationality" of expectations in the special sense of that term, at least much of the time.

Rational expectations remain an interesting idea (which we will illustrate in several contexts); but it is not clear that it has wide application. We shall have occasion to dispute some of its proposed applications (particularly by "monetarists") at several points in subsequent chapters.

The third strand of theorizing about expectations is at an opposite remove from that of rational expectations. It is the work of "psychological" or "behavioral" economists, who may see the action of economic agents occurring in a sociopsychological context of perceptions, attitudes, and expectations, formed individually, and formed, as well, through social interaction (via interpersonal contacts and individual and mass communications). This context is subject to change, in response to news and events, and reflecting individual and social knowledge and experience. The perceptions, attitudes, and expectations which comprise this "context" are often seen to carry considerable affective content. The economic situation may sometimes be seen as familiar, permissive, and reinforcing—generating confidence, optimism, feelings of well-being, aspirations for individual and group improvement. At other times it may be seen as threatening or limiting—generating fear, resentment, anxiety, insecurity, protective rather than creative or ambitious conduct. These perceptions, attitudes, and expectations which help determine economic behavior are seen as influenced not only by economic but very importantly as well by political, social, and international events and trends.

This sociopsychological view of expectations may well exaggerate the importance of attitudinal factors; yet it has undoubtedly made some contribution to the thinking of many macroeconomists. We shall illustrate some of its applications in a later chapter.

APPENDIX TO CHAPTER 7
STABILITY CONDITIONS

A. Stability Conditions for the Simple Keynesian Model

Chapter 7 showed that the stability condition of the simple Keynesian model, incorporating a consumption lag, was that the MPC be less than 1. No rigorous demonstration was provided for this finding. However, it can be derived quite directly, by simple algebra. We generalize the model, as follows:

$$Y_t = C_t + A_t$$
$$C_t = c_0 + c_1 Y_{t-1}$$

By substitution,

$$Y_t = c_1 Y_{t-1} + c_0 + A_t$$

The equilibrium consistent with any given constant level, A_0, of investment is found by letting

$$Y_t = Y_{t-1} = Y_E$$

or, substituting in the previous expression,

$$Y_E = c_1 Y_E + c_0 + A_0$$

$$Y_E = \frac{1}{1 - c_1}(c_0 + A_0)$$

which is, of course, the familiar formulation obtained earlier for the static model.

If, for any period, income is at its equilibrium level, it will remain there, for, if

$$Y_{t-1} = Y_E = \frac{1}{1 - c_1}(c_0 + A_0)$$

then

$$
\begin{aligned}
Y_t &= c_1 Y_{t-1} + c_0 + A_0 \\
&= \frac{c_1}{1 - c_1}(c_0 + A_0) + c_0 + A_0 \\
&= \left(1 + \frac{c_1}{1 - c_1}\right)(c_0 + A_0) \\
&= \frac{1}{1 - c_1}(c_0 + A_0) \\
&= Y_E
\end{aligned}
$$

This condition obtains whether or not the equilibrium is stable. However, suppose that income is, even for one period, different from its equilibrium level. That is, suppose that

$$Y_{t-1} = Y_E + X$$

where X is either positive or negative, but not zero. Then, in the following period,

$$
\begin{aligned}
Y_t &= c_1 Y_{t-1} + c_0 + A_0 \\
&= c_1(Y_E + X) + c_0 + A_0 \\
&= \frac{c_1}{1 - c_1}(c_0 + A_0) + c_1 X + c_0 + A_0 \\
&= \frac{1}{1 - c_1}(c_0 + A_0) + c_1 X \\
&= Y_E + c_1 X
\end{aligned}
$$

In the period that follows, we have

$$Y_{t+1} = c_1(Y_E + c_1 X) + c_0 + A_0$$

$$= \frac{c_1}{1 - c_1}(c_0 + A_0) + c_1^2 X + c_0 + A_0$$

$$= \frac{1}{1 - c_1}(c_0 + A_0) + c_1^2 X$$

$$= Y_E + c_1^2 X$$

And, in the following period:

$$Y_{t+2} = Y_E + c_1^3 X$$

The income series, then, is,

$$(Y_E + X), (Y_E + c_1 X), (Y_E + c_1^2 X), (Y_E + c_1^3 X), \ldots$$

If X is positive, that is, if income in period $t - 1$ exceeded equilibrium, it is clear that the excess will grow if c_1 is greater than 1. That is, the equilibrium is unstable. But the excess will shrink toward zero if c_1 is less than 1. If X is negative, which means that income in period Y_{t-1} was less than equilibrium, the negative deficiency will grow if c_1 is greater than 1, and shrink toward zero if c_1 is less than 1.

Consider now the case $c_1 = 1$. In this case our dynamic income equation becomes

$$Y_t = Y_{t-1} + c_0 + A_0$$

If $c_0 + A_0 = 0$, we have the result that income always equals its previous value. Although this is a kind of equilibrium ("neutral equilibrium"), it implies no economic explanation for the level of income. Income is whatever it has been. But if $c_0 + A_0$ is either positive or negative, no equilibrium is possible. Successive values of Y_t will differ by a constant amount—income either shrinking toward zero (if $c_0 + A_0 < 0$) or growing without limit (if $c_0 + A_0 > 0$).

Our conclusion thus is that stable equilibrium requires that the marginal propensity to consume be less than one.

B. Stability Conditions of Metzler Inventory-Cycle Model with (a) Desired Stocks Proportional to Sales, and (b) Expected Sales Projected on Basis of Recent Change.

The equations of this model can be written as follows (using the notation of Chapter 7):

$$Y_t = \bar{C}_t + A_t$$

$$C_t = c_0 + c_1 DI_t$$

$$DI_t = d_0 + d_1 Y_t$$

$$\bar{C}_t = \mu_t + r_t + s_t$$

where

μ_t = anticipated sales = $C_{t-1} + \eta(C_{t-1} - C_{t-2})$

r_t = replacement for unintended inventory depletion of last period (actual sales less anticipated sales)

$= C_{t-1} - \mu_{t-1}$

$= C_{t-1} - [C_{t-2} + \eta(C_{t-2} - C_{t-3})]$

s_t = pure "accelerator" investment—that desired adjustment of inventories to respond to expected sales

$= \alpha[\mu_t - \mu_{t-1}] = \alpha[(1 + \eta)C_{t-1} - (1 + 2\eta)C_{t-2} + \eta C_{t-3}]$

From the above, by successive substitution, once can easily derive the following dynamic income equation:

$$y_t = (c_0 + c_1 d_0) + A_t + [(\alpha + 1)(\eta + 1) + 1]c_1 d_1 y_{t-1}$$
$$- [(\alpha + 1)(1 + 2n)]c_1 d_1 y_{t-2} + (\alpha + 1)\eta c_1 d_1 Y_{t-3}$$

As briefly noted in the text, this model can produce various kinds of movements, including unstable movements, depending on the values of the parameters c_1, d_1, η, and α. The necessary conditions for this movement to approach a constant value—that is, the "stability" conditions are that

$$(1 + \alpha)(2 + \alpha)\eta(c_1 d_1)^2 - (1 + \alpha)(1 + 2\eta)c_1 d_1 + 1 > 0$$

and

$$3 - c_1 d_1(2\alpha + 3) > 0$$

REVIEW QUESTIONS

1.

(a) Show how the following "multiplier" (applicable to a change of government purchases) is derived algebraically from a simple macroeconomic model:

$$\frac{dY}{dG} = \frac{1}{1 - c_1(1 - t_1 - r_1)}$$

where Y is real income or output, G is real government expenditures, c_1 is the slope of an aggregate consumption function, t_1 the slope of an aggregate tax function, and r_1 the slope of an aggregate transfer payment function.

(b) Derive the multiplier applicable to an increase in the constant term of the tax function. Explain in words why (ignoring sign) it is (larger than), (smaller than), or (equal to) the multiplier applicable to a reduction in G.

2.

(a) What is the "balanced-budget-multiplier"?

(b) Present a derivation (algebraic or otherwise) of the balanced-budget-multiplier, indicating the assumptions necessary for its derivation.

3. In 1975 President Ford proposed that the Congress simultaneously enact tax cuts amounting to $28 billion, and a ceiling on expenditures of $395 billion for fiscal year 1977, which was $28 billion less than the expenditures that he estimated would otherwise be made in that year.

(a) Ignoring the *timing*—i.e., the fact that the tax cuts would be effective Jan. 1, 1976, and the expenditure ceiling was for the fiscal year beginning October 1, 1976—what would probably be the ultimate effect on the level of equilibrium GNP if this program were adopted?

(b) Assuming that this were going to be done, how would you evaluate the proposed timing, knowing that the economy in 1976 would still be in the relatively early stages of recovery from our deepest postwar recession?

4. In the section on "Numerical Examples of Fiscal Operations," three different policies were illustrated. Note, however, that there is another policy available to raise Y to Y_P. This is the policy of increasing both taxes (estimated at the previous level of income) and purchases by the same amount. Compute values of all variables that would result if this policy were applied, and compare with the results shown for the other policies.

5. Briefly define each of the following concepts:

(a) built-in stabilization

(b) fiscal drag

(c) full-employment surplus

(d) tax-cut multiplier

(e) stability condition

(f) adaptive expectation

(g) rational expectation

6. Below are data on federal government finances (national-income-accounts basis) for the second quarter of each of five years. All data are in billions of dollars at seasonally adjusted annual rates.

Year and Quarter	Revenues Actual	Revenues Full-employment basis	Expenditures Actual	Expenditures Full-employment basis	Surplus Actual	Surplus Full-employment basis
1968-2	169.8	165.6	181.8	181.2	−11.2	−15.7
1969-2	199.7	199.6	187.6	187.8	12.0	11.8
1970-2	194.2	212.9	207.5	206.1	−13.4	6.8
1971-2	198.2	219.9	221.2	217.7	−23.0	2.2
1972-2	224.9	245.5	246.5	243.2	−21.6	2.3

(a) Explain the differences (1) between the two concepts of expenditures; (2) between the two concepts of revenues.

(b) By studying the changes in federal finances which occurred during each of the four one-year intervals, indicate—*for each such interval*—

(1) what changes were occurring *in the economy*—output, employment, unemployment, and *how can you tell*;

(2) what changes occurred *in federal fiscal policy* (both on the expenditure and revenue sides of the budget), and *how can you tell*;

(3) judging from your answers to parts (1) and (2), were these fiscal policies appropriate or inappropriate?

(c) What are the major flaws of the full-employment surplus as a measure of fiscal policy?

7. The multiplier is a "comparative-statics" concept. But the multiplier effect cannot possibly be instantaneous; to understand how the multiplier operates, we really need a "dynamic" analysis. Explain and illustrate (verbally, diagrammatically, or algebraically)

(a) How an increase of government spending from one steady level to another higher level must create a gap either between "actual" and "desired" investment or between "actual" and "desired" saving or consumption;

(b) How this gap leads to increased production, which in turn creates a new gap, leading to a further increase in production; and

(c) How such a gap disappears only when production has finally risen by the full amount indicated by the (static) multiplier.

SELECTED REFERENCES

Council of Economic Advisers, "The Effects of Tax Reduction on Output and Employment," *Annual Report of Council of Economic Advisers*, 1963, pp. 45–51, reprinted in Smith and Teigen (eds.), *Readings in Money, National Income and Stabilization Policy* (R. D. Irwin, 3rd ed., 1974), pp. 310–314.
(A simple summary of how tax reduction affect economic activity.)

A. P. Lerner, "Functional Finance and the Federal Debt," *Social Research*, 10 (February 1943), 38–51, reprinted in N. F. Keiser (ed.), *Readings in Macro-economics* (Prentice-Hall, 1970), pp. 371–378.
(An early and influential effort to spell out the implications of Keynesian economics for the theory and practice of fiscal policy.)

W. A. Salant, "Taxes, Income Determination, and the Balanced Budget Theorem," *Review of Economics and Statistics*, 39 (May 1957), 152–161, reprinted in J. Scherer and J. A. Papke (eds.), *Public Finance and Fiscal Policy* (Houghton Mifflin, 1966), pp. 346–361.
(The classic statement of the balanced budget theorem.)

R. A. Musgrave and M. H. Miller, "Built-In Flexibility," *American Economic Review*, 38 (March 1948), pp. 122–123. reprinted in A. Smithies and J. K. Butters (eds.), *Readings in Fiscal Policy* (R. D. Irwin, 1955), pp. 379–386.
(A landmark exposition of the built-in stabilization concept.)

Council of Economic Advisers, "The Full Employment Surplus Concept," *Annual Report of Council of Economic Advisers*, 1962, pp. 78–81, reprinted in W. L. Smith and R. L. Teigen (eds.), *Readings in Money, National Income and Stabilization Policy* (R. D. Irwin, 3rd ed., 1974), pp. 297–299.
(A simple introduction to the full employment surplus.)

W. Lewis Jr., *Federal Policy in the Postwar Recessions* (Washington: The Brookings Institution, 1962); and

C. Brown, "Fiscal Policy in the Thirties: A Reappraisal," *American Economic Review*, 46 (December 1956), pp. 857–879.
(Two early applications of a version of the full employment surplus concept to the interpretation of economic history.)

A. M. Okun and N. H. Teeters, "The Full Employment Surplus Revisited," in *Brookings Papers on Economic Activity*, 1:1970, pp. 77–116.
(A full discussion of the strengths and weaknesses of the full employment surplus.)

A. S. Blinder, R. M. Solow, "Analytical Foundations of Fiscal Policy," in A. S. Blinder, R. M. Solow, G. F. Break, P. O. Steiner, and D. Netzer, *The Economics of Public Finance* (The Brookings Institution, 1974), pp. 3–45, especially pp. 11–36.
(The most sophisticated review of literature on the measurement of fiscal policy impact.)

G. Ackley, "The Multiplier Time Period: Money, Inventories, and Flexibility," *American Economic Review*, 41 (June 1951), 350–368, reprinted in W. L. Smith and R. L. Teigen (eds.), *Readings in Money, National Income and Stabilization Policy*, (R. D. Irwin, 3rd ed., 1974), pp. 104–114.
(A nontechnical exposition of Keynesian dynamics.)

L. A. Metzler, "The Nature and Stability of Inventory Cycles," *Review of Economic Statistics*, 23 (August 1941), 113–129, reprinted in R. A. Gordon and L. R. Klein (eds.), *Readings in Business Cycles* (R. D. Irwin, 1965), pp. 100–129; and L. A. Metzler, "Factors Governing the Length of Inventory Cycles," *Review of Economic Statistics*, 29 (February 1947), 1–5.
(The classic works on inventory cycles.)

W. J. Baumol, *Economic Dynamics*, (Macmillan, 3rd ed., 1970), Chapters 9–13, 15, 16.
(The economics and mathematics of dynamic analysis.)

Chapter 8

Extensions of the Keynesian Model: Investment and Economic Growth

The Keynesian Model with Endogenous Investment
The investment decision of the firm
Investment, too, depends on income
The acceleration principle
The Hansen–Samuelson model
Further modifications of the acceleration principle
A simple capital-accumulation model

The Acceleration Principle, Potential Output, and Economic Growth
The ceiling of potential output
A "Harrod–Domar" Model of Balanced Growth

At the end of Chapter 7, we quietly slipped an explanation for some investment expenditures into the Keynesian model. This occurred once we admitted the existence of changes in inventories (in connection both with the production-lag model of the multiplier and with the inventory model of Lloyd Metzler). So long as we were considering the change of inventories only as something that happened involuntarily and presumably temporarily, this presented few problems. But once we introduce a target level of inventories, and particularly when (as in the more advanced version of the Metzler model) we make the size of desired inventories depend on Y, we already have introduced an investment theory, relating to at least one part (and the most volatile part) of investment.[1]

The broader category of investment includes, of course, the purchase or construction by businesses of new plant and equipment of all kinds, along with construction of new residential structures, whether by businesses or households. The sum of these, plus additions to business inventories, is called **private gross domestic investment** in the United States national income accounts. It has in recent decades constituted roughly between $13\frac{1}{2}$ and 18 percent of United States GNP. (During the Great Depression, however, it fell in 1933 to as little as 2.5 percent of a greatly shrunken GNP. Of the four major categories of GNP, this is the most volatile, and its variations contribute strongly to the fluctuations commonly called "business cycles."

On a net basis—that is, after deducting estimated depreciation from private gross domestic investment—investment has normally (since the early 1950s) ranged from about $5\frac{1}{2}$ to $9\frac{3}{4}$ percent of NNP (**net national product**). However, net investment reached an unusual 13.0 percent of NNP in 1948 and 12.4 percent in 1951 (when deficiencies of capital

---

[1] Making the size of desired inventories dependent on Y in fact introduces a version of the "acceleration principle," which is to be considered shortly as applicable to total investment.

resulting from wartime and depression were being made up, while depreciation was still based on the shrunken stock). And in 1933 net investment had sunk to an astounding −11.5 percent of NNP.

By international standards, the recent percentages are relatively low, at least when compared with the fast growing economies of Western Europe and Japan. In the latter country, for example, private gross investment has exceeded 30 percent of GNP in some postwar boom years.

THE KEYNESIAN MODEL WITH ENDOGENOUS INVESTMENT

Despite the importance of investment to fluctuations in GNP (as well as to long-term economic growth) and the extensive attention which economists have therefore given to its study, our understanding of the factors that determine the amount of investment remains far from satisfactory—either on a theoretical or empirical basis. Chapters 18 and 19 will review what we think we know and what we clearly do not know about investment; here our principal purpose is to explain the basis for the treatment of investment in the simple macromodels developed in this section of the book. This discussion will also serve as an introduction to the more thorough treatment of Chapters 18 and 19. We will ignore changes in inventories.

The Investment Decision of the Firm

Considering the nature of the investment decision by the individual firm immediately suggests some of the reasons why, in a world in which the future is uncertain, investment is such a complex matter and why generalizations simple enough to be understandable yet reasonably accurate in their predictions may be difficult to achieve. Even if we can achieve a reasonably satisfactory understanding of an individual firm's investment, the problems of explaining *aggregate* investment are still far from solved: first, because many things that the individual investor can appropriately take as given turn out to be variables in an aggregate analysis; second, because many of the variables crucial to any single firm's investment decisions tend to cancel out when we look at the entire economy.

Still, it is useful to start with the firm. The entrepreneur confronting an investment decision is attempting to assess what will be the profitability (if any) of a prospective newly purchased asset over a future period as long as the life of the asset—which may extend 30 years or more. The firm knows what it will cost to purchase (or build) and install the asset now, what funds it has on hand available for investment and what they are earning, and what it will have to pay in interest over the life of a loan taken out now to help to finance this purchase. It also has much information about the asset's probable *physical* performance and *physical* durability over its life. But it certainly cannot know with any degree of certainty the *prices* and *quantities* sold (or even the price-quantity relationship—the demand curve) that will prevail in the future for the output of the asset; nor the prices of raw materials, labor, power, and so on, necessary to be used along with the asset in producing and selling the product; nor the taxes that will in the future be imposed on ownership of the asset, the sale of the product, or the profits earned. To be sure, it can know quite accurately the current values of almost all of these things; but the *future* values are subject to wide variation as the result of both foreseeable and unforseeable future changes in the structure of product demand and competition, in technology, in the degree of general prosperity or recession in the economy as a whole, and in the political and social factors affecting the firm.

The investor thus must calculate profitability on the basis of *expected* (that is, anticipated) values of all of these variables. His expectation for each element determining profitability may ultimately be subjectively reducible to some single, "most probable," value, but this value is surrounded by a wide band of uncertainty.[2] And, as J. M. Keynes pointed out many years ago, in a treatment which every student of macroeconomics should read (and every student of investment behavior should frequently reread), such subjectively determined values may be drastically affected by the "political climate" of the day and "by the nerves and hysteria and even the digestions and reactions to the weather" of those who make investment decisions. "Only a little more than an expedition to the South Pole," said Keynes, can the investment decision be "based on an exact calculation of benefits to come."[3] Moreover, guesses about the future profitability of a new investment are strongly influenced by the current valuations placed on *existing* investments of the same or similar kind, which also extend into the same future. The stock market is continually making such valuations (not of particular assets, to be sure, but of the firms which own them). However, for reasons that Keynes most entertainingly and penetratingly explains, the stock market's valuations may bear little relationship to the "true" value of such firms or assets. And we know that the market's valuations can double—or be cut in half—within a relatively short period of time.

How, then, can any rational, economic explanation be offered either of an individual investment or of the aggregate volume of investment?

To start with, we recognize that many things are *known* at the time of an investment decision. We also recognize that these known values may recently have changed, perhaps quite independently of the expected future values of those variables (whatever these may be), in a way that could substantially alter the profitability of the investment (whatever that profitability would previously have been estimated to be). For example, a

---

[2] Here, as elsewhere in this volume, "expected" and "expectation" are used in the sense of "anticipated" and "anticipation," not in the sense of mathematical expectation, unless so specified.

[3] *General Theory of Employment, Interest and Money* (Harcourt-Brace, 1936), Chap. 12 ("The State of Long-Term Expectation"), pp. 147–164.

reduction (or increase) in the cost of the asset, relative to prices generally and to the prices of the particular outputs which the investment would supply, might be expected substantially to increase (or decrease) the expected profitability of an investment, even though the *level* of that future profitability may be most imperfectly known. Likewise, a reduction (or increase) in the rate of interest at which loans can now be contracted may well change the expected profitability. The availability of recent technological improvements, increasing the physical productivity of the asset, or reducing its costs of operation, or extending its durability, will presumably enlarge the possibility of profit, whether or not the *level* of that profit can be accurately foreseen. An increase in the firm's own funds available for investment will not itself increase the profitability of investment. However, inasmuch as many firms are unable, due to the imperfection of capital markets, to borrow, or to borrow as much as they would like, an increase in the availability of "internal funds" may enable the firm to undertake prospective investments already believed to be profitable but which it could not previously finance. The above factors—relating to present or recent facts—are all quite objective matters, not heavily influenced by guess or sentiment. Another relevant magnitude, reasonably well known to the firm, is how many of its *existing* assets (similar to the one being considered) currently need to be replaced (or the rate at which their physical productivity is currently declining). From one year to the next this quantity also changes, at least for the firm.

Furthermore, some of the recent changes in objective economic circumstances affecting the market for the prospective output or the costs of future operation can often reasonably be expected to indicate changes that may prevail during at last some appreciable part of the relevant future. We refer not only to recent one-time changes but also to recent trends or recent changes in trends. For example, if the demand for a certain product has recently been growing, or its growth has accelerated, this may very well alter previous expectations either of future sales or prices or both, presumably raising the expected profitability. Or, if profits taxes have recently been reduced, it may be reasonable to expect that they will remain lower during some or all of the life of any newly purchased assets, and thus increase expected after-tax profitability of investment—unless such a tax cut had previously been expected!

Thus, certain *current facts* are relevant to investment decisions (because they are relevant to expected profitability); changes in these should cause changes in the volume of investment. Even so, it is often only the expectation, not directly observable, that some *recent change will continue* that affects investment.

Unfortunately, many of the recent changes that may reasonably affect the investment decisions of an individual firm cancel out, or largely cancel out, in terms of their effects on aggregate investment. Such changes may involve mere shifts of demand from one product to another, shifts in the relative efficiency of competing firms, or relative shifts in the expected profitability of one kind of capital equipment over another. Moreover, although variations in the availability of internal funds or in the need to replace existing productive assets about to wear out may account for large differences in investment as among firms or may account for large fluctuations in any particular firm's investments, the effects of these variables on aggregate investment may be slight because only modest changes may occur from year to year in their aggregate amounts.

As we shift our consideration from the firm to the aggregate economy, we also must note that some important "facts" that are known to the firm need to be treated as variables when the entire economy is considered. For example, the costs of new capital equipment are rather precisely ascertainable by the firm and are largely independent of the volume of any firm's (except possibly the largests') investments; yet the level of these costs may vary considerably for different amounts of aggregate investment currently made. Similarly the interest rate: each firm knows it, but for the economy it is a variable, depending, among other things, on the aggregate amount of investment. Moreover, while the time lag, often substantial, between an investment *decision* and the expenditures for the *production* of the equipment is essentially independent of the amount of investment by any firm, it may well be a variable (and perhaps a quite important one) as the aggregate volume of investment changes.

The preceding comments suggest the complexity of the investment decision of the firm, as well as a few of the further problems encountered in moving from the micro to the macro level. It should be clear, then, that any generalized model of the investment process is unlikely to be both (a) sufficiently simplified so that it is readily understandable and its implications easily traceable, yet (b) conform reasonably accurately to what actually happens in the "real world." Many earlier theories, some of which we will review, met the first test but failed the second. More recent theories, some of which we will also review, often seem to fail both.

Nevertheless, even simple macro models need to say something about the determination of investment. What they say usually involves one, or some selected combination of one, or two, or three of the elements mentioned in the previous section. One possibility is simply to assume that the amount of investment is "exogenously" or "autonomously" determined. It varies, and it does so for many and complicated reasons; but the most important of these reasons are essentially independent of any of the variables that the models incorporate or that could readily be incorporated in such models. Investment is thus the product of some "deus ex machina"; it is determined "outside the model." Exogenous determinants of investment surely include changes in technology, that at least for economies already at or close to the "technological frontier," are obviously an important factor in investment, and no set of macroeconomic variables "explains" technological developments. Also exogeneous are the "political climate" and "the nerves and hysteria and even the digestions and reactions to the weather" of entrepreneurs, as well as the speculative manias that run stock prices up and down.

Assuming investment to be exogenous does not necessarily deny that changes in "objective" variables included (or includable) in simple macro models may also affect the volume of investment. The assumption, however, may be that the systematic effects on investment of any such changes are swamped by the exogenous elements, and that it is thus unnecessary, perhaps even silly, to include them. A more common treatment of investment in simple models is to include the recognition of possible large unexplained or autonomous shifts in investment and to incorporate as well some systematic effects of other variables on investment, which modify or qualify the "purely exogenous" view of investment. (Unfortunately, once the systematic elements get included, it is all too easy—and very common—simply to forget about the exogenous elements.)

The most venerable of the inclusions is the notion that investment depends on the interest rate—a variable that can be appropriately "explained" within a relatively simple macro model. (This was the investment theory of classical economics; and the classical model which incorporated it also explained the determination of the interest rate. It remains an important, if not dominant, factor in modern macroeconomic models of the "Keynesian-classical synthesis" type.) Since interest is either a cost incurred in financing most investment (to the extent that borrowed funds are used) or is an "opportunity cost" of investment (to the extent that owners' funds are used) it seems evident that, *ceteris paribus*, there should be an inverse relationship between interest rate and investment: the higher the interest rate the smaller the amount of investment. Since the simple Keynesian model does not incorporate the determination of the interest rate, we are unable to use this theory of investment until we also enlarge the Keynesian model so that the interest rate becomes an endogenous variable, which we shall do subsequently. However, two other simple theories of investment *can* be incorporated in a simple Keynesian model, although the second of them requires a dynamic rather than merely static form of analysis. We turn to the first of these.

Investment, Too, Depends on Income

One rather simple theory of investment argues that its amount depends on the level of income or output. (This can of course be combined with the idea that exogenous shifts also occur). Several alternative explanations for such dependence are at least implicit in the foregoing description of a firm's investment consideration. One explanation is based on the idea that investment depends on the hope or expectation of profits, and that the best information which the businessman has as to the future level of profits is their current level. This, indeed, is the usual microeconomic explanation of how production is adapted to demand. If demand shifts from product *A* to product *B*, price changes will lead to profit changes that, in the short run, will cause output rates to be adjusted with given equipment, and, in the longer run, will induce extra investment in product *B* and disinvestment in product *A*. This investment and disinvestment will continue until profit rates are again equalized (assuming free entry and perfect competition) at zero pure profit.

The usual microeconomic discussion is carried out under the assumption of a constant level of aggregate demand, thus, any shift of demand towards one product—creating profits and stimulating investment—must be fully at the expense of other products. However, once we admit variations in aggregate demand, profits can increase (or decrease) in many or all lines of production, stimulating (or depressing) investment in them all. We have already noted that profits are highly sensitive to the level of *Y*; thus investment will respond to changes in *Y*.

A rather different version does not stress the role of current *Y* and current profits as creating expectations of future *Y* and profits; rather it sees the role of profits—or, in particular, of *undistributed* profits—as a source of "internal funds" for financing investment. This source becomes of greater importance the less perfect are the capital markets available to the firm. Withdrawals of current profits to provide for the consumption expenditures of the proprietor or the dividends that must be paid to keep stockholders satisfied ordinarily absorb only a fraction of any variation in profits. Thus, when total national income and total profits are high, retained earnings are high, and vice versa, with retained earnings fluctuating rather violently (from negative to large positive quantities) in response to moderate output changes. The effect of changes in retained earnings is particularly important in the case of small businesses, whose access to capital markets is typically very limited, and many of which are perennially short of capital facilities—that is, unable to take advantage of clear opportunities to increase their profits. Even large corporations may sometimes prefer to reinvest extra profits in enlarging their businesses rather than to pile up useless bank accounts, to buy securities, or to give stockholders a taste of dividends at a rate that possibly cannot be maintained. Likewise, even the large corporation may pass up or cut back promising investment projects when falling profits mean that they cannot be financed internally.

Even if we recognize the existence of capital markets that permit *external* as well as internal financing of investment, we can still relate total investment to current (or recent) profits. We assume that the amount of outside capital that a firm can attract depends positively upon its demonstrated recent profitability and/or that the amount of funds lenders are willing to supply depends partly upon the amount of internal financing that its owners can supply (or, at least, that increases in the *ratio* of external to internal financing involve appreciable increases in the cost of the outside capital).

We can state this investment theory in linear form (for simplicity) as

$$I = b_0 + b_1 Y$$

where b_0 is some (probably negative) constant, and b_1 some positive slope, presumably considerably less than 1. We can incorporate exogenous shifts in investment (reflecting the influence of all *other* factors affecting I) through considering the constant, b_0, as subject to exogeneous increase or decrease. Adding the other equations of the simple Keynesian model, we have the system:

(1) $$Y = C + I + G$$
(2) $$C = c_0 + c_1 DI$$
(3) $$DI = d_0 + d_1 Y$$
(4) $$I = b_0 + b_1 Y$$

from which we obtain, by successive substitution, the expression for equilibrium Y:

(5) $$Y = \frac{1}{1 - c_1 d_1 - b_1} (c_0 + c_1 d_0 + b_0 + G)$$

This differs from our earlier solution by the further subtraction of b_1 in the denominator of the multiplier and by the inclusion of b_0 instead of I in the multiplicand.

The solution of the model is shown graphically in Figure 8-1, for the case in which $G = 0$.

Notice first the effects on the multiplier. An increase in G, or additional autonomous investment (represented by an increase in the constant term b_0 in the investment function) will lead to an increase in income equal to the amount of the shift times a new "super-multiplier," $1/(1 - c_1 d_1 - b_1)$. Since b_1 is necessarily positive, this multiplier is larger than the one previously derived. The common sense of this is easy to grasp. If a rise in income not only leads to increased consumption but as well to increased investment (creating the basis for further expansion of income, consumption, and investment, in endless but diminishing chain), the ultimate increase in income will be greater than if only consumption so responded.

Suppose, for instance, that our functions were as follows:

$$C = 5 + 0.8DI$$
$$DI = 100 + 0.6Y$$
$$I = 10 + 0.2Y$$
$$G = 33$$
$$Y = C + I + G$$

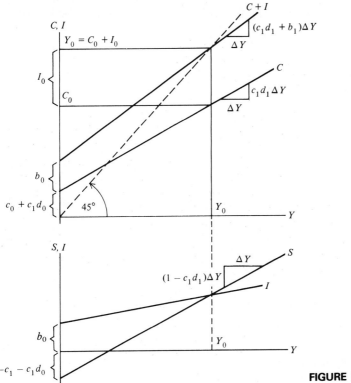

FIGURE 8-1

Substituting, we obtain

$$C = 5 + 0.8(100) + 0.8(0.6)Y$$
$$= 85 + 0.48Y$$
$$Y = 85 + 0.48Y + 10 + 0.2Y + 33$$
$$= 400$$
$$DI = 340$$
$$C = 277$$
$$I = 90$$

If the constant in the investment function rose from 10 to 20, the new equilibrium would be found as follows:

$$Y = 85 + 0.48Y + 20 + 0.2Y + 33 = 431.25$$

Comparing the two solutions shows the super-multiplier to be 3.125, whereas, if investment had been entirely autonomous, the multiplier would have been only 1.92.

Among other things, this model is the source of the so-called **paradox of thrift**. An increased propensity to save, in the simpler Keynesian model, left total saving (and investment) unchanged, although reducing income. In the present model the effort of the community to save more is actually self-defeating; the new equilibrium involves not only lower income but lower saving as well. Yet a community that loses its thrifty habits succeeds in saving more than it did previously. Although these results are more "interesting" and dramatic than those of the simple Keynesian model, this does not necessarily make it a "better" model, nor is the difference much more than one of degree.

It is also easy to see that the stability condition of this model is altered from the previous one. Instead of having it that the marginal propensity to consume (c) times the marginal share of disposable income in GNP (d_1) must be less than 1, we now have that the sum of this product plus the b_1 (the "marginal propensity to invest," or slope of the investment function) must be less than 1.

A variant of this investment theory is to make investment depend not directly on Y, but instead on profits; but profits are then made to depend on Y (and perhaps other factors). Some models further assume that there are only two income shares—wages and profits, the sum of which equals Y. If it is further assumed (as it sometimes is) that all wage income is consumed, then stability depends on the coefficient of the profits term in the investment equation being less than one.

Some business-cycle models (or even growth models) in this mold in fact assume that this coefficient is greater than one. Thus, no meaningful equilibrium exists; expansions and contractions cumulate in an unstable process. Turning points then come either (1) because the relation of profits to total output changes as the expansion or contraction proceeds (profit margins begin to shrink toward the end of expansions, begin to rise toward the end of depressions) for special reasons that the theorist may develop, or (2) because some external event or limit checks and reverses the process.

We can now ask whether there is any empirical evidence suggesting the plausibility of the theory that investment, like consumption, depends on Y. In Figure 8-2, we present data on NNP and net private domestic invesment in the United States for the years 1946–1976, both measured in constant dollars. Although the points do not fall on, or even close to, a single line of relationship, it is clear that a strong correlation exists. (The upward-sloping line drawn in the figure is not a statistical regression, but a free-hand approximation.) Almost every time NNP rose or fell, investment did too. Attempts have been made to estimate statistical investment functions from just these data. But critics quickly pointed out that the relationship may be entirely specious, merely a misinterpretation of the direction of causation. For if, as we have generally accepted, consumption is a function of income, we should *expect* to find this kind of a relationship between investment and income, *even if investment were entirely independent*

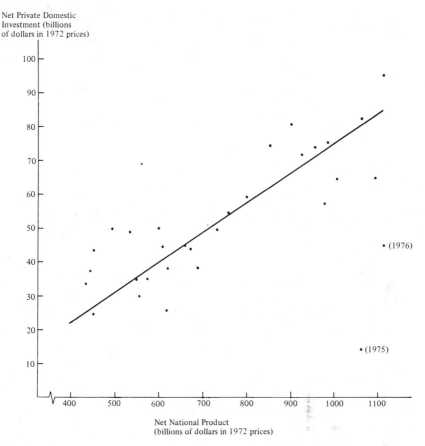

Net Private Domestic
Investment (billions
of dollars in 1972 prices)

FIGURE 8-2 The Relationship of Net Investment to Net National Product in the United States, 1946–1976.

of income. Does not the causation run the other way: high investment *causes* high income (directly and via the multiplier), low investment, low income?

The criticism of statistical procedure is well taken, but reflection as to its import immediately suggests what may be a troublesome thought. The data do indeed seem consistent with the theory that investment is independent of income, and only consumption depends on income. But they would also be consistent with the reverse theory: namely, that consumption is independent of income and only investment depends on income! This is merely a reminder that statistics can never "prove" a theory or hypothesis. The best that we can ever say is that a body of data is consistent with a hypothesis. It may also be consistent with another hypothesis, too, as might seem to be the case here.

The data might seem to be inconsistent with a third possible hypothesis: that *both* consumption *and* investment are reasonably stable functions of income; for if, in a simple model, this were the case, no change in income would ever occur—stable consumption and investment functions would always produce the same level of equilibrium income. However, the observed fact that income does change does not necessarily dispose of the hypothesis that both consumption and investment depend on income, so long as either function, or both, is presumed also to be subject to exogenous shifts. Moreover, there may also occur changes in fiscal policy, that could produce changes in Y even if both C and I were completely stable functions of Y.

Successful statistical estimation of any systematic dependence of both C and I on Y—permitting the identification as well, of shifts in either or both of these functions and the existence of other influences on C and I—may require the simultaneous estimation of these (and other) equations of a complete model. Elementary statistical methods using pairs of variables in isolation do not permit us to test the plausibility of a model involving both saving (consumption) and investment as functions of income. This does not mean that the investment theory is to be rejected— indeed, on this ground, one might equally well reject the consumption theory. Rather, it means that, as always, the economic theorist must first decide (on other grounds) what he considers to be a plausible model.[4] Then, if the model is capable of statistical testing (and not all models are), the statistician can tell him if it needs to be rejected. However, he can never "prove" it to be "the" correct theory.

The hypothesis that investment depends on the level of income or output is the simplest of all available theories of aggregate investment. This is insufficient reason to dismiss it. To be sure, no simple and direct statistical test of the theory is possible. And even its supporters admit the relationship probably to be erratic and unstable. However, after examining other, more complicated theories, the reader will observe that economists have as yet no thoroughly satisfactory theory of investment.

The Acceleration Principle

The idea that investment depends on income is sometimes explained by an allegedly technological argument, which instead actually supports a quite different theory. The argument is that more or less output *requires more or less capital equipment to produce it*, just as it requires more or less labor and

---

[4] The "other grounds" that determine plausibility to a theorist presumably are its consistency with *a priori* postulates. Such postulates are either derived from (1) accepted existing bodies of theory, already judged consistent with available empirical data or observations, or (2) the assumption of "rational behavior," thus tacitly reflecting an empirical observation (more casual than scientific) that men behave "rationally," at least with respect to certain kinds of decisions. These comments are not intended to derogate *a priori* analysis. In the present state of our knowledge such analysis may often be superior to such statistical tests as are available—which sometimes means none.

material. Thus, any increase in total output requires higher investment in additional plant and equipment with which to produce the added output; investment is thus a function of output. However, this chain of reasoning is incorrect.

A higher aggregate output and income of course imply an increase in the demand for the product of almost every entrepreneur. In response to this increase in demand, each needs to employ more productive services of all kinds, and probably in amounts which increase more or less in proportion to the increase in output. Some of these productive services are purchased currently—labor, power, parts, raw materials, and so on. A rise in demand will require greater purchases of all of them. The entrepreneur will also need a larger current flow of the productive services rendered by plant and equipment. Assuming that he has no idle plant and equipment, a rise in demand (corresponding to higher aggregate income) may induce each entrepreneur who experiences such a rise to purchase more plant and equipment (over and above mere replacement).

But with his purchase of a larger flow of capital-goods services *now*, the entrepreneur automatically also purchases an enlarged future flow of such services, over some period to come. This is exactly what distinguishes the building or machine from the raw material "used up" in production. This means that, if demand rises and then merely remains at the higher level, entrepreneurs will probably not need, again, to buy still more new buildings and machines (although there may ultimately be higher replacement requirements associated with their larger stocks of capital goods). Only if demand *continually rises* will they need to *continue adding to their net stock of capital goods*. That is, it might be more plausible to assume, as a first approximation, that net demand for new capital goods (and thus net investment) depends on the *change* of aggregate output rather than on its *level*. This theory of investment, or, more appropriately, this *family* of theories is (perhaps somewhat inaptly) known as the **acceleration principle**. It asserts that the most significant factor affecting the amount of capital goods used in production is the physical volume of production—of a particular product, if we are explaining the capital used in a firm or industry, or of aggregate GNP or NNP, if we are explaining the total capital used. As the production of a firm or industry grows (or declines) so should its capital stock—not its investment—and in much the same proportion as the variation in its production. Extended to the entire economy the theory asserts that changes in the aggregate stock of capital goods will parallel any variation of national product.

As just stated, the acceleration principle is a theory of the size of the desired or optimum capital stock rather than a theory of (net) investment; the latter, of course, constitutes the *change* of the capital stock. It is the wide variety of possible ways in which the transition can be made from a theory about stocks of capital to one about flows of investment that produces the large and diverse family of investment theories (some of them exceedingly complex) which share the "acceleration-principle" concept and label. Some version of the acceleration principle is an almost unavoidable element in the more complex theories of investment treated in Chapters 18 and 19. However, even the simple macroeconomic models developed in the next few chapters can include one or another of the simpler versions of the acceleration principle as their theory of investment. We begin with some rather rigid versions, at first *limited to an economy with no long-run growth.* We also assume that whatever income variation occurs takes place *entirely within the range of less than full employment.* These are crucial assumptions which will be relaxed in the next section of this chapter.

The simplest of Keynesian models to include an acceleration theory of investment assumes that there exists for each consumer good some fixed proportion between the rate of production of that good and the stock of capital needed for its production. Each machine, that is, can turn out only so many units of output; in order to turn out more units more machines are required. Abstracting from other possible influences on the stock of capital, and aggregating to the entire economy, the necessary or desired or equilibrium stock of capital (measured in physical terms) depends on the demand for consumer goods (also in physical terms). Then, given the prices of consumer and capital goods, any change in consumer goods' output will call for a change in the stock of capital in an amount x times the change of output, where x is the dollar value of the capital needed or desired to produce \$1 worth of consumer goods. This number is often called the "accelerator", or the **acceleration coefficient**. That is, net investment equals $x \Delta C$.

If $I = x \Delta C$, then I will equal zero whenever ΔC equals zero; that is, whenever C (and thus whenever Y) is constant. But whenever Y and C change, by a positive or negative amount, net investment (or disinvestment) will occur, at a rate which is small or large depending on whether the change of consumption is small or large. We incorporate this simple acceleration theory into our macro model by starting with a definition of income or product in any period as

(1a) $$Y_t = C_t + I_t + G_0$$

where G_0 is some constant amount of government purchases, and add a consumption function, without lag,

(2a) $$C_t = c_0 + c_1 DI_t \qquad (c_0 \geq 0,\ c_1 < 1)$$

a disposable income function, also without lag,

(3a) $$DI_t = d_0 + d_1 Y_t \qquad (d_0 > 0,\ d_1 < 1)$$

and an accelerator investment function

(4a) $$I_t = w + x(C_t - C_{t-1}) \qquad (w \geq 0,\ x > 0)$$

Equation (4a) asserts that investment in any period will occur in an amount sufficient to supply the added capital goods required to produce any increment of consumer goods which has occurred since last period, plus a constant, w, which may be zero. (We may treat w as representing any exogenous element or portion of investment, or that explained by another variable or variables.)

Substituting from (3a) into (2a), then into (4a), and finally into (1a) gives

$$C_t = c_0 + c_1 d_0 + c_1 d_1 Y_t$$

$$I_t = w + x(c_0 + c_1 d_0 + c_1 d_1 Y_t - c_0 - c_1 d_0 - c_1 d_1 Y_{t-1})$$

$$= w + x c_1 d_1 Y_t - x c_1 d_1 Y_{t-1}$$

$$Y_t = c_0 + c_1 d_0 + c_1 d_1 Y_t + w + x c_1 d_1 Y_t - x c_1 d_1 Y_{t-1} + G_0$$

$$(5a) \ Y_t = \frac{-x c_1 d_1}{1 - c_1 d_1 (1 + x)} Y_{t-1} + \frac{1}{1 - c_1 d_1 (1 + x)} (c_0 + c_1 d_0 + w + G_0)$$

We can also compute the steady-state equilibrium value of Y, by substituting into (5a),

$$Y_{t-1} = Y_t = Y_E$$

and solving, to obtain

$$Y_E = \frac{-x c_1 d_1}{1 - c_1 d_1 (1 + x)} Y_E + \frac{1}{1 - c_1 d_1 (1 + x)} (c_0 + c_1 d_0 + w + G_0)$$

or

$$(5) \ Y_E = \frac{1}{1 - c_1 d_1} (c_0 + c_1 d_0 + w + G_0)$$

which is the usual multiplier formulation of the simple Keynesian model (with government and other leakages), except that w (the constant element of investment) here replaces I.[5] It will be noted that the acceleration coefficient x drops out of the expression for equilibrium income. The reason is simple enough: net investment occurs, under the acceleration principle, only when Y is changing, equilibrium is defined in terms of an unchanged income, and the acceleration principle produces zero net investment at equilibrium income.

If, for example, we assume particular numerical values, such as

$$c_0 = 0 \qquad x = 2$$
$$c_1 = 0.9 \qquad w = 0$$
$$d_0 = 10 \qquad G_0 = 37$$
$$d_1 = 0.6$$

[5] Note that, unless c_0, d_0, w, or G_0 is greater than zero, the equilibrium level of Y is zero. However, we can see from equation (5a) that there still exists some constant, steady growth of Y:

$$\frac{Y_t}{Y_{t-1}} = \frac{-x c_1 d_1}{1 - c_1 d_1 (1 + x)}$$

we can compute that

$$Y_E = \frac{1}{1 - 0.54}(9 + 37) = 100$$

If G now changes from 37 to 42, Y_E rises from 100 to 110.8696. The change equals the change in G times the usual multiplier.

We can satisfy ourselves that the initial Y_E is truly an equilibrium position by inserting $Y_{t-1} = 100$ into equation (5a) and solving for Y_t. Given our numerical assumptions, equation (5a) becomes

$$Y_t = \frac{-1.08}{1 - 0.54(3)} Y_{t-1} + \frac{1}{1 - 0.54(3)}(0 + 9 + 0 + 37)$$

$$= 1.741935 Y_{t-1} - 74.1935$$

If $Y_{t-1} = 100$

$$Y_t = 1.741935(100) - 74.1935 = 100$$
$$Y_{t+1} = 100$$
$$Y_{t+2} = 100$$
$$\vdots$$

Suppose, however, Y_{t-1} was not the equilibrium value. For example, suppose

$$Y_{t-1} = 98$$

Then

$$Y_t = 1.741935(98) - 74.1935 = 96.5161$$
$$Y_{t+1} = 1.741935(96.5161) - 74.1935 = 93.9313$$

Similarly,

$$Y_{t+2} = 89.4288$$
$$Y_{t+3} = 81.5856$$
$$Y_{t+4} = 67.9233$$
$$Y_{t+5} = 44.1244$$
$$Y_{t+6} = 2.6683$$

Thereafter, Y becomes increasingly negative!
On the other hand, suppose

$$Y_{t-1} = 105$$

Then

$$Y_t = 108.7097$$
$$Y_{t+2} = 115.1719$$
$$Y_{t+3} = 126.4281$$

and, after a few more periods,

$$Y_{t+8} = 523.8640$$
$$Y_{t+9} = 838.3437$$
$$Y_{t+10} = 1386.1472$$
$$Y_{t+11} = 2340.3854$$
$$\vdots$$

Equilibrium exists (at $Y = 100$), but it is unobtainable: if Y has any value in $t - 1$ other than 100, it will immediately gallop off in one direction or the other and never return. Of course, sequences of progressive, self-perpetuating declines or increases of income are not unknown in real-world economies; but progressively accelerating changes that have only the limits of zero and infinity do not seem very relevant to the economies we know.

One may appropriately ask whether this result depended on the particular numerical values selected. The answer is yes; but the alternatives—with other values—are no more comforting. The particular example used was one for which

(6) $$1 - c_1 d_1 (1 + x) < 0$$
$$(\text{e.g., } 1 - 0.9(0.6)(1 + 2) = -0.62 < 0)$$

The particular pattern shown in the example we used—galloping off without return—holds for all values of c_1, d_1, and x which satisfy inequality (6).

If, however, we use values which do not satisfy this inequality—for example, values for which

(7) $$1 - c_1 d_1 (1 + x) > 0$$

we find a different pattern of unstable movement emerging whenever $Y_{t-1} \neq Y_E$. It involves a saw-toothed pattern of variation around the equilibrium level: one period above the equilibrium level, the next below it.[6] And the distance above or below increases steadily and without limit. Also a condition not observed in real-world economies.

---

[6] For example, the reader might try these values:

$$c_1 = 0.9 \qquad d_1 = 0.5 \qquad x = 1$$

producing

$$1 - c_1 d_1 (1 + x) > 0$$
$$1 - 0.9(0.5)(1 + 1) = 0.1 > 0$$

The reader should compute the equilibrium income, then compute a sequence of subsequent incomes, given $Y_{t-1} \neq Y_E$.

In the intermediate case, in which

(8) $$1 - c_1d_1(1 + x) = 0$$

there still exists a positive equilibrium for Y, which, if attained, is indefinitely repeated. But if $Y_{t-1} \neq Y_E$, all subsequent values of Y, will be zero.[7]

In short, the combination of a simple acceleration theory of investment with an unlagged consumption function produces a dynamic model—which has an equilibrium solution; but the equilibrium is a meaningless one, because unattainable; and the dynamic patterns resemble no real-world experience. There is no simple intuitive explanation available why this must be the case. An extremely laborious verbal explanation can be attempted; but it essentially involves translating the algebraic calculations into verbal form—hardly a useful exercise.

Nevertheless, this result does not necessarily mean that the accelerator–multiplier combination has no relevance to the kind of economy we know. For quite different results emerge if we vary the model in other respects, as we begin to do in the section that follows.

The Hansen–Samuelson Model

As a young graduate student at Harvard, Paul Samuelson was stimulated by his teacher Alvin Hansen to work out in rigorous form what has become the best known of the multiplier–accelerator models.[8] We present it briefly before indicating some of its analytical limitations.

As usual we start with a definition of income as

(1a) $$Y_t = C_t + I_t + G_t$$

but this time we use a *lagged* consumption function

(2b) $$C_t = c_0 + c_1 DI_{t-1}$$

along with the same disposable income function

(3a) $$DI_t = d_0 + d_1 Y_t$$

and the investment function

(4a) $$I_t = w + x(C_t - C_{t-1})$$

Note that the period we use in (4a) is clearly defined as having the length of the consumption lag.

---

[7] For example, try $c_1 = 0.5$; $d_1 = 0.1$; $x = 1$.
[8] P. A. Samuelson, "Interaction between the Multiplier Analysis and the Principle of Acceleration," *Review of Economic Statistics*, XXI (May 1939), 75–78 (reprinted in the AEA *Readings in Business Cycle Theory*, pp. 261–69).

Substituting from (2b) into (3a), then into (4a) and into (1a) gives these results:

$$C_t = c_0 + c_1 d_0 + c_1 d_1 Y_{t-1}$$

$$I_t = w + x(c_0 + c_1 d_0 + c_1 d_1 Y_{t-1} - c_0 - c_1 d_0 - c_1 d_1 Y_{t-2})$$

$$= w + x c_1 d_1 Y_{t-1} - x c_1 d_1 Y_{t-2}$$

$$Y_t = c_0 + c_1 d_0 + c_1 d_1 Y_{t-1} + w + x c_1 d_1 Y_{t-1} - x c_1 d_1 Y_{t-2} + G_t$$

$$(9) \quad Y_t = c_1 d_1 (1 + x) Y_{t-1} - x c_1 d_1 Y_{t-2} + c_0 + c_1 d_0 + w + G_t$$

Equation (9) tells us that this period's income depends in a particular way on the incomes of the two previous periods, plus the current level of government expenditures. The equilibrium income level of this model associated with any given values of c_0, c_1, d_0, d_1, w, and x, and any given constant level, G_0, of government expenditures can be found by setting

$$Y_t = Y_{t-1} = Y_{t-2} = Y_E$$

or, substituting into equation (6),

$$Y_E = c_1 d_1 (1 + x) Y_E - x c_1 d_1 Y_E + c_0 + c_1 d_0 + w + G_0$$

or

$$(5) \quad Y_E = \frac{1}{1 - c_1 d_1} (c_0 + c_1 d_0 + w + G_0)$$

This is, of course, again the familiar multiplier formulation (and identical with that for the previous model), in which income equals the expenditures that are independent of income times the multiplier.[9] It should be noted that, once again, the acceleration coefficient, x, drops out of the expression for equilibrium income.

However, the dynamics of the model are now considerably changed. To illustrate, assume

$$c_0 = 0 \qquad\qquad x = 2$$
$$c_1 = 0.75 \qquad\qquad w = 0$$
$$d_0 = 20 \qquad\qquad G = 45$$
$$d_1 = 0.6667$$

[9] However, as in the case of the nonlagged accelerator-multiplier model reviewed earlier (see footnote 5), equation (5) shows that equilibrium is at zero if all of the constants—c_0, d_0, w, and G_0—are at zero. However, once again, equation (9) shows that this model can, with the constants at zero, produce steady growth of Y—in fact two such rates. These rates can be found by solving equation (9), with the last four terms set a zero, for

$$\frac{Y_t}{Y_{t-1}} = \frac{Y_{t-1}}{Y_{t-2}}$$

We compute equilibrium income as

$$Y_E = \frac{1}{1 - 0.5}(60) = 120$$

If G now changes from 45 to 50, regardless of the magnitude of the accelerator, x, the new equilibrium is

$$Y_E = \frac{1}{1 - 0.5}(65) = 130$$

Suppose, however, we start with $Y_{t-2} = 120$ and $Y_{t-1} = 120$ (corresponding to an equilibrium with $G = 45$; then cause G to increase to 50, and trace the movement of income through successive periods. Substituting our assumed numerical values in equation (9) above gives

$$Y_t = 0.5(1 + 2)Y_{t-1} - 2(0.5)Y_{t-2} + 65$$

or

$$Y_t = 1.5Y_{t-1} - Y_{t-2} + 65$$

Substituting 120 for Y_{t-1} and Y_{t-2}, we have

$$Y_t = 180 - 120 + 65 = 125$$
$$Y_{t+1} = 1.5(125) - 120 + 65 = 132.5$$
$$Y_{t+2} = 1.5(132.5) - 125 + 65 = 138.75$$
$$Y_{t+3} = 1.5(138.75) - 132.5 + 65 = 140.625$$
$$Y_{t+4} = 1.5(140.625) - 138.75 + 65 = 137.875$$
$$Y_{t+5} = 1.5(137.875) - 140.625 + 65 = 130.15625$$
$$Y_{t+6} = 1.5(130.15625) - 137.875 + 65 = 122.359375$$
$$Y_{t+7} = 1.5(122.359375) - 130.15625 + 65 = 118.3828125$$
$$Y_{t+8} = 1.5(118.3828125) - 122.359375 + 65 = 120.21484375$$

Continuing to trace out the income movement for successive periods beyond $t + 8$, we would find that income continues to move upward for several more periods, again rising above the new equilibrium; then it reaches a maximum, declines, reaches a minimum, rises, in a never-ending cycle. The amplitude of the fluctuation (which is centered on the new equilibrium level of 130), however, will neither increase nor shrink.

This particular result depends, of course, on our particular selection of values for the several parameters. Specifically, it depends on the absolute and upon the relative magnitudes of c_1d_1 (the marginal propensity to consume times the marginal disposable-income share in Y) and x (the acceleration coefficient). The reader might test this by trying, instead, the following pairs of values: $c_1d_1 = 0.8$, $x = 0.1$; $c_1d_1 = 0.5$, $x = 3$; $c_1d_1 = 0.8$, $x = 4$; and so on. He would find that none of these produces the

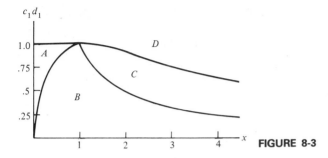

FIGURE 8-3

previous stable cycle! However, trial and error is a rather painful way of discovering the possible solutions of the model. A mathematician can easily solve the generalized equation (9) to determine its stability conditions—that is the possible types of movement and the conditions under which each type occurs. The results for this particular model are summarized in Figure 8-3.

Figure 8-3 shows a variety of possible combinations of values of c_1d_1, measured vertically, and x, measured horizontally. Any point in the quadrant represents some pair of values of the two variables. For any such combination of values that falls in region A, the equilibrium of the model is a stable one, and is approached by a monotonic path, as is shown by line A in Figure 8-4. In region B, the path to equilibrium is that of a damped cycle, as line B in Figure 8-4. In region C, the equilibrium of the model is unstable: if income is at its equilibrium level it will stay there; but if there is a change in any of the determinants of equilibrium (for example, in G, c_0 or w), a cyclical movement will be generated, which, centering on the new equilibrium value, will oscillate around it in ever widening cycles, as in line C. In region D, the movement is simply an explosive one. Also shown in the figure is the path of adjustment if the accelerator is zero—that is, if only the multiplier is operating (through a lagged consumption function).[10] Again we have an example of the principle that a system may have an equilibrium, yet be dynamically unstable, at least for some values of its parameters.

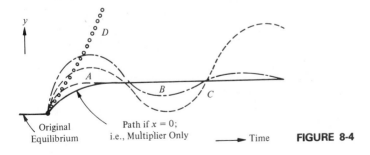

FIGURE 8-4

[10] With $c_1d_1 < 1$.

This model (or a variant) has had great appeal for economists, as offering a simple yet logical explanation of the essential mechanism of the business cycle. Presumably, it is region B that is relevant; for cycles in the real world are not unstable. To be sure, if the values of c_1 and x were such as to lie exactly on the borderline between zones B and C (in Figure 8-3), the cycle would perpetuate itself with neither diminution of its amplitude ("damping"), nor increase ("explosion"). (Our first numerical example used values that lay precisely on this borderline.) But it would be too much of a coincidence for the "real-world" values to be just such as to lie on this borderline. However, it can be shown that if there is an erratic element of disturbance, a damped cycle can be kept oscillating. In fact, in an interesting experiment, using a set of random numbers for his "disturbance," G. H. Fisher showed how this cycle model would produce a synthetic "time series" that looks convincingly like the familiar series used to show the business cycle, and with no apparent tendency for the cycle to die out, even after several hundred successive periods.[11]

Further, Hansen argued that the probable values of c_1 and x were such as to place the economy in region B (although fairly close to the B–C boundary). The marginal propensity to consume, he suggested, was surely not far from 0.5, when adjusted for the leakage into taxes (that is, $c_1 d_1$). The accelerator's value, he argued, must be about 2, perhaps a little less. The total capital stock of a modern industrial economy is close to 3 times its national income. This may suggest an accelerator of 3, too high for stability. However, much of this is truly fixed capital, in the sense that its value is quite independent of current output. What is relevant is the *marginal* capital to output ratio—the added capital necessary to produce an added dollar's worth of output. This might reasonably be expected to be close to $2.

This reasoning is fairly convincing, at first sight. But more careful examination discloses a serious fallacy. When we say that the ratio of capital to output is two (or any other number), we must specify the period over which the rate of output is to be measured. The comparisons Hansen had in mind were between the capital stock and *annual* output. The same data would make the ratio not 2 but 4 if output were expressed in half-yearly rates; or it would be 8 if output were expressed per calendar quarter; 24 if output were expressed in monthly rate. Which manner of expression is called for by the model? The answer is that the way in which the rate of ouptut must be expressed depends on the length of the period of the model. What is the length of the period in this model? It is the length of the consumption lag. This lag is certainly not a year. At most, it might be a calendar quarter. This would convert an accelerator of 2 expressed in terms of annual output into an accelerator for model purposes of 8. But this puts

---

[11] See "Some Comments on Stochastic Macroeconomic Models," *American Economic Review*, XLII (September 1952), 528–39.

us into the unstable region—actually into region D, where there is not even a cycle!

We can reduce this apparent instability somewhat by correcting one feature of the model which reflection shows to be quite implausible. This is the requirement that the investment called for by the accelerator be completed in the same period as that in which the additional consumer goods output occurs which required the investment. Suppose the output is of shirts. If income rises, people buy more shirts. To make more shirts requires more sewing machines. But what our last model required was that, when *this* quarter's demand for shirts turned out to be higher than last quarter's demand, more sewing machines (and more steel, and so on to make sewing machines) had to be made, *this quarter*, in time to be used, *this quarter*, to make the extra shirts. This seems to require an impossible speed of construction and installation of plant and equipment. To get away from this difficulty, some have *lagged* the accelerator effect, making it

$$(4b) \qquad I_t = w + x(C_{t-1} - C_{t-2})$$

This change turns out to reduce the instability of the model, that is, increases the range of levels of $c_1 d_1$ and x consistent with the achievement of an equilibrium position.[12]

However, another modification which many prefer works in the opposite direction—to make the stability requirements more restrictive. This change involves making the accelerator apply to changes in *total output*, not merely in the output of consumer goods. For added output of capital or government goods should, by the same logic, also require added investment (unless we assume that the capital goods industry always has excess capacity). Thus we have:

$$(4c) \qquad I_t = w + x(Y_t - Y_{t-1})$$

or

$$(4d) \qquad I_t = w + x(Y_{t-1} - Y_{t-2})$$

By using various combinations of lags in consumption and investment functions, and different formulations of the change in output to which the accelerator applies, we can construct a variety of models. However, many such models have the property that, if we make realistic assumptions about the duration of lags (hence the probable numerical magnitude of x), and the size of $c_1 d_1$ and x, we seem to get an unstable result.

---

[12] Using this form of the accelerator with an *unlagged consumption function* (as was used in our first experiment with accelerator and multiplier) reproduces exactly the equations of the Hansen–Samuelson model.

Further Modifications of the Acceleration Principle

One trouble probably is that the accelerator relationship is given too fixed and rigid a form. The acceleration principle is usually presented as a technological or engineering relationship: more output requires more machines, and more output is thus impossible until more machines have been produced. The difficulty with this technological formulation is apparent when we consider, as we did a few paragraphs back, the necessity for some lag in the relationship. Without such a lag, the implication is that the customer's order (if it involved *added* business) cannot be filled until the new machines are built, installed and operating.

Actually, the relationship is much looser, and, once its looseness is recognized, we see that it is not strictly a technological relationship at all but a truly economic one. Even if all regular equipment is in use when there is a rise in demand, the rise can still be met, temporarily, by drawing down inventories, by working overtime, by extra shifts, by pressing into service standby equipment. But inventories cannot be drawn down below zero, and production through overtime, extra shifts, or standby equipment is more costly. If the rise in business is expected to endure long enough to make it worth while, new equipment will be ordered. On the other hand, if the rise in business is not expected to be permanent, the added demand will be met in the ways already suggested, or perhaps by raising the price. Only if the rise in demand is considered to be permanent will the pursuit of maximum profit lead the entrepreneur to install the added equipment.

This way of thinking about the accelerator is obviously more realistic, but it also suggests that the value of the accelerator is not necessarily fixed over the period of the business cycle and that its value will be affected by calculations of future profitability extending over the life of the new assets. The strict accelerator theory, in a sense, calls for the entrepreneur to assume, in his calculations, that future demand (in physical terms) is always precisely equal to current demand. Instead, we know that entrepreneurs may expect future levels of demand to differ materially, in either direction, from the current level. Calculations of future profitability might also involve the expectation of a changed relationship between the prices at which future production can be sold, the current prices at which the machines can be bought, and the current interest rates at which their purchase can be financed. In our later discussion of investment theory (Chapter 18), we will find that several of the principal competing investment theories emphasize precisely these elements: expectations of longer-term *future* demand—whether generated by past experience or by foresight; as well as expected future price levels for output in relationship to current prices for capital goods and current interest rates.

However, for the present, we are not ready to introduce these additional variables. Nevertheless, still other modifications of the strict acceleration principle, also in the direction of greater realism, can easily and usefully be made at this point. The first of these is to recognize that there may be limits on the rate of investment—both of positive and of negative investment.

The strict accelerator theory ignores any limit on the rate of production of capital goods. No matter how rapid the increase in the demand for final products, the necessary capital goods can be immediately produced, so that the *desired* or *optimum* stock and the actual stock of capital always coincide, or do so within a single short period. Suppose, instead, that we use the basic idea of the accelerator—that the capital stock depends on output—but only as a *theory of the desired or optimum capital stock*: $K^* = xY$, where K^* is the desired or optimum stock, in contrast with K, the actual stock. We then recognize that whenever the desired stock K^*, exceeds the actual stock, K, investment occurs, but that its rate may be limited by the economy's ability to produce capital goods, which is relatively fixed in the short run. If so, the capital stock grows through positive net investment, but may remain for some time below the desired stock.

And what happens if the desired stock is less than the actual stock—for example, because Y is declining? The simple acceleration theory assumes that net investment will be negative (that is, capital goods wearing out will not be replaced), and that this rate of negative net investment can take on whatever value is necessary to adjust the actual to the desired stock. But this is obviously not true. There is a lower limit of zero on *gross* investment that means a lower limit on negative net investment equal to the rate at which capital goods wear out. If the actual stock is 100 and the desired stock is 80, and depreciation is only 5 per period, net investment cannot exceed a lower limit of -5. Thus, if there is no change in the desired stock, investment will be at a rate of -5 for four periods, until the actual stock shrinks to equal the desired. Thus, there may often be *idle* plant and equipment, which does not disappear simply because it is not used. This factor has the further important consequence that, if, for some reason, demand for products then increases, no new investment may occur, at least until the idle equipment is first brought into use. Thus the accelerator makes no contribution, during such periods, to the growth of demand. We can combine both the upper limit on gross investment (because of capacity limits in the capital goods industry), and the lower limit of zero on gross investment, to produce further interesting variants of accelerator-multiplier interaction. One of these is described in the following section. It can be attributed to economist Richard Goodwin.[13]

---

[13] See *Econometrica*, 19 (1951), 1–17. An essentially similar mechanism, however, appeared in earlier models of M. Kalecki and N. Kaldor.

A Simple Capital Accumulation Model

Suppose we start from a situation of complete equilibrium, in which all firms[14] have just the stock of capital necessary to produce the amount of output currently demanded. Gross investment thus equals depreciation; net investment is zero. The capital goods industry is producing only for replacement purposes, and has idle capacity. Suppose that this equilibrium is disturbed by some increase in the optimum stock (or decrease in the actual stock) of capital. This could result, for example, from even a small increase in *G*. Will equilibrium be restored?

The resulting shortage of capacity will lead to an immediate increase in orders to the capital goods industries and, therefore, to an increase of production by these industries, up to their capacity level. The increased employment and income in these industries leads to a higher level of consumption demand and, thus, to a further increase in the desired stock of capital, intensifying the capital shortage, and prolonging the period of capacity operation in the capital goods industries. Eventually, however, the shortage of capital is made up. At this point desired stock and actual stock are equal. Does this represent the new equilibrium for the economy? Obviously it cannot. For, once the actual stock reaches the desired level, orders for new capital goods must decline to a mere replacement level. This means reduced employment and income in the capital goods industries, and therefore reduced consumption demand. A drop in total demand must therefore necessarily occur once the actual stock of capital has accumulated to its desired level. This drop of demand itself reduces the desired level of the capital stock. Thus, to get *enough* capital goods necessarily means to get *too many*.

Production of capital goods now drops to zero, for not even replacement expenditures will now be made. Consumption, income, and total demand drop further, causing still further shrinkage in the desired stock of capital, thus intensifying and prolonging the redundancy of capital, that can only slowly be worked off through depreciation.

Finally, however, the stock of capital will have shrunk to the point at which, even with low total demand, it is no longer redundant. Normal replacement expenditures are now in order. But this means a rise in income and employment (as operations commence in the capital goods industries), and thus a (multiplied) increase in total demand, and an immediate rise in the desired stock of capital, turning what had been a just adequate capital stock into one that is too small, leading to increased orders for capital goods, further rises in income, total demand, and in the optimum stock, and so on.

Assuming no lags (except the necessary lag in capital accumulation or capital shrinkage), we can represent this model graphically as in Figure 8-5. Here time is measured on the horizontal axis, and, in the three panels,

[14] Except firms in the capital goods industry.

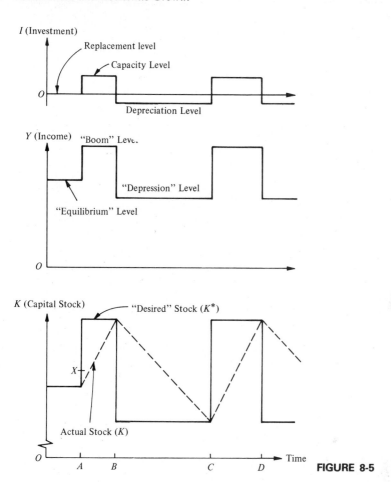

FIGURE 8-5

investment, income, and capital on the vertical axis. We start with a hypothetical period of equilibrium in which the actual and optimum stocks are equal. At time A this condition is disturbed, we assume, by a very slight increase (say to X) in the desired stock. This sets off a boom, as investment, income, and thus the desired stock all rise. The limit of the boom is set by the productive capacity for capital goods. During the boom, while investment continues at the maximum possible level, the actual stock of capital gradually accumulates up to the point of saturation of backlog demands for capital goods (at time B), and thus to the crisis.

The reader can easily discern some violently unreal aspects of the model (for example, the rectangular shape of the cycle; the apparent necessity for depressions to be longer than booms; and so on). He may also be able to see intuitively, however, that introduction of lags—for example, in consumption—could eliminate some of these objectionable features.

Another complication, easily enough introduced, is to allow the capacity of the capital goods industry itself to vary, through investment and disinvestment in this industry.

It is interesting and instructive to contrast the mechanism of the upper turning point of the business cycle in the Goodwin and in the Samuelson models. In the Goodwin model, the turning point comes because, at last, the actual stock of capital has caught up with the desired stock, leading to a drop of investment, income, and thus of the desired stock. This clearly cannot be the problem in the Samuelson accelerator model, for there the desired and actual stocks are always the same because no limit on the production of capital goods is recognized. It is rather that (at least in regions *B* and *C* of Figure 8-3) the *increase* of income and demand must at some point begin to taper off. This means that the *increase* in desired stock begins to taper off, leading to a decline in investment and, with one period lag, in income. Both rest on a similar notion—that of a relationship between output and required or desired capital stock. But they are very different theories.

Simultaneously with Goodwin's work, J. R. Hicks[15] had developed a modified accelerator theory that brought the simple Hansen–Samuelson model much closer toward the Goodwin model. In the first place, Hicks incorporated the same limitation on the operation of the accelerator that Goodwin used (and that many earlier writers on the acceleration principle had noticed but not incorporated into a formal model)—namely, that the accelerator does not operate symmetrically in the upward and downward directions if changes of demand are at all large. That is, if the level of final demand drops so fast that the desired stock of capital declines more rapidly than capital depreciates, then the strict accelerator relationship is upset. Excess capital goods accumulate; then, even if final demand levels off or rises, investment will not occur until the idle machines have first been brought back into use.

Goodwin's theory also had an upper limit on the rate of investment—one set by the productive capacity of the capital goods industry. Hicks did not recognize any such limit on production of capital goods, but he incorporated an upper limit on business cycle booms. Hicks postulated a ceiling on total output, $C + I + G$—a limit set by the size of the total labor force. (It was essentially the concept now ordinarily described as "potential output.") When, through the operation of the accelerator and multiplier, aggregate demand would be generated at a rate beyond the limit of aggregate productive capacity, this limit would in fact prevail. This is not, of course, a specific limit on investment as such, but only on the total of investment *plus other kinds of output*. When consumption and total output are low (for example, early in the recovery phase), investment could occur at whatever rate was called for by the strict operation of the accelerator.

---

[15] *A Contribution to the Theory of the Trade Cycle* (Oxford, 1950).

Hicks' capacity limitation—as a constraint on the accelerator–multiplier process—was more or less simultaneously and independently recognized, in various forms and contexts, by other economists. This recognition points attention toward a new and different set of analytical problems, which we now introduce, in elementary form, in the final section of this chapter.[16]

THE ACCELERATION PRINCIPLE, POTENTIAL OUTPUT, AND ECONOMIC GROWTH

Up to this point, our discussion of the simple Keynesian model incorporating the acceleration theory of investment has been subject to two highly restrictive assumptions: (1) that all output variation occurred in the zone of less than potential output; and (2) that potential output was constant over time—the economy experienced no growth. We are now ready to relax both assumptions.

The Ceiling of Potential Output

The first assumption—that booms do not run into the "ceiling" on total output represented by the concept of potential—is clearly necessary for an *unrestricted* operation of the acceleration principle. To see this, suppose that in the course of an expansion of output and income, involving the interaction of multiplier and accelerator, actual output runs into potential. The very reason for the *high level* of output is the high level of net investment; and the reason for the high net investment is the fact that *output is increasing.* As actual output reaches potential, *aggregate demand* may *still* be increasing but, now, *actual output* can no longer expand (or can do so only at the cost of substantial inflationary pressures). Something has to give. Some attempted or desired expenditures will necessarily be crowded out by others. How this occurs, and to what extent it may be investment or consumption spending that suffers, are matters we are not ready to consider. However, so far as the operation of the acceleration principle is concerned, it makes little difference. The expansion of total output must stop or slow down, and, under the acceleration principle,

[16] Before leaving the subject of simple, unconstrained accelerator–multiplier models, we may note two other modifications sometimes introduced. One is to insert depreciation explicitly into the model—usually making it proportional to the size of the capital stock (which is manageable, though not entirely realistic). A second is to assume that when there is a gap between the actual and desired capital stocks (the latter proportional to output) investment in that period is not *equal* to the amount of the gap but some fixed proportion—less than one—of that amount. This assumption produces what are often called "capital-stock adjustment models." For an excellent illustration both of the incorporation of depreciation as a fraction of the capital stock and of the partial filling of gaps between desired and actual stocks, see W. L. Smith, *Macroeconomics,* (R. D. Irwin, 1970), pp. 182–189.

either a stop or a slowdown means a *decline* in investment demand—which will shortly be followed by a decline in income and consumption—leading to further decline in investment. In other words, when an expansion (involving the accelerator) bumps into the ceiling, it cannot just cling to the ceiling like a gas-filled balloon, instead, it "bounces off." In this case, the upper turning point of the business cycle is not an endogenous one, occurring through the uninhibited interaction of accelerator and multiplier. It is instead one forced by the interaction of capacity limits and the accelerator.

We do not propose to explore extensively the consequences of this for the acceleration principle. However, it can be demonstrated, and probably can even be seen intuitively, that the existence of a "ceiling" on total output, along with the "floor" of zero for gross investment, will convert what would otherwise be an explosive cycle or even an accelerating monotonic movement (because of high values of x and $c_1 d_1$) into a stable "limit cycle": the processes of expansion and contraction are unstable, but the system does not explode. The possibility is not to be exluded, *a priori*, that the real-world business cycles may have essentially this mechanism.

The consequences of the second assumption—that there is no growth of potential output—has another and perhaps even more important consequence for the operation of the acceleration principle. For, whether or not the ceiling is reached during booms, if the ceiling is flat, *average net investment* over any considerable period of time cannot exceed zero. It will be positive when output is rising toward the ceiling; it will be negative when output is falling; and, if the economy were ever in equilibrium at constant income, whether at or below the ceiling, net investment would be zero.

Actually, it is not merely that the acceleration principle could not explain positive net investment (on the average) in a no-growth economy; it is hard to imagine *any* very solid basis for continuing positive net investment in such an economy. With a constant labor force, net investment is not needed to equip added workers with capital goods like those already in use by the existing labor force. In an economy without technological change, no new methods of production are becoming available that increase output by using more capital but less labor per unit of output. Positive net investment in such an economy would have to involve providing the average worker with steadily more capital than he used before, but only in ways that were already known, yet—up to that time—unprofitable to use. Although increased capital per worker might occur in such circumstances, perhaps through a fall in interest rate, the interest rate would have to fall steadily in order to keep net investment prevailingly positive; and there might well be limits both to its fall (it certainly cannot fall below zero!), and to the responsiveness of investment to lower interest rates. (These are matters we will take up later, in Chapter 18.) Here we need only to observe that, in modern real-world economies, interest rates have not fallen secularly but have rather moved in cyclical fashion. A macro model in which the *only source* of net investment is falling interest rates thus has not much relation to the investment we observe.

But once we dispense with the assumption of a no-growth economy, the role of investment immediately becomes very different. There are a number of reasons why it could be prevailingly positive. And, of course, a fairly steady growth of potential output—and a less steady but persistent growth of actual output—are dominant characteristics of modern economies. And so is positive net investment! Theoretical macro models that "simplify" the "real world" by omitting growth, and the changes that account for growth, surely cannot hope to explain investment in a way that is relevant to modern real-world economies.

Growth of potential output, and the changes that account for it, may help to explain positive net investment in a number of ways. But even the simple acceleration principle takes on new and dual significance in a growing economy. First, the additional capital accumulated through prevailingly positive net investment, induced by the accelerator, can itself contribute to the growth of potential output. But second, and perhaps even more important, the acceleration principle is a possible source not only of prevailingly positive investment but also of *growing* investment, the effects of which on aggregate demand can permit the utilization of a growing potential. Indeed, some economists have built exceedingly simple growth models in which the acceleration principle both (a) contributes to growth of potential, and (b) assures the utilization of precisely that growing potential to which it contributed, thereby inducing still further investment and growth. Called Harrod–Domar models, after two of their earliest developers, such simple models attracted considerable interest for a number of years, until the special and very artificial nature of their structure finally became fully apparent. Still, it is worth a brief digression to describe one of this family of models.

The "Harrod–Domar" Model of Balanced Growth

The particular model that follows is a slight variant of one presented by Harrod, himself.[17] It assumes that growth of potential output occurs only through labor force expansion and growth of the capital stock, technology remaining unchanged. Assume, for simplicity, that the technology permits

---

[17] The original Domar and Harrod publications were: E. S. Domar, "Expansion and Employment," and "The Problem of Capital Accumulation," *American Economic Review*, 37 (March 1947), 34–55 and 38 (December 1948), 777–794. These and related essays are republished in Domar's *Essays in the Theory of Economic Growth* (Oxford University Press, 1957). R. F. Harrod "An Essay in Dynamic Theory," *Economic Journal* XLIX (March 1939), 14–33, expanded and revised in *Toward a Dynamic Economics* (Macmillan, 1949), especially pp. 63–100. These original works are reprinted in various collections, and called forth a large literature of comment, criticism, and further development.

no substitution between labor and capital in production: each unit of output requires fixed inputs of labor and capital, and extra units of output thus require increments of both labor and capital in the same proportion as the increment of output. (On the side of capital, this is obviously the assumption that underlies the acceleration principle.) And if we assume the simple unlagged form of the accelerator, the demand for extra output simultaneously generates net investment in the amount necessary to supply the necessary extra capital. We assume further that consumption is proportional to income, with a one period lag, and that the labor force grows at a constant percentage rate.

   Having made these assumptions—and given certain precise numerical relationships among the assumed rate of growth of the labor force, the size of marginal propensity to consume, the size of the acceleration coefficient, and the initial size of both capital stock and labor force—it is possible to portray a self-generating growth process which has extremely desirable properties. With an initial level of output equal to potential output and the recent growth of output at the same rate as the growth of the labor force, and with an initial level of capital equal to that required for the initial output level, smooth growth will occur "along the ceiling." That is, actual output will grow in parallel with potential output, maintaining the initial full employment and generating neither capital shortage nor idle capital.

   Table 8-1 illustrates this process with specific numerical assumptions. The underlying equations are:

(10) $$L_t = 1.05L_{t-1}$$

that is, the labor force grows at a steady 5 percent a year; the definition

(11) $$K_t \equiv K_{t-1} + I_{t-1}$$

where K_t represents the capital stock at the beginning of year t and I_t the

TABLE 8-1
Illustrative "Harrod–Domar" Sequence

(1)	(2)	(3)	(4)	(5)	(6)	(7)	(8)
				Aggregate Demand			
Period	Labor Force (L)	Capital Stock (K)	Actual Output (Y)	Consumption (C)	Investment (I)	Employment (N)	Potential Output (Y_P)
$t-1$			952.38095				
t	500.000	2000.000	1000.000	900.000	100.000	500.000	1000.000
$t+1$	525.000	2100.000	1050.000	945.000	105.000	525.000	1050.000
$t+2$	551.250	2205.000	1102.500	992.250	110.250	551.250	1102.500
$t+3$	578.8125	2315.250	1157.625	1041.8625	115.7625	578.8125	1157.625
$t+4$	607.753	2431.0125	1215.506	1093.956	121.551	607.753	1215.506

investment during the year;

(12) $$Y_{P_t} = \text{(the lower of)} \begin{cases} 2L_t \\ 0.5K_t \end{cases}$$

which makes potential output proportional to whichever factor is in shorter supply given the fixed technology;

(13) $$C_t = 0.945\,Y_{t-1}$$

that is, consumption is proportional to income, with a one-period lag;

(14) $$I_t = 2.1(Y_t - Y_{t-1})$$

that is, investment is determined by an unlagged accelerator mechanism, with an acceleration coefficient of 2.1;

(15) $$N_t = 0.5\,Y_t$$

that is, employment is proportional to current output; and, of course,

(16) $$Y_t = C_t + I_t$$

The reader can ascertain that, for every period shown in Table 8-1, the numbers in each column conform exactly to the above equations. Moreover, he will observe that N is continuously equal to L, and Y to Y_P.[18]

However, before we get too carried away by this result, we need to recognize that it depends on very carefully selected assumptions, both as to the initial situation and as to the coefficients of the structural equations. For example, if the marginal propensity to consume were changed to 0.95, the results of the table are destroyed. To be sure, there exists another set of coefficients in the other equations, another set of initial values, and another steady growth pattern consistent with the higher marginal propensity to consume. However, while the economist can readily assume whatever values he wants, an economy (or its policy-makers) cannot very easily revise its technology, its labor-force growth rate, or its own past history to fit its citizens' consumption behavior.

---

[18] The data in the table would also be consistent with alternative specifications. For example, an unlagged consumption function

(13a) $$C_t = 0.9\,Y_t$$

or a lagged accelerator

(14a) $$I_t = 2.205(Y_{t-1} - Y_{t-2})$$

or an accelerator applicable only to consumer goods demand

(14b) $$I_t = 2.333(C_t - C_{t-1})$$

However, alternative systems using one or more of these substitute equations have the same disabilities as the model shown above.

Moreover, with the model shown above, any minor random fluctuation of any element of aggregate demand would divert the economy from its path of balanced growth, causing output to fall progressively faster below that path, or to bounce against the ceiling and then fall progressively below it. Further, if we complicate the model, for example, by inserting government spending, a constant in the consumption function, or autonomous (as well as induced) investment, balanced growth is impossible *no matter what the history and the structure* (unless each of these further elements happens to grow exogenously at exactly the same rate that the labor force grows). Moreover, there is no model of this kind which can adjust to change in technology, alteration in the rate of labor-force growth, or shifts in structural equations.[19]

In short, it is a mirage to believe that any simple accelerator-multiplier mechanism, which we have seen to be the potential source of such violent instability, can be tamed to produce smooth and steady growth in any real economy.

The preceding difficulties do not mean that stable, balanced growth—with Y and Y_P rising together—is utterly impossible in the "real world," merely that a *simple* accelerator-multiplier process will not produce it except under most exceptional circumstances. More complex accelerator-multiplier models can be developed, which build in a variety of "stabilizers" to dampen the violent instability of the particular model illustrated here. Yet, so long as the model is framed completely in "real" terms—that is, one in which variations in the price level, if they occur, do not affect either consumption or investment, or in which there is no disaggregation of sectors (even if only of consumer goods and capital goods production) whose *relative* price levels can vary, or no interest rate which affects any type of expenditure, or wage rate that can vary relative to prices—the possibilities of *stable* growth, whether balanced or unbalanced, are not very promising. And prices and interest rates would have to be exceedingly flexible to avoid real problems so long as the acceleration principle plays an important role in investment.

To be sure, if government has a fiscal policy which it can use freely, it may, in principle, be able to counterbalance the instability of an economy in which investment depends on some version of the acceleration principle. But it should be evident that an accelerator-multiplier model implies strong forces making for instability. Fiscal policy makers would need to

---

[19] The careful reader may note that the aggregate demand side of this model (equations 13, 14, and 16) is essentially identical with that of the Hansen–Samuelson model (which, however, has no "supply side"). In fact if we substitute equation (14b) from footnote 18, our equations are exactly in the form specified in that model if we assume $c_0 = 0$, $d_0 = 0$, $d_1 = 1$, $w = 0$, and $G = 0$. As was pointed out in footnote 9, the Hansen–Samuelson model (with all these constant terms set at zero) can produce steady growth at a constant rate—indeed, steady growth at *two* constant rates. (Here the second rate of steady growth is at 110 percent a year; not, however, very consistent with a labor force growth of 5 percent a year!)

discern the makings of future instability well in advance, and to adjust forcefully even to temporary and random fluctuations to keep the economy on the growth path.

This is not to say that such steering is impossible, merely that it is very difficult. One reason why it may not be impossible, however, is the fact that, in the real world, the working of the acceleration principle does appear to be heavily dampened by various lags and constraints—some of which have been referred to previously (and others of which will be developed in Chapter 19)—*and* because the price system (including interest rates) does operate to some (uncertain and possibly changing) extent to provide automatic counterbalance against instability. To understand these, we now must begin to introduce additional elements into the Keynesian model, elements that were contained in the pre-Keynesian macroeconomics and were assumed by Keynes' classical predecessors to be capable of maintaining stable, full-employment growth quite without need of fiscal interference.

REVIEW QUESTIONS

1. Inclusion of an endogenous investment function in a simple Keynesian model produces several important changes in the model's implications. Assume that investment depends on income in linear form,

$$I = b_0 + b_1 Y \tag{1}$$

and that

$$C = c_0 + c_1(Y - T) \tag{2}$$

$$T = t_0 + t_1 Y \tag{3}$$

$$Y = C + I + G \tag{4}$$

where all notations are as used in the text.

(a) Explain the theory which might support the equation (1).

(b) Derive the government expenditure multiplier and compare it with that which would have obtained if investment were exogenous.

(c) State the stability condition of the model, and compare it with the one for exogenous investment.

(d) Show the derivation of the balanced budget multiplier. Is it greater than, equal to, or less than 1?

(e) Repeat part (d) with an alternative investment function;

$$I = b_0 + b_1(Y - T)$$

What is an implication of the comparative results obtained for parts (d) and (e)?

(f) What is "paradox of thrift"? Show either algebraically or graphically that equation (1) is indeed the source of the paradox.

2. Another simple theory of investment is the "acceleration principle." Explain carefully the simplest accelerator theory of investment; indicate its principal weaknesses, and how they may be corrected in a more comprehensive theory. (Do not deal with the interaction between the accelerator and the multiplier.)

3. Identify and contrast the upper limits on the rate of investment that are implied in the Hansen–Samuelson model, the Goodwin model, and the Hicks model.

4. "Many investment theories devote most of their attention to explaining the size of the *desired stock of capital*; but this is only a part of the problem for the investment theory."

(a) What factors might determine the size of the desired stock of capital?

(b) What is the other part of the problem?

(c) "The simple accelerator theory makes the rate of investment equal to the difference between the desired and actual stocks." Explain.

(d) "However, this assumption of the simple accelerator theory is quite untenable." List and briefly explain a number of respects in which it is untenable.

(e) Present some theories that possibly relax this assumption.

5. Assume the following model:

$$Y = C + I + G \tag{1}$$

$$Y = W + \Pi \tag{2}$$

$$\Pi = a_0 + a_1 Y \quad (a_0 < 0, \quad a_1 > 0) \tag{3}$$

$$C = W \tag{4}$$

$$I = b_0 + b_1 \Pi \quad (b_0 \geqq 0, \quad 1 > b_1 > 0) \tag{5}$$

$$G = G_0 \tag{6}$$

where

Y = national product = national income

C = consumption (only by wage earners)

I = investment (only by nonwage earners)

Π = nonwage income

W = wage income

G = government purchases

(a) Explain verbally each equation.

(b) Solve the model algebraically for Y.

(c) Compute the government expenditures multiplier.

(d) Assume

$$a_0 = 0 \qquad b_0 = -8 \qquad G = 5$$
$$a_1 = 0.5 \qquad b_1 = 4$$

Solve for all variables.

(e) What is the government expenditures multiplier? (To check, solve again with $G = 6$.)

(f) What is the stability condition for this model?

SELECTED REFERENCES

J. M. Keynes, *The General Theory of Employment, Interest, and Money* (Harcourt, Brace, 1936), Chapters 11 and 12.

(Keynes' famous exposition of the marginal efficiency of capital and the reasons for its instability.)

A. D. Knox, "The Acceleration Principle and the Theory of Investment: A Survey," *Economica*, 19 (August 1952), 269–297, reprinted in E. Shapiro (ed.), *Macroeconomics: Selected Readings*, (Harcourt, Brace and World, 1970), pp. 49–74.
(A review of fifty years analysis of the acceleration principle.)

P. A. Samuelson, "Interaction between the Multiplier Analysis and the Principle of Acceleration," *Review of Economic Statistics*, 21 (May 1939) 75–158, reprinted in J. Lindauer (ed.), *Macroeconomic Readings* (Free Press, 1968), pp. 153–175, and in M. G. Mueller (ed.), *Readings in Macroeconomics* (Holt, Rinehart, and Winston, 2nd ed. 1971), pp. 259–264.
(The introduction of the multiplier-accelerator model.)

R. Goodwin, "The Non-linear Accelerator and the Persistence of Business Cycles," *Econometrica*, 91 (January 1951) pp. 1–17; and J. R. Hicks, *A Contribution to the Theory of the Trade Cycle* (Oxford University Press, 1950).
(Two sophisticated applications of multiplier and accelerator to explain business cycles.)

R. F. Harrod, "An Essay in Dynamic Theory," *Economic Journal*, 49 (March 1939), 14–33; and E. D. Domar, "Capital Expansion, Rate of Growth and Employment," *Econometrica*, 14 (April 1946), 137–147, both reprinted in J. E. Stiglitz and H. Uzawa (eds.), *Readings in the Modern Theory of Economic Growth* (M.I.T. Press, 1969), pp. 14–44.
(The original statements of the Harrod and Domar Models.)

Chapter 9

The Keynesian Theory of Interest

Adding the Consumption Function to the Classical Model
The classical double defense against unemployment remains
If the double defense fails?

An Interest-Elastic Demand for Money
A precautionary demand for money
The speculative demand for money
Speculation and the "liquidity trap"
Other sources of an interest-elastic demand for money: mere uncertainty
An interest-elastic transactions demand

The Interest Rate and the Supply and Demand for Bonds
The effects of monetary and fiscal policies on interest rates

It was remarked earlier that modern macroeconomic theory constitutes a synthesis of Keynesian and classical elements. To this synthesis Keynesian theory brings (a) the distinction between actual and potential output; (b) the aggregate demand approach to the explanation of actual output; together with (c) the consumption function as determinant of the largest element of aggregate demand. In the synthesis, these elements are, in one way or another, married to theories of the interest rate, investment, money, and the determination of wages and prices, partly or largely derived from classical ideas.

Keynes, himself, made just such a synthesis—using many ideas lifted bodily from classical analysis, some in unchanged form, others with substantial alterations. In this Chapter, we discuss one of the classical elements—the theory of interest—that Keynes believed needed crucial revisions before being included in a complete macroeconomic model. We present it more or less as Keynes first developed it, then in a somewhat different, more modern interpretation. In Chapter 10 we shall fit this theory—together with other Keynesian elements—into a modernized *Keynesian* version of the Keynesian-classical synthesis. Chapter 12 will present a more *classical* version of the same synthesis.

First, however, we show that the mere addition of the consumption function, by itself, to the classical model really modifies the nature and conclusions of that model very little.

ADDING THE CONSUMPTION FUNCTION TO THE CLASSICAL MODEL

At the end of Chapter 5, we summarized the classical model in the form of eight simultaneous equations, as follows:

(1) $\qquad Y = F(N) \qquad$ (employment–output relationship)

(2) $\qquad N = N\left(\dfrac{W}{P}\right) \qquad$ (demand for labor function)

(3) $\qquad L = L\left(\dfrac{W}{P}\right) \qquad$ (supply of labor function)

(4) $\qquad N = L \qquad$ (equilibrium in labor market)

(5) $\qquad M = mPY \qquad$ (equilibrium in money market)

(6) $\qquad S = S(i) \qquad$ (saving function)

(7) $\qquad I = I(i) \qquad$ (investment function)

(8) $\qquad S = I \qquad$ (equilibrium in goods market)

We can now add Keynes' consumption function to that equation system, as

(9) $$C = C(Y)$$

specifying that

$$0 < \frac{dC}{dY} < 1.$$

This adds one variable, C, and one equation. It is obvious that equations (1) through (4) still determine Y, and thus, through (9), now determine C, all other variables remaining unaffected. Thus nothing essential is changed by adding the consumption function.

However, this is a bit *too simple*. The classical model, as it stands, already has a hidden (and not very good) theory of the determination of aggregate consumption, namely equation (6):

$$S = S(i)$$

Given Y, determined from equations (1) through (4), and S, determined from equations (6) through (8), the classical model has clearly already determined C; thus, adding equation (9) is either redundant or conflicting. However, we can avoid this difficulty by reformulating (9) and using it to replace equation (6); as

(6a) $$S = S(Y, i)$$

specifying that $0 < \partial S/\partial Y < 1$, and $\partial S/\partial i \geq 0$. In so doing, we add neither a new variable nor another equation. If we take $\partial S/\partial i = 0$, equation (6a) makes saving depend on Y alone—this is the purely Keynesian form; if we take $\partial S/\partial i > 0$, (6a) makes saving depend on both Y and i. Given the Y determined by equations (1) through (4), equation (6a) now operates along with (7) and (8) to determine i, S, and I (and by implication C).

However, the difference made by this inclusion of the consumption function is hardly consequential. The rest of the model requires that equilibrium Y be at Y_P [corresponding to the solutions of equations (1) through (4)]; adding equation (5) still determines the price level. Thus, nothing important has really changed, at least so far as the equilibrium solution of the model is concerned.

Graphically, we can represent the equilibrium model, including the Keynesian saving function, as in Figure 9-1. Here assume $\partial S/\partial i = 0$, both for simplicity and because, even on classical grounds, it is not clear whether the slope of the saving function with respect to the interest rate should be positive or negative. (Moreover, there exists little or no valid empirical support for either positive or negative response of saving to the interest rate.)

Parts a, b, c, and d of Figure 9-1 are exactly the same as for the classical model (see Figure 4-7), but now the determination of saving, investment, and the interest rate have been integrated into the model. Recognizing that all output must be sold, either for consumption or investment, we show this division in the new parts e and f.

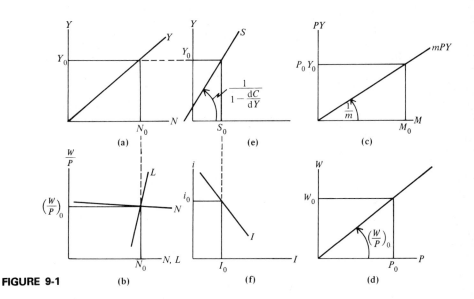

FIGURE 9-1

Part e shows the amount that would be saved (and thereby implicitly the amount consumed) at every level of income. It is simply the Keynesian saving function with vertical and horizontal axes reversed. That part of aggregate production which is not consumed—that is, which is saved—must, in equilibrium, be matched by investment. Part f shows what the interest rate must be to produce the amount of investment needed to offset saving. We can still think of saving as a demand for (new) bonds, and investment as the (new) supply of bonds, and the price of bonds (or the interest rate) as equating them. (If we believe that the amount of saving also depends on the interest rate, this makes only modest changes in the results, but it cannot be shown in two-dimensional graphs.)

The Classical Double Defense Against Unemployment Remains

So long as wages, prices, and interest rates are freely flexible, however, the basic classical conclusions are thus unaltered by inclusion of the Keynesian consumption function. Changes in M alter only wages and prices; changes in the supply of labor or in the production function alter all variables, including, now, interest rates. (This last is the only important substantive change from the classical model.) The reader can easily confirm these results by manipulating the graphs. He can also find the effect of a shift in the investment schedule, which, in the short run, is only to change the interest rate and the division of total output between consumption and investment. For example, an increase in investment demand raises as well the supply of new bonds issued; but since saving—and thus the demand for bonds—is not changed, interest rates must rise until the extra investment is choked off. Similarly, a shift in the saving schedule changes the composition of total output but not its aggregate amount. For instance, an increase in saving (drop in consumption demand) increases the demand for bonds; with no increase in the supply schedule, bond prices rise (interest rates fall), until businesses increase investment by as much as consumption has fallen. So long as the other classical assumptions hold, output is always at the full employment level—*in equilibrium.*

This conclusion is not altered if we make one other change in the classical model—not strictly Keynesian, but not inconsistent with Keynesian ideas—namely, by adding the acceleration principle. Suppose we revise equation (7) as

(7a)
$$I = I(i, \Delta Y)$$

where

$$\frac{\partial I}{\partial i} < 0 \quad \text{and} \quad \frac{\partial I}{\partial \Delta Y} > 0$$

This obviously has no effect on the equilibrium of the model, for, in equilibrium, by definition, $\Delta Y = 0$. At best it could contribute something to the nature of the disequilibrium adjustment of the economy.[1]

The classical model—although expanded to include the Keynesian consumption function and even the accelerator—still has only one equilibrium solution, and that equilibrium is always at full employment. This is the case because it still incorporates two basic forces tending always to move the economy toward full employment. The first "line of defense" against unemployment is the flexible interest rate. The second line of defense comes into play if and only if the first one fails. If, for some reason, the interest rate does not fall, or falls too slowly, or falls not enough, there will indeed be at least a temporary drop in aggregate demand, thereby in the demand for labor, and thereby in employment. However, so long as the money wage is flexible downward, and responds by declining when there is unemployment, a second stimulative force comes into play. With lower wages, prices fall, too; and, with a given stock of money, idle balances will be created. If these idle balances are used to buy additional goods and services (as some quantity theory discussions imply), they directly increase aggregate demand. If the idle balances are instead used to buy bonds, they reduce interest rates, thereby stimulating investment (and possibly consumption). So long as there is any unemployment resulting from an insufficiency of demand, one or both of these defenses will be working to eliminate it.

Thus, it is clear that the addition of the consumption function to the classical model does not, by itself, significantly change the classical results. These results are altered only if one, or both, of the classical defenses against unemployment fail to work—that is, only if there were some reason why the interest rate fails automatically to equate saving and investment at the full employment level of income and/or if there is some reason why wage rates fail to decline to whatever extent is necessary to maintain full employment. The classical economists, however, saw no reason to assume that either defense might fail. Thus, they never asked what might happen if the defenses didn't work, or didn't work at once. But we can.

---

[1] If, however, we should assume steady growth in the labor force and/or a steady trend of technological improvement—permitting steady growth of output—some investment would be continuously generated by some form of the acceleration principle. Models can be developed which rely on the classical defenses of flexible prices and interest rates to maintain continuous full employment of labor (and capital) in the presence of economic growth. Such models, however, embody relationships far more complex than investment and production relationships used in the simple accelerator-multiplier ("Harrod-Domar") models of Chapter 8. For an introduction to such models (usually described as neoclassical growth models), see R. M. Solow, "A Contribution to the Theory of Economic Growth," *Quarterly Journal of Economics* LXX (February, 1950), pp. 65–94; J. Tobin, "A Dynamic Aggregative Model," *Journal of Political Economy* LXIII (April 1955) pp. 103–115; *ibid.*, "Money and Economic Growth," *Econometrica* 33 (Oct. 1965), pp. 671–684. These and related essays are reprinted in J. E. Stiglitz and H. Uzawa, *Readings in the Modern Theory of Economic Growth*, The M.I.T. Press, 1969.

If the Double Defense Fails?

Suppose, for a moment, that one or both of the double defenses should fail, even temporarily. Suppose, in the face of an increased propensity to save, or a drop of investment, interest rates did not decline, or, at least, did not drop by enough to maintain constant consumption plus investment. Then, presumably, production would drop instead, by the amount of the deficiency of demand. This would clearly mean some unemployment. And suppose that wage rates did not immediately fall in response to the unemployment. What would then happen?

Clearly, the multiplier process would immediately begin to work; the initial reduction in employment and income would reduce consumption demand, producing further declines in employment. Suppose that we also admit the acceleration principle into the model. In equilibrium, with Y constant at Y_P, the acceleration principle plays no role; but once Y should start to decline, its decline would then be reinforced by further drops in I—which might be limited only by the lower limit on negative net investment that involves gross investment of zero.

A particularly important short-run application of the acceleration principle relates to investment in inventories. If final demand drops, even temporarily, sellers who seek to maintain stocks of materials and parts, work-in-process, and finished goods more or less proportional to their production and sales, will find that they need smaller inventories. They may seek to reduce inventories by cutting back rates of purchases and production below current rates of production and sales. (This is the one type of net investment which can easily be negative.) But reducing purchases only further reduces the sales of other firms; reducing production reduces employment and incomes of workers (and owners as well), further reducing sales of consumer goods.

This self-feeding process of inventory reduction coud be the more serious if the initial reduction of aggregate demand was unexpected by sellers, and (because of lags in production decisions) had the *initial* result of giving them an unplanned accretion of inventories just at the time when they would in any case have wanted to reduce them. (A downward spiral of production based on efforts to adjust inventories to production and sales is indeed an essential part of every "business-cycle" recession.)

Such a recession might be further extended and prolonged through its effects in exposing (and in creating) positions of strained "liquidity" for some or many businesses that had committed themselves to future payments that they now found difficult or impossible to make, leading to business failures, loss of confidence, and further reductions of consumption and investment. If the liquidity crisis affected banks, as it sometimes does (and often did before the structural and legislative changes of the 1930s) this might also lead to sharp declines in the stock of money, that, in the classical model, would add new pressures of deflation.

Thus, at least in periods of disequilibrium, when the classical correctives failed—or even *if*, and *while*, the classical correctives were working—we find that the classical model, amended by the inclusion of multiplier and acceleration effects, would produce something that looks strangely like the simple Keynesian model, with original small deficiencies of demand producing much larger ones. This means that the strain that would be placed on the automatic stabilizers of the classical model (flexible interest rates and wage rates) would be far greater than might have appeared to the classical economist who thought in terms of minor and temporary rather than *cumulative* departures from equilibrium. Indeed, the stabilizers might for a considerable period prove quite inadequate to restore equilibrium.

However, we shall not pursue the question further. Keynes showed that there were reasons why the defenses would not work as the classical economists assumed, no matter how much time was allowed for them to function. He significantly modified the classical theory of the interest rate to show that it would not automatically fall enough fully to correct a saving-investment gap, and he pointed out that it was empirically incorrect to assume the full and immediate downward flexibility of wage rates in the presence of unemployment. The remainder of this chapter explores the modification Keynes proposed in the classical theory of interest. And the following chapter investigates the consequences both of this modification and of the assumption that wage rates are not fully flexible.

AN INTEREST-ELASTIC DEMAND FOR MONEY

We consider now a major modification that Keynes made in classical analysis—one he considered as important a break with classical ideas as was his aggregate-demand approach to the determination of national product or income and his invention of the consumption function as the explanation for the largest component of aggregate demand. This was his concept of **liquidity preference**—a demand for money that depends, among other things, on the interest rate. Specifically, he argued that the demand for money is inversely related to the interest rate: the higher the interest rate the less the demand.

It should not be difficult to grasp why and how this dependence of the demand for money on the interest rate limits the effectiveness of the classical "first-line defense" against a reduction in aggregate demand. According to classical interest theory, an increase of thriftiness or a decrease in investment would naturally tend to reduce interest rates: the former by increasing the demand for bonds, the latter by reducing their supply. Both clearly tend to raise the price of bonds, which is another way of saying that they tend to reduce the interest rate. In the classical theory, this decline stimulates investment and may reduce saving (that is, increase consumption), thereby offsetting the initial tendency of aggregate demand to decline.

But if Keynes is correct that the demand for money depends, inversely, on the interest rate; any decline in the interest rate increases the public's demand for money. That is, it makes some wealthholders wish to substitute money for their existing or future holdings of bonds. Their sale of bonds already held—or their failure to buy new bonds with their new saving—thus limits the fall in the interest rate, or, in extreme cases might even stop it entirely beyond some point. Thus it emasculates the automatic "first-line defense."

Like Wicksell's theory, Keynes' new approach involved an integration of monetary theory and interest theory. His analysis of the demand for money, although in many respects incomplete, nevertheless went far beyond the classical theory's simple view of money's role in the economy. Keynes, for the first time, looked seriously at the holding of money not merely as a *medium of exchange*, but as an *asset*.

We showed in Chapter 4 that the "quantity theory of money", originally formulated in terms of "velocity," can easily be restated as a theory about the demand for money balances. This theory says that money is demanded for use as a medium of exchange and that the amount of this "transactions demand for money" depends in stable fashion on the money value of output or income. Keynes accepted this as *one* element of his "liquidity preference," but he broke with the quantity theory by arguing that there were at least two other components of the demand for money—a "precautionary demand" and a "speculative demand." Each of these was a demand for money *as an asset*, not as a medium of exchange.

Classical monetary theory had considered the individual essentially as a current "transactor," selling his productive services for intermittent payment in money, then using that money over the period until his next income payment arrived to purchase needed goods and services. This is clearly a valid way of looking at the role of money. But it is also valid, indeed necessary, to consider the individual in his role as current saver, and because he has saved in the past, a *current wealthholder*. If we do, we recognize that one of the things he does with the income that flows into him in intermittent money payments may be to save, that is, to add to his wealth. Now, this does not *necessarily* imply any demand for money as an asset. Because money is barren of yield, whereas securities produce income, classical theory implied that money is universally dominated by securities as a form of wealthholding. If so, the classical quantity theorist can easily take account of saving by noting that—in its role as a medium of exchange—money "mediates" still another kind of transaction. Not only is money used (in place of barter) in the sale and purchase of current productive services from consumers to businesses, in the purchase and sale of intermediate goods among firms in the business sector, and in the purchase and sale of final output, it is also used in the purchase and sale of securities issued by businesses to obtain the money with which to finance their investment purchases. (It is again used as a medium of exchange when securities are later resold among wealthholders, as their preferences among different types of securities may change.) In this way, the demand for money still is a "transactions demand" for a "medium of exchange": at recurrent points in time (the minimum points in the "payment cycle") money balances could still be assumed to be zero for every transactor. It was this assumption that Keynes denied, opening up the fuller consideration of money as an asset—as part of people's wealth.

In Chapter 2, when accounting for the wealth of individuals, we noted that their assets could be classified as (a) *money*; (b) a wide variety of claims or *securities*—representing the financial obligations of businesses, governments, and financial institutions; along with (c) certain stocks of durable *goods*.[2] We noted, however, that the borderline between "money" and "securities" need not always be drawn at the same point. The definition of money includes, almost always, government currency and demand deposits. These are the only forms that are commonly usable as "means of payment," but sometimes the definition is extended further to include certain other kinds of claims against financial intermediaries, such as time and savings accounts, or even savings-and-loan shares. When we restated the quantity theory as the explanation of *why* people hold money, we obviously were talking about money as medium of exchange, that is, as currency and demand deposits only. If that is how money is defined, time deposits, savings and loan shares, and so on, must remain in the category of securities. For now, we shall continue to mean by "money" the narrow definition—currency and demand deposits—often designated as M_1.

When discussing the classical theory of saving and investment, we assumed, for simplicity, that there was only one kind of security ever issued to finance investment, which we called a bond, and that bonds were sold directly by investors to savers. By referring to "demand deposits" as part of the money supply, we did assume, at least tacitly, the existence of one kind of financial intermediary, a commercial bank. Such banks issued claims against themselves in the form of demand deposits (money), which they used to buy those bonds issued by businesses that were not bought directly by savers. For the present, indeed until Chapter 20, we are going to continue the assumption that bonds are the only kind of security, and that commercial banks, with demand deposits only, are the only form of financial intermediary. We thus lump together—and continue to represent by the concept of "bond"—everything from time and savings deposits, savings and loan shares, pension fund claims, through every kind of loan, note, bond, share, even including equity claims. This makes for considerable unreality in our description of the world, but it greatly simplifies our theorizing. When, in Chapters 20 and 21, we consider a model with many

---

[2] Money also appeared, of course, in the balance sheets of businesses of every type.

financial assets, we shall see that the simple one-financial-asset-other-than-money model nevertheless captures many of the main aspects of the roles of money and securities.

We shall also continue to assume, to keep things simple, that all production takes place in business firms. This implies that consumers own no residences or other durable goods: they rent the *services* of houses and other durables from the business sector. In this simplified world, then, consumers' wealth takes the form only of "money" and "bonds."

A Precautionary Demand for Money

The first of Keynes' *additional* sources of "liquidity preference," or demand for money, was a **precautionary demand**. This demand—on the part of an individual or a business—consisted of a cache of money set aside for use in some potential emergency that unexpectedly might deprive him of income, delay its receipt, or impose sudden requirements (or favorable opportunities) for extra purchases. Such a demand for money as an asset could not be satisfied by the holding of securities, presumably for two reasons: first, because, in the feared emergency, securities might lose some appreciable part of their value; and, second, because it would take at least some time to dispose of the securities for money, whatever their price.

The aggregate amount of such a demand for money would obviously depend on the degree of fear or confidence with which businesses and consumers regarded the future. When they lost confidence, their precautionary demand for money might swell considerably; when everything seemed rosy, it would shrink. By generating (in the first case) "hoarding," and (in the second) "dishoarding," a *changing* precautionary demand, he contended, might well deepen recessions and heighten booms. To be sure, the mere *existence* of a precautionary demand was not seen by Keynes as necessarily playing any *systematic* continuing role in determining the level of aggregate demand; it did not ordinarily generate the booms or recessions to which it might often respond. However, an increased or decreased precautionary demand can be brought about not only by changing economic circumstances, such as booms or recessions, but also by news, rumors, or threats that made people and businesses more or less fearful of the future—for example, by news or threats of public disturbance, crop failure, political uncertainties, and so on, or by the disappearance of such threats. In that context, the precautionary demand can be seen as a more important independent source of possible exogenous economic disturbance.

Because some uncertainty *always* exists, the precautionary demand is presumably positive at all times. This means that people will normally hold *minimum* cash balances greater than zero even at the minimum point of each of their payment cycles. For an income recipient with a completely regular series of income payments, with consumption needs spread evenly

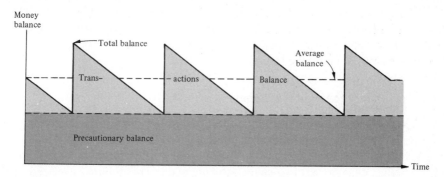

FIGURE 9-2

over time, the pattern of a cash balance that includes a precautionary demand would look like that in Figure 9-2, which can be contrasted with Figure 4-1, in Chapter 4.

If there were only a constant, "normal" degree of uncertainty, the size of the precautionary balance that any consumer or businessman might need would probably depend mainly on the size of his normal income or transactions and would thus be at least roughly proportional to the money value of national product, PY. Thus, the systematic role of precautionary balances in determination of national income would not differ appreciably from that of the transactions demand, and might even be included as a part of that demand for money. As such, it requires no substantive change in classical conclusions. Only as precautionary demands unsystematically changed would they (unsystematically) affect income determination.

However, fuller consideration of the nature of the precautionary demand can lead us to the perception of other sources of an asset demand for money. We noted that a demand for precautionary balances arises when one fears unknown and unexpected developments that might deprive him of income or impose sudden requirements or opportunities to purchase at a time when he fears either (a) that such a circumstance would occur so quickly that he would not have time to find a buyer for his securities or (b) that this circumstance, whatever it was, might also seriously depress security prices.

This calls attention both to two attributes of money as an asset and to two attributes of bonds as an asset: (1) money is completely "liquid," instantaneously available for use, and (2) money's value is fixed and certain (at least in nominal terms). Securities, on the other hand, are (1) not perfectly liquid, they must be sold in order for their value to be usable in purchase of other things, and (2) their value may fluctuate.[3] Both of these attributes of money—the insurance of instantaneous usability, and the

---

[3] These two differences between bonds and money are additional to that difference previously recognized, which was that securities provide a yield, while money is barren.

absence of price fluctuation—have obvious value to individuals or businesses, value that can be derived only from holding money as an asset instead of holding securities. Each of these attributes suggests a further source of demand for money as an asset.

The Speculative Demand for Money

Modern macroeconomics identifies several reasons for an "asset demand" for money, and, what is most important, an asset demand that is interest-elastic. We begin with Keynes' own original version: an asset demand for money that he terms a **speculative demand**. This theory is related to the useful attribute of money just noted that its price is *fixed*, as opposed to the *variability* of the price of securities. We of course continue to represent all securities by a single type—a consol bond.

Since bond prices are subject to change, they may either rise or fall. When they rise, the bond-holder can congratulate himself: in addition to the interest yield he receives from holding the bond (instead of holding money) he also has made a capital gain, which he can realize whenever he sells the bond, now or in the future. Anyone holding money as an asset, however, must view a rise in bond prices (once it has occurred) with some dismay: by holding money he has not merely lost interest, he has missed the opportunity for a capital gain.

On the other hand, bond prices can also fall. If so, the bondholder incurs a capital loss, which he must subtract from his interest return. If the loss should be sufficient to wipe out (or more than wipe out) his interest return, he will be worse off than if he had held money instead. However, just because bond prices have recently fallen is no reason for him now to sell his bond and hold money instead (unless he expects the bond's price to fall again). That would only lose him future interest.

Any money holder who had observed the decline in bond price that was large enough to wipe out the interest return on bonds could, of course, congratulate himself; he may have received no interest, but at least he still has all of the original value of his wealth. That does not, however, give him reason to continue to hold money and lose interest. Unless he expects a *further* fall in the bond price, he may now wish to acquire a bond to hold. Indeed, if he should think that the new, lower bond price is only temporary, by buying a bond he will receive not merely interest but a future capital gain.

Why, then, might one hold money as an asset in place of a bond? Because he feels that current bond prices are "too high" and likely to fall: that is, because he believes the current interest rate is "too low," and likely to rise. Keynes pointed out that an expected rise in the rate of interest by the square of itself will wipe out the expected gain from holding a bond. If the price of a consol paying \$5 a year coupon and now selling for \$100 (that is, with a current yield of 5 percent) should drop in a year to \$95, the capital loss of $5 would wipe out the $5 of interest. (A fall to $95 means a rise in the current interest yield to approximately 5.25 percent—that is, by the square of itself). If the price were expected to fall by more than this, the net advantage would clearly be to sell the bond at the present price, and to hold cash instead. If his expectation proved correct, the seller could purchase that same bond after its price had fallen, at a price at least $5 lower than the price he sold it for, and still receive (after the repurchase) the same stream of coupon payments and right to repayment of principal as before.

Keynes argued that each wealthholder inevitably develops and has at all times some concept of a "normal" or "expected" range of bond price movements. This is not fixed for all time, but neither does it change in the exact proportion that actual bond prices change. Whenever the price reaches his upper limit of safety, he sells out, moving into cash instead. His sale, of course, tends to limit the rise in price (fall in interest rate). And if bond prices nevertheless should continue to rise, more and more bond holders or prospective bondholders would find their limits of a "safe" price reached and exceeded. As each one reached that point, he would retreat to holding money instead. Ultimately, bond prices might approach a level so high that no one would feel safe holding bonds. Despite the positive return on bonds, all would fear that the return would be more than wiped out by a future decline in bond prices. The price could go no higher, interest rates no lower.

Thus, Keynes described a smooth market schedule showing the demand for speculative money balances at various interest rates. It might appear as curve DM_S in part a of Figure 9-3. At some rather high interest rate, I_s, the speculative demand would be zero. But it would become positive, and thereafter increase, as progressively lower interest rates were to prevail. At some low rate, i_t (that is, the highest safe limit of the bond price for anyone), the demand for money would become infinitely elastic (what came to be called the "liquidity trap" case). The curve is shown as concave upward, on the assumption that the distribution of concepts of normal is rather bunched around a prevailing level, few holding extreme views on either side of this range. Clearly, the more alike are the "normal" interest rate concepts of wealthholders, the flatter the curve would be; the more diverse their expectations of future interest rates, the steeper the curve.

We have been describing in these paragraphs the demand for money as an asset—as an alternative to holding bonds. This demand for money is, of course, additional to the "transactions demand for money" (in which we can include the normal precautionary demand). The total demand for money thus has two parts—a transactions demand, which is proportional to the level of money national product (or income), and an "asset" or "speculative" demand, which is a function of the interest rate.

Equilibrium with respect to money holding requires that the *actual* money holdings or cash balances of the public should in the aggregate

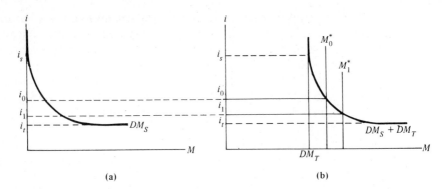

FIGURE 9-3

equal the total of *needed* or *desired* cash balances. When only the transactions demand was considered, equilibrium required a certain level of PY,
money national income or product. That is, the price and output levels had
to be such that people willingly held the entire stock of money. Now we
hypothesize that the demand for money depends both on the level of
money national income and on the level of the interest rate. This means
that the combination of PY and i must be such as to make the public
willing to hold the money stock.

We can begin our further analysis of this matter, so long as we do not
stop there, by assuming the transactions demand as temporarily given, and
consider the interest rate as the variable which equates supply and demand
for money. In part b of Figure 9-3, we represent the total demand for
money $DM_T + DM_S$ as the sum of a transactions demand DM_T, which
depends on PY, and a speculative demand DM_S, which depends on the
interest rate. Given the total supply of money (M_0^*), and given DM_T, there
is only one interest rate (i_0), at which total supply and demand are equal.
Remember that, while the central bank or government can alter the supply
of money, the public cannot. Whether the public desires more or less
money, the actual amount it holds is the amount the central bank and
government have supplied.[4] Every individual can readily acquire more or
less money by selling or buying bonds (or goods) for money. But if one
person thereby acquires more money, another has less.

However, through "open-market operations" (or in other ways that
we shall not now consider) the central bank can quickly and substantially
change the amount of the public's stock of money. Whether it sells or buys
bonds for money, members of the public are persuaded—through the
change in bond prices which the bank's efforts directly produce—to hold

[4] There are some exceptions to this statement—which we will explain in Chapter 21.
However, they are not relevant here. And, in any case, those fluctuations in the supply of
money which respond to changes in the demand for it can ordinarily be offset by the central
bank

the smaller or larger money stock that the bank desires to achieve; thereby, it directly alters the rate of interest. If the bank desires to increase the money stock, by buying bonds, it cannot compel any bond holder to give up bonds and take money in exchange; it can only make someone, previously a bond holder, desire to become a money holder instead. It does this by bidding up the price of bonds in the open market to the point where more and more wealthholders find that, at the new level of bond prices, they now prefer money to bonds.

We illustrate this result in part b of Figure 9-3, where we show a second and larger money stock M_1^*, created by open-market purchases, that has reduced the interest rate from i_0 to i_1, at least on the assumption that the transactions demand remains at DM_T. Thus, we conclude that, given the transactions demand for money, and given people's expectation of the future level of interest rates, the actual interest rate depends on the supply of money in such fashion that the larger the supply of money the lower the interest rate.

We can, however, turn the previous statement around to say that, given the supply of money and given the transactions demand, the interest rate depends on people's expectations of the future level of rates. Thus, if some event or piece of news were to change people's expectation of future interest rates, the rate would change in the same direction and by an amount equal to the characteristic change in expectation.

Suppose, for example, that whatever expectation each wealthholder previously had of future interest rates—on the basis of which he had decided whether to hold bonds or money—each one now believes that future rates will be 1 percentage point higher than he had previously expected. Essentially, this will shift the speculative demand for money schedule vertically upward or downward by the amount of the expected change, as in part a of Figure 9-4. As will be seen, with transactions

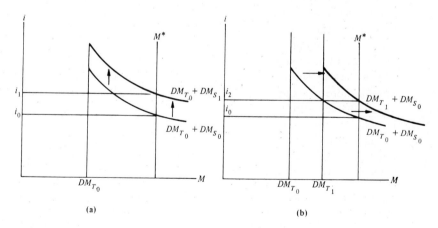

(a)   (b)

FIGURE 9-4

demand and quantity of money both unchanged, a shift of the speculative demand for money schedule from DM_{S_0} to DM_{S_1} raises the interest rate from i_0 to i_1, that is, by the amount of the altered expectation.

In part b of Figure 9-4 there is illustrated the case of a shift in the transactions demand—for example, as the result of an increase either in P or Y, or both. As DM_{T_0} shifts to DM_{T_1}, the total demand for money shifts horizontally from $DM_{T_0} + DM_{S_0}$ to $DM_{T_1} + DM_{S_0}$, raising the interest rate from i_0 to i_2.

In the previous paragraphs, we have considered each of the three elements in the determination of the interest rate on a *ceteris paribus* basis. Obviously, however, this is not a legitimate procedure in analyzing the determination of the interest rate, at least other than in the short run. Because, to whatever extent a change in any one or more of the three elements considered alters the interest rate, if the level of private investment (and perhaps of consumption as well) depends on the interest rate and if, via the multiplier, a change of investment alters Y (or perhaps both Y and P), there will occur further repercussions on the interest rate through an altered transactions demand for money. We will obviously need to take account of this "feedback" in our more complete analysis. For the present, however, we neglect it, in order to permit a further exploration of several other considerations so far skirted.[5]

We can thus summarize our argument and conclusions to this point as follows:

1. At any given point in time, the number of units of each type of financial wealth in the hands of the public (here limited to bonds and money) is given. In equilibrium, members of the public must be satisfied with the composition of their holdings. The equilibrium price of bonds in terms of money (the interest rate) is therefore determined by people's preferences for holding wealth in one form versus the other at various bond-price levels. These preferences reflect the level of transactions in the economy ("transactions demand for money"), and the public's expectations of future bond prices ("speculative demand for money").

2. The equilibrium bond price (interest rate) can be expected to prevail at almost every moment of time because the bond market is one in which current price information is widely available, and any unsatisfied wealthholder can almost immediately trade the one form of wealth for the other.

---

[5] At times, in his *General Theory*, Keynes appeared to assume that a change in the supply of money would have no effect, direct or indirect, on the transactions demand—despite the fact that, in his analysis, a change in i affected I, and, therefore Y and PY. This led to his rather peculiar view of the interest rate as a "purely monetary phenomenon"—the rate of interest depending only on the supply of money and on people's expectations of future rates of interest. Many critics found this a strange doctrine. Actually, Keynes' whole analysis, sympathetically interpreted, does not at all support this view. He did, in fact, take account of the "feedback" referred to.

3. A shift in prevailing expectations about future bond prices will be largely self-fulfilling. This occurs through attempts by wealthholders to alter their portfolios to profit from or to avoid loss from the expected change. In the aggregate they cannot change their portfolios, but their effort to do so can change the price of one part of it in terms of the other.

4. An increase or decrease in the transactions (or precautionary) demand for money (for example, as a result of a changed money value of total output) will, given the supply of money, produce an increase or decrease in interest rates. Thus, for instance, a reduction of output or a deflation of wages and prices in the face of reduced aggregate demand, will lower the interest rate by reducing the transactions demand for money.

5. The central bank—which does have the ability to alter the money stock—by increasing the supply, can lower the interest rates, or, by reducing the supply, can raise them.

Speculation and the "Liquidity Trap"

As we will see in the next section of this chapter, *post*-Keynesian economists have shown that there are other reasons, in addition to interest-rate expectations, why the demand for money should be interest-elastic. These other reasons are, in a sense, more general reasons, which reflect basic properties of money. As a result, Keynes' reason for the interest-elasticity of demand often tends nowadays to be omitted completely or relegated to a historical footnote. The writer happens to diagree with this judgment, believing that speculation indeed may, at least at critical times, be the most important source of some of the macroeconomic and public-policy consequences of this interest-elasticity.

In understanding this point of view, we need, in the first place, to remind ourselves that the slope of the speculative demand for money schedule described by Keynes reflects the extent of *differences* in wealth-holders' expectations of bond prices. If these expectations are highly diverse, the schedule will be very steep; even modest changes in the transactions demand for money or in the stock of money would produce large changes in the rate of interest. If wealthholders' expectations are more similar, the curve will be flatter; in the extreme case, in which all wealthholders have precisely the same interest rate expectation, the curve becomes completely horizontal. No change in the transactions demand or quantity of money could then alter the interest rate at all; it would remain where people expected it to be.

In fact, Keynes postulated, there might well be some interest-rate (bond-price) level at which all wealthholders would have an identical expectation about interest rates, at least in one respect. At a low enough interest rate (high enough level of bond prices), everyone might consider that the interest rate would go no lower (bond prices no higher). The rate could go no lower so long as this expectation remained.

Of course, we do not need to assume that every wealthholder has expectations about future interest rates, other than the expectation that future rates will be whatever they now are or that they are equally likely to rise or to fall. Any one holding the expectation that today's interest rate is the best estimate one can make of future rates should, Keynes assumed, hold bonds rather than money.[6] If all wealthholders held this expectation, none would hold money as an asset, and the speculative demand for money would disappear.

Now we may well ask *why* any wealthholder possesses any expectation other than that the best estimate. of the future rate is the present rate. What, indeed, does determine any wealthholder's interest-rate expectation, and what explains the existence of diverse expectations? Clearly people are not *born* with interest-rate expectations, whether similar or diverse. Rather, any expectations they possess must be the result of their experience and their analysis. People's perceptions of their experience, and of what range of experience is *relevant* to the current situation, clearly may differ considerably. Moreover, even people with the same experience and similar perceptions of that experience may still envisage different *future* developments that might affect future interest rates; they may have different information, or listen to different "experts." Thus, at a time when the market interest rate was 5 percent, some might expect a large rise, others a small increase, and still others no change or a decline.

Nevertheless, there may be some particular very low level of interest rates—high level of bond prices—that almost everyone would judge unsafe or abnormal. Few may ever have observed higher bond prices, and none may see anything in past experience or conceivable future developments that at least in the reasonably near term, would cause bond prices to be even higher. (They might of course still have very different expectations as to the lower bond price level at which it would be safe to hold bonds.) If bond prices ever were to approach the level universally considered unsafe, anyone not already holding only money would stand ready to sell his bonds were the price to move even fractionally higher. This is the "liquidity trap" situation: no increase in the supply of money nor any reduction in the transactions demand for money could further reduce the interest rate.

Now, the existence of price expectations—expectations that may have considerable significance for the determination of actual prices—is not something peculiar to the bond market. Indeed, Keynes was calling attention to a general phenomenon of whose existence and consequences economists have long been aware. In markets for durable, standardized commodities, where stocks are large relative to current new supply and demand, speculation inevitably occurs, and its role is agreed to be highly beneficial in ordinary circumstances. Its role consists of reducing temporary price fluctuations, as speculators buy when prices fall below "nor-

[6] However, see the next section.

mal" and sell when above, thus reducing the amplitude of the price fluctuations which would otherwise occur.

In the wheat market, for instance, the annual supply comes on the market at harvest time, whereas demand—by ultimate consumers—has little, if any, seasonal pattern. But the price does not go nearly to zero right after harvest, which it would have to do in order to increase consumption sufficiently to take all this glut of wheat off the market. Nor does it soar high enough to choke off all demand in the months when no new supply is forthcoming. Rather, seasonal price fluctuations are almost completely smoothed out by speculators, who buy during the crop months, when prices fall below levels expected to prevail later, and use or sell (from inventory) during the remainder of the year, when prices are higher than their normal average. As a result of this action the seasonal pattern of wheat prices is smoothed out, until (ideally) the difference between low and high is little more than the cost of carrying wheat in inventory, including interest.

Speculation in the wheat market not only smooths out prices and consumption over the course of the year but over longer periods too. A bumper crop in one year, due to unusually favorable weather, will lead to some price decline. But speculators, sensing (or guessing) that prices will be higher in subsequent years, buy wheat and thereby prevent as large a price decline as would otherwise have occurred. In the year of a relatively small crop or unusually large consumption, prices rise; but, to the extent that stocks exist, the rise will be moderated by the release of inventories, to get the benefit of the higher-than-normal prices.[7] And, so long as inventories last, prices will not rise above an upper limit beyond which no market participant believes the price can remain. It can go no higher—so long as price expectations are unchanged.

As the wheat example may remind us, however, speculators may sometimes be wrong in their estimates of future prices. They may expect higher (or lower) future prices than can in fact be justified by underlying supply and demand conditions. In response to this expectation, they may hold the present price too high (low), by absorbing wheat into inventories (selling from stocks). Thus, in Figure 9-5, SS and DD may represent the long-run supply and demand conditions for wheat. An average price of P_N would keep production and consumption in balance. Speculators, however, because of mistaken views about either supply or demand (underestimate of future demand, overestimate of future supply), may hold the price in the neighborhood of P_S, standing ready to sell from inventories the current average excess, AB, of consumption over production. So long as the conviction prevails that the long-run normal price is at or below P_S,

---

[7] It is probably unnecessary to remind the reader that the wheat "speculator" ordinarily is a person who also has other interests in the wheat business—a farmer, a dealer, or a flour miller, for instance—who needs to hold inventories of wheat in connection with his other activities but can easily alter the size of his inventories in response to speculative considerations.

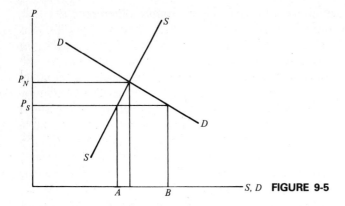

S, D **FIGURE 9-5**

speculators may continue to release inventories, and keep the price below the level which can adjust consumption to production.

Of course, sooner or later, if this view is mistaken, it must eventually be abandoned, and prices will rise. The continued depletion of inventories will sooner or later convince speculators that current prices are too low, and that, instead of selling at such prices, they probably should be buying. Expectations of "normal" prices will be revised to or toward P_N. As they are so revised, the actual price may rise even above P_N for a time, until normal stocks are rebuilt. But in order for anyone to be willing to hold any portion of the wheat that always exists, he must have an expectation that the price is not about to fall substantially.

Mistaken price expectations like those just described do not often arise from a *changed expectation* by speculators as to the normal price level for a commodity. More frequently, it is the normal price that changes, while speculators, not appreciating the extent of the fundamental changes in supply or demand conditions, cling to a now obsolete view of the normal price. Thus they tend to delay the readjustment of price levels, up or down, by selling from or buying for inventory at price levels close to those that have previously been considered normal.

What Keynes asserts is that the bond market is a perfect example of a speculative situation of this kind. The "commodity" involved is highly durable. The existing stock is extremely large relative to the new flows of investment and saving; that is, relative to the new supply and demand for bonds (which, in principle, can be zero). The market is close to a perfect market, in which a definite price always exists and any individual can buy or sell to the limit of his resources without appreciable influence on the price. "Inventories" of existing securities are probably larger relative to the current new supply and demand than is the case for almost any other good, unless it be gold (where the new supply over any short period is a tiny fraction of the stock) or land (where the new supply is zero). Moreover, unlike most commodities, bond prices have had essentially no long-term price trend. Interest rates, abstracting from risk differential, have for several centuries (in the developed world) essentially varied between 2 or 3 percent and 10 to 12 percent. They may occasionally reach one limit or the other but never go beyond. In any given decade, the limit between the highest and lowest conceivable interest rate is far narrower than that. Prices of wheat, soybeans, copper, or nickel in any given year or short period of years may have been kept within relatively narrow limits by stable supply and demand conditions and purchases for or sales from inventories, but the limits of reasonable price expectation have been successively extended (in one or the other direction) over the decades in a way that makes them at any time far less limiting of the range of future price variation than is the case for bond-price expectations.

Of course, at times, people's concepts of the "normal" price level of a commodity, or of bonds, may change discontinuously when new information is received. In the case of bonds, this is often information (including rumors, guesses, or rational analyses) that support the prediction of a changed policy by the central bank. If the public's guesses or analyses regarding the central bank's change of policy are correct, the central bank may need neither to sell nor buy bonds to accomplish its desired change in the interest rate; the shift in the public's demand schedule for money may accomplish the rate change without any help from the central bank.

Thus, speculation, resting on price expectations, may surely play a major role in determining not only commodity prices but bond prices; and, for considerable periods of time, it can significantly limit the fall of interest rates. Keynes called this phenomenon a **speculative demand for money**, which could be infinitely elastic at low—but still well above zero—interest rates.[8]

Other Sources of an Interest-Elastic Demand for Money: Mere Uncertainty

Earlier we referred to three differences between bonds and money as assets: (1) bonds have a yield, whereas money is barren; (2) the value of

---

[8] This very phenomenon of speculation, which Keynes developed to explain the behavior of *nonbank* lenders, actually provides the most cogent rationale for the kind of behavior that Wicksell described for the commercial banks. Why do the banks tend to sell from their portfolios as interest rates start to fall and to buy when they start to rise (thus, in each case, limiting the fall or rise)? Because banks, too, like to avoid capital losses and make capital gains. They, too, have developed concepts of normal rates of interest, and behave rationally in the light of these concepts. Thus Keynes' theory is broad enough to include Wicksell's (although Keynes made no reference to this).

There is, of course, the difference that bank operations involve the creation or destruction of money, those by nonbank lenders its activation or inactivation. The difference is not as great as might appear at first sight, however. In fact, before it became common to count banknotes or bank deposits as "money," changes in their volume were often referred to as causing changes in the effective velocity rather than in the volume of "money" (that is, reserve money, usually gold).

bonds may vary, whereas that of money is stable; and (3) bonds cannot be used as a medium of exchange—they must first be converted to money, which involves time, inconvenience, and cost—whereas money is instantaneously usable. Keynes' "speculative demand" for money takes note of one particular aspect of the variability of price, namely the prospect of capital gain or loss as a function of whether bond prices are considered high or low relative to "normal."

However, James Tobin has expanded and generalized a demand for money that rests on the price variability of bonds, somewhat as follows: Suppose that no individual wealthholder has any reason to assume that the rate of interest is more likely to change in one direction than the other, but many or all recognize that it will probably change. If they hold cash, they can neither benefit nor lose by whatever change may occur in the interest rate. If they hold bonds, they stand either to lose or to gain; that is, they take a risk. Suppose further that the majority of individuals have an aversion to risk: they would rather have $1 "for sure" than a fifty-fifty chance of having either $0.50 or $1.50. The mathematical value of the risky alternative is exactly the same as the "sure thing"; but they prefer the latter to the former. Other things equal, they would always choose the fixed-price asset (money) to the variable-price asset (bonds).

But other things are not equal: holding bonds, whose prices may change, not only involves risk but also involves return. The higher the available return, the more individuals will be willing to assume the risk for the prospect of return, or, for any individual, the higher the return, the larger the percentage of his wealth he is willing to commit in the risky form and the smaller percentage he will prefer to hold in cash. Once again, the demand for cash as an asset—the demand for idle balances—bears an inverse relationship to the rate of interest.[9]

Keynes' speculative demand analysis assumed that every wealthholder, depending on his own particular interest rate expectations, was either a bond holder or a cash holder. There were no "mixed portfolios:" those who felt safe with current bond prices held only bonds, those who felt unsafe at those prices held money instead. Differences among the expectations of individual wealthholders accounted for the nonzero slope of Keynes' money demand schedule. In Tobin's analysis, however, mixed portfolios are easily explained. Uncertainty about the expected interest rate—even if the mean of the distribution of possible future rates is perceived as the same as the current level—will produce mixed portfolios in the presence of risk aversion. And the proportions of bonds and money in these mixed portfolios will vary with the interest rate.

It should be clear that Tobin's analysis, although more general, does not necessarily displace Keynes'. Indeed, Tobin's analysis relies on interest

---

[9] For an elegant demonstration, see James Tobin, "Liquidity Preference as Behavior Towards Risk", *Review of Economic Studies*, 25 (February 1958), 65–86. Reprinted in M. G. Mueller (ed.), *Readings in Macroeconomics*, 2nd ed. (Holt, Rinehart and Winston, 1971) pp. 173–191.

rate expectations: it is merely that he dispenses with any assumption that the mean value of the uncertain rate expectations differs from the current rate.[10] In the more complete analysis of Chapters 20 and 21, we can evaluate Tobin's more general approach.

An Interest-Elastic Transactions Demand

We turn now to the property of money that is usually designated as **liquidity**: the advantage (as contrasted with other forms of wealth) that it is instantaneously useful as a medium of exchange. The advantage consists of avoiding the time and inconvenience—and the transactions costs (for example, brokers' fees)—of frequent conversions of cash into bonds and bonds into cash. However, to the extent that one obtains these advantages by holding cash, he loses the interest he could otherwise obtain by holding bonds. How much it costs him to obtain the liquidity advantages of cash thus depends on the interest rate. The higher the interest rate, the more he may be willing (and the more easily he can afford) to incur the costs and inconvenience of needed conversions between cash and bonds. Thus, the higher the rate of interest, the less the demand for money.

What is really at issue here involves what we have up to now described as the transactions demand for money. We explained that money is held in transactions balances because it is needed to bridge the gap in time between one's intermittent cash receipts and noncoincident cash payments. We assumed that one had no choice about this: how much he needs to hold depends on an institutionally determined time schedule of his income payments or other cash receipts. But if one is paid on the first of January and will not be paid again until February 1, he *could* buy a bond with that part of his income which he does not need to use at once, and collect interest for a few days before selling it to enable him to pay the rest of his monthly expenses. For example, he might buy a bond on payday with half of his income, selling it on the fifteenth to obtain the funds to use for the rest of the month. That way, he could receive 15 days' interest on half of his monthly income; on the other hand, there would be some inconvenience and two brokers' charges to pay. If the interest rate were high enough and brokers' fees not too expensive, it might be profitable.

If his income were large enough or the interest rate high enough, it might even pay him to buy a bond with all of his income that he doesn't plan to spend until the third of January or after; then, on the morning of the third, sell that bond, hold back what money he needs to use on the third and fourth, and buy a smaller denomination bond with the rest; and repeat that transaction 14 more times during the month. That way, he would receive 14 days' worth of interest on his total monthly income each

---

[10] The final paragraph of Tobin's classic paper makes clear his own view that, at least at times, wealthholders' expectations are definitely not neutral.

month—less brokerage charges on 15 purchases and 15 sales. (He gets interest on $\frac{1}{15}$ of his monthly income for 2 days, on $\frac{1}{15}$ of his income for 4 days, on $\frac{1}{15}$ for 6 days, and so on, which adds to 14 days' interest on his monthly income. From this, brokerage—and the costs of associated inconvenience—would be subtracted.) Of course, if his income were small and brokerage expensive, this might not pay at any interest rate. However, given his income, the higher the rate of interest the larger the number of conversions it would pay to make: the less his demand for money.[11]

If one's income and expenditures were $1 million a month, he might easily find that it paid to buy or sell bonds every day! The loss of interest for even one day on all or a fraction of one million dollars could make 30 or more asset transformations a month quite worthwhile. But given one's income, how frequently it is worthwhile to incur the costs and inconvenience of asset conversions clearly depends on the level of the interest rate. The same considerations apply, of course, to businesses as well as individuals. The higher the interest rate, the more assiduously the corporate treasurer attempts to minimize the firm's cash balances by seeing that funds not immediately needed are "invested" at interest in short term securities. Thus, the transactions demand for money depends not only on the level of income, but also on the interest rate; the transactions demand for money is interest-elastic! This further reason for an interest-elastic demand for money was first set forth by economist William Baumol.[12]

We have now introduced two additional reasons for an interest-elastic demand for money, which can be added to Keynes' original speculative demand. As noted earlier, some economists indeed prefer to *substitute* one or both of these in place of Keynes' version. One can do so and still leave most of the analysis that follows at least formally unchanged. This writer prefers to retain the Keynesian version, along with the others, for two reasons.

First, because nothing like the "liquidity trap" case (at least at an interest rate *above zero*) can be derived from either the Baumol or Tobin reasons for an interest-elastic demand for money. As will be seen below, the writer is not prepared to deny the existence of at least temporary liquidity traps and their possible occasional relevance. Second, because

---

[11] In the real world, of course, one does not need to buy and sell bonds: one can simply deposit excess funds in a savings account, withdrawing as needed, with no brokerage fees, but only the inconvenience of frequent trips to the bank. The higher the rate paid on savings deposits, the more it pays to keep one's checking account as small as possible and his savings account as large as possible. However, we are still trying to describe a world with only one kind of security—a consol bond.

[12] For an elegant and convincing mathematical demonstration see W. J. Baumol, "The Transactions Demand for Cash: An Inventory Theoretic Approach," *Quarterly Journal of Economics*, November, 1952; reprinted in Edward Shapiro, *Macroeconomics: Selected Readings* (Harcourt, Brace and World, 1970) pp. 172–183; and/or James Tobin, "The Interest-Elasticity of the Transactions Demand for Cash," *Review of Economics and Statistics*, 38 (August, 1956), pp. 241–247.

omission of the speculative element has the consequence that we must picture the liquidity preference schedule as a stable schedule, the level of which changes only very slowly over time. For its slope and level depend, in this view, only upon relatively stable characteristics of economic structure (for example, the size distribution of individual wealthholdings and the costs of buying and selling securities), or of basic attitudes (for example, the degree of aversion to risk).

Keynes' speculative demand requires no such stability of the schedule. If the rate of interest has commonly been in the 8 to 15 percent range, the level of the demand-for-money schedule will reflect this; if it has commonly varied in the 1.5 to 5 per cent range, its level will be much lower because wealthholders will have very different expectations as to its probable future range of variation. Yet the shape and elasticity of the schedule may be very much the same in either case. If past variation has been in the 8 to 15 percent range, it is very unlikely that the rate can, in the short run, be moved outside of these limits because the expectations of the speculators will lead them to act in a way that will hold it in this range. The schedule might become almost infinitely elastic at 8 percent. But in the other case, it might become highly elastic only at a level of 1.5 percent.

Keynes' view as to the significance of speculation does not rest upon the previous existence of any particular range of interest rates. His point is, simply, that, *at any given time*, wealthholders will have, quite reasonably, formed certain expectations as to rates of interest likely to prevail in the near future. These expectations alone are enough to prevent the rate of interest from operating in the way classical economics assumed; that is, they prevent it from in the first instance automatically adjusting to stabilize the aggregate demand for goods. If the interest rate varied automatically and freely to equate saving and investment, shifts in saving or investment schedules could have no effect other than to change the rate of interest and the division of a given total output between investment and consumption. But, as we will see, if the adjustment of the rate of interest is limited by speculation, the impact of shifts in saving or investment schedules will be on the aggregate demand for goods, leading, if wages and prices are flexible, to inflation or deflation or, if they are rigid, to an increase or decrease in output and employment.

THE INTEREST RATE AND THE SUPPLY OF AND DEMAND FOR BONDS

Keynes' interest rate theory—as now modified or expanded by subsequent contributions—has thus far been described in terms of the supply and demand for money. Nevertheless, it may seem plausible that this theory should somehow involve the supply and demand for bonds as well. Given our simple assumptions, individuals hold wealth only in the form of bonds and/or money. For there to be equilibrium in the community's asset holdings, each wealthholder must be satisfied not merely with the amount of *money* he holds but with his entire portfolio of assets—the particular combination of amounts that he holds of bonds and/or money. We have noted that any wealthholder who is not satisfied can always immediately trade some of his bonds for money (or vice versa) with some other wealthholder who wants to make the reverse trade. Such trades are constantly occurring, at a market price for bonds (an interest rate) that is independent of the amount that any individual may wish to trade. And, since the bond market is close to a perfect market with continuous trading and full and immediate price information avilable to all participants, it can be assumed that the market is almost always in equilibrium: individuals hold what they want to hold at the price that prevails—both the quantity of money they want *and the amount of bonds they want*.

Although any individual can always change the composition of his portfolio by selling or buying bonds for money, it is, of course, not possible for wealthholders as a group to change the composition of their holdings. At any given time, not merely is the total stock of money fixed but so is the number and coupon value of the bonds the public owns. Thus, any alteration in the public's preference for bonds versus money—that is, any net desire of the public to change the composition of its wealthholdings—will not (in the short run) change the aggregate quantity of either one. It will, however, immediately change the price of bonds in terms of money, the reciprocal of which is the interest rate. Can we not thus equally well describe the interest rate as determined by the supply and the demand for bonds?

We earlier described the speculative demand for money as an asset, as a desire *not* to hold bonds because of the fear that bond prices might fall (to which we can now add the other reasons suggested in the previous section). The desire *not* to hold money as an asset is, equally, a desire to hold bonds. Thus, corresponding to the interest-elastic demand for money in part a of Figure 9-6, we can describe in part b a corresponding implied demand for bonds, labelled *DB*. This demand would be zero at interest rates below i_t, increasingly positive as interest rates rose above i_t, reaching its maximum at interest rate i_s.

The demand for money *DM* is of course measured, in part a (along the horizontal axis) in units of money, for example, dollars; but how do we measure the demand for bonds? If all bonds were identical in principal and coupon, the amount of the demand for them could be measured simply by their number. If they are not identical, a better measure is the aggregate dollar amount of the annual coupons on the bonds held. For simplicity, we shall assume that all bonds are identical and that we can measure the demand for them in part b of Figure 9-6 by their number.

Earlier, we used Figure 9-3 to describe the determination of the interest rate by the intersection of a total demand for money schedule

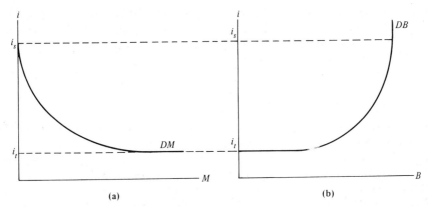

FIGURE 9-6

$(DM_T + DM_S)$ and the supply of money (M_0^*). At the equilibrium interest rate so determined, people wanted to hold—either for transactions (including precautionary) purposes or for speculative purposes—exactly the amount of money that they were in fact holding. Equilibrium would similarly seem to require that the number of bonds people are holding—that is, the total number that exists—exactly matches the number which they desire to hold.

In Figure 9-7, we show, in part a, equilibrium in money holding at interest rate i_0. This reproduces exactly part b of Figure 9-3. However, this equilibrium seems to imply that, in part b of Figure 9-7, where we show the implied demand for bonds (DB), there exists some particular stock of bonds (B_0) that people are holding and is exactly the number of bonds *that they desire to hold.*

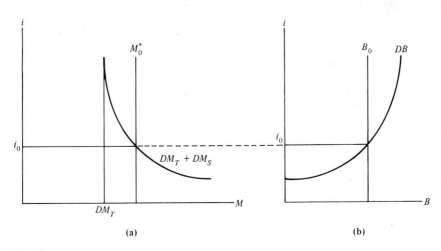

FIGURE 9-7

In fact, it is easy to show that B_0 must be the number of bonds that exist, and thus the number that people are actually holding. We may define the community's total wealth at some particular time as

$$(10) \qquad W \equiv M_0^* + \frac{Q_0}{i} B_0$$

where Q_0 is the coupon per bond, i the rate of interest, and B_0 the number of bonds outstanding. It is clear that Q_0/i is the price per bond, and thus that $Q_0/i \times B_0$ represents the total money value of bonds.

We earlier described the determination of the interest rate in terms of equality between the supply and demand for money:

$$M_0^* = DM_T + DM_S$$

where DM_T was proportional to PY, and DM_S depended (nonlinearly) on the interest rate i. However, once we admit that the transactions demand also depends on the interest rate, we should abandon the distinction between the two demands, and write the total demand for money

$$(11) \qquad DM = mPY + f(i)$$

where mPY represents the (linear) dependence of the total demand on the money value of national product, and $f(i)$ represents the interest-elastic portion of that total demand. We assume that

$$\partial DM/\partial i \equiv f_i < 0$$

$$\frac{\partial^2 DM}{\partial i^2} \equiv f_{ii} > 0$$

We can now describe a demand for bonds DB that is the *nondemand* for money. That is, the demand for bonds is represented by that part of total wealth which people do not wish to hold in money form:

$$(12) \qquad DB = W - mPY - f(i)$$

Note that DB is here expressed in money terms, as the *value* of total bonds demanded. We can set this demand for bonds equal to the supply of bonds, as the condition for equilibrium in bondholding. However, since B_0 represented the supply of bonds *in number*, we must multiply it by the price per bond in order to get the desired money value of bonds:

$$(13) \qquad B_0 \frac{Q_0}{i} = W - mPY - f(i)$$

We can easily show that this condition for equilibrium is identical to that previously derived. Substituting from (10), the definition of wealth into (13), we have

$$B_0 \frac{Q_0}{i} = M_0^* + \frac{Q_0}{i} B_0 - mPY - f(i)$$

Clearly, the terms in B_0 cancel out, leaving the familiar

$$(14) \qquad\qquad M_0^* = mPY + f(i)$$

Thus, we can describe the determination of the interest rate either in terms of the supply and demand for money, as we earlier did, or alternatively in terms of the supply and demand for bonds. But either approach implies exactly the same equilibrium rate. That is, if the interest rate is such that the supply and demand for money are in equilibrium, it is necessarily true that, at that same interest rate, the demand for bonds will also equal the supply of bonds. The one equality is merely a trivial arrangement of the other.[13] Moreover, *it appears that the stock of bonds can be neglected in the determination of the interest rate.*

However, the last sentence is too simple a conclusion; indeed, it is probably incorrect. For what we assumed was that the demand for money (and thus by implication the demand for bonds) was dependent only on i and PY and was independent of the value of total wealth. This might be all right if the total stock of wealth could be counted on as constant—in value terms, as well as in numbers of each asset. But once we admit changes in interest rates (that is, bond prices), which is what the analysis is all about, the *value* of this constant stock will also change. Moreover, of course, over time, total wealth may change *both* in physical and in value terms, as the result of a positive value for net investment plus government deficit. Further, its composition is changed through the operation of monetary policy.

We have assumed, so far, that the demand for bonds equalled the value of total wealth less the demand for money, *which in turn was independent of the value of total wealth*. This implies that, whenever any increase (decrease) occurs in the value of total wealth, wealthholders will (*ceteris paribus*) want to hold the entire additional value exclusively in bonds. There is probably no more reason to assume this than there would be to assume the reverse—that the entire amount of any increase in the value of wealth would be desired to be held in money form.

Once we begin to think of money as a kind of financial *asset* (along with bonds), it seems clear that we must consider the possibility, indeed the plausibility, that the demand for each type of asset also depends on the total value of wealth available to be held in one or the other form.

We may, for instance, assume that the demand for money depends not only on the money value of the national product and the interest rate but

---

[13] Students of economic theory will recognize this as simply an application of "Walras' Law," although (the author would assert) a more legitimate one than the usual statements that involve the demand for goods, the demand for money, and the demand for bonds, and point out that any two of them imply the third. (Such statements usually fail to deal adequately with the fact that "goods" need to be treated as a flow variable, not a stock, as are bonds and money.)

also, linearly, on the value of total wealth. That is,

(11a) $$DM = mPY + f(i) + \alpha W \qquad 0 < \alpha < 1.$$

where α is the fraction of any increment of wealth which would be preferred to be held in money form if both PY and i were constant. As before,

(10) $$W = M_0^* + B_0 \frac{Q_0}{i}$$

If we use the equality of demand and supply for *money* as the condition for equilibrium,

$$M_0^* = DM$$

we derive

(15) $$M_0^* = \frac{mPY + f(i) + \alpha B_0(Q_0/i)}{1 - \alpha}$$

We can think of the right side of equation (15) as representing an **adjusted demand schedule for money** which takes account of the number and the coupon value of the bonds outstanding. If, given M_0^* and PY, we attempt to solve this equation for i, we will find that i depends also on B_0 and Q_0: the number of bonds and the coupon value per bond. That is, the interest rate does depend *both* on the stock of money *and* on the stock of bonds.[14] And, *ceteris paribus*, the larger the stock of bonds, the higher the interest rate. Similarly, the larger the stock of money, the lower the interest rate.

The Effects of Monetary and Fiscal Policies on Interest Rates

Very important differences exist, especially in the longer run, between the effects of monetary and fiscal policies on wealth, and on interest rates. Monetary policy does not directly change aggregate wealth, but merely alters its composition. To be sure, the altered composition does affect interest rates and thereby indirectly changes the value of the bond portion of wealth. Fiscal policy, on the other hand, directly alters total wealth, by adding to (or reducing) the public's stock of one asset, without reducing (adding to) the stock of the other. Because this also changes the relative composition of wealth, it, too, will alter interest rates, and the value of the bond portion of total wealth. To the extent that the change of interest rates from *either* policy affects investment and therefore income, there will be still further feedbacks on interest rates which need to be taken into account.

---

[14] It remains true (by Walras' Law) that, if we specify the equality of supply and demand for *bonds* (rather than money) as the condition for equilibrium, we derive exactly the same expression as (15). Rearranging (15) in terms of supply and demand for bonds, we have

(15') $$B_0 = \frac{(1 - \alpha)M_0^* - mPY - f(i)}{\alpha(Q_0/i)}$$

Analyzing all of these effects is fairly complex, but the following paragraphs attempt to sort them out.

Monetary Policy. Earlier, we analyzed the effects of changes in the supply of money on interest rates, but that was before we had recognized that the stock of bonds (their number and aggregate coupon value) also affects the outcome. Although the differences will turn out to be modest, we can now repeat the analysis of money supply changes, taking into account our latest findings. Once again we assume that monetary policy is conducted entirely through open market operations. As noted earlier, such operations consist of a substitution, in the aggregate portfolio of the public, of bonds for money or money for bonds. The effects of this substitution on interest rates can be alternatively described in terms of an increase (decrease) in the supply of money, with a given demand schedule for money; in terms of a decrease (increase) in the supply of bonds, with a given demand schedule for bonds; or (perhaps best) in terms of an imposed substitution of bonds for money in the face of given schedules of preferences on the part of the public for holding wealth in one form or the other.

The very process by which this substitution is accomplished of course affects bond prices, that is, interest rates. Since it is a voluntary swap, the way in which the bank gets (say) more bonds into the public's portfolio (and money out of it) is by forcing down the price of bonds through its sales, thus inducing some persons who previously were money holders to decide that, at lower bond prices, they now prefer bonds to money (or now prefer to hold a larger portion of their wealth in bonds).

Now in each such sale (or purchase), the values exchanged are identical: each sale of $100 of bonds reduces someone's wealth by $100 in the form of money balanced by an increment of his wealth in the form of bonds also worth $100. Thus, open market operations, per se, do not directly alter the public's total wealth.[15] Nevertheless, the change in interest rates which is necessary to induce the public to accept a different composition of its wealth between bonds and money also changes the value of each bond in the public's portfolio. Thus, it is not only the composition of wealth that changes but, as well, the total money value of the public's wealth. In the case of a sale of bonds by the bank, wealth declines, for the value of the bonds already in the hands of the public is now reduced by the rise in interest rate. This reduction in wealth reduces (*ceteris paribus*) both the

---

[15] The reader who has been introduced to the process of "multiple" deposit creation based on central bank open-market purchases will object that (in a fractional reserve banking system) the quantity of money will increase by several times the amount of the initial purchase, as the proceeds of that purchase add to bank reserves, and thus permit an expansion in commercial bank lending. And that is correct. However, in terms of the resulting addition to the wealth of the nonbank public, the statement in the text is exactly correct. Until we return to this subject in Chapters 20 and 21, one who is puzzled by this apparent contradiction can pretend that we are discussing a banking system subject to a 100 percent reserve requirement.

demand for money and that for bonds—the former in the proportion α, the latter in the proportion $(1 - \alpha)$. This adds to the necessary fall in the price of bonds because the *supply* of bonds in the hands of the public is increased at the same time that the *demand* for them is decreased.

Of course, to the extent that the resulting lower bond prices (higher interest rates) depress investment, lowering income and the (transactions) demand for money, this will constitute a partial offset to the effect of the increase in supply and reduction in demand for bonds.

We can present these results graphically, as in Figure 9-8. Here, the demand for money schedule, *DM* of part a, is the **adjusted demand schedule** which takes account of the number of bonds. (This appears on the right side of equation (15)). Similarly, in part b, the demand for bonds schedule, *DB*, is the adjusted schedule shown in footnote 14, which takes account of the quantity of money. The initial interest rate i_0 is obtained in either part of the figure by the intersection of the initial supply and demand schedules, $DM(B = B_0)$ and M_0^*, and $DB(M = M_0^*)$ and B_0.

We now consider the effects of an open market operation which involves the sale of bonds to the public. This increases the supply of bonds from B_0 to B_1 while reducing the supply of money from M_0^* to M_1^*. The initial (solid line) demand schedules, $DM(B = B_0)$ and $DB(M^* = M_0^*)$ assumed the initial composition of wealth. The broken schedules, however, assume the new composition of wealth, M_1^* and B_1. As the supply of money schedule moves to the left (decreases), the demand schedule for money moves to the right by the amount (see equation 15):

$$\frac{\alpha(Q/i)}{1 - \alpha} \Delta B$$

This raises the interest rate from i_0 to i_1. The same facts are shown in part b. Here, as the supply of bonds schedule moves to the right, the demand for bonds schedule moves to the left (to reflect the decreased supply of money),

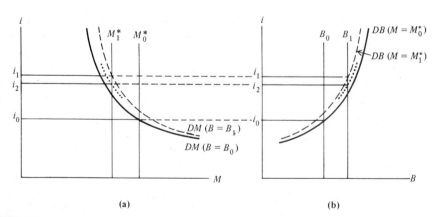

(a)   (b)

FIGURE 9-8

by the amount (see equation 15', footnote 14)

$$\frac{1-\alpha}{\alpha(Q_0/i)}\Delta M^*$$

The interest rate is thereby raised from i_0 to i_1 (at least before taking account of any feedback on investment). If and to the extent that an interest rate higher than i_0 reduces investment, and thus Y, the adjusted *DM* schedule moves to the left, and the adjusted *DB* schedule to the right (as shown by the dotted lines), with the final equilibrium at the intermediate interest rate i_2. Here, the *slopes* of *DM* and *DB* schedules depend on the interest elasticity of the two demands, reflecting (1) the $f(i)$ function; and (2) the effects on the demand for each of the changed value of wealth which is associated with each interest rate. The position of each schedule, however, reflects the amount of the supply of the other asset, and the level of money income *PY*.

The reader can easily repeat the analysis for the case of open market operations that *increase* the supply of money, and should do so to make sure that he understands it.

Fiscal Policy. The effects of fiscal policy on the interest rate can be analyzed in a similar way. For convenience, we assume that the government's budget had previously been exactly balanced; but a stimulative fiscal policy is now introduced, creating a budgetary deficit (for example, through an increase of expenditures without change in tax rates, a reduction in tax rates without change in expenditures, or any other combination which lowers revenues relative to expenditures). Assume, in the first instance, that this deficit is financed entirely through the sale by the government in the open market of newly printed bonds. (We shall then consider alternative means of financing it.)

However this deficit is financed, its existence leads directly to an increase in wealth. The mere sale of the new bonds by the government does not, of course, itself increase wealth, for it essentially involves a swap of money for bonds, in which the values exchanged are equal. (To the extent that bond prices are bid down in the process, wealth will actually decline.) But the money received by the government is in turn used to finance a deficit—either taxpayers pay less than otherwise or sellers of goods or services to the government receive more, or both; the money borrowed thus returns to the public's hands. When the transaction is concluded, the public has the same stock of money as before, but it has more bonds than before; its wealth has increased, all in the form of bonds.[16]

---

[16] The only exception to this statement would be if the deficit were used to purchase existing inventories from the private sector, producing a matching disinvestment in inventories, thus reducing wealth. However, on the assumption that the sellers had some reason for holding those inventories, they will now set out to replace them, at which point wealth will have risen. If the deficit is used to hire extra workers or to make transfer payments, the rise in wealth is immediate.

The fiscal policy obviously also has the effect of raising income, output, and perhaps prices, thus increasing the (transactions) demand for money. Given no change in the supply of money, interest rates should therefore rise for this reason alone. By affecting investment adversely, this rise of i provides a partial offset to the fiscal stimulus (this is the "crowding out" effect to be considered more fully in Chapter 11). Most analyses simply stop with this. But this is not the full effect of fiscal policy on the interest rate.

To see that a stimulative fiscal policy will raise interest rates by more than merely the effect of the increased transactions demand—let us assume that the central bank automatically increases the supply of money (buying bonds) by exactly the amount of any increased transactions demand for money. If the increased transactions demand were the only reason for a rise in interest rates, this should take care of it. But it does not.

To see this, consider Figure 9-9. In part a, M_0^* is the supply of money, as already increased to supply the extra transactions balances, and $DM(W = W_0)$ is the initial demand for money, increased to include the extra transactions demand. In part b, B_0 is the public's initial supply of bonds as reduced by the central bank's purchases made to supply the extra transactions demand for money; but it does not include the new bonds sold to finance the deficit; and $DB(W = W_0)$ is the demand for bonds before taking account of the extra wealth which accrues from the deficit.

B_1 in part b, however, includes the new bonds sold to finance the deficit. And $DB'(W = W_1 > W_0)$ is the demand for bonds, reflecting the increased wealth created by the deficit finance. The value of this increase in wealth equals B_1 minus B_0 valued at interest rate i_0, *minus* the effect of higher interest rates in reducing the value of the bonds already in the public's hands.

This higher value of wealth increases the demands both for bonds and for money. However, the shift in the demand for bonds (part b) is neces-

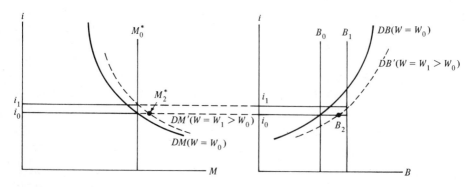

FIGURE 9-9

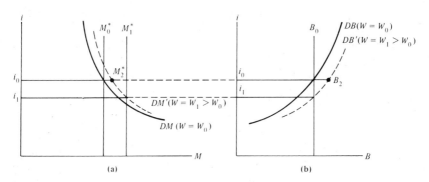

FIGURE 9-10

sarily less than the increase in the supply, because the public wishes to hold some fraction α of its extra wealth in the form of money. Thus, the interest rate rises (bond prices fall) from i_0 to i_1. Showing the same phenomenon in part a, the new demand for money, DM' ($W = W_1 > W_0$), lies to the right of the previous demand schedule, and, with no further increase in supply of money, can only be satisfied at the same higher interest rate i_1.

It is clear that this effect on interest rates is *additive* to the effect of the increased transactions demand resulting from the stimulative fiscal policy. *If* it were desired to keep the interest rate from rising, as a result of the fact that the public is provided more additional bonds than the additional amount it wishes to hold at the old interest rate, further open market purchases of bonds by the central bank would be needed, raising the supply of money from M_0^* to M_2^*, and thereby reducing the supply of bonds from B_1 to B_2.

It will be useful to contrast this result with another case, in which the same deficit is created, with the same increased transactions demand (again fully offset by central bank open market purchases). But this time the deficit is financed not by selling new government bonds but by running the government's printing press for money. This means that no change occurs in the public's stock of bonds, but, instead, an increase occurs in the public's money stock, from M_0^* to M_1^* in part a of Figure 9-10.[17]

Once again the stock of wealth increases, by the amount $M_1^* - M_0^*$, *plus* any extent to which a lower interest rate may raise the prices of the public's bonds. This increase in wealth again raises the demand both for bonds and for money. But the increased demand for money is less than the increase in wealth (because $\alpha < 1$). Thus the increase in demand for money is clearly less than the increase in supply of money, and the interest rate falls. For the interest rate to be maintained at i_0, the central bank

---

[17] Once again M_0 and B_0 and DM ($W = W_0$) and DB ($W = W_0$) are drawn *after* taking account of open market purchases made to supply the increased transactions demand for money, but before taking account of the wealth effect.

would have to engage in further swaps, selling enough bonds to raise B_0 to B_2 and absorbing enough money to reduce M_1^* to M_2^*.

We may make this description of fiscal policy effects more realistic by not assuming that the government has its own printing press that it uses to finance deficits. Exactly the same total effect could be achieved if, as is the traditional usage, the government finances its entire deficit in all cases by selling newly issued bonds. The central bank, faced with this action, might follow a highly restrictive monetary policy, keeping M^* constant, thus requiring a rise in the interest rate not merely in response to the increased transactions demand but to the disproportionate growth of the public's wealth entirely in the form of bonds. At the opposite extreme, the central bank could, at the same time as the government sold its bonds in the open market, purchase enough bonds in that market to keep the interest rate constant, in spite of both the increase in transactions demand *and* the increase in wealth. Or, it might follow some intermediate policy, allowing some rise in interest rate but not the maximum rise. We thus can have the combination of a stimulative fiscal policy with a range of alternative monetary policies from completely "easy" (or "accomodative") to restrictive. But in this or in any case, our analysis needs to consider separately the three elements affecting the supply and demand for money and bonds: (1) the effects due to any increased (decreased) transactions demand for money; (2) the effects on the demand for money and on the demand for bonds due to the rise (fall) in wealth associated with the fiscal policy—this is the same however the deficit is financed and whatever the monetary policy followed; and (3) the effects due to the method of financing and/or the monetary policy adopted by the central bank.

The reader who believes that he understands the preceding discussion can confirm that understanding by analyzing the opposite case of a restrictive fiscal policy—on the one extreme assuming that the government uses the resulting surplus to repurchase debt from the public, and on the other extreme assuming that it accumulates the surplus in cash.

Before closing this discussion we need to note an important point. Our analysis of the supply and demand for money has been consistently framed entirely in stock terms—quantities of money and bonds existing as of some point in time and the quantities demanded (that is, desired to be held) at that point of time. These quantities can, of course, be massively changed, in the very short run, by central bank open market operations. We have shown the effects of such changes on interest rates.

However, when we discuss government deficit or surplus, we are, of course, dealing with flow magnitudes—rates of flow at a point in time, expressed in terms of some time unit (for example, a year). Thus, when we talk about *financing* deficits or surpluses through the issuance or retirement of bonds or money and the resultant changes in the stocks of these assets resulting from this financing, we are necessarily referring to *rates of change* in stocks at a point in time that gradually, over some period of time, would cause the stocks of money and bonds to *accumulate*. Assume, for example, that a fiscal-policy change creates a deficit (or additional deficit) of $12 billion a year (annual rate), financed entirely by money creation. After 1 month, the money stock will have grown by $1 billion, after 7 months by $7 billion. And, if the same deficit rate were maintained, and the same method of financing continued, after 3 years the money stock would be $36 billion higher, still increasing at $1 billion a month. (If bond financing had been used, it would have been the stock of bonds that increased by $1 billion a month.) However, within any moderately short period of time, these cumulative changes in stocks would be so small—relative to the total size of these stocks—as to be insignificant.

At the same time, of course, the public's demands for money and for bonds would also be continuing slowly to grow, reflecting the increase of wealth at the rate of $1 billion a month *plus* the effects of any continuing fall (or rise) of interest rates on the value of outstanding bonds. (What we have just demonstrated was that, with α less than 1, the increase in the demand for money would, *ceteris paribus*, be less than the increase in supply if the deficit were financed entirely by money; greater than the increase in supply if financed entirely by bonds.) But none of these stock effects has yet occurred as of the initial *point* in time that we were analyzing, and only insignificant changes will have occurred during any reasonably short period of time.

The increase in the transactions demand for money resulting from the added fiscal stimulus, on the other hand, will have been a one-time (although not necessarily instantaneous) affair. For a higher, but *constant*, fiscal stimulus will produce not a continually growing level of PY, and thus of mPY, but a one-time increase, maintained for so long as the higher stimulus continues.

In the relatively short run, the transactions demand effect is thus the dominant one; even though, as time passes, future short-run equilibria will be changing in a different way than they had been changing previously. In a short-run equilibrium analysis, we can therefore appropriately ignore the changed rate of stock accumulation, just as we had been ignoring any effects of stock accumulation at the *initial* rate, before the policy change.

This is entirely analogous with the analysis of the effects of a change in the rate of investment from, say, one constant positive level to a higher one. Just as we ignored the stock effects at the *initial* level of investment, we can, for a short-run equilibrium analysis, ignore the fact that stocks are now accumulating at a somewhat different rate. To be sure, once the multiplier effect has worked itself out, the level of income will have undergone a once-and-for-all rise. But the accumulation of business plant and equipment and of consumer wealth (and the effects on the *composition* of wealth arising from alternative ways in which investment may be financed) continue to occur, and *at a rate different from that at which they were occurring before*. Whatever the *long run* effects of stock accumulation, they will now be different from before; yet this is appropriately ignored in short-run analysis.

We return to this discussion only in Chapter 20, but adapted to the case of an economy with multiple financial assets. The interested reader can skip directly to the first half of that chapter.

REVIEW QUESTIONS

1. What are the two crucial premises on the basis of which economists in the classical tradition can argue that introducing the Keynesian consumption function and the accelerator principle into the classical model does not alter the important conclusion that the economy tends always toward full employment? What would be the consequence if either premise fails to hold?

2. Explain carefully the "why" and "how" of each of these three statements:

(a) The coupon rates on today's *new* bond issues do not differ appreciably from the yields-to-maturity reflected in the prices at which previously issued bonds with similar maturity dates and degrees of default-risk are trading today.

(b) The level of today's bond prices is significantly influenced by traders' expectations of future bond prices.

(c) The above two relationships, taken together, mean that interest rates will often not be at a level consistent with full employment of productive resources.

3. Present several reasons why many economists think the demand for money is interest-elastic.

4. "'Speculation' has an important influence on price in any market in which the outstanding stock is large relative to current additions to the stock over any relatively short period of time."

Explain this proposition; illustrate it in the case of the bond market; indicate its macroeconomic significance in that market.

5. Although the majority of individuals was assumed (in the text) to have an aversion to risk (that is, they prefer a "sure thing" to the risky alternative with the same expected value), some asset holders enjoy risk. Analyze how a change in the interest rate would affect the demand for money by an asset holder who preferred risk to safety, other things equal.

6. Analyze the effect on the rate of interest, with and without taking account of wealth effects

(a) of open market operations tht increase the supply of money;

(b) of an increase in government expenditure that is financed by selling new government bonds;

(c) of an increase in government expenditure that is financed by printing money.

SELECTED REFERENCES

J. M. Keynes, *The General Theory of Employment, Interest and Money* (Harcourt, Brace, 1936) Chapters 13–15.
(Keynes' statement of the Keynesian theory of interest.)

W. J. Baumol, "The Transactions Demand for Cash: An Inventory Theoretic Approach," *Quarterly Journal of Economics* 66 (November 1952) 545–556, reprinted in E. Shapiro (ed.), *Macroeconomics: Selected Readings* (Harcourt, Brace and World, 1970), pp. 172–183; and J. Tobin, "The Interest-Elasticity of the Transactions Demand for Cash," *Review of Economics and Statistics*, 38 (August, 1956), 241–247.

(Both articles show why the transactions demand for money is interest-elastic.)

J. Tobin, "Liquidity Preference as Behaviour Towards Risk," *Review of Economic Studies*, 25 (February 1958), 65–86, reprinted in M. G. Mueller (ed.), *Readings in Macroeconomics*, 2nd ed. (Holt, Rinehart, and Winston, 1971), pp. 173–191.

(Broadens and generalizes the speculative demand for money.)

A. Leijonhufvud, *On Keynesian Economics and the Economics of Keynes* (Oxford University Press, 1968), Chapter V, part 3, pp. 354–385.

(A sympathetic interpretation and analysis of Keynes' speculative demand for money.)

D. Laidler, *The Demand for Money* (International Textbook Co., 1969).

(A modern restatement.)

Chapter 10

A Keynesian Version of the Synthesis

Macroeconomic Consequences of an Interest-Elastic Demand for Money
A diagrammatic summary
Weakening the "first-line defense"
The liquidity trap and its significance
An "inconsistency" of saving and investment
Summary: Keynesian-classical synthesis with flexible wages

Rigid Money Wages
Equilibrium at less-than-full employment?
Diagrammatic analysis of a Keynesian-classical model with rigid wages
Government policy in the rigid wage model
Some mistaken views of wage-price effects

Full Employment and Inflation

Appendix: A Numerical Model for the Analysis of Wage Changes

The major part of the preceding chapter was devoted to elucidating a modernized and somewhat extended version of Keynes' theory of an interest-elastic demand for money. This chapter presents the full Keynesian-classical synthesis, Keynesian style. It starts by considering what difference it makes when we incorporate Keynes' demand-for-money theory into the classical model, in place of the previous classical "quantity theory." In this enlarged version we include, as well, the Keynesian consumption function (introduced into the classical model at the beginning of Chapter 9); but, for the present, we retain the classical assumption of perfectly flexible wage rates. In the second major section of the chapter, we replace the flexible-wage assumption with the assumption of rigid wages.

MACROECONOMIC CONSEQUENCES OF AN INTEREST-ELASTIC DEMAND FOR MONEY

At the beginning of Chapter 9, we added Keynes' consumption function to the classical model, by changing equation (6) of that model

(6) $$S = S(i)$$

to

(6a) $$S = S(Y, i)$$

We found that this change, taken by itself, altered the classical model very little, and its most basic conclusions not at all: (1) the economy still automatically generated full employment; (2) changes in the quantity of money still affected only prices (and wages) but no "real" magnitudes; (3) shifts in saving and investment schedules still affected only the interest rate, but not employment, output, or prices.

What difference does it make in these classical results if we now also add the interest-elastic demand for money to the model? This would change equation (5) of Chapter 9 from

$$(5) \qquad\qquad M^* = mPY$$

to

$$(5a) \qquad\qquad M^* = mPY + f(i)^1$$

As we can easily show, this added change makes only modest further alteration in the classical results; and it does not challenge the first or second of what were referred to just above as the "most basic conclusions" of the classical model, *so long as money wage rates are still assumed to be perfectly flexible, and so long as we still confine our discussion to positions of full equilibrium.*

As before, equations (1) through (4) of Chapter 9 still constitute a subset that can be independently solved to find the equilibrium levels of output, employment, and the real wage; and this solution is necessarily at the full-employment level. These four equations

$$(1) \qquad\qquad Y = F(N)$$

$$(2) \qquad\qquad N = N\left(\frac{W}{P}\right)$$

$$(3) \qquad\qquad L = L\left(\frac{W}{P}\right)$$

$$(4) \qquad\qquad L = N$$

contains four unknowns: $Y, N, L, W/P$. Therefore (if there is no inconsistency among them—that is, so long as N and L functions intersect at a positive real wage) these relationships determine equilibrium levels of these variables to which all other variables must adjust. And since L is defined as the (full-employment) labor supply, the equilibrium level of employment necessarily provides jobs for all who want them.

---

[1] Since the classical model as formulated earlier did not include any variable for wealth, we will not explore the addition of

$$(5b) \qquad\qquad M^* = mPY + f(i) + \alpha W$$

However, if we did add this and other equations in wealth, it would not significantly alter the results to be shown from use of (5a) (at least in the short run).

Consider next the (modified) equations (6a) through (8):

(6a) $$S = S(Y, i)$$

(7) $$I = I(i)$$

(8) $$S = I$$

The Y determined from equations (1) through (4) can now be inserted into equation (6a), leaving three equations in S, I, and i. This subset, therefore, uniquely determines equilibrium values of S, I, and i. Since i and Y are already determined, equation (5a)

(5a) $$M^* = mPY + f(i)$$

uniquely determines the price level, P, given the stock of money, M^*, exogenously determined by the central bank. The money wage W will then equal W/P determined by the first four equations, times the price level P.

The only significant change from the previous conclusions seems to be that a shift of saving and/or investment schedules can now (given M^*) alter P and W. To see this, start with the saving–investment subset: given Y, a shift of the I or S schedule affects i; and i so determined affects the demand for money (right-hand side of Equation 5a); thus, given Y and M^*, a shift of the I or S schedules affects P and thereby W. Since a given M^* can now be associated with more than one P and W, the "quantity theory" of the price level clearly no longer holds, even with a constant Y. On the other hand, it is still true that a change of M does not affect i, nor, of course, any other real magnitude: only P and W are altered when M changes. But P and W are now also altered by shifts in S or I schedules.

It will be noted that this version uses as its investment theory the simple classical equation, $I = I(i)$. Thus, it fails to incorporate the substantial modifications of investment analysis discussed in Chapter 8, that, although not Keynesian—in the sense of having been specifically introduced or even discussed by J. M. Keynes—are nevertheless very Keynesian in spirit and reflect a long nonclassical, or even *anti*classical, tradition of work in "business-cycle" and "monetary" economics. This tradition emphasized the volatility of investment and its role as a major source of instability in aggregate demand, as well as its role in permitting secular growth in both potential output and aggregate demand.

We could, without difficulty, extend the investment function to include the level of income as a determinant, making it

(7a) $$I = I(i, Y)$$

as we will do exactly that in Chapter 11. However, so long as this is thought of as a stable function, its addition changes the results very little, and we shall not bother to include it at this point. Nor, since the model we are developing is an equilibrium model, will we formally include any variant of the acceleration principle, even though, in some form or other, it clearly "belongs" in any realistic macro model. We shall, however, remind ourselves that the investment function may be subject to large shifts and consider briefly their consequences for the "synthesis" model.

A Diagrammatic Summary

We can also summarize these results diagrammatically through an expansion of the diagram (Figure 9-1) used in Chapter 9 to present the classical model, when expanded to include the consumption function. We now add an interest-elastic demand for money but still assume perfectly flexible wages, and confine attention to positions of full equilibrium. The diagram, naturally, is drawn in such a way that an equilibrium does exist. (To permit two-dimensional representation, we assume $\partial S/\partial i = 0$, that is, saving independent of the interest rate.)

Parts a, b, d, e, and f of Figure 10-1 are essentially identical with their counterparts in Figure 9-1, although the position of part d is now changed. But part c of Figure 9-1—which represented the classical monetary equilibrium with a transactions demand for money only—is now replaced by parts g and h, which incorporate the Keynesian interest theory. Part g shows the influence of P and Y on the demand for money DM_1, and part h shows the influence of the interest rate on the demand for money DM_2, along with the total demand for money $DM_1 + DM_2$. (If one wishes to simplify by calling DM_1 the transactions demand, and $DM_1 + DM_2$ the total of transactions and asset demands, he can; but we know that the transaction demand also depends on the interest rate.)

Clearly, parts a and b uniquely determine Y, N, L, and W/P. The broken line from part a to e shows how Y determines S; and that from e to f shows how S and I determine i. The broken line from part f to part h shows how M_0^*, and the interest-elastic portion of the demand for money, DM_2, determine what DM_1 must be. The broken line from part h to part g shows what mPY must be; and, since Y is already determined and m is a constant, this necessarily determines P. Carrying this P and the W/P from part b, into part d shows what W must be. In using the diagram, exactly the above sequence must always be followed in finding equilibrium values: b–a–e–f–h–g–d.

In this way, we can easily show the effects of any of numerous possible changes in economic structure or economic policy. (Although we have not yet complicated either the model or the diagram to permit introduction of fiscal policy at this point, we shall do so later.)

The diagrammatic apparatus allows us to predict the effects, in comparative statics terms, of a shift in any parameter of the model. For example, assume that an increase in thriftiness occurs. That would be represented by a shift to the right of the saving schedule in part e. At the same Y_0 (from part a), S would now be larger. Given the same I schedule

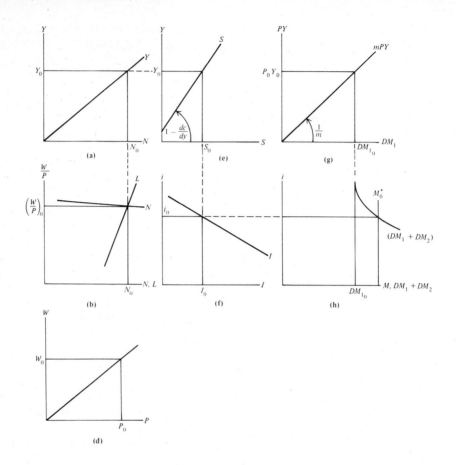

FIGURE 10-1

in part f, i must then be lower. In order for M_0^* to intersect $DM_1 + DM_2$ at a lower i, DM_1 must shift to the left, carrying the $DM_1 + DM_2$ schedule with it. Given the same Y, and a lower mPY, P must fall. From part d we can find that, with a lower P, W must decline in proportion to P.

The reader should himself draw the diagrams with an initial equilibrium, then draw a new saving schedule and show the new equilibrium values. He should also explain in words why each change is necessary. He can then try some other parameter shift, for example, an increase in the quantity of money or an increase in the supply of labor schedule. Table 10-1 summarizes the comparative statics predictions of this model for three cases. The reader should first confirm for himself the result shown in cases (a) through (c), then attempt to fill in the missing lines (d) through (g).

TABLE 10-1

Parameter shift	Change in Equilibrium Values of											
	Y	N	L	$\dfrac{W}{P}$	i	DM_1	DM_2	P	W	I	S	C
(a) Saving schedule shifts to right	—	—	—	—	↓	↓	↑	↓	↓	↑	↑	↓
(b) M^* increases	—	—	—	—	—	↑	—	↑	↑	—	—	—
(c) L schedule shifts to right	↑	↑	↑	↓	—	—	—	↓	↓	—	—	—
(d) I schedule shifts to right												
(e) m increases (mPY schedule rotates downward)												
(f) Production function shifts upward (both level and slope increasing)												
(g) DM_2 schedule shifts upward (more M desired at each i)												

Although the diagrams may permit us to find and to understand the comparative statics results—the changes in variables necessary to produce a new equilibrium—we may also want to have some idea how these results are brought about. Are we sure that prices, wages, and interest rates will in fact tend to fall in the case of an increased propensity to save, so that the new equilibrium will be achieved? This is asking, of course, for some explanation of the dynamics of the model. Without being at all rigorous in our presentation, we can sketch several possible varieties of disequilibrium behavior that may satisfy curiosity on this point.

Suppose that, in the case of an increased propensity to save, neither output, the interest rate, nor the price level should immediately fall but temporarily stayed at Y_0, P_0, and i_0. Would forces develop that would require them to fall? The demand and supply of money would still be equal, since the demand (which depends on PY and i) would not have changed. But saving would now exceed investment (I_0). One interpretation of what might now happen would run thus: A drop in consumption demand for current output (increase in saving), with no increase in investment demand and no decrease in the supply of output, would cause unsold goods to pile up. The excess of amounts supplied over amounts demanded would cause a reduction of prices. This would, if money wages remains unchanged, mean a higher real wage and thus create a deficiency of demand for labor as compared with supply. To avoid unemployment, wages would rapidly be bid down, preventing any rise in W/P and any decline in employment or output. But if wages and prices fall, this reduces the transactions demand for money, leaving the public with larger balances than they would want to hold as an asset at the initial rate of interest. In the effort to get a return on these idle balances, some people will buy securities, forcing up their prices and forcing down the rate of interest. Until P,

W, and *i* have each fallen, there will, therefore, be disequilibrium in one or all of the goods, labor, or money markets. In each case, disequilibrium produces a movement in the proper direction: toward lower *W*, *P*, and *i*—that is, in the direction that will eliminate the disequilibrium.

A slightly different sequence might assume that employers could and would cut back output as fast as demand (consumption plus investment) declined. The increased saving (reduced demand for consumer goods) would thus cause a reduction of output, throwing workers out of their jobs. For example, if *i* did not immediately fall, output might be cut back by the excess of the new *S* over the old *I*. This would create unemployment, as employment was reduced in proportion to the decline in *Y*. This would also reduce the transactions demand (as *Y* fell even though *P* did not). The idle balances thus created would flow into the capital market, reducing the rate of interest. A downward pressure on money wages resulting from unemployment would simultaneously reduce costs, and competition would then force employers to reduce prices. In the new equilibrium, output, employment and the real wage would be restored to their initial values, but money wages and prices and the interest rate would all be lower.

Still other sequences can be imagined. These sequences differ as a result of the assumptions made concerning the relative speeds with which the various adjustments occur; consequently they differ with respect to other aspects of the disequilibrium process, for example, who gets hurt in the meantime. If employers lag in cutting back output and wages don't at once decline, their selling prices will fall faster than their costs and profits will turn to losses. Consumers will gain, as prices fall ahead of incomes. On the other hand, if output is cut back fast enough, profit margins may be protected even though wages are temporarily maintained; but workers will be unemployed until *W* declines. However, we do not plan a systematic and rigorous analysis of dynamic processes.

Weakening the "First-Line Defense"

So far as the equilibrium model with an interest-elastic money demand is concerned, the main difference from the purely classical model relates to the required variability of price and wage levels in response to changes in aggregate demand. If, in the strict classical model, the quantity of money is held constant, prices (and wages) will change only in response to (a) increases in the supply of labor or in its productivity, or (b) changes in "velocity"—that is, changes in the fraction of money income that is needed to be held in cash to mediate transactions. Growth in the supply of labor and in the economy's aggregate production function could be expected to occur rather slowly and predictably. The necessary price level changes would be slow and smooth and not apt to cause trouble. And, if it were desired to stabilize prices (or money wages) in the face of these shifts, deliberate changes in the quantity of money seemed quite capable of doing the job. Changes in the structural determinants of velocity were of the same character—slow and smooth, offering no challenge that either price level fluctuations or monetary policy could not meet. The only source of sudden or sharp trouble might be changes in velocity reflecting irrational shifts in the demand for money. One could easily enough argue that either (a) since people are rational, this will not occur—no one ever wants to acquire a barren cash balance (and, since they are not acquired, they could not be released), or (b) hoarding or dishoarding do occur, but they are a product of instability that has some other origin (for example, a badly functioning banking system.)

Changes in saving propensities or investment incentives, it must be emphasized, would be taken care of in the strict classical model by the interest rate alone, assuming a stable money supply. This was the "first line of defense" against unemployment arising from any increased propensity to save or decreased incentive to invest. And it should do the entire job.

Thus the economy could be counted on to work pretty successfully, if only the banks were not allowed to cause trouble of the kind that Wicksell discussed. Of course, the worst trouble they could cause would be price level instability. But it was generally agreed that instability of prices was always unfortunate, and, if it were a downward movement, likely to cause some transitional unemployment because of the temporary stickiness of money wages.

Now what significant change does the interest-elastic demand for money make? Simply that, even if the quantity of money does not decrease, declines in investment and consumption propensities require price and wage reductions for full employment to be maintained. The first line of defense is breached, throwing some of the burden on the second line, wage-price flexibility.

This is important, for the instability of incentives for investment (if not saving) has long been recognized. Investment is essentially postponable; it depends on an uncertain estimate of future demand stretching many years ahead; it is strongly affected by technological change and other "external" factors. Thus, to show that the interest rate cannot be counted on to handle saving-investment disturbances means that a much heavier load is placed on the wage-price mechanism to avoid unemployment. To be sure, monetary policy could, in principle, always avoid the necessity for wage-price changes; but the instability and unpredictability of investment pose a more severe challenge to monetary policy than do productivity changes or alterations in the structural determinants of velocity, which presumably occur smoothly and slowly. Thus, the interest-elastic demand for money, which shows the fallibility of the interest rate mechanism, exposes a possible weakness in the supposed smoothly self-regulating character of the economy.

The Liquidity Trap and Its Significance

But this is not the worst of it. Keynes further pointed out that, in an extreme form, his speculative demand for money might make automatic full employment impossible, *even if wages and prices were entirely flexible.* It is possible, Keynes argued, that, at times, the speculative demand for money schedule becomes infinitely elastic, or nearly so. Suppose, for sake of argument, that the speculative demand for money is infinitely elastic at a rate of 3 percent. This means that bond prices higher than a level which reflects 3 per cent yield are considered by every wealthholder as prohibitively high. No one would be willing to hold bonds (in preference to cash) at a bond price level any higher than this. At this level many wealthholders are right on the margin, holding cash or bonds indifferently but ready to sell their bonds and unwilling to buy at bond prices any higher than those which presently prevail. Suppose, further, that, at present, the investment outlook is such that there is less investor demand for funds at 3 percent than savers wish to supply at that rate. This means that 3 percent is too high a rate for full employment. Insufficient aggregate demand means unemployment and falling wages and prices, releasing funds from transactions balances, funds which should bid down the rate of interest and restore full employment. But the interest rate expectations of wealthholders rule out this result. No amount of deflation and release of cash from transactions balances can drive the interest rate below 3 percent, and 3 percent is too high for full employment. In other words, there is an impasse, a "trap". Moreover, in this case, monetary policy is also helpless. Instead of, or in addition to, the effects of whatever deflation of prices and wages might occur, the central bank could seek to increase the stock of money by open market purchases. But, if the demand for money were truly infinitely elastic at an interest rate too high for full employment, it could be driven no lower.

The case just described is, admittedly, an extreme case, but it dramatizes the problem posed by the speculative demand for money. Suppose, instead, that the money demand schedule is not infinitely elastic with respect to the rate of interest but only highly elastic. Under these circumstances, full employment is theoretically possible, but only through an extreme deflation of prices, enough to release from transactions balances the very large amounts necessary to depress the rate of interest sufficiently to restore full employment and thus remove the necessity for further deflation. The more elastic the speculative demand, the greater the burden placed upon wage–price adjustments. And, as we have seen, as the elasticity increases, we approach the extreme case in which no amount of deflation would be adequate.

Now there are several important counter arguments to fears about liquidity trap. For one thing, the fall in interest rates induced by deflation (or by monetary policy) raises considerably the value of the public's wealth.

Even if this would not raise the demand for bonds sufficiently to reduce interest rates to the level required for full employment (because of firm and universal concepts of maximum "normal" or "safe" bond-price levels), it may have direct effects on aggregate demand of a sort we have not so far considered but will discuss in Chapter 12.

Second, is it plausible to assume that speculative concepts of "normal" bond price levels can really survive very long if actual bond prices are pushed up to and held at these levels? Will not those individual wealth-holders who chose to move their portfolios into money as bond prices approached the unsafe level, eventually conclude—as bond prices continue to hold at these high levels—that such prices are not as "unsafe" as they thought? They gave up an interest return because they feared it would be more than wiped out by a capital loss. But so long as the yield on bonds remains positive, will that not come to appear better than a zero return, as fears of capital loss fade? In other words, how can the liquidity trap survive as an equilibrium situation?

The answer, of course, is that it cannot. But this does not really destroy the significance of the argument. The real world is not one in which equilibrium commonly prevails. If there is a collapse of private investment demand, which greatly reduces production and the demand for labor, creating unemployment and (assuming for the moment that it does) a deflation of wages and prices and falling interest rates, it is not very interesting to know that there is (or may be) some new full-employment equilibrium at some very low price level and interest rate.

This is particularly the case if there is no reason to expect that, even if this equilibrium were reached, it would long prevail. Wealthholders (like workers, entrepreneurs, and consumers, who may also have expectations that interfere with needed price adjustments) have had experience with recessions and booms. They have seen bond prices climb in recessions and then fall back when prosperity returned. It is not surprising that they fear after some point to hold bonds at ever higher prices and that they increasingly sell out to take their capital gains and avoid probable future losses. Their doing so may well prevent the interest rate from falling enough to maintain full-employment equilibrium during the recession, in the face of a collapse of investment demand.

An "Inconsistency" of Saving and Investment

Now let us stretch the case of the previous section a little further in another direction. Suppose that the speculative demand schedule is not infinitely elastic at some low but positive interest rate—that it is possible by sufficient deflation (or by sufficient increase in M) to push the rate of interest down to zero. Nevertheless, it is clearly not possible, either by deflation or by ordinary tools of monetary policy, to push it *below zero*. For this would imply a willingness on the part of the public to hold bonds that have a negative yield in place of cash with a zero yield. Thus, whether or not the demand for money becomes infinitely elastic at a rate above zero, it certainly becomes infinitely elastic at zero rate. What is the significance of this? Simply that, at times, saving might exceed investment even at a zero rate of interest. That is, full-employment saving might exceed investment at an interest rate of zero. (In Figure 10-1, the I schedule in part f would cut the horizontal axis to the left of I_0.) In this case, full employment would be quite impossible, regardless of the speculative demand for money. Full employment would then be prevented not by expectations of future rates of interest that were inconsistent with the conditions of saving and invest-ment. Rather, it would be prevented by an inconsistency between saving and investment at any (positive) rate of interest.

What is the probability that investment at zero interest rate might (at least at times) fall short of full-employment saving? If one believes that there is little or no interest elasticity of saving (that is, of consumption) and that the investment schedule is only moderately interest elastic, but subject to substantial shifts for other reasons—for example, through accelerator effects or exogenous causes—the possibility of inconsistency surely cannot be ruled out.

One may ask whether interest rates of zero have ever been observed. It is arguable that, after allowance for transactions costs and default risk, rates of interest did in effect reach zero during a period of the Great Depression. However, one would not need to observe interest rates of zero for an inconsistency of saving and investment to have been the basic cause of unemployment in some particular time period. For, if wage rates were rigid, or slow to adjust in the presence of unemployment, or if M had not been increased sufficiently, interest rates might still have remained above zero, even though there was no *equilibrium* level of the interest rate above, or even at, zero, and therefore no possibility of a full-employment equilibrium for the economy. If the investment schedule had then sub-sequently moved to the right, the inconsistency would never need to have become apparent through an *observed* interest rate of zero, even if wages were, at least slowly, flexible downward in the presence of unemployment.

Again, we need not labor the extreme case to see the relevance of the considerations advanced. What this view emphasizes is the relative interest inelasticity of saving and investment schedules. If both are fairly inelastic, moderate shifts in either one can cause substantial changes in the rate of interest which would equate S and I at any given income level. This means that a larger burden is placed on wage and price adjustments than would be the case were saving and investment schedules highly elastic. In order for wide changes to occur in the interest rate in the face of speculative concepts of "normal" rate, large changes must occur in the transactions demand for money, changes requiring very extreme inflation or deflation of the price level. Thus there may be situations in which the reductions in the interest rate necessary to maintain full employment are simply not feasible, even without formal inconsistency.

The view that saving and investment schedules are relatively inelastic to interest rates is, of course, an empirical judgment. It could be a very mistaken one. However, it has been many years since the idea of an appreciably interest-elastic saving schedule gained much support, and the available empirical evidence, as we shall see in Chapter 19, does not give overwhelming support to the hypothesis of a high degree of interest elasticity of investment. Specifically, it was Keynes' own empirical judgment that the investment schedule, although somewhat interest-elastic, was not highly so; even at a zero rate of interest, investment would be at a limited, not an infinite, rate—a rate possibly appreciably less than the rate of full-employment saving at a zero interest rate.

Keynes referred in his *General Theory* to still another possible kind of failure of the classical full-employment mechanism. Suppose that wages and prices are perfectly flexible and fall rapidly in the presence of unemployment. But suppose that such deflation produces expectations of still further declines in wages and prices—which cause both investors and consumers to postpone purchases awaiting still lower prices, leading not to higher but to lower aggregate demand in real terms. Although our modern unfamiliarity with situations of wage–price deflation may make this sound a bit fanciful, it is only the obverse of an idea which finds a certain amount of adherence today: namely, that in the presence of inflation, people come to expect its continuance, which in turn causes them to act in ways that assure it. If deflation did engender such expectations, once again, no amount of wage and price decline could restore full employment.

Summary: Keynesian–Classical System with Flexible Wages

We have now successively added to the classical model two of J. M. Keynes' major innovations: the idea that consumption depends on income and an interest-elastic demand for money. However, we have continued to assume that wages are perfectly flexible. This makes certain differences in the results of the classical equilibrium model, but only in rather extreme circumstances does it seem to raise serious questions regarding the theoretical validity of the principal conclusions of classical macroeconomics: namely, (a) that a competitive market economy contains automatic forces driving the economy always toward an equilibrium at full employment, and (b) that the quantity of money affects the equilibrium levels only of wages and prices but of no "real" magnitudes.

The exceptions to or serious problems with this conclusion appear to be the following:

1. The possibility that investment and saving schedules are quite inelastic with respect to the interest rate, perhaps even (at times) not having a positive intersection (with Y at the full-employment level). In that case, a full-employment equilibrium is not even *theoretically* possible in the model as so far presented.

2. Even if there always remains a positive intersection for S and I, unless either or both of these variables is highly interest-elastic, maintaining full employment in the face of even modest shifts in saving or investment schedules will require large fluctuations in interest rates in order to avoid changes in aggregate demand. So would large shifts of investment or saving schedules, even if the schedules were fairly elastic.

3. Given an interest-elastic demand for money and a constant supply of money, achieving fluctuations in interest rates at the constant (full-employment) real income necessarily requires changes in the wage and price level. If, as indicated under item 2, large interest rate changes are required to equate full-employment S and I, large changes in levels of wages and prices may therefore be necessary to maintain full-employment equilibrium. These may, in practice, be nonachievable.

4. It is possible that (in the liquidity trap case) interest rates may have a lower limit, at least in the short run, regardless of how far wages and prices fall.

The convinced "Keynesian" is likely to play down the interest-elasticity of both saving and investment schedules, especially in the short run; he tends to believe that expectations based on past interest-rate experience are likely to engender speculative responses by wealthholders that prevent or at least greatly delay wide swings in interest rates; he is typically impressed with the volatility of the investment schedule in response to such factors as technological change or sudden shifts in business confidence, and stresses the importance of accelerator effects when income is not in equilibrium. To him, the problems listed above seem formidable, indeed.

On the other hand, today's economist of more classical bent has possible answers for most of these Keynesian worries—certainly so long as wage rates are permitted to vary flexibly. Chapter 12 will present his response to the Keynesian position.

RIGID MONEY WAGES

We turn now to Keynes' third major analytical innovation: the proposition that money wage rates are typically rigid against downward pressures resulting from unemployment. This proposition may be put forth in either of two senses: (a) In the strict form of the proposition, that wage rates are *in fact* completely rigid downward. Or (b), in the weaker form that, although not necessarily absolutely or permanently rigid, regardless of the amount or duration of unemployment, money wage rates respond slowly and inadequately to unemployment. Thus, any analysis that assumes them fully flexible produces erroneous or, at best, irrelevant conclusions; thus, an analysis that assumes wages rigid instead produces more relevant and useful information about how the economy works and can better suggest appropriate policies to improve its performance.

A sympathetic and careful reading of *The General Theory*[2] shows that Keynes' own view was much closer to the second than the first of these senses. Essentially, Keynes' treatment held that the money wage level was dependent upon institutional and historical forces, subject to some influence also from the state of the economy. Money wages at any point in time are at the level they are mostly because it is close to where they have recently been. To be sure, they may have recently risen or fallen somewhat in response to institutional pressures, such as minimum wage laws or the efforts of trade unions. Further, the state of employment will make some difference. As an economy moves closer to full employment, the strenth of trade unions is likely to increase and the resistance of employers to wage increases to fade. Further, as full employment is approached, particular employers, in certain localities or occupations, will encounter shortages of labor. They will be unable to hire as many men as they need at the going rate of wages. They will, therefore, tend to seek additional employees by offering slightly higher wages, even apart from trade union efforts. Conversely, when employment is very slack, trade unions will press less hard for wage increases, employers will find no need to bid against each other for labor and may even try to get their workers to accept lower money wages in order to reduce costs and strengthen their competitive position. There may even be some competition, open or concealed, among workers for the available jobs.

Thus, Keynes saw the wage level as tending to rise (from wherever it had been) when employment was nearly full, rising perhaps faster the closer the economy was to full employment and stronger and more efficient was trade union organization. Money wage rates would tend to sag when unemployment was widespread, again perhaps sagging faster the weaker were the unions and the greater the level of unemployment. But, at any given time and place, the money wage rate level was, more or less, a matter "historically" or "autonomously" determined.

This concept of the money wage level is a very different one from the "flexible" wage level assumed by classical writers. If the wage level is truly flexible, it falls continuously and without limit whenever there is any unemployment and is stable only if all workers seeking jobs can find them. Keynes' concept has the money wage level stable at some point below full employment, a point at which upward and downward pressures are in balance. At lower levels of employment, wage rates may sag, but only at a limited, predictable rate—a rate that depends on the *extent* of unemployment, which would not be the case with truly flexible wages. Spelled out a bit more rigorously, this describes the so-called **Phillips curve**, a version of which we shall formally introduce into the model in Chapter 12.

[2] Especially Chapter 19.

Equilibrium at Less-Than-Full Employment?

Empirically, there can be little argument with at least the weaker proposition about money wage rates—that they do not decline immediately and without limit in the presence even of substantial unemployment. (Indeed, we know that they sometimes even rise in these circumstances!) Partly, this failure of wage rates to decline reflects institutional obstacles: minimum wage laws, the resistance of powerful trade unions, the existence of fairly long-term contractual agreements between workers and their employers, or the problems and costs involved in revising complex wage structures at frequent intervals. However, quite apart from legal or other institutional barriers to wage cutting, there is usually a general social reluctance—on the part of employers as well as the general public—to condone money wage reductions, even if the cost of the failure to cut wages should be seen to be a loss of jobs for some of the workers involved.

Economists sometimes characterize this reluctance as "irrational," since a cut in the average money wage is almost sure to be followed by a decline in prices, so that *real* wages would then decline by less than might appear—or perhaps not even decline at all. Thus the loss of jobs would be avoided in whole or in part. Since we assume people are rational, the argument sometimes is even that wage rigidity therefore does not exist. This view seems to assume that the average wage rate can be changed through some single act or agreement that affects all workers simultaneously and equally. Instead, it requires tens of thousands of bilateral wage negotiations (or unilateral employer actions) to alter the average wage significantly; and each such act is quite independent of the others. Neither any single organized group of workers nor any single nonunion employer is large enough to take account of any effect on the prices those workers will pay that will stem from the reduction of their own wage rates. No worker group or employer can be sure that other wages will be similarly cut or that prices generally will fall. Instead, workers and employers both correctly recognize that a 10 percent money wage cut is a 10 percent real wage cut for the workers involved; for whatever happens to the price level would have happened anyway. Thus, it is not clearly irrational to oppose or to attempt to delay money wage reductions—unless, perhaps, the failure to do so would clearly cause a wholesale and permanent loss of jobs for the workers immediately involved. However, to the workers, and to the public, the notion that wage cuts will avoid or reduce the loss of jobs seems clearly contradicted by the common observation that wage cuts in the past have not reduced unemployment. On the contrary they have been accompanied by rising unemployment and business recessions. The argument that this only proves that the wage cuts were too slow or too small may be theoretically correct but seldom convinces.

Even if there were no resistance or reluctance to cut wages, a general reduction in a level of wage rates too high for full employment would still take a long time. Existing wage contracts may last up to 3 years and expire at different times. Those workers whose contracts are up for renewal at any given time are a small fraction of the total; even if their wages were severely slashed, this would not immediately reduce the average money wage very much. Of course, in the meantime, it would reduce those workers' real wages severely.

Thus, for whatever reason, it is hardly debatable that wage rates are very imperfectly flexible downward. From this it follows that the money wage level that exists at any given time can often be too high for full employment, and less-than-full employment may therefore very well exist. What remains debatable is only whether—if wages *were* truly flexible and fell without limit in the presence of unemployment—unemployment would, in fact, be avoided. Another way of putting this question is whether, when unemployment exists—either because wages have failed to decline enough or because no amount of decline could have been enough—this situation should be described as an "equilibrium at less than full employment." That would seem to depend entirely on what one chooses to mean by "equilibrium." One would probably say that it is not an equilibrium if wages are in fact still falling. But suppose that they are falling at a rate of only 2 percent a year. Or suppose that unemployment is producing clear downward pressures on wage rates, yet this pressure is "artificially bottled up" by a minimum wage law, union contracts, or social or political opposition to wage cuts. In these cases, one might still argue that this should be called a disequilibrium situation. However, if the law, the contracts, or the attitudes have so molded worker and employer behavior that no one is being "forced" to do anything that he does not expect to or want to do, then should one call it an equilibrium, or at least a "quasi–equilibrium," at less than full employment?

As noted earlier, it will be shown in Chapter 12 that, at least in principle, there exist other economic forces, not yet considered, that might ultimately operate to overcome even an inconsistency between saving and investment or a liquidity trap, *so long as the price level shows any continuing downward responsiveness in the presence of unemployment.* Moreover, as was recognized earlier, the existence of a *permanent* "liquidity trap" at any rate of interest above zero is highly implausible. A Keynesian, determined to prove that, at times, there may exist a macroequilibrium at less-than-full employment, may thus ultimately be cornered into relying on wage rigidity as the sole source of that equilibrium. But what's new about that? The classical economists argued all along that wage rigidity could create unemployment! Moreover, semantic disputes about whether relative or absolute wage rigidity in the presence of unemployment can be described as a "true" or even a "quasi" equilibrium have no real answers. One may well conclude that the buckets, nay, tanks, of ink spilled over the question posed in the subhead above have had, at best, an inconclusive outcome. Indeed, they have been largely wasted.

Wasted, because the question is really unimportant. Whether or not the economy is in a situation of "equilibrium," it is often at less than full employment; and, without policy intervention, it often, or perhaps usually, makes little or slow progress in getting out of that situation other than through stimulative government policies or through a basically exogenous, or at least largely unpredictable, favorable shift of investment. Thus, putting aside questions of what words we may use to describe such periods, our real interest must be in developing theoretical models that adequately explain how actual economies really behave, and in providing the basis for decisions about public policy when we are dissatisfied with such an economy's performance. Whether or not it is ever appropriate to describe these periods as "equilibrium at less than full employment," we do have periods of unemployment, accompanied by more or less rigid wages, and we do need theories that are relevant to them. The Keynesian rigid-wage model seems to be such a model.

Diagrammatic Analysis of a Keynesian-classical Model with Rigid Wages

We are thus concerned with a macro model in which we assume more or less rigid wages, and we want to know what the effects will be of various parameter shifts. We can easily determine this graphically, using a diagram like Figure 10-1. As can be seen by the broken lines in Figure 10-2, part b, full employment would be N_F, to which would correspond a full-employment real wage, $(W/P)_F$. The corresponding full-employment output (part a) would in turn be Y_F. At Y_F, saving would be S_F (part e); thus, investment would need to be I_F (part f). This, in turn, would require an interest rate of i_F. From parts g and h, we can see that an interest rate of i_F would, given M_0^* and the schedule DM_2, require a DM_1 of DM_{1_F}. Instead, the actual DM_1 is DM_{1_0}, corresponding to the existing less-than-full employment output, Y_0, and the existing price level P_0. Given the rigid money wage W_0 (part d), and the less-than-full employment real wage $(W/P)_0$, P_0 is the lowest price level that can prevail. It will prevail because a higher price level than P_0 would, given W_0, mean a lower real wage than employers require to produce Y_0: marginal units of output thus are more profitable than necessary to induce their production. Competition would thus reduce prices to P_0.

To reduce the interest rate to i_F, making possible investment of I_F, equal to saving of S_F, thus to permit the full-employment output and employment, Y_F and N_F, it would be necessary for PY to reach P_FY_F—substantially below P_0Y_0; and, since Y_F is *larger* than Y_0, this means that P would have to fall considerably. But P cannot fall unless W falls. A decline of W_0 to W_1, with P unchanged at P_0, would establish the full-employment real wage $(W/P)_F$. But this would not produce full employment. For that, P must fall to P_F, and that requires that W fall not merely to W_1 but all the

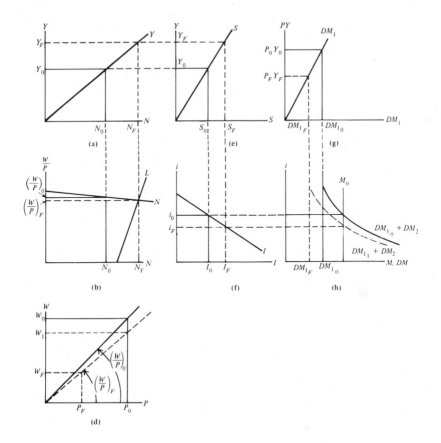

FIGURE 10-2

way to W_F. By definition, this it will not do, at least not quickly enough to be relevant.

Instead, or in the meantime, Y_0, N_0, and so on, have all the characteristics of an equilibrium or quasi-equilibrium at less than full employment. Investment equals saving at the prevailing income Y_0 and interest rate i_0. Given the supply of money and the price level P_0 the demand for money is just satisfied at the same interest rate and income. Given the too-high and rigid money wage W_0 and the wage-price ratio $(W/P)_0$ which is appropriate for the existing employment N_0, the appropriate—that is, the competitive—price level is P_0. In turn, employment at N_0 implies output of Y_0 that produces saving of S_0 equal to investment I_0 appropriate to i_0.

In this situation, no firm, wealthholder, consumer, investor, or employed worker is dissatisfied with his economic behavior; none has any reason to want to change what he is doing. Doubtless the unemployed are dissatisfied, but this does not lead them effectively to offer their services at a lower money wage, thereby to bid the wage level quickly down to W_F.

Note again that full employment would require both a lower real wage $(W/P)_F$ and a lower absolute wage W_F. But it should be recognized that the latter requirement is the more fundamental. To see this, suppose, for example, that the demand curve for labor were horizontal, as we have argued that it well might be. Then there would be no need for *any* decline in the real wage. But the money wage would still need to fall. Or suppose that the government provided a wage subsidy to employers equal to $W_0 - W_1$, reducing the effective real wage to employers, given P_0, to $(W/P)_F$. There would still be unemployment because P_0 is too high.

Given an equilibrium or quasi-equilibrium at less than full employment, how is that equilibrium displaced by shifts in the functional relationships of the system or changes in policy variables? Consider first a shift in the consumption (saving) function. For example, assume an increase in the propensity to consume—a reduction in saving relative to income. In Figure 10-3, this shift is represented by a rotation to the left of the saving function, from S to S'. The initial equilibrium, before the saving shift, is represented by variables with subscript zero. In the new equilibrium, represented by variables with subscripts 1, the value of every variable has changed except (a) the money wage, which is stable by assumption, and (b) the money supply, which is changed only by government action. Employment, income, prices, and the interest rate rise; investment and the real wage decline.

One familiar with the simple Keynesian model and the concepts of aggregate demand and the multiplier, should have no trouble understanding why income and employment increase with a rise in consumption demand. And one familiar with classical economics has no trouble understanding why, *given a rise in output*, prices might rise (because of the assumption of diminishing returns in the traditional version of the model or of rising markups over unit labor costs as demand increases in a more contemporary version). He may also recall that, in the classical analysis, a decline in the saving schedule raises the interest rate, reducing investment (and perhaps stimulating saving) thereby equating amounts saved and invested. However, that analysis was conducted on the assumption that income was constant—or, at least, that saving was independent of income. With saving a function of income, a sufficient rise in Y (see part e) could cause saving, even with the new, reduced saving schedule, to remain unchanged or even to rise. Thus, the classical explanation is now inadequate. However, Keynesian interest theory supplies the explanation. Higher Y and higher P both raise the transactions demand for money (part g), which—given the asset demand-for-money schedule DM_2—raises the interest rate (part h), in turn reducing investment (part f). The higher interest rate, stemming from increased output, and thus higher transactions demand for money, depresses investment, thus limiting the rise in output.

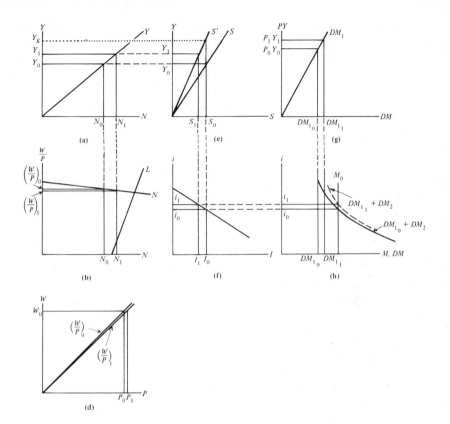

FIGURE 10-3

Put differently, the effect of increased aggregate demand for goods and services on the demand for money produces a negative feedback on investment that limits the rise in income.

Note also the differences from the simple Keynesian model. There, investment was autonomous; it did not depend on the rate of interest. In part f, it would be represented by a vertical line through I_0. In that case, a downward shift of the saving function would have raised income to Y_K, actual saving remaining at $S_0 = I_0$. Instead, in this model, the rise in Y (and any induced rise in P) prevents the famous "paradox of thrift" from being fully realized.

The case of an upward (on the graph, rightward) shift of the investment function involves essentially the same considerations and produces essentially the same results as the previous case. The reader should confirm this by drawing the diagram with an initial equilibrium, then showing the new equilibrium with stronger investment. The results should be: higher Y and N, somewhat higher P (unless the N function is taken as horizontal), higher i, and, notwithstanding the higher i, higher I and S (and by implication, C).

What would be the result of a growth of the labor force—a rightward shift of the L function? The reader should convince himself that, in this model as it stands, nothing happens except that unemployment rises and the gap between actual and potential output increases.

And what of an increase in the aggregate production–employment relationship: a higher Y for any and every N (accompanied, of course, by some upward shift of the demand for labor function)? Assume an upward rotation of the Y function from Y to Y' as shown in part a of Figure 10-4. (Figure 10-4 differs from the previous figures in that the labor demand

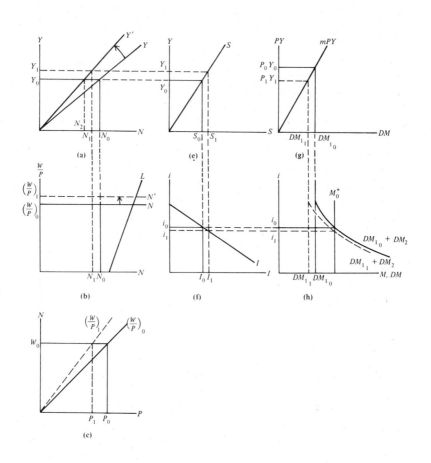

FIGURE 10-4

function is made horizontal, for simplicity, and, perhaps, for realism. However, it makes no significant difference in results if the N function is taken as sloping downward to the right.)

With the new production-employment relationship, any given employment is associated with larger output or any given output can be produced with lower employment. For example, the initial equilibrium output Y_0, which formerly required employment of N_0, can now be produced with employment of N_2. Is there any force that will produce a higher aggregate demand $C + I$, and thus permit a higher Y than Y_0? Since the C function (S function) is unchanged, it is clear that investment must rise if Y is to increase. Given the I schedule, that requires a lower i. But, given M^*, and the DM_1 and DM_2 functions, i can fall only if PY does. Since we are trying to discover whether Y will rise, not fall, PY can fall only if P falls considerably. And P, indeed can be expected to fall. With less labor input required for any output and the wage rate fixed, costs will be lower and P should decline. Indeed, the counterpart of the upward rotation of the Y function in part a, is a rise of the N function in part b—from N to N'. This means that, in part d, P can fall to P_1 with W_0 unchanged. A lower P permits PY to fall even though Y rises. This permits a lower i, higher I, and thus higher Y in the new equilibrium. Employment, however, declines (and unemployment thus rises) even though the real wage and aggregate real income are higher. The gap between actual and potential output again increases.

Thus, this model shares with the simple Keynesian model the property that growth of potential output—whether occurring through an expansion of the labor force or a growth in labor's productivity—only results in a wider margin of unused resources. Realized economic growth in this model thus requires either autonomous growth of aggregate demand, stimulative government policy, or the existence of some self-maintaining dynamic process analogous to the multiplier-accelerator models presented in Chapter 8.

Government Policy in the Rigid Wage Model

The results of an increase in M are straightforward, and not shown graphically. There results a decline in i, despite an increase in DM_1, the result of a higher Y, and, depending on whether the N function is horizontal or downward sloping, possibly a higher P as well. The higher Y reflects the increase in investment associated with lower i, with given consumption function; that is, C increases as well as I.

Since we grafted the Keynesian consumption function and interest theory on to a classical model that had no government expenditure or taxes, we cannot easily show the results of fiscal policy changes. However, an increase in government expenditures can be regarded as having the same effects as that of a *parallel* rightward movement of the investment function; and a tax cut can be regarded as having the same effects as leftward rotation or shift of the saving function. However, in Chapter 11 we will provide an alternative diagrammatic apparatus which permits the explicit introduction of government fiscal policy variables.

We might also consider the money wage as a policy variable in this model. Even though the wage rate is not automatically flexible, falling in the presence of unemployment, it might be capable of being pushed up, or down, by government action or encouragement, undertaken in an effort to affect the volume of employment and output or, perhaps, the price level. Such an analysis of the effects of a finite one-time change in the money wage, induced by government, also permits us to predict the effects of any other *autonomous*, finite rise, or fall, in the average wage rate, occurring without the help of government policy.

Figure 10-5 illustrates this for the case of a rise in the money wage, whether secured by a higher minimum wage, government pressures on

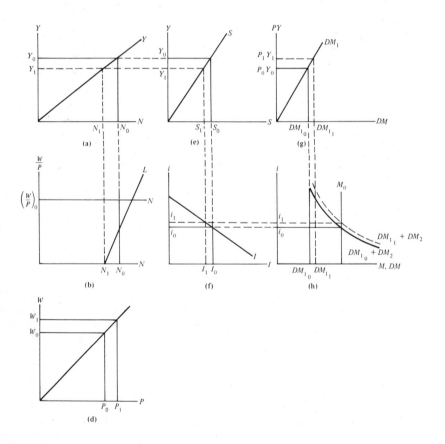

FIGURE 10-5

firms to raise wages (including a rise in the wages of its own employees), or merely through private wage setting without government influence or approval. The effects of a wage *cut* will be exactly the opposite of those we will find for a wage increase. Figure 10-5, for simplicity, continues to assume a horizontal N function.

The rise in the money wage from W_0 to W_1 is shown in part d. Since there is no change in the N function, it is clear that the real wage cannot change, and that prices must therefore rise in the same proportion as wages, from P_0 to P_1. The only effect of this can be a rise in mPY, in DM_1, and thus in the interest rate, i, which will reduce I, and therefore Y. The new equilibrium values are shown with subscripts 1.

It is clear that Y does not fall in proportion to the rise in P; for, if it did, there would be no rise in i, and thus no reason for Y to decline. But, other things equal, the extent of the decline in Y will be the less, and the extent of the rise in i will be the greater, if investment is relatively insensitive to the interest rate. On the other hand, the more sensitive the demand for money is to the interest rate, other things equal, the less, again, will be the decline in Y but also the less the rise in i.

If the N function sloped downward to the right, the direction of all changes would be the same as indicated. But, to the extent that Y declined, P would not rise in the same proportion as W, and all other effects of a given ΔW would therefore be smaller than if W/P were constant.[3]

Thus, a rise in the money wage—unless its effects on the interest rate are offset by a simultaneous rise in M—will tend to reduce employment and output. The converse is that a cut in the money wage will tend to increase employment. (This is why and how fully flexible wages—always falling in the presence of any unemployment—would ultimately produce full employment in the absence of special cases previously reviewed.)

It is important to understand clearly *why* the *inverse* connection exists between ΔW and ΔN. Essentially, it arises from, and *only* from, the impact of the wage level on the price level and of the price level on the demand for money. If the reader turns back to Chapter 4, he will see that these same two relationships are essential to the simple, Say's Law results of the classical model. To be sure, in the classical "quantity–theory" context, there was no explicit theory of aggregate demand, and changes in the price level affected output directly rather than via the rate of interest. But the basic mechanism of price effects on the transactions demand for money is identical.

It is also clear, in this model, as in the simple classical model, that the effects of changes in the money wage level are exactly parallel to the effects of changes in the money supply. In either model, the negative effect on

---

[3] The explanation for a rise in W/P with a decline in employment and output can be considered, in classical terms, as stemming from a rise in the marginal (and average) product of labor as less labor is used; expressed otherwise, this means a movement back down along rising marginal cost schedules.

employment of a rise in the money wage can be precisely offset by an appropriate rise in M, leaving the interest rate, and thus investment, unchanged. Or the positive effects from a fall in W can be equally well secured—and through the same interest rate-investment channel—through a rise in M. Indeed, some economists prefer to talk about a "real money supply" M^*/P, which is equally affected by a 10 percent rise in M or a 10 percent fall in P.

This does not mean that there may not be effects of changes in W on employment, other than through the interest rate. It is just that this channel is the only one incorporated in this model. Economists or others who may propose to use the wage level as a tool of employment policy should understand that they require a different model if they are to support other kinds of effects. Yet there continue to be proposals to use wage policy to affect employment, which are said to be or interpreted to be identified with a "Keynesian" approach yet find no justification in the Keynesian model, at least as developed to this point. Consideration of the error of these views helps us better to understand the nature of the Keynesian version of the Keynesian-classical synthesis.

Some Mistaken Views of Wage–Price Effects

Each of these arguments assumes that there can be some *direct effect* of wage rate changes on aggregate *consumer demand*, in this context often called "purchasing power." One line of argument is frequently used by those who oppose flexible wages as a means of stabilizing demand. It is often put forward by them in the mistaken impression that they are thereby explaining Keynes' analysis of wage cuts. The argument runs this way: From the standpoint of employer incentives, wage cuts would appear to be favorable to the employment of labor, but this neglects the demand side. Wages are not only a cost of production, but an element of income. If wages are cut, incomes fall, and therefore, the demand for consumer goods will fall. As a result of the drop in demand, prices must fall, too, perhaps even as much as wages, thus eliminating the employer incentive.

Now this is a strange doctrine, indeed. Whether *total wage income in money terms* (W times N) falls or not clearly depends not only on what happens to money wages W but also on employment N. Only by *assuming* no increase or a lesser (percentage) increase in employment than the cut in wages can one be sure that there is a fall in money wage income. But we should not *assume* what it is that we want to discover. Further, what is relevant to demand for consumer goods (and thus, indirectly, for the demand for labor) is not money income but real income. If prices fall, then that is relevant too. Indeed, if prices fall in the same proportion as wages (which is the conclusion of the above argument) there will be no reduction in *real* wage income even if employment does not increase, and thus no cut in workers' real consumer demand.

This argument also seems to imply that wage income is the only kind, or the only kind that is relevant to the demand for consumer goods. In fact, nonwage income, for example, profits, must also be considered. Entrepreneurs eat too. If prices fall in the same proportion as wages, then there has been no redistribution between wage and nonwage income; if they fall by less, any loss by wage earners is a gain by someone else, *relatively*. But what happens to *total* real income, and total demand, remains dependent upon what happens to employment and output—which is exactly what we are trying to discover and therefore must not assume. We cannot reach any conclusion about total demand for goods except by considering all of the relationships in our model that this argument attempts to short cut.

A second line of argument has been used by those who have supported wage reductions as a means of increasing demand. This argument is one stage superior to the previous one, for it recognizes that what happens to total wage income depends on what happens to employment as well as what happens to wages. There must be cases, this argument insists, in which the demand for labor has an elasticity greater than 1. If so, then total wage income will increase as a result of a wage cut. Even if prices do not fall, this means an increase in the aggregate *real* as well as the money income of labor, and therefore an increase in the demand for consumer goods. Thus, we do not have to rely on an "indirect" effect operating on investment through the demand for money and the interest rate. A wage cut may have a *direct* effect on aggregate consumer demand.

Now this argument is all right as far as it goes, but it does not go far enough. To see what is missing, refer to Figure 10-6.

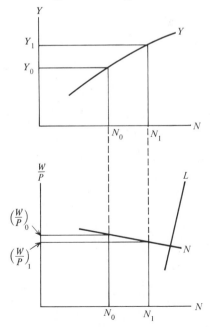

FIGURE 10-6

In the lower half of the figure is clearly a highly elastic demand for labor schedule (N). A cut in W/P will increase real wage income, for the product $(W/P)_1 \times N_1$ is greater than $(W/P)_0 \times N_0$. If wage-earner demand for consumer goods depends on real wage income, then aggregate wage-earner demand for goods will rise when the real wage declines. We may even assume that the marginal propensity to consume of wage earners is 1. But the argument is incomplete unless we compare this potential increase in *demand* with the increase in *supply* of goods. The increase in supply is equal to $Y_1 - Y_0$ in the upper half. Will the increase in demand be that great, even with a wage-earner MPC = 1? It will be *only if the entire increment of income earned from the production of this increment of output goes to wage earners.* But this is impossible under the assumption of profit-maximizing behavior by entrepreneurs, or, indeed, of any other reasonable kind of price and output behavior.

Output Y_1 and employment N_1 were chosen by entrepreneurs, we assume, as representing some kind of an optimum, this optimum point of operations having been shifted from the previous one involving output Y_0 and employment N_0. Unless output Y_1 involves a larger profit income, it will not be chosen; for employers still have the option of producing the previous output Y_0 which, with lower wages, would clearly mean a greater profit than originally. Thus, for employers to prefer output Y_1, it must offer greater profit at the new wage rate than the previous output. This means that some part of the increased real income associated with the larger output must go to nonwage earners. Unless the MPC of profit recipients is also equal to 1, the increase in demand must be less than the increase in supply. The correct conclusion from our model is that, regardless of the elasticity of the demand for labor, prices must fall in proportion to wages. The real income positions of both wage earners and profit recipients will be restored to their initial levels with no change in real output or demand, *except* as there may be some "indirect" effect via the interest rate or some similar "indirect" route not considered by this argument, or unless we use some dynamic argument.

Still a third line of fallacious equilibrium analysis is used by those who support wage *increases* as a means of reducing unemployment. It relies on the probable fact that the marginal propensity to consume of wage earners is higher than that of profit recipients. Thus, a rise in wages, which is assumed to redistribute income in favor of wage earners, will cause an increase in aggregate demand, the increase in wage-earner demand being greater than the decrease in profit-recipient demand. Now there will be a redistribution in favor of wage earners only if prices rise less than in proportion to wages. If they rise in equal proportion, everything is as before, in real terms. Why is it assumed that employers will not raise prices in the same proportion? Without going through the argument in detail, it can be shown that the assumption of profit-maximizing behavior by entrepreneurs will require an equal percentage increase, unless there is some "indirect" effect that produces a rise or fall of aggregate demand through some other means—for example, via the interest rate. If prices were at first advanced in smaller proportion, the real wage would be higher than initially, and employment and output therefore reduced. This reduction in real income would reduce demand, but by less than the decrease in supply (because the MPC is less than 1). Prices would therefore rise, until the initial wage-price ratio was restored. If there were any "indirect" effect, it would presumably be unfavorable, causing prices to rise by less than wages, and employment to decrease rather than increase as the argument tried to prove. If there were no "indirect" effects, the wage increase would merely inflate prices in equal proportion.

These, and other similar erroneous lines of argument all try to prove that wage changes can have some *direct* influence, favorable or unfavorable, on aggregate consumer demand. The fact is that no direct effects on consumer demand are possible so long as we accept three assumptions: (a) that real consumption, in total and of each group, is a function of *real* not money income; (b) that the average MPC of the community as a whole (wage earners and nonwage-earners taken together) is less than 1; and (c) that employers maximize, or at least are concerned about, profits. Of course, we continue to reason in terms of a static model.

A specific numerical model in terms of which the problem can be analyzed is presented in an appendix to this chapter. Each of the three mistaken analyses here considered can be tested through this example, which incorporates the assumptions listed.

We have been concerned in this section with some incomplete or mistaken analyses, each of which has been used as the basis of a policy recommendation. Although we think it important to show the errors of these arguments, we do not necessarily reject or approve any particular policy recommendation merely because a certain argument proceeds or does not proceed logically from assumption to conclusions. The static Keynesian analysis appears to be *logically* faultless, and argues that, although wage reductions can have no direct effect on demand, they should probably have some favorable indirect effects, except in limiting cases. But Keynes himself rejected general wage cuts as a policy for increasing employment, largely on the grounds that whatever good wage cuts might accomplish could be obtained more quickly and efficiently in other ways, in particular, by monetary or fiscal policy. To be sure, the conviction of classical thought that unemployment could arise only from too high a money wage and could always be cured by wage cuts obviously rested on an oversimplified and unrealistic analysis. However, the crude "underconsumptionist" arguments of trade unions for money wage increases are equally flawed.

Nevertheless, it is probable that there may be particular times and places where a general wage cut would (if it could be secured) have a pronounced favorable effect and be the most efficient among alternative policies. There may even be times and places where a general wage *increase* would be helpful. But the justification of any such policy must rest on other considerations than are incorporated in the static theories so far analyzed, as well as upon administrative or strategic considerations that may be of crucial significance. In particular, dynamic relationships which our static theories neglect, are of overriding importance in the design of short-run economic stabilization policies. Thus our interest has been primarily that of indicating erroneous or incomplete arguments in support of one or another policy, not in arriving at a particular recommendation.

For example, once we introduce expectations and a dynamic analysis, the effect of a wage cut might be highly favorable. We know that a wage cut for one firm (all other wages and prices unchanged) will lead that firm to expand output[4] in the (correct) expectation that the demand curve for his own product will be unaffected. Total output in the economy will not necessarily rise, for his increased sales will be at the expense of other products; but a wage cut will raise *his* production, sales, and profits.

Suppose that, even though a wage cut is general in the economy, each employer (not having learned "Keynesian economics") *assumes* that he will be able to sell more and steps up his production. If the consumption function is stable and investment does not increase, we know that the increased output cannot all be taken off the market. Increased output means more income and hence more consumer buying; but so long as the marginal propensity to consume is less than 1, demand will expand by less than supply. Suppose, however, that the desired stock of inventories of each employer (or, at least, of many employers)—or even his desired stock of plant and equipment—is tied to his output level. Then increased output (in the *expectation* of increased sales) will engender investment in inventories or plant and equipment and, hence, an increase in demand that may, in the aggregate, justify the increased output.

Since we postulated that this investment depended on an *increase* in output, it may only be maintained if there is now a further increase in output. Thus, in the absence of another favorable "shock," the economy might then fall back, after this short spurt, to its initial position. But this is not the only possibility. If, for example, investment depends heavily on business confidence, a rise, once begun, may easily cumulate. In effect, the marginal propensity to spend (MPC + MPI) may exceed unity during expansion periods, once the expansion is touched off.

What we have sketched in the preceding discussion is only one of numerous possible developments, not a general dynamic theory of the effect of wage cuts in a depression. As indicated, the effect might equally well be highly unfavorable; to decide when one might expect favorable and when unfavorable results takes us beyond the scope of this book (and, one may suggest, beyond the firm "knowledge" of economists).

---

[4] Unless its demand curve has zero elasticity or its marginal cost curve is vertical.

It is, nevertheless, fair to state that the theoretical developments of the past 40 years have probably brought about as complete a reversal of the general tenor of informed judgment on the matter of wage cuts as on any other single major question of stabilization policy. Fifty years ago the opinion of economists would have been close to unanimous that wage cuts (if they could be achieved) would have a favorable effect on employment when there was general unemployment. Today, the overwhelming judgment would be to leave money wages alone, or to put a heavy burden of proof on one who would propose to remedy unemployment by any kind of manipulation of the general level of wage rates.

FULL EMPLOYMENT AND INFLATION

The discussion of this and the preceding several chapters has concentrated almost exclusively on situations involving unemployment and a national income and output short of what the economy is capable of producing. It should be easy to see, however, that there is nothing inherent in the Keynesian model that makes unemployment inevitable. What Keynesian theory stresses is rather the absence or weakness of those *automatic stabilizers* relied upon in classical theory to prevent deficient aggregate demand or quickly to eliminate a deficiency if it should arise. Keynesian doctrine suggests that the external forces shaping aggregate demand—the position of the C and I functions and the level of G—*may be such* as to yield less than full employment. But, by the same token, they *may yield* a level of aggregate demand sufficient for full employment or even a level of demand *more than sufficient*. Actually, a level of demand just sufficient for full employment would represent an unusual case, for this is only one possible point in a wide band of possibilities, a dividing line between the case of unemployment and inflation. For aggregate demand more than sufficient for full employment would imply inflation.

We shall consider the analysis of inflation in detail in a later chapter, but the outline of the Keynesian analysis of inflation is implicit in all that has been developed for the unemployment case. If the demand for final goods, and therefore for resources (including labor) that produce final goods, should exceed the supply when all workers are employed, there will be a bidding up of both P and W. This bidding up will occur if we assume prices and wages flexible to upward pressure, whether or not they may be so to downward pressure. Such upward flexibility (with full employment) was what Keynes assumed; and, in general, one can take little exception to this asymmetry of his hypothesis.

The question then arises as to the possible effects of rising wages and prices on aggregate demand. Will inflation tend to remove the excess demand that causes it, or will it leave the excess untouched, causing prices and wages to rise in endless spiral?

Keynes argued that flexible wages, *on the downside*, might remove a **deflationary gap**—a margin between actual demand and full employment— but that the effects were uncertain and weak and, in any case, of doubtful relevance. By the same token, an **inflationary gap**—an excess of demand over the full-employment level—will generate an upward price and wage movement that might have some tendency to remove the excess, although the effects were, again, uncertain and weak. The analysis of effects in the inflation case is exactly parallel with that in the deflation case. The one effect built into the basic Keynesian model is the interest rate effect: higher wages and prices, with no change in M, raising interest rates and thereby reducing real aggregate demand. (In the next chapter, we will introduce some further effects of rising as well as falling prices.)

Oversimplified and therefore mistaken analyses are as dangerous and as likely to arise in the inflation case as in the case involving deflation. If one argues that higher prices will directly reduce real consumer demand, thus eliminating the inflation, he is reasoning illegitimately from a single commodity to the aggregate economy. For, in this model, money incomes rise in whatever proportion prices rise, leaving consumers in the same real-income position as before. Unless it affects expectations or interest rates, inflation in the cost of capital goods should not deter real-investment demand, for the prices of the final products made with capital goods will have risen too. A rise in money wages will not reduce employer demand for labor if prices also are moving up. Attempting to derive some "direct" effects on consumption or investment or on the willingness of employers to bid for labor by introducing particular elasticities of demand for labor or differences in MPC between workers and owners can be no more successful in this case than in the analysis of deflation, so long as we assume no money illusions and employers' concern about profits.

If the net effect of the interest-rate change (and other effects yet to be considered) should be for aggregate real demand to fall as prices rise, there would be some rise in prices just sufficient to eliminate the entire excess demand, producing a level of demand just equal to productive capacity when all resources are employed and a cessation of the price rise, with prices stable at their new, higher level. If the net effect of all of the indirect effects were not to reduce real demand, then aggregate demand in excess of full-employment output would only create a disequilibrium *process* of continuing inflation. An equilibrium analysis can say little or nothing about the speed or nature of that process.

One final paragraph on the relation of the quantity of money to inflation will terminate this discussion. Given an initial equilibrium at precisely full employment, an increase in M will ordinarily lead to a rise in prices. It will do so by causing i to fall, thus stimulating investment and creating an *excess* of demand in place of the previous just-adequate level. If the only source of the excess demand were a reduced i arising from an expanded M, a cessation of the increase in M should cause the inflation to terminate, with a price level higher in the same proportion as *M*. This higher price level would generate an increase in transactions demand equal to the increase in *M*, allowing only the previous level of asset balances, and thus the same interest rate as initially. So long as prices had risen in smaller proportion than *M*, there would remain idle balances to depress *i* and thereby to manufacture further inflation. Wages, too, must have risen in the same proportion as prices. If they had risen by less, employers would be trying to hire more workers (at the lower real wage) than were willing to work, thus further bidding up the money wage. One may note that this analysis of inflation is practically identical to that which, in Chapter 5, we attributed to Wicksell. The identity between quantity theory and Keynesian reasoning in this particular case should not, however, confuse us. The Keynesian analysis also shows how inflation can be produced without *any* increase in *M* or how an inflation can occur the extent of which bears no necessary relationship to the extent of any increase in *M*.

Nevertheless, it is now obvious to most observers that neither the Keynesian nor quantity theory explanation of inflation is highly relevant to the modern phenomenon of widespread and persistent inflation. Thus, we shall not pursue the subject further at this point but will take it up separately in Chapters 13, 14, and 15.

APPENDIX
A NUMERICAL MODEL FOR THE ANALYSIS OF WAGE CHANGES

This model is designed only to make it easier to see that the *direct* effects of a money wage increase or decrease on consumer demand are nil, given certain basic assumptions, no matter whether the demand for labor is elastic or inelastic, and whether the marginal propensity to consume of wage earners is or is not higher than that of profit recipients. This conclusion follows so long as our argument is static and we accept the three basic assumptions: a consumption function stable in real terms; an average MPC < 1; and profit maximizing behavior.

The model consists of six equations and an (autonomous) money wage level.

$$(1) \qquad \frac{C_w}{P} = \frac{WN}{P} \qquad (\text{or, } C_w = WN)$$

This equation describes the consumption of wage-earners (C_w). We assume that both marginal and average propensities equal one; workers spend their entire money incomes—that is, the entire money wage bill (WN).

$$(2) \qquad \frac{C_r}{P} = 10 + 0.6 \frac{PY - WN}{P}$$

This equation describes the consumption of profit recipients (C_r).[5] We assume their real consumption to be a function of their real income, with a marginal propensity to consume of 0.60. Profit in money terms is equal to the money national income, PY, less the wage bill, WN.

(3)
$$\frac{I}{P} = 30$$

This embodies the assumption of constant (intended) real investment.

(4)
$$PY = C_w + C_r + I$$

Total expenditure or income consists only of consumption plus investment.

(5)
$$Y = 50 + 7N - 0.02N^2$$

This is an aggregate production function. It shows diminishing marginal returns as employment increases.

(6)
$$\frac{dY}{dN} = \frac{W}{P}$$

This is the familiar assumption of profit maximization, assuming perfect competition. Given the production function of equation (5), $dY/dN = 7 - 0.04\,N$.

(7)
$$W = \$5$$

This is the initial money wage, which we can alter to find the effects on other variables.

It can be seen that we assume only a single commodity, one which can either be consumed or invested. This is equivalent to using an index number of outputs of a number of commodities on the assumption that the *composition* of output either remains constant, or at least makes no difference.

Simultaneous solution of these seven equations is possible by successive substitutions. This process yields a cubic equation, which has, however, only a single solution with economic meaning (that is, a single solution involving positive prices and quantities). The reader need not attempt to reproduce the solution, but he may wish to test the values shown below to see that they satisfy each of the equations. He can take it on faith that there is no other set which will also satisfy all of them.

$$N = 50$$
$$Y = 350$$
$$\frac{W}{P} = 5$$
$$P = \$1$$

[5] Profit here really means nonwage income; specifically it includes interest and rent. We are assuming no government transfer payments or taxes.

$$PY = \$350$$
$$WN = \$250$$
$$PY - WN \text{ (profits)} = \$100$$
$$C_w = \$250$$
$$C_r = \$70$$
$$I = \$30$$

This system involves an elastic demand for labor. If the real wage could be reduced from 5 to 4.4, employment would expand from 50 to 65 [substitute in equation (6)], causing real wage income (WN/P) to increase from 250 to 286.[6] Suppose that the money wage were cut from \$5 to \$4.40. Suppose, further, that prices did not change. (In a moment we shall show that they must change, but assume that they do not in order to see why they must!) This would mean a reduction in the real wage from 5 to 4.4. Such a reduction would, as already noted, lead to an increase in employment from 50 to 65, and an increase in money wage income from \$250 to \$286. Wage earner consumption would therefore also increase from 250 to 286 units of output [see equation (1)]. But how much would output increase if employment went from 50 to 65? It can be seen that Y would rise from 350 to 420.5 [equation (5)], and the money national income, PY, from \$350 to \$420.50 (still assuming unchanged prices). Wage earners, then, would provide a market for 36 additional units, but production would have risen by 70.5 units. Could profit recipients be counted on to consume the balance? Profit income has risen from \$100 to \$134.50 (\$420.50 − \$286). On this basis, $C_r/P = 10 + 0.6(\$134.5/P) = 90.7$. This is an increase of 20.7 units from their previous demand of 70, but it is not enough. Total demand is now (C_w/P) 286 + (C_r/P) 90.7 + (I/P) 30 = 406.7, compared with a total supply of 420.5. If, in fact, employers had assumed that prices would stay unchanged when wages were cut, and had immediately raised employment from 50 to 65 in this expectation, they would now find unsold goods piling up.

Suppose that, in response to this inability to sell what they produced, entrepreneurs reduced prices, but in smaller proportion than wages had fallen, say, to \$0.94. This means a real wage of 4.68, employment of 58 [equation (6)], and output of 388.72 [equation (5)]. With a money national income of \$365.40 (388.72 × \$0.94), the wage bill would be \$255.20 (58 × \$4.40), leaving a profit income of \$110.20. Wage earner consumption would be 271.5 (255.20 ÷ \$0.94), and consumption from profits 80.3 [10 + 0.6(\$110.20/\$0.94)]. Adding investment of 30 gives total demand of 381.8. This is still short of the output of 388.7. The gap has been reduced by half, from 13.8 to 6.9. But a gap remains, and will remain at any price level higher than \$0.88, at which point prices will have fallen in

---

[6] At the equilibrium point, the elasticity of demand for labor is 2.5.

the same proportion as wages, the real wage will again be 5, with employment back to 50, and output back down to 350. Wage income will be $220 (50 × $4.4); the money national income $308 (350 × $0.88); and profits $88. Consumption by wage earners will be 250 ($220 $0.88); by profit recipients 70 [10 + 0.6($88/$0.88)]; making total demand 350, once again equal to the supply. Of course, interest-rate effects would be favorable to employment (and other indirect effects to be considered later). But these are not part of the simpler arguments considered here.

The reader can test the effect of a money wage increase by an analogous procedure.

REVIEW QUESTIONS

1. Complete Table 10-1.

2.

(a) Assuming prices are constant, but *taking account of the feedback on private investment* through the interest rate, explain why the effect on Y of a reduction in G will be less than G times the multiplier that would have been obtained if the feedback on investment were ignored. (Assume that the cut in G does not involve a reduction in the money supply). You are not required to use diagrams, but if you do use diagrams, label and explain them.

(b) (1) The cut in G of part (a) may, however, reduce the price level (even at a constant wage rate), and may reduce the wage rate as well. Why and how?

(2) If it does reduce the price level, show that Y will decline by less than the result described in part (a) and explain why.

(3) If wage rates are "perfectly flexible," the decrease in G may not reduce Y at all. Explain carefully.

(c) However, if there exists a "liquidity trap," the answer to part (b) (3) may have to be changed. Explain what is meant by a liquidity trap, and why its existence changes the answer to (b) (3).

3. "The fact that actual interest rates have never reached zero (except possibly during a brief period in the Great Depression) refutes the argument about an 'inconsistency' between saving and investment." Briefly explain what is meant by the inconsistency and evaluate the statement.

4. An essential difference between Keynesian and classical macroeconomics consists of their different assumptions regarding the effects of involuntary unemployment on wage rates.

(a) What are the assumptions of each about wage rates?

(b) Show that if truly flexible wage rates are inserted in the Keynesian model, there is no equilibrium position other than at full employment.

(c) However, with flexible wages, there may still be no equilibrium in the Keynesian model. Indicate several possible circumstances in which wage deflation might fail to produce equilibrium at full employment.

5. Identify and contrast the sources of inflation under the Keynesian macroeconomic theories and the classical economic theories.

6. Carefully evaluate each of the following statements (considered separately):
(a) If hourly wages rates increase more rapidly than the advance of output per labor hour, either prices must rise or profits will decrease.
(b) If the marginal propensity to consume of wage earners exceeds that of capitalists, a wage increase will raise income and employment.
(c) Proposition (b) is correct only if the elasticity of demand for labor with respect to wage rates is greater than one.

SELECTED REFERENCES

J. M. Keynes, *The General Theory of Employment, Interest, and Money* (Harcourt, Brace, 1936), Chapter 19.
(Keynes' views on wage determination and the classical model.)

A. Leijonhufvud, *On Keynesian Economics and the Economics of Keynes* (Oxford University Press, 1968), pp. 35–48.
(A summary of a sophisticated reinterpretation of Keynesian theory; the entire book can be read with profit.)

J. Tobin, "Money Wage Rates and Employment," in *The New Economics*, S. E. Harris (ed.) (Knopf, 1947), reprinted in M. G. Mueller (ed.), *Readings in Macroeconomics* (Holt, Rinehart, and Winston, 2nd ed., 1971), pp. 215–225.
(An early and authoritative analysis of the relation of wage rigidity to unemployment.)

D. Patinkin, "Price Flexibility and Full Employment," *American Economic Review*, 38 (September 1948), 543–564, reprinted with revisions, in *Readings in Monetary Theory* (selected by a committee of the American Economic Association, Blakiston, 1951), pp. 252–283; and in M. G. Mueller, *Readings in Macroeconomics*, (Holt, Rinehart, Winston, 2nd ed., 1966), pp. 226–244.
(A classic review of the role of wage rigidity in unemployment and of how price-wage flexibility promotes full employment.)

Chapter 11

The "IS-LM" Form of the Model

The IS-LM Form of the Synthesis Model
The *IS* curve
The *LM* curve
Combining *IS* and *LM* curves

Relationships to the Multiplier and Quantity Theory
Special cases of the *IS-LM* model
"Crowding-out"
Growth in the rigid-price *IS-LM* model

Simple Dynamics of the *IS-LM* Model
Lags and the *IS* curve
The *LM* curve
More complex dynamic elements

The principal task of this chapter is to present an alternative formulation of the synthesis model that was put together in Chapter 10. It differs substantively only in that it expands that model explicitly to take account of government taxes, transfers, and purchases, so as to permit consideration of fiscal policy effects. However, the main contribution of this formulation of the model is a simpler kind of graphic presentation, replacing the seven part diagrams used in Chapter 10. This graphic version (although without explicit introduction of fiscal policy) was first developed by J. R. Hicks,[1] and later popularized by Alvin Hansen;[2] thus, it has sometimes been called the "Hicks-Hansen" analysis. Since the two functions used in the graphic analysis are usually labelled *IS* and *LM* curves, the analysis is most commonly known today simply as the **IS-LM model**.

In its most frequently used form, this model assumes rigid prices; it thus represents a strongly Keynesian version of the Keynesian-classical synthesis. We will so present it. However, in Chapter 12, we will show how the classical wage-price-employment analysis can be incorporated into the *IS-LM* model.

THE *IS-LM* FORM OF THE SYNTHESIS MODEL

Although prices are taken as rigid in this form of the model, the price level is explicitly incorporated so that it is possible to see what difference the

---

[1] See "Mr. Keynes and the Classics," *Econometrica* (1937), reprinted in *Readings in the Theory of Income Distribution*, selected by a committee of the American Economic Association (Blakiston, 1946); in M. G. Mueller, ed., *Readings in Macroeconomics*, 2nd ed. (Holt, Rinehart & Winston, 1971); in E. Shapiro, ed., *Macroeconomics: Sected Readings* (Harcourt, Brace & World, 1970); and in J. Lindauer, ed., *Macroeconomic Readings* (The Free Press, 1968).

[2] *Monetary Theory and Fiscal Policy* (McGraw-Hill, 1949).

price level makes and to consider the effect of one-time shifts in the price level. However, since prices (and wages) are not assumed flexible and there exists no mechanism (except government policy) to assure full employment, we suppress equations (1) and (4) of the model used at the beginning of Chapter 10. In effect, we start with the model presented graphically at the end of Chapter 10, except that we incorporate fiscal variables, and that we present it in the $C + I = Y$ form instead of the $S = I$ form. The model thus consists of these relationships:

(1) $\qquad Y \equiv C + I + G_0$

(2) $\qquad C = C(DI, i) \qquad\qquad 0 < \dfrac{\partial C}{\partial DI} < 1; \quad \dfrac{\partial C}{\partial i} \gtreqless 0$

(3) $\qquad DI \equiv Y - T$

(4) $\qquad T = T(Y) \qquad\qquad 0 < \dfrac{dT}{dY} < 1$

(5) $\qquad I = I(i, Y) \qquad\qquad \dfrac{\partial I}{\partial i} < 0; \quad \dfrac{\partial I}{\partial Y} \gtreqless 0$

(6) $\qquad M^* = mPY + f(i) \qquad \dfrac{df}{di} < 0; \quad \dfrac{d^2 f}{di^2} > 0$

where, as usual,

$\qquad Y =$ net national product
$\qquad C =$ consumer purchases
$\qquad I =$ investment purchases
$\qquad G_0 =$ government purchases (exogenous)
$\qquad T =$ taxes less transfers
$\qquad DI =$ disposable income
$\qquad i =$ rate of interest
$\qquad M^* =$ money supply (exogenous)
$\qquad P =$ price level (exogenous)

Since only in equation (6) have we specified the sign of other than a first derivative, that is, anything other than the direction of slope of any function, we can without loss of generality take the functions of (2), (4), and (5) as linear, giving us the subsystem:

(1) $\quad Y \equiv C + I + G_0$

(2a) $\quad C = c_0 + c_1 DI - c_2 i \qquad\qquad c_0 \gtreqless 0; \quad 0 < c_1 < 1; \quad c_2 > 0$

(3) $\quad DI \equiv Y - T$

(4a) $\quad T = t_0 + t_1 Y \qquad\qquad\qquad t_0 \gtreqless 0; \quad 0 < t_1 < 1$

(5a) $\quad I = b_0 + b_1 Y - b_2 i \qquad\qquad b_0 > 0; \quad b_1 > 0; \quad b_2 > 0$

The *IS* Curve

By successive substitutions involving equations (1), (2), (3), (4), and (5), we can readily reduce these five to a single equation:

$$(7) \qquad Y = [C\{Y - T(Y)\}, i] + I(i, Y) + G_0$$

Using, instead, the linear forms, (2a), (4a), and (5a), this becomes

$$(7a) \quad Y = \frac{1}{1 - c_1(1 - t_1) - b_1}[c_0 + b_0 - c_1 t_0 - (b_2 + c_2)i + G_0]$$

This can be seen to be an expanded version of the fiscal-policy model of Chapter 7, where the term outside the square brackets is a multiplier and that within the brackets a multiplicand. There we were implicitly assuming $c_2 = 0$, that is, no interest elasticity in the consumption function; and, most of the time, we assumed both b_1 and b_2 also as zero, that is, investment as simply autonomous.

Setting these three parameters at zero reduces equation (7a) to its Keynesian special case:

$$(7K) \qquad Y = \frac{1}{1 - c_1(1 - t_1)}[c_0 + b_0 - c_1 t_0 + G_0]$$

Except for the use of b_0 in place of I_0, this equation, both multiplier and multiplicand, is identical with equation (22) developed at the end of Chapter 6, and then used to develop the fiscal-policy model of Chapter 7. In Chapter 8, we also briefly explored a model involving a $b_1 > 0$ ("investment, too, depends on income"); that produced a multiplier similar to that of (7a), which we called a "super-multiplier."[3]

In its more general form, with c_2, b_1, and b_2 not arbitrarily set at zero, equation (7a) makes Y depend not merely on the parameters of the consumption function and the fiscal variables but, as well, on the parameters of the investment function and—as a further determinant of both consumption and investment—on the interest rate. Since the interest rate is itself a variable, we can equally well rearrange (7a) in a form that makes i depend on the same parameters and on Y:

$$(7a') \qquad i = \frac{c_0 + b_0 - c_1 t_0 + G_0 - [1 - c_1(1 - t_1) - b_1]Y}{b_2 + c_2}$$

---

[3] We shall arbitrarily assume that the denominator of the term we have called the multiplier is positive, that is, that $1 > c_1(1 - t_1) + b_1$. In discussing the multiplier and super-multiplier (in earlier chapters) we showed that, in a simple Keynesian model, the failure of this condition to be satisfied meant that any equilibrium was unstable. Although that is not *necessarily* the case for the *IS-LM* model, we are not going to construct an explicitly dynamic version of the *IS-LM* model. Since any discussion of the case of $1 < c_1(1 - t_1) + b_1$ in an equilibrium framework seems essentially meaningless (and some existing discussions of it wrong), we will suppress the problem by assuming $1 > c_1(1 - t_1) + b_1$.

In fact, rather than to think of the causation as running either from Y to i or i to Y, equation (7a) in either form really expresses a mutual interdependence between i and Y; it says that, given the relationships expressed in equations (1) through (5a), the equilibrium values of i and Y are related as in (7a) or (7a').

Using (7a') we can easily show that equation (7a) comprehends, as a special case, not merely the simple Keynesian theory of income determination (7K), but, as well, the classical theory of interest. The classical theory clearly had no reference to fiscal variables: thus we take t_0, t_1, and G_0 as zero. Moreover, neither saving nor investment was assumed dependent on income; thus c_1 and b_1 were, in effect, taken as zero. Making these changes reduces equation (7a') to its classical special case:

(7C)
$$i = \frac{c_0 + b_0 - Y}{b_2 + c_2}$$

It is easy to show that this corresponds to the classical saving-investment theory of the interest rate. If we define saving as $S = DI - C$, and take $c_1 = 0$ and $DI = Y$ (because T is zero), we get the classical saving function,

$$S = Y - c_0 + c_2 i$$

Using the simplified investment function,

$$I = b_0 - b_2 i$$

and setting $S = I$, we again derive (7C).

Thus, depending on which parameters of the model we choose to ignore (or suppress), equation (7a) can be seen to include, as special cases, alternatively the "simple Keynesian model," or the "classical theory of interest"! This should not completely surprise us. For when the classical theory argued that "saving and investment determine the interest rate," it (implicitly) took income as given (or as determined elsewhere in the model at the constant full-employment level) and thus ignored any effects of changes in Y on S. When Keynes argued that "saving and investment determine the level of income," he (implicitly) took the interest rate as given, thus ignoring any effects of changes in i on I. Equation (7) says that both statements are correct but incomplete. In fact, saving and investment determine neither income nor interest rate, but rather *what combinations of Y and i* are consistent with an equality of *I*nvestment and *S*aving (which is why equation (7a) is called the "*IS* curve").

Plotted in a quadrant with the axes i and Y, equation (7a') appears as in Figure 11-1. Setting $Y = 0$ in (7a') produces the vertical intercept shown on the figure; setting $i = 0$ in (7a) produces the horizontal intercept shown; and letting Y change by ΔY in (7a') gives the slope shown in the figure.

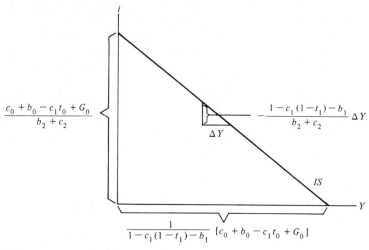

FIGURE 11-1

It is clear that increases in any of the terms that determine the intercepts and slope will shift the *IS* curve. The reader should learn (and not have to figure out every time the question arises) what these shifts will be. For example, looking at the horizontal and vertical intercepts and the slope shown in Figure 11-1, it is clear that an increase in G_0 shifts the *IS* curve to the right without changing its slope. The amount of the rightward shift can be seen to be

$$\frac{1}{1 - c_1(1 - t_1) - b_1} \Delta G_0$$

That is, Y will increase at any and every level of i by the change in G_0 times the multiplier (or super-multiplier, so long as $b_1 > 0$). The same is true of an exogenous increase in c_0 (constant in the consumption function). Such an upward shift of the consumption function will raise Y (at any and every i) by an amount equal to the shift times the same multiplier. The same is true for an increase in b_0, the constant in the investment function. If both investment and saving are unresponsive to the interest rate ($c_2 = b_2 = 0$), it can be seen that the *IS* curve is vertical. This gives us the "simple Keynesian model" with super-multiplier; if, investment is also unresponsive to income, we have the "simple Keynesian model" with the regular (consumption) multiplier. In either case, whatever the rate of interest, income is the same; and it changes only for reasons unrelated to the interest rate.

The *leftward shift* of the *IS* curve in response to an (algebraic) increase in t_0 (the constant in the tax-transfer function) is seen to equal

$$\frac{-c_1}{1 - c_1(1 - t_1) - b_1} \Delta t_0$$

Except for the b_1, this is the tax increase multiplier of Chapter 7 (equation 1).

On the other hand, it is clear that any change in c_1, t_1, b_1, b_2, or c_2 changes both the *slope* of the *IS* curve and one or both of its intercepts. A reduction in the interest elasticity of either investment or saving (b_2 or c_2) rotates the *IS* curve toward the vertical, without changing its horizontal intercept. An increase in the income sensitivity of consumption or investment (c_1 or b_1) rotates it upward while reducing its vertical intercept (by $\Delta c_1 t_0$) and increasing its horizontal one. An increase in the marginal tax rate t_1 rotates the *IS* curve downward without changing its vertical intercept, while reducing its horizontal one.

An excellent exercise is to attempt to *explain* each of these shift effects in words. For example, an increase in government expenditures, *ceteris paribus*, raises income at any and every rate of interest because it brings about extra production and incomes, which when spent (and respent) further raise both consumer and investment spending. To be sure, if the rate of interest should also simultaneously rise, the net increase in spending would be less because this would deter both consumer spending and business investment.

The *LM* Curve

The *IS* curve summarizes all the relationships involved in equations (1) through (5a). There remains equation (6), which is the *LM* curve (presumably an abbreviation for "Liquidity preference–Money"). A *linear* version of equation (6) could be written as

(6a) $$M^* = m_0 + m_1 PY - m_2 i$$

or

$$Y = \frac{M^* - m_0}{m_1 P} + \frac{m_2}{m_1 P} i$$

Rearranged with i as the left-hand variable, this is

(6a′) $$i = \frac{m_0 - M^*}{m_2} + \frac{m_1 P}{m_2} Y$$

Graphed in Figure 11-2, this is either of the straight lines, the intercepts and slope of which are indicated. Whether the horizontal intercept is positive or negative (the vertical intercept negative or positive) depends on the relative magnitudes of m_0 and M^*.

Clearly, if m_2 were zero (the demand for money independent of the interest rate), the *LM* curve would be vertical, and Y would be independent of the interest rate, but would depend on M^*, m_0, m_1, and P.

However, we specified equation (6) as *nonlinear*, with $\partial^2 f/\partial i^2 > 0$. To reason about the appearance of (6) and the factors that cause it to shift, we

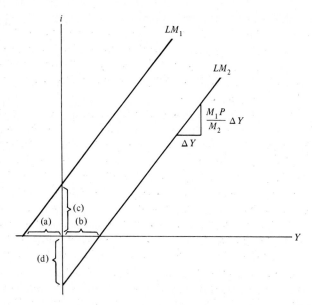

Horizontal intercept ($i = 0$): $Y = \dfrac{M^* - m_0}{m_1 P}$: shown as

(a) where $M^* < m_0$
(b) where $M^* > m_0$

Vertical intercept ($Y = 0$): $i = \dfrac{m_0 - M^*}{m_2}$: shown as

(c) where $M^* < m_0$
(d) where $M^* > m_0$

FIGURE 11-2

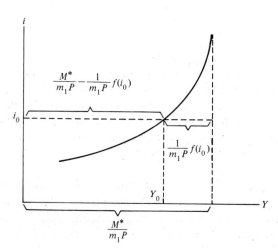

FIGURE 11-3

can rearrange (6) as

(6')
$$Y = \frac{M^*}{m_1 P} - \frac{1}{m_1 P} f(i)$$

This permits us to visualize (6) graphically as in Figure 11-3.[4]

---

[4] The following discussion can perhaps be clarified by making a specific assumption about the shape of $f(i)$, the interest-elastic portion of the demand for money, which we earlier labelled DM_2. Assume, for example, that

$$DM_2 = \frac{m_3}{i - m_4} \qquad m_3, m_4 > 0$$

Graphically, this appears as in Diagram A,

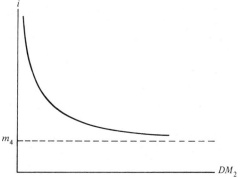

DM_2 **DIAGRAM A**

a rectangular hyperbola asymptotic to m_4 and to the vertical axis. Substituting in equation (6),

$$M^* = m_0 + m_1 PY + \frac{m_3}{i - m_4}$$

and rearranging, we get

(6b)
$$Y = \frac{M^* - m_0}{m_1 P} - \frac{1}{m_1 P} \cdot \frac{m_3}{i - m_4}$$

This makes the *LM* curve of Figure 11-3 appear as in Diagram B.

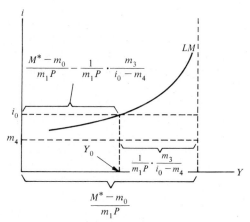

DIAGRAM B

It is clear that m_4 is the rate of interest at which the demand for money becomes infinitely elastic—that is, at which the "liquidity trap" appears.

The expression for Y in (6′) consists of two terms, the first of which is independent of the interest rate. This first term is shown on the horizontal axis and by the broken vertical line of Figure 11-3. The second term in (6′) is negative and is equal to the interest-elastic portion of the demand for money $f(i)$ times the fraction $1/m_1 P$. Thus, given m_1 and P, the *subtracted* term has the *shape* of the interest-elastic money demand. But its *extent* is horizontally stretched or compressed as $1/m_1 P$ may change.

Thus, it is easy to see that an increase in M^* moves the entire LM curve to the *right* with its shape unchanged—that is, the rightward shift is the same at any interest rate. Put otherwise, the slope of LM remains the same at each interest rate. On the other hand, an increase in P moves the curve to the *left*, while compressing it horizontally—that is, making it steeper than before at every interest rate. An increase in m_1 has exactly the same effects as an increase in P. Returning to the version of Figure 11-2, it is clear that each of the above propositions applies equally to the linear version. An effort to *explain* each of these propositions verbally will again test one's understanding of the economics of the model.

We characterized the IS curve as showing all of the possible combinations of interest rate and income at which saving would equal investment. Similarly, we can characterize the LM curve as showing all of the possible combinations of i and Y at which the supply and the demand for money are equal. The IS curve is described as showing all possible positions of "equilibrium in the goods market", the LM curve as showing all possible positions of "equilibrium in the money (bonds) market."

Combining *IS* and *LM* Curves

Since IS and LM curves each represent combinations of Y and i consistent with equilibrium in one "market," their intersection clearly must determine the *one* combination of Y and i that is consistent with simultaneous equilibrium in *both* markets. Figure 11-4 illustrates such a total model equilibrium position. At (i_0, Y_0), not only is the demand for money equal to the exogenous supply M^* but aggregate demand for goods and services also equals the production of goods and services. That is, income earned from production is such that aggregate consumer demand at income level Y_0 (taking account of taxes at that income level) and at interest rate i_0, plus aggregate investment demand at interest rate i_0 and at production level Y_0, plus the given government demand G_0 just equal Y_0.

Corresponding to i_0 and Y_0, there are, of course, equilibrium levels of C, I, T, and DI. These are not shown in the diagram itself. Each can, however, be calculated once Y_0 and i_0 are known. The inability to see these amounts (and changes in them) directly in the diagram is perhaps one disadvantage of this form of the model as compared with the seven-part diagrams used in the last major section of Chapter 10. It should be stressed, however, that the IS-LM model is essentially identical with that

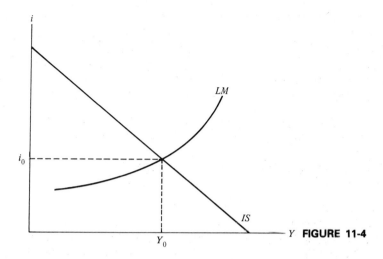

FIGURE 11-4

of Chapter 10, with two minor differences: (a) the seven-part diagrams of Chapter 10 did not expressly take account of fiscal policy variables (and there is no simple way of incorporating them); and (b) instead of taking the price level as exogenous, the earlier presentation "explained" it in terms of an exogenous wage level and a demand-for-labor (or price-determination) function. However, all major conclusions from the *IS-LM* model are identical with those derived from the Chapter 10 model.

The intersection of *IS* and *LM* curves represents graphically, of course, the simultaneous solution of equations (6) and (7). This solution can also be found algebraically by setting as equal the right hand sides of equations (6) and (7), or (6a') and (7a'), and solving for i or Y. If we assume the linear versions of both curves, this is relatively simple. From (7a') and (6a'), we get, by laborious manipulation, this expression for equilibrium Y:

$$
(8) \qquad Y = \frac{c_0 - c_1 t_0 + b_0 + G_0 + \left(\dfrac{M^* - m_0}{m_2}\right)(b_2 + c_2)}{1 - c_1(1 - t_1) - b_1 + \dfrac{m_1}{m_2}(b_2 + c_2)P}
$$

By inserting this expression for Y into either (6a) or (7a) we can solve for equilibrium i. Then, using the equilibrium values of Y and i, we can solve for equilibrium values of T, DI, C, and I.

Equation (8) shows Y to depend on the parameters of the consumption, tax, investment, and money-demand functions, and on G, M^*, and P. It is easy to see directly from (8) that

1. An increase of G_0 or a reduction of t_0 or t_1 will necessarily increase Y—that is, Keynesian fiscal policy "works" in this model.
2. An increase of M^* necessarily raises Y—that is, monetary policy also "works."

3. An increase in c_0 or b_0 (upward shifts in consumption or investment functions) increases Y, as in the simple Keynesian model.
4. An increase in m_1 (the amount of money balances needed for each dollar of transactions) reduces Y.
5. An increase in P lowers Y.
6. The effects of increases in c_1, m_2, and $b_2 + c_2$ require further analysis.[5]

By deriving the expression for i corresponding to equation (8)—that is, by substituting (8) into (6a) or (7a) and solving for i—we also can directly determine the effect on i of some of the shifts considered above, although several are again not obvious. However, we can reach *all* of these conclusions graphically once we recall how shifts in the various exogenous variables and parameters move either *IS* or *LM* curve (there is *no* parameter a change in which shifts *both* curves).

For conclusions 1 and 3 above, we need merely recall that increases in G_0, b_0, or c_0, or a reduction in t_0 or t_1 shift the *IS* curve to the right. This necessarily moves its intersection with the *LM* curve to a higher Y and i.

For conclusions 2, 4, and 5, we need merely recall that an increase in M^* shifts the *LM* curve to the right; increases in P or m_1 shift it to the left. Thus the former raises Y and lowers i; the latter lowers Y and raises i.

As to conclusion 6 (the need for further analysis of shifts in c_1, m_2, and $b_2 + c_2$), graphic analysis permits immediate conclusions. From Figure 11-1, we see that (provided $t_0 < 0$, as is probable) an increase in c_1 raises the vertical intercept of the *IS* curve and raises as well the horizontal intercept—increasing both the multiplier and the multiplicand. Thus, *IS* shifts to the right, and both Y and i increase. Also from Figure 11-1 we can see that an increase in $b_2 + c_2$ lowers the vertical intercept of *IS* without reducing the horizontal intercept—rotating the *IS* curve downward, reducing both Y and i (unless the *LM* curve is either vertical or horizontal in the range of their intersection). From Figure 11-2, it is easy to see that whether an increase in m_2 shifts the *LM* curve to left or right depends on the relative size of M^* and m_0, producing (for the leftward shift) lower Y and higher i (vice versa for the rightward).

For the *nonlinear* version of the *LM* curve, it is equally clear, from Figure 11-3, that an increase in M^* shifts the entire *LM* curve to the right, again lowering equilibrium i and raising Y, and an increase in m_1 or P does just the opposite. One can also conclude that an increase in the $f(i)$ schedule—that is, a shift of it to the right (or upward)—moves the *LM* curve to the left (or upward), reducing equilibrium Y but raising i.

Thus, the *IS-LM* apparatus provides an exceedingly convenient tool for analyzing questions of monetary and fiscal policy or the effects of

---

[5] However, so long as t_0 is negative—as seems likely (at least in the United States)—an increase in c_1 will clearly raise Y, because it will both increase the numerator and reduce the denominator of (8).

parameter shifts. It is widely used in the literature of macroeconomics for these purposes, and we shall use it frequently in our subsequent analyses. Several cautions, however, are necessary:

1. We should recall that the apparatus (in this form) has suppressed the production–employment relationship and the supply of and demand for labor functions. Therefore, we are not automatically reminded that Y cannot exceed potential output. No matter how far to the right the *IS-LM* curve intersection may move, such an intersection, beyond some level Y_P, is meaningless. Another way of putting the same proposition is to note that we have taken P as given. This may not be an unreasonable assumption for $Y < Y_P$. But increases of demand when $Y = Y_P$ clearly must lead to increases in P. We shall return to this problem shortly.

2. The mechanical simplicity of the graphics makes it easy to forget the economic underpinning of the model and to leave under-developed the user's ability to explain complicated interactions in *words* that could be understood by someone not familiar with the graphics. Thus, it is urged that everytime the *IS-LM* model is used to reach a conclusion, the user attempt to explain fully, in words, the underlying logic which is summarized in his use of this apparatus.

3. We have so far excluded wealth effects from the apparatus, although we can insert them crudely by first asking in what direction, if at all, they shift *IS* and/or *LM* curves.

RELATIONSHIPS TO THE MULTIPLIER AND THE QUANTITY THEORY

Figure 11-5 helps us to visualize the relationship of the *IS-LM* model to the multiplier.[6] Consider, for example, the effects of an increase in government purchases, ΔG. As noted earlier, the effect is to shift the *IS* curve to the right by ΔG times the multiplier (or super-multiplier, if $b_1 > 0$, that is, if investment also increases with higher Y). Thus, if i remained at i_0, Y would increase from Y_0 to Y_2—the full multiplier amount. However, i cannot remain at i_0. For any rise in Y increases the (transactions) demand for money, and, with a constant supply of money, some money previously held as an asset must be used in mediating the larger volume of money payments. Persons holding no asset balances of money, that is, holding only bonds, will sell some of their bonds to acquire the larger transactions balances (or not buy bonds with all of their current saving). This reduces the demand and increases the supply in the bond market, lowering bond prices or raising interest rates. Persons holding asset balances of money

---

[6] Note that, in Figure 11-5, we have inserted on the horizontal axis the level of potential output, Y_P, to remind us that we are still dealing only with equilibrium levels of Y less than Y_P.

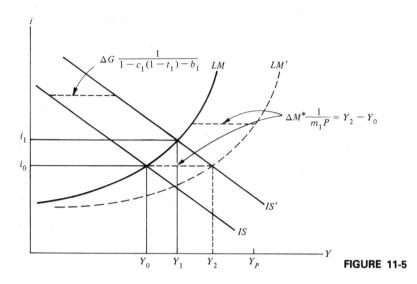

FIGURE 11-5

need not sell bonds to meet their extra transactions needs; but, assuming that they previously held cash idle for some good reason—that is, had deliberately sacrificed an available interest return—they should, at the same interest rate, still want such idle balances. They, too, will sell bonds if they have them or buy fewer from current saving. The interest rate thus must rise to maintain equilibrium in asset holdings as income rises.

This rise in interest, however, pares back the rise which otherwise would have occurred, as Y rose, in I and C. The new equilibrium, at (Y_1, i_1) in Figure 11-5, involves higher Y but not to the full extent of the multiplier. We can either say that the size of the effective multiplier is reduced or that the multiplicand is reduced by the effect of the higher interest rate. If we take the former approach, we can describe the effective multiplier as equal to one divided by the denominator of equation (8). Since this denominator exceeds that of the simple multiplier by $(m_1/m_2)(b_2 + c_2)P$, it is clear that the effective multiplier applicable to G_0, b_0, c_0, or $-c_1t_0$ is less than that derived when we ignored or suppressed any effect of Y on the demand for money, and thus on the interest rate, and any effect of the interest rate on consumption and investment. If we take the latter approach, we merely note that, in equation (7a), the multiplicand within the square brackets is reduced by the rise in i.

As Figure 11-5 shows, the full multiplier effect would be secured only if the LM curve were simultaneously shifted to the right, for example, by an increase in M^*, so that the new LM curve (LM', shown as a broken line) intersects the IS' at the original interest rate i_0. How large would the increase in M^* need to be? To secure a rightward shift sufficient to keep the interest rate constant obviously requires providing all of the extra transactions balances needed at income Y_2. This necessary increase ΔM^* equals m_1P

times ΔY. Clearly, a stimulative change in fiscal policy (ΔG) can have its "full multiplier effect" only if accompanied by a stimulative (or "accomodative") monetary policy to prevent i from increasing.

Note, however, that the monetary policy of increasing M^* by an amount sufficient to shift the LM curve from LM to LM' will not, by itself, achieve income level Y_2. If the IS curve were not simultaneously shifted to IS' but remained in its original position, Y would not increase to Y_2 but only to Y_1.

This calls attention to the fact that just as the simple multiplier theory is now modified, so is the crude "quantity theory." In a world with rigid prices, an increase in M should—according to the simple quantity theory— raise Y by ΔM^* times $m_1 P$:

$$M^* = m_1 P Y$$
$$\Delta M^* = m_1 P \, \Delta Y$$
$$\Delta Y = \Delta M^* \frac{1}{m_1 P}$$

That is, Y should rise from Y_0 to Y_2, rather than merely to Y_1. Instead, Y will rise to Y_2 with this increase in M^* only if fiscal policy is also used, involving an appropriate increase in G (or cut in taxes). If one wishes to say that fiscal policy needs to be supplemented by monetary policy "in order to be fully effective," it is equally correct to say that the reverse is true.

However, reflection shows that these are really quite meaningless expressions. If the economy is really described by all the relationships which enter into the IS and LM curves, then neither the simple multiplier nor the crude quantity theory is correct. And it is a rather meaningless exercise to compute what it would take to realize the forecast of an incomplete, and therefore incorrect, model. Only if one asserts that the simple multiplier or simple quantity-theory model is in fact the correct model does the simpler concept have meaning or deserve further attention. There are, however, some special cases in which the simple multiplier model would still adequately summarize what happens, just as there are some special cases in which the crude quantity theory might hold.

There are two special cases in which the "simple" Keynesian multiplier theory would hold without qualification. Both are shown in Figure 11-6.

In part a, we have the IS curve intersecting a horizontal portion of the LM curve. This obviously represents the case of a liquidity trap, where the equilibrium rate of interest i_T is at its minimum, given prevailing expectations of higher future interest rates. Here, a horizontal shift in the IS curve raises income by an amount equal to ΔG (or Δc_0 or Δb_0 or $-c \, \Delta t_0$) times the simple multiplier (or super-multiplier $1/(1 - c_1(1 - t_1) - b_1)$). Fiscal policy "works" without any "negative feedback" from higher interest rates. In the same case, it is clear that monetary policy is powerless. An

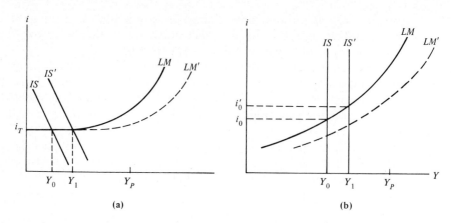

FIGURE 11-6

increase in M^*, shifting the LM curve to the right—to LM', has no effect on either the interest rate or income.

In part b, we have a vertical IS curve, which would occur if $b_2 + c_2 = 0$, that is, if both I and C were completely insensitive to the interest rate. The shift in the IS curve still equals the change in G (or c_0 or b_0 or $-c_1t_0$) times the preceding multiplier; and Y would increase by exactly this amount. In this case, i will rise; but, since Y is unaffected by i, this makes no difference. In the first case, the extra transactions balances are pulled out of asset balances without raising i; in the latter case, it requires an increase in i to pull out the necessary extra transactions balances. However, the rise in i does not reduce either I or C. Again in this case, monetary policy is powerless. An increase in M^*, shifting the LM curve to LM', lowers the rate of interest; but so long as the IS curve is not changed, nothing happens to Y.

Figure 11-7 illustrates two special cases in which the crude quantity theory holds. In part a, the LM curve is vertical, whereas the IS curve has its usual properties. This means that the interest-elasticity of the demand for money is zero. No one holds "idle balances" whatever the interest rate. Here, fiscal policy is powerless; a shift from IS to IS' through fiscal stimulation yields a higher interest rate, but no change in Y. On the other hand, monetary policy is all powerful. An increase in M^*, shifting the LM curve rightward by $\Delta M^* \cdot 1/m_1P$, raises Y in exact proportion to the increase of M^*.

Part b illustrates what may also be considered a special case of the IS-LM model in which the original equilibrium was at full employment—$Y_0 = Y_P$. Here, a stimulative fiscal policy, shifting the IS curve to the right as shown by the arrow labeled 1, creates a demand for labor and other resources in excess of their supply. Even if wages and other resource prices fail to fall in the presence of unemployment, we can be almost sure that

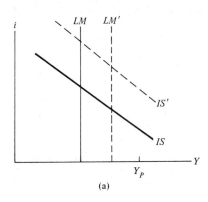
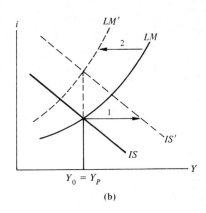

(a)   (b)

FIGURE 11-7

they will rise in the presence of excess demand. The rise in resource prices—and therefore in goods prices—must continue to the point at which rising P has shifted the LM curve left to LM', as shown by arrow 2, until the excess demand is eliminated by rising interest rates paring back consumption and investment.

"Crowding Out"

Whenever a stimulus to aggregate demand occurs, whether from fiscal policy or from an upward shift of either consumption or investment functions (all of which move the IS curve to the right), the resulting rise of production will be partly restrained by rising interest rates. The term **crowding-out** is sometimes used to describe this phenomenon. In the case pictured in Figure 11-5, in which the IS curve shifted to the right, while intersecting a fixed, and rising, LM curve (because M^* was constant), the interest rate rose, "crowding out" some part of an increase in demand that would otherwise have occurred (and that would have occurred with an "accommodative" monetary policy). The most common use of the term, however, is restricted to the case of a fiscal stimulus, when higher interest rates crowd out a certain amount of private investment (and consumption, if that is sensitive to interest rates) which would otherwise have taken place. This crowding out occurs because extra transactions balances are needed at a higher Y, and these will be released from asset balances only as i rises. (In addition, as we have noted in Chapter 9, as wealth gradually rises as the result of increased bond issues, private plus government, there will also be a gradual rise in the asset demand for money.)

Unfortunately, the term "crowding out" can be used to describe several quite different phenomena; and it is important to understand each usage, and to see the relationships among them. In its most fundamental sense the term could refer to a crowding out which results from a *shortage of real productive resources*. Had the economy been at full employment when G rose (or when consumption was stimulated by a cut in taxes), any rise in G or C must inevitably crowd out an equivalent volume of I. This is the situation pictured in Figure 11-7, part b. Here, it is the higher P— resulting from a competition for real resources—which requires larger transactions balances, raises i, and crowds out I. This crowding out is real and unavoidable; the rise in i is only a symptom of the resource shortage, which is more fundamentally reflected in the rise in P and W. Had the extra transactions balances been supplied by the creation of new money, the crowding out would have occurred in some other way: resources used to produce one kind of output cannot be simultaneously used to produce another kind.

But at *less* than full employment, what one hopes will be crowded out by a stimulative fiscal policy is only unemployment. For an economy with idle resources has no real limitation on its capacity to create and to absorb new government bonds, any more than on its capacity to create extra investment goods or government goods. The reason why the interest rate rises if monetary policy is not accommodative, and why investment is thereby pared back, is because—if all of the added deficit is financed by bonds, none by new money—the division of the public's aggregate portfolio of bonds plus money gets twisted in the direction of bonds. Instead, with higher incomes and increased wealth, the public would prefer that part of its added saving accrue in money form, in order to facilitate its increased transactions as income rises, and to accommodate the structure of financial assets to that desired as wealth grows. If only the financing of the increased government deficit had been different—involving more new money and fewer bonds—the interest rate would not have risen; investment would not have been crowded out; and Y would have risen by more. This is crowding out not by shortage of resources but *by a relative shortage of money*.

To be sure, as we will analyze at length in later chapters, even at considerably less than full employment (in the sense of that term used so far), any increase in aggregate demand and employment may still generate a certain amount of "premature" inflation. How does this modify the conclusion just reached? Clearly, if prices rise, the crowding out will be greater than if prices had not risen: the transactions demand will increase not only because of higher Y but also because of higher P. Thus, the resulting rise in i will be larger, and the net gain in Y will be reduced. But this is still not a resource problem. No other use of resources crowds out I; it is just that a rise in aggregate demand is now less effective in crowding out unemployment. But it is still a problem of transactions demand and portfolio preference, and one that can be solved by an accommodative monetary policy or a different financing of the deficit. It is still crowding out as the result of a shortage of money, not of resources.

But would it not be inflationary in these circumstances to supply the extra money? Yes, to the extent that this permits a greater rise in Y than would otherwise have occurred. But it is not an inflation based on a shortage of productive resources. And the crowding out which occurs if the extra M is not supplied is still not "real" or "necessary."

There is a third sense in which the term crowding out is sometimes used (but not often by economists). This usage suggests that investment can be crowded out by a stimulative fiscal policy because of a *shortage of saving*. Here, crowding out is described as a capital-market phenomenon. The bonds which need to be sold to finance extra government spending compete with the bonds being sold to finance private investment. The government and private firms are by implication competing for a fixed flow of private saving; the outcome of the competition is a higher interest rate. This higher interest rate is assumed to have no effect in reducing the planned increase in government spending; thus it is the financing of private investment which is crowded out. Only if the central bank creates new money, and uses it to purchase the extra government bonds—thereby "artificially" holding down interest rates—will private investment fail to be crowded out. But that involves creating extra money, and that is "inflationary."

The author is unable to find any useful meaning for this third conception of crowding out. If there are unemployed resources, the flow of saving surely should not be taken as fixed, regardless of investment spending or government purchases, and, therefore, of income. If output and income are permitted to rise with no paring back of investment—by an accommodative monetary policy which supplies the added transactions balances necessary to keep i from rising—saving will rise *pari passu* with whatever level of investment plus government deficit may emerge.

To be sure, *if* the initial position of the economy were one of full employment, one can equally well describe the situation that we have called a "shortage of resources" as a "shortage of saving." A shortage of resources means that

$$\bar{C} + \bar{I} + \bar{G} > Y_P,$$

where the bars indicate "planned" or "desired" purchases at $Y = Y_P$, and with some particular interest rate and price level. If we define saving, $\bar{S}$, as $Y_P - \bar{C}$, and substitute in the above inequality, we get

$$\bar{C} + \bar{I} + \bar{G} > \bar{C} + \bar{S};$$

or

$$\bar{I} + \bar{G} > \bar{S}$$

But this all relates to a full-employment situation, and has no significance at other levels of output.[7]

Growth of Potential Output in the Rigid-Price *IS-LM* Model

The rigid-price *IS-LM* model seems to share the property of the simplest Keynesian model of Chapter 7 that growth in labor force, as well as capital accumulation and technological change that raise labor's productivity—all of which increase Y_P—have no effect on equilibrium Y because it does not affect either *IS* or *LM* curve. All that happens is that the gap between Y_P and Y grows by whatever growth occurs in Y_P. However, this simply reflects the suppression in the *IS-LM* presentation of the relationship between wages and prices—that remnant of classical supply-and-demand for labor analyses that we retained in the "synthesis model" of Chapters 9 and 10. To the extent that labor's productivity improves through technological change or capital accumulation, prices should fall even with the money wage rigid, shifting the *LM* curve to the right, reducing the interest rate, and producing some expansion of Y. However, as was shown in Chapter 10, the expansion of output will be insufficient to maintain the previous level of employment. Thus unemployment must rise even if the labor force does not grow; and, to the extent that the labor force also expands, unemployment grows all the more.

Fiscal and/or monetary policy could, of course, be used to keep Y growing in line with Y_P.

SIMPLE DYNAMICS OF THE *IS-LM* MODEL

Much earlier, we analyzed the rudimentary dynamics of a simple Keynesian model with exogenous investment, involving lags in the adjustment of consumption to changes in income as well as lags in the adjustment of production to changes in aggregate demand (the latter

---

[7] In the spring of 1975, when the unemployment rate was around 9 percent, and the gap between actual and potential output was on the order of 12 percent of potential, the then Secretary of the Treasury declared that a prospective Federal deficit of $50 billion during the next fiscal year would have either of two consequences. It would either *crowd out* an equivalent volume of private investment (because the government would pay whatever interest rate was necessary to sell its bonds, which private investors could not afford to do), or else the Federal Reserve system would have to buy the extra Federal bonds, the result of which would be the revival of rampant inflation.

In fact, the deficit in the 1975–1976 fiscal year was not $50 billion but $77 billion. Nevertheless, interest rates declined steadily and so did the rate of inflation; the percentage increase in the money supply was lower than in all but one of the previous five years. What the Secretary failed to understand was that, with abundant idle resources, output and income would rise as the result of the government deficit, thereby generating the extra saving used to buy the extra bonds which financed that deficit.

involving the possible unintended accumulation or decumulation of inventories and the efforts of sellers to restore inventories to desired levels). Later, when we introduced the possible dependence of investment on income, and still later on the interest rate (both of which effects are incorporated in the *IS-LM* model), we did not consider the possible extent or nature of the lagged adjustment of investment to changes in *these* variables. (To be sure, we did consider the purely dynamic "accelerator" theory of investment—its responses to *changes* in income.) There can be no doubt, however, that, to whatever extent investment responds to interest rates and *level* of income, this adjustment, too, is subject to very substantial lags.

Lags and the *IS* Curve

Thus, the *IS* curve, which incorporates these responses of both consumption and investment to income and to the interest rate and of production to changes in demand, is concerned only with equilibrium positions. The *IS* curve shows those combinations of Y and i that represent full equilibrium in the "goods market," with production exactly equal to purchases and with all purchases at desired levels, *given the prevailing Y and i.* Thus, the *IS* curve ignores any lag in any of these adjustments. Because this is the character of the *IS* curve, there is no reason to assume that actual levels of Y and i that are observed at any given point of time in any economy not in full equilibrium, fall on (or even near) the *IS* curve—to say nothing of falling on the particular point of the *IS* curve that corresponds to its intersection with the *LM* curve.

Given some underlying consumption function, investment function, and tax function and the existing exogenous G, the *IS* curve in Figure 11-8 shows all possible values of Y and i that might exist *in goods-market equilibrium.* Similarly, the *LM* curve shows the values of Y and i that might coexist, given M, in *money-market equilibrium.* Yet at any point in time, actual observed values of Y and i might correspond to points such as

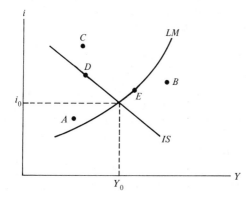

FIGURE 11-8

A, *B*, or *C*; or, by accident, to points like *D* or *E*—each of the latter satisfying one of the two sets of equilibrium conditions but not the other. If all underlying functions and exogenous variables remained unchanged, we assume that values of *Y* and *i* corresponding to positions such as *A* through *E* will presumably gradually adjust toward (Y_0, i_0), and then remain there, so long as none of the determinants of either *IS* or *LM* changes. But can we say anything in general about the nature and direction of the path of such adjustments?

Obviously, we could specify a fully dynamic version of the *IS-LM* model that incorporated some particular pattern of lagged adjustment of each variable to the others (and/or some other specification of the dis-equilibrium—as well as the equilibrium—behavior for each class of decision makers). This would permit us to derive an exact time path from any particular disequilibrium position to the corresponding equilibrium (assuming that equilibrium remains unchanged). Likewise, we could describe the way in which actual values might chase a continually changing equilibrium set. Of course, there is an almost infinite variety of such possible disequilibrium models. We are interested in that one that presumably gives the closest approximation of the adjustment processes of a real-world economy of the type in which we are interested. Do economists know which is the most *relevant* of the possible range of dynamic models?

Most modern macroeconometric models (about which we will say a little in later chapters) consist of greatly elaborated and highly dis-aggregated versions of an *IS-LM* model. Such models incorporate lags in many of the equations that comprise the model—presumably those *par-ticular* lags that the statistical processing of the data has revealed to display some acceptable degree of regularity. Lags are used particularly widely in models based on quarterly (as opposed to annual) data and used for quar-terly forecasts or simulations. (Lags are even more important in the one or two *monthly* models.) However, most of these models are so complex that it becomes exceedingly difficult, if not impossible, to derive anything useful for understanding the basic nature of the presumed dynamic adjustment of an *IS-LM* model, at the level of generality of *that* model. (Or, at least, they have not been studied with this objective.)

The *LM* Curve

There is, however, one possible generalization that is broadly consistent with most macroeconometric models known to the author, as well as consistent with purely *a priori* analysis. In Chapter 9, in discussing wealth-holders' adjustment of their portfolios between alternative assets of bonds and money it was suggested that, "The equilibrium bond price (interest rate) can be expected to prevail at almost every moment in time because the bond market is one in which current price information is widely available, and any unsatisfied wealthholder can almost immediately trade the one form of wealth for the other." Since the demand for money is simply the inverse of the demand for bonds, this would suggest that the *LM* curve—which is in turn merely a rearrangement of the supply and demand for money equation—holds almost continuously; that is, all observed combinations of *Y* and *i* lie on or very close to the *LM* curve.

To be sure, this is not conclusive. Whereas there is almost instant knowledge of market interest rates and bond trading is fast and highly efficient, there may be lags in the perception of changes in factors that affect the firm's or individual's transactions demand for money or in the *response* to such perceptions. (For example, it apparently took some time for corporate treasurers to recognize that, at the higher interest-rate levels prevailing in the late 1960s and 1970s, there was substantial gain to be made by any means of economizing on cash balances—and to learn all the available ways to do it or even to invent new ways. Indeed, if one thinks of the development of new types of financial institutions and new credit markets as part of the response to changes in prevailing levels of interest rates, the lags are even longer.) Moreover, the same may be true of the asset demand for money, particularly to the extent that concepts of "normal" interest rates may be gradually modified by experience. (To be sure, this learning process might also be described as producing shifts in the *LM* curve rather than deviations from it. But the point is still valid.)

Nevertheless, taking institutional forms and expectations as given, it is commonly believed by economists that the lag in the adjustment to equilibrium in the money and capital markets is far shorter than in the goods markets; indeed, the lags may be short enough (relative to the production and purchase lags) that it may be a fair approximation to argue that *LM* adjustment is essentially instantaneous. This suggests that most observed combinations of *Y* and *i* lie close to whatever may be the current *LM* curve—which, of course, is stable in the absence of changes in M^*, P, m_1, or $f(i)$. Thus, given *Y*, which adjusts slowly, *i* adjusts immediately to whatever level is necessary to equate the supply and demand for money.

We may then envisage an adjustment process like that illustrated in Figure 11-9. In part a of that figure we show an initial full equilibrium at (Y_0, i_0), which is disturbed by a sudden one-time increase in M^* (or a sudden one-time reduction in P), that is thereafter maintained in its new value, moving the *LM* curve rightward to *LM'*. Since *Y* can be assumed slow to move, the initial response is a drop from i_0 to i_1 while *Y* remains unchanged at Y_0. At i_1, however, both investment and (possibly) consumption are lower than would be desired, given Y_0 and i_1. As *I* and *C* gradually increase (an increase that feeds on itself through the multiplier or supermultiplier process), *Y* grows as well. As it does so, the transactions demand increases; with no (further) change in M^*, this requires a somewhat higher interest rate. Thus, *i* gradually rises as *Y* does. Still, at any levels of *Y* and *i* below Y_N and i_N, investors and consumers will still be

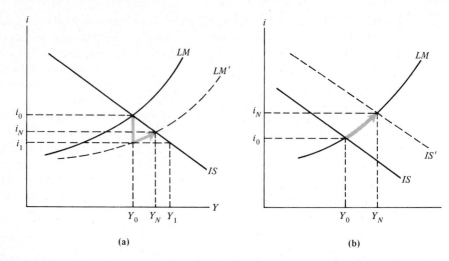

FIGURE 11-9

adjusting spending upward, forcing both variables further upward toward Y_N, i_N. However, after the initial drop to i_1, the subsequent movement will be along the *LM* curve, with the money market in full equilibrium at all times. Thus, *i* "overshoots" its new equilibrium: at first drops below it, then gradually rises toward it; *Y* grows smoothly toward its new equilibrium. The path is shown by the heavy arrow.

In part b, we show an initial equilibrium displaced by a once-for-all upward shift in *IS*. Here the movement of both variables would at all times be along the *LM* curve, again as shown by the gray arrow.

But we need not assume that movement always starts from an initial position of full equilibrium. Suppose that the process of adjustment in either part of Figure 11-9 had been interrupted, before its completion, by a new shift in either *IS* or *LM* curve (or both). From whatever levels of *Y* and *i* then existed, they would now take off on a path toward the still newer equilibrium.

Thus, in Figure 11-10, part a, we can imagine that at some point in time, *Y* and *i* were alternatively at points *A, B,* or *C* when *LM* and *IS* curves came to rest in the positions there shown. If *IS* and *LM* now remain at rest for a sufficient time, the adjustment would occur along the heavy lines shown. Note that the path from *A* starts *downward* to a lower rate of interest, even though the new equilibrium will be at a higher *i*, that from *B* involves an overshoot in *i*, that from *C* a monotonic movement in both variables.

However, we do not need to assume that the money market equilibrium is entirely instantaneous. We may instead suppose it takes some time—but not nearly as much time as the goods market adjustments. Then, as *i* falls toward the *LM* curve in part b of Figure 11-10, lower

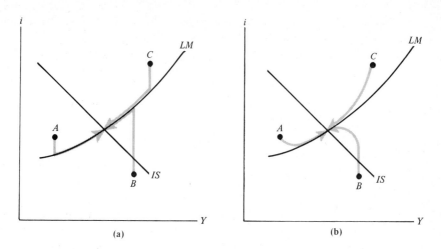

(a)   (b)

FIGURE 11-10

interest rates begin to affect demand and production, causing Y to start increasing even before i reaches the LM curve. The rise in Y means an increase in the demand for money, which slows the drop in i, and soon begins to reverse it, with the adjustment following the heavy line shown. Similar paths are shown beginning with points C and B.

More Complex Dynamic Elements

Although moderately complex, this is still miles away from reality. If we consider the possibility of inventory adjustments arising from a production lag, we have the clear possibility of overshooting in the Y direction as well as in the i direction. The same is clearly also the case if we assume the acceleration principle at work during any process that involves a *change* in Y.

The interested reader should return to the inventory cycle model of Chapter 7 and the accelerator models of Chapter 8 and consider what is changed about them when one assumes that investment (and possibly consumption) depends not only on the variables considered there but *also* on the interest rate, and, if one then adds an interest rate theory involving a demand for money, responsive to both Y and i. Clearly, the important change is the addition of a new *stabilizing influence*—upswings in Y moderated not only by the relationships embodied in those models but now by rising interest rates as well, downswings in activity similarly moderated by falling interest rates. Indeed, all possibilities for nonreversing dynamic processes would seem removed once one introduces such an interest theory, together with an inverse dependence of investment (or consumption) on the interest rate, and an assumed unwillingness of the monetary authorities indefinitely to "accommodate" (or at least *fully* to accommodate) rising or falling transactions demands for money.

With these quite inadequate and incomplete remarks, we leave the subject of dynamic versions of the *IS-LM* curve model.[8]

REVIEW QUESTIONS

1. Assume that the following model adequately summarizes the major economic forces at work in the economy:

$$Y = C + I + G_0 \tag{1}$$

$$C = c_0 + c_1(Y - T) - c_2 i \tag{2}$$

$$T = t_0 + t_1 Y \tag{3}$$

$$I = b_0 + b_1 Y - b_2 i \tag{4}$$

$$M_d = m_0 + m_1 PY - m_2 i \tag{5}$$

$$M_d = M^* \tag{6}$$

where all notations are as used in the text.

(a) Explain in a few sentences the theory which might support equation (5).

(b) Represent this model graphically in a quadrant whose axes are i and Y. Explain what each line in your diagram represents and what their intersection represents.

(c) Solve algebraically the model for equilibrium values of i and Y.

(d) This model has the advantage in that it includes several models (or situations) as special cases. Provide the values of parameters of the model that would reduce it to each of the following special cases. Then show each special case graphically in the i-Y quadrant.

(1) the simple Keynesian model

(2) the simple classical model

(3) the liquidity trap

(4) an inconsistency of saving and investment in the classical model

(5) an infinitely interest-elastic investment function

(e) Use the above model to analyze the effect on the lines in your diagram, and equilibrium values of i and Y, of an increase in $c_1, t_1, b_2, m_1,$ and m_2 (each taken separately).

2. Explain each of these three statements:

(a) In the classical economics, an increased propensity to save affects the amounts saved and invested and the rate of interest, but not aggregate output and employment;

(b) In the simplest Keynesian model, an increased propensity to save affects aggregate output and employment, but not the amounts saved and invested;

(c) Most modern macroeconomic theorists see the result of an increased propensity to save as dependent on whether money wage rates are flexible or rigid.

---

[8] For a simple, explicitly dynamic algebraic version, see W. L. Smith, *Macroeconomics* (R. D. Irwin, 1970), pp. 267–79.

3.
(a) If the simple Keynesian model is broadened to include an investment function and interest rates, the "multiplier" of the simple model becomes limited to a special case requiring a particular kind of monetary policy. Explain what monetary policy and why. (Assume substantial unemployment throughout.)

(b) If a different monetary policy is followed—e.g., a constant money supply—the effect of a tax cut or increase in government spending may be significantly offset by a "crowding out" of private investment. Explain carefully (still assuming substantial unemployment).

(c) Are there circumstances (still assuming substantial unemployment) in which the "crowding out" of part (b) would fully offset the fiscal stimulus?

(d) How does your answer to (c) change if the fiscal stimulus is given with the economy close to full employment?

4. The fact that the interest rate tends to "overshoot" might explain the often observed phenomenon that an increase in money supply raises rather than lowers interest rates. Comment briefly.

SELECTED REFERENCES

J. R. Hicks, "Mr. Keynes and the 'Classics', A Suggested Interpretation," *Econometrica*, 5 (April 1937) 147–59, reprinted in W. Fellner and B. F. Haley (eds.), *Readings in the Theory of Income Distribution* (Blakiston, 1946), pp. 461–476; in M. G. Mueller (ed.), *Readings in Macroeconomics* (Holt, Rinehart, and Winston, 2nd ed., 1971), pp. 137–145; in E. Shaprio (ed.), *Macroeconomics: Selected Readings* (Harcourt Brace, Jovanovich, 1970), pp. 197–209; and in J. Lindauer (ed.), *Macroeconomic Readings* (The Free Press, 1968), pp. 53–60.
(Hicks' original (1937) translation of Keynesian ideas into the IS-LM form.)

W. L. Smith and R. L. Teigen (eds.), *Readings in Money, National Income and Stabilization Policy* (R. D. Irwin, 3rd ed., 1974), Introduction to Chapter 1, pp. 1–38.
(A superb and detailed exposition of IS-LM analysis.)

R. W. Spencer and W. P. Yohe, "The 'Crowding out' of Private Expenditures by Fiscal Policy Actions,' *Federal Reserve Bank of St. Louis Review*, 52 (October, 1970), 12–24.
(One of the first explicit discussions of the crowding-out hypothesis.)

K. M. Carlson and R. W. Spencer, "Crowding Out and Its Critics," *Federal Reserve Bank of St. Louis Review*, 57 (December, 1975), 2–17.
(A review of the technical literature on crowding out.)

D. P. Tucker, "Dynamic Income Adjustment to Money-Supply Changes," *American Economic Review*, 56 (June 1966), pp. 433–449.
(A thorough, theoretical discussion of dynamic income adjustment.)

W. L. Smith, *Macroeconomics* (R. D. Irwin, 1970), pp. 267–279.
(A simple, algebraic, dynamic version of the IS–LM curve model.)

Chapter 12

More-Classical Versions of the Synthesis

A Modernized Classical Macroeconomic Model
The *IS-LM* model with flexible wages
Wealth effects on consumption
Other channels through which deflation may increase spending
Dynamic adjustment to the classical equilibrium
The classical defenses against unemployment with growing potential output
Equilibrium at less than full employment?

Monetarism: A Special Variant of Classical Macroeconomics
Basic tenets of monetarism
Policy implications of monetarism
Positive contributions of the monetarist view
Evidence supporting the monetarist position
Monetarist econometric models
An interest-elastic velocity

Classical Versus Keynesian Versions of the Synthesis
The more-classical versions
More-Keynesian versions

This chapter has three main purposes. First, it shows how full or partial wage flexibility can be inserted into the *IS-LM* model, and then introduces some additional relationships among variables not previously considered. Both changes strengthen presumed tendencies for the economy to approach equilibrium at full employment. They thus lead to an interpretation of the model far more classical in spirit than the Keynesian version presented in the previous chapter. Second, the chapter presents and evaluates that special version of modern classical macroeconomic theory known as "monetarism." It concludes by weighing considerations that support the more Keynesian or more classical versions of the synthesis and by suggesting rather different, but perhaps complementary, roles for the two versions.

A MODERNIZED CLASSICAL MACROECONOMIC MODEL

Now that the *IS-LM* curve apparatus has been introduced, we can use it, among other purposes, to clarify some of the relationships between more Keynesian and more classical versions of the Keynesian-classical synthesis. The *IS-LM* model, as it was developed in the preceding chapter, possesses a heavily Keynesian bias through its assumption of rigid prices (based on rigid wages). It takes on a still more Keynesian flavor to the extent that one considers the interest elasticity of the demand for money to be relatively high, making the *LM* curve approach the horizontal. If one is inclined to minimize the interest elasticity of investment and consumption, making the *IS* curve approach the vertical, the Keynesian bias becomes even stronger. Under either of these circumstances, or both in combination, the "negative financial feedbacks" generated by shifts in aggregate demand shrink toward insignificance (at least in terms of their effects on output and employment), and the simple multiplier version of Keynesian economics comes much closer to providing an adequate approximation of macro-economic reality. Obviously, too, in these circumstances, fiscal policy becomes a far more powerful tool, monetary policy a weaker one.

The *IS-LM* Model with Flexible Wages

We take a major step back toward a basically classical view of the world once we dispense with the clearly extreme assumption that wages and prices are completely rigid. The economist of more classical leanings is unlikely to insist that wages are in fact highly flexible downward in response to any trace of unemployment (in excess of that which exists at "full employment"). But he contends that there is clearly some tendency for wage rates to fall (or, as we shall show later, to rise by less than the exogenous increase in labor's average productivity) in situations of unemployment. Any tendency for wages to decline in the absence of full employment clearly implies a tendency for the economy to move toward full employment—a tendency that is the stronger the greater the responsiveness of wages to unemployment. The tendency for wages to decline may be slight when unemployment is small; but, the more extensive the unemployment, presumably the stronger is the tendency for wage rates to decline, and the faster they would decline.

It is not difficult to amend the *IS-LM* model to incorporate wage flexibility, although the simplicity of the graphics is thereby considerably lessened. Figure 12-1 suggests how this may be done. (For the present, ignore broken *LM* curves and those with bars over the symbols, for example, $\overline{LM}(P = P_0)$.) Part a shows *IS* and *LM* curves, with *LM* initially in such position that (given *IS*) full employment is impossible (at the given wage level, and other conditions). This impossibility is shown by the fact that the *IS-LM* intersection at (i_0, Y_0) lies considerably to the left of Y_P.

Now, however, instead of taking Y_P as given, we can show its relationship to the supply and demand for labor and to wages and prices. The intersection of the supply and demand curves for labor in part c defines the point of full employment N_F. The aggregate production–employment relationship of part d shows that N_F implies a potential output, Y_P. Converting this measurement of Y_P from a vertical to a horizontal one through the 45° angle line of part b establishes the Y_P level for the *IS-LM* curve diagram.

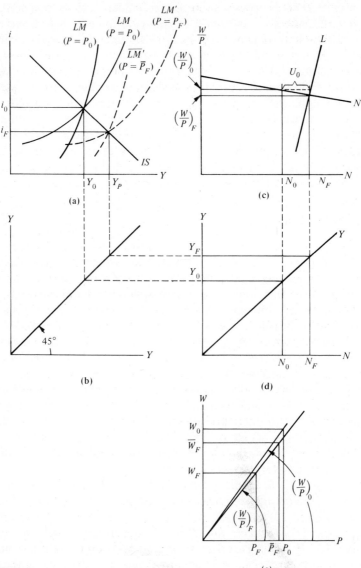

FIGURE 12-1

Running back in the opposite direction from the initial output level Y_0, found at the intersection of $LM(P = P_0)$ and IS, we find that this implies in part d an initial level of employment N_0, and, in part c, an initial price–wage relationship $(W/P)_0$ and an initial unemployment level U_0. If we now suppose that this unemployment induces some continuing decline in wages, and thus in prices, we can calculate how far wages must fall to reach full employment. Returning to part a, we see that full employment will require an *LM* curve that has shifted to $LM'(P = P_F)$, which intersects the *IS* curve at (i_F, Y_P). This shift of *LM* can be achieved if the price level declines from P_0 to P_F. Inserting this P_F in part e, along with the full employment wage-price relationship from part c, gives us the extent to which the wage rate must fall to achieve full employment, that is, to W_F. Any lesser extent of wage decline will still shift the *LM* curve to the right, causing Y to expand toward Y_P.

It should be relatively easy to see that the steeper the *LM* curve and the flatter the *IS* curve, the greater will be the effect of any given decline in prices and wages on the interest rate and thus on output. The alternative steeper $\overline{LM}(P = P_0)$ curve in part a, drawn to intersect the *IS* curve at the same initial i_0 and Y_0 as did the original $LM(P = P_0)$, illustrates this. The deflation necessary to achieve full employment—by shifting it to $\overline{LM}'(P = \overline{P}_F)$—is now far more modest than before. If a decline from W_0 to W_F was too drastic to be achieved or would take to long to be tolerated, the decline to $\overline{W}_F$ may be more feasible. The reader can ascertain that a flatter *IS* curve (with the original *LM*) produces similar results.

It should be clear that the slopes of the *IS* and *LM* curves (reflecting the interest elasticities of investment and consumption purchases and of the demand for money) are basically empirical matters. But they are matters on which the empirical evidence remains highly debatable (some of this evidence will be referred to in Chapters 16 through 21). In the absence of agreement on the interpretation of the evidence, economists favoring a Keynesian or a classical view inevitably may make somewhat different assumptions about these elasticities—assumptions that, perhaps unconsciously, tend toward compatibility with their preconceived positions on public policy. (Economists' views about how much wage flexibility really exists can also involve some element of conscious or unconscious wish fulfillment.) The way in which economists (including this writer) draw their *IS-LM* curves in a textbook or on a blackboard reveal their hunches about the elasticities of those curves. Those inclined to a classical position tend to draw the *IS* curve as quite elastic and the *LM* curve as fairly inelastic. Of course, it is the actual elasticities that are important; but these are not well established.

Nevertheless, there is somewhat more basis for the support of a classical view than merely a particular set of hunches about disputed empirical matters. As the next sections show, the classical economist can argue that the analysis embodied in the *IS-LM* model, as so far presented, and as commonly used, remains seriously incomplete in its assessment of the forces pushing the economy toward full employment.

Wealth Effects on Consumption

It needs to be recalled that, in the *IS-LM* model as so far presented, there is only *one way* in which a reduction in the wage and price level can affect the volume of real spending on goods and services. This mechanism operates through (a) the effect of lower prices in reducing the (transactions) demand for money, which (b) lowers interest rates, which (c) stimulates investment and (possibly) consumption. Since economists cannot be entirely certain whether, by how much, or how quickly lower interest rates increase real spending, it can be argued that this channel provides a weak basis for the classical economist's rejection of active policy measures to promote full employment. However, the classical view does find added support for the effectiveness of deflation in the identification of at least *three other channels* by which wage rate deflation, in the presence of unemployment, may automatically raise aggregate demand.

The first—and, theoretically, the one of greatest interest (judging by the volume of professional literature which deals with it)—is through the effects of wage and price reductions on the real volume of individual wealth and of an increased real volume of individual wealth on consumer demand. The theoretical and empirical basis for the view that wealth—rather than, or in addition to, income—is a major determinant of consumer purchases will be developed in some detail in Chapters 16 and 17. Some modern writers argue that this view was already at least *implicit* in classical economic analysis—a claim that this writer finds difficult to sustain.[1] In any case, to follow the argument, let us assume it to be the case that changes in wealth (income given) will produce changes in the same direction in consumer spending. That is, we assume that *increases* in real wealth will *increase* real consumer purchases.

We turn then to the question of how changes in the general wage and price level can increase the real volume of individuals' wealth. In Chapter 2, we saw that aggregate wealth, in the sense of the total net worth of members of a society, can be measured by the sum of (a) the value of all of the community's physical wealth—land, plant, machinery and equipment, residences and other structures, and inventories—plus (b) the outstanding amount of government bonds and government money, regardless of by whom it is held. General changes in the price level of goods and services should not change significantly the real value of existing physical assets. For the prices of existing assets should approximate the prices of identical newly produced goods and services. Thus, "deflated" by any general price index, the real value of this part of national wealth will not appear to have fallen or risen appreciably.[2] But the nominal value of that portion of wealth that consists of government bonds and money is fixed; changes in the price

---

[1] Nevertheless, Keynes appears to have recognized the wealth effect on consumption. See *General Theory*, pp. 217–18.

[2] Except to the extent that the price level of new capital goods moves differently than the general price level.

level therefore produce opposite changes in the real value of this portion of wealth, and thus in the real value of total wealth.[3]

Substantial changes in the general price level, of course, also considerably affect the real value of the great mass of *private* debts outstanding (including all the liabilities of financial institutions). For the debtor (or financial institution), a fall in the price level on which his money income depends, even if it leaves his real income unchanged, increases substantially the real value of his liability for repayment of the loan, as well as of his liability for interest payments at the rate set in the debt contract. This increase in his real liability produces a decline in the debtor's real net worth. But the person or institution *to whom the debt is owed* experiences, by the same token, an equivalent gain in real net worth. Thus, the *aggregate* real value of wealth of private debtor plus private creditor remains unaffected. To the extent that consumption is affected by wealth, the debtor may well reduce his spending, the creditor increase his. Although the two changes may not be identical in amount (they are, of course, opposite in sign), we can assume that they roughly cancel out. But in the case of the government debt (and the outstanding stock of government money) the private creditor of the government is enriched as prices fall. The burden of this government debt, on the government, may be correspondingly increased; but this is not presumed (in ordinary circumstances) to affect government purchases. Thus, to the extent of government obligations to the private community, a deflation of prices increases private real wealth (and an inflation reduces it) thereby producing a change in the same direction in the volume of real private consumption spending.

Since the first economist to spell this out explicitly was British economist A. C. Pigou, the effect has ever since been called the "Pigou effect."[4]

One can, of course, argue as to the importance of the Pigou effect in practice. A rough calculation shows that it is probably not very great, at least in terms of the extent of the deflation that might be expected to occur during any reasonable period of time. Suppose, for example, that wages

---

[3] In the case of government bonds, the repayment obligation and the coupon payment are fixed in nominal terms; however, as noted below, the market value of such bonds will nevertheless change somewhat with the rate of interest.

[4] See A. C. Pigou, *Employment and Equilibrium* (London, 1941), especially pp 96–130. See also D. Patinkin, *Money, Interest, and Prices* (Row, Peterson, 1956). A shorter version of Patinkin's highly influential views is found in his "Price Flexibility and Full Employment", originally published in *American Economic Review*, XXXVIII (1948); republished in a revised version in *Readings in Monetary Theory* (Blakiston, 1951) pp. 252–83, and reprinted in J. Lindauer, ed., *Macroeconomic Readings* (The Free Press, 1968), pp. 120-36, in E. Shapiro, ed., *Macroeconomics: Selected Readings* (Harcourt, Brace and World, 1970) pp. 245–71, and in M. G. Mueller, ed., *Readings in Macroeconomics* (Holt, Rinehart, Winston, 1971) pp. 226–44.

were sufficiently flexible that, within a reasonable period, the price level might fall 20 percent in the presence of substantial unemployment. This would produce a 25 percent increase in the value of that portion of real wealth that represents government obligations. In 1973, that portion amounted to about 17 percent of total United States national wealth, or approximately $441 billion valued in 1968 prices. A 25 percent increase in real value would thus be an increment of $110 billion. We might guess the corresponding figure for 1977, and valued in 1977 prices, might be twice that—$220 billion.

To estimate the effect of a change in wealth on consumption, we use a recent empirical consumption function estimated by Franco Modigliani,[5] that implies that each $1 billion addition to real wealth increases real consumption by 0.053 billion. Applying this coefficient to a $220 billion increase in real wealth implies an increase in consumption of $11.6 billion. This equals about 0.7 percent of GNP in 1977—hardly a major contribution to the reduction of any substantial unemployment! (And recall that this assumed a 20 percent wage reduction. To be sure, a price level decline of 80 percent would produce a 15 percent increase in real spending, but an 80 percent deflation is rather difficult to imagine!) This, of course, is *in addition to* the interest rate effects of the deflation on investment and consumption and other effects to be noted shortly.

Surely, the practical importance of the Pigou effect can well be doubted (at least in the deflation case). The importance of the Pigou effect is, instead, primarily theoretical—as proof that full-employment equilibrium, at *some* price level, in principle, is always available to an economy organized on competitive principles. This importance reflects the fact that the Pigou effect would also overcome a liquidity trap (because its working does not depend on the rate of interest), or an inconsistency even at a zero interest rate between full-employment saving and investment (because the rising real value of wealth would reduce full-employment saving). However, because the opportunities for effective deflation seem so modest in today's world, the relevance of the Pigou effect may actually be greater for the case of inflation than for that of unemployment, as will be pointed out in Chapter 13.

Still, there is an additional way in which the wealth effect on consumption may also contribute to an increase in aggregate demand in the presence of unemployment and falling wages. Although not properly described as the Pigou effect, because that operates independently of the interest rate, it may well be appreciably more important than the Pigou effect. To the extent that a deflation of wages and prices induced by unemployment also reduces the interest rate (as it should unless M

---

[5] Franco Modigliani, "Monetary Policy and Consumption," in *Consumer Spending and Monetary Policy: The Linkages* (Federal Reserve Bank of Boston, 1971) p. 75.

declines proportionately), it thereby raises the value of consumer wealth, and in that way, also, stimulates consumer spending. A substantial part of consumer wealth is represented directly or indirectly by bonds and other fixed coupon and fixed repayment obligations, the prices of which vary inversely with the interest rate. (And, in the process of adjustment of the values of fixed-coupon obligations, this should also induce increases in the values of other securities, including shares, as will be explained in Chapter 20.) Thus, as interest rates fall (because prices fall), wealth rises; consumer spending then rises as well.

This effect obviously applies to a decline in interest rates engendered by monetary policy as much as to a decline in interest rates engendered by deflation. From recent econometric models developed by Franco Modigliani (for which the consumption function referred to earlier was developed), it is concluded that "consumption is one of the most important, if not *the* most important, single channel through which [the tools of monetary policy] affect directly and indirectly the level of aggregate real and money demand and thus, the level of output, employment and prices."[6] If it is one of the most important effects of monetary policy, it may also be one of the most important effects of any deflation arising from unemployment.

Other Channels through which Deflation May Increase Spending

The comment that wealth effects on consumption may be more relevant to the analysis of inflation than to the analysis of unemployment applies as well to the additional effects about to be considered. Nevertheless, they are relevant to the classical view that deflation provides a potential automatic solution for unemployment. The first effect to be considered is that of a changing price level on the posture of fiscal policy.

Given a tax system, like that of the United States, with heavy dependence on a progressive income tax, a reduction of the price level, if substantial, moves many taxpayers from higher to lower tax brackets, even if their *real* incomes have not fallen. This reduces the real burden of taxation, and, as well, raises the real purchasing power of existing transfer payments and increases some people's eligibility for transfers. Thus real disposable income is raised and real consumption is thereby increased, at any level of real GNP. On the other side of the fiscal equation, if prices decline after government budgets have already been set (in money terms), the same sums buy more real goods and services than originally planned, thereby adding further real stimulus to production and employment.

The impact of these effects may be considerable. A recent study estimated that a 10 percent inflation increases United States income tax

[6] *Ibid.* pp. 9, 10.

revenues (under rate structures in effect in 1974) by 14.7 percent.[7] This permits a calculation that a 20 percent increase in the price level would reduce real disposable income by 1.13 percent and real consumer purchases by perhaps 1.0 percent. Assuming symmetrical effects from deflation and inflation, this suggests that the fiscal effect on one side of the budget alone (neglecting the effect both on real transfer payments and on real purchases) would be about as important as the estimate of the Pigou effect made earlier.

Another automatic effect of price level changes relates to their impacts on foreign trade, and thus on a nation's net exports—a component of GNP, and, like any other component, a source of employment. Assume a deflation of a country's domestic price level in a world in which other countries' price levels do not change and in which exchange rates are fixed. This will, other things equal, reduce the deflating country's imports—causing domestic buyers to prefer the now cheaper domestic products—and stimulate exports to other countries as substitutes for their own now relatively higher priced products or replacing their imports from third countries. Depending on the importance of exports and imports relative to the deflating counry's GNP and on the sensitivity of both imports and exports to changes in relative international prices, the effects can be substantial. (In the relatively new world of flexible exchange rates, much of the impact of a change in a country's internal price level may be reflected in its exchange rate rather than its net exports. However, some impact may remain.) At least in the fixed-exchange-rate world, the effects of deflation or inflation on aggregate demand, in a country with substantial foreign trade, might well dwarf the impact either through interest rates or through wealth effects. Of course, like the latter, all of this depends on the existence of *some significant degree of downward wage rate flexibility* in the face of unemployment.

Dynamic Adjustment to Classical Equilibrium

All of the equilibrating effects discussed above, which reinforce the classical version of macroeconomic theory, depend for their operation on changes in the level of money wage rates in the presence of unemployment (or in the presence of "over-full" employment). It may be convenient explicitly to build a process of wage adjustment into the model, making it to that extent a dynamic model.

We suggested earlier that the *speed* with which wage rates would adjust to labor market imbalance might depend on the *extent* of unem-

[7] J. M. Buchanan and J. M. Dean, "Inflation and Real Rates of Income Tax," a paper presented at the Sixty-Seventh Annual Conference on Taxation of the National Tax Association-Tax Institute, 1974, as reported in *Inflation and the Consumer in 1974*, A Study Prepared for the Use of the Joint Economic Committee, Congress of the United States, February 10, 1975.

ployment. We have defined potential output, Y_P, as the output corresponding to full employment. And we have defined full employment as the highest level of employment consistent with stable prices. Thus, potential output is the highest level of *output* consistent with price stability. But full employment does not mean the highest possible level of employment, nor does potential output mean the highest possible level of output. And since our model implies an essentially proportional relationship between changes in wage rates and changes in the price level, we can identify stability of the price level with stability of the wage level (at least in a world without growth). Thus, if the speed of wage-rate adjustment depends on the extent of unemployment, then the speed of price-level adjustment must depend on the size of the gap between actual and potential output. If we define $\dot{P}$ as the percentage rate of price change per time unit (for example, percentage change in GNP deflator, expressed at annual rate), then the hypothesis is that

$$\dot{P} = \Phi(Y - Y_P) \qquad \frac{d\dot{P}}{d(Y - Y_P)} > 0$$

such that $\dot{P} = 0$ (that is, the price level is stable), when $Y = Y_P$; $\dot{P} > 0$ (that is, prices rise), when $Y > Y_P$; $\dot{P} < 0$ (that is, prices fall), when $Y_P < Y$. We may further specify that the larger the positive (or negative) output gap, the faster will be the rate of price increase (or decrease). Thus the relationship between direction and rate of price change, on the one hand, and the level of output, on the other, might be represented as in panels a, b, or c of Figure 12-2.[8]

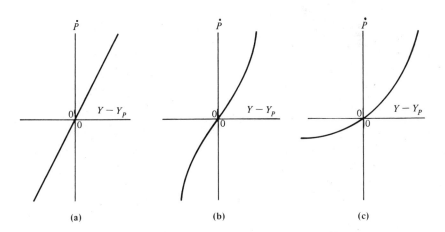

FIGURE 12-2

[8] Later, in Chapters 13 and 14, we will consider some of the factors that might explain the existence of such price adjustment functions. Here, we simply postulate their existence.

We may call the functions shown in Figure 12-2 "price adjustment functions." Functions in panels a and b exhibit symmetry in the responsiveness of prices to a negative or positive output gap. This, however, need not be the case. Panel c shows a response that is nonsymmetrical, in that even quite large negative gaps produce only slow deflation, whereas even relatively small positive gaps produce sharp inflation. (We shall see still other possibilities a bit later.)

We can easily combine "price adjustment functions," like a, b, or c, with the *IS-LM* curve diagram in the way shown in Figure 12-3. Here, a price adjustment function is aligned with an *IS-LM* diagram in the following way: The level of Y_P on the *IS-LM* diagram is aligned with the zero point on the $(Y - Y_P)$ scale of the price adjustment diagram. In panel a, for example, suppose that the initial *IS* curve IS_1 and initial *LM* curve LM_1 intersect at a less-than-full employment output Y_1, that is, to the left of Y_P. Reading down to the price adjustment function, we see that price adjustment is negative, at rate $\dot{P}_1$. As P falls, at rate $\dot{P}_1$, the *LM* curve, of course, begins to shift to the right (because deflation reduces transactions demands

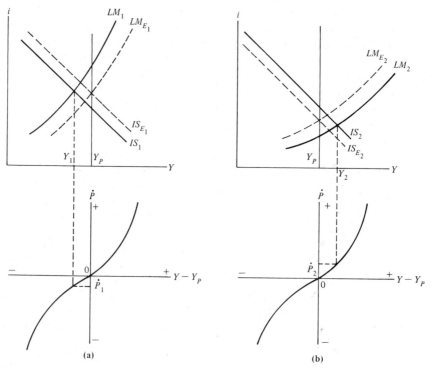

(a)   (b)

FIGURE 12-3

for money), and the *IS* curve may also begin to shift to the right, because deflation (a) increases real wealth directly (Pigou effect), (b) increases real wealth indirectly as i begins to fall, (c) increases exports and reduces imports, and (d) reduces the restrictiveness of the government budget. Obviously, as this adjustment starts to occur, the $Y - Y_P$ gap begins to narrow, and the rate of deflation slows down to less than $\dot{P}_1$. This means that the rate of equilibrating movements of *LM* and *IS* curves slows down too. But so long as the price adjustment is negative at all outputs below Y_P, there will continue to be (ever slower) movement of the economy *toward* full-employment equilibrium, approaching the limiting positions of the *IS* and *LM* curve at IS_{E_1} and LM_{E_1}, intersecting at Y_P, where $\dot{P} = 0$.

In panel b, the initial position is taken as one of over-full employment, producing inflation at an initial rate $\dot{P}_2$, which, in turn, pushes both *IS* and *LM* curves to the left, approaching, as a limit, positions IS_{E_2} and LM_{E_2}, intersecting at Y_P and consistent with price stability at $\dot{P} = 0$.

We have implicitly assumed in the preceding discussion that the lags discussed earlier (in Chapter 11)—of spending to income and to interest rates, and of interest rates to changes in demand for money—are both rather short, relative to the speed with which prices change. Thus, Y and i at all times during the adjustment process essentially correspond to those given by intersections of the current positions of *IS* and *LM* curve. It is easy to see that this is not necessarily the case, and to recognize that, if it were not, it might introduce "overshoots" into the adjustment of some or all of the variables. Still, the equilibrating force of the price adjustment (as the functions are drawn in Figures 12-2 and 12-3) is such that equilibrium will necessarily eventually be established (or at least approached).

Equilibrium at full employment would not be established, however, if the price-adjustment functions were as shown in Figure 12-4. The reader should be able to establish that if the price adjustment function were like that of panel a, an initial *IS-LM* equilibrium to the right of the origin

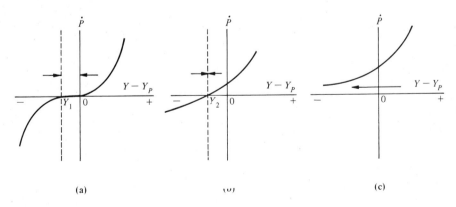

(a)   (b)   (c)

FIGURE 12-4

would create inflation which would reduce Y to Y_P. But an initial equilibrium *below* Y_1 would create deflation which would raise Y only to Y_1; whereas an initial equilibrium between Y_1 and Y_P would produce no price movement in either direction, and thus no tendency for Y to move in either direction. Here we have wage rigidity (and, thus, price rigidity) at levels between Y_1 and Y_P.

In panel b, prices would rise at any initial Y in excess of Y_2, shifting *LM* and *IS* curves to the left, and Y toward Y_2; if the initial Y were less than Y_2, prices would fall, and the movement would be toward Y_2. (In that case, one might well ask whether Y_P had been properly defined!) In panel b as in panel c, the basic condition initially proposed for price-adjustment functions is not met, namely, that $\dot{P} = 0$ when $Y = Y_P$. However, in case c prices tend to rise at *any* Y—faster at higher levels of Y, less rapidly at lower levels—but always to rise. This means that *IS* and *LM* curves tend to shift continually to the left, and without limit, as inflation steadily reduces aggregate demand and raises interest rates. No equilibrium at full-employment (nor at any other output level) is possible.

Worse than the case of mere "wage rigidity," b and c are cases in which wage rates, and thus prices, actually rise at less-than-full-employment levels of employment and output. Clearly, this is a very unclassical world. Yet some economists have suggested that it may be something like the world in which we now live!

One might well suggest that we have, in the concept of the "price adjustment" function, a means for specifying more concretely the *degree* and *pattern* of price (that is, wage) rigidity or flexibility. If the price adjustment function is very flat (approaching coincidence with the horizontal axis), we have extreme wage rigidity, approaching the complete rigidity assumed in the Keynesian model. If the function rises (and falls) steeply (approaching the vertical axis), we have extreme flexibility approaching the assumption of the classical economists.

Although this may be one way of giving more precise content to discussions of wage rigidity-flexibility, it is not the only one. Nor, indeed, does it do much more than to frame the same old questions in new terms; it does not answer them, nor even suggest new avenues for finding such answers.

The discussion in Chapter 13 of the "Phillips curve" will further develop these questions; we defer further treatment to that point.

The Classical Defenses against Unemployment with Growing Potential Output

The preceding discussion has been conducted in the context of the automatic equilibrating forces at work in a stationary, nongrowth world. Now we need to consider whether these equilibrating tendencies might operate differently in the more realistic setting of a world in which economic growth occurs. By growth, we again mean a situation in which potential output steadily rises over time, through the effects of a growing labor force, productivity-enhancing technological change, and capital accumulation from past positive net investment. The general picture for such an economy—as earlier analyzed in terms either of the simple Keynesian model or by the *IS-LM* version of the Keynesian-classical synthesis—was not an encouraging one. A growth of productive capability seemed mainly to mean that more productive capability would be unused. To be sure, we have identified several effects that *falling wage rates*, induced by growing unemployment, might have in stimulating aggregate demand: operating through interest rates, the volume of wealth, the tax structure, or the foreign trade balance. These effects would be triggered as much by the unemployment resulting from growth as by unemployment arising from a decline in demand. But any and all of these defenses require effective deflation of the wage level, induced by unemployment; and the "real-world" may not offer an extent or degree of wage flexibility appropriate to the magnitude of the requirement.

Nevertheless, there are *other aspects of the growth process*, neglected, because irrelevant—in the artificial analytical model of a no growth economy—that might make the prospects for achieving and maintaining full employment appear somewhat less dismal than has so far been implied. Although ignored in classical stationary equilibrium theory, they may provide somewhat better support for the classical optimism about the ability of a competitive market economy to achieve full employment with a constant money supply and no government intervention—*even of an economy handicapped by substantial downward wage rigidity.*

To be sure, mere growth in the labor force, lacking the elements of technological change and capital accumulation, would not make the job for the classical correctives any easier. Its direct effect is a growth of the number of unemployed, thus apparently requiring a steadily falling wage and price level (given a constant money stock) in order to reach and maintain full employment, by inducing continuing declines in the interest rate, continuing increases in the value of consumer wealth, further decreases in the restrictiveness of fiscal policy, or further growth in net exports.

On the other hand, to the extent that the elements of technological progress and capital accumulation contribute to growth of potential (and, in most countries, they provide the largest contributions) the outlook is more favorable. To see how this might operate, assume only technological progress and capital accumulation (no labor force growth). These, too, in the first instance, might seem only to create unemployment (unless aggregate demand simultaneously rises), for they permit the same volume of output to be produced using fewer worker hours. But there are now important new reasons why aggregate demand might rise, *even if wage rates do not decline.*

In the first place, technological improvement reduces costs, permitting prices to be reduced even if wage rates do not decline. Competition among producers should translate declines of costs into lower prices. Indeed, prices may still fall even if wage rates rise somewhat, so long as the rise in wages is less than the increase in output per employment hour resulting from technological improvement. The effects of capital accumulation are essentially similar. This means that, in a growing economy, *a declining wage level is not necessary for prices to decline*. Wage rates, for institutional or social reasons, may be exceedingly difficult to reduce; but a declining price level might not be unachievable, if only money wages *increase* by less than the rise in output per hour.

A second, and often neglected kind of technological process is the steady improvement that occurs in the efficiency of the management of money balances, reducing the transactions demand for money (at least as defined by M_1) that accompanies any given PY—that is, reduces the coefficient m (in mPY). Other things equal, this reduces interest rates below what they would otherwise be, with direct and indirect stimulative effects on aggregate demand.

Together, these two aspects of growth could permit the following changes to occur simultaneously:

1. With no decline, or even a small *rise*, in money wage rates, the price level might still fall.
2. With falling prices, and a declining transactions demand per dollar's worth of output, the aggregate transactions demand for money might still fall even in the face of some rise in real output and employment.
3. A fall in the aggregate transactions demand, along with a constant quantity of money, would permit interest rates to decline, thus providing net stimulus to aggregate demand, in addition to any stimulus provided by falling prices through wealth, trade, or fiscal effects.[9]

[9] For the United States economy the trend rise in output per manhour (resulting from technological and managerial improvements and capital accumulation) is around 2.5 percent a year; the trend increase in "velocity" of the narrowly defined money stock (M_1) is also around 2.5 percent a year (some part of which may, however, merely represent the effects of an upward trend in interest rates). It is a simple piece of arithmetic to show that, with a constant money stock, and the money wage rate unchanged, this would still permit (for example) a rise of one-half percent in employment and of 3.0125 percent in output; a decline of 2.5 percent in prices; and thereby a fall of 2.074 percent in aggregate transactions demand. The extent of the resultant reduction of interest rates (money stock unchanged) and of increased demand both for goods and services would depend on the uncertain interest elasticities of the demands for money and for consumer and investment goods (and on the extent of the rise in consumer wealth which might accompany it). But it is not inconceivable that the increase in aggregate demand could be of the same order of magnitude as the output increase (in the example, 3.0125 percent). The arithmetic follows:

Thus, in a setting of some economic growth (including increases in the efficiency both of production and of the use of money), the need for extensive declines in the wage level in order to correct or to prevent the emergence of unemployment would appear to be considerably reduced. If it is the inability to achieve absolute declines in money wage rates which is judged to be the main obstacle to full employment, that, at least, seems less of an obstacle when we take account of the facts of economic growth. However, we shall not develop that case further in the present context.[10]

Equilibrium at Less-Than-Full Employment?

In Chapter 10, we concluded that it was problematical whether Keynes or Keynesians had demonstrated or could demonstrate that, given some downward flexibility of wage rates, a true macroeconomic equilibrium at less than full employment could exist. Now that we have added wealth effects, fiscal effects, and international trade effects, and the possible effects of economic growth, it seems clear that, in principle, there exists at all times in a market economy with even moderately flexible wages and prices, some theoretically attainable price and wage levels which would permit full employment with *any* quantity of money and *any* government budget, however restrictive.

In Chapter 10 we concluded, nevertheless, that the question (whether there always exists an equilibrium at full employment) is really an unimportant one, the interminable debate about it a waste of time. "Whether or

---

Assume that column (1) below represents an initial situation, and column (2) represents the effects, after one year, of a 2.5 percent increase both in the velocity of money and in the productivity of labor. Here, we *assume a* 0.5 percent increase in employment in order to explore its consequences, and thus its feasibility.

(1)	(2)
$M_{T_0} = 3PY$	$M_{T_1} = 2.925PY$
$Y_0 = 2N_0$	$Y_1 = 2.05N_1$
$W_0 = \$5$	$W_1 = \$5$
$P_0 = \$3$	$P_1 = \$2.925$
$N_0 = 100$	$N_1 = 100.5$
$Y_0 = 200$	$Y_1 = 206.025$
$Y_0 P_0 = \$600$	$Y_1 P_1 = \$602.623$
$M_{T_0} = \$1800$	$M_{T_1} = \$1762.673 \, (-2.074\%)$
$M_0 = \$2500$	$M_1 = \$2500$
$M_0 - M_{T_0} = \$700$	$M_1 - M_{T_1} = \$737.33 \, (+5.33\%)$

[10] Perhaps the most relevant effect of technological change in creating additional aggregate demand is none of those considered here, but rather the opportunities it creates for innovators to take advantage of new possibilities for profit by increased investment, an effect emphasized in the final section of Chapter 19.

not the economy is in a state of 'equilibrium,' it is often at less than full employment; and without policy intervention, it often, or perhaps usually, makes little or slow progress in getting out of that situation other than through stimulative government policies or through a basically exogenous, or at least largely unpredictable, favorable shift of investment." Nothing that we have been able in this chapter to add to this more classical version of the macroeconomic synthesis would appear to require a change in this judgment. Few classically leaning economists today argue that, in the modern world, downward wage and price flexibility is sufficiently effective to be relied on to prevent or quickly to eliminate unemployment arising from inadequate demand for labor. Thus, most of those who insist that there always exists some full-employment equilibrium, without govern- ment intervention, are nevertheless prepared to accept some use of monetary and/or fiscal policy, at least where achievement of equilibrium would otherwise require substantial price and (especially) wage-rate reductions.[11] There is, nevertheless, one school of modern macroeconomic thinking which comes close to arguing (a) that the current real-world economy is, most of the time, very close to full employment; (b) that it is kept there by reasonably effective wage and price flexibility, which can and should be relied upon (and strengthened); and (c) that inflation is basically what the classical economists saw it to be, a purely monetary phenomenon. The ideas of these classically oriented economists—the "monetarists"—are set forth in the major section which follows.

MONETARISM: A MODERN VARIANT OF CLASSICAL MACRO-ECONOMICS

Monetarism is a modern variant of classical macroeconomics, sufficiently specialized in its views to require separate treatment. Emerging in the United States in the period since World War II, it has attracted a relatively small but highly devoted and vocal following among economists, and achieved, as well, a certain popularity among noneconomists. One can easily describe monetarist ideas in terms of the special shapes which are

[11] To be sure, in the modern world of apparently endemic and continuous inflation, many of those who agree that the classical automatic correctives are quite ineffective in promptly eliminating unemployment nevertheless also argue that expansionary monetary and fiscal policies, intended to prevent or reduce unemployment, either must be avoided or used sparingly and with great moderation, lest they also worsen inflation. We should emphasize, however, that the modern dilemma of simultaneous inflation and unemployment (which we will take up in detail in Part V) was in no sense one contemplated in earlier Classical economic analysis any more than it is explained in traditional Keynesian terms. Thus it has little direct relevance to the question whether the classical automatic correctives have practical relevance in today's world, and, if not, whether fiscal and monetary policies provide an adequate substitute.

implied for *IS* and *LM* curves (the *LM* curve essentially vertical, or nearly so; the *IS* curve perhaps rather flat; prices sufficiently flexible that the vertical *LM* curve usually stands at Y_P). To be sure, that is not the way many monetarists prefer to describe their views; and to do so misses some of the special flavor of monetarist doctrine. For monetarism is a *doctrine*, with all of the connotations suggested by that term. As almost everyone knows, Professor Milton Friedman is the founder of and principal spokesman for that doctrine.[12]

In recent years, monetarist economists have made interesting and important new contributions to theories of inflation, unemployment, and interest rates, which will be considered in Chapters 14 and 15. And they have somewhat modified some of their earlier views. Here, however, we are concerned essentially with the earlier development of monetarist ideas, up to approximately 1970. These are the ideas that one *can* readily fit into a discussion of the *IS-LM* model. They are also the ideas incorporated in the widely popularized versions of monetarism.

Basic Tenets of Monetarism

1. The most fundamental tenet of monetarism is the conviction that the "velocity" of money is essentially constant. Professor Friedman prefers to express this constant velocity in terms of the ratio of GNP or NNP to M_2, a definition of money that includes, along with currency, all types of commercial bank deposits other than large denomination certificates of deposit. (Many other monetarists, more faithful to the quantity-theory origins of the concept of constant velocity, still prefer the narrower definition, that is, M_1, which limits money to currency and *demand* deposits.) Most agree, however, that the definition makes little difference. Since M_1 is the concept we have consistently used up to this point, we shall continue to do so. The essential constancy of velocity—except for a steady upward trend reflecting increased efficiency in money use[13]—is not derived from any theoretical analysis which proves that it must be so; rather it is asserted

---

[12] Friedman's ideas are summarized in a number of provocative articles. An early formulation is found in his "A Monetary and Fiscal Framework for Economic Stability," *American Economic Review*, 38 (1948), 245–64, reprinted in several books of readings, including those edited by F. A. Lutz and L. W. Mints (1951), J. Lindauer (1968), and M. G. Mueller (1970). Vintage Friedmanism is well summarized in his "The Role of Monetary Policy", *American Economic Review*, 58 (1968), pp. 1–17, reprinted in books of readings edited by W. L. Smith and R. L. Teigen (1974), W. L. Johnson and D. R. Kamerschen (1970), E. Shapiro (1970). See also the lively debate, Milton Friedman and Walter W. Heller, *Monetary vs. Fiscal Policy* (W. W. Norton, 1969); and the article by R. L. Teigen "A Critical Look at Monetarist Economics," *Federal Reserve Bank of St. Louis Review* (January 1972) 10–25, reprinted in Smith and Teigen, *op. cit.* pp. 123–40.

[13] If, however, M_2 is used as the definition of money, the trend of velocity is instead downward, leading Friedman to the conclusion that money is a "superior good", one which has an income-elasticity of demand in excess of unity.

as an incontestable empirical fact. For example, many monetarists, Friedman included, admit that there are good theoretical reasons why velocity should be influenced by interest rates. But they assert that the evidence supports only the view that velocity is (essentially) constant. (We will briefly present and evaluate some of that evidence below.)

Constant velocity means that the m in the quantity theory equation, $M^* = mPY$, does not fluctuate. Therefore, $PY = (1/m)M^*$; the money value of national income or product is a constant multiple of the quantity of money. Thus, money is all powerful—for good, but also, alas, for evil. Since we observe considerable instability in output and employment and prices, this can only reflect an unfortunate instability of the money supply. However, if the (growth rate of the) money supply were only stabilized, production, employment, prices, and incomes would be, too.

2. There are many possible channels through which money might exert its powerful control over PY—through interest rates affecting investment (or consumption), through direct or indirect wealth effects on consumption, through influencing the liquidity of business or personal balance sheets, or simply because people receiving money are unable to refrain from immediately spending it on something, whether goods, services, property, or securities. Some monetarists specify one or more of the above channels as more important than the others. Friedman, however, has (except for one or two lapses) continued to express his own view that money may operate through any one or all of these channels (or others not yet dreamed of); but *how* it operates is irrelevant and unimportant. The empirical "fact" is that velocity is constant.

3. Monetarists usually believe that wages and prices are quite flexible, more flexible than you (Keynesians) think! Or, at least, they would be flexible if it were not for government meddling in the economy (setting legal minimum or maximum prices, encouraging, or even helping to enforce, monopolies in labor or product markets). But even if some prices or wages are indeed inflexible, this merely throws the burden of price or wage adjustment on other products or groups of workers—whose prices must and will move by more to offset the failure of some to move freely. Thus, the economy is usually at or close to full employment (or, as we will explain in Chapter 14, at or close to the monetarist equivalent of full employment: the "natural rate of unemployment.")

This is why changes in M mainly alter P rather than Y. To whatever extent that P fails immediately to adjust, Y will do so—but only temporarily, and only until the P adjustment is completed. Thus, the basic cause of any and all inflation is inappropriate growth of M. "Inflation is a purely monetary phenomenon."

4. The economy is inherently highly stable. Underlying propensities to spend are not subject to wide or sudden swings, as Keynesians often imply. The principal instability that exists (or the appearance of instability) is the result of government actions undertaken to offset alleged underlying

instability in the private economy. Monetary and fiscal policy should be called the exercise not of "stabilization policy", but of "destablization policy." The "business cycle" would probably not exist in the absence of measures taken allegedly to "compensate" for it.

5. Business, worker, and consumer expectations are important and generally rational—that is, economic agents are capable of correctly anticipating the effects of their own and others' actions. Decisions taken on the basis of such expectations will cause the anticipated future results to occur even more quickly, if not at once. Thus, intelligent expectations are self-reinforcing and stabilizing, so long as the government does not create false signals by erratic and irrational intervention. That is, expectations are "rational" in the sense described at the end of Chapter 7.[14]

Belief in rational expectations fits well with an essentially classical view of the world, where there is little inherent disturbance (other than slow and steady growth trends), and external disturbance arises mainly from often unwise (but highly visible) government actions. In such a world, equilibrium is at full employment; and it is easily and promptly achieved through price and wage flexibility. If the money supply changes, only the equilibrium price level is altered; and, since the money supply is readily measurable and observed, economic agents can anticipate the equilibrium effects (which are only on prices) of changes in it, and can and will act in a way which brings these price changes about extremely quickly.

6. As is already clear from points 3, 4, and 5, political action in the economic field is inevitably destabilizing and counterproductive. The reason is that politicians, concerned only with being reelected, try to create temporary conditions that will make the economy appear to be even better than it is. Since, without such intervention, the state of the economy is usually at or close to the best that is permitted by existing resources and technology, attempts to make it appear even better (usually shortly before elections) may provide extra rewards for strategic political groups; but these are necessarily false and temporary, and can only create additional instability in the future, and a poorer *average* performance over longer periods of time. Almost invariably, of course, this deliberate intervention is of a kind that creates inflation rather than deflation—that is, it involves excessive monetary growth. However, because the central bank has great power over the money supply, but often seems not really to understand how money (or the economy) operates, it may create instability (at least of prices) even with the best of intentions.

---

[14] To be sure, not all monetarists are advocates of rational expectations. Indeed, Friedman's earlier work clearly implied adaptive expectations. For example, he long argued that the expected rate of inflation can ordinarily be taken as equal to the current rate. And his consumption theory (described in Chapter 16) implied income expectations which adapted quite slowly to past values of income. But the principal proponents of rational expectations tend also to be monetarists.

Policy Implications of Monetarism

Most of the implications for policy of the preceding basic ideas are probably obvious. The fundamental policy prescription, of course, is that the money supply should be held constant or (in a world of growth) should be made to expand at some low constant rate, say, 1 or 2 percent a year for M_1 (in the current United States economy). Given the steady upward trend in the velocity of M_1, the steady growth of the labor force, the gradual improvement of technology, and the substitution of capital for labor through net investment, a money supply (M_1) growing at 1 or 2 percent a year might produce a growth of Y roughly consistent with the growth of potential output at basically stable prices. However, *stability* of money growth is more important than the choice of precisely the correct growth rate to achieve price stability. If the stable rate of increase in money turns out instead to be consistent with a steady slight inflation (or deflation) this is unimportant because, being steady, it will be fully anticipated and will bother no one. Prices being reasonably flexible downward as well as upward, a steady, slight downward trend would create no problem.

Despite the high degree of underlying stability, some slight shifts or irregularities may occur, of course, in the underlying trends in velocity or productivity or in propensities to consume or invest. Although in principle, even these elements of instability might be offset by small variations in the rate of growth of M, the temptation to try to do so should be resisted at all costs, given our inability to forecast such fluctuations and given the propensity of politicians to overreact—or to use minor fluctuations as the excuse for trying to induce a false sense of well being through inflationary money supply growth.

It should be obvious that the tenets of monetarism leave no room for fiscal policy. Fiscal policy is, indeed, without effect on the economy unless—and then only to the extent that—it is accompanied by, or serves as the excuse for, changes in the supply of money. But these can be accomplished without using fiscal policy. Since the economy tends already to be at full employment, expansionary fiscal policy necessarily involves a 100 percent "crowding out" of other private expenditures.

A corollary of the monetarist view of monetary policy is Friedman's idea that a central bank cannot influence interest rates (other than perhaps very temporarily) through changes in the quantity of money. If it tries to reduce, or to hold down, the interest rate, by creating money at a faster rate, this will (since the economy is already essentially at full employment) only cause inflation, which will reduce the real quantity of money and raise interest rates. (Visualize a vertical LM curve, intersecting the horizontal axis at Y_P, shifted right by an increase in M, leading to higher prices that continually push the LM curve back to its initial position.) Money is all powerful, but the central bank cannot use it artificially to reduce interest rates or to attempt to maintain them too low.

Given the fact that United States interest rates were pegged by the Federal Reserve System at exceedingly low levels from 1937 through 1946 and then at a slightly higher level through 1950, this is a strange doctrine indeed![15] Surely, what Professor Friedman means is not that it can't be done, but that *the side effects* of doing it are so unthinkable that no sane central bank would long pursue such a policy (although Friedman does not usually give most central banks much credit for sanity!)

One such side effect would be continuing inflation—assuming the interest rate were pegged below the level at which the *IS* curve intersects a vertical *LM* curve drawn at the full employment level. To be sure, there was a considerable amount of inflation between 1941 and 1951 (usually attributed not to the pegging of interest rates but to a 5-year war that, at its peak, saw United States government purchases taking more than 50 percent of GNP). However, during most of this period the inflation was held to quite moderate proportions—perhaps mainly through the use of widespread direct controls over production, prices, wages, distribution, material use, inventories, imports and exports, hiring of labor, and so forth. So it may be that what Friedman really means is that the interest rate can only be pegged at the high cost *either* of unacceptable inflation *or* of highly unpalatable direct controls.

There is still another alternative, one that was considerably employed during World War II, along with direct controls: namely, higher taxes. Keynesians, at least, argue that a more restrictive government fiscal policy (pushing the *IS* curve to the left through higher taxes and reduced expenditures) could permit the central bank to reduce the interest rate below a level that would be inflationary in the absence of the restrictive fiscal policy. Maybe Professor Friedman means that this alternative, too, is so unthinkable that it need not be considered.

In any case, this writer will assert that Friedman's proposition, as stated (although perhaps so stated in order to be deliberately provocative), and as it is widely believed by many noneconomist monetarists, is simply wrong. We may not *wish* the central bank to hold the interest rate "artificially low"; each of the possible consequences of such a policy may be difficult or distasteful; but it can be done. And such countries as Japan, France, Belguim, and many others, have run rather successful monetary policies, over considerable periods, with interest rates pegged for much of the time at what are clearly "artificially" low levels—presumably to encourage investment and economic growth—using *other instruments* (in-

---

[15] This was done by essentially standing ready to buy, at fixed prices, all government securities offered to it by private holders.

cluding especially extensive direct controls over extension of credit) to prevent unfavorable consequences.[16]

Positive Contributions of the Monetarist View

Many of the criticisms that monetarists have made of monetary policy are very well taken. Clearly, monetary policy has often been destablizing rather than stabilizing. Central banks have speeded up their rates of money creation during inflationary boom periods either through a failure to recognize that they were, in fact, speeding up the growth of M, or through a failure to understand the consequences of what they knew they were doing, or simply because they didn't want to spoil the party. They have allowed the quantity of money to decline in periods of recession or depression, either by mistake or by default, or by failure to understand the consequences of letting M decline, or in order to fight a nonexistent inflation or unreasonable fears of future inflation.

In particular, monetarists point out that central bankers' concentration on the level of interest rates or on the "condition of credit markets" as appropriate targets or indicators of monetary policy has often been the source of perverse monetary influence. In recessions, because interest rates were low and falling and credit markets were "easing," they have assumed that their "easy money" policies were countering recession. In fact, the quantity of money may have been declining. It was just that the demand for money was falling even faster as the result of declining output and/or prices. In booms, high or rising interest rates or tight credit markets were assumed to be evidence of restrictive monetary policy when, in fact, the supply of money was growing rapidly but the demand growing even faster. Clearly, a steady, slow rise in M would have been a *better* (although perhaps not optimal) policy in both recession and boom.

Other useful contributions of monetarists (to be discussed later) relate to their emphasis on expectations of inflation, and to the impact of inflation (and price expectations) on interest rates.

[16] In a recent study of Japanese monetary and fiscal policy, this writer concluded that, "Government policy makers ... have been able to exercise a more precise—and, on the whole, more effective—management of overall economic developments than have their counterparts in most other free market countries ...

"During booms the banking system has been permitted—indeed, assisted and encouraged—to supply whatever volume of money and credit was demanded at low and stable interest rates (rates set progressively lower in each period of easy money). During intermittent periods of restraint, interest rates rose only slightly; instead, credit was effectively rationed ..."

"Obviously, use of rationing instead of price ... means that the average rate of interest could be kept considerably lower than it would otherwise have been .... This actually may be the most fundamental reason for the buoyancy of investment demand in Japan." (Gardner Ackley, with the collaboration of Hiromitsu Ishi, "Fiscal, Monetary, and Related Policies", in H. Patrick and H. Rosovsky, editors, *Asia's New Giant: How the Japanese Economy Works*, The Brookings Institution, 1976, pp. 153–247. Quotations are from pages 240 and 205.)

Evidence Supporting the Monetarist Position

The fundamental tenet of monetarism is the constancy of velocity (except for a smooth trend which occurs entirely exogenously). Several kinds of evidence have been adduced in support of this view.

The simplest kind is that illustrated in Figure 12-5. This shows annual data, on a ratio scale, over the period from 1949 to 1974, for the United States money stock (M_1), for GNP in current prices, and for the observed velocity of M_1 (GNP ÷ M_1). The movements of GNP and M_1 clearly follow very similar patterns, although the growth of GNP is somewhat faster than of M_1. This impression is largely confirmed when we look at the ratio of these two series, V_1. This does show a clear upward trend over the years, although it is also clear that the upward trend has not been constant but rather has tended to diminish as the period progressed. Moreover, noticeable year-to-year variations appear in the growth of V_1, indeed,

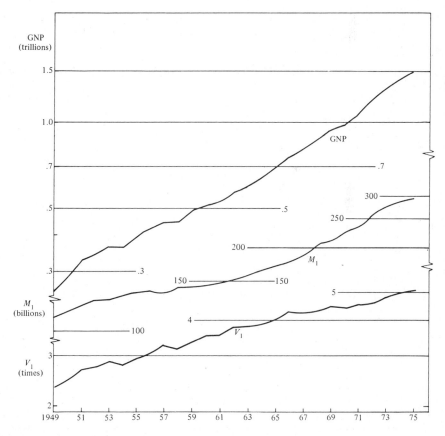

FIGURE 12-5 Gross National Product (GNP), Money Stock (M_1), and Velocity of M_1 (V_1), 1949–1975.

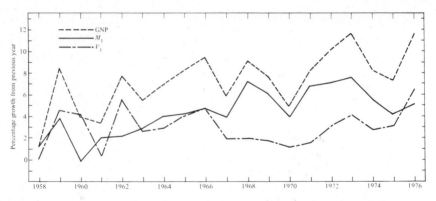

FIGURE 12-6　Annual Growth Rates of GNP, M_1 and V_1, 1958–1976.

possibly somewhat wider year-to-year variations than in the growth of M_1 or GNP.[17] Still, one gets the impression of considerable correlation of M_1 and GNP, that would be consistent with the view that changes in M_1 caused changes in GNP.

Figure 12-6, however, conveys a somewhat different picture. Here, the same data are plotted (although for a somewhat shorter period, 1958–1976), but they are now expressed in terms of percentage rates of growth from the previous year. The chart shows that growth rates of M_1 and GNP have been generally similar (although always higher for GNP than for M_1) and that both growth rates have risen over the period. Both observations are consistent with monetarist doctrines.

If we compare the shorter run movements in M_1 and GNP, these, too, seem to have been rather similar. Eight of the year-to-year changes in the growth rate of GNP were decreases, ten were increases. Of the eight decreases, six are seen to have occurred in years when M_1 growth also decreased. Of the ten increases in GNP growth rate, all ten occurred in years when M_1 growth rate also increased. Thus, sixteen of the eighteen year-to-year changes are conforming, only two nonconforming. Again, quite consistent with the monetarist conclusion.

However, now compare year-to-year growth rates of GNP and V_1. Over the period as a whole the growth rate of GNP tended to increase, and that of V_1 to be without substantial trend. But the year-to-year correspondence of changes in growth rates is about as striking as in the case of GNP and M_1. Of the ten years in which the growth rate of GNP increased, the growth of V_1 also accelerated in nine years and was unchanged in the

---

[17] If we consider years prior to the late 1940s, we get a very different impression of the behavior of velocity. It was highly irregular between 1915 and the late 1920s, then descended sharply until about 1932, fluctuated substantially around this much lower level in the 1930s, then descended sharply further through 1946—before beginning the relatively smooth and steady rise shown in Figure 12-5.

tenth; of the eight years in which GNP growth decelerated, V_1 growth also decelerated in seven. Thus, sixteen of the eighteen movements were conforming.

Moreover, the growth rate of V_1 appears at least as unstable as that of M_1. If the V_1 growth rate were believed to be completely exogenous, one would have to conclude that variations in V_1 were about as important as variations in M_1 in causing changes in GNP. On the other hand, the evidence would also be consistent with a view that something else, in addition to M_1 (perhaps another systematic variable or variables, perhaps mere random fluctuations), was contributing substantially to changes in GNP and that velocity was merely a residual element that moved passively to reflect the variation of this other factor and M.

Surely, crude comparisons of GNP, M_1 and V_1 do not provide evidence overwhelmingly consistent with the view that M_1, and only M_1, explains annual movements in GNP.

When we turn to shorter-term, for example, quarterly movements, the evidence is even more ambiguous. Figure 12-7 shows *quarter-to-quarter* percentage rates of change of GNP, M_1, and V_1 over the years 1972–1976. Here, variations in the growth rate of V_1 are considerably larger than those of M_1. Moreover, changes in GNP growth rates conform considerably more closely to changes in V_1 growth rates than to changes in M_1 growth. Of the eighteen quarter-to-quarter movements, the direction of changes in V_1 growth conform in seventeen cases with the direction of GNP growth, only one nonconforming. Comparing M_1 and GNP growth rates, noncon-

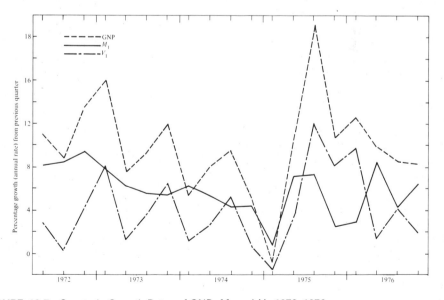

FIGURE 12-7 Quarterly Growth Rates of GNP, M_1 and V_1, 1972–1976.

forming movements are found in ten instances, conforming movements in only seven.

One might be tempted to conclude that the monetarists' complaints about the instability of monetary growth rates as the source of instability of output and prices are misplaced. Even if the growth rate of M_1 were maintained absolutely steady, there would still be wide swings in GNP growth resulting from the irregularities of velocity. But this is not the only possible conclusion. Indeed, crude confrontations such as these between monetarist doctrines and the data are not fair to the monetarist position (although monetarists sometimes invite such tests by a certain tendency toward overstatement). For most monetarists do argue that there exists a substantial (perhaps distributed) lag in the short-run relationship of M and GNP. Changes in M during one year or one quarter have some of their effects on GNP immediately—that is, within the same time period—with further effects during one or more subsequent periods. If this is correct, then, with irregularities in the growth rate of M, one would expect to find irregularities in *observed* velocity, when velocity is measured as a ratio of *current M* to *current* GNP. Thus, a judgment based on data like those plotted in Figures 12-5, 12-6, and 12-7 would not constitute a fair test of the monetarist hypothesis.[18]

Moreover, say the monetarists, stability of velocity need not be thought of as an absolute but a relative matter. To test the monetarist model should mean to test it *in comparison with some alternative*; obviously, the only current relevant alternative is the Keynesian model. By this they usually mean a simple Keynesian model that ignores all "monetary feedback." (Keynesians might well disagree with that choice!)

Monetarist Econometric Models

One comparative test of a simple Keynesian versus a monetarist model, which attracted much attention, was that published in 1963 by Friedman and David Meiselman.[19] This essentially purported to show that the "fundamental constant" of the monetarist system of thought (velocity) was more stable and predictable than the "fundamental constant" of the Keynesian system, the simple consumption multiplier. Another, more recent, and in many ways more interesting study, is that made by Leonall

---

[18] For a recent monetarist recognition of, and proposed explanation of, irregularities in velocity, see Leonall Andersen, "Observed Income Velocity of Money: A Misunderstood Issue in Monetary Policy," *Federal Reserve Bank of St. Louis Review*, 57 (August, 1975), 8–19.

[19] "The Relative Stability of Monetary Velocity and the Investment Multiplier in the United States," in Commission on Money and Credit, *Stabilization Policies* (Prentice-Hall, 1963), pp. 168–268. For a good brief summary and critical discussion, see Paul Wonnacott, *Macroeconomics* (R. D. Irwin, 1974), pp. 217–227; for more detail see A. Ando and F. Modigliani, "The Relative Stability of Monetary Velocity and the Investment Multiplier," *American Economic Review* 55 (September, 1965), 693–728.

Andersen and Jerry Jordan of the Federal Reserve Bank of St. Louis. (The St. Louis Bank is a strong outpost of Monetarist thought within the Federal Reserve System itself.)[20]

The Andersen-Jordan model is an econometric investigation in which a single equation containing a number of variables is statistically fitted to recent quarterly United States data. The model makes the current quarter's change of nominal GNP depend on the current quarter's and the three previous quarters' changes in a money-supply variable *and* on the current quarter's and the three previous quarters' changes in one or more fiscal variables. (Since several alternative definitions of monetary and fiscal variables are tried, the result is not a single equation but a family of them.) The general form of all equations is

$$\Delta Y_t = a_1 \Delta M_t + a_2 M_{t-1} + a_3 \Delta M_{t-2} + a_4 \Delta M_{t-3} + b_1 \Delta F_t + b_2 \Delta F_{t-1}$$
$$+ b_3 \Delta F_{t-2} + b_4 \Delta F_{t-3} + c$$

where Y is nominal GNP, M is some measure of money stock, F some measure of fiscal influence, and c is a constant. By statistical regression methods, the data determine the "best" numerical values of a_1, a_2, a_3, a_4, b_1, b_2, b_3, b_4, and c—best in the sense of producing a computed ΔY which conforms most closely to the actual ΔY. The equations thus purport to embody both the monetarist and the Keynesian hypotheses, leaving it up to the data to indicate whether, to what extent, and how quickly, monetary or fiscal policy changes, or both, produce changes in GNP.[21]

The results of their study are interpreted by Andersen and Jordan to show (a) that the effects of changes in the money supply are stronger, more predictable, occur with shorter lag, and are far more durable than the effects of changes in fiscal variables. Indeed, such effects as fiscal variables have on GNP are not only relatively weak but unpredictable and evanescent, disappearing after a few quarters. For example, one of the family of empirical equations presented by Andersen and Jordan is the following:

$$\Delta Y_t = 1.57^* \Delta M_t + 1.94^* \Delta M_{t-1} + 1.80^* \Delta M_{t-2} + 1.28 \Delta M_{t-3}$$
$$+ 0.15 \Delta(E - R)_t + 0.20 \Delta(E - R)_{t-1} - 0.10 \Delta(E - R)_{t-2}$$
$$- 0.47^* \Delta(E - R)_{t-3} + 1.99^* \qquad (R^2 = 0.56)$$

---

[20] "Monetary and Fiscal Actions: A Test of Their Relative Importance in Economic Stabilization," *Federal Reserve Bank of St. Louis Review*, 50 (November 1968), pp. 11–24. For excellent summaries and devastating critiques, see Wonnacott, *op. cit.*, pp. 228–37; and A. S. Blinder and R. M. Solow, "Analytical Foundations of Fiscal Policy," in A. S. Blinder and R. M. Solow, G. F. Break, P. O. Steiner, and D. Netzer, *The Economics of Public Finance* (Brookings Institution, 1974), pp. 65–78.

[21] Note that the equation makes no provision for the possibility that shifts in investment or consumption schedules (nor in the demand for money) might affect changes in GNP. We shall comment on this aspect below.

where:

> Y = nominal GNP (in billions of dollars at annual rates)
>
> M = narrowly-defined money supply, M_1 (in billions of dollars)
>
> $E - R$ = high-employment government expenditures minus high-employment government receipts (in billions of dollars at annual rates), where "high-employment" means levels estimated at 4 percent unemployment
>
> $t, t - 1, t - 2, \ldots$ represent the current quarter, the previous quarter, the second previous quarter, and so on
>
> Δ means change from previous period
>
> * signifies that the coefficient is statistically significant at the 5 percent level.

To understand the implications of this equation, note that the constant term (+1.99) implies a basic upward trend in GNP of $1.99 billion a year, regardless of monetary or fiscal policy. To this is added (or subtracted) the effects of concurrent and earlier changes in the money supply and in the "high-employment" deficit. To keep it simple, suppose that M_1 and $E - R$ have been constant for some time, with Y growing only by the $1.99 billion a year trend. Then, in quarter t, assume that M_1 rises by $1 billion and remains at the higher level (fiscal policy remaining unchanged). In that same quarter, the annual-rate rise of GNP will be $1.57 billion (in addition to the $1.99 billion trend); a quarter later, the change in GNP will be a further +$1.94 billion (the total annual-rate rise over two quarters thus being $1.57 + 1.94 billion, plus trend); in the third quarter, a further GNP change of $1.80 billion (plus trend); and in the fourth quarter, an additional $1.28 billion (plus trend). Over the four quarters, the total increase in GNP as the result of $1 billion more of M_1 will be $1.63 billion ($1.57 + 1.94 + 1.80 + 1.28) ÷ 4 (plus the $1.99 billion trend). (Division by four is necessary because the actual rise in GNP in any given quarter is one fourth of the rise in GNP at annual rate. That is, the rise of $1.57 in the first quarter is a rise which, *if it continued for four quarters*, would add $1.57 billion to GNP.)

Now suppose that, *instead*, the high-employment budget deficit rises by $1 billion and stays at the higher level (money supply unchanged). GNP will simultaneously change (in addition to trend) by +$0.15 billion, by a further +$0.20 billion in the second quarter, then in the third by −$0.10 billion, and in the fourth by a further −$0.47 billion, ending up $0.05 billion below where it started (0.15 + 0.20 − 0.10 − 0.47) ÷ 4 (exclusive of trend). Without a concurrent increase in M, this result may be attributed to "negative financial feedbacks," or "100 percent crowding-out" at work.

The fact that the first three of the coefficients of ΔM are statistically significant, whereas only the fourth (negative) coefficient of the change in high-employment deficit meets this test, is interpreted to imply that monetary effects are more regular and predictable than fiscal effects, and the only fiscal effect one can be reasonably confident about is the lagged *negative* effect of an (alleged) fiscal stimulus.

Evaluating the meaning and significance of statistical studies such as this one (or that of Friedman and Meiselman) is a complex matter; competent experts do not fully agree on the appropriate tests to apply. Almost needless to say, Keynesians—although initially somewhat impressed with the results of these particular studies—have had no trouble finding serious problems with the interpretations given by the monetarists. (References in earlier footnotes to analyses by Wonnacott, Ando and Modigliani, and Blinder and Solow provide much fuller evaluation than will be attempted here, as well as references to still other evaluations.)

However, this writer is particularly impressed with three points made by critics of the Andersen-Jordan study (both, in essence, applicable also to the Friedman-Meiselman study). First, finding a high degree of statistical association between changes in money stock and changes in GNP does not prove the direction of causation. (Not even the fact that changes in GNP are found correlated with *earlier* changes in M is conclusive with respect to direction of causation; note as well that the study did not test for the existence of correlation between current changes in M and *earlier* changes in GNP.) The question of direction of causation is significant because (as noted earlier) a major recurrent theme of monetarist attacks on the Federal Reserve has been its tendency, either by design or default, to follow a policy of adjusting the supply of money to the demand for it, for example, by stabilizing interest rates. Moreover, as will be shown in Chapter 21, there is a clearly identified and readily explainable mechanism by which (unless policy-makers deliberately offset it) increases in the demand for money tend automatically to increase the supply (through raising the volume of demand deposits supported by any given volume of bank reserves as well as the volume of reserves itself). Thus, what the equation shows may mainly be a reflection of the way in which M adjusts to GNP, not the reverse. Such an incorrect specification of the direction of causation of the money-GNP relationship (if it is incorrect) could also result in a failure to identify statistically the true, underlying fiscal-GNP relationship.

Second, although the monetarist view is that money affects nominal income, Keynesians argue that the stable relationships which they postulate exist between real, not nominal variables.

Third, assume, as many Keynesians argue (but monetarists deny), that there is an inherent instability in private spending propensities, perhaps especially in the case of investment. This, in turn, would create instability in GNP—*unless deliberately offset* by stabilization policy measures. Indeed, the Keynesians would say that countering such instability is what monetary and fiscal policy are all about. Thus, if one is seeking a statistical representation of "the Keynesian model," many will argue that investment should have been included as an autonomous variable. (Failure to do so could strongly bias the coefficients found for the fiscal policy variables.)

Moreover, to the extent that monetary and/or fiscal policy had been used (during the period to which the data relate) so as to offset some or all of the instability originating in private investment (or consumption), this use would have destroyed the statistical evidence of the effectiveness of such policies (at least such evidence as could be found through tests like that of Andersen and Jordan). To see this, suppose that, in the absence of policy, the time pattern of changes in GNP during some period would have been highly irregular. But because fiscal policy (say) had been perfectly designed and completely effective, the time pattern of changes in GNP had been smoothed out to a perfectly smooth trend. Since this would have been accomplished through large and irregular variations in fiscal-policy variables, looking back, *ex post*, one would find no correlation between these large and irregular changes in fiscal policy and the concurrent smooth change in GNP. (Only if one were aware of, and could measure, the underlying instability in investment spending would he be able to discover the power of the fiscal stabilization.)

Now no one contends that United States fiscal policy was perfectly stabilizing during the 1950s and 1960s (the period covered by the Andersen-Jordan data). However it should also be clear that if, *some* of the time, fiscal policy was used in a stabilizing direction (with wholly or partially stabilizing effects), whereas at *other* times no stabilizing changes were made in fiscal variables and, as a result, there were irregular changes in GNP due to instability of private demand, during *neither* period would any correlation appear between fiscal changes and GNP changes. In the one period, wide variation in fiscal policy measures would have accompanied relatively stable GNP; during the other, no variation in fiscal policy measures would have accompanied irregular changes in GNP. Thus, even if there were still other periods when fiscal policy was the main factor creating instability, evidence of the effectiveness of fiscal policy would be obscured.

Perhaps there is a country in which, over some period, it is appropriate to hypothesize that aggregate demand would have been essentially flat in the absence of changes in fiscal and monetary policy. In that case, any and all growth and fluctuations that appeared might appropriately be attributed only to policy changes. In that special circumstances, the Andersen–Jordan tests might correctly measure the effectiveness of monetary and fiscal policies. We may doubt that there is any such case.

Earlier, in discussing the "tenets" of monetarism, we noted the assumption that the underlying economic structure is stable. The importance of this assumption should now be apparent. If correct, it means that any and all instability in GNP arises only from policy changes—presumably purposeless, random, or mistaken. If that were the nature of the world, we would expect data to reveal clear correlation between changes in observed GNP and changes in any policy variables that was "*effective*"; failure to find such correlation would then prove that policy variable to have been "*ineffective.*" But underlying stability is not the Keynesian's assumption; he should not therefore be expected to accept as definitive a statistical analysis that implicitly assumes this to be the case.

An Interest-Elastic Velocity

Before leaving the subject of the empirical validity of monetarist doctrines, we should note that there is a large volume of econometric research which establishes very strongly the existence of an interest-rate elasticity of the demand for money. Of all the many econometric investigations made of this subject, only one (which happens to have been made by Milton Friedman) fails to find a significant negative relationship between some interest rate variable and the demand for money.[22] This finding, of course, directly contradicts the monetarist position regarding the constancy of velocity. Rearranging the demand-for-money equation used in Chapter 11 and elsewhere

$$M = mPY + f(i)$$

we obtain

$$PY = \frac{M}{m} - \frac{f(i)}{m}$$

Dividing through by M produces an expression for velocity

$$V \equiv \frac{PY}{M} = \frac{1}{m} - \frac{1}{mM} f(i)$$

which clearly is not constant if i varies, or, indeed, if M varies.

Some monetarists are willing to accept a dependence of the demand for money on the interest rate. This means, in *IS-LM* terms, that the *LM* curve is not vertical, but slopes upward to the right. However, if the interest-elasticity of the demand for money is only moderate, and if one accepts the *other* monetarist tenets (especially, reasonably effective wage-price flexibility, and the inherent stability of private demand), most fundamental monetarist doctrines are only slightly modified. Nevertheless, the clearly distinctive character of monetarist positions begins to be blurred. If, then, the monetarist is also willing to specify the *channels* through which he thinks money affects the economy—usually through interest rate and wealth effects on investment and consumption—he ends up propounding only what we have called a "more classical version" of the Keynesian-

---

[22] For a list of such studies, and a characterization of their conclusions, see A. Okun, *The Political Economy of Prosperity* (The Brookings Institution, 1970), pp. 146–47. An excellent later study is by S. M. Goldfeld, "The Demand for Money Revisited", in *Brookings Papers on Economic Activity*, 3:1973, pp. 577–638. A more recent survey is found in E. L. Feige and D. K. Pearce, "The Substitutability of Money and Near-Monies: A Survey of the Time Series Evidence," *Journal of Economic Literature*, 15 (June 1977), 439–69.

classical synthesis. Not all economists who hold such views choose to call themselves monetarists.

CLASSICAL VERSUS KEYNESIAN VERSIONS OF THE SYNTHESIS

As should by now be abundantly clear, the Keynesian-classical synthesis—as represented (somewhat inadequately) by the *IS-LM* apparatus—is not a single model but a family of submodels. Although we can, and do, describe some of these submodels as "more classical" in spirit, and others as "more Keynesian," there is no single version which we can definitively describe as *the Keynesian* or *the classical* model. And since the submodels differ in several dimensions, there is not even a single meaningful scale running from most classical to most Keynesian.

Despite all this, it is not entirely meaningless to talk about and to attempt to evaluate "more classical" and "more Keynesian" versions, and we shall do so here. Mainly we will be pulling together observations scattered through this and the two preceding chapters.

Since all of these submodels have been repeatedly analyzed and widely used, we can safely assume that all are logically faultless; that is, their different results follow inescapably from their different assumptions. (To be sure, the assumptions may not always be fully or accurately stated by model users, or some users may confuse which results go with which assumptions. But these are not faults of the models.) Thus, evaluating the various models requires evaluating the assumptions—which assumptions are more *appropriate* and for what purpose?

Note that we said "appropriate," not "realistic." "Realism" may be an important criterion of appropriateness, but it is not necessarily the main or only criterion and it is not entirely clear what it means. In the first place, models are not useful, and used, only as descriptions of today's or yesterday's "real world." We may be interested not only in understanding how some existing or historical economy works but how some modified or alternative economy might work.

In any case, no model can aspire to complete descriptive realism. The very nature of a model is that it gives a *simplified* picture of some economy, isolating what are believed to be the important characteristics of its structure and operation. What is "important," of course, is a relative matter: it depends on what characteristics the user (or society) judges to be important (often reflecting subjective or social values) and on how much detail is thought to be needed or of interest, which, in turn, depends on what kinds of questions the economist, or society is interested in.

Moreover, what is realistic, and useful, and interesting may well depend on the time span of our concern. Are we interested in understanding only broad tendencies believed to work out over considerable periods of time, or do we care about what happens in the interim? Thus we may well ask about more-classical or more-Keynesian models: What kind of questions do they appropriately help us to answer, and are we interested in those questions? To what kinds of situations do they correspond, and are these of interest or relevance?

The More-Classical Versions

Like the original classical model, the more-classical versions of the synthesis model describe an economy that automatically achieves equilibrium at full employment. For these versions to have much descriptive relevance to any real-world economy, that economy would seem to require one or more of the following characteristics: (a) a high degree of wage and price flexibility, downward as well as upward, and/or (b) a high degree of stability of its underlying structure, so that achieving equilibrium does not require large movements (at least downward) in wages and prices; and/or (c) a strong and relatively steady exogenous upward trend in investment (or in the consumption function) which would reduce the need for interest rate *reductions* secured through price reductions; and/or (d) rapidly occurring technological improvements, reducing unit costs and/or the amount of money needed per transaction, both of which reduce the need for the difficult wage-rate reductions. If one or more of these characteristics is missing, the economy, left to itself, is likely to experience substantial periods of disequilibrium—to which the classical model has relevance primarily as a standard of comparison.

Most observers do not find that modern Western economies possess these necessary characteristics in sufficient degree to make the classical model relevant, other than as descriptive of some ideal or imaginary alternative world. To be sure, indisputable direct empirical evidence on the presence of these characteristics is essentially impossible to present. However, the indirect evidence, for example, that employment in these economies appears frequently (and often substantially) to exceed what can be identified as a "frictional" or "structural" minimum—seems inescapable. Yet some classical–leaning economists (for example, Milton Friedman) would even dispute this empirical generalization (or its relevance).

There is, however, an alternative and more limited descriptive role that might be claimed for the more-classical versions. One may observe that, although most modern Western economies experience serious and sometimes prolonged "lapses from full employment," they ordinarily do return from time to time to something approximating full employment. The trend of GNP is essentially parallel with the trend in potential output. Thus, one could interpret the recurrent high-employment intervals as approximating recurrent positions of full-employment equilibrium. To be sure, these positions may not, and probably will not, have been achieved "automatically" through the classical wage-price-interest rate adjustments.

They may reflect, instead, booms in private investment not explained by the automatic classical mechanisms of adjustment, or occasional upsurges in government spending or tax reductions, or accidental or deliberate increases in the money supply. Still, in a comparative statics sense, we might still use the classical model to analyze changes between successive "bench-mark" periods of approximate full employment and thus to explain longer term trends and adjustments.

More Keynesian Versions

For relatively short-run analysis, we are clearly better able to use the more Keynesian versions of the synthesis, which take wages and prices as essentially given rather than endogenous, and permit us to focus more sharply on exogenous factors affecting investment, on dynamic mechanisms such as inventory adjustments and the acceleration principle, and on the short-run effects of fiscal and monetary policy measures, which may be used in an attempt to achieve reasonable stability, reasonably close to potential output.

We may think of the more-classical versions as concerned with recurrent positions of full-employment equilibrium, whether secured by fully flexible wages, prices, and interest rates, or otherwise. Then we can identify the more-Keynesian versions as describing the adjustments of an economy in which equilibrium, for whatever reason, is not secured through wage, price, and interest-rate adjustments, and in which, instead, quantities adjust: quantities of employment, output, consumption, investment, incomes, transfers, taxes, and so on. Whether we want to call the resulting positions "equilibria" is a matter of taste; "quasi–equilibria" will do as well.

As these quantity adjustments occur (the price adjustments having failed to occur), evidence of disequilibrium, and resulting pressures for equilibrating price movements, may not appear in most markets. Because saving is reduced (through falling incomes) when investment declines, downward pressure on interest rates will be absent, even though the interest rate is too high for full employment. Because production is cut back (rather than prices reduced) as demand falls, there is no excess production overhanging most markets for goods and services, which would tend to drive down prices. Evidence of disequilibrium remains in only one market—the labor market, where supply clearly exceeds demand. However, if this excess fails to reduce wage rates (or to reduce them far enough or fast enough), the money and goods markets will show no excess of supply over demand and no pressures for equilibrating interest rate or price adjustments.

What might have been a relatively minor exogenous drop in aggregate demand is thus "multiplied" to become a bigger one. And when we take account of accelerator and inventory effects, what might appear to be minor and temporary departures from equilibrium become cumulative departures, with large quantity adjustments occurring because relatively small price adjustments failed to occur in time to avoid them.

In recent years, a new emphasis has been given to the *disequilibrium* character of the Keynesian model by a group of economists led especially by Robert W. Clower and Axel Leijonhufvud.[23] They argue that the *IS-LM* models—especially those that incorporate some degree of wage flexibility (like those summarized in Figure 12-1 or 12-3)—lose the entire message of the "Keynesian Revolution", which they believe was that the price system does not and, probably, cannot conceivably be made to work to maintain full-employment equilibrium, which is the only equilibrium of these models. Given the absence of some effective equivalent of Walras' auctioneer (see Chapter 1) in every market—and most of all in the labor market—there is simply no way for full-employment equilibrium to be achieved (except by accident) or maintained in a complex modern economy using money rather than barter, with extensive division of labor, and with substantial separation of the activities of saving and investment.

Instead, in the real-world economies of today, few prices and almost no wage rates are made to, or allowed to, "clear" their respective markets; knowledge and foresight by participants in most of these markets are notably imperfect; given modern technology, investment decisions committing vast resources for decades ahead must be made on the basis of precarious information and hunches; contagious moods of optimism or pessimism can sweep financial and other markets; participants in most markets form expectations which, much of the time, are surely not "rational" in the special sense of that term. Any or all of these circumstances can lead to decisions which, instead of pushing the economy toward equilibrium, may cause it to move for considerable periods away from equilibrium.

Clower and Leijonhufvud, and others who think in these terms, berate most of their fellow-economists' preoccupation with equilibrium, and their lack of concern with analyzing at all realistically the dynamic processes that may, but usually will not, carry the economy toward equilibrium. They deplore the "domestication" of investment into a wholly endogenous variable, automatically stabilized by interest rate movements, which (in the models) are in turn heavily dependent upon the occurrence of stabilizing price level changes. And they argue that the economists who insist on constraining Keynes' message into the straightjacket of an *IS-LM* model have never understood or have forgotten the main burden of that message.

[23] For examples of this work, see R. W. Clower, "The Keynesian Counterrevolution: a Theoretical Appraisal," in F. H. Hahn and F. P. R. Brechling, eds., *The Theory of Interest Rates* (London: Macmillan, 1965); and A. Leijonhufvud, *On Keynesian Economics and the Economics of Keynes* (Oxford University Press, 1968). Somewhat similar ideas are expressed by a group of economists at Cambridge University, led by Joan Robinson, whose attacks on "bastard Keynesianism" carry especial weight since she was one of Keynes' own pupils.

As can be seen from many parts of this book, this writer is highly sympathetic to this point of view. He differs, if at all, mainly in thinking that it may put excessive emphasis on identifying as "equilibrium" only the full macroequilibrium of the classical full-employment economy. Moreover, he holds that no harm—and perhaps some good—can be accomplished by organizing one's reasoning about the "real–world" economy into relatively simple models which might be imagined to achieve at least a *quasi*-equilibrium, so long as one remembers that even these *quasi*-equilibrium positions are likely to be continually changing, and rarely, if ever, in practice fully achieved or long maintained.

REVIEW QUESTIONS

1. Show either algebraically or graphically that the flatter the IS curve the greater will be the effect of a change in prices and wages on output.

2. Explain the "wealth effect" on consumption, and illustrate its possible significance in connection with each of the following:

(a) the effects of price level deflation;

(b) the effects of monetary policy.

3. It was noted in this chapter that there are at least four channels through which a change in wage and price level can affect the volume of real spending on goods and services. Name these channels and show how a reduction in price level is transmitted through the channels to a change in real output. Explain fully to what extent these channels provide support for the classical conclusion that the economy will automatically provide full employment, without need for policy intervention.

4. "If downward wage rigidity is the main obstacle to full employment, it is less of an obstacle when the facts of economic growth are taken into account." Explain fully this proposition.

5. "A distinguishing feature of monetarists and nonmonetarists is the role that each group assigns to stabilization policies. Nonmonetarists hold that a private economy *needs* to be, *can* be, and therefore *should* be stabilized by appropriate monetary and fiscal policies. Monetarists take the view that there is no serious need to stabilize the economy; that even if there were a need it could not be done; and, that even if it could in principle be done, it cannot be done in practice and we should not try." Present a brief argument that supports each position, with particular emphasis on the question whether the economy *needs* to be stabilized, whether it *can* be stabilized, and whether we should try to stabilize it, using monetary and fiscal policies.

6.

(a) Briefly explain what Andersen and Jordan found in their famous empirical study of the relative effectiveness of monetary and fiscal policies.

(b) Explain several of the leading criticisms of this study and its conclusions.

7. Explain how one might support the view that the more classical versions of the "synthesis model" are concerned principally with the long-run consequences of economic events, while short-run consequences are the main concern of Keynesian versions.

SELECTED REFERENCES

R. Holbrook, "The Interest Rate, the Price Level, and Aggregate Demand," in W. L. Smith and R. L. Teigen (eds.), *Readings in Money, National Income, and Stabilization Policy* (R. D. Irwin, 3rd ed., 1974), pp. 38–60.

W. L. Smith, "A Graphical Exposition of the Complete Keynesian System," *Southern Economic Journal*, 23 (October 1956), 115–125, reprinted in Smith and Teigen (*op. cit.*), pp. 61–68.
(Two versions of the IS–LM model with flexible prices.)

A. C. Pigou, *Employment and Equilibrium* (Macmillan, 2nd (rev.) ed.), 1949), Parts I and II, esp. pp. 131–134.
(Pigou's original statement of the wealth effect on consumption.)

L. A. Metzler, "Wealth, Saving, and the Rate of Interest," *Journal of Political Economy*, 59 (April 1951), 93–116, reprinted in R. S. Thorn (ed.), *Monetary Theory and Policy* (Random House, 1966), pp. 324–357.
(A technical discussion of the implications of the wealth effect.)

M. Friedman, "A Monetary and Fiscal Framework for Economic Stability," *American Economic Review*, 38 (June 1948), 245–264, reprinted in J. Lindauer (ed.), *Macroeconomic Readings* (Free Press, 1968), pp. 275–286; and in M. G. Mueller (ed.), *Readings in Macroeconomics* (Holt, Rinehart, and Winston, 2nd ed., 1971), pp. 337–352.
(A famous early statement (1948) of Friedman's ideas.)

M. Friedman, "The Role of Monetary Policy," *American Economic Review*, 58 (March 1968), 1–17, reprinted in Smith and Teigen (*op. cit.*), pp. 412–421; and in E. Shapiro (ed.), *Macroeconomics: Selected Readings* (Harcourt, Brace, and World, 1970), pp. 488–424.
(Friedman's Presidential Address to the American Economic Association, detailing his views on monetary and fiscal policy.)

K. Brunner, "The 'Monetarist Revolution' in Monetary Theory," *Weltwirtschaftliches Archiv*, 55 (No. 1, 1970), 1–30.
(A presentation of basic tenets of monetarism.)

R. L. Teigen, "A Critical Look at Monetarist Economics," *Federal Reserve Bank of St. Louis Review*, 54 (January 1972), 10–25, reprinted in Smith and Teigen (*op. cit.*), pp. 123–140.
(An excellent, critical review of monetarists' tenets.)

F. Modigliani, "The Monetarist Controversy or, Should We Forsake Stabilization Policies?," *American Economic Review*, 67 (March 1977), 1–19.
(Modigliani's Presidential Address to the American Economic Association, providing a Keynesian answer to monetarist views on policy.)

M. Friedman and D. Meiselman, "The Relative Stability of Monetary Velocity and the Investment Multiplier in the United States," in Commission on Money and Credit, *Stabilization Policies* (Prentice-Hall, 1963), pp. 168–268.
(One of the earliest modern empirical works presented as evidence in support of monetarism.)

L. Andersen and J. Jordan, "Monetary and Fiscal Actions: A Test of Their Relative Importance in Economic Stabilization," *Federal Reserve Bank of St. Louis Review*, 50 (November 1968), 11–24.
(An empirical work on the effectiveness of policies that most monetarists regard as proof of the validity of their arguments.)

A. S. Blinder and R. M. Solow, "Analytical Foundations of Fiscal Policy," in A. S. Blinder, R. M. Solow, G. F. Break, P. O. Steiner, and D. Netzer, *The Economics of Public Finance* (The Brookings Institution, 1974), pp. 57–78.
(Presenting critical reviews of the monetarists' position, including their empirical works.)

S. M. Goldfeld, "The Demand for Money Revisited," in *Brookings Papers on Economic Activity*, 3, 1973, pp. 577–638.
(A thorough discussion and estimation of the demand for money in as many aspects as possible.)

R. W. Clower, "The Keynesian Counterrevolution: A Theoretical Appraisal," in F. H. Hahn and F. P. R. Brechling (eds.), *The Theory of Interest Rates* (Macmillan, 1965).

A. Leijonhufvud, *On Keynesian Economics and the Economics of Keynes* (Oxford University Press, 1968).
(The foundations of a newer, "disequilibrium" interpretation of Keynesian economics.)

PART V

INFLATION

Chapter 13

Elements of a Theory of Inflation

Excess-demand Inflation
Keynesian "inflationary-gap" analysis
The dynamics of demand inflation

"Cost-push" Inflation

The Simple Phillips Curve
A price-Phillips curve
A cost-push theory of the Phillips curve
A purely competitive explanation: Lipsey
Search unemployment: Phelps
Alternative theories of a simple Phillips curve

In the 1961 predecessor of this book, the second sentence of the chapter on inflation reads as follows: "It may well be argued that inflation is currently, has been for a decade or more, and threatens to be in the future one of the most crucial macroeconomic problems for most countries of the world." During the 5 years, 1955–1960, the United States inflation rate (measured by the Consumer Price Index) had averaged 2.0 percent, and public concern with inflation was minimal. During the 5 years 1970–1975, it averaged 6.7 percent; similar accelerations occurred in most other countries. Everywhere, inflation is now popularly, and usually officially, regarded as a major economic problem. If the words quoted were appropriate in 1961, they are considerably more so in 1977.

With the intensification of inflation there has been an explosion of interest in the subject, not only among ordinary citizens and their political leaders but, quite naturally, also among economists. This chapter and the next two cannot pretend to summarize more than a tiny fraction of the research on this subject, much of which has occurred in the past 15 years. Still, as will be seen, there is far from complete agreement among economists on the nature and causes of inflation.

We have been able to avoid saying much about inflation in the first 12 chapters of this book by the not very satisfactory device of explicitly limiting our concern in those chapters to variations of aggregate output in the range below **potential output**, where potential output was defined as the real GNP associated with "full employment" of the labor force, and **full employment** was defined as the level of employment beyond which unit labor costs, and thus the price level, were almost sure to rise, for a number of reasons that we briefly sketched.

We recognized that this level of employment might not appropriately be described as a point but was perhaps instead a range. Still, in many countries, official or unofficial "full-employment targets" had often been set, which represented "some uneasy compromise between what are seen to be the social and economic costs of inflation and the clear social and economic advantages of high employment". *Until this chapter*, we have (with brief exceptions) discussed only variations in employment below and up to such target levels and variations in output below and up to the corresponding potential output.

We further qualified our procedure with the following words: "This is not to say that the only explanation for a general rise in the price level is 'over-full' employment; there may well be others. It *is* to say that, in any case, such levels of employment are almost sure to generate 'inflationary pressures,' whether other forces do or not. And, if other forces are generating inflation, over-full employment will magnify their impact."

As rickety as this device was, we have used it to hold off a whole range of problems while we settled others. Now we will need to face up squarely to the nature and meaning of "full-employment," and its associated "potential output." Before we begin doing that, however, we will survey briefly some simple, earlier theories of inflation that dealt with what happens when full-employment limits are breached—a situation usually described as one of **excess-demand inflation**, or, sometimes, **demand-pull inflation**. These theories ordinarily paid no attention to the meaning of the term "full employment," perhaps assuming it meant zero (involuntary) unemployment, even though that condition has never been recorded.[1] This starting point has the advantage of providing a bridge from earlier treatments of inflation, which had fundamentally changed very little between the origins of modern economics in the eighteenth century and the late 1950s, and all of which treated inflation as a phenomenon of excess demand.

EXCESS-DEMAND INFLATION

We can define **inflation** as a persistent and appreciable rise in the general level of prices. This clearly makes inflation a *process*: *rising* prices, not *high* prices. Thus, in some sense, inflation is a disequilibrium state; it must be analyzed dynamically rather than with the tools of statics. The latter may tell us something about the conditions under which an inflation may emerge or possibly define its limits (by describing the conditions of price level equilibrium). But to analyze the *rate* of inflation, to explain why it is 1 percent rather than 15 percent a year, is essentially a problem of macrodynamics.[2]

In the classical analysis, the price level depended directly and proportionately on the quantity of money. Inflation occurred when the quantity of money increased and stopped when the quantity of money was stabilized. The rate of inflation thus presumably depended on the rate of new money creation. If $\Delta M/M$ was 3 percent a year, prices would tend to rise at 3 percent a year (adjusted for any trends in full-employment output and in velocity).

[1] At least in the United States. Other countries—especially Switzerland—have often come close.

[2] Although we can and will define an **equilibrium rate of inflation** as one in which the rate of price change is constant.

In its cruder forms, however, the quantity theory was defective in failing to explain the channel by which an increase in M produced an increase in money spending, which, with constant output (at the maximum level permitted by the economy's resources), bid up prices. This deficiency was remedied by Wicksell, who saw new money flowing into the economy in the form of bank loans to businessmen to finance investment in excess of the current rate of saving. This represented, then, a net increase in the aggregate demand for an unchanged total supply of goods (since the economy was already at full employment), bidding up the prices of goods (and of the resources to produce goods), and at the same time extracting "forced saving" from the consumers, whose money incomes were based on an earlier price level. This explanation thus clearly made monetary inflation an excess-demand phenomenon. Wicksell clearly saw that the rise in prices would not itself reduce aggregate demand, because, after a brief lag, money incomes would rise in proportion to prices, leaving consumers in the same position as before to compete with investors for the limited supply of goods. If the banks stood ready to supply the investors with further new loans, the process would continue. If, on the other hand, the banks ceased to expand the money supply, the market rate of interest would have to rise to the "natural rate," choking off the extra investment demand (and perhaps stimulating saving, that is, reducing consumption demand), thus halting the inflation.

The theory of inflation implied in Keynes' analysis is only a little more than an extension and generalization of Wicksell's. Suppose that there is already full employment and investment demand increases. This means a total demand for goods in excess of the available supply. Prices are thus bid up. Since consumer demand depends on real income, which is not reduced by rising prices (because the sale of output at higher prices creates an equivalent rise in money incomes), the excess of demand is not directly eliminated by the process of inflation itself. However, Keynes broke the close tie between the quantity of money and the level of aggregate demand. An economy could experience inflation even with a constant money supply, if consumption or investment propensities increased under conditions of full employment. To be sure, if M were constant, higher prices would raise the transactions demand for money and thus push up interest rates, tending to choke off some investment (or consumer) demand and thus to moderate the inflationary pressure. But it would not completely avoid a rise in the price level. The reason is that the rise in interest rates would also release money from idle balances to supply the added transaction needs at higher prices. Thus some inflation would still occur, until the interest rate rose enough to eliminate excess demand.

The two analyses, and the differences between them, can also be illuminated by considering the case of increased government demand in a situation of full employment. If government spending increases with no rise in taxes, the difference (deficit) must be financed either (a) by borrowing from the general (nonbank) public or (b) by running the printing press, borrowing from banks with excess reserves, or by the central bank buying bonds in the open market to offset sales by the government. All methods under (b) directly increase the money supply. In the classical analysis method (b) would raise the price level but not method (a). In the Keynesian analysis, even solution (a) is inflationary. Still, despite their differences, both the Keynesian analysis and the quantity theory (as expanded by Wicksell) explained inflation, when it occurred, as arising from an *excess of aggregate demand over potential output*, causing prices to be bid up until markets were cleared at a price level high enough to eliminate excess demand.

Keynesian Inflationary-Gap Analysis

Keynesian demand-inflation analysis has frequently been summarized in the concept of an **inflationary gap**. This can easily be pictured as in Figure 13-1. Here we represent consumption C as a function of real income Y in the customary manner. Assuming a high level of $I + G$ (investment plus government spending) and assuming this level of real spending independent of the price level, the total desired real expenditures at each possible level of income are shown by the solid line $(C + I + G)$. If there were no limit on real output, income would rise to Y_0 where real expenditures would equal real output. But if there exists a full-employment limit on real output, Y_P, real income cannot reach Y_0. At Y_P, total demand $(C + I + G)$ exceeds total output, leaving an "inflationary gap" equal to AB in the figure. This is the amount by which aggregate demand at full employment exceeds output at full employment.[3] This inflationary gap causes prices to rise, but the price rise does nothing *directly* to eliminate the gap.

However, there are a number of "indirect effects" of rising prices on real demand, most of which do reduce the gap. These are precisely parallel to the analysis of the "indirect effects" of deflation:

1. If M is constant, or rises in smaller proportion than prices, i will rise, tending to reduce I (and possibly shifting the C function downward).

2. To the extent that the "Pigou effect" exists, higher prices may reduce C by reducing real wealth held in the form of government money and government debt. Moreover, to the extent that i rises, this, too, will reduce wealth by lowering bond prices and thereby restrain consumption.

3. If there is international trade, higher domestic prices will tend to encourage imports and reduce exports (an effect which can be put into the diagram by including "net foreign investment" in I).

[3] Although the concept of an inflationary gap is implicit in the *IS-LM* analysis of this case, the extent of that gap is not measurable in that kind of diagram because effect number 1 in the following list is built into the *IS* curve.

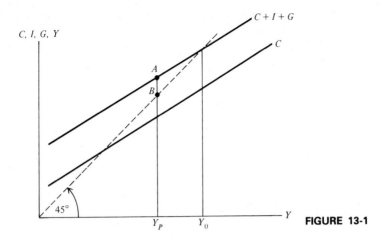

FIGURE 13-1

4. If tax collections rise faster than prices (as they are almost certain to do under existing tax systems), this shifts the C function downward by reducing the real disposable income associated with any given level of Y. Transfer payments fixed in dollar terms also become less significant in real terms, further reducing the C function. Real government purchases will also be reduced if budgets are fixed in money terms.

5. If rising prices engender expectation of further rise, causing consumers to step up their normal buying of durable goods and investors to try to "beat the rise" by investing more or sooner than otherwise, the inflationary gap may be widened. If speculators try to build up inventories to beat the rise or to profit by resale, this will further widen the gap. On the other hand, if the current rise in prices is expected to be temporary and to be followed by later reductions in prices, consumer buying of durables and investment in plant and equipment may be delayed and inventories drawn down, thus narrowing the gap.

Many "Keynesian" analyses of inflation have also attempted to build in effects on aggregate demand resulting from redistributions of income between wages and profits that may occur as the result of inflation. If money wage rates were fixed, higher prices would go entirely to profits. (A wage ceiling without price ceilings might have this effect.) Assuming that the MPC + MPI (marginal propensity to invest from increases in income) of profit recipients is less than the MPC of wage earners, a redistribution of income toward profits would tend to reduce aggregate demand and to narrow the inflationary gap. However, on customary assumptions of profit-maximizing behavior and a free labor market, there should be no permanent redistribution against labor. For any fall in the real wage should make individual employers anxious to increase their employment and output, resulting in a competitive bidding for labor which (with full employment) would cause money wage rates to rise along with prices. If there were a *lag* of wage adjustment, income would be temporarily redistributed against labor, *during the inflation*, thus narrowing the inflationary gap. The wage lag could not, by itself, however, reduce the inflationary gap. For, if prices stabilized as a result of reduced consumer demand arising from a wage lag and a redistribution toward profits, wages could then "catch up," reopening the gap.

An inflationary gap can obviously arise when a government, for whatever reasons, chooses to use the printing press (or the sale of bonds to the central bank) to finance even its normal expenditures in a time of full employment. Inflation from excess demand could also occur during a strong private investment boom (such as might result from massive innovations, opening of new territory, and so on), especially if monetary policy were willing to "accommodate" increased demands for money (or, before the existence of central banks, if the banking system were such as to allow the increase in demand for money to produce its own increased supply). However, the important cases of excess-demand inflation are surely those associated with war or preparations for war, when government expenditure typically increases far more than private expenditures are reduced by higher taxes.

The Dynamics of Demand Inflation

During the 1940s and 1950s a number of models were constructed that attempted to describe the dynamic behavior of an economy with excess demand, and thus to explain not merely the ultimate extent of inflation but also the *rate* of inflation in the presence of an inflationary gap. Since modern inflation analysis tends to obliterate any sharp distinction between excess-demand inflation and other kinds, these earlier dynamic analyses are of interest mainly as introduction to more recent analyses. We therefore give them only brief attention.

Inflationary-gap analysis contributes nothing directly to the analysis of the rate of inflation. Knowing the approximate size of an inflationary gap may tell us that, under certain conditions, a price rise of 20 or 50 or 100 percent is necessary to remove an inflationary gap, through interest rate, wealth, fiscal, or international trade effects, or whatever; but it tells us nothing about how fast prices will rise. We know that prices will not rise 20, 50, or 100 percent instantaneously, but over some period of time. If that period is 5 years, the inflation rate accompanying any one of these gaps will be only 1/20 as fast as if that period is 0.25 years. In any case, long before the gap is eliminated, it is probable that the basic conditions determining its size and the circumstances under which it might be closed will have altered; thus, our static analysis may have little relevance even for a medium run. But a useful theory of the inflationary *process*—in the presence of a gap—would contribute to our understanding of the current rate of inflation and of the factors that affect it.

A natural hypothesis for a dynamic theory of demand inflation is that the rate of price increase is functionally related to the size of the inflationary gap. (This is the hypothesis we used in Chapter 12—see Figures 12-2 and 12-3.) The larger the gap, the faster prices rise; the smaller the gap, the more slowly they rise. In some very general sense this must be true. At the microeconomic level, this hypothesis might imply that firms with unsatisfied customers raise their prices more frequently or by larger amounts the larger the number of their unsatisfied customers; that wage contracts are revised more often or by larger amounts the greater the number of job vacancies. However, this is inconsistent with the strict form of the demand-inflation concept, which asserts that prices are bid up by buyers (of goods or of labor) to whatever extent is necessary to clear markets. If we stick strictly to the idea that perfectly flexible prices and wages are bid up by buyers, why are prices not bid up to the point at which markets are completely cleared? With an aggregate inflationary gap, this would mean that the price level should immediately "explode" upward to the point (if any exists) at which the inflationary gap is eliminated through the indirect effects we have mentioned.

This would, indeed, seem to be the case *unless* for some reason the *ability* of buyers to bid prices up is, at any given time, limited. Some theories of the rate of demand inflation imply just such a limit on buyers' ability to bid up prices.

Implicit in Wicksell's analysis, for example, is the idea that market demand for goods is at any one time *limited by the money income accruing from previous production.* Consumers come into the market with money incomes derived from the earlier sale of output at the price level then prevailing. Their demand competes with that of businessmen supplied with new bank money. Given the total of this available purchasing power, prices at any given time are bid up to the point at which all markets are cleared— that is, the point at which there are no unsatisfied demands. Given the available purchasing power, "excess demand" is zero. However, with some lag, money incomes rise as a result of the sale of output at the new higher prices, recreating excess demand and requiring progressively higher price levels for markets to remain cleared.

Since spelling this process out rigorously almost requires the use of a consumption function of some kind, we may sketch a Keynes-Wicksell analysis of the inflation process somewhat as follows:

$$(1) \qquad\qquad Y_t = C_t + I_t = Y_P$$

where Y_t is current real demand for output, made up of real consumer demand C_t and real investment demand I_t, and where Y_P is a fixed potential output. (We can, if we wish, include government spending in I. We could also specifically take account of taxes, perhaps with a lag in the tax function. However, we shall for the present ignore taxes.) Setting $Y_t = Y_P$ means that we are assuming no unsatisfied demand; that is, all markets are cleared. Our consumption function makes current real consumption proportional to current real consumer income:

$$(2) \qquad\qquad C_t = c_1 \frac{Y_{t-1}P_{t-1}}{P_t}$$

where c_1 is the marginal propensity to consume, and $Y_{t-1}P_{t-1}$ is the money income arising from sale of output at an earlier date. Dividing by P_t converts it to real income.

$$(3) \qquad\qquad I_t = I_0$$

where I_0 is a (constant) real investment demand. Equation (3) states that all real investment demands are carried out regardless of current prices. In Wicksellian terms, the banks currently provide whatever new funds are necessary for borrowers to be able to buy the investment (or government) goods demanded at whatever price it takes.[4]

By substitution of equations (2) and (3) into (1), we obtain the following simple result:

$$(4) \qquad\qquad \frac{P_t}{P_{t-1}} = \frac{c_1 Y_P}{Y_P - I_0}$$

This tells us that the rate of price increase depends positively both on c_1 (the marginal propensity to consume) and on I_0 and uncertainly on Y_P (depending on the relative size of c_1, Y_P, and I_0).

For example, if $Y_P = 100$, $c_1 = 0.75$ and $I_0 = 40$,

$$\frac{P_t}{P_{t-1}} = \frac{0.75(100)}{100 - 40} = 1.25$$

That is, prices rise by 25 percent per period. What *annual rate* of price increase this implies depends on the length of the period, which has been defined by the length of the income-payments lag. If this lag is 6 months, prices rise by (approximately) 50 percent per year. If the lag is 2 years, prices rise by (approximately) 12.5 percent per year. Obviously, the longer this lag, other things equal, the slower the rate of inflation.

---

[4] Alternatively, we might have assumed that the banks supply a fixed amount of purchasing power to investors (and/or government), based on past prices of the goods they propose to buy, and that the current *real* amount of investors' current real purchases also depends on the rise in prices. That would give

$$(3a) \qquad\qquad I_t = \frac{I_0 P_{t-1}}{P_t}$$

where $I_0 P_{t-1}$ is thus a predetermined amount of purchasing power.

This model has the result that the rate of inflation is a direct function of the size of the inflationary gap.[5] This, however, does not depend upon any assumption that the rate at which *individual businessmen* increase their prices depends on the size of the unsatisfied demands of their buyers. There are no unsatisfied demands at any time. Rather, the gap is continuously translated into forced saving by consumers.

A variant of this theory of the rate of inflation is to postulate a lag only in the adjustment of wage rates. For example, assume that price increases clear markets continuously and that (through continuous accounting) the entire receipts are recognized immediately as income. However, assume that wage rates are advanced in some relation to the price level (for example, the cost of living), with a lag. If this is the case, the emergence of an inflationary gap immediately raises prices and profits; but, until wage rates are raised, it reduces real wage income. The "clearing" of the goods market at any given time will then be secured by sufficient temporary redistribution of real income, through inflation, against labor (assuming a lower marginal propensity to spend by profit recipients than by workers). Other lags—for example, of the adjustment of government budgets to inflation or of consumption to income changes—have similar effects.[6]

These dynamic models, then, are models of a true demand-inflation process in which either *all* markets are instantaneously and continuously cleared, or, in the case just cited, the goods market is so cleared but wages are set by some formula. This calls attention to a crucial but often neglected difference among inflation theories, some of which (as we will note) even today assume continuous and instantaneous market clearing and others of which involve pricing by some rule of thumb or adaptive or learning process.

---

[5] To measure the size of the inflationary gap we merely consider the equilibrium position of the consumption function

(2a) $$C_E = c_1 Y_E = c_1 Y_P$$

The gap, then, is measured as

$$IG = c_1 Y_P + I_0 - Y_P$$

or

$$IG = I_0 - (1 - c_1) Y_P$$

which can be interpreted as the excess of investment over intended or desired saving. It can easily be seen from equation (4) that any parameter change that enlarges IG also raises P_t/P_{t-1}. The gap is obviously zero when

$$Y_P = \frac{I_0}{1 - c_1}$$

and it can be seen from equation (4) that $P_t/P_{t-1} = 1$ when that condition is satisfied.

[6] A model using all three of these lags was developed by Arthur Smithies, in a well-known article, "The Behavior of Money National Income Under Inflationary Conditions," *Quarterly Journal of Economics*, LVII (November 1942), 113-28; reprinted in American Economic Association, *Readings in Fiscal Policy* (R. D. Irwin, 1955), pp. 122–36. It, too, has the result that the rate of inflation depends on the size of the inflationary gap and the length of the lags.

Beginning in the late 1950s, various new currents began to emerge in the analysis of inflation, many of which moved away from simple excessive aggregate demand as the exclusive source of a rising price level. Some of these new currents were apparently mutually inconsistent or contradictory; yet many of them contribute to the more eclectic theory of inflation which emerged in the 1970s. This theory cannot be limited to situations of excessive demand at full employment—and thus mainly relevant only to situations of war, fiscally irresponsible governments, or defective monetary or banking systems—although it must include these as special cases. Although most of the new strands of inflation analysis to which we now turn make some contribution to the more general theory of inflation that we shall attempt to summarize at the end of the next chapter, they cannot all be fully integrated. Thus, to some extent, they remain as competing explanations, or at least competing emphases, in inflation theory.

"COST-PUSH" INFLATION

One obvious reason for the emergence of new ideas about the sources and nature of inflation was the fact, or what appears to be the fact, that inflation has come increasingly to occur in periods that do not, at least to superficial appearances, resemble the circumstances presumed to generate demand inflation. When price levels increase with unemployment substantially in excess of a frictional or structural minimum, or when wages and prices rise at the same time as unemployment during a business-cycle recession, it is difficult to postulate excess demand. On the microeconomic level, we observe that most labor unions can secure pay raises even when many of their members (or potential members) are out of work, and that many firms not only often fail to cut prices during periods of slack demand but sometimes even raise them (even though some of their plant and equipment seems clearly to be unused or underused, and when, equally clearly, they would have no problem finding extra workers at going wage rates). These situations seem to call for a different explanation of price level changes than that given by any demand-inflation model.

The first of the new currents in inflation theory was the suggestion, which began to be widely advanced in the mid-1950s (although there are earlier instances), that many sellers of labor and/or products possess sufficient "market power" to "push up" their wages and/or prices in periods of moderately high, but clearly not excessive, demand to an extent that can cause the average price level to rise. The resulting inflation was variously described as **cost-push**, **administered-price**, **sellers'**, **markup**, or **income-shares** inflation. This basic idea was, in part, no more than a logical extension of Keynesian views about the existence, importance, and effects of wage rigidity. If wages and prices can resist rapid and unlimited decline in the presence of unemployment and unused capacity, and thus not clear their respective markets, may not some of the same factors that explain this phenomenon also explain how wages and prices could *rise* in these circumstances?

To be sure, some important elements in wage rigidity—for example, the element of pure inertia due to lagged perceptions or responses, or the existence of contractual arrangements, or the costs involved in making *any* change—may explain why wages do not immediately fall in the presence of excess supply; yet they certainly do not explain why wages might rise in these circumstances. However, the "market power", that may permit trade unions to resist wage cuts, together with sentiments about workers' right to a "just," or "socially-desirable" standard of living—held not only by workers, but by society generally, by important political forces, and even by employers—could perhaps explain wage rate *increases* as well as they explain downward rigidity. Wage rates which, by formula or otherwise, rise (but often do not fall) with changes in the cost of living are examples of the same kind of non-market-clearing pricing as are rigid wages in a recession; so are wage rates that more or less routinely rise in reflection of some presumed (or even measured) rise in productivity. Wage rates that rise because a contract signed 1 or 2 years ago requires it or because employers can "afford" to pay higher wages are of the same kind, as are wages that rise because employers want their workers to be happy or because a legal minimum wage is raised. Wage rates that rise to preserve "parity" with wages elsewhere or for other kinds of labor are in this class, along with wage rates that rise simply because organized workers are able, by successful strike or threat of strike, to compel employers to pay the higher rates. The crucial difference from the demand inflation case is that, here, rising wages are not, for each and every type of labor and in each and every labor market or even in the typical case, confined to the situation in which there is an actual, experienced market scarcity of labor that forces employers to compete for workers by bidding wages upward.

In the case of business—in industries that account for a substantial fraction of total output of goods and services—it has long been observed that many firms appear not to set their prices (or, more precisely, not to allow the "market" to set their prices) at whatever level will clear the market. Many firms change prices only occasionally. Normally, they appear to reduce or increase output rather than to cut or raise prices when demand declines or increases. Often they report that they have raised (or lowered) prices because their costs have risen (or fallen), thus to preserve a mark-up designed to yield some "target" rate of return. Frequently they have large fixed costs for plant and equipment, along with important indirect costs for research and development, advertising, and administration, which are not directly allocable to particular sales or even to particular products (and thus not part of marginal cost), but which are administratively so assigned and made an element in price-determining formulas.

Frequently firms' beneficial owners have little or no genuine control of management decisions, and the managers often seem more concerned with growth than with profitability. Many such firms also seem more concerned about the "image" they present to public opinion (both nationally, and in the local communities where they operate), to their workers, and to the government. They seek to appear technologically progressive, responsible, humane, and concerned with the "public interest." Instead of being "market-determined," their prices and outputs are clearly "administered" in accordance with policies, principles, and formulas determined by their professional managers. These prices can be and are administered upward (and sometimes downward) at least somewhat independently of the state either of demand for their own products or aggregate demand in the economy. Although these forms of behavior do not necessarily cause prices to rise, much of the time they may have this result, and particularly so when costs are rising—perhaps as a result of the same kind of pricing by their suppliers or because of wage increases in excess of productivity gains.

If groups of workers, or individual firms or industries, have the market power to raise wages or prices, even when resources are unemployed, it is not "irrational" for them to use it, even if their combined actions should raise the prices that they pay. For whatever happens to the prices that individual workers or firms and their owners pay for what they buy would have happened whether or not their *own* wages or prices were pushed up. Of course, if demand for their individual services or products were highly elastic, raising wages or prices might reduce rather than raise real income. However, it is often extremely difficult for workers or firms to know the elasticity of their market demand. Moreover, the reasons that cause them to raise wages or prices are likely to be simultaneously affecting the prices of competititve products or services in the same direction, which greatly reduces any loss of employment or sales. And even if raising wages or prices did reduce employment or sales somewhat, much or all of the unfavorable impact might well be borne by nonmembers of the union, those with lowest seniority, or weaker firms in the industry.

The distinction is sometimes made between the "aggressive" use of market power, in an effort to enlarge some group's share of the national income, and its "defensive" use to protect existing shares from erosion by rising costs (including a rising cost of living), but the distinction is often meaningless, as, for example, if the shares desired to be protected add up to more than 100 percent of the national income. (Of course, almost no group frames income objectives in terms of shares of the national income; but, if they are framed in terms of comparisons with other wages or with profits, they can always be translated into those terms.) In a growing economy, all incomes can grow simultaneously in absolute or per capita terms; but, if the desired shares do add up to more than 100 percent, the only result of an effort by all parties to secure their "fair" shares can be to produce inflation.

Obviously, not all segments of society possess market power. Some that don't have it are nonetheless able to protect their income shares, at least to some degree, by *political* means; for example, "parity incomes" (or worse, "parity prices")[7] for farmers or escalation of minimum wages or social security benefits with the cost of living or of public employees' wages with "prevailing wages."

It is not necessary that all segments of society possess either the market *or* political power to raise the particular prices which determine their incomes. If some groups' incomes are determined by purely market processes, the demand for their services or products will still rise (in money terms) as money incomes rise through inflation and as prices of competing services or products rise in the rest of the economy. These groups may be powerless to initiate an inflationary spiral, yet their shares are not squeezed indefinitely in such a process.

One serious problem with this simple "cost-push" explanation of inflation without excess demand is, of course, its inability to explain why inflation does not occur continually, and why the rate of inflation is what it is, and why it varies—unless one assumes that there are exogenous fluctuations in the extent of market power, which seems thoroughly implausible. However, as we shall see shortly, consideration of the Phillips-curve phenomenon provides a possible simple answer to this problem.

THE SIMPLE "PHILLIPS CURVE"

A second factor that contributed significantly to the emergence of a new view of inflation was the discovery of an interesting empirical regularity. In 1958, a British economist, Professor A. W. Phillips, published a study of annual changes in British wage rates over a period of almost 100 years.[8] Over at least the first 52 years of this period (ending in 1913), there appeared to be a fairly stable inverse relationship between the annual percentage change of the average wage rate in any year and the average level of unemployment. Phillips "fitted" (by informal methods) an equation to this apparent relationship:

$$\dot{W} = -0.9 + 9.638U^{-1.394}$$

where $\dot{W}$ is the percentage change in average wage rate in any year and U the rate of unemployment that year; this equation appears as the *solid*

---

[7] Worse, because, with productivity rising faster in agriculture than in the economy generally, protecting parity prices means guaranteeing a rising share of income.

[8] "The Relation Between Unemployment and the Rate of Change of Money Wage Rates in the United Kingdom, 1861–1957," *Economica*, XXV (1958) 283–300; reprinted in J. Lindauer, ed., *Macroeconomic Readings* (The Free Press, 1968), pp. 107–19.

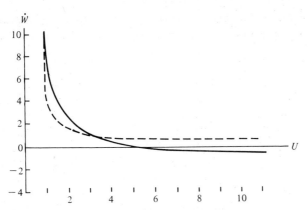

FIGURE 13-2 Empirical "Phillips-Curves" as Fitted by R. G. Lipsey (solid line to data for 1861–1913; broken line to selected years from 1914–1957).

curve in Figure 13-2.[9] Although actual values of $\dot{W}$ in some years were rather far from those computed by this equation, the visual impression from a plotting of all of these individual points was that the relationship was fairly strong. Later, Richard Lipsey fitted the relationship by standard statistical regression techniques to the very same data, obtaining the very similar equation (for the 52 years ending in 1913)[10]

$$\dot{W} = -0.44 + 0.023U^{-1} + 12.52U^{-2}$$

Lipsey's method permitted the calculation of a measure of the "goodness of fit"—the coefficient of determination (R^2)—which was 0.64 (meaning that 64 percent of the variance of money wage changes from their mean was "explained" by the level of unemployment, leaving 36 percent unexplained). Using additional variables (which Phillips had informally

---

[9] This may be more easily understood as

$$\dot{W} = -0.9 + 9.638\frac{1}{U^{1.394}}$$

An equation in the form

$$\dot{W} = a_0 + a_1\frac{1}{U}$$

is, of course, the equation for a rectangular hyperbola, with its horizontal asymptote at a_0. The term $1/U^{1.394}$ makes this the equation for a somewhat elongated hyperbola.

[10] Or,

$$\dot{W} = -0.44 + 0.023\frac{1}{U} + 12.52\frac{1}{U^2}$$

The equation for Lipsey's curve is thus somewhat different in algebraic form from Phillips' but, when plotted, they are barely distinguishable. See R. G. Lipsey, "The Relation Between Unemployment and the Rate of Change of Money Wage Rates in the United Kingdom, 1862–1957: A Further Analysis," *Economica*, XXVII (February 1960); reprinted in R. A. Gordon and L. R. Klein, eds., *Readings in Business Cycles* (R. D. Irwin, 1965), pp. 456–87.

experimented with) so as better to explain wage movements over this same period, Lipsey obtained

$$\dot{W} = -1.21 + 6.45U^{-1} + 2.26U^{-2} - 0.019\dot{U} + 0.21\dot{P}$$

where $\dot{U}$ is the percentage change of the unemployment rate from the preceding year and $\dot{P}$ the percentage change of consumer prices. The negative sign of the $\dot{U}$ term indicates that a 1 percent *rise* in the unemployment rate tends to reduce the rate of increase in wage rates by about 0.02 percent for any *level* of the unemployment rate; and the positive coefficient for $\dot{P}$ means that a 1 percent rise in consumer prices tends to raise the rate of wage increase by 0.2 percent, whatever the level and rate of change of unemployment. Adding these variables raises the R^2 to 0.76, meaning that taking account not only of the level but also of the change in U as well as of the change in P permitted the equation to explain substantially more (that is, 76 percent) of the observed variation in the rate of wage increase.

Phillips did note that his relationship seemed considerably loosened, and perhaps altered in shape, in years subsequent to 1913, even after he omitted nonconforming data for war and immediate postwar periods and for the Great Depression; but he did not attempt to describe the relationship for this period mathematically. Lipsey, omitting several more years with extreme values, obtained a fitted regression equation for selected years between 1913 and 1957:

$$\dot{W} = 0.74 + 0.43U^{-1} + 11.18U^{-4} + 0.038\dot{U} + 0.69\dot{P}$$

Holding $\dot{U}$ and $\dot{P}$ constant (at their average values), this function is represented by the broken curve in Figure 13-1. This shows the level of unemployment to make essentially no difference in the rate of wage increase over most of its range, but to cause the rate of wage increase to shoot up almost vertically once U reaches a certain minimum. The R^2 for the preceding equation is 0.91, leaving only 9 percent of the variance unexplained. But almost all of the explanatory power of the equation now resides in the $\dot{P}$ variable![11] It will also be noted that the constant term is much higher and the coefficient of $\dot{U}$ changed in sign.

The notion that there is some rough relationship between the unemployment rate and the existence and speed of inflation of course was not new with Phillips.[12] Other scholars were also looking at the relationship of unemployment and wage increases as reflected in other data sets about the

---

[11] The "coefficient of partial determination" for $\dot{P}$ is 0.76, indicating that price changes *alone* explain 76 percent of the variation of $\dot{W}$; U and $\dot{U}$ together account for only $0.91 - 0.76$, that is, about 15 percent.

[12] A paper by Irving Fisher has recently been discovered that anticipated Phillips by 32 years: "A Statistical Relation Between Unemployment and Price Changes," *International Labour Review*, 13 (June 1926), 785–92. Reprinted in *Journal of Political Economy*, 81 (March/April 1973), 496–502.

same time as Phillips was and independently of Phillips' work.[13] However, many of these scholars were, at first, mainly impressed not with the regularity of the phenomenon but with its irregularity and looseness. Mainly, they were using data that related to more recent years than Phillips used, and, of course, even Phillips found a much different and far looser relationship for the United Kingdom in the years following 1913. Phillips, himself, treated his findings as essentially a set of facts in search of an explanation, which he did not himself try to provide beyond some casual, common-sense references to supply and demand factors. Lipsey, however, in addition to refining Phillips' empirical treatment, also tried to develop a more formal model that might explain the phenomenon. Other theorists were quick to follow, as we shall see in the next section. First, however, we should note that Phillips' work touched off an extensive effort to establish whether "Phillips curves" could be found in empirical data for other economies. Apparently they could, at least if you selected the right years. By the late 1960s, Phillips curves were identified for almost every major economy, including, of course, that of the United States.[14]

One reason for the sudden popularity of the notion that a highly regular relationship existed between unemployment and inflation was the fact that United States data for the period following 1954 seemed to be tracing out an extremely regular Phillips-curve pattern. Thus, the idea of a fixed and dependable "trade-off" between unemployment and inflation naturally attracted the attention and interest of economists and, before long, even of public officials, journalists, and the general public.[15] We shall see in Chapter 14 that the stability of the Phillips-curve was to prove a delusion. But the belief in its stability in the 1960s led a series of theoretical and empirical studies which economists have subsequently built upon.

The 1960s were also the period when the notion began to take hold that fiscal and monetary policies, used flexibly and aggressively, could make—and keep—the unemployment rate whatever policy makers wanted it to be. Thus, all that seemed necessary was for the public, through the political process, to express its preference among the alternative combinations of U and $\dot{P}$ offered by the Phillips curve; then policy could achieve that preferred combination. (This preferred combination might be thought to represent that "uneasy compromise between what are seen to

[13] For references, and an example of an early statistical Phillips curve for the United States, see the writer's *Macroeconomic Theory* (1961), pp. 443–44.

[14] The best of the early empirical studies of the wage-employment relationship for the United States economy was by George L. Perry, first as a 1961 Ph.D. thesis at MIT, later published in articles, and finally in *Unemployment, Money Wage Rates, and Inflation* (MIT Press, 1966).

[15] However, the notion that there was a *stable* Phillips curve tradeoff did not capture the support of the economists most closely associated with formulating monetary and fiscal policies, at least in the United States. The writer believes that a careful study of the *Annual Reports* of the Council of Economic Advisers for the years 1961–1968 will discover no reference to any such stable trade-off. (However, it did creep into the 1969 *Annual Report*— see Chart 8, page 95.)

be the social and economic costs of inflation and the clear social and economic advantages of high employment," which defined the concepts of "full-employment" and, thereby, of "potential output," first introduced in Chapter 3 and used thereafter to confine the analysis of this book until the present chapter.)

A Price-Phillips Curve

The original Phillips curve was a relationship between unemployment and the rate of wage increase. However, the rate of wage increase had long been taken to be the primary determinant of the rate of price increase (or vice versa); so that a Phillips curve could easily be restated as a relationship between unemployment and the rate of price inflation. The close tie between wage rates and prices (on the macroeconomic level) rests both on classical price theory (somewhat questionably, to be sure) and on empirical observation. And we have, in previous chapters, frequently used this connection to go from one to the other.[16] Expressing the relationship among wage and price levels and productivity (for an economy with progressive technology and capital accumulation) in terms of percentage changes it becomes

$$\dot{P} = \dot{W} - A\dot{P}L$$

where APL represents the average product of labor (real GNP per worker hour), and the dots indicate percentage changes per time unit. Given the questionable theoretical basis for this aggregate relationship, it may be regarded as no more than an accident that it exhibits a very high degree of empirical stability, at least in the United States.[17]

Thus, if a Phillips curve explains wage changes in terms of unemployment, an analogous curve (usually also called a Phillips curve) relates price changes to unemployment. The presumed relationship between the two curves can be shown as in Figure 13-3. Here we have one hypothetical Phillips curve, but two vertical axes, one representing the rate of change of wages, the other of prices. However, the zero points on the two vertical axes are not the same; each rate of price change corresponds to a rate of wage change 3 percent higher. Thus, at U_0 (5 percent), the rate of wage change (left axis) is $\dot{W}_0$ (3 percent), but the corresponding rate of price change (right axis) is zero. The reason is that average output per hour is increasing by an (assumed constant) $A\dot{P}L$ of 3 percent. At a lower unemployment level, U_1 ($2\frac{1}{2}$ percent), the rate of wage increase is $\dot{W}_1$ (7

---

[16] The reader may wish to review the discussion of the relationship of wages and prices in the classical theory of the firm (and some of the problems of aggregating it to the entire economy) that appears in Chapter 4.

[17] By adjusting the equation further for changes in import prices, indirect taxes, and other factors, confining it to the private nonagricultural sector and introducing distributed lags, it becomes an even more stable relationship.

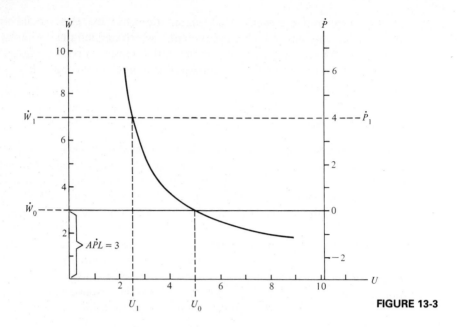

FIGURE 13-3

percent), while the corresponding rate of price increase $\dot{P}_1$ is $\dot{W}_1 - A\dot{P}L$ (7% − 3% = 4%).

An empirical representation of a simple price–Phillips curve for the United States, ignoring all variables other than $\dot{P}$ and U, is shown in Figure 13-4—as it would have appeared to an observer in, say, 1970 (based on data for the years 1955–1969). Here, each dot represents paired observations on the average unemployment rate for all workers in some year,

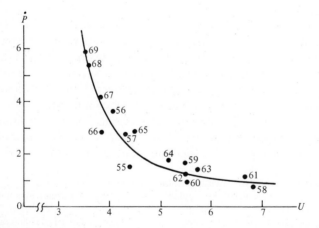

FIGURE 13-4 Consumer Price Index Changes and Unemployment in the United States, 1955–1969.

and the percentage increase in the consumer price index between that year and the following year (essentially assuming a lag of six months). The dates next to the dots indicate the year to which the unemployment data relate. The solid line is a free-hand representation of what appears to be an underlying stable relationship.

A Cost-Push Theory of the Phillips Curve

As noted, the Phillips curve relationship is an *empirical phenomenon* seen (or believed to be seen) in various bodies of data. But what explains its existence? What determines its position and shape? *Why* can we not choose to have 99 percent employment and 1 percent inflation? What would have to be changed to make that combination possible? Clearly, we need a theory of the Phillips curve.

As hinted earlier, it seems fairly easy to explain the Phillips curve in institutional terms, largely as a cost-push phenomenon similar to (and related to) the downward rigidity of wage rates. Is it not reasonable to assume that market power—which helps to explain downward wage rigidity, even with substantial unemployment—increases substantially as labor markets become tighter and unemployment shrinks? As the number of unemployed falls beyond some point, does not wage rigidity translate into upward wage push? It may take the discipline of (say) 7 percent unemployment to neutralize unions' market power sufficiently that wages on the average do not rise at all, and perhaps 5 percent unemployment to dampen market power enough that wages rise no faster than productivity so that costs and prices are stable. However, as unemployment falls progressively below 5 percent, organized labor's market power increases sufficiently to permit progressively faster rates of wage inflation. This could explain a Phillips curve in wage rates; and if prices merely reflect costs, it would explain the price–Phillips curve.

Market power on the employer side works as well, either alone or in combination with union power, to explain faster inflation as unemployment falls. Falling unemployment ordinarily accompanies a decline in idle plant and equipment. May there not be a inflationary bias built into business pricing formulas, a bias that is progressively curbed only as excess capacity increases? As capacity-utilization rates begin to exceed those corresponding roughly to, say, 5 percent unemployment, prices may on the average tend to rise, even with stable labor costs. And, at progressively higher rates of capacity utilization, that bias may cause prices to rise relative to wages more than in proportion to the excess over the utilization rate consistent with stable prices. With substantial excess capacity in their industries, firms are unable fully to realize their target prices (like the golfer who achieves his "average" score only occasionally). But as markets strengthen, they are able, increasingly, to meet the pricing standards they have set for themselves.

Moreover, a rise in capacity utilization generates an increased demand for labor. Even if the labor market were purely competitive, increased employer demand would tend to *pull* wage rates up as employment and prices rose. If the labor market, too, is partially monopolized, increased employer demand for labor combines with the increased market power of unions to *push* wages up. Thus, at relatively low unemployment, costs rise along with prices. Because workers want to be recompensed for a rising cost of living and because most business pricing formulas call for prices to reflect costs, levels of employment and capacity utilization that are high enough to cause wages to rise more rapidly than productivity and/or to induce efforts to raise prices relative to costs, produce not a one-time price rise but an interacting spiral of wages pushing up prices, prices pushing up wages (and other prices). The speed of this spiral will be related to the intensity of aggregate demand, as reflected in the unemployment and capacity-utilization rates.

To be sure, a rising price level, unless continually "ratified" by growing government deficits and/or increases in M, will reduce real demand and employment through the many channels previously considered. If this ratification fails to occur, the inflation will eventually "burn itself out" as unemployment gradually rises and capacity-utilization gradually shrinks. But there will be strong pressures on monetary and fiscal policy-makers to accept some inflation as the price for maintaining lower unemployment and larger output. Thus some degree of ratification is likely to occur.

The writer would hold that there is some valid basis in the preceding sketch of an argument for a cost-push explanation of the Phillips curve and would argue that, indeed, the Phillips-curve relationship, to the extent that it exists, can *best* be explained by a theory that includes cost-push elements. However, a number of faults can easily be found with this sketch of a cost-push plus downward-rigidity explanation of the Phillips curve. Moreover, many microeconomists hold that the power of unions and firms (other than a few monopolists) to raise wages and prices is greatly exaggerated. What appears to be the market power of a union to raise wages is merely the rhetoric of union organizers. Even though many wages are formally set by a collective bargaining process, it is really the underlying demand and supply, including the direct and indirect competition of unorganized workers, that determines whether or not wages rise and by how much. And even though many firms appear to be setting their prices by administrative procedures and standards, we should not be misled by the *process*. It is really supply and demand, in the light of the direct and indirect competition of other firms, of potential new entrants, and of substitute products, that determine whether prices rise and by how much.

Such considerations led many economists to jump to the other extreme, and to seek to explain the Phillips-curve phenomenon *in the complete absence of any and every departure (in either labor or product markets) from pure competition.* In effect, such explanations attempt to describe all inflations as an excess-demand phenomenon. We turn to consideration of such efforts.

A Purely Competitive Explanation: Lipsey

As noted, R. G. Lipsey was one of the first to provide a theory for the phenomenon of the Phillips curve, a theory that made no essential reference to any absence of competition. Lipsey's theory begins with the concept of a "wage-adjustment function," based on the existence of disequilibrium in a competitive labor market, as pictured in Figure 13-5.

Part a of the figure represents supply and demand curves for labor. At W_E the labor market would be in equilibrium. However, because of recent shifts in S or D curves, or for other reasons, the wage rate need not be at W_E. Suppose it is at W_1. Here there is a gap between amounts demanded and supplied equal to $b - a$. Part b of the figure shows how wages change in response to supply-demand gaps—positive or negative (expressed as a percentage of supply). Using the symmetrical wage adjustment function shown by the solid line in b, a gap equal to $b - a$ will produce a current (positive) rate of wage change equal to $\dot{W}_1$. If the wage adjustment function is nonsymmetrical, as seems plausible, and as is the case with the broken curve in part b, then negative gaps produce only a slow wage decrease, while equivalent positive gaps produce more rapid wage increases.

Returning to part a, this means that the wage rate, *over time*, moves upward from W_1 toward W_E. If the S and D curves remain fixed, the demand-supply gap will shrink as W rises; but it will remain positive, producing still positive but ever slower rates of wage increase as W

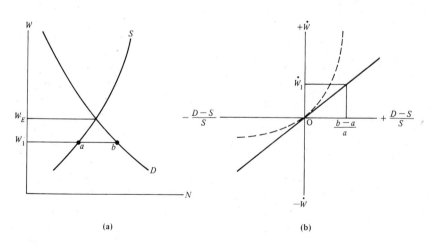

(a)   (b)

FIGURE 13-5

approaches W_E. However, there is no reason to assume S and D curves fixed. (Indeed, on a macroeconomic basis, presumably the rise in employment, along the supply curve, as W rose would increase Y and thus the demand for labor!) However, if the speed (and direction) of the wage movement at any time depends only on the size of the gap between supply and demand and if we can find some index of the size of this gap, the relationship can be assumed stable even though supply and demand curves are continually changing.

It seems natural to take unemployment as a good index of the supply-demand balance in the labor market, but, since unemployment *rises* as $(D - S)/S$ declines, the positive and negative directions on the horizontal axis in part b are reversed. Turned around, the nonsymmetrical adjustment curve immediately resembles a Phillips curve! To be sure, there might seem to be problems. For one, the zero point of unemployment is clearly not where Phillips found that wage rates began to rise; rather (for the period 1857–1913), that point appeared to lie between 5 and 6 percent unemployment! Indeed, at $U = 0$, all empirical Phillips curves suggest that wage inflation should be at an infinite rate.

But, declared Lipsey, equality of supply and demand for labor *does not occur at zero unemployment*. Rather, equality of supply and demand implies only that there are *as many job vacancies as there are numbers unemployed* (which can be measured either in absolute numbers or as percentages of the labor force). Lipsey used $u = U/LF$, $v = V/LF$, where U, V, and LF mean, respectively, the numbers of unemployed, vacancies, and the labor force. Thus, in Figure 13-6, we show $\dot{W} = 0$ at $u - v = 0$ (on the upper horizontal axis). However, given v, $u - v$ increases directly with u. Therefore, we may equally well change Figure 13-6 by substituting the alternative (broken) axis on which we measure merely u. This axis has the zero point for u at the origin, and makes $\dot{W} = 0$ where $u = v$. From

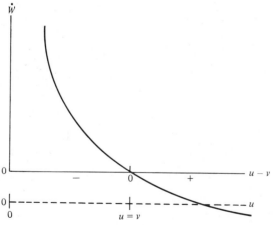

FIGURE 13-6

there, Lipsey went on to consider problems of aggregating a series of *local* or *specialized* labor markets into an economy-wide aggregate, reaching some interesting results which we shall not take time to summarize.

Derivation of the Phillips curve from a wage-adjustment function reflecting gaps between supply and demand retains a basic tie between inflation and excess demand. Prices rise because (and only because) demand exceeds supply. All that is changed is that the influence of demand on prices has now become a matter of degree. Too much demand raises prices, but how fast it raises them depends on how large the excess of demand is. A small inflationary gap raises prices slowly, a larger one more rapidly.

Reflection will show that this is not *demonstrated* in Lipsey's model, it is merely *assumed*. The assumed underlying wage-adjustment function *already embodies that idea*; but no explanation is given for such a relationship. In that sense, Lipsey's theory of the Phillips curve is inferior to the Keynes-Wicksell and later dynamic models of the inflationary gap. For, rather than merely *assuming* that the rate of inflation varies directly with the size of the gap, they derived this result from theories about lags and/or differential marginal propensities to spend of workers and capitalists in the presence of a wage lag.[18] And it should be clear, on reflection, that a wage-adjustment (or price-adjustment) function of the kind assumed by Lipsey is not a market-clearing phenomenon, but can only be explained, at the economic level, as some kind of an adaptive or rule-of-thumb response to a noncleared market.

Moreover, Lipsey's theory raises a great many questions about its identification of the particular unemployment level at which aggregate demand equals aggregate supply. Why do we identify $u = v$ with labor market equilibrium and thus with $\dot{W} = 0$? And, even more fundamentally, how do we explain why vacancies and unemployment can simultaneously exist—the one a measure of excess demand for labor, the other of excess supply? Moreover, does not v almost necessarily change when u does, meaning that the position of the curve in Figure 13-6, using the alternative (u) scale, shifts with every change in u?[19]

---

[18] Somewhat earlier, economist Bent Hansen, in *A Study in the Theory of Inflation* (Allen and Unwin, 1951), had developed an elegant model of the inflationary process under conditions of excess demand, embodying some of the elements contained in the Wicksell-Keynes and Smithies' models, along with new elements of his own. His model incorporated two separate aggregated "markets"—one for labor, the other for goods—and made the rate of price change in *each market* depend on the amount of excess demand in that market in the manner specified by Lipsey. (The two markets were related by the fact that the supply of goods implies the demand for labor.) Although a Phillips curve is implied, or could be explained, by Hansen's theory, the basic reasons for the relationship between the *speed* of inflation and the size of the (two) inflationary gaps are never made explicit.

[19] Some of these questions are partially, or at least implicitly, answered in a remarkable condensed (and largely unexplained) algebraic model contained in a Lipsey footnote, which, to some extent, anticipates the Phelps' model presented in the next section.

These last questions seem indeed to be the crucial ones for a theory of the Phillips curve. What precisely does define that level of labor and capital utilization beyond which further increases of aggregate demand begin to create rising prices? Clearly, this point is not 100 percent employment and 100 percent use of physical capacity. But is it where $u = v$, and, if so why? What determines the point at which prices begin to rise, or begin to rise at a rate sufficiently high to excite public and therefore government concern? Thus, what lies behind and explains the choice of the unemployment rate at which social consensus or government policy defines the existence of "full employment" and establishes a "target" for monetary and fiscal policies? This is the problem we ducked for 12 chapters and now hope to answer. But Lipsey appears to have assumed the answer rather than to have explained it. Perhaps the first to grapple seriously with the problem in these terms was Professor E. S. Phelps.

Search Unemployment: Phelps

Edmund S. Phelps saw that this problem had to be approached in micro-economic terms.[20] His argument was originally presented in highly mathematical and abstract form, but its essence can perhaps be grasped from the far less rigorous summary presented here. In order to insure that no noncompetitive or institutional elements might contribute to this explanation, all such elements are assumed not to exist. Employers always maximize profits in their decisions on employment, output, wages, and prices; workers always maximize the net utility of the wage less the dis-utility of work; firms in every industry are numerous and of similar size; they offer employment in labor markets in which none has any monopsony power; there are no unions, no minimum wage laws, no "irrational" preferences for higher money wages or prices, or against lower money wages or prices.

It is assumed that workers are of different quality and that different jobs require different worker attributes, but there are large numbers of competing employers who can use each type of worker. In addition, combining proportions are assumed sufficiently flexible that, at some positive wage rate, all workers of every type who want to work at such wages can be employed. Prices clear all goods markets daily, and workers are hired in a labor market in which wage rates adjust freely up or down to the point where the market for each class of worker is cleared daily. To be sure, because of the high costs involved, individual firms do not adjust their wage rates every day but only periodically. (They can, of course, freely lay off workers or hire more on any day, and workers can quit at any time.) We

---

[20] "Money Wage Dynamics and Labor Market Equilibrium," in E. S. Phelps, ed., *Microeconomic Foundations of Employment and Inflation Theory* (W. W. Norton, 1970), pp. 124–66, and elsewhere.

can assume that these wage-setting dates are staggered so that a representative sample of the firms set new wage rates (or reaffirm previous rates) every day. Any worker who enters the labor market, quits, or is laid off, can thus immediately find a job simply by making himself part of the supply of labor for one or more of the firms setting wage rates that day. In determining his wage, each employer seeks to offer the lowest wage rate that, on the average over the period for which his wage rates are to be set, is likely to attract to his firm the number of workers needed to produce the output that, given expected product prices, will maximize his firm's profits.

Under these circumstances one might assume that (1) a nearly uniform wage rate would be paid by all employers for each type of labor; (2) that there would be no involuntary unemployment, in the sense that all persons for whom the marginal utility of the market wage was greater than the marginal disutility of working would have jobs; (3) there would be no employer vacancies—that is, given each firm's existing wage rate for each type of worker, it would be able to hire exactly the number of workers it wished to hire.

However, *one* and only one factor prevents these three conditions from being fully achieved: a lack of complete information on the part of each worker of all available jobs and the associated wage rates and a lack of complete information on the part of employers of available labor supplies and wage rates paid by other employers for each type of labor. Lack of complete information means lack of information *available without cost.* Workers acquire much information about wages and availability of jobs from employers without cost. They can always get more, but this requires spending time and money "shopping around." Employers, too, acquire much free labor-market information from the job inquiries of workers, but it requires expenditures for advertising and recruiting to learn more about worker availability and wages. And extra information is available to workers and employers only at increased unit cost, as extra information needs to be sought at greater distances, in greater detail, or with greater frequency.

Because labor-market information is imperfect (that is, costly) for units on both sides of the market, wage rates will not be completely uniform for all workers of any given labor quality. Because wage rates are not uniform, workers who believe or suspect that they are qualified for available, better paying work may rationally refrain from accepting the first available employment they encounter on the first day they enter the labor force or are laid off. Moreover, at times, workers may quit their jobs—even though the available wage exceeds their marginal disutility of labor—in order to search for jobs in which this excess is even greater. This means there will always be some unemployment, which we may call "search unemployment." For the same reason, employers may fail to fill some jobs because the workers who show up in search of work may not include as many as they would want to hire at the wage rate they have set and believe they need to pay; there will thus be some job vacancies and some expenditures on advertising or "recruiting" seeking to fill those vacancies.

Obviously, if all conditions were stationary, both in the aggregate and for every firm and worker, the search activity on both sides of the market would ultimately succeed in permitting an equilibrium to be reached in which every worker was in his best job, in the sense that the chances he could find a better one were so small that no further expenditure on search was justified. Thus there would be no unemployment, and wages for every type of labor quality would approach complete uniformity. There would also be no vacancies and no recruiting by employers—because the chances of finding better qualified workers at the same wage or equally qualified workers at a lower wage would not justify any employer's expenditure on advertising or recruitment.

However, there are always changes occurring in consumer tastes, affecting the demands for particular products and the labor requirements for producing them; there is always some labor turnover, even in a labor force of constant size, as workers retire or die and new workers enter the labor force; and there could be differentiated technological change affecting various firms unevenly. Given imperfect information, the above changes mean that there is always some nonuniformity of wages, justifying some search activity by both workers and employers, and giving rise both to vacancies and unemployment. If the intensity of this ceaseless change ("stochastic disturbance") which affects the internal structure of supply and demand remains constant over time or changes only slowly in response to exogenous elements, the total numbers of unemployed and of vacancies might be essentially constant for any given level of aggregate demand. And the numbers both of unemployed and of vacancies and the volume of search activity might be fairly substantial.

We are now ready to ask what happens in this situation if a change occurs in aggregate demand? What will happen to the unemployment rate u, the vacancy rate v, the price level P, and the wage level W? We can assume that the economy has been in a particular equilibrium situation with some particular volume of unemployment and vacancies and with a steady volume of search activity both by workers and employers. And we can further assume, for convenience, that this equilibrium involved a stable P and W (although we will shortly see that this is only a very special case).

Assume that an increase occurs in aggregate demand. This might occur through an exogenous increase in the propensity to consume or invest or a shift toward a more expansionary monetary or fiscal policy. For simplicity, assume that it is a policy shift, intended to reduce the unemployment rate by increasing the demand for labor. Assume, further, that policy makers, seeking to achieve some specific (lower) unemployment rate, are prepared and able to adjust their policy instruments continuously to whatever extent is necessary to get the unemployment rate to their target and to keep it there.

With this increase in aggregate demand, some or all employers of course experience an increase in the demands for their products. As most of these employers attempt to hire more workers at their existing wage rates, the number of their vacancies will increase, as workers with particular skills fail to appear in sufficient numbers. Thus, employers increase their search activity, increasing the sums spent for advertising and recruiting. This extra search succeeds in finding some unemployed workers who have the desired characteristics and are searching for such jobs but whose own search (plus that of employers) had not previously brought worker and employer together. The increased search, of course, also turns up employed workers with required characteristics, working for wages below what the employers who now discover them offer to pay. Each such worker's shift to a new job removes one vacancy but creates another, and so continues the recruiting activity—which continues to locate more of the unemployed, although at the same time also creating other vacancies. Vacancies remain higher than before, as does search activity by employers, but unemployment is reduced and total output increased. Although the extra employer search costs at the higher level of search activity might entail a once-and-for-all higher level of prices, we have so far not shown why it should affect wage rates.

That becomes clear only when we examine the implications of the crucial assumption that labor-market information is obtained under conditions of increasing unit cost. As the price of a unit of employers' search activity rises (the unit of search activity being defined as the amount necessary to hire each additional worker) it now pays some employers among those who are setting new wage rates each day to consider an alternative means of enlarging their work force: namely, raising their new wage schedules above prevailing rates. To the extent that this promises to be a cheaper way of getting extra workers than engaging in extra units of recruitment activity, employers will choose this method. (Presumably, they do both: raise wages and increase their recruitment).

Raising their wage offers will attract to them more than their normal share both of new entrants and of the unemployed whose search activity brings them into touch with their offers, and will discourage search by their own employees. Nevertheless, some (or even most) of the workers attracted will inevitably merely be pulled away from other firms. This creates new vacancies for those firms, inducing them both to increase their recruiting activity, and, when *their* wage-setting dates arrive, also to raise wage rates. Their adjustments will also catch some of the unemployed, but mainly they will force still other firms to raise their wage rates (and increase recruiting), affecting still other firms.

As these impulses work their way through the economy, there will be some new equilibrium reached, involving lower unemployment than before, higher vacancies, and a higher level of recruiting activity. However, this equilibrium can only be maintained by a steady increase in wage rates—which, of course, requires a steady increase in prices.[21] If later on there were to occur a further increase in the level of aggregate demand, it would justify still larger expenditures on recruiting, along with a larger reliance on wage increases in the effort to pull workers away from other employers and to avoid losing workers to other employers. Thus, it involves a faster rate of wage and price inflation, along with some further reduction in search unemployment. Thus, the inverse relation between unemployment rate and inflation rate.

There is, of course, some lower level of aggregate demand, and resulting lower level of recruiting activity—producing a lower level of unit information costs—which generates no rise in the average wage rate or price level. It also, of course, involves higher unemployment. And for still lower levels of aggregate demand and still higher levels of unemployment, employers will find that, even with zero recruiting, there are more workers seeking their jobs than they want to hire, and wage rates decline in the daily auctions. This, of course, is the Phillips-curve relationship.[22]

Why is this relationship nonlinear? (That is, why is the Phillips curve concave upward?) The reason inheres in the nature of information exchanges. As aggregate demand increases, unemployment declines and vacancies necessarily increase—because it is only the increased recruiting (related to the increased vacancies) that adds to available information and reduces search unemployment. But this very process reduces the effectiveness of further increases in recruiting. This effectiveness of recruiting and of employee search depends on the ability to bring about new and additional contacts between firms having vacant jobs and workers qualified for and seeking such jobs.

We can think of recruiting activity by employers as constituting an essentially random process of shooting off arrows containing information in all directions, and we can think of search unemployment by workers as setting up more or less random targets for employer search. When vacancies are few and unemployed are numerous, a large proportion of the small number of arrows sent out by employers encounter one of the relatively numerous targets. Thus, employers' recruiting activity is very effective and thus relatively cheap (although workers' job search is costly and relatively ineffective).

But as unemployment declines and recruiting increases, there are fewer and fewer targets and more and more arrows; the shooting effectiveness declines (and the effectiveness of workers' search increases). Although more workers may quit jobs as unemployment falls, the time that

[21] This means, of course, that, if policy makers are to maintain this higher level of aggregate demand, they must steadily increase their stimulus to offset the demand-reducing effect of rising prices.

[22] A falling price level means, of course, that in order for policy makers to maintain the same high unemployment rate in the face of falling prices a continually more restrictive setting of fiscal or monetary policy is required.

it takes each unemployed worker to find a new job declines even faster than the increase in quits, which permits unemployment to decline. This increasingly costly search activity by employers induces rising numbers of them to make the more frequent or larger advances in wage rates when their wage-setting date comes round (and they may also decide to revise wages more frequently), which means faster inflation.[23]

One can well suggest that search unemployment, which is the only unemployment in Phelps' model, is really *voluntary unemployment*; thus the phenomenon he describes might be considered to affect the size of the labor force, rather than the existence and amount of unemployment. Certainly, the search unemployment he describes is planned, rational, and voluntary. But it is not voluntary unemployment in the sense that the unemployed do not want work, that they are unwilling to take jobs at the available real wage. They merely want and think they can get, and most of them do ultimately get, better jobs through search. In United States practice such persons would be counted as unemployed, and the economist might call their unemployment "frictional."

Thus, as search unemployment falls, aggregate economic welfare improves—aggregate production and income are higher; and both productive efficiency and social justice are improved through greater wage uniformity among workers of identical endowments. Thus, Phelps himself was quite ready to "trade off" lower search unemployment for a certain amount of inflation.

Alternative Theories of the Simple Phillips Curve

There can be little doubt that considerable numbers of workers are voluntarily unemployed as they search for jobs. However, it can be doubted that all of the job search activity that occurs in an actual economy consists of the kind of rational search activity described by Phelps; it can also be doubted that search unemployment constitutes a large fraction of total unemployment in such an economy (a great many workers who voluntarily change jobs do so without interruption of employment.)[24] Even granted that some

[23] The relationship described—present but somewhat obscure in Phelps' presentation (reflected in his reasoning about the probable signs of several partial second derivatives)—was explicitly introduced in Lipsey's simple footnote algebraic model, when he proposed (without explanation) that $N = \beta UV$, where N is the number of new hires per period, β a constant, and U and V the numbers of unemployed and of vacancies. N thus increases with an increase in either U or V, with the other held constant; but the increase in either one raises N by more, the higher is the other. If this equation is instead written $N = \alpha U + \beta V$, the resulting relation between $\dot{W}$ and U in Lipsey's model becomes linear. Lipsey provided no explanation for the multiplicative relationship of U and V, but it presumably reflects the arrow-and-target reasoning sketched previously.

[24] Martin Feldstein has recently shown that a large proportion of unemployment consists of workers on "temporary layoff"—workers waiting to return to a specific job who have not quit to look for work, and few of whom do look for alternative or temporary employment while waiting. See his "The Importance of Temporary Layoffs: An Empirical Analysis," *Brookings Papers on Economic Activity*, 3:1975, pp. 725–44.

kind of Phillips curve relationship exists in actual economies, one may well doubt that changes in search unemployment explain very much of the total variation in unemployment. Indeed, it is not even clear that search unemployment *declines* as total unemployment does. Thus, the rising cost of labor market information may not provide the major explanation for the Phillips-curve phenomenon which is thought to be observed.

Nor is it hard to find other possible explanations for the Phillips curve which, like Phelps', do not require market power or "irrational" worker behavior. For example, instead of unemployment associated with imperfections of labor market *information*, there are theorists who stress instead imperfections of labor *mobility*—geographic, occupational, inter-employer—and the rising costs of overcoming such immobility. The problem, thus, is not that workers don't know about job opportunities or employers about pools of unemployed; rather, it reflects the high and rising costs of taking advantage of this knowledge. Otherwise, the argument is essentially the same as Phelps, with the substitution of rising costs of movement rather than of information. Once again, we need "stochastic disturbance" to keep renewing the need for movement, and probably some element of downward wage rigidity.

It is difficult to see why so many economists insisted for so long on assuming away any element of downward rigidity of wages. Even apart from unions, downward rigidity is provided by minimum wage laws, unemployment insurance, and private or public welfare benefits—phenomena hardly unknown or nonexistent in most modern societies. Moreover, as a number of microeconomic theorists have recently shown, some degree of wage rigidity reflects a rational response of individual employers to circumstances of uncertainty, costs of hiring and training, and either stochastic or cyclical movements in product demand.

Indeed, a significant degree of downward wage rigidity, from whatever cause, plus "stochastic disturbance" seems adequately to explain a Phillips-curve relationship without specific need for *rising costs* either of information or of mobility. Assume merely that there are imperfections, *time lags*, perhaps, in information and/or movement. Suppose that the inter-industry, and/or interfirm, and/or intergeographical-area pattern of consumer, investment, and government demand is continually fluctuating at any given level of aggregate real demand. This means that some more or less random assortment of firms, localities, and industries is always losing customers, as others are always gaining them. Some employers are always laying off workers, others seeking (partly unsuccessfully) to hire more workers. To the extent the latter are unsuccessful (because of imperfect information and mobility), output of such firms fails to rise in line with increases in the demand for their products. Thus, their prices, and the wages they are able and willing to pay, are bid up. And this happens under purely competitive assumptions; no monopolies or unions are needed. Prices may fall somewhat in the declining demand set, but if wage rates merely fail to decline, prices cannot fall very far. Thus, output and employment decline there, as they rise in the expanding sectors. The shift in the structure of a constant level of demand requires a change in relative prices, but, if prices cannot fall appreciably, changes in relative prices require a rise in the average level of prices. (Had wages and prices been fully flexible downward in the labor surplus sectors, *average* wages and prices need not have changed and the reallocation of labor, even if not instantaneous, would not have raised the average wage or price level.)

Altered relative wages and prices (and the passage of time) will gradually achieve further response of production to the altered structure of demand. More resources are shifted toward the expanding sectors and away from the contracting ones. This would limit any further rise in prices for an initial disturbance or even eventually reverse it. However, the prices that had risen would not return to their initial level because of downward wage rigidity. What converts this one-shot upward movement of average prices and average wages (in response to any single rearrangement of a constant aggregate demand) into a steady price rise is the fact that stochastic disturbance continues—always creating new instances of shortage and surplus of labor or goods. And, because wages and prices do not decline as easily as they rise, the shortages continually raise wages and prices more than the surpluses depress them.[25]

To convert this into an explanation of the Phillips curve we need merely to note that the closer the overall economy is to 100 percent utilization of its labor and capital resources—that is, the higher is aggregate demand—the more situations of temporary and localized shortage will be created by stochastic disturbance, and the fewer situations of surplus. Thus, the more prices that must rise to clear particular product markets and the faster the rate of overall inflation created by continuing shifts in the structure of demand. With lower levels of aggregate demand, fewer shortages are created by stochastic disturbance and surpluses remain almost everywhere. These surpluses may produce *some* downward pressure of unemployment on wage rates—or there is some continuous progress of productivity—which can keep average prices stable at some particular high level of unemployment even with continuous reshuffling of the inadequate level of demand. And this may perhaps even generate a slow deflation of average prices at a still higher level of unemployment.

We can, of course, be eclectic in our explanation of the Phillips curve of the "real world." We may use any or all of the foregoing elements and perhaps still others as well (including elements of market power on the part of unions and firms—a power that is reinforced by increased labor and

---

[25] An explanation in essentially these terms was provided for the United States' inflation in the boom of 1956–57 by Charles L. Schultze in *Recent Inflation in the United States*, Study Paper No. 1, prepared in connection with the Study of Employment, Growth, and Price Levels for the Joint Economic Committee, Congress of the United States, September 1959 (Government Printing Office).

product demand) to explain the apparent inverse relationship between unemployment rate and inflation, giving particular emphasis to any that seem most relevant to our own observation and experience.[26] Indeed, it is ironic that economists have found so many quite simple explanations for a Phillips curve, just at a time when the Phillips curve seems to have disappeared.

In the next chapter, after documenting the "disappearance" of the simple Phillips curve, we will review the recent search for new (and the revival of older) aspects of inflation analysis, that have been advanced in an effort better to explain the *Age of Inflation* in which (some contend) we now live.

REVIEW QUESTIONS

1. "Most pre-Keynesian macroeconomic theories saw the only source of inflation to lie in an excessive rate of expansion of the money stock. Keynes' theory saw inflation's source in an excess of aggregate demand over full-employment output, which might arise from an autonomous surge in investment or consumer demand, or from an overly expansionary fiscal (or monetary) policy. Current inflation theory denies none of the above possible sources; but it also finds still other possible origins for a rising price level." In relationship to the above, answer the following questions.

(a) Why did pre-Keynesian economic theory rule out an "autonomous" increase in either investment or consumer demand as a source of inflation (unless accompanied by an increase of M)?

(b) What is different in Keynesian macroeconomics which means that autonomous increases in private demand are *not* "ruled out" as sources of inflationary pressure?

(c) Keynes' theory was, properly speaking, a theory of the conditions under whch inflation would occur, not a theory of the rate of inflation. Explain.

(d) Although current inflation theories allow for autonomous surges in private demand or increased government purchases as a source of inflationary pressure, "excessive" aggregate demand is now seen as very much more a matter of *degree* than was the case in Keynes' or earlier theories. Explain.

2. "The original Phillips curve was a set of facts looking for a theory." Explain. What were the facts?

3. Present the theoretical assumptions on the basis of which Lipsey explained the Phillips curve. What are the weaknesses of his analysis?

4.

(a) Present a purely "cost-push" explanation for the Phillips curve.

(b) Present the "search-theory" basis for the short-run Phillips curve as proposed by Phelps.

---

[26] For a good example of such an eclectic theory, see James Tobin, "Inflation and Unemployment," *American Economic Review*, LXII (March 1972) 1–18, especially parts IV and V.

(c) Explain how one can derive the Phillips curve from the assumption that wages are rigid downward and that aggregate demand shifts randomly among business firms.

5. The Phillips curve relates wage changes to unemployment; yet it is used to explain price inflation. What is the link between the two?

SELECTED REFERENCES

A Smithies, "The Behavior of Money National Income Under Inflationary Conditions," *Quarterly Journal of Economics*, 57 (November 1942), 113–128, reprinted in A. Smithies and K. Butters (eds.), *Readings in Fiscal Policy* (R. D. Irwin, 1955), pp. 122–136.
(A pioneering study of the dynamics of demand inflation.)

A. P. Lerner, "Inflationary Depression and the Regulation of Administered Prices," and G. Ackley, "A Third Approach to the Analysis and Control of Inflation," both in *The Relationship of Prices to Economic Stability and Growth*, Compendium of Papers Submitted by Panelists Appearing before the Joint Economic Committee, March 31, 1958. U.S. Government Printing Office, pp. 257–268 and 619–636. The Lerner paper is reprinted in M. H. Mueller (ed.), *Readings in Macroeconomics* (Holt, Rinehart, and Winston, 2nd ed., 1971), pp. 361–371; and the Ackley paper in N. H. Keiser (ed.), *Readings in Macroeconomics* (Prentice-Hall, 1970), pp. 495–523.
(Relatively early statements of the "cost-push" inflation thesis.)

M. Friedman, "What Price Guideposts?" in G. P. Schultz and R. Z. Aliber (eds.), *Guidelines: Informal Controls and the Market Place* (University of Chicago Press, 1966), pp. 17–39.
(An attack on the "cost-push" inflation thesis.)

C. L. Schultze, *Recent Inflation in the United States*, Study Paper No. 1, *Study of Employment, Growth and Price Levels*, Joint Economic Committee, 86th Congress, 1st session, 1959; summary chapter is reprinted in E. Shapiro (ed.), *Macroeconomics: Selected Readings* (Harcourt, Brace, and World, 1970), pp. 368–383.
(An influential analysis of the inflation experience of the 1950s.)

A. W. Phillips, "The Relation between Unemployment and the Rate of Change of Money Wage Rates in the United Kingdom, 1861–1957," *Economica*, 25 (1958), 283–300, reprinted in J. Lindauer (ed.), *Macroeconomic Readings* (The Free Press, 1968), pp. 107–119.
(One of the best-known empirical studies in macroeconomics.)

I. Fisher, "A Statistical Relation Between Unemployment and Price Changes," *International Labor Review*, 13 (June 1926), 785–792, reprinted in *Journal of Political Economy*, 81 (March/April 1973), 496–502.
(A recently discovered early study on the subject that precedes Phillips' work by 32 years.)

R. G. Lipsey, "The Relation Between Unemployment and the Rate of Change of Money Wage Rates in the United Kingdom, 1862–1957: A Further Analysis," *Economica*, 27 (February 1960), reprinted in R. A. Gordon and L. R. Klein (eds.), *Readings in Business Cycles* (R. D. Irwin, 1965), pp. 456–487.
(The first attempt to explain theoretically the Phillips curve phenomenon.)

G. L. Perry, *Unemployment, Money Wage Rates, and Inflation* (M.I.T. Press, 1966).

(An early empirical study of the Phillips' type of wage–employment relationship for the United States.)

E. S. Phelps, "Money Wage Dynamics and Labor Market Equilibrium," in E. S. Phelps (ed.), *Microeconomic Foundations of Employment and Inflation Theory* (W. W. Norton, 1970), pp. 124–166.

(A thorough, technical presentation of a possible microeconomic basis for the Phillips curve.)

J. Tobin, "Inflation and Unemployment," *American Economic Review*, 62 (March 1972), 1–18, reprinted in W. L. Smith and R. L. Teigen (eds.), *Readings in Money, National Income and Stabilization Policy* (R. D. Irwin, 3rd ed., 1974), pp. 147–160.

(Tobin's Presidential Address to the American Economic Association, offering an eclectic but antimonetarist approach to the explanation of inflation.)

Chapter 14

Recent Developments in Inflation Theory

The Elaboration of the Phillips Curve
Cost-of-living influences on wage rates
A long-run Phillips curve
Expectational models: Friedman, Phelps
Expectations and the Friedman model
Welfare implications of the Friedman model
Multiple feedbacks

Inflation as a Self-Maintaining Process
Institutional influences on the inflationary process

Longer term Pressures toward Inflation or
    Stability
Institutional, social, and political factors
The state of aggregate demand: labor markets
Aggregate demand: product markets
The feedbacks from inflation to aggregate demand

The State of Inflation Theory

Around 1970, the economy not only of the United States but of the entire world began to experience an acceleration of inflation unprecedented in peacetime. In many countries, inflation, its cause and control, became a major political issue. Not only the general public but political leaders seemed to find the previous explanations of inflation provided by economists no longer satisfactory. And so did a great many economists. The most embarrassed, and the most puzzled, were those economists who, in the 1960s, had accepted most enthusiastically the hypothesis of a stable Phillips-curve trade-off and had developed simple or elaborate theoretical explanations for the phenomenon. For the most striking fact about the new and frightening inflation of the 1970s was that it appeared to bear little relationship to the rate of unemployment.

Essentially, three major strands emerged from the consideration of the inflation experience of the 1970s and from the *re*consideration of the earlier explanations for inflation. One strand attempted to find an acceptable extension or elaboration of the Phillips curve analysis by including additional variables, and/or more complex lag structures, while still retaining the idea of a strong structural relationship between rate of price change and the degree of demand pressure on the economy as reflected in the unemployment rate (or in an "adjusted" unemployment rate).

A second strand was provided by the monetarists (who never were enthusiastic about the Phillips curve), and who found in the experience of the 1970s further confirmation of Friedman's view that "inflation is always and everywhere a purely monetary phenomenon." However, they developed a new framework for their argument in the concepts of "natural rate of unemployment", a "vertical long-run Phillips curve," and the "accelerationist" principle.

A third strand explained the increased tendencies toward inflation more in terms of institutional and sociopolitical forces; they refined and elaborated, in various ways, ideas related to earlier "cost-push" explanations. Often, the first and second, or first and third, of these strands were woven together (the second and third, never).

In the compass of this chapter, it is impossible to do justice to more than a few examples of the recent explosion of theoretical analyses of inflation.[1] And, inevitably, the presentation will reflect, though not excessively it is hoped, the predilections of the writer.

THE ELABORATION OF THE PHILLIPS CURVE

First, however, we need to document the "disappearance" of the simple Phillips curve phenomenon. This can be illustrated by Figure 14-1, showing data (unemployment rate and percent change in consumer prices) for the United States for the period 1950–1975. This figure is exactly the same as Figure 13-4, presented earlier, *except* that the earlier figure incorporated only data covering the years 1955–1969 (here plotted in black). Now, data for 1970–1975 have been added (in light gray) as well as for 1950–1954 (in dark gray). Whereas data for the years 1955–1969 lie close to the freehand Phillips curve of Figure 13-4, data for the immediately previous and subsequent years appear to belong to a different universe. Actually, what is truly unusual is probably the period 1955–1969! Certainly, Phillips' own original data for the United Kingdom for the period after 1913 showed very little relationship to the earlier data for 1861–1913, which had traced out the now-familiar shape.

We could, of course, say that the Phillips curve has not disappeared but merely that its position is not as stable as it appeared to have been for those 15 years from 1955 to 1969. We can imagine, that is, that the Phillips curve—its shape accurately traced out by data for 1955 through 1969— had been shifting before 1955, and has again been shifting since 1969. In each of these earlier or subsequent years its position was such that the observed plotted point in Figure 14-1 lay right on the curve. Such shifts could have been the result of purely random and entirely noneconomic factors that (in addition to the unemployment rate) also influence the rate of inflation. On the other hand, the shifts might instead have been entirely due to the systematic influence of other economic variables in addition to

---

[1] For admirable (but demanding) surveys of the recent literature, see D. Laidler and M. Parkin, "Inflation: A Survey," *Economic Journal*, 85 (December 1975), 741–809; and R. J. Gordon, "Recent Developments in the Theory of Inflation and Unemployment," *Journal of Monetary Economics*, 2 (April 1976), 185–219.

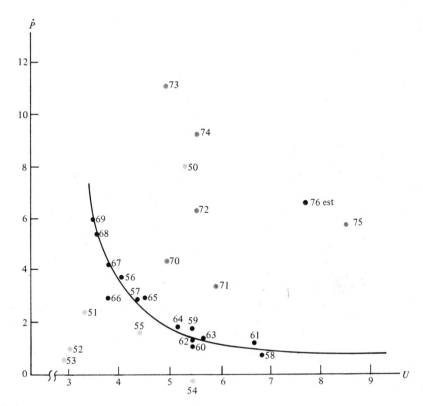

FIGURE 14-1　Consumer Price Index Changes and Unemployment in the United States, 1950–1975.

unemployment, that also influence wages and prices but, for some reason, either did not themselves vary during 1955–1969 or else happened to vary during that period in such a way that their net impact almost exactly cancelled out in each year. In that case, all that we would then need to do is to discover what these other economic variables are and measure their separate influence and we would have a complete and adequate explanation for all of the variations in rates of price and wage change over the entire period from 1950 to 1976. Using this explanation, we could then accurately predict subsequent rates of inflation, once we were given current or expected values of all of these explanatory variables.

Actually, of course, the search for influences, other than the unemployment rate alone, began with the birth of the Phillips curve. Phillips, himself—and, shortly afterward, Lipsey—had attempted to measure the further influence of *changes* in the unemployment rate $\dot{U}$ and of changes in prices (the cost of living) $\dot{P}$. We begin with the Phillips-Lipsey suggestion that changes in the cost of living also affect changes in wage rates.

Cost-of-Living Influences on Wage Rates

The simple Phillips-curve models discussed in the previous chapter could be expressed, alternatively, as theories of the rate of wage increase or of the rate of price increase, the only difference between the two rates representing the change in productivity. But this relationship neglected the possibility of any interaction between wages and prices *other than* that involved in the proposition that unit labor costs (wage rates adjusted for productivity gain) determine prices.

As just noted, Phillips, himself, had suggested that changes in consumer prices, as well as changes in the unemployment rate, might help to explain the observed variation in United Kingdom wage rates. Lipsey, adding these further variables to his statistical regression, found that they substantially improved the "goodness of fit" of the Phillips curve relationship for the United Kingdom. As reported previously, for the period prior to 1913, the coefficient of the variable for change in consumer prices was 0.21—meaning that, for every 1 percent change in consumer prices, the rate of wage change would be 0.21 percent higher than otherwise. For the period after 1913, Lipsey found the coefficient for price change to be 0.69, and that the price-change variable "explained" by far the largest part of the variance of wage-rate changes.

It was quite natural to think of this relationship from price change to wage change as reflecting the "cost-of-living" case for wage increases, which has a long history in wage determinations—whether wages are negotiated with unions or administered by employers. In many union contracts—and in some entire national wage systems (for example, that of Italy)—automatic adjustment of wage rates for cost-of-living changes is required. And, indeed, many economists (the writer included) believe that a significant line of causation almost everywhere runs from cost-of-living changes to wage-rate changes.

However, we have to be extremely careful not to confuse this line of causation, running from changes in prices (the cost of living) to wages, with the reverse causation running from changes in wages (as the major element in costs of production) to prices. This becomes apparent when we convert a Phillips curve in wage rates to one in prices. We then have the rate of price change determined by unemployment and the rate of price change! Distinguishing these separate directions of causation statistically is impossible unless we can assume that there is some lag between price changes (as cost of living) and wage changes, and/or some lag between wage changes (as cost of production) and price changes; even in this case, identifying the separate influences is very difficult, especially if the lags are distributed lags. For simplicity, we will illustrate the nature of the interaction assuming a lag in only one of these relationships, not both (although in the "real world" both relationships are surely lagged).

Suppose that we assume that any period's wage-rate change depends on the current unemployment rate and on the previous period's price (cost of living) change, for example,

(1) $$\dot{W}_t = a_0 + a_1\frac{1}{U_t} + a_2\dot{P}_{t-1} \qquad (a_0 \gtrless 0; a_1, a_2 > 0)$$

where P is a cost-of-living index. We will assume that the current $\dot{P}$ depends (for simplicity) on the current $\dot{W}$, and on a (constant) increase in productivity, X, as follows,

(2) $$\dot{P}_t = \dot{W}_t - X$$

By substitution, we can also derive

(3) $$\dot{W}_t = a_0 + a_1\frac{1}{U_t} + a_2\dot{W}_{t-1} - a_2X$$

which makes the current rate of wage change depend (in part) on its previous rate. Alternatively, we can derive

(4) $$\dot{P}_t = a_0 + a_1\frac{1}{U_t} + a_2\dot{P}_{t-1} - X$$

which makes the rate of price change depend (in part) on its previous rate.

We can represent equations (1) and (2) as in figure 14-2; in panel a, equation (1); in panel b, equation (2). They are here drawn on the assumption that $a_0 = 0, a_1 = 12, a_2 = 0.75, X = 3$. Thus, their equations are

(1a) $$\dot{W}_t = \frac{12}{U_t} + 0.75\dot{P}_{t-1}$$

(2a) $$\dot{P}_t = \dot{W}_t - 3$$

Corresponding to (3) above, we then have

(3a) $$\dot{W}_t = \frac{12}{U_t} + 0.75\dot{W}_{t-1} - 2.25$$

which we shall use shortly; and, corresponding to (4),

(4a) $$\dot{P}_t = \frac{12}{U_t} + 0.75\dot{P}_{t-1} - 3$$

Since $\dot{W}_t$ depends not only on U_t, but also on $\dot{P}_{t-1}$, there should be a whole family of parallel curves drawn in panel a, one for each possible level of $\dot{P}_{t-1}$. We have drawn only three such curves, those corresponding to $\dot{P}_{t-1} = 0$, $\dot{P}_{t-1} = 4$, and $\dot{P}_{t-1} = 7.2$. The second curve lies 3 percentage points above the first, because $0.75\dot{P}_{t-1} = 0.75(4) = 3$; the third lies 5.4

units above the first, because $0.75\dot{P}_{t-1} = 0.75(7.2) = 5.4$. If we are concerned only with the effect of unemployment on wage-rate changes (that is, *ceteris paribus*), we can take any one of these Phillips curves that corresponds to whatever has been the rate of price change. However, we clearly cannot *stop there*, because whatever wage change we determine (given U_t) will itself shortly affect the rate of price change and thereby feed back on the future rate of wage change.

Table 14-1 illustrates some possible time sequences (with various assumed constant rates of unemployment) reflecting this *double* relationship of $\dot{W}$ and $\dot{P}$, all figures based upon the specific equations used in Figure 14-2.

In periods 0 and 1, we show results with the unemployment rate stabilized at 4 percent, and with the past rate of price change taken as zero. Given these conditions, the rate of wage increase is 3 percent and the rate of price change remains at zero. (This combination is represented as point A in both parts of Figure 14-2.) So long as unemployment remains at 4 percent, prices will continue to show no change, and wages will rise by just the rate of productivity increase which permits prices to remain stable. (Had we started with some previous rate of price change other than zero, $\dot{P}$ would have approached zero over a number of periods, so long as U remained at 4 percent.) However, this is a unique situation, applicable at no rate of unemployment other than 4 percent.

Thus, in period 2, we assume that public policy, using fiscal or monetary stimulus to aggregate demand, reduces the unemployment rate to 3 percent, and thereafter keeps it there. This has the short-run effect of causing $\dot{W}$ to rise to 4 percent (even though the previous rate of $\dot{P}$ is still zero) and the current $\dot{P}$ to rise to 1 percent. (This short-run combination is

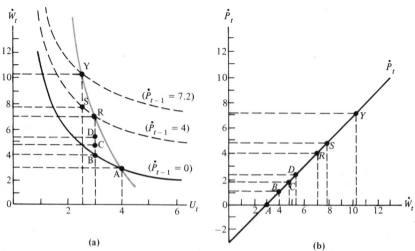

FIGURE 14-2

TABLE 14-1

Period	U_t	$\dot{P}_{t-1}$	$\dot{W}_t$ $\left(=\dfrac{12}{U}+0.75\dot{P}_{t-1}\right)$	$\dot{P}_t$ $(=\dot{W}_t-3)$	Reference in Figure 14-2
0	4	0	3	0	Point A
1	4	0	3	0	
2	3	0	4	1	Point B
3	3	1	4.75	1.75	Point C
4	3	1.75	5.3125	2.3125	Point D
5	3	2.3125	5.7344	2.7344	
$\vdots$					
n	3	4	7	4	Point R
$n+1$	2.5	4	7.8	4.8	Point S
$n+2$	2.5	4.8	8.4	5.4	
$n+3$	2.5	5.4	8.85	5.85	
$n+4$	2.5	5.85	9.1875	6.1875	
$\vdots$					
$n+n$	2.5	7.2	10.2	7.2	Point Y

shown as point B in Figure 14-2.) Reducing the unemployment rate by 25 percent at the cost of only 1 percent inflation of prices may seem to be a quite acceptable trade-off. Policy makers, and their public, may be pleased with the accomplishment. However, rejoicing is premature. For now, because prices are rising at a 1 percent rate, cost-of-living wage increases are in order, which, in period 3, brings about a further rise in wages by 0.75 times $\dot{P}_{t-1}$, or to 4.75; this in turn raises $\dot{P}$ to 1.75 (shown at point C). But this is not the end. An accelerating "price-wage spiral" (with $U = 3$ percent) continues indefinitely, although the rate of acceleration continually slows. After a long time (period n), with U maintained at 3 percent, the rate of wage increase ultimately approaches a stable rate of 7 percent, and price increases a stable rate of 4 percent. (Point R in the figure.) Policy makers and their public may not be as happy with this trade-off. But at least unemployment was reduced and the rate of inflation has stabilized.

How do we find the "equilibrium rate of inflation" that corresponds to 3 percent unemployment (or any other stable U)? Simply by solving our dynamic model for the special case of $\dot{W}_t = \dot{W}_{t-1}$, that is, for a stable rate of wage increase. We can define an equilibrium rate of wage increase as

$$\dot{W}_E \equiv \dot{W}_t = \dot{W}_{t-1}$$

Substituting from this definition into (3a), we can find equilibrium rates of wage and price increases for any given U as follows

$$\dot{W}_E = \frac{12}{U} + 0.75\dot{W}_E - 2.25$$

$$0.25\dot{W}_E = \frac{12}{U} - 2.25$$

or

(5a)
$$\dot{W}_E = \frac{48}{U} - 9$$

And, from (2a), we have

(6a)
$$\dot{P}_E = \dot{W}_E - 3$$

where $\dot{P}_E$ is the equilibrium rate of price change.

At the original equilibrium, with $U = 4$,

$$\dot{W}_E = 12 - 9 = 3; \qquad \dot{P}_E = 3 - 3 = 0$$

At the new equilibrium, with $U = 3$

$$\dot{W}_E = 16 - 9 = 7; \qquad \dot{P}_E = 7 - 3 = 4$$

If the unemployment rate is now reduced to $2\frac{1}{2}$ percent, this new equilibrium of $\dot{P} = 4$ is once again disturbed. The inflation rate (of wages) rises (after one period) to 7.8 percent, and, of prices, to 4.8 percent (point S). Then, with U maintained at $2\frac{1}{2}$ percent, $\dot{W}$ and $\dot{P}$ further increase, but at a decreasing rate, ultimately approaching a new equilibrium inflation rate of 7.2 percent in prices and 10.2 percent in wages (point Y), which can be found by solving (5a) and then (6a) using $U = 2.5$. The last 0.5 percent reduction in the unemployment rate has ultimately cost a further 3.2 percentage points in the inflation rate.

A Long-Run Phillips Curve

Neglecting any feedback of the cost of living on wage rates, we had (in effect) postulated a *short-run Phillips curve*, like any one of the black curves shown in part a of Figure 14-2. But once we recognize this feedback, we find that there is a whole family of such short-run curves, one for each past rate of price change. And, across these, we can trace out a *long-run Phillips curve*, shown in gray, consisting of points like A, R, and Y: each an equilibrium rate of (wage) inflation associated with a long-maintained constant level of unemployment. Other points on the long-run curve can be found from the equation for the long-run curve, equation (5a), using any other rate of unemployment: for example, if $U = 6$, $\dot{W}_E = 8 - 9 = -1$; and, from (6a), $\dot{P}_E = -1 - 3 = -4$.

Thus, once we admit a feedback of prices on wages, we find that there are two Phillips curves, not one, and the long-run curve is always steeper than the short-run curve. There is, of course, a limiting case, as the coefficient of lagged prices in the wage equation approaches zero. In that case, instead of a family of short-run Phillips curves, there is only one; and that is also the long-run Phillips curve.

However, we should also note that, if the coefficient of lagged prices in the wage equation were 1.0, there are still multiple short-run Phillips curves but there is no unique equilibrium rate of inflation. Assume

$$\dot{W}_t = \frac{12}{U} + 1\dot{P}_{t-1}$$

and

$$\dot{P}_t = \dot{W}_t - 3$$

Substituting, we find

(3a′)
$$\dot{W}_t = \frac{12}{U} + \dot{W}_{t-1} - 3$$

In equilibrium, defining $\dot{W}_t = \dot{W}_{t-1} \equiv \dot{W}_E$, and substituting, $\dot{W}_E$ disappears, leaving only

$$\frac{12}{U_E} = 3$$

From this, however, we still derive some characteristics of the equilibrium, namely,

$$U_E = 4$$

and, from (6a)

$$\dot{W}_E = 3 + \dot{P}_E.$$

But this equilibrium is not determined in terms of an inflation rate. In this case, the curves shown in Figure 14-2, panel a, becomes as in Figure 14-3. The long-run Phillips curve is now vertical, at some unemployment rate, U^* (in our example, 4 percent).

What this says is that, if U is stable at U^* (4 percent in our example), the equilibrium rate of wage inflation can be anything (from plus to minus infinity); and, of course, the equilibrium rate of price inflation will be 3 percentage points less than that. So long as U remains at 4 percent, any rate of inflation, once established, will continue without change. For example, if $U = 4$ percent, and $\dot{W}_{t-1} = 10$, we can substitute into (3a′) to find

$$\dot{W}_t = \frac{12}{4} + 10 - 3 = 10$$

and, from (2a)

$$\dot{P}_t = 10 - 3 = 7$$

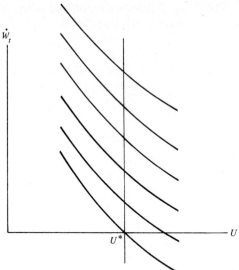

FIGURE 14-3

If $\dot{W}_{t-1} = -5$

$$\dot{W}_t = \frac{12}{4} - 5 - 3 = -5$$

and

$$\dot{P}_t = -5 - 3 = -8$$

Any rate of inflation or deflation once established is forever maintained.

The fact that the long-run curve is vertical at 4 percent does not, of course, mean that rates of unemployment below (or above) U^* are impossible. Suppose $U = 3$, $\dot{P}_{t-1} = 4$, $\dot{W}_{t-1} = 7$, then, from (3a') and (2a)

$$\dot{W}_t = 4 + 7 - 3 = 8; \qquad \dot{P}_t = 8 - 3 = 5$$

And, in subsequent periods,

$$\dot{W}_{t+1} = 4 + 8 - 3 = 9 \qquad \dot{P}_{t+1} = 9 - 3 = 6$$
$$\dot{W}_{t+2} = 4 + 9 - 3 = 10 \qquad \dot{P}_{t+2} = 10 - 3 = 7$$
$$\dot{W}_{t+3} = 4 + 10 - 3 = 11 \qquad \dot{P}_{t+3} = 11 - 3 = 8$$

In short, the rate of inflation accelerates without limit at all unemployment rates below U^* (here 4 percent). Experiment will also show that the acceleration will be the faster the lower the rate of unemployment (for example, try $U = 2$, $\dot{P}_{t-1} = 4$, $\dot{W}_{t-1} = 7$).

At rates of unemployment above 4 percent: for example, $U = 6$, $\dot{P}_{t-1} = 4$, $\dot{W}_{t-1} = 7$, we get from equations (3a′) and (2a):

$$\dot{W}_t = 2 + 7 - 3 = 6 \qquad \dot{P}_t = 6 - 3 = 3$$
$$\dot{W}_{t+1} = 2 + 6 - 3 = 5 \qquad \dot{P}_{t+1} = 5 - 3 = 2$$
$$\dot{W}_{t+2} = 2 + 5 - 3 = 4 \qquad \dot{P}_{t+2} = 4 - 3 = 1$$

$$\vdots$$

$$\dot{W}_{t+6} = 2 + 1 - 3 = 0 \qquad \dot{P}_{t+6} = 0 - 3 = -3$$
$$\dot{W}_{t+7} = 2 + 0 - 3 = -1 \qquad \dot{P}_{t+7} = -1 - 3 = -4$$
$$\dot{W}_{t+8} = 2 + -1 - 3 = -2 \qquad \dot{P}_{t+8} = -2 - 3 = -5$$

In short, $U > U^*$ produces indefinitely decelerating inflation (and then accelerating deflation). The higher the unemployment rate, the faster the deflation rate accelerates (for example, try $U = 12$, $\dot{P}_{t-1} = 4$, $\dot{W}_{t-1} = 7$).[2]

Expectational Models: Friedman, Phelps

The cost-of-living feedback from prices to wages (and thus to prices) is only one of several types of feedback that may contribute to the process of inflation, and, in particular, to a "long-run" relationship between the unemployment rate and the inflation rate that is very different from the short-run relationship. This section considers briefly another such feedback, associated mainly with the name of Milton Friedman (although E. S. Phelps independently developed essentially the same ideas).

We have noted that the long-run Phillips curve would be vertical if there were a unitary feedback from current cost-of-living change to future wage change (and thus to future price change); that is, if a 1 percent faster price change now produces a 1 percent faster wage change (and thus price change) later. Friedman argues that the feedback from present price change to future price change may well be less than unitary in the short run, thus accounting for short-run Phillips curves of the familiar variety. But, in the longer run, the feedback has to be unitary. To be sure, the particular feedback channel that Friedman has in mind is completely different from the one we have been considering. Rather than a feedback from the cost of living to wage rates and thereby to prices, Friedman sees it as a feedback from prices directly to future prices, and it operates exclusively through expectations. Nevertheless, although the feedback mechanism is different, its longer run unitary character compels a vertical long-run Phillips curve, with all the properties previously derived. It is

---

[2] It is conceivable, at least, that the coefficient of $\dot{P}_{t-1}$ in equation (1a) could exceed 1. Although this produces a dynamic system even more explosive than that with a coefficient of 1, the equilibrium implications are economically meaningless (that is, the equilibrium is unstable—not approached by the dynamic process).

vertical at an unemployment rate, U^*, which Friedman calls the "natural rate of unemployment." We need now to develop these ideas in more detail. To keep the story simple, we will assume, for the present, that the growth rate of productivity is zero: thus $\dot{P} = \dot{W}$.

The cost-of-living feedback previously discussed was essentially an institutional connection, recent cost of living changes affecting, with a lag, the bargained or otherwise administratively determined future wage rate. The impact of wage increases on prices is also usually visualized as an administrative, "mark-up" form of price setting: costs rise, and prices are directly raised to offset the rise of costs (*not* that costs rise and amounts supplied are then reduced until the goods market again clears at a higher price level). Friedman's feedback, in contrast, operates through purely competitive markets, both for goods and for labor, with prices that instantly and continually clear these markets to reflect impersonal, atomistic adjustments of amounts supplied and demanded. In determining the amounts they wish to supply and demand, both suppliers and demanders necessarily take into account their expectations of future prices for what they buy or sell today. In particular, if workers (or sellers of other factor services) expect that the prices of the goods they must buy tomorrow will be higher than they are today, this affects the marginal utility of today's money wage and thus the amount of labor offered today (or the willingness to supply other factor services today). Marginal units of factor supply will continue to be offered by their sellers only if the wage (or other income) payable today is advancing as fast as any expected future rise in prices of goods to be bought tomorrow. *Buyers* of factors today, facing rising factor prices, will agree to pay those rising prices only if they expect future prices of outputs to rise as fast as factor prices now are. If the expectation were that future prices would rise more rapidly than today's price, marginal workers (and suppliers of other factor services) would tend to withdraw their supplies; buyers of factor services, on the other hand, would tend to increase their demands. Thus, today's rate of price rise would necessarily increase toward tomorrow's expected rise. If today's prices were rising faster than tomorrow's expected prices, suppliers would tend to increase their current offers, and buyers would tend to reduce their current demands, causing today's rate of price increase to fall toward tomorrow's expected rate.

Thus, today's inflation rate depends upon—and, in equilibrium, must equal—yesterday's expected rate for today, ${}_{t-1}P_t^e$. If this were *not* the case, expectations would invariably be found erroneous, which is surely inconsistent with the concept of equilibrium. But what determines the expected rate of inflation? Mainly, the current rate of inflation. If prices have been stable ($\dot{P}_{t-1} = 0$), they will ordinarily be expected to remain stable $({}_{t-1}\dot{P}_t^e = 0)$; if they have been rising at a 10 percent rate—or falling at a 5 percent rate—they will ordinarily be expected to continue to do the same. And this expectation will tend to make buyers and sellers act in such a way that the expectation will be confirmed. However, it will be fully confirmed only if the economy is at the natural rate of unemployment.

Friedman's natural rate of unemployment corresponds precisely to what the classical economists described as full employment; everyone who wants any work at the prevailing real wage rate has exactly the amount he wants. To be sure, that does not mean that some nonemployed workers do not *consider* themselves as unemployed (or as involuntarily working part time). Although the real wage offered for any work that they can find is less than required to induce their work, they believe that there *should* be work available for them at a higher real wage than they are offered; thus, they do not accept that real wage, but look for the higher one. Not only do many of these nonemployed call themselves "unemployed" but society may also regard them as such. They are allowed to register at the employment exchange as seeking jobs (for which they are not sufficiently qualified); they are counted in the monthly labor force survey as "in the labor force" seeking work but not at work. Many of them may be drawing unemployment insurance or on welfare because they are "unable to find work." Officially, there is unemployment—in an amount usually equal to the "natural rate of unemployment" (which may not be constant). Friedman regards this as the normal state of affairs—or it would be if it were not for politicians, whether well-meaning or cynical.

Suppose that the economy is in this "natural" state, with the money wage level not being bid down by the job seeking of those nominally unemployed nor being bid up by the competition of employers, who have all the workers they want to hire at the current wage. Prices are stable, have been stable, and are expected to remain stable. This requires, of course, that the amount of money is also stable: $\dot{M}_t = 0$, where $\dot{M}$ is the percentage rate of change in M.

Seeing the "unemployed," politicians conclude that the economy needs "stimulus." They induce the central bank (if they are not themselves running it) to increase the money supply (or to buy bonds issued to finance a fiscal deficit). This does increase the demand for goods and for labor to produce them. Wage rates begin to rise. Some of the "unemployed," expecting that prices will remain stable and thus that the rise in the money wage is also a rise in the real wage, now take jobs; unemployment declines.

However, rising wage rates, after some lag, raise costs and prices, violating the workers' expectation of stability. The formerly unemployed will thus remain at work only if nominal wages increase by more—which, of course, takes a larger $\dot{M}$. The "stimulus" must be increased, just to keep unemployment constant. But this only causes prices to rise faster. In short, over-full-employment ($U < U^*$), can be maintained only by an ever-accelerating inflation, fed by an ever-accelerating increase in M. There had appeared to be a short-run Phillips curve through U^*, which sloped upward to the left—based on yesterday's expectation for today, $_{t-1}\dot{P}_t^e = 0$. But, as with the previous model, the short-run curve moves to a higher level as inflation ensues and as this inflation gets built into workers' and employers' expectations. But in this case, inflation progressively accelerates, approaching no equilibrium rate (the so-called "accelerationist principle"). The long-run Phillips curve is vertical at U^*.[3]

Finally, in our story, the monetary authorities catch on (or the public rebels). With the inflation rate having accelerated to, say, 20 percent a year, and promising to rise ever faster, they cease trying to hold U below U^*. But, now, merely to hold U at U^* requires not $\dot{M} = 0$, but $\dot{M} = 20$. For, with today's expectation for tomorrow, $_t\dot{P}^e_{t+1} = 20$, workers would no longer supply even their full-employment effort unless $\dot{W}_t$ remains at 20; whereas employers, expecting $_t\dot{P}^e_{t+1} = 20$, are willing to employ all of those full-employment labor hours with $\dot{W}_t = 20$. (At $\dot{W}_t < 20$, they would want to hire even more; but the supply would not be available; so $\dot{W}_t$ would instantly rise to 20.)

Of course, the rate of inflation can now be reduced—but only at the cost of some *real* unemployment. With $\dot{M}$ below 20 (if 20 is the prevailing rate of $\dot{P}$) the demand for labor will fall short of the supply; $\dot{W}$ will decline. The economy will move southeast along the short-run Phillips curve based on yesterday's expectation for today, $_t\dot{P}^e_{t+1} = 20$. As inflation—and then inflationary expectations—are gradually revised downward, it requires a gradually lower $\dot{M}_t$ (remaining less than $\dot{P}_t$) in order to maintain the above-natural-rate level of unemployment. As inflation and inflationary expectations finally reach zero (with $\dot{M}$ now < 0), the monetary authorities can restore $\dot{M}$ to 0, letting U fall to U^*; and all can then live happily forever after at $U = U^*$, $\dot{M} = 0$, $\dot{P} = 0$, and $\dot{P}^e = 0$. (Knowing politicians, Friedman hopes for the best but fears that it will all happen again before long.)

---

[3] The story gets somewhat confusing here, and sometimes inconsistent. Why were employers willing to hire the (unqualified) workers at a higher money wage but, at first, no higher prices? Were they fooled into it, and if so how? Friedman's version sees employers (but not workers) *expecting* the equivalent price rise which will follow from the higher wages and the faster growth of M. However, on classical assumptions, employers should need to expect a *reduced* real wage in order to induce them to hire more workers. Thus, as others tell the story, it gets turned around. The initial increase of M causes goods *prices* to rise (or causes employers to expect them to rise). With *unchanged* money wages, this appears to reduce the real wage that employers now have to pay to hire the below-standard workers. At this lower real wage, employers believe it profitable to hire these workers, not realizing that their own collective bidding for them will soon raise the money wage. But it does. Then, in order to keep employers *willing* to continue to hire these workers, the monetary authorities must generate a progressive inflation, which will keep employers thinking that it pays to hire workers whose productivity is less than the real wage which will induce them to work. However, this version implies that there was *genuine* unemployment: there were workers without jobs willing to work at the going real wage, which Friedman's version does not assume. In either version of the story, however, someone—workers or employers (but it is hard to see how it can be both)—are being fooled: fooled by always expecting continuation of *today's* rate of inflation for what they buy (consumer goods or labor), but discovering when it gets to be tomorrow that inflation is at a higher rate.

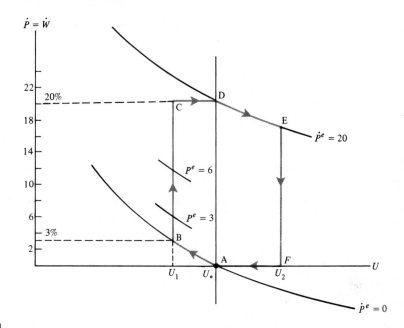

FIGURE 14-4

We can schematically map the odyssey just completed in Figure 14-4. At point A, with $U_t = U^*$, $\dot{P}_{t-1} = 0$, the initial bliss is disturbed by the temptress who promises to move the economy along the $\dot{P}^e = 0$ short-run trade-off to point B—by a suitable monetary policy of $\dot{M}_t = 3$, which will generate a 3 percent inflation but will reduce U to U_1. Unfortunately, once the temporarily fooled workers (or employers?) shift their expectations to $\dot{P}^e = 3$, inflation has begun to accelerate, fed by the ever-increasing $\dot{M}$. Only when $\dot{P}$ and $\dot{M}$ have reached point C(20 percent) does our hero recognize the error of his ways. Instead of further increasing $\dot{M}$, the authorities allow unemployment to rise as we move to point D. Here, it takes a continuation of $\dot{M} = 20$ to keep $U = U^*$. At least things aren't getting any worse! But there is no need for $\dot{M} = \dot{P} = 20$ merely to keep $U = U^*$. By revising the inflationary expectations, we can get back to original bliss at A. Unfortunately, this takes some temporary unemployment (real, this time). The route to A thus leads through E and F.

Expectations and the Friedman Model

Now there can be no doubt that expectations relating to future prices— whether they are for price level stability, or for price level change and of the speed of that change—have an important impact on the myriad decisions that affect today's (and tomorrow's) price and wage level. Expectations clearly cannot be left out of any satisfactory theory of inflation; it is to Friedman's credit (and that of his monetarist associates) for having brought expectations back into inflation analysis.[4]

Nevertheless, there are several crucial aspects of Friedman's use of expectations that can and should be challenged. Expectations of future prices surely influence the decisions that determine today's price and wage changes. But Friedman holds that these decisions exclusively affect *quantities* (of labor services, products, and so on) supplied and demanded, with prices and wages then immediately assuming whatever level is necessary to "clear" those markets. Market-clearing prices, however, characterize a miniscule fraction of labor markets and a small minority of product markets (although the remaining flexible-price markets may play a fairly crucial role in inflation). Thus, the more important ways in which inflationary expectations affect the current rate of inflation may be quite different. Instead of affecting quantities bought and supplied, and only thereby affecting prices, they may principally affect the decisions about future wages and prices that will be made today by those who participate in setting that small fraction of all wages and prices which will be set today, but that are set *on the assumption*, and often with the *contractual commitment*, that they will be *unchanged for a considerable term*. As other wages and prices come up for consideration, they, too, will reflect the (then) current expectations for inflation or stability. (Over a longer period of time, moreover, inflationary expectations—as well as the *uncertainty* of price expectations—may also affect the institutional arrangements for wage and price setting: for example, the standard length of contracts, the use of escalator provisions, and so on).

To be sure, price expectations will also affect the *amount*, and the *timing* of spending decisions—quantities to be bought, ordered to be bought, or planned to be bought—by consumers (especially for durable goods), and by businesses (for additions to inventories and for additions to and replacements of plant and equipment). The resulting aggregate impact of these spending decisions on the volume of employment and output—and unemployment—then has subsequent macroeconomic impacts on administrative price and wage decisions, as well as on those few prices which are set by market clearing processes. We shall refer to some of these specific impacts at a later point.

The second crucial assumption of Friedman's that needs to be challenged is that expectations of future price movements are formed mainly by some simple adaptive process which merely extrapolates the recent and current rate of inflation.

Obviously, current and recent values provide much of the basis on which expectations are formed. But this experience is interpreted and

---

[4] "Brought back," because Irving Fisher (and others) recognized their importance more than 75 years ago. Moreover, discussions of "hyperinflations" have always emphasized the vital importance of inflation expectations.

qualified by people who will have observed that, in the past, any such simple extrapolation would have produced extremely erroneous forecasts of (then) future inflation (or stability)—forecasts that would have been (and sometimes were) exceedingly costly if (or when) they had formed the basis for economic action.

Such individuals may, therefore, have learned not to rely on any kind of extrapolative or adaptive expectations, but instead develop ideas or "theories"—simple or sophisticated, correct or incorrect (and almost no one's have been close to correct)—about what will determine future prices. Such theories are presumably based on observation, learning, and reasoning; they take account of current and recent events; and they do not always, or even often, give the same prediction as simple extrapolation.

Indeed, one striking extension of Friedman's theory of the vertical Phillips curve is the "rational expectations" version. This holds that rational individuals have observed (or perhaps have learned from Friedman) that past increases in prices (and in the rate of change of prices) have invariably been accompanied or closely preceded by equal proportional changes in M (and $\dot{M}$). When all economic agents act on this knowledge, this produces the result that the vertical Phillips curve becomes not a long-run tendency, but something that happens almost instantaneously and continually.

There are many problems with this version, which we do not have space to consider in detail. Note, however, that, in this version, an increase in M does not need to create an *actual* increase in the real demand for labor or products—reducing U below U^*, generating excess demand, and thus bidding up wages and prices. Rather, it is "all done by mirrors," to use a Galbraithian phrase, or, in his more recent and irreverent characterization, "inflation by immaculate conception." It is "excess demand inflation" without any actual excess demand.

It also implies that we never observe inequalities between U and U^*, because these would lead to instantaneous hyperinflation or hyperdeflation. Thus, whenever U changes, it must be that U^* has changed, too. Increased unemployment in a recession then must occur because the supply of labor has contracted: fewer people want to work.

The rational expectations view also conflicts seriously with the monetarist complaint that politicians, trying to please the public, persist in mistaken monetary policies in the effort to increase employment through inflationary increases in M. Where are our "rational" individuals when that happens? Or is it that all of the *economic* decisions are made by a minority of rational business leaders and wealthholders, but most votes are cast by the irrational masses? But the behavior of every worker is supposed to be represented in the employment decisions underlying the analysis.

Whatever one may think of Friedman's original theory of extrapolative price expectations, or of the amended "rational expectations" version, one should have no doubt of the important role of inflationary expectations in creating inflation. But these expectations are not based merely on past rates of inflation nor only on observations of changes in M. This is dramatically illustrated by the events following July 1950, when North Korean troops invaded South Korea, and, shortly thereafter, armed forces first of the United States, and then of People's Republic of China entered the fighting on behalf of South and North Korea, respectively. Everywhere, the outbreak of World War III was anticipated, the United States and its allies to be pitted against China and Russia (then still closely allied). With memories of World War II still fresh in people's minds, such a development meant only one thing for the price level: rapid inflation followed by direct controls.

The economy was then just emerging from recession during which (the last time it has happened) the consumer price level declined. Nevertheless, the expectation of inflation (and of attendant shortages and controls) led to an explosion of price and wage increases and scare buying. In administered-price markets, sellers of goods and services, and both buyers and sellers of labor attempted rapidly to raise their prices to beat the expected controls (which were remembered to have started in World War II with a freeze of existing prices and wages). Scare buying by consumers and producers to beat the expected shortages caused a rapid expansion of aggregate demand and production, and a sharp explosion of flexible prices (mainly in wholesale markets for raw commodities). Expected inflation clearly created current inflation. But the expected inflation was not the mere extrapolation of a preexisting inflation; prices were steady or declining before the North Korean invasion. Nor was it based on observed changes in M. Rather, the expectation reflected people's memories of past events and their reasoning about the economic impact of current events.

Nor did the realized inflation create an irresistible expectation of further inflation, which would inevitably cause the inflation to continue. After a brief episode of makeshift (but fairly tough) wage and price controls—almost all removed at or before the end of 1952—the United States economy then enjoyed almost perfect price stability for the next three years, despite an unemployment rate at a historical low. (Except for the peak of World War II, it was the lowest in U.S. records or estimates).

Price expectations played a major role in 1950–1954; but the expectations were not extrapolative. Nor, indeed, was any aspect of this episode consistent with any simple (nor, so far as this writer is aware, with any sophisticated) version of the Phillips curve. (See the dots for 1950, 1951, 1952, 1953, and 1954 in Figure 14-1). Although a number of attempts have been made to find evidence directly supporting the hypothesis of extrapolative as well as of rational price expectations, this writer regards them as most charitably described as inconclusive. Further research may well lead to better theories of how expectations are formed; but, for now, we probably should conclude that expectations are extremely important for inflation, but their origin is not fully understood.

Welfare Implications of the Friedman Analysis

Deriving directly from Friedman's assumption of uniformly market-clearing price and wage behavior are his fundamental propositions involving the amount and character of the unemployment which exists at the "natural rate" of unemployment. However, if we reject the assumption of universally market-clearing prices, we destroy the welfare implications of the entire Friedman argument. This argument implies that inflation is not only unnecessary, but in a real sense is a pure evil—causing people to do things which are not in their interest to do: workers fooled into taking jobs when really they prefer leisure at the real wage which they can (and in fact do) earn; or employers fooled into investing in payrolls (and perhaps even in plant and equipment) to produce goods which society values at less than their real cost of production. If we believe that a long-run Phillips curve exists (and has enough stability to make the concept interesting), it might conceivably be vertical—and, whether vertical or not, it will surely intersect the horizontal axis at some positive level of unemployment. This is, presumably, the lowest level of unemployment consistent with maintained price stability. Yet, if Friedman is wrong about the character of U^*, the real costs of inflation (which we shall briefly analyze in Chapter 15) could be far less than the real costs of unemployment when $U = U^*$.

We can presume that a period like that of, say, 1973–1974 is one that Friedman would say involved the U.S. economy operating below its natural rate of unemployment. Inflation was not only nonzero, but accelerating from an annual rate of 8.2 percent in the CPI in the first half of 1973 to one of 12.5 percent in the first half of 1974. Except for one month, the unemployment rate held steady between 4.8 and 5.0 percent during the eighteen months from January 1973 through June 1974.

But can one really believe that *all*—or even *many*—of the more than $4\frac{1}{2}$ million workers reported as unemployed in the first half of 1974 were really *voluntarily* unemployed because the marginal utility of the real wage available to them was less than the marginal disutility of the work available? Can one seriously argue that the 4.5 percent unemployment rate of those classified as (ordinarily) "full-time workers" represented only or even mainly voluntary idleness? Or that 2.3 percent of "married men" (living with their wives) didn't need to work? Or that all of the roughly two million unemployed who were *not* receiving unemployment insurance really preferred daytime television to a regular income? The prevailing real wage was higher than that of one, two, five, or ten years earlier. Can it be that many of those who *were* at work later regretted it because they really required a still higher real wage to make it worthwhile?

Multiple Feedbacks

A number of economists have, in effect, fitted statistical regressions to United States quarterly data (usually for the period beginning in 1955) more or less in the form

$$\dot{P}_t = a_0 + a_1\frac{1}{U_t} + a_2\dot{P}_t^e$$

where P_t^e is taken as equal to P_{t-1}. Although regressions in this form made prior to the early 1970s invariably found the coefficient a_2 to be clearly less than one, studies which include data for the early 1970s often found the coefficient to be at or close to unity. This latter finding has frequently been interpreted, and not only by monetarists, as evidence in support of the existence of unitary price expectations and thus of a vertical long-run Phillips curve. It surely does imply a vertical long-run curve. But to use it as support for the expectations hypothesis is entirely gratuitous, for there are other feedback channels from past price change to current price change in addition to the expectational one. One alternative interpretation, for instance, would be as evidence for the operation of a unitary "cost-of-living principle" in wage negotiation—every percentage point of extra cost-of-living increase producing an extra 1 percentage point increase in wage rates and thus in prices: popularly known as the **wage-price spiral**.

There are also theories of feedback involving the effects of current wage-rate changes by groups setting wages today on the future wage-rate changes of other groups (the so-called **wage-wage spiral**). There are also theories of how current price changes, with most wage rates predetermined, affect the size of business profits, which in turn influence future labor-union bargaining targets and strategies. Any of these theories could be imagined to produce a unitary coefficient for the past change of prices. More importantly, these (and other) feedback channels *need not be thought of as mutually exclusive*—the feedback from present to future wage and price changes may operate through all of these channels: expectations, cost of living, wage imitation, profits, and others. The estimated coefficient for past prices in a simple "reduced-form" dynamic price-change equation (like that in the text above) thus may well reflect the sum of a number of partial coefficients representing each of several feedback channels. However, as we will see later, it is plausible that some of these coefficients may be variable, and even somewhat unstable.

INFLATION AS A SELF-MAINTAINING PROCESS

Most theories of inflation continue to be formulated in the way outlined previously, as an extended or elaborated Phillips curve. In one way or another, today's inflation rate is made to depend (a) inversely on unemployment (or some adjusted measure of unemployment)—usually current unemployment, but sometimes both current and lagged unemployment, and (b) directly on lagged prices changes. But since the influence of lagged prices is extremely large, possibly even unitary, and prices are largely determined by wages, one can equally well describe these as theories of a (largely) self-maintaining inflationary process or spiral, in which today's wage or price change depends on earlier rates of price change, but with its current speed somewhat modified by the influence of current (or current and lagged) unemployment.[6]

Indeed, it seems to this writer that it is more useful to think of current inflation theories in this way: as theories of an *inflationary process with a life of its own*, which, once started, is almost bound to continue for some period of time. Of course, its rate is not independent of the state of aggregate demand or external factors. But it is clear that the *current* level of aggregate demand is only one, and probably relatively minor, determinant of the current rate of inflation; a wide variety of current rates of inflation can coexist with any current level of aggregate demand.

As we have seen, there are many different versions of this process. For Friedman, it is essentially a self-reinforcing process of expectations affecting flexible, market-determined wages and prices, in turn determining expectations of future wages and prices. One is accustomed to think of Friedman's inflation theory as implying that aggregate demand (as determined by M) is everything. And, surely, Friedman's analysis does involve the sharpest possible line between a state of zero excess demand and a state which implies an unlimited acceleration of inflation. Still, Friedman's inflationary process is substantially self-maintaining at any given unemployment rate (so long as the necessary M is supplied to maintain that rate of unemployment); and, except in the rational-expectations version, any level of unemployment can be associated with a wide variety of rates of inflation (or deflation). At the natural rate of unemployment, *any* rate of inflation—positive, negative, or zero—will exactly maintain itself; at unemployment levels below the natural rate, any rate of inflation is not merely self-maintaining but accelerating; at unemployment above the natural rate, any rate of inflation will not quite maintain itself, but it will still generate future inflation.

Other theories of the inflationary process emphasize different channels of feedback from past inflation rates to present rates. Most of them imply that the effects stem not only from expectations of future events but from the influence of past or present events. Of course, since expectations are usually represented in empirical work as functions of past events, there is no real operational difference between the two kinds of theories. But there is a world of difference for the policies these theories may imply.

---

[6] Whether or not lagged unemployment is directly introduced as a determinant, lagged unemployment enters indirectly into the determination of current inflation rates through its influence on past rates of wage—and therefore of price—change.

Most of these theories do not assume market-clearing wages and prices but rather administered wages and prices, although they may recognize an occasionally crucial role played by flexible-price markets, as we shall see shortly.

This way of thinking about inflation suggests that a wide variety of factors may set off an inflation (or alter its rate): bursts of aggregate demand; dramatic changes in expectations of future inflation; "wage explosions" reflecting economic, social, or political resentments; sharp increases in prices of imports; supply failures in flexible-price markets; sharp increases in indirect taxes. Whatever the initial cause, the inflationary process, once begun, possesses a strong inertia that tends to keep it rolling and makes it extremely difficult to halt. By the same token, price stability (an inflation rate of zero) also possesses the same inertia, providing resistance to the initiation of inflation.

The writer's own vision of this process emphasizes a combination of backward-looking, forward-looking, and sideways-looking perceptions and responses that tend to maintain an inflation—including the special case of a zero inflation. And it sees these factors as operating mainly, though not exclusively, on the administrative determination of wage rates, whether set through negotiation, political action, or employer decision. Those making wage decisions on any particular day or month are determining wage rates for only a small fraction of the labor force. They do so in the light of their perceptions of an ongoing rate of wage and price change, of what has been happening to other wages and prices, of what is currently happening to them, and what is thought likely to happen in the future. The response to these perceptions is a mixture of attempts to "catch up" with past price-level increases, to "keep up" with other current increases, and to "anticipate" future increases. (The anticipations of the future increases are surely significantly influenced by past price changes, but they are unlikely to represent simply a unitary extrapolation. They may be nonlinearly related to the size, duration, and stability of past price changes, and they may be generated, or altered, by news and perceptions of current, past, and future developments which have not yet affected the price level.)

Any one set of decision makers can only take the ongoing inflationary environment as given—entirely beyond its control. It attempts to make an adjustment of its own wages or prices that may keep them up with, catch them up with, move them ahead of, or, in some cases, let them fall somewhat behind the parade. The adjustments, however, are always *relative to the perceived speed of the parade.* On the average, or in the aggregate, these individual current responses will ordinarily be such as to keep the parade moving in the future at something close to its present rate. Of course, changes in the current rate of unemployment and capacity utilization will also have some effect, but at first this can only influence the wages and prices being set today. Only gradually does it affect other wages and prices, and, by the time all of these first-round effects will have been fully felt, they will have merged with (or even been swamped by) the secondary repercussions originating in the areas where the influence was first felt.

Institutional Influences on the Inflationary Process

The fundamental sources of the circular or spiral character of the inflationary process relate (a) to the basic economic fact that suppliers of factor services are interested in the "real" return from their employment, and thus—whether through adjusting the quantities of their services supplied or in other ways—increases in prices of final products must ultimately be reflected in factor prices; and (b) to the equally basic economic fact that enterprises essentially finance continued factor purchases from the sale of final products, and thus factor cost changes must ultimately be translated into intermediate and final product prices. However, a number of institutional factors relating to the manner in which wages and prices are set and changed considerably affect the character of the inflationary process.[7]

Duration and Character of Contracts

One important institutional factor affecting the nature of the process is the standard duration and character of negotiated wage contracts, as well as the standard frequency of revision of price lists. Labor contracts in the United States are now typically of 2 or 3 years duration (ordinarily providing wage increases in steps over the life of the contract), and are exceedingly difficult to reopen. The standard frequency of price changes, of course, is typically substantially greater than for wage changes, nor is it as rigidly set as is the case for negotiated wage rates. Still, it has some significant stability. For example, United States automobile prices are ordinarily altered only once a year, although they *can* be changed more frequently and sometimes have been. Steel prices are rarely changed more than two or three times a year—mainly because the price structure is so exceedingly complicated and because large buyers tend to order their requirements for considerable periods ahead. Frequent changes would thus disturb competitive relations both within the steel industry and among customers in steel-using industries. Nevertheless, steel prices *can* be changed more frequently. Annual, or even multiyear, contracts are customary in many industries—between producers and their customers, or with their suppliers of materials and parts—which, in many cases, do not permit interim price adjustments. Public utility rates and other regulated

---

[7] To be sure, in the longer run some of these institutions are themselves gradually altered by the extent and character of inflation or stability. A good example is the historical variation in the use of escalator clauses in United States wage contracts—which has greatly expanded during each recent prevailingly inflationary period, and contracted in periods of relative stability.

prices and the prices of public enterprises are changed only through extremely lengthy processes. At the consumer level, rents are usually set for a year at a time or longer, and there is considerable stickiness in charges for many consumer services. Of course, wages and prices that are only adjusted intermittently often change by fairly substantial "steps," when they do change.

Those engaged in setting wages, and in setting those prices set on the assumption or agreement that they will not be revised for some period ahead, are adjusting wages or prices that were last adjusted some time ago—as long as 3 years earlier in the case of many wage rates. If the price level has been rising, the sellers may need to catch up with the interim rise of the cost of living or of production costs; while the buyers' ability to pay has been increased by their own past or now contemplated price or income increases. If the price level is expected to rise, buyers and sellers may need to and may be prepared at least partially to anticipate it in the prices set today. If the last wage or price determination had reflected some anticipation of changes in the cost of living or production costs, the ensuing inflation may have been greater than expected, so that the new wage or price must both again anticipate future developments but also include a "catch-up" adjustment, thus making a double allowance for inflation. (This is particularly likely to occur in the second or third years of any new inflationary episode.) Even if the allowance for inflation in the previous wage or price had been about "right," taking the contract period as a whole, during most or all of the time since the last change, the nominally fixed wage or price will have been falling behind in real terms. Thus, a catch-up almost always appears, at least to the seller, to be justified, whether it is or not. The upward bias that results is particularly difficult to avoid because the extent of the anticipated inflation that was built into the previous contract is almost never explicitly formulated, and the seller will always claim that it was less than the inflation which has occurred.

Whatever new wages or prices (and further future wage or price increases) are set in the contracts revised today, these, along with all the prices set earlier, will have collectively determined the extent and nature of the inflationary process tomorrow, the next day, and next year. Thus, they will determine the perceptions and responses of those who will then be revising wages and prices.

As noted, the same factors that produce the inertia which makes inflations difficult to stop also makes them difficult to start. The 2- or 3-year stability of labor costs assured by major labor contracts negotiated during the years 1962–1965 and the prices then set in long-term contracts for many basic materials helped to delay and restrain inflation during the excess-demand years of 1966–1968. However, the labor agreements negotiated and contract prices set in the inflationary years 1972–1974 helped to assure the continuance of inflation during the recession and early recovery years of 1974–1976.

Escalator Clauses

To be sure, the relative stability of labor or materials costs provided by long-term contracts negotiated during noninflationary periods is at least potentially compromised if those contracts provide escalator clauses, as a large and increasing number of United States agreements do. Of course, escalator provisions have no impact on wage rates if prices do not rise, but they quickly generalize and perpetuate upward movements of prices that have originated elsewhere.

The full impact of the use of escalator clauses in wage or price contracts is not easy to assess. Although there is some evidence that, in inflationary periods, the basic wage increase included in contracts with escalators tends to be less than in contracts without escalators, it often appears to be less by an amount smaller than a reasonable expectation of future inflation would have called for. Thus, escalator contracts may provide an extra upward bias during inflationary periods. One can imagine that the results would be quite different in an economy in which escalator clauses were universally used, and always provided 100 percent pass through of rising costs of living or costs of production. Then, periodic wage and price determinations might be understood to relate mainly to the sharing between employer and workers, or between supplier and customer, of past and expected productivity gains (or of past and expected gains or losses from shifts in relative supply and demand conditions). Under such circumstances, there would presumably be a great deal less inertia to the inflationary process. The rate of inflation would respond much more readily to changes in aggregate demand; unfortunately, it would also respond much more readily to every external inflationary impulse—such as an increase in import prices, a major crop failure, and so on. And if, as is now the case, most escalator provisions operated only in one direction, temporary bulges in, say, farm prices, would immediately get permanently embedded in the structure of wage costs.

Of course, wage rates, without escalators, respond to rising prices and to changes in the rate of price rise, and prices of goods and services respond in any case to increases in costs of production. However, the response is more nearly complete, and is more prompt and automatic, where escalator provisions are used; whereas, in their absence, it is likely to be partial, delayed, and to require negotiation. Thus, wide-spread use of escalators is sure to make inflation rates more unstable, and it is almost sure to increase the longer-term average rate of inflation.

Where wage agreements are made for an unspecified term, as for example in the United Kingdom, the institutional forces are somewhat different. Such agreements provide little assured stability of labor costs. Whether a new agreement has embodied a large or a small wage increase will only be determined by how long it lasts before it is again revised. To the extent that current economic conditions affect negotiated wage changes, the British agreement can be more responsive than the United States contract: in a less inflationary environment, reopening of the agreement can be delayed; in a more inflationary environment it will be speeded up and the size of the new increase enlarged over the previous one. Because of this, in the inflationary environment, the British system seems to build in a tendency toward double counting of price increases: an early contract reopening that increases the average size of the last wage increase and a large new increase to reflect current and expected conditions.

Use of Wage Comparison

Another important institutional practice, somewhat more difficult to define and assess, is the frequent use of wage comparisons to determine the size of wage increases. Often, in the bargaining between a large employer and a powerful union—the latter usually with some degree of monopoly power, the former with some degree of at least temporary monopsony power—there is no economically determinate outcome for their wage level other than through bargaining ability and bluff or through the ability to survive a strike. In the absence of another way of resolving otherwise irreconcilable claims in bargaining, recourse is frequently had, often quite explicitly, to wage rates recently set (or wage increases recently given) elsewhere in the same or another industry. For small unions and smaller employers, use of the most comparable wage rates in the same labor market is a natural way of determining wage levels and thus wage increases; but that is rather different from the "pattern bargaining" which crosses industrial and geographic boundaries. Of course, where there are no explicit or effective economic pressures on the employer—as in public employment, or public utilities—use of wage comparisons is exceedingly common, sometimes even prescribed by law.

Through the use of wage comparisons, the pattern of wage rates both in and between industries, occupations, and labor markets tends to assume a certain loose institutional structure: every wage rate is more or less closely tied to other wage rates—and rather more rigidly than would emerge merely from competitive market forces (which, of course, do tend to produce uniformity of wages for uniform qualities of labor). This strengthens the inertial force of wage-price stability or of any positive rate of inflation (the "wage-wage spiral").

Moreover, in practice, the institutional process of setting wages by comparison often seems to produce a bias toward faster wage inflation. There seems to be an almost inevitable tendency to ignore wage rates (or wage increases) that are lower and to choose wage models from among employers that pay higher wages (or give larger increases). Even where the process of wage comparisons is most highly formalized and "scientific," for example, for the United States Civil Service, many observers report that the bias is always upward.

Some employers, of course, prefer to have their wage rates always set a bit above the prevailing market level so as to insure (in the face of uncertainty about future demand conditions) that in a tight labor market they will always be able to recruit workers or, in a normal or loose labor market, so that they can always choose the best among numerous job applicants. But unions dealing with employers who have no such preference, by pointing to the higher wage level of the employers who do, seem frequently able to force or persuade their own employers to match the higher wages.

Wage setting by comparison also gives an upward bias to the rate of wage inflation whenever particular groups of workers receive especially large wage increases for microeconomic reasons—whether because of a sharp rise in the demand for their particular services, because they have recently increased their ability to exclude others from entering their trade, simply because their trade union has become more aggressive or effective in its bargaining tactics, or because their particular union leader is trying to achieve notoriety by showing how tough he can be. The king-size wage increases so negotiated seem to create a strong tendency for wages in other, often unrelated, industries and occupations to be similarly raised, especially in periods of moderately high demand for labor.

LONGER-TERM PRESSURES TOWARD INFLATION OR STABILITY

Inertia arising from the character of the wage-price determining process causes any rate of inflation to tend to maintain itself with considerable independence from more basic pressures toward inflation or stability. But these more basic forces will ultimately determine whether the inflationary process speeds up, slows down, disappears (or, possibly, even becomes a deflationary process). Perhaps the most fundamental of these forces is the state of aggregate demand in the economy, and we shall turn back to that in a moment. First, however, we may briefly note that certain factors related to the institutional structure of labor and product markets and to existing social and political arrangements and attitudes may also play a role, sometimes a crucial one, in determining how inflationary any given level of aggregate demand will be.

Institutional, Social, and Political Factors

The nature and structure of labor union organization in a country or in an epoch surely can affect the extent of cost-push pressures toward inflation or stability. Relevant aspects of union organization seem to include, for instance, the extent of centralization of control (for example by top union officers versus by the "rank and file"), the existence of competitive unions with the same or overlapping jurisdictions, organization by craft versus industry, the power and influence of national union federations, union affiliation with political parties that may be in (or out of) the government, and many others.

Systems of centralized national bargaining—such as those in the Netherlands or Sweden—permit, indeed, almost require, that negotiators be conscious of the effect of their negotiated wage increase on the level of prices. Thus, it is a little easier for those on the labor side to recognize that much or all of what workers might appear to gain from an excessive settlement is illusory: whatever extra amount workers may gain in higher wages, beyond some point, will be lost through higher prices. The highly decentralized bargaining practiced in the United States and some other countries, on the other hand, makes the size of any individual settlement essentially irrelevant for the prices the workers involved will pay. Thus, the interest of the negotiators on the labor side in any given wage bargain in getting the largest possible increase in money wages is not appreciably compromised by any consideration of its effects on prices.

The belief that what happens to prices is independent of the size of any, and thus of *every*, wage settlement is also nourished by the myth that, since the wage bargain is in the first instance made between a union and an employer, a wage dispute can only be an argument about the division of the "pie" between wages and profits and not about the division of the "pie" among this group of workers, its employer, and its employer's customers— most of whom are other workers. (This myth may be reinforced by economic doctrines that assert that the level of prices depends on competition, or the level of demand, the money supply, or some other outside force.) That each group of workers believes or at least perpetuates this myth about the effect on prices of its own bargaining is not strange, for it is obviously so comforting and self-serving a doctrine. What is more difficult to understand is how workers often can appear to believe that gains obtained in other workers' bargaining—even those much better paid than themselves—come only from their employers' pockets. Still more difficult to explain is how this myth continues to be unquestioningly accepted—at least in the United States—by many highly educated middle-class "liberals" in the professions, government, the universities, and the information media. But the fact that it is so accepted suggests a still wider set of influences on the process of wage determination.

Many economists have increasingly been recognizing the importance of social and political forces affecting the initiation and perpetuation of inflation. Such explanations seem particularly appropriate with respect to the phenomenon known as a **wage explosion**—a sudden, discontinuous upward thrust of wage rates—experienced in several countries in recent years (first, and perhaps most dramatically, in France in 1968). Most of these explosions seem to lack any clear economic explanation. That in

France, for example, came during a period of prolonged and increasing economic slack. Nor can the similar experiences in Italy and Germany in 1969, and in the United Kingdom in 1970, be explained by demand forces (although it is the writer's view that the wage explosion in Japan in 1973 probably can be so explained).[8] It was with respect to such events that economist Roy W. Harrod declared that the "new wage-price explosion is altogether unprecedented ... the causes [of which] are sociological [and] first cousins to the causes of such things as student unrest."[9] Indeed the French wage explosion was closely associated with a sociopolitical near-insurrection, touched off as students occupied their universities and strikers their factories and as dissident political groups mounted massive demonstrations of social and political protest, much of it aimed at unseating President De Gaulle. The massive wage increases, designed in part to separate the workers from their allies in discontent, were negotiated not by employers but by the government.

Quite apart from wage explosions, wage determination in most major countries takes place in a highly political environment. Public attitudes of sympathy or antagonism toward unions, the public's perception of unions' role in inflation, their tolerance for strikes, picketing, and boycotts, all affect labor's bargaining position—as do the attitudes expressed both publicly and privately to the parties by government officials. This sociopolitical environment can, of course, change; but, like most such attitudes, it is likely to change slowly, to be somewhat responsive to strong (and unresponsive to weak) political leadership, and to reflect any ties—or antipathies—between unions and the political party or forces in control of the government. There are, however, instances in which public or political *opposition* to labor's wage objectives generates a determination to achieve sufficiently extravagant settlements as to bring down a government (or a particular government policy)—as the British miners union brought down a Conservative Government in 1974, as French workers almost did to DeGaulle in 1968 (and contributed significantly to his resignation a year later), or as the New York subway workers and airline machinists did to the U.S. government's "wage guideposts" in 1966. These are instances of the almost explicit use of economic means to achieve political objectives. And even when not so blatant, political influences and attitudes profoundly affect the bargaining climate, and thus the rate of wage increase, much of the time in many countries.

[8] See the exploratory study by William Nordhaus, "The Worldwide Wage Explosion," and subsequent "Discussion," in *Brookings Papers on Economic Activity* 2: 1972, pp. 431–65; and George L. Perry, "Determinants of Wage Inflation Around the World," with "Comments" by Gardner Ackley and William Nordhaus, and "Discussion," in *Brookings Papers on Economic Activity*, 2:1975 403–47; and G. Ackley, "Fiscal, Monetary, and Related Policies," in *Asia's New Giant: How the Japanese Economy Works* (The Brookings Institution, 1976), pp. 153–247.

[9] See "The Issues: Five Views," in R. Hinshaw, ed., *Inflation as a Global Problem* (London, Johns Hopkins Press, 1972), quoted in Parkin, *op. cit.*, p. 742.

The State of Aggregate Demand: Labor Markets

We return now to a subject far more comfortable for the economist to handle: the state of aggregate demand. In most countries and periods, the influence of aggregate demand is probably far more important for the presence or absence and, in the longer run, the speed of inflation than are sociopolitical attitudes or changeable institutional arrangements.

Up to now, we have dealt with the pressure of aggregate demand as measured essentially by the over-all rate of unemployment. However, the rate of unemployment is clearly an imperfect measure because any given level of over-all unemployment can have quite different inflationary implications in terms of relevant supply–demand pressures in labor markets. Perhaps the most basic source of different pressures at a given unemployment rate is the degree of correspondence, or lack of it, between the "structure" or "composition" of the demand for labor, on the one hand, and the structure or composition of the labor force, on the other.

Workers differ with respect to age, sex, intelligence, physical strength and coordination, attitudes, education, specific skills, experience, degree of "attachment" to the labor force, preference for part-time versus full-time work, and in many combinations and permutations of these and other respects. They also reside in particular areas, with limited and lagged accessibility, at rising costs, to more distant places. Employers may, at any given pattern of relative wage rates, seek to hire a different set of worker characteristics and locations than then exists in the labor force, thus implying surpluses of some particular types of labor and shortages of others.

It is clear that perfect correspondence between the composition of labor demand and supply is both impossible to expect and quite unnecessary. For many substitutions or adaptations among categories of workers are easily made. Many of these adaptations require only a short time to be achieved, as untrained or inexperienced workers learn the job and gain experience while doing it, and with only a minor and temporary cost to be shared between employer and worker or assumed by one or the other. Other substitutions or adaptations may impose more significant or more permanent costs and will require some nontemporary, yet still feasible, changes in relative wage rates (or even in relative product prices). Any such changes in relative wages or prices, of course, are likely to produce or to be accompanied by some moderate inflation in the average level of wage rates, for reasons considered earlier. Still other substitutions would require changes in relative wage rates that are feasible only at the cost of a sharp rise in the average wage level; and some are not achievable at all.

Constant changes occur both in the structure of the supply of labor— as the result of changing demography and social patterns and institutions of all kinds; constant changes occur, as well, in the structure of the demand for labor—as the result mainly of evolving technology and the changing composition of final product demand. These continuous changes may in some periods greatly increase the disparity between patterns of labor demand and supply and may thus increase the degree of inflationary pressures at any given level of aggregate demand relative to aggregate supply.[10]

In recent years, at least in the United States, there have been substantial and progressive changes in the composition of the labor force, reflecting partly demographic and partly social changes, mainly in the direction of a substantially larger proportion of the labor force consisting of women and young workers. Among other characteristics, such workers clearly have lower labor force attachment than adult males. They typically enter and leave the force far more frequently and often have periods of unemployment at one or both transition points. They also tend to be less experienced and to have fewer specific skills than adult males, more of them may prefer part-time jobs, and many have lower incentives to work and to seek to improve their qualifications than do adult male "heads of households."

To be sure, there have also been other structural changes in labor *supply*, some of which might be assumed to be associated with improved labor force flexibility and better job performance—for example, a steady rise in the average number of years of education (which is negatively correlated with unemployment rates for any cross section of the labor force), as well as improvements in labor training and information systems, and in interarea labor mobility. One could argue that these changes should have improved the overall supply-demand balance. In any case, however, it is difficult to characterize or to measure the speed and extent of changes in the structure of job *demand*, although we know it too has been changing steadily and rapidly and perhaps in ways that have created steadily larger imbalances between the composition of labor supply and of demand.

United States data are at least roughly consistent with the now widely accepted hypothesis that recent trends in United States male-female and adult-teenager proportions of the labor supply have been associated with a net worsening of the labor-market compositional imbalance, such that whatever upward pressure on the average wage rate was exerted in the mid-1960s by a 4 percent overall unemployment rate was in the mid-1970s exerted by a $4\frac{3}{4}$ percent or even 5 percent unemployment rate.[11] It is implicit in this conclusion that whatever improvements have occurred in other aspects of labor supply have not been sufficient to offset the com-

---

[10] Note that we are here referring to systematic, trend-type changes in the composition of supply and demand—not the mere stochastic rearrangements that account for the fact that the rate of change in (and not just the level of) average wage rates is related to the aggregate supply–demand balance. We continue to assume stochastic disturbance as well, so that internal or structural equilibrium is never established.

[11] It has been noted earlier that the Council of Economic Advisers (of the outgoing Ford Administration) estimated in January 1977 that the rate corresponding to 4 percent in 1965 was 4.9 percent in 1977.

bined effects of demographic and social changes affecting the proportions of women and young workers in the labor supply, given the progressive changes in the composition of labor demand.[12]

A second set of factors that might alter the impact on the price level of any given aggregate labor-market supply–demand balance could arise from changes in the availability and level of financial support to unemployed workers from unemployment insurance and welfare systems. Changes in the direction of more extended coverage and higher levels of support (relative to average job earnings) suggest, although only impressionistically, that these factors, too, may have contributed in the United States and perhaps other countries to a greater inflationary impact from any given level of reported unemployment.[13]

It might be noted that both the demographic-social changes and the more liberal support systems might be expected also to have contributed to a lesser degree of pressure on government to maintain constant high employment through active use of fiscal and monetary policy. (On the other hand, increased social sympathy and concern for the particular social and racial groups always hardest hit by unemployment could have partially neutralized the influence just cited.) In any case, numerous competent observers have expressed surprise at the extent of public tolerance of, and relative absence of sociopolitical protest against 40-year-record-high levels of unemployment during 1974–1976.

Aggregate Demand: Product Markets

In considering the longer run impact on the inflation rate of movements in the level of aggregate demand in product markets, it is necessary to divide such markets into at least two major categories: administered-price markets and flexible-price-markets—the latter relevant mainly for certain raw materials, including most agricultural products. In administered-price markets, the basic response of firms to a change in the level of market demand is simply to alter the volume of production; hence, also, to alter the level of orders for purchased materials and services, the hours of employment offered, and (possibly) the rate of investment in new plant and equipment and in inventories ("acceleration principle"). If supplies of purchased materials and services and capital goods are also purchased in administered-price markets, the prices of these purchases will not change with an alteration in their volume. Thus, a change in aggregate demand will, in the first instance, mainly affect real and nominal GNP, in essentially

[12] The first and most important study was by George L. Perry, "Changing Labor Markets and Inflation," *Brookings Papers on Economic Activity* 3: 1970, 411–41.

[13] See Martin Feldstein, "Unemployment Compensation: Adverse Incentives and Distributional Anomalies," *National Tax Journal*, 27 (June 1974) 231–44; and Stephen T. Marston, "The Impact of Unemployment Insurance on Job Search," *Brookings Papers on Economic Activity* 1: 1975, 13–60.

equal proportions, employment, and real and nominal incomes (although disposable income less than national income because of the effects on taxes, transfers, and undistributed profits). Changes in productivity associated with changes in the rate of capacity utilization will, of course, somewhat affect the level of costs. And some of these cost changes may affect selling prices and thus the general price level. However, the macroeconomic evidence, and some scattered microeconomic evidence, strongly suggests that productivity changes associated with short-run changes in the level of production are mainly absorbed by changes in profits and are not passed along in changes of selling prices.

On the other hand, if changes in the volume of economic activity in the administered-price sectors should affect the prices of raw materials (or other products) sold in flexible-price markets or the level of wage rates (because the economy is relatively close to full employment), these changes in cost are almost invariably passed along in altered administered prices. (Also, of course, if materials prices or wage rates change exogenously for whatever reason, or if indirect taxes are altered, or if the prices of imported materials rise or fall, the price level will be affected.) Because administered prices are not changed continuously, cost increases or decreases are not passed along at once. After an interval, however, the general price level will begin to reflect these higher or lower costs.

This much of the description of how prices change in administered price sectors is now widely accepted by economists (with minor embellishments or qualifications). What is not fully agreed is whether, or to what extent, the average "markup" over costs, used in determining administered prices, also tends systematically to widen or to shrink with increases or decreases in the level of economic activity. Some empirical studies do find such variation to be significant; others fail to do so. If average markups rise and fall with volume, it may reflect changes in what we earlier called "market power" associated with alterations in the volume of unused productive capacity. Or it could merely reflect changes in the mix of products produced, associated with changes in the level of output, or still other influences.[14]

In contrast, the response of prices in flexible-price markets for goods and services to an increase or decrease in aggregate demand is likely to be substantial and immediate. Supplies of such products tend to be quite inelastic in the short run because of the substantial time lapse between production decisions and the emergence of output (for example, most crop products are on annual cycles; some, such as animal or tree crops, on even longer cycles) and because direct costs tend to be relatively small. Short-run supply curves are thus steep, and prices quite responsive to changes in demand.

[14] Increases of aggregate output normally involve a rise in the proportion of durable goods, and gross markups in durable goods pricing probably are considerably wider than in nondurables.

On the other hand, many such products—especially but not exclusively the agricultural ones—are subject to random supply shifts reflecting weather, political disturbance to production or marketing, or longer term cycles in invested capital, which tend to generate price instability for these products even with stability in aggregate demand. Thus, price level instability may originate in the flexible-price markets quite independently of changes in aggregate demand. Given the response of wage rates, through cost-of-living escalators of otherwise, substantial fluctuations (especially upward) of flexible-price products tend to be generalized, expanded, and prolonged over time through the spiral inter- actions in the administered-price sectors, and thus are not fully reversible when the flexible prices later decline.

One other aspect of the flexible price markets is, however, also important. Because most of these products are (a) highly durable, (b) relatively easily stored, and (c) their production is often seasonal or otherwise irregular over time, inventories of these products tend to be high relative to annual production rates. Because most of these products are traded in near-perfect markets, such inventories are excellent vehicles for speculation—by producers, users, middlemen, and professional traders. This speculation ordinarily tends to be stabilizing, as stocks are absorbed into or released from inventories as supplies rise or fall relative to demand. Thus, ordinary fluctuations in aggregate demand, of an expected duration of no more than a year or two, may be substantially absorbed by inventory changes with only modest changes in price level. On the other hand, once market price levels begin to press too long or hard against established concepts of the "normal" range of price variation, discontinuous changes in expectations may occur and commodity prices may embark on extreme and exaggerated swings as speculators attempt to profit or to avoid loss by unloading or acquiring inventories. Given the bias toward inflation in the administered sectors, upward displacements of the commodity price level have more permanent effects than downward ones. (The reader may wish to look again at the discussion of "speculation" in Chapter 9.)[15]

The Feedback from Inflation to Aggregate Demand

This section is intended only as another reminder to the reader that, throughout Chapters 13 and 14, the level of aggregate demand has been taken as given. Although we have dealt extensively with the implications for the price level of different (or of changing) levels of aggregate demand (relative to potential output), we have either explicitly or implicitly taken the level of aggregate demand in turn to be unaffected by the inflation (or price stability) which that level of demand might generate.

[15] For an early, and considerably fuller discussion, of many of the points made in this and the previous section, see G. Ackley, "Administered Prices and the Inflationary Process," *American Economic Review*, 49 (May, 1959), 419–20.

Here we remind ourselves that such a feedback exists and that it is important. Although it is exactly the mirror image of the feedback from deflation to aggregate demand, the feedback from inflation is a lot more important simply because inflation is a far more pervasive and extensive phenomenon than is deflation. Although a 10 percent cumulative deflation of the price level would be almost unthinkable and has not occurred since the Great Depression, cumulative inflation of more than 10 percent has recently occurred in a single year in almost every country, often in several successive years. In the United States, the cumulative increase of the price level between 1945 and 1975, as measured by the GNP deflator, was 194 percent (that is, 1975's price level was 2.94 times that of 1945). Almost every other major market economy experienced a considerably greater inflation over those same 30 years.

Automatic feedbacks from inflation to aggregate demand—through interest rate effects (with M unchanged), wealth effects (both with or without M unchanged), international trade effects, and fiscal effects of inflation—can thus be exceedingly important, either in a single year or over any relatively short period of years. All of these impacts of inflation on aggregate demand are negative.

Thus, inflation will usually ultimately "burn itself out" by reducing the level of aggregate demand, if allowed to proceed long and far enough without policy intervention (that is, without supplying more money or lowering tax rates). This is, however, about as useful a conclusion as is the corresponding conclusion about deflation inevitably producing full employment. For the evidence accumulates (as will be briefly reviewed in Chapter 15) that, once an inflation is underway, its control either through an active policy of monetary or fiscal restraint (*reducing M, raising* taxes), or through letting inflation burn itself out (in the presence of *unchanged* policy settings) may well involve economic and social costs that society is simply unwilling to pay. For, given inflation's inertial force, the level of unemployment and lost production that would be necessary immediately and completely to suppress an inflation which had reached the rate of 25 percent a year, or even 6 percent a year, is probably something no government (or independent central bank) could possibly contemplate.

Still, in theory, both possibilities are important. And, in practice, the feedbacks from inflation to aggregate demand are sufficiently important that they must be taken into account in whatever policy is adopted to control inflation, or to influence employment and output in the face of inflation.

THE STATE OF INFLATION THEORY

It should be obvious to the reader that inflation theory has come a long way from the simple quantity theory of money of the classical economists or

Wicksell, from the Keynesian "inflationary gap" analysis of the 1940s, and even from the simple Phillips curve of the 1960s. To be sure, reference has here been made only to a small fraction of recent economic literature on the subject and to only a few of the specific hypotheses advanced. But it should be clear that inflation is now recognized, at least by many economists, as an exceedingly complex process, involving numerous elements of economic organization and structure, social and political institutions and attitudes, along with levels (and composition) of aggregate supply and demand.

Two major developments in (or perhaps merely implications of) much recent inflation analysis have here been particularly stressed. The first is the recognition of inflation as a "process with a life of its own"—or, if one prefers, a process "with a significant element of inertia." Once underway, any rate of inflation (including that of zero) has a strong tendency to perpetuate itself.[16] The second element stressed here has been the proposition (contrary to the approaches of Lipsey, Phelps, Friedman, and others) that, although inflation might well occur in a purely competitive economy with perfect flexibility of all wages and prices, the nature of actual inflation in the modern economy is closely tied to the nature and functioning of the administrative processes through which almost all wages and the majority of all prices are set.

What has been most neglected in this summary has been the vital question of why and how "administered pricing" has developed in the modern economy—what needs it serves, what advantages it has. A brilliant start on this analysis has recently been made by Arthur Okun—which would have required too much space to have been adequately summarized here.[17]

In recognizing the crucial importance of institutional elements associated with "administered pricing," this emphasis has merely extended a point of view already developed in earlier chapters. In analyzing and contrasting Keynesian and classical models of income and output determination, we pointed out that the essential difference between classical and Keynesian models stems from the implicit or explicit rejection by Keynesians of the classical assumption that price changes occur instantaneously

---

[16] This vision of "inflation as process" is one that this writer has pressed for a long time, in opposition to much of the earlier analysis of economists. In 1958, he wrote: "Too much of our thinking about inflation has concentrated on how it starts rather than how it proceeds. Inflation might start from an initial 'autonomous' increase in either business or labor markups. Or it might start from an increase in aggregate demand which first and most directly affected some of the flexible, market-determined prices. But, however it starts, the process involves both demand and markup elements." ("A Third Approach to the Analysis and Control of Inflation," *The Relationship of Prices to Economic Stability and Growth*, Compendium of Papers Submitted by Panelists Appearing before the Joint Economic Committee, March 31, 1958, pp. 630–31.)

[17] "Inflation: Its Mechanics and Welfare Costs," *Brookings Papers on Economic Activity* 2: 1975, pp. 351–401.

in response to demand changes—or at least occur sooner than the dis-equilibrium adjustment of quantities. Thus, the quantity adjustments take place instead of price adjustments in a state that might be regarded as disequilibrium but does not appear to be. For the quantity adjustments obscure the disequilibrium character of the results and eliminate the pressure for price changes, by eliminating excess supply or demand (other than in the labor market). It is this absence of perfect price flexibility that fundamentally accounts for involuntary unemployment, and associated gaps between actual and potential output. *This* is why fluctuations in aggregate demand, or changes in monetary or fiscal policy, affect mainly output and not the price level. *This* is what accounts for the crucial importance of the Keynesian consumption function (which plays only a trivial role in an otherwise classical model).

And now we have seen that this same absence of flexible, market-clearing prices (except in a few sectors) determines, as well, the character of inflation in the modern economy: how it is affected by changes in aggregate demand, and why and how it develops its spiral character, and its self-maintaining inertia. And, as will be shown in Chapter 15, this also has implications for the welfare costs of inflation, and for the policies chosen to deal with it.

REVIEW QUESTIONS

1. "During the decade of the 1960s, the Phillips curve tended to monopolize the attention of most economists concerned with the problem of inflation."
(a) What facts supported this attention?
(b) Why did the simple Phillips curve lose favor after the end of the 1960s?
(c) Most efforts to rescue the Phillips curve involved distinguishing short-run and long-run curves, the latter embodying some form of "feedback" of previous rates of inflation on the current rate. Explain some alternative forms of this feedback.
2. Assume that the following model appropriately describes the wage and price adjustment behavior of an economy:

(1) $$\dot{W}_t = a_0 + a_1 \frac{1}{U_t} + a_2 \dot{P}_{t-1}$$

(2) $$\dot{P}_t = b(\dot{W}_t - X)$$

where all notations are as used in this chapter.
(a) Briefly explain the theory that might lie behind equation (1).
(b) What range of values for a_2 and for b are most likely to prevail in the real world, and why do you think so?
(c) Derive both short-run and long-run Phillips curves. Show why the long-run Phillips curve is steeper than the short-run except in a special case. What is the special case? Interpret the special case in words.
(d) Under what condition does the long-run Phillips curve become vertical?

(e) Find the noninflationary level of the unemployment rate for the model.

(f) Given a fixed quantity of money, and investment dependent on the rate of interest, what is the long-run equilibrium rate of inflation given the above wage–price model?

3. "The natural rate of unemployment hypothesis implies that both monetary and fiscal policies are ineffective even in the short run when people's expectations are rational, whereas with adaptive expectations both policies are effective at least in the short run." Evaluate thoroughly.

4. What is the phenomenon of "wage explosion," and how have such explosions been explained? What do they imply for inflation theory and for inflation policy?

5. What are some of the "institutional aspects" of labor markets that seem to contribute to an inflationary bias in most modern economies?

6. "Escalator clauses do not cause inflation, because they only operate when prices are rising." Evaluate.

7. Explain how one might take a view that inflation may very well begin in "flexible-price" markets for goods and services but is perpetuated through the "administered-price" markets.

SELECTED REFERENCES

D. Laidler and M. Parkin, "Inflation: A Survey," *Economic Journal*, 85 (December 1975), 741–809; and R. J. Gordon, "Recent Developments in the Theory of Inflation and Unemployment," *Journal of Monetary Economics*, 2 (April 1976), 185–219.

(Admirable but demanding surveys of the recent literature on inflation theory.)

M. Friedman, "The Role of Monetary Policy," *American Economic Review*, 58 (March 1968), 1–17, reprinted in W. L. Smith and R. L. Teigen (eds.), *Readings in Money, National Income and Stabilization Policy* (R. D. Irwin, 3rd ed., 1974), pp. 412–421; and in E. Shapiro (ed.), *Macroeconomics: Selected Readings* (Harcourt, Brace, and World, 1970), pp. 488–524.

M. Friedman, "A Theoretical Framework for Monetary Analysis," *Journal of Political Economy*, 78 (March/April 1970), 193–238.

(Groundwork of Friedman's expectational model.)

J. Tobin, "Friedman's Theoretical Framework," *Journal of Political Economy*, 80 (September/October 1972), 852–863.

(Critical review of Friedman's theoretical basis.)

W. Nordhaus, "The Worldwide Wage Explosion," *Brookings Papers on Economic Activity*, 2: 1972, pp. 431–465.

(An introduction to the "wage-explosion" phenomenon.)

G. L. Perry, "Determinants of Wage Inflation Around the World," *Brookings Papers on Economic Activity*, 2: 1975, pp. 403–447.

(An attempt to test empirically alternative theories of wage inflation using data from ten countries.)

M. N. Baily, "Contract Theory and the Moderation of Inflation by Recession and by Controls," *Brookings Papers on Economic Activity*, 3: 1976, pp. 585–634.

(A sophisticated analysis of the influence wage contracts on wage flexibility.)

R. Flanagan, "Wage Interdependence in Unionized Labor Markets," *Brookings Papers on Economic Activity*, 3: 1976, pp. 635–682.
Economic Activity, 3: 1970, pp. 411–441.

G. L. Perry, "Changing Labor Markets and Inflation," *Brookings Papers on Economic Activity*, 3: 1970, pp. 411–441.
(One of the first and most important empirical studies of structural changes in labor markets as affecting the inflationary threshold.)

M. Feldstein, "Unemployment Compensation: Adverse Incentives and Distributional Anomalies," *National Tax Journal*, 27 (June 1974).

S. T. Marston, "The Impact of Unemployment Insurance on Job Search," *Brookings Papers on Economic Activity*, 1: 1975, pp. 13–60.
(Two papers on the effect of unemployment insurance on the inflationary threshold.)

A. Okun, "Inflation: Its Mechanics and Welfare Costs," *Brookings Papers on Economic Activity*, 2: 1975, pp. 351–401.
(An important paper analyzing the theoretical basis for administered-price inflation.)

R. J. Gordon, "Can the Inflation of the 1970s Be Explained?" *Brookings Papers on Economic Activity*, 1: 1977, pp. 153–279.
(One of the leading proponents of the "extended Phillips curve" approach testing his pre-1971 empirical models against the subsequent experience.)

R. J. Gordon, "The Theory of Domestic Inflation," *American Economic Review*, 76 (February 1977), 128–134.
(The same author's brief and brilliant attempt to summarize current inflation theory.)

Chapter 15

Empirical and Policy Aspects of Inflation

Why Inflation Has Accelerated

The Costs of Inflation
Income redistributions from inflation
Inflation and the distribution of wealth
Effects of accounting and taxes
Expected and unexpected inflation
Effects on aggregate production and efficiency

Inflation and Interest Rates

Policies against Inflation
Demand management policies
Policies to "shift the Phillips Curve"
Altering inflationary institutions
Building a counterforce against inflation

As recently as 1971, it was still possible to reserve final judgment on the question whether there had developed a world-wide trend toward faster inflation during the post World War II period. There were enough special explanations available for events in particular countries and enough examples of countries in which inflation had either slowed or not clearly accelerated to qualify or question the implications of global averages that pointed toward the acceleration diagnosis.

The first three columns of Table 15-1 are taken from a study made by this writer in early 1971;[1] they show a faster inflation in 1965–1970 than in the previous decade. However, considered along with other, more detailed evidence, these data then failed to support a clear judgment that inflation was accelerating. The new fourth column, however, leaves no doubt of a near-universal acceleration; more inclusive evidence further supports the conclusion. To be sure, the price explosion of 1973 and 1974, which brought "double-digit" inflation to almost every country, had special causes, perhaps not likely to be repeated. But even in the recession or weak-recovery year, 1975 to 1976, inflation rates remained well above earlier averages, especially when compared with previous recession periods.

Other studies show that some aspects of this acceleration of inflation have been regular and progressive. For example, a recent study by Phillip Cagan[2] shows that there has been a progressive pattern of change in United States price behavior during recessions, beginning with the end of

[1] With minor corrections for subsequent data revisions. The study was *Stemming World Inflation* (The Atlantic Institute, Paris, 1971).
[2] "Changes in the Recession Behavior of Wholesale Prices in the 1920's and Post World War II," *Explorations in Economic Research*, 2 (Winter 1975) 54–104). See also his *The Hydra-Headed Monster: The Problem of Inflation in the United States* (American Enterprise Institute, 1974).

TABLE 15-1
Price Changes in Major Countries, 1955–1976, as Measured by GNP Deflators

	Average annual percentage increase						Cumulative percentage increase, 1955–75
	1955–60	1960–65	1965–70	1970–75	1976	1955–75	
Germany	2.7	3.6	3.4	6.9	3.0	4.1	125.0
France	6.5	4.2	4.6	8.7	9.6	6.0	219.8
Italy	2.0	5.8	7.4	11.8	17.8	6.7	265.3
United Kingdom	3.2	3.5	5.0	12.9	15.6	6.1	225.4
Canada	2.6	1.9	4.1	8.4	9.5	4.2	128.6
United States	2.6	1.6	4.2	6.9	5.1	3.8	111.1
Japan	3.3	5.1	5.1	9.6	6.4	5.8	205.9
Average, seven countries*	3.0	2.7	4.5	8.1	6.9	4.5	147.7

* Weighted by 1970 GNP at 1970 exchange rates.
** Increase from 1975; preliminary data, from *OECD Economic Outlook*, 21 (July, 1977).

World War II, and moving progressively from appreciable price decline, to substantial stability, to appreciable increase.

WHY INFLATION HAS ACCELERATED

Since it now seems clear that a progressive and nearly universal acceleration of inflation characterizes the last three decades, it becomes important to ask what wide-spread and progressive changes may have occurred to bring this about. There is no single, widely agreed answer.

For monetarists, the answer lies in a progressively looser, more inflationary management of money supply in some or most countries, with the excessive money creation of the "least responsible" ones spilling over (through international monetary mechanisms that we shall not describe) to countries that tried to maintain a more responsible monetary management. There is no doubt that the rate of increase of the world's money stock has accelerated. But most non monetarists will say that this increase was mostly the by-product of the breakdown of the Bretton-Woods system of fixed exchange rates, and, in any case, mainly *effect*, not *cause*, of an inflation that monetary policy could never have prevented—even through a measure of restrictiveness that would in most countries have proved socially and politically intolerable.

Others, who may share the monetarists' view that the inflation has been, basically, the result of "excessive demand", will nevertheless put the case quite differently. They will argue that powerful social and political groups in many countries, not adequately disciplined—perhaps because of a decay in the quality of intellectual and political leadership—have become progressively less tolerant of unemployment, and steadily more insistent on a continuous growth of incomes, and at a rate beyond the capacity of their economies to support; this social and political pressure to obtain impossible objectives has generated fiscal policies, and supporting monetary policies, that have proved too expansionary, too much of the time.

Other observers are more sympathetic with the evolution of social goals toward greater emphasis on full employment and steadily growing *per capita* incomes; they are likely to celebrate rather than to deplore the new "activism" of government policies, which they see as produced or encouraged by a more modern and "correct" economic analysis that has liberated policy makers from obsolete and meaningless shibboleths. Yet they may basically agree with the previous groups in recognizing that the increasing tendency to inflation is a by-product of a *higher average degree of pressure on economic resources*,[3] which has, however, also produced higher and more rapidly growing real incomes, and, on balance, has been highly rewarding.

However, the case supporting any of these three diagnoses is far from obvious; for, although it is clear that the average rate of utilization of labor and capital resources in the post-war period is appreciably higher than in the prewar era, it is not easy to substantiate a case that utilization rates everywhere, or on the average, have progressively expanded since 1950 (or 1955). If such a case is to be made, it must rest, in many countries, on an interpretation that notes that the usual simple measures of resource utilization fail to take account of progressive changes in the "quality" of the labor force or capital stock,[4] and holds that there is evidence that such changes have appeared in a number of countries.[5]

Still other economists argue that, whether or not there has been a progressive increase in pressures of aggregate demand in some or many countries, this is only part of a much broader set of changes that have occurred, and perhaps are still occurring, a number of which contribute to the explanation of the acceleration of inflation. Consistent with his own more eclectic view of the inflation process, presented in Chapter 14, this writer is inclined to view the acceleration of inflation as a far more complex phenomenon, and one not solely dependent on any trend toward higher pressures of demand on capacity—which may (or may not) have occurred.

---

[3] Along with some admitted, and perhaps understandable mistakes of economic diagnosis or policy formulation on the expansionary side, as well as some special circumstances affecting the supplies of food and energy in the 1970s.

[4] For example, for the United States, the thesis pioneered by George Perry, explained in Chapter 14.

[5] In his study, "Determinants of Wage Inflation around the World," *Brookings Papers on Economic Activity*, 2:1975, 407–47, Perry found the statistical evidence compatible with this hypothesis for a number of the countries studied.

He would argue that the acceleration of inflation reflects the presence in many, if not all, countries of somewhat similar progressive changes in economic ideas, policies, and roles; in institutions, attitudes, and aspirations; in procedures, practices, and styles of leadership in labor, business, and government; in information, knowledge, and experience. Among these changes, this writer has, on occasion, listed some or all of the following, for most of which he could provide at best very subjective and impressionistic evidence.

1. The increasing acceptance of the idea that steadily rising real incomes are not only theoretically possible but achievable.
2. The increasing acceptance of "full employment" as an appropriate goal of government fiscal, monetary, and other policies.
3. The decay of conventional and sometimes irrational fears of the consequences of deficits both in government budgets and in a country's balance of payments.
4. The progressive shift from almost completely fixed to almost universally variable exchange rates, which largely removed pressures on governments to reduce or avoid inflation in order to protect international reserves.
5. In many countries, a rise in government expenditures as a share of GNP, and increases in taxes, often price-raising indirect taxes, to finance them.
6. The increasing recognition that members of every group in society are entitled to protection from adverse economic developments, and previously disadvantaged groups to a larger share in general prosperity, a recognition which both encourages and tolerates increasingly aggressive collective action, economic and political, by such groups to achieve these goals; perhaps an increasing truculence by all groups in demanding and defending their "rights".
7. An increase in the proportion of all prices that are set in large corporations, by essentially bureaucratic methods which make prices respond mainly to changes in unit costs; perhaps an increasing recourse to mechanical rules of thumb, and especially to income or price formulas or comparisons, to avoid or resolve business and labor disputes.
8. An increasing volume of statistical information and an increasing awareness of, and ability to use such information to measure changes in the relative economic position of individuals and groups.
9. An increasing experience with inflation, which makes people both more conscious of inflation in the present and more likely to expect it in the future.

Several of these changes tend to assure high levels of aggregate demand most of the time, which means that policy mistakes will more often be in the direction of excessive than of deficient demand. Other changes have reduced downward flexibility of wages and prices in markets where and in periods when there is excess supply. Several changes have weakened resistance to efforts to raise incomes by raising costs and prices. And some changes have produced rising costs of government which taxpayers seek to pass on to others by raising wages or prices.

Perhaps most important, these changes have led to actions, public and private, that inevitably *exaggerate and prolong* the impacts on the price level of temporary and accidental inflationary events, including, of course, policy mistakes. Thus, there are fewer periods of price stability or slow inflation; thus, new inflationary impulses are more likely than before to build on an already rising price level, producing a tendency for cumulative acceleration of inflation.

THE COSTS OF INFLATION

We are concerned in this section with the costs of inflation, *per se*. That is, we are not attempting to consider the net balance of costs and benefits stemming from an inflation itself *plus* the benefits (or costs) of whatever conditions may have "caused" the inflation or are associated with it. To be sure, in considering policies to deal with inflation we obviously need to consider the net balance of benefits from reducing inflation with the costs of the policies proposed. Here, however, we are concerned only with the costs of inflation—that is, the benefits from reducing it.

It seems clear that the general public typically has a mistaken or exaggerated view of the costs of a moderate inflation. The popular view is that inflation impoverishes everyone: a dollar (or yen or lira or mark) buys less when prices rise; therefore, we all have less. What this view misses is the fairly obvious fact that the inflation which raises the prices people pay also inevitably raises the money incomes people receive—they receive *more* dollars, yen, lire, or marks. This has to be so because for every buyer there is a seller; when a buyer pays more some seller receives more. Since almost everyone is both buyer and seller, and in the aggregate, purchases and sales are identical in amount, it has to be true that, if *some* lose— because the prices which *they* pay rise on the average by more than the prices which *they* receive—*other* individuals or groups must equivalently benefit. Thus, on the average, real income is not altered by inflation. This generalization is to be qualified only by the recognition that there are many international transactions, which means that the individuals or groups benefited and hurt may be in different countries; and that there are transactions between the private sector and government, in which the government may be gainer or loser relative to the private sector. Since the government-related effects are quite important, we will reserve their discussion to a separate subsection and abstract from them in the prior discussion.

Thus, ignoring international and (for the present) governmental transactions, inflation may *redistribute* real income, as well as real wealth, within the private sector, but it does not automatically reduce it. Only as it is shown that inflation somehow affects the real volume of aggregate production and thus the real incomes arising from that production can we find an effect of inflation on aggregate real income. There are, indeed, some effects of inflation on total production and real wealth. But, before considering them, we need to deal with the effects of inflation on the *distribution* of income and wealth.

Income Redistributions from Inflation

It is clear that, during particular historical periods of inflation, *relative prices* have changed in such a way as to alter the distribution of real income between wages and profits, between individuals with higher versus those with lower incomes, between urban and rural groups, between salaried workers and wage earners, between organized and unorganized workers, or between other such categories. But changes in income distribution also occur in periods of a stable price level, as relative prices change even though the average of all prices does not. Is there any reason to expect systematic changes in *relative* prices to occur *as the result* of a change in *average* prices? If so, what particular kinds of relative price changes? Is there any empirical evidence that this happens? That is, does inflation, *per se*, systematically redistribute income?

The answer is that, taking broad groups such as those referred to in the preceding paragraph, there is almost no theoretical reason to expect such redistributions to occur on any large scale and very little empirical evidence that they do occur. To be sure, in some inflationary periods, wages have risen faster than profits, but in others the reverse is true; in some periods real farm incomes have risen relative to urban incomes, in others the reverse. It used to be believed that real salaries—and, in particular, public salaries—lagged behind real wages during inflations; but, at least recently, this seems not to have occurred.

In general, inflation does not seem clearly to favor property incomes over labor incomes or the reverse. However, *within* the property incomes, interest incomes tend to lag behind profit-type incomes, mainly because most interest incomes are set by long-term contract— and because many short-term interest rates, especially those on deposits, are subject to inflexible government ceilings. To be sure, dividend rates for stockholders also tend to be sticky in nominal terms but this is counterbalanced by higher retained earnings, which tend to raise stock values. And, to the extent that corporations tend to be long-term debtors at contractually fixed interest rates, the equity owners of corporations receive the benefit of whatever bondholders may lose from inflation.

One type of income distribution that is of special interest is that by age groups, particularly that between the retired and the still active. By definition, most income of the retired consists of property income or transfer payments. However, within the retired population, different types of property and transfer incomes are received in quite different proportions; and these several types of income respond differently to inflation. Also, many retired persons are dissaving, consuming their wealth, which mixes up the effects of inflation on income with its effects on wealth. Members of one group, which tends to include many of the higher income and wealthier retired persons (though it is not confined to the well-off), receive most of their income directly or indirectly from interest payments fixed by long-term contracts, either directly from portfolios of bonds or from annuities, insurance policies, trust funds, or similar arrangements, the principal of which is mainly invested in bonds. Bond income clearly is eroded by inflation. The receipt of many such incomes is combined with some element of dissaving—the simultaneous gradual withdrawal of the principal sum; being fixed in nominal value, this wealth also is eroded by inflation.

Such people are, clearly, seriously hurt by inflation. Since well-off persons, retired or approaching retirement, tend to have substantial social and political influence, they provide much of the political pressure on governments to avoid or to curb inflation.

Another category of retirement income is based on property income from stock ownership and/or real estate—also often combined with gradual capital consumption. Many well-off retired persons directly own portfolios of stocks. And the private pension funds provided by corporations for the benefit of their retired executives and workers are largely invested in stocks, of which both income and capital value are far more responsive to price level changes. Such pension funds will be providing an increasingly important share of all retirement incomes in the future; their beneficiaries are and will be less concerned about inflation.

Finally, there is the Social Security System, and other transfer payments to older persons. Almost from the beginning of the system, United States social security benefits (for any given duration and scale of contributions) have risen considerably faster than the price level—both through legislative adjustments of benefit scales and, in recent years, through an automatic cost-of-living escalator. Thus, the retired who are primarily dependent on social security—usually lower income people—are not seriously disadvantaged by inflation.[6]

[6] The view of the (U.S.) Social Security System reflected here sees it basically as a system for current transfers from the active population, paying a tax (which reflects any inflation of its incomes) to support the currently retired, at incomes that can thereby also reflect the inflation. One can take another view of the system—which is the legal and traditional view—as a state-administered private pension fund. Workers (and their employers) pay into this fund during each worker's active years, building up a capital sum that is invested in government bonds and which, together with interest earned on the capital, is then distributed over the worker's retirement years. Under this conception, the participants must receive less real income and consumption of capital in an inflationary period than if there were no inflation. For many reasons, the first conception seems more realistic.

Inflation and the Distribution of Wealth

In earlier chapters we have already discussed the effect of inflation on the aggregate of real wealth under the heading of the "Pigou effect." Since all private financial wealth in the form of private debts or equities fully cancels out against the corresponding private liabilities, aggregate wealth consists only of the value of the stocks of real goods, government debt, and government money (bank money is both a private asset and a private liability). The money value of physical property tends to move closely with the price level of newly produced goods, and its real value is thus little affected by inflation. But inflation does shrink the real value of government debt and money.

However, in considering the effects of inflation on the *distribution* of wealth, the private debts and equities clearly do not cancel out, and, indeed, dominate the effects of inflation on wealth distribution. Private debtors obviously gain through inflation; the creditors (whether of private or governmental debtors) correspondingly lose. These include the private debtors to and creditors of the many kinds and layers of financial inter-mediaries.

The principal classes of private debtors in American society are (1) home-buyers, carrying a massive aggregate mortgage debt, and (2) the beneficial owners of businesses of all kinds. Both groups benefit from inflation in the proportion that the value of their *physical* assets exceeds their *equity* (their total assets, physical and financial, less their debts). Since houses often constitute a substantial share of the wealth of younger middle-income families, who often have large mortgages and thus a small equity, an important fraction of the younger middle income group proba-bly benefits—at least on wealth account—from inflation. The beneficial owners of most businesses are, of course, the stockholders, who include financial institutions, especially mutual funds and pension funds, and (ty-pically high-income) individuals. These owners should benefit from inflation on wealth account as well as income account, even though stock prices, which presumably measure the value of their wealth, are often slow to reflect inflation and are substantially affected by other factors.[7]

Owners of fixed-income, fixed-principal assets, including money balances (where the income is fixed at zero) clearly lose from inflation to the extent of their ownership. These fixed-income, fixed-principal assets include most of the liabilities of financial institutions as well as the direct debts of businesses. Although most financial intermediaries (other than perhaps pension funds) might benefit from the fixity of the money value of their obligations, their assets, too, are mainly of the fixed-principal, fixed-

---

[7] The long recent debate in the popular and business press about whether inflation raises stock prices mainly proves that inflation is only one of many determinants of changes in stock prices. The fact that stock prices can change drastically even in the absence of price level changes can hardly be denied.

income variety, which rules out much net benefit. To be sure, the assets of *banks* are mostly *short-term* loans and securities, so that, as one set of assets is rapidly replaced by another, the banks at least benefit from the higher interest rates that accompany inflation (see next major section). Moreover, although many of the liabilities of financial institutions are also short-term, or even payable on demand, government ceilings prevent or greatly delay increases in interest rates paid on many of these short-term liabilities. To be sure, such ceilings often result in the occurrence of "disintermediation" during inflations, as deposit holders withdraw their noninterest bearing or controlled-interest funds in order to buy obligations whose interest rates are free of control. However, there are limits to the extent to which most holders of deposits can economize on them; also many small holders cannot or do not know how to invest in other interest-bearing securities.

Savings and loan institutions and mutual savings banks are hardest hit both by the fixity of their incomes during an inflation and the loss of their share accounts and deposits. They mainly own long-term, fixed-interest mortgages; and their short-term liabilities are interest-regulated. The latter regulation does them little good when deposit funds are withdrawn, and they are forced to sell their mortgages at prices reduced to reflect the rise in open-market interest rates in order to find the funds to pay off their depositors. Insurance companies, too, with their prevailingly long-term bond and mortgage assets, and a contractual commitment to lend to their policy holders at low fixed interest rates, are disadvantaged by inflation.[8]

Effects of Accounting and Taxes

The effects of inflation on the distribution of income and wealth described above unfortunately are not revealed by the standard accounting records of private firms. Indeed, because these records are also used by governments both for levying taxes and for government price regulation, *e.g.*, of utility rates, these accounting procedures create further significant redistributions of income and wealth. Traditional business accounting, used both to measure a firm's wealth and ownership (balance sheet) and to record its income (profit and loss statement), is based on certain conventional methods of valuing assets and liabilities, sales, costs, and profits. The conventions have generally required that fixed assets—land, structures, and equipment—be carried at initial purchase cost (regardless of subsequent changes in prices of such assets) less (except in the case of land) depreciation based on (a) the initial cost, (b) standard "useful lives" of assets, and (c) prescribed acceptable methods for spreading the initial cost

---

[8] However, the beneficial owners of most savings and loans, mutual savings banks, and insurance companies include many of each institution's debtors, most of whom benefit, at its expense, from inflation.

over the useful life. Thus, because they are valued at initial cost, business assets are typically undervalued during an inflation. And the depreciation that is charged as a cost of current production is therefore also typically understated, raising the reported profit. Financial assets are ordinarily required to be carried at purchase price, thus failing to reflect any subsequent increase or reduction of market value, including those reductions caused by the effect of inflation in raising interest rates, and, of course, not reflecting the effects of price level changes on real value. (By itself, this tends to overstate reported business net worth, but it does not affect profits.) Debts are usually carried at face value, thus failing to reflect the fact that they will be paid off (in an inflation) with dollars worth less than the dollars borrowed.

Although inventories, when acquired, are recorded at purchase cost, when used in production or resold they may be valued (as a component of cost of goods sold) in any of several ways, so long as one method is used consistently. The value of the remaining stock—that purchased, less that used or sold—then reflects the particular method of valuation of that which is used or sold. With stable prices, all of these methods give essentially the same results. When prices change, however, each method reflects these changes at different times, in quite different amounts, and with quite different results for the calculation both of net worth and of profit.[9]

Managers, stockholders (and potential purchasers of stocks), lenders, public officials, and others could, in principle, all make their own private inflation adjustments of the public accounting records of firms in which they are interested, in order not to let their decisions be warped. In fact, most of them have no idea how to do this and (except perhaps for the managers) lack most of the detailed data necessary to do it. Thus, reforms of accounting standards would appear necessary in an inflationary age merely to promote the efficiency of private decisions, and thus a rational allocation of resources. But the situation is made much worse by the fact that these private accounting records are used as the basis for the levying of business taxes (and sometimes for price controls, especially of utility rates).

Most of the inadequacies of current accounting lead to a serious increase in the real taxation of business income during inflation.[10] Moreover, the extent of these tax increases is very uneven among firms and industries, depending on their particular asset structures, methods of inventory valuation, and so on. Given that the marginal rate of United States corporate profits taxation, federal plus state, is around 50 per cent, the effects on after-tax income can be considerable. Quite unintentionally

[9] During the recent inflation many firms have shifted to one of the permitted methods—"last in, first out" (LIFO)—which essentially values inventories used in production at replacement cost.

[10] But not all. Accounting for business debt at face value obviously works in the opposite direction and, to the extent that physical properties are appraised on the basis of accounting records rather than market or replacement value, property taxes may be understated.

and arbitrarily, taxation based on standard accounting may well reduce and distort investment incentives.

Given the complexity of the problems involved and the fact that many of them have not been thoroughly thought through by accountants and economists, it is here inappropriate to discuss possible reforms of accounting.[11]

The effects of inflation on the taxation of personal income are similar to those on corporate income, insofar as income from unincorporated enterprises are concerned. And, as we have noted earlier, given the existence of fixed deductions, exemptions, and tax brackets in the United States personal income tax (and that of most states), the effect of inflation is also to raise effective rates of taxation on individuals—unintentionally and arbitrarily—thus, tending to reduce real incomes and to depress aggregate demand. As we have also noted earlier, to the extent that government budgets are fixed in money terms with no allowance or inadequate allowance for inflation, the occurrence of inflation also reduces real government purchases and, again, aggregate demand. These results may be desirable if inflation is clearly the result of excess demand, or, however caused, if it can be effectively curbed by reductions of demand. If not, the effect of inflation on government budgets merely creates unnecessary personal hardship both through reducing the consumption (or saving) of those employed and through increasing unemployment.

Expected Versus Unexpected Inflation

The effects of inflation in distorting the distribution of income and wealth have so far been analyzed essentially in terms of an inflation that is unexpected, or not fully expected. A similar (but obviously less relevant) analysis could be made of a price level *deflation* that is unexpected or not fully expected.

It is a famous proposition in economics that a fully expected inflation (or deflation) hurts no one. For, given the expectation that inflation (deflation) will occur and its expected amount, every individual will be able to make contracts for the future sale, whether of his factor services or of his products, that take account of the changes which will occur in other prices and costs. He can thus protect himself from losses (and deny windfall gains to others at his expense). In the management of his wealth, he will recognize that future fixed-price interest payments and repayments of principal will change in real value, and can adjust the price he will pay now for such financial assets in order to reflect those future changes. Or, on a new loan, he will require an interest rate that will compensate him for whatever

---

[11] See, however, the analysis and proposals of J. B. Shoven and J. I. Bulow, "Inflation Accounting and Nonfinancial Corporate Profits," in *Brookings Papers on Economic Activity* 3:1975, pp. 613–70; and 1:1976, 15–66.

future changes in the real value of interest and principal he expects to occur.

Buyers who contract to pay for goods and services to be delivered in the future, expecting the changes in the prices at which they in turn will sell their own goods and services, will be willing to schedule parallel changes in prices for future deliveries to them, and competition from other buyers with similar expectations will force such changes. Those currently borrowing will be willing to pay interest rates that will recompense the lender for the expected inflation or deflation, because they know that they will pay the interest, and repay the principal, in dollars of altered value; competition will force them to pay such interest rates.

Thus, a fully expected inflation (deflation) hurts no one. It is only an unexpected *increase or decrease* in the rate of inflation (deflation) that creates redistributions of income and wealth.

As with many other such facile generalizations, the proposition that fully expected changes in the price level are painless is both true and essentially meaningless. Confining attention to the relevant case, that is, inflation, it seems to be agreed that it is necessary that inflation be at a steady rate for it to be fully expected. But no inflation has ever been at a steady rate. Indeed, it may very well be a contradiction in terms to speak of a fully expected *and* steady rate of inflation. For, whatever may be the *causes* of the inflation—whether on the side of demand, or cost, or both—they will still be operating, and they should induce behavior which, given the firm and universal expectation of one rate of inflation, would seem inevitably to produce a higher rate.

Thus, it may be the case that, for an inflation to be at a steady rate, it must be expected to occur at a declining rate so that expectations are continually disappointed. Moreover, even if inflationary expectations are, on balance, ratified by the event, there will surely have been a variety of expectations, almost all disappointed—but some in one direction, some in the other, with windfall gains and losses to most individuals. In any case, all propositions about the costs of a fully anticipated inflation seem utterly metaphysical, given that there has never been a steady rate of inflation for any appreciable period in any country, and that no evidence has ever been presented that any inflation was accurately expected, even on balance, whereas there is much (admittedly casual) evidence that the rates of particular inflations have been unexpected.

Propositions about the costs of expected and unexpected inflations do, however, have the virtue of reminding us that whatever expectations people have about future changes in the prices that affect them—including the expectation that these will be zero or negative—do influence their behavior. For everyone who enters into contracts calling for future payments or receipts is making a bet on the future that requires some kind of expectation, consciously formulated or not. Such bets are implied by almost any future-oriented economic decision, for example, to change residence, to prepare for a career, to buy a durable physical asset, whether or not an explicit contract is involved. And it is the failure of those expectations to be fully realized—*in either direction*—which thereby creates unexpected, and therefore "unjust," changes in the distribution of income and wealth, whether the unexpected increments are positive or negative.

The high productivity and resulting high incomes of modern economic society require that people make many such bets: that they participate in large, impersonal markets, and make actual or implied contracts for the continuing sale of their services and/or their products; that they participate in capital markets that permit separation of the acts of saving and investment; that firms (and governments) plan their activities and thus make or require commitments (or impose obligations) which occur *over time*.

Although even a stable average price level imposes windfall costs and disposes windfall benefits as relative prices unexpectedly change (thus preventing all expectations from being fulfilled), changes in the general price level multiply the societally imposed windfall costs and benefits. All such gains and losses increase personal insecurity, lessen personal satisfactions (even on the part of the beneficiaries of inflation), heighten interpersonal tensions, and are thus destructive of the fabric of social and political coherence and ultimately of economic efficiency.

Talking about fully expected inflation (or deflation) is thus essentially irrelevant. It is the nature of the case that expectations are uncertain; yet actions are required that must be based on expectation; the results of many of these actions will necessarily turn out differently than expected. Changes in the level of prices greatly increase the number of these surprises and disappointments.

Whether or not these surprises and disappointments imposed by unexpected changes (in either direction) of the rate of inflation affect social or economic classes or groups taken as a whole (suppliers of labor versus suppliers of property services, organized versus unorganized workers, farm versus urban communities, and so on)—and such systematic changes do not seem to be large—the existence of price level changes multiplies uncertainties at the individual level and reduces the sum total of human satisfactions, whether or not it also reduces aggregate real production or per capita real income as these are traditionally measured. Whether, or to what extent it also reduces these is the subject to which we next turn briefly.

Effects on Aggregate Production and Efficiency

In the course of a number of chapters, we have accumulated a considerable list of probable effects of inflation on *aggregate demand*, and thus, *ceteris paribus*, on total production and incomes. All of these effects except the last two in the list below are negative:

1. By increasing the demand for a constant money supply, interest rates are forced up.
2. By reducing the real value of aggregate consumer wealth, consumer spending is inhibited.
3. By raising effective tax rates and reducing real government purchases, fiscal policy is made more restrictive.
4. By raising domestic prices relative to foreign, exports are inhibited and imports stimulated.
5. By increasing consumer fears and feelings of insecurity, the propensity to save is increased.
6. By increasing future prices of output relative to current costs of capital goods, investment is stimulated.
7. By encouraging purchases now instead of later, investment and consumption are moved forward in time.

The first five are effects of actual inflation; the last two of expected inflation. Presumably, all of these effects on aggregate demand could, in principle, be offset by appropriate adjustments of monetary and/or fiscal policies.

Here we will additionally refer to some possible effects of inflation on the *supply side* of the economy, which, even in principle, are not so easily offset. Essentially, these are effects that reduce the real output (or the value to consumers of the mix of real output) which can be produced with any given input of productive resources. These include the following.

1. Inflation, or at least the expectation of inflation, tends artificially to increase the production of goods as opposed to services and of more durable as opposed to less durable goods. This occurs because these goods are seen to cost less today than they will tomorrow and they will still be there tomorrow. In a sense, this is the same point as 7 in the previous list, but it is seen here in its aspect as a distortion of production, and thus as a reduced real value of production to consumers. More concretely, firms are encouraged to carry larger inventories than they really need, to build plants and buy equipment sooner than really necessary. In countries with continuous, very rapid inflation, people try to turn money into goods as soon as they get it, before it further depreciates: Incomplete buildings are visible everywhere, awaiting gradual completion as their owners can gradually finance it; new machinery rusts awaiting use; coal piles are far larger than needed. These are gross examples of inefficiencies created by inflation, more subtle ones are everywhere.

The economist may say that this behavior reflects the absence of suitable financial investments that could produce the same yield—perhaps because ceilings are placed on interest rates—or the absence of institutional structures for providing other forms of income-producing use of savings in units small enough for low or moderate-income savers. But this is not always easy, and often not *economical*, to provide.

2. In a sense the complement of item 1, money and other deposit balances are excessively economized, requiring more frequent trips to the bank, smaller transactions than are economical, more frequent settlement of accounts than is reasonable, and so on, in order not to hold depreciating money. Again, the economist will say that this particular problem can be solved by removing the ceiling of zero on the interest payable on demand deposits and the interest rate ceilings on other deposits. But in some economies, demand deposits are not used by most of the population, and it is impossible to pay interest on holdings of cash.

3. Scarce managerial talent is diverted from managing production, maintaining efficiency, seeking economy, innovating, and other productive activities, in favor of maneuver, speculation, and the search for protection against (or benefit from) inflation. Investment in human capital is slighted in favor of investment in physical capital or merely in stocks to be sold later.

4. Because long-term contracts of all kinds involve more risk in inflationary periods and places, people refuse to enter upon them, sacrificing the many real production efficiencies and economies which are made possible by such contracts, as well as wasting resources in more frequent negotiation.

5. Inflation destroys or weakens the usefulness of all kinds of market information which people accumulate merely through repeated transactions at a given price level. Every transaction requires new information-gathering, to find the cheapest source, the most suitable quality at the price, and so on. Shopping for the family or the firm is made more difficult, in the same way that occurs when one suddenly begins using a new currency. What is a "good buy" requires laborious calculations of what this price means in the familiar currency and how it compares with prices of other goods, which requires finding out what other goods are selling for before deciding to buy the first.[12]

Economists do not know how to measure the extent and significance of the effects of inflation on distribution or on production. Clearly, they occur; yet they do not necessarily stand in the way of reasonable economic performance or even of economic progress. Some countries, for example in Latin America, have lived with inflation rates of 30 to 150 per cent a year for decades without complete breakdown (or even highly visible impairment) of production and living standards; some have even been able to achieve economic growth despite high inflation. This writer, however, would argue that the immensely more complex and completely market-oriented economies of the major Western countries could never survive so well under these conditions.

[12] In a brilliant analysis, referred to earlier, Arthur Okun has developed this point in detail in his "Inflation: its Mechanics and Welfare Cost", *Brookings Papers on Economic Activity* 2 : 1975, pp. 351–90.

INFLATION AND INTEREST RATES

Irving Fisher, writing in 1896 (and further refining his argument in other works),[13] first clearly formulated the view that inflation tends to raise interest rates and that a steady and fully anticipated inflation is eventually fully reflected in interest rates. In that event, the actual rate of interest would consist of the "real rate," determined (in a classical, full-employment equilibrium only by "productivity" and "thrift"), plus the expected rate of inflation. Since the determinants of the real rate change very little, most changes in actual rates of interest reflect changes in expected rates of inflation.[14]

Fisher himself saw the expected rate of inflation as adapting slowly and gradually to changes in the actual rate, and he found the historical evidence consistent with this view. But modern theorists of "rational expectations"[15] insist that the present rate of inflation must at all times equal the expected rate—both, in turn, being determined by the rate of change of *M*. This implies that the current rate of interest should equal the roughly constant real rate *plus the current rate of inflation*. The fact that the data seem grossly inconsistent with this theory troubles them less than this writer believes it should.[16] Why and how the expected inflation rate and the actual inflation rate are supposed to be kept equal was explained in the section on "expectational models" in Chapter 14. Why and how the expected inflation rate should get embodied in the interest rate was suggested in the last section: both lender and borrower base their behavior on the confident expectation that any nominal interest paid to borrower (and the final nominal repayment of principal) deteriorate in real value at the expected inflation rate; thus the lender will only be willing to lend, and the borrower has no reason not to offer to pay (if competition requires it) an interest rate that incorporates that expectation. In the background seems to be an implied assumption that all lenders or borrowers or both have the available alternative of buying capital goods at present prices, and watching them, and their output, appreciate in nominal value even as they

---

[13] "Appreciation and Interest," *AEA Publications*, Series Three (II) (August, 1896) 331–42; for later treatment see his *The Theory of Interest* (Macmillan, 1930) pp. 399–451. (Reprinted, 1965, by A. M. Kelley.)

[14] Fisher's own theory of the real rate emphasized "time preference," the extent of savers' preference for present over future satisfactions. And this was surely highly stable, even from one generation to another.

[15] Described in Chapter 7, and briefly referred to in the section of Chapter 14 describing Friedman's expectational inflation theory.

[16] It is easy to subtract percentage changes (at annual rate) in the Consumer Price Index, the Wholesale Price Index, or the GNP Deflator from any interest rate series (for example, Treasury Bonds, Moody's Aaa Corporate Bonds, Average (or Prime) Bank Lending Rate) to establish this fact. However, rational expectations theorists fight accepting it. For a good example, see T. J. Sargent, "Rational Expectations, the Real Rate of Interest, and the Natural Rate of Unemployment," *Brookings Papers on Economic Activity*, 2:1973, pp. 429–72.

produce their *real* return, which is the marginal product of capital. They are also all assumed to be purely competitive "price-takers."

In fact, most lenders (that is, savers, directly, or the financial institutions that receive their saving) have no such option; nor does each business borrower face unlimited competition from a host of potential competitors who share his knowledge of his own market and his assumed confident expectation that *the present rate of inflation will continue over the entire life of capital assets purchased today*. But unless the current rate of inflation is expected to continue over the entire life of the assets to be purchased today (or, at least, the life of the loan to finance that purchase); and unless there are numerous competitors of every potential borrower sharing that information and conviction and possessing the knowledge, experience, and ability of each actual borrower to manage each potential investment effectively, there is no reason why the full inflation adjustment should get incorporated in the interest rate.

Some who recognize the lack of full incorporation of current inflation into the interest rate attempt to explain the failure—or the delay—by hypothesizing that, at low rates of inflation, it does not pay economic agents to inform themselves of the true rate of inflation and to take the trouble of negotiating loan contracts which compensate for it. Only as inflation accelerates to higher rates, and thus becomes more visible, do lenders and borrowers begin to take account of inflation, or of changes in the rate of inflation—or take account of it with shorter lag. This is clearly not the "rational expectations view"; but a proponent of "adaptive expectations" can well argue that the speed with which and the extent to which the expected inflation rate adapts to the actual rate is a function of the level of the inflation rate, the adaptation becoming complete and instantaneous as inflation approaches hyperinflation. These are plausible hypotheses, but need further empirical study to be fully evaluated.

Perhaps the best judgment is that Irving Fisher had it about right. Inflation tends to raise interest rates because it tends to increase the expected rate of inflation. But the expected rate adapts slowly and gradually to the actual rate, and competition among business borrowers incorporates this expected rate of inflation only slowly and gradually into the actual market rate of interest. In the meantime, inflation does redistribute wealth and income between borrower and lender.

POLICIES AGAINST INFLATION[17]

Whatever may be the true economic costs of inflation, some of which, in principle, should be discernible in standard statistical measurements of

---

[17] Several parts of this section borrow substantially from two of the writer's earlier publications: *Stemming World Inflation* (Atlantic Institute, 1971); and "Roles and Limits of Incomes Policy," *The Oriental Economist*, 42 (April 1974), also published in Japanese.

aggregate production and income and in the distribution of each, it is an obvious fact that inflation is exceedingly unpopular. In part, this may merely reflect the myopia that permits almost every individual to blame some impersonal force called "inflation" for raising the prices he pays yet, at the same time, to credit the extra rise in his money income that accompanies it to his own cleverness or hard work, the success of his trade union, the policies of his government, or just to the smiles of fortune. But, whatever caused his higher income, it would have happened anyway; thus inflation has robbed him of what was rightfully his. Someone or something is to blame; and the government should "do something" about it. Political leaders have little choice but to be "against inflation" and, at least, to appear to be doing something about it. Since there are, clearly, *real* costs of inflation, it would be wise if the things public policy tries to do should also have some effects. This section considers four general types of policies— not mutually exclusive—that might "do something" to reduce or control inflation.

Demand Management Policies

If inflation always and only reflected an excess of aggregate demand over some acceptable level of unemployment, the control of inflation would, in principle, be simple: use fiscal and/or monetary policies so to "manage" demand that the unemployment rate is kept at or as close as possible to its acceptable level.

If, instead, there is some stable "trade-off" between inflation and unemployment—a nonvertical "long-run Phillips curve"—then policy makers have a more difficult assignment; they must attempt to minimize the combined loss due to unemployment plus inflation. This might be done by assigning *quantitative* costs to each unit of unemployment and inflation, costs that are assumed to rise, per unit of each, the larger the number of units experienced. Adding these two costs together for each possible combination of U and $\dot{P}$ on the Phillips curve, one obtains a **loss function**, from which, in principle, one can calculate the combination of U and $\dot{P}$ at which the aggregate loss is minimized.

The unit cost functions may be approximated by the intuition of political leaders or estimated by some kind of a polling process in which samples of voters are asked to rank, as equivalent, or as one higher than the other, alternative hypothetical combinations of U and $\dot{P}$; or, conceivably, the cost functions might be found by statistical analysis of time series on election returns or on measures of political unrest.[18]

[18] For a simple introduction to the "theory of economic policy," just summarized, see J. Tinbergen, *On the Theory of Economic Policy* (North-Holland, 1952). For more advanced discussion of various aspects, see R. S. Holbrook, "Optimal Economic Policy and the Problem of Instrument Instability," *American Economic Review*, 62 (March 1972), 57–65; A. M. Okun, "Fiscal-Monetary Activism: Some Analytical Issues," *Brookings Papers on Economic Activity*, 1:1972, pp. 123–63.

If, as is now widely believed by many economists, the current inflation rate depends on a series of past unemployment rates, the calculus becomes more complex—adding the need to discount to the present future inflation costs associated with the unemployment determined by today's demand management and past unemployment rates. And if, realistically, the effects of today's demand management on unemployment are also lagged, then a series of future (discounted) unemployment costs must also be included in the loss function to be minimized. Given, further, the presence of uncertainty about both the relationship between today's monetary and fiscal policy decisions and the future series of unemployment rate and, in turn, between past, present, and future unemployment rates and present and future inflation rates, the calculation becomes still more complex. Still, in principle, economists can construct mathematical models of the decision process and minimize the value of present and future loss—given some way of estimating the social costs attributed to each inflation rate and unemployment rate, and given economists' knowledge of the relevant economic relationships and of the probability distribution of each outcome. Needless to say, only hypothetical experiments have so far been made with such calculations.

Many economists, however, no longer believe that there is any very stable relationship between aggregate demand and inflation. Or, at least, they believe that they discern a number of other factors that also influence the rate of inflation, some of which might be influenced by public policies other than of demand management. The writer is of this group. This greatly widens the scope of an anti-inflation policy.

Nevertheless, no one can deny that much of the historical and recent record of inflation can be attributed either to the pursuit of overambitious and unrealistic objectives with respect to unemployment, or to mistakes of fiscal and/or monetary policies that pushed and held unemployment below existing targets which may have been quite reasonable and appropriate. In the United States, for example, the failure to raise tax rates (or sharply to cut other Federal expenditures), when military spending in connection with the Vietnam conflict was sharply accelerated beginning in late 1965, was a fiscal policy mistake of serious proportions and was clearly inconsistent with the government's own expressed targets regarding the unemployment rate.

Given the inertia of the inflationary process, which earlier pages have emphasized, this was a most costly mistake. A full account of the origins, the nature, and the consequences of this mistake has not yet been published. But it is clear that the economists who were advising policy makers both in the White House and in the Federal Reserve System gave ample warning of the consequences, at least to their principals. There was time to have raised taxes sufficiently to have avoided much of the inflation of 1967, 1968, and 1969.

In a larger sense, however, it may simply not have been possible, politically, to have avoided the inflationary mistake, once the decision was made to widen the United States military involvement in Vietnam. President Johnson and his senior political advisers were convinced of the inflationary dangers of their policy; but they also believed—probably correctly, judging by subsequent events—that public opinion would not then support a tax increase. They may still be judged to have failed in their responsibility by not having immediately made the inflationary consequences clear to the public and recommended the correct course of action, even though they believed that the recommendation would be rejected.

Instead, a year passed before more than a token tax increase was recommended (in January 1967, and then only to become effective in the second half of 1967); and another year-and-a-half elapsed before the increase could pass the Congress and be made effective, in July 1968. By that time no warning was needed of the inflationary consequences—they were fully evident. By that time, the momentum of inflation was also well established, and the tax increase (and associated highly restrictive monetary policy) generated (with some lag) an extended recession, which, however, produced only small and gradual effects in reducing the inflation.

Even though demand management policies may often be quite inadequate, used *alone*, to minimize inflation at acceptable levels of unemployment—particularly, once inflation becomes established—they are surely an essential element of any effective anti-inflation policy.

Policies to "Shift the Phillips Curve"

Economists disagree whether there exists a short-run or long-run trade-off between inflation and unemployment or whether, as Friedman and others hold, there is only a single unemployment rate (the "natural rate") that divides a zone of indefinitely accelerating inflation and one of indefinitely accelerating deflation. They also disagree whether the terms of any trade-off, or the level of any natural rate, are stable or highly variable, and what are the other factors at work. Nevertheless, most economists can agree that any measures which might lower the unemployment rate associated with any particular degree of inflation ought to be considered an appropriate and important part of an anti-inflation policy. In this section, we briefly consider some policies that are believed to alter some of the "structural" (as opposed to "institutional") factors that determine the locus of the threshold between inflation and price stability.[19]

[19] Our distinction between structural and institutional factors is far from clear cut, but the sense in which these terms are here used (for want of better ones) will become somewhat more clear from the context of this and the following subsection.

As we have argued, limitations on and imperfections of labor-market *information* and worker *mobility* may not be the only or even the principal source of a Phillips curve (short-run or long-run, vertical or sloping, stable or shifting). Yet almost all economists would agree that more effective labor-market information and an increase in labor mobility should reduce the unemployment rate associated with any given degree of inflation.

The information network dealing with vacancies and available workers is almost nowhere as good as it might be, and in many countries it is exceedingly poor. It involves word-of-mouth, advertising, and private and public placement services and labor exchanges. There is a strong case to be made for having a single (and therefore public) agency as the source of all job information and placement activities. Requiring that employers report all vacancies to the public labor exchange, and that they hire only workers who had registered with the exchange, would greatly increase the availability of information to workers about jobs and to employers about job seekers. Modern computers can also vastly speed the matching of qualifications sought and available. Advance information on forthcoming lay-offs, given to workers and—through a labor exchange—to prospective alternative employers, can greatly reduce the time lag between discharge and reemployment. Prohibition of lay-offs without substantial advance notice to the worker and to the labor exchange would be costly to employers; yet it might greatly reduce the net social cost of frictional unemployment, and at the same time reduce inflationary pressures at high employment.

The case for large-scale manpower training and retraining programs can rest alone on human considerations and on considerations of productive efficiency. Yet there is also a powerful case, too little understood, for large-scale training and retraining programs as an important means of increasing the effective mobility of labor, thereby reducing inflationary pressures at low levels of unemployment.

Persistent regional disparities of unemployment rates reflect another reason why low over-all unemployment rates lead to inflation. Demand-management policies sufficiently expansionary to reduce unemployment to an acceptable level in regions with persistent labor surplus must first create severe inflationary pressures in areas of persistent labor shortage. Improved labor market information and manpower training will help to even out regional disparities; but more positive measures are surely needed, designed to assist and encourage workers to leave surplus areas and/or to assist in creating new jobs in these areas. Government payment of transport and moving expenses for workers and their families and assistance in acquiring new housing (and in the disposal of housing in the old location) may be expensive. Yet, by reducing the costs of frictional unemployment to workers and to society they may easily pay for themselves, permitting higher levels of employment, output, and real incomes, along with a lower rate of inflation.

To the extent that the particular design of unemployment insurance and public assistance programs (for example, food stamps) either provide unintended incentives not to return to work or are subject to serious abuse (as they appear to be in the United States), they also contribute to inflation at unnecessarily high rates of unemployment. Correcting such deficiencies is also an important ingredient of anti-inflation policy.

In societies that accept full employment as an urgent goal of social policy, it should hardly need to be said that artificial barriers, public or private, that needlessly prevent unemployed workers from filling vacant jobs have no excuse for existing. Yet a vast array of such barriers exists in almost every country—the relic of a day when there was no commitment to full employment, when unemployment was in fact often massive and prolonged, and when a desire to "protect" jobs from the competition of "outsiders" was a quite understandable if never fully justifiable objective of workers. Such barriers exist in central government and local government legislation and regulations, in trade-union requirements, and in employers' hiring practices. They often take the form of the insistence upon irrelevant qualifications of age, sex, color, residence, education, training, or experience, enforced through eligibility requirements, entrance examinations, union membership, licensing, or other methods. They have some impact on the price level even when unemployment is not unusually low. But by further restricting the ability of employers to hire from among the much smaller number of available job seekers when unemployment is low, they exert strong inflationary pressures on wages, costs, and prices.

It seems to be a fact that in many economies there are substantial numbers of "marginal" or "submarginal" workers who, because of physical or other handicaps or weaknesses, can find (or hold) jobs in large numbers only in periods of inflationary boom. Public policy is always under pressure to overstimulate the economy in order to reduce the number of such unemployed. This is both a costly and ineffective way of solving this problem. Some of these workers could benefit substantially from job training, and thereby become fully employable in any ordinarily prosperous period; others should perhaps be provided decent incomes, and relieved of any need to find work. But many can perform useful work, want to work, and can contribute both to the needs of society and to their own support, provided that they are not expected to be able to *earn* a standard income from a regular private employer. One way of increasing the *private* employment of such workers is through wage subsidies paid to the employers who hire them. An alternative is a system of residual *public* employment, *at below-standard wage rates*, which guarantees jobs to any who fail to find ordinary employment. Such methods can supply most of marginal workers' income needs, and, at the same time, contribute either market output or useful public services. And this can be done at a lower budgetary cost, and with far less inflation, than by attempting to create private employment for submarginal workers through stimulating aggregate demand.

Immobilities and frictions in the labor market undoubtedly have some counterparts in the goods markets, although they are probably far more limited. However, better consumer information about products and prices might reduce the inflationary significance of bottlenecks in the production of particular goods and services at times when no bottleneck limits the production of substitute goods or services. Unnecessarily restrictive procurement specifications or production standards (as, for example, in building codes) can also prevent feasible substitutions of alternative materials when a bottleneck at high employment limits production of the one specified.

Moreover, some bottlenecks on the production side may be unnecessary and avoidable. Such bottlenecks may arise from inadequate investment, explained by insufficient information or appreciation by producers of what has been happening to stocks (at all levels), by inadequate attention to trends in internal and external demand, by unfavorable developments in the supply of necessary materials or highly specialized labor, or as a result of some legal or institutional limitation on investment or the profitability of investment. The fact that such bottlenecks due to inadequate investment may have contributed in some degree or in some countries to the inflation of 1972–1974, has led, in the United States, to calls for some system of "national planning". Without getting into details, the writer will only give his opinion that so elaborate a system is quite unnecessary to deal with such problems; that, given the techniques and the data presently available for such planning, it would be unlikely to give warning of most of the kinds of problems that arose in 1972–1974; and that, to the extent that it had *any* effects, they would in the long-run probably be to increase rather than reduce the number of bottlenecks.

There is a strong case to be made for a much earlier awareness of potential future bottlenecks arising from inadequate investment. This could be achieved by creating a relatively small research and advisory staff for this purpose, attached (in the United States) to the Council of Economic Advisers. It would be assigned to look out for such problems, to investigate, and to propose *ad hoc* measures to deal with them in advance of trouble.

Altering Inflationary Institutions

In Chapter 14, considerable reference was made to "institutional factors" that either help to generate inflation or to perpetuate it. Although many of the institutions there referred to are deeply rooted in modern economic society and many clearly serve important social and political purposes, there may be some marginal changes which could make these institutions less inflationary.

Many of these possible changes relate to the legal status and organizational structure of trade unions. Many legal provisions can be found that appear artificially to support or strengthen the market power of unions, permitting them sometimes (or often) to impose excessive and inflationary wage claims on employers. Such legislation may include rules that give direct or indirect support to restrictive apprenticeship programs, high initiation fees, or other methods that limit union membership; permit the "closed shop" or something close to it; tend to make union wage scales the minimum wage for nonunion establishments; permit secondary boycotts or strike pressures on firms not involved in a particular labor dispute; fail to enforce contract provisions equally as between employers and unions; or set irrelevant qualifications for public procurement. The standards used by public agencies in the enforcement of, or administrative determinations under, such legislation may be as important as the legislation itself and may also need careful review.

An excessively restrictive scope for wage bargaining, and an absence of adequate influence or control by national unions over their locals or by national federations over member unions, may encourage myopic bargaining that appears to be in the economic interest of small groups of workers taken separately, but is against the interest of workers generally. Whether or not the structure of internal union organization can be constructively influenced by legislation may be questionable, but there are provisions for legal determination of appropriate "bargaining units" which might be reconsidered. In any case, the influence of national political and labor leaders might be constructively brought to bear *within* the labor movement to encourage reorganizations that would permit a broader view of labor's true economic interests to be reflected in wage determination and related contract provisions.

Legally required or encouraged automatic escalation of wages with living costs undoubtedly strengthens the inflationary spiral, especially where (as is the case in Italy) escalation is nearly universal, nearly complete, and almost immediate. Consideration might, more generally, be given to legislation limiting the scope of automatic escalation to lower wages only, perhaps limiting the frequency of adjustments and excluding the effect of tax increases or costs of imports.

Minimum wage laws and determinations made under them might also be examined in terms of possible inflationary effects. Similarly, laws that determine wages in public employment by inappropriate comparisons with private wages may need review. In fact, laws that permit collective bargaining for public employees, where there is no effective countervailing market pressure from the employer and where strikes can dangerously threaten the public welfare, may well be judged to be inflationary, both in terms of their influence on rates of indirect taxation and, more importantly, in terms of the model they may set for private wage determinations. In countries with a large public industrial sector, wage determinations by nationalized industries may set the pace for the entire national wage level. Although public workers should not be discriminated against, the public interest in avoiding inflation should certainly be considered in such wage determinations. The timing, if not the ultimate extent, of revisions in prices for goods and services sold by government enterprises also needs the careful attention of government officials concerned with overall economic policy.

Policies to strengthen business competition strike directly at the market power which underlies cost-push inflation. Such policies could thus contribute direct, although probably marginal, benefits in weakening the sources of inflation. However, in many cases, the real significance of competition policies is that such policies can permit the one-time reduction of, or curb the increase in, particular costs or prices and thereby help to offset increases in the general price level that stem from the more basic mechanisms of an inflationary spiral. Included here are a strengthening of the conventional approaches of "antitrust" policy (conspiracy in restraint of trade, market sharing, mergers, and so on); the reexamination of laws relating to trade practices, price discrimination, and similar matters in order to eliminate unnecessary restrictions on competition; the elimination of most or all regulation of *minimum* prices in such areas as transport and retail trade; and the elimination of any unnecessary and anticompetitive effects of licensing provisions, building codes, government procurement regulations, and similar governmental interventions.

Finally, there is a wide range of industries in every country which, although inefficient and technologically backward, survive because they provide important or irreplaceable goods or services for which no alternative source is available. Their prices, however, are unnecessarily high, and, in many cases rise more rapidly than others. They include building construction; medical care; many kinds of personal and business services, particularly repair services; some branches of retailing. Available remedies include financial assistance for rationalization, removal of obsolete legal requirements, encouragement or financial support for the development and dissemination of improved technology, alteration of structures of fees or methods of payment that provide incentives for inefficiency, and many similar possibilities.

Building a Counterforce Against Inflation

Although something can doubtless be done to lessen the inflationary impact of existing economic structures and institutions, this route is exceedingly difficult and is unlikely in any short period of time substantially to reduce the inflationary bias which seems to prevail in modern industrial economies. Many of the institutions involved are seen to serve important social, political, and even individual needs, and can thus be altered only with great difficulty in a democratic society. Labor unions, for example, clearly contribute in most countries to the inflationary process; yet their abolition is unthinkable. Even substantial modifications in their legal status, organizational structure, and certainly in their institutional objectives can only come slowly and must reflect substantial prior alterations in the perceptions and attitudes of their leaders and members; attempting to impose them by law without that is almost sure to be counterproductive.

Moreover, whatever can be done to improve the functioning of labor and product markets, there will still occur fiscal mistakes, serious crop failures, tax increases that raise costs, sharp rises in the prices of imports, declines in exchange rates reflecting international capital movements, and public support for efforts to raise incomes of some particular groups through political or market action, but without readiness on the part of any other group to sacrifice any of its own potential income gains to permit it. These impulses to inflation will still feed back upon the price level through affecting price expectations, the cost of living, wage comparisons, profits targets, and so on.

Thus, beyond some point, further efforts to alter market structures and institutions may need to be supplemented by attempting to influence wage and price behavior directly—through some kind of an "incomes policy." This may be fully as effective as altering structures or institutions. For, as we have argued, in modern industrial societies, most wage- and price-setting behavior does not simply reflect inevitable market pressures: almost no wage rates, and very few prices are either automatically allowed, or deliberately adjusted, to "clear the market." Rather, they are adjusted by organizational "decision makers," on the basis of various perceptions, expectations, and assumptions, and in accordance with institutionalized standards of what is "reasonable," "fair," or "expected of them." The perceptions, expectations, and assumptions, and the standards of what is reasonable, fair, or expected can be influenced by an active and aggressive incomes policy.

Such a policy may be defined as a deliberate, organized, and continuing government effort to persuade—or, in the extreme case, to require—businesses, workers, and others to avoid, reduce, or delay increases which they might otherwise have made in prices, wages, rents, dividends, or other forms of money incomes.[20] Although this organized effort may be primarily confined to certain sectors of the economy, the purpose of an incomes policy is not to affect selectively particular prices and incomes—that is, to change income distribution—but it is rather to prevent, slow down, or stop a rise in the general price level and the general level of (money) incomes.

The fundamental requirement for the success of an incomes policy is the government's ability to convince a majority of the general public and of

[20] Use of the word "require" means that wage-price controls are included in the concept of incomes policy; however, the use of wage and price controls *during a major war* involves such special considerations that it needs to be treated quite separately.

the leaders and members of the major economic interest groups (1) that the large nominal income gains achieved during inflation are ephemeral, and that inflation in fact imposes social costs; thus (2) that slowing or preventing inflation is in the general social interest and thus in theirs; (3) that, if restraint in wage- or price-setting in accordance with government standards on one's part were matched by a parallel restraint on the part of others, the objectives of the policy could be realized; (4) that one's adherence to the policy will have some influence on the adherence of others, and that the government will also be promoting the adherence of others; and (5) that one's failure to adhere will be noticed unfavorably by the government, by others in the same social or economic group, and by the general public, and that this will involve some costs.

If this conviction can be widely achieved, the perceptions, expectations, and assumptions about the behavior of others and about the general economic environment will have been altered in a way which makes adherence to the standards seem to be reasonable, appropriate, and even rewarding.

Some writers have distinguished between (a) incomes policies based essentially on a "social contract," negotiated among the main economic interest groups and the government, and (b) policies based essentially on a unilateral government determination. Under the former, leaders of each participating interest group make more or less formal commitments with respect to matters under their control or influence in return for reciprocal commitments by leaders of other interests and the government. Under the latter, the government may consult with the parties, but does not seek their agreement or consent. It merely promulgates the policy and calls upon all parties to adhere to it. This distinction may perhaps be more formal than substantive, since it seems clear that, in a democratic society and in peacetime, no incomes policy can long succeed that does not have the essential consent of the major economic interests, whether formal or tacit. In particular, no democratic government is likely to succeed in imposing for long either a voluntary restraint or a mandatory control on wages unless workers regard what it asks of them as essentially fair and reasonable— both in terms of the expectations that workers have developed with respect to absolute levels of income and working conditions and in comparison with the severity of the restraint requested or control imposed on other major economic groups, including particularly on the prices charged and profits earned by their employers.

To be sure, there are probably few countries in which leaders of the major economic interest groups have sufficient confidence in their ability to represent and to discipline their respective memberships that they are willing and able openly to endorse and commit their support to a policy that limits their members' freedom to pursue whatever the members may regard as their fundamental economic self-interest. Still a government may be able to build an informal understanding and consensus in support of its policy, even though leaders of the interest groups may be quite unwilling to subscribe to it publicly and may even publicly oppose it. What is required is sufficient tacit agreement with the policy or at least willingness to tolerate it, so that open confrontation is avoided and leaders privately advise their respective partisans that an open challenge to the policy would be unwise.

Securing the consent or consensus without which an incomes policy cannot succeed is undoubtedly the major problem for any government which wishes to introduce such a policy. Conditions that seem to increase the chances of success may include the following, among others: (a) a tradition of national unity in support of the nation's economic and social objectives; (b) a political system in which the political parties are not primarily identified with separate interest groups (for example, labor identified with one party, business with another); (c) a traditionally law-abiding public; (d) an able, effective, and respected government bureaucracy; and (e) recent experience with a costly inflation.

Whatever the degree of consent that may exist or be created in support of an incomes policy, the policy cannot be self-executing. Government will thus have administrative responsibilities for securing adherence to it in particular situations by members of some or all of the economic interests involved. Most such adherence must be self-imposed; government officials can directly intervene in only an insignificant fraction of all wage and price determinations. But it is important that it be ready to intervene to avoid too many cases of obvious and well-publicized flouting of the policy. Methods used to secure this adherence range from mere exhortation, at the one extreme, to legal compulsion, enforceable by fine and imprisonment, at the other, with a wide variety of intermediate positions along this scale.

Toward the "purely voluntary" end of this scale are methods variously described (in the United States) as "ear twisting," "jaw boning," or "finger pointing." They include face-to-face discussion between government officials and leaders of particular firms or unions, in which the government officials explain the importance of conforming to the policy and appeal for cooperation; the focussing of public attention on the decisions made by the firms or unions in the expectation that public opinion may demand adherence; explicit public criticism by government spokesmen of decisions inconsistent with the policy, and commendation when they do conform; and the threat of withdrawal (by administrative or legislative action) of special privileges or benefits which these groups may enjoy if they fail to adhere.

The processes of "education" and "persuasion" in behalf of "voluntary" adherence may be strengthened if the government has the legal authority to do some or all of the following: to appoint prestigious permanent or *ad hoc* boards of inquiry that will issue public evaluations of disputed private actions; to require formal advance notice to the government of price or wage changes; to suspend such changes for a period while their justification is investigated; to require testimony and the supplying of detailed evidence by those subject to such investigation; to make specific formal recommendations with respect to the wage or price changes reviewed.

Intermediate between "voluntary" and "compulsory" schemes of incomes policy lies a method, often proposed but up to now untried, namely, to impose a special tax on wage payments and/or price increases in excess of specified standards; or, alternatively, to provide special tax reductions for those firms and for those workers whose prices and wages comply with stated standards.[21] As one who participated in planning and administering the U.S. price- and wage-control programs both for World War II and the Korean War, the writer is skeptical whether all of the complex exceptions and special provisions that would be necessary to make such a tax even reasonably fair and effective can (or should) be legislated into the United States Tax Code. However, the approach has so many attractive features that it surely deserves intensive study.

Choice among the many possible methods of securing adherence to an incomes policy and decisions on the explicit coverage of the policy must obviously depend on national traditions and experience, on the seriousness of the inflationary problem, on the extent to which the problem is focussed in certain sectors, and on the sense of urgency about solving it. If inflation is rapid and its momentum well established, it is probably almost impossible to slow it down quickly without mandatory controls, effective for at least a temporary period. On the other hand, a largely voluntary policy, undertaken when the price level is fairly stable, may be reasonably effective in preventing inflation from developing and is surely more viable in the longer run.

To stop an inflation quickly by mandatory controls requires a tough policy, with few loopholes or exceptions; otherwise, the control system will be found merely to provide a formal means of administering an inflationary spiral. Yet mandatory controls on a broad scale, even if not rigid in character, seem almost impossible to administer successfully for any extended period. The essential reason is that, even though aggregate demand may not put heavy pressure on the economy's over-all resources of labor, capital, and natural resources, there are always particular markets in which labor, products, or services will be in excess demand. And, over time, a changing assortment of markets will experience this condition. Inflexible restraints, long-maintained, (a) would prevent shifts in relative prices that would redirect resources and demand in ways which would relieve these pressures and (b) require some system either of formal or

---

[21] For examples of proposals of this type see H. C. Wallich and S. Weintraub, "A Tax-Based Incomes Policy", *Journal of Economic Issues*, 5 (June 1971), 1–19; A. P. Lerner, "Stagflation—Its Cause and Cure", *Challenge*, 20 (September-October 1977), 14–19; M. A. Okun, "The Great Stagflation Swamp", *Challenge*, 20 (November-December 1977), 6–13; and G. Ackley comments in *Economic Outlook, USA* (Winter 1978).

private rationing to avoid inequitable and inefficient distortions of distribution (and perhaps of production at subsequent levels). Yet flexible restraints, which could permit the needed alteration of relative prices and are capable of objective and equitable administration, are exceedingly difficult to design.

This is not to say that price and wage restraints, mandatory or otherwise, are inappropriate for markets in which there is excess demand, particularly if the excess can be expected to be of relatively short duration. Rather, the problem of restraints in such markets is that of providing equitable and objectively administrable ways of permitting an increase in relative prices where it is needed for purposes of efficiency, and of denying increases not so needed, thus maintaining appreciable downward pressure on the price level.

The particular standards proposed or required for prices and wages under an incomes policy (other than wartime controls) are usually essentially built around the arithmetic of the relationship between wage and price changes which will leave the distribution of the income from production between wages and profits unchanged. This relationship can be summarized in the equation: $\dot{P} = \dot{W} - \dot{\Pi}$ where the dots indicate percentage changes, P prices, W wages, and Π productivity. Thus, if wage rates can be restricted to advance at the average rate of productivity gain for the entire economy, with exceptions (in both directions) for special cases, the *average* price level can be held stable, with individual prices allowed to advance (or expected to decline depending on whether and by how much the particular productivity advance for the good falls short of or exceeds the average. The detailed problems of further defining such standards, finding the information necessary to apply them, and providing necessary exceptions are too complex to be discussed here.[22]

Almost every developed Western country has had some experience with incomes policy during the postwar period. In the Netherlands, for instance, some kind of incomes policy has been in effect almost continuously over this period—including at various times compulsory price controls, compulsory wage controls, voluntary "guidelines," requirement of government approval of private decisions before they become effective, or authority for government to invalidate private decisions after they were made.

The Scandinavian countries all have a strong tradition of highly centralized wage bargaining, encouraged but not formally participated in by government, through which national wage levels are negotiated and which sometimes involve commitments by employers about their price policies. Given the great importance of international trade for these countries, the

---

[22] See, however, E. F. Denison, *Guideposts for Wages and Prices: Criteria and Consistency*; W. S. Woytinsky Lecture No. 2 (Department of Economics and Institute of Public Policy Studies, The University of Michigan, 1968), 32pp; J. Sheahan, *The Wage-Price Guideposts* (Brookings, 1967).

parties to this centralized bargaining have usually paid considerable attention to the national interest in reasonable price stability. Thus, the process has sometimes been described as a "private incomes policy." Still, Scandinavian governments at various times have intervened in this process to reinforce the weight given to price stability rather than merely to industrial peace or export success.

Among the larger European countries, the United Kingdom has had the most extensive experience with incomes policy, including wage "stops" and price freezes, government authority to review and delay wage and price changes, and voluntary appeals and agreements. France and Germany have had relatively less experience, but began to experiment in the late 1960s. The United States instituted "guideposts" for wage and price stability in 1962, and used persuasion, public criticism, and private negotiations in an effort to influence wages and prices through 1968.

However, the most extensive and drastic peacetime use of incomes policy in Western countries occurred after 1970. At one time or another after then, almost every country in Western Europe and North America instituted some form of incomes policy, in many cases involving formal wage and/or price controls. In the United States, such controls were in continuous use from August 1971 to Spring 1973, although their coverage and severity varied considerably during the various "phases" of the policy.

Most students of incomes policies agree that such policies have had a certain degree of success in avoiding or slowing down inflation, at least in some countries and for limited periods. Although this conclusion is, by its nature, difficult to prove or to quantify, careful observation by qualified scholars does often support it. What needs to be added at once is that, in almost every case, the policy has sooner or later been removed or has broken down, followed by an upward surge of wages and prices.

This, of course, does not prove that incomes policies have been useless, for the price level may have been lower after the removal or breakdown and subsequent price surge than if no effort had been made, although this conclusion is even harder to prove. Moreover, it can be plausibly argued that in some cases the policy breakdown was an avoidable result of incorrect monetary or fiscal policies, which created inflationary pressures beyond the capability of the particular incomes policy to resist. Indeed, one familiar criticism of incomes policies is precisely that they divert public and official attention from the necessity also to pursue adequately noninflationary fiscal and monetary policies.

The fact that many countries have returned again and again to the use of incomes policies after earlier attempts that ended in "failure" may suggest that national political leaders believe that such policies, properly conceived and administered and used in conjunction with other appropriate anti-inflationary policies, can contribute to price stabilization. However, the fact of repeated use has instead been interpreted by more skeptical observers as evidence either that "politicians never learn" or that they cynically adopt such policies in full knowledge of their uselessness because the public likes to think that its leaders are "doing something" about inflation. As should be evident from this discussion, this writer does believe that incomes policies can—at least in some countries and in some periods—make a useful contribution as part of a broader attack on inflation.[23]

REVIEW QUESTIONS

1. Which of the following gain or lose from inflation and why?

(a) homeowners

(b) landlords

(c) stockholders

(d) farmers

(e) savings and loan institutions

(f) bondholders

(g) retired persons dependent upon annuities

(h) insurance companies

(i) fixed wage and salary earners

(j) businessmen

(k) beneficiaries of the Social Security system

(l) commercial banks

(m) business firms that adopt LIFO for inventory valuation

2. "A fully expected inflation hurts no one. It is only unexpected changes in the rate of inflation that hurt some people."

(a) Explain why no one is hurt by a fully expected inflation.

(b) "But this is meaningless." Why?

(c) Describe some of the effects on income distribution which might be created by an unexpected decrease in the rate of inflation.

3. It is often argued that maintaining a continuing moderate inflation is conducive to economic growth, especially in developing countries. What aspects of inflation are emphasized by this proposition? In light of other aspects of inflation, how would you evaluate the proposition?

4. During the year 1976, the interest rate on ordinary savings deposits in commercial banks averaged less than 5 percent; on Treasury bills it averaged 4.99 percent, on "prime" bank loans 6.84 percent, and on the best corporate bonds 8.43 percent. During that year, consumer prices rose by 4.8 percent, the GNP deflator by 5.3 percent. How can these facts be reconciled with the proposition that inflation invariably gets "embodied" in interest rates?

5. Demand management policies, manpower policies, efforts to strengthen competitive forces, and incomes policies represent alternative methods of attempting to reduce inflation. Explain how each method purports to reduce inflation, and what particular theoretical view of the inflation process supports each method.

---

[23] For a full review of United States experience with incomes policies see J. Sheahan, *op. cit.*; C. D. Goodwin, editor, *Exhortation and Controls: The Search for a Wage-Price Policy, 1945–1971* (Brookings, 1975); and the several Brookings volumes on the wage-price controls of 1971–1973. For a summary of this writer's views on the Kennedy–Johnson experience and some suggestions for the future, see his "An Incomes Policy for the 1970's," *Review of Economics and Statistics*, 54 (August 1972), reprinted in W. L. Smith and R. T. Teigen, *Readings in Money, National Income, and Stabilization Policy* (R. D. Irwin, third edition 1974).

6. Explain why mandatory controls of prices and wages is usually effective only for a relatively short period of time. Does this mean that mandatory controls should never be used as a policy against inflation?

7. "That 'incomes policies' will not work is proved by the fact that prices often rise faster when incomes policies are in effect than when they are not." Evaluate.

SELECTED REFERENCES

G. L. Bach, "Inflation: Who Gains and Who Loses," *Challenge*, 17 (July/August 1973), 48–55.
  (A nontechnical discussion of the costs of inflation.)
W. Fellner, M. Gilbert, B. Hansen, R. Kahn, F. Lutz, and P. de Wolff, *The Problem of Rising Prices*, Organization for European Economic Cooperation and Development, 1961.
Inflation: The Present Problem, Report by the Secretary General, Organization for Economic Cooperation and Development, 1970.
P. McCracken, G. Carli, H. Giersch, A. Karaosmanoglu, R. Komiya, A. Lindbeck, R. Marjolin, and R. Matthews, *Towards Full Employment and Price Stability*, Organization for Economic Cooperation and Development, 1977.
  (Three reports, over 16 years, on inflation—causes and remedies—by the OECD, the first and third involving international panels of private experts.)
J. Sheahan, *The Wage–Price Guideposts* (Brookings Institution, 1967).
L. Ulman and R. J. Flanagan, *Wage Restraint: A Study of Incomes Policies in Western Europe* (University of California Press, 1971).
C. D. Goodwin (ed.), *Exhortation and Controls: The Search for a Wage–Price Policy, 1945–71* (Brookings Institution, 1975.)
  (Three scholarly analyses of noncompulsory incomes policies in the United States and Europe.)
C. C. Holt, C. D. MacRae, S. O. Schweitzer, and R. E. Smith, *Manpower Programs to Reduce Unemployment and Inflation: Manpower Lyrics for Macro Music* (The Urban Institute, 1971).
  (The role of labor market frictions in inflation and policies to combat them.)
J. L. Pierce, "Quantitative Analysis for Decisions at the Federal Reserve," *Annals of Economic and Social Measurement*, 3 (January 1974), 1–19.
  (A Federal Reserve official reflects on how the Fed weighs the costs of inflation versus those of unemployment in setting monetary policy.)
J. Rutledge, "Irving Fisher and Autoregressive Expectations," *American Economic Review*, 67 (February 1977), 200–205.
  (A needed clarification of what Irving Fisher really said about inflation and interest rates.)
G. Ackley, "The Costs of Inflation," to be published in *American Economic Review*, 68 (February, 1978).

Part VI

CONSUMER SPENDING

Chapter 16

The Theory of Aggregate Consumption

The Meaning of Consumption

The Theory of Individual Consumption
Particular products and services
Total consumption
Graphical exposition of consumption theory
The effect of interest rate changes

Significance of the Theory for Cross-Section Analysis

Applications to Aggregate Consumption

Importance of demographic factors
The role of lifetime resources:
    Modigliani and associates
Lifetime resources: Friedman
Importance of interest rates

Shortcomings of the Standard Theory
Extent of consumer knowledge and calculation
The estate motive for saving
Liquidity constraints
Uncertainty of expectations
Consistency with "the facts"

Alternatives to the Standard Theory

The idea that consumption is a stable function of income was given its first full and clear statement by J. M. Keynes, in his *General Theory of Employment, Interest, and Money.*[1] It is easy, however, to find others who had come close to stating the same idea earlier. As Pigou points out,[2] Alfred Marshall expressly recognized the existence of a relationship between aggregate income and saving, although admittedly in the context of long-term growth, rather than short-term fluctuation. Others may have stated the idea in the latter context, but failed to recognize its crucial relevance. However, J. M. Clark, in his *Strategic Factors in Business Cycles* (1934), not only specifically formulated the idea in the context of income fluctuations, but was quite clear as to its relevance.[3] Nevertheless, the "consumption function" is properly considered a Keynesian invention, for it lies at the heart of Keynes' theoretical system.

---

[1] Chaps. 8, 9, 10.
[2] A. C. Pigou, *Employment and Equilibrium*, 2nd (rev.) ed. (Macmillan, 1952) p. 100.
[3] National Bureau of Economic Research (1934), esp. pp. 80–85, but also 48–49, 167–69, 177–78, 188, 202–03.

Had earlier economists been specifically asked how they might suppose a person's consumption expenditures would behave as his real income changed, it is likely that they would have given an answer like Keynes': consumption will increase as income increases, but by less. But, in the short run, *aggregate* real income was simply not a variable with which they needed to be concerned. Flexible interest rates and wage rates would keep real income constant at the limits set by the economy's productive power. In the longer run, aggregate and *per capita* income might increase as the productive power of the economy grew. But with many other factors operating in the long run, there was hardly any occasion to isolate for particular scrutiny the relationship of consumption to income. Thus the novelty of the consumption function lay as much in the question as in the answer.

Keynes' specific formulation of the relationship between consumption and income on the individual (and also on the aggregate) level contained several propositions, advanced with different degrees of definiteness and not considered to be equally essential. Two points were definite and essential:

1. Real consumption expenditures are a stable function of real income.
2. The marginal propensity to consume is positive, but less than 1.

Not essential to his argument, and less positively stated, were the further hypotheses:

3. The marginal propensity to consume is less than the average propensity (which means that the latter declines with rising income).
4. The marginal propensity, itself, probably declines as income rises.

Although Keynes refers incidentally in the course of his discussion to a few bits of statistical evidence, one who reads his argument can only conclude that his consumption hypotheses were based largely upon introspection and the most casual observation. On no more solid base he propounded what he called his "fundamental psychological law." Keynes may also have seen intuitively that his function is broadly consistent with the behavior of a "rational" consumer of given tastes; nevertheless, he failed to provide any detailed *a priori* argument showing how the behavior he described would necessarily follow from the usual psychological assumptions which economists make. However, numerous later economists have sought to derive the consumption-income relationship from or integrate it with the general analysis of consumer preference which constitutes an important cornerstone of microeconomics.

THE MEANING OF CONSUMPTION

Consumption clearly involves the drawing of physical or psychological satisfactions from the use or ownership of consumer goods and services, not their mere purchase. Yet the data used earlier to represent consumption, which come from the national income and product accounts, basically represent the *purchase* by consumers of consumer goods and services, together with a few items of "imputed consumption," the most important of which is the rental value of owned residences. Quite obviously, purchase must *precede* consumption, but the time interval between purchase and enjoyment can vary. Consumption of a concert occurs simultaneously with its production, as does that of many other services.[4] The interval between purchase and consumption of "nondurable" goods may be somewhat longer, especially to the extent that consumers carry inventories; still, identifying consumption of nondurables and services with purchases is not unreasonable. However, in the case of consumer durable goods, the interval between purchase and the derivation of satisfactions from use may extend over a considerable period of time. This has led many economists to seek to refine the national-accounts data on consumer expenditures—at least insofar as consumer durable goods are concerned—for use in the empirical formulation and testing of theories of consumption.

As noted above in Chapter 2, the usual procedure for this correction is to remove purchases of new durable goods from the national-accounts total for "personal consumption expenditures," and to replace it with an estimate of the value of the *current services* of the stock of durable goods, usually estimated as the sum of depreciation on the existing stock of durables (a stock continually built up by new purchases and reduced by depreciation) plus an imputed interest income or rental return on the stock.[5] This last component is also added to disposable income.

This treatment argues that a *purchase* of consumer durable goods is an act of investment and needs to be explained in a different way than is *consumption* (of nondurables and services, including the services of durable goods). Income is undoubtedly a major determinant of the demand for the *services* of durable goods, and, as such, it helps to determine the desired stock of consumer durable goods. The size of this desired stock, together with the size of the actual stock, and other factors, is held to determine the

---

[4] Unless it is a recorded concert, in which case it becomes a consumer durable good, rendering its services over a number of years.

[5] In recent versions of the consumption equations for the "Federal Reserve-MIT Econometric Model," Modigliani and associates estimate depreciation of consumer durables as equal to 22.5 per cent of the value of the stock, and assume an imputed income or rental rate on the stock of about 15.2 per cent. See F. Modigliani, "Monetary Policy and Consumption: Linkages via Interest Rate and Wealth Effects in the FMP Model," in *Consumer Spending and Monetary Policy: The Linkages*, Conference Series No. 5 (Federal Reserve Bank of Boston 1971) pp. 9–84.

rate of purchase of durable goods in a manner that will be discussed at a later point for the case of business investment.[6]

This treatment of durable goods consumption makes little difference in the average *level* of estimated aggregate consumption (or of net national product or national or disposable income); but it does change appreciably the *time pattern* of consumption, while changing only moderately the time pattern of disposable income (through the inclusion of the imputed interest or rental income). Such a change in timing is surely important in the case of an individual consuming unit, which may purchase a car or refurnish the living room only every few years. If its purchases of durables are counted as consumption, it will appear, perhaps, to dissave substantially in the years of those purchases and save in the intervening years. If only the current services of its durables are considered consumption, its time pattern of consumption and saving will be far more stable. The difference between the two concepts is much smaller for a total population, obviously, than for an individual; but, even in the aggregate, purchases of durables do fluctuate considerably more than those of nondurables and services. (Unfortunately, trips to Europe or the Caribbean may distort individual time patterns of consumption and saving in the same way as do purchases of automobiles, reminding us that it is not only durable physical objects that yield their satisfactions over a period of time rather than at or close to the moment of their purchase.) In what follows, we will use "consumer purchase" interchangeably with "consumption," on the assumption that corrected data for purchases provide an adequate representation of consumption.

THE THEORY OF INDIVIDUAL CONSUMPTION

Aggregate consumption by United States consumers is the sum of the consumption by perhaps 70 or 80 million spending units: families, unrelated individuals, and nonprofit institutions mainly serving individuals. In the course of a year or more, most of these spending units purchase or use a thousand or more individual products or services—some products or services once or even several times a day, others only occasionally. In the aggregate, consumers make hundreds of billions of separate purchases a

[6] A simpler and almost equally satisfactory alternative treatment is to disaggregate consumption expenditures, that is, purchases, at least to the extent of providing separate consumption functions for durable goods purchases and for other consumer spending. Then the special factors believed to explain purchases of durable goods (including the desired and actual stocks of durables) can be used in the durable goods consumption function, which continues to constitute a component of total consumption and thus of GNP. Purchases of nondurables and services are then separately explained, but without the revision of disposable income described above and without including the imputed consumption of durable goods as an element of such consumption. This is, for example, the treatment in recent econometric models of the Research Seminar in Quantitative Economics, The University of Michigan.

year, acquiring tens of thousands of different consumer commodities and services (if defined narrowly, hundreds of thousands or even millions). The macroeconomic theory explaining aggregate consumption should somehow build upon the microeconomic theory which explains the ultimate unit of consumption: the single spending unit's demand for (requiring the purchase of) an individual product or service.

Particular Products and Services

An individual spending unit's decisions to purchase each particular good or service which it does purchase are surely influenced by such factors (to suggest only the more important categories) as (a) its demographic characteristics (number, age, and state of health of the unit's members)—which affect its "needs"; (b) its members' educations, tastes, experiences, life styles, place of residence, and so on—which affect the "values" it places on various goods and services; (c) its income, wealth, and debt positions and the recent and expected changes in each of these—which affect its "ability to buy"; (d) its present ownership of durable goods or stocks of nondurables and their ages and states of repair—which determine the services it gets without purchase; (e) the relative prices of all the goods and services available to it—which determine its ability to trade off one kind of purchase for another—and its knowledge of the prices, availability, and qualities of all these goods and services; (f) the current and past purchases made by other consumers—which provide "social" or "competitive" pressures to consume in particular ways; and (g) the persuasive efforts of sellers. Microeconomic theory, in attempting to explain an individual unit's purchases of any single good or service, takes most of these factors as "given" and concentrates on relatively few of the others—in particular, the prices and qualities of particular goods, and, occasionally, sellers' efforts to persuade. Some theory has also related the composition of a consumer unit's expenditures to its income (for example, in explaining the empirical observations described as "Engel's Law").

When, however, we aggregate across individual products and services, in order to deal with a spending unit's total consumption, factors which are of the greatest importance in explaining the *composition* of a unit's spending largely cancel out. This is particularly true for the one determinant which receives most attention in microeconomic theory—relative prices. However much particular relative prices may change, their average change for all products is bound to be zero.

Microeconomic theory tells us that the amount of consumer purchases of any commodity is a function of its price, given consumer income and the prices of other commodities (and all the other factors listed above). A reduction of the price of any commodity will generally increase its sales for two reasons: (a) a "substitution effect," and (b) an "income effect." The substitution effect occurs because this product's price is now lower relative to the prices of other commodities, leading to its substitution (at the margin) for the purchase of other goods. Purchase of this good is increased, whereas purchases of other goods are reduced. The income effect operates because any price reduction (given money income) increases real income. This leads to increased purchases, of the particular commodity and of all other commodities (except of "inferior goods," in which case the income effect will be negative). Thus the effect of a price reduction on purchases of the particular good is ordinarily positive for both income and substitution reasons. The effect on purchase of other goods will be negative through the substitution effect, but positive through the income effect.

It is not difficult to see how the income effect of microeconomic theory is related to the consumption function of macroeconomics. The latter holds that a rise in real income (which comes about either through a rise in money income, the price level constant or rising by less, or through a fall in prices, money income constant or falling by less) will increase consumer demand for commodities in general—the amount of the increase in demand for each commodity depending on its individual income elasticity. The aggregate marginal propensity to consume can thus be thought of as the sum of all of the individual commodity "income effects."

But how is the *substitution* effect of microeconomics to be handled in macroeconomic theory? If all individual prices rise or fall in the same proportion as the general price level, then there are only income but no substitution effects to worry about. But suppose that individual prices rise or fall unequally. This will produce substitution effects on the demands for particular commodities. How does it affect aggregate consumer demand?

To keep our treatment of the problem as simple as possible, assume that consumers can buy only two commodities, real quantities of which are indicated by C_a and C_b, and their prices by P_a and P_b. Microeconomic theory then tells us that (in a linear approximation) the following relationships hold:

$$C_a = a_0 + a_1\frac{Y}{P} + a_2\frac{P_a}{P_b}$$

$$C_b = b_0 + b_1\frac{Y}{P} + b_2\frac{P_b}{P_a}$$

where Y is total money income, P is the average price level, a_1 and b_1 are the income coefficients of demand, and a_2 and b_2 are the coefficients of relative price response. Ruling out inferior goods, we assume that a_1 and b_1 are each positive, whereas a_2 and b_2 each are negative.

Now we wish to derive the consumption function for a single consumer, using C as the sum of $C_a + C_b$. By substitution we derive:

$$C = a_0 + b_0 + (a_1 + b_1)\frac{Y}{P} + a_2\frac{P_a}{P_b} + b_2\frac{P_b}{P_a}$$

Except for the final two terms, this resembles the customary aggregate consumption function (except that microeconomic price theory does not tell us whether the sum $a_1 + b_1$—the marginal propensity to consume—is greater than, equal to, or less than 1). It would appear from this, however, that relative prices should also be included in the aggregate consumption function, unless we could be sure that the sum of the final two terms were constant.

In order to isolate the substitution effect, let us suppose that P_a and P_b both change, but in such fashion that P remains unchanged. (This assumption lets us avoid confusing income and substitution effects).

It is clear that any such change in relative prices will produce results that are at least partly offsetting, for a rise in P_a/P_b necessarily means a fall in P_b/P_a. Consumption demand for one commodity will increase and for the other will decrease. But is there any reason to suppose that the two effects are completely offsetting? Is it necessary that the values of a_2 and b_2 should be such that any change in relative prices leaves total C unchanged? The answer is that there appear to be no *a priori* reason why this should be the case.[7] Yet apparently this, at least roughly, is the case, so far as the record of experience indicates. At least, no microeconomic theorist has postulated any significant effect on a family's total consumption (or saving) as a result of any specific type of relative price change, and no statistician has improved the "fit" of an aggregate consumption function through including any term for relative price effects. (It should be added, however, that few have really tried!) In any case, we shall follow the customary practice in macroeconomics of aggregating consumer demand across all commodities and services without reference to the structure of relative consumer prices.

Thus, conventional microeconomic theory provides support for the notion that an individual consumer's aggregate consumption is affected by the relationship between his money income and the average of the prices he pays, that is, by his real income, thereby providing a major building block for macroeconomic consumption theory. But to explain *why* and *how* and *by how much* income affects consumption—that is, what is the sum of the income coefficients of demand for all individual products—we need to go behind the demand curves of price theory to examine the kind of behavior that underlies the income effect.

Total Consumption

The microtheory that is relevant to the relationship of income to aggregate consumption focuses upon the choice which a consumer must continually make between consumption, identified as present satisfactions, and saving

[7] See G. Ackley and D. B. Suits, "Relative Price Changes and Aggregate Consumer Demand," *American Economic Review*, XL (December 1950) 785–804.

or dissaving, which affect potential future satisfactions. The basic body of theory that deals with this choice is not in any respect new; much of it was carefully worked out by Irving Fisher in the first two decades of this century.[8] But its applicability to the explanation of aggregate consumption was proposed only in the 1950s—although in form and emphasis somewhat different from Fisher's—by Franco Modigliani and Richard Brumberg and by Milton Friedman.[9] The Modigliani approach is usually referred to as the **life-cycle theory**, that of Friedman as the **permanent income theory**. In either theory, the consuming unit is visualized as having not only a current income from work and wealth but meaningful expectations and plans about its future incomes from work and wealth. Its future income from wealth will, of course, be higher to the extent that the unit chooses to save today, thus adding to wealth and its earnings; future income from wealth will be lower to the extent that the unit now reduces its wealth through dissaving. Moreover, if it dissaves by borrowing, some part of its future earnings will have to be used to repay the borrowing with interest. (In principle, the unit can also affect its expected future income from work through investing in human capital—education, training, health care.) The unit also has a vision of its future "needs" and "wants," as affected by the changing number and character of its members, by the changing satisfactions which its members expect to receive from their consumption, and by expected changes in the social or commercial pressures upon it to consume.

Given this vision of its future needs and wants, the consuming unit's decision on its current total consumption and saving can be described as reflecting a more or less conscious effort to achieve an optimum time pattern of total consumption over the remaining life cycle, subject to the constraints imposed by the expected amount of the resources available to it over its life, the anticipated time pattern of its receipt of those resources, and its desire to leave an estate when the spending unit comes to an end. "The rate of consumption in any given period is a facet of a plan which extends over the balance of the individual's life, while the income accruing within the same period is but one element which contributes to the shaping of such a plan."[10] More precisely, how a rational spending unit may make its choices and plans—and what factors may affect them—can be easily described algebraically, or shown graphically, for the artificial case of a consumer with a two-period horizon. (For example, we can assume that at the end of the second period the world is expected to come to an end; alternatively, we can think of the two periods as two halves of a life

---

[8] And later summarized in his *The Theory of Interest* (Macmillan, 1930).
[9] F. Modigliani and R. Brumberg, "Utility Analysis and the Consumption Function: An Interpretation of Cross-Section Data, in K. Kurihara, ed., *Post Keynesian Economics* (Rutgers University Press, 1954); and M. Friedman, *A Theory of the Consumption Function* (Princeton University Press, 1957). See also A. Ando and F. Modigliani, "The Life-Cycle Hypothesis of Saving," *American Economic Review*, 53 (May 1963), pp. 55–84.
[10] Modigliani and Brumberg, *op. cit.*, p. 392.

cycle—for example, from now until the children finish college and leave home, and from then until death of the parents—on the further assumption that there is no desire to leave an estate.)

We first develop the theory algebraically for the simple two-period case, (assuming that the periods are such that nothing changes within them, but only between them).

Define Y_1 as the unit's income *from work and wealth* in period 1, and Y_2^e its expected earnings *from work only* in period 2. The unit's wealth in period 1 is represented as W_1; *and i* is the rate of interest at which it can both lend and borrow (and which it assumes will be constant). Consumption in the two periods is represented by C_1 and C_2^e, respectively. The total resources available to the unit in period 1 are

$$R_1 = Y_1 + W_1 + Y_2^e \frac{1}{1+i}$$

respectively, its income, its wealth, and its borrowing power. The expected resources available to it in period 2 are equal to all resources not consumed in period 1, plus interest on that carryover:

$$R_2^e = (R_1 - C_1)(1 + i)$$

$$= (Y_1 + W_1)(1 + i) + Y_2^e - C_1(1 + i)$$

or, if we define its saving in period 1, S_1, as $Y_1 - C_1$,

$$R_2^e = (S_1 + W_1)(1 + i) + Y_2^e$$

The sum $S_1 + W_1$ represents the wealth carried over from period 1. If S_1 is positive, the first period's wealth has been augmented by saving, and this sum, plus interest on it, becomes part of its second period's resources, along with its earnings. If S_1 is negative, wealth has been reduced by dissaving, but, so long as $S_1 + W_1$ is positive, total available resources in period 2 will still exceed the unit's earnings in that period. However, if $S_1 + W_1$ is negative, the unit has borrowed in period 1 to finance its dissaving, and the negative sum $(S_1 + W_1)(1 + i)$ represents the repayment, with interest, of that borrowing in period 2, reducing its resources below its expected second-period earnings.

As the simplest case, we assume that some fixed relationship exists between the unit's expected consumption "needs" and "wants" in the two periods. For example, if it regards the expected needs and wants of the second period exactly as important as those of the first period, we can specify that $C_1 = C_2^e$, or $C_1 = 0.5(C_1 + C_2^e)$. On the other hand, if it regards its needs and wants in the first period as twice as urgent as in the second, $C_1 = 0.667(C_1 + C_2^e)$. More generally, we can specify $C_1 = k(C_1 + C_2^e)$, where k equals the desired ratio, $C_1/(C_1 + C_2^e)$.[11] Moreover, since the unit has no reason to save in period 2, nor to conserve any previous saving,

$$C_2^e = R_2^e$$

Thus,

$$C_1 = kC_1 + kR_2^e$$

or

$$C_1 = \frac{k}{1-k}R_2^e = \frac{k}{1-k}[(Y_1 + W_1)(1 + i) + Y_2^e - C_1(1 + i)],$$

which reduces to

$$C_1 = \frac{k}{1 + ki}[(Y_1 + W_1)(1 + i) + Y_2^e]$$

By substituting into equation (1) various assumed values of Y_1, Y_2^e, W_1, k, and i, we obtain the illustrative results for C_1, S_1, and C_2^e shown in Table 16-1. The bottom section of the table spells out the financial transactions that accompany the results shown in the middle section. The additional symbols used are W_2^e, for wealth expected to be carried over into the second period, Y_2^{we} for the expected income from wealth in the second period, B for first-period borrowing, and P^e for the required second-period repayment, including interest.

By comparing various pairs of columns, we can see what effects various changes in incomes, wealth, "needs," and interest rate may have on consumption, saving, and the unit's economic welfare. Some conclusions of this analysis are listed below, referring in each case to the column comparisons in the table which illustrate them.

1. A spending unit that expects declining income tends to consume less and save more than does another unit—with the same current income, wealth, and pattern of "needs"—that expects rising income (A versus B).
2. With the same income, income expectations, and needs, a spending unit with greater wealth will consume more and save less (A versus C).

---

[11] It is usually assumed that consumers exhibit a quality called "time preference"—a preference for present over future satisfactions, with satisfactions farther in the future discounted progressively more than nearby ones. We could thus write

$$C_1 = k\left(C_1 + \frac{1}{1+m}C_2^e\right) = \frac{k}{(1-k)(1+m)}C_2^e$$

where m is a rate of time preference discount, distinguished from k, the factor reflecting changes in situation associated with stages in its life cycle. In the two-period case, it is, of course, not only difficult to distinguish the two factors, but mathematically unnecessary.

TABLE 16-1
Numerical Examples of C_1, C_2^e, and Related Magnitudes

	A	B	C	D	E	F	G	H	I	J	K
Assumptions											
Y_1	200	200	200	100	250	300	200	100	200	300	300
Y_2^e	100	300	100	200	100	150	100	200	100	100	150
W_1	0	0	50	50	50	50	50	50	0	0	0
i	0.1	0.1	0.1	0.1	0.1	0.1	0.2	0.2	0.1	0.1	0.1
k	0.5	0.5	0.5	0.5	0.5	0.5	0.5	0.5	0.667	0.667	0.667
Results											
C_1	152.4	247.6	178.6	173.8	204.8	254.8	181.8	172.7	200	268.8	300
$S_1 = R_1 - C_1$	47.6	−47.6	21.4	−73.8	45.2	45.2	18.2	−72.7	0	31.2	0
C_2^e	152.4	247.6	178.6	173.8	204.8	254.8	181.8	172.7	100	134.4	150
Financial transactions											
$W_2^e = (W_1 + S_1)$	47.6	0	71.4	0	95.2	95.2	68.2	0	0	31.2	0
$Y_2^{we} = W_2^e(1 + i)$	4.8	0	7.1	0	9.5	9.5	13.6	0	0	3.1	0
$B_1 = (W_1 + S_1)$	0	47.6	0	23.8	0	0	0	22.7	0	0	0
$P_2^e = (W_1 + S_1)(1 + i)$	0	52.4	0	26.2	0	0	0	27.3	0	0	0
$R_2 = Y_2 + W_2^e + Y_2^{we} - P_2^e = C_2$	152.4	247.6	178.6	173.8	204.8	254.8	181.8	172.7	100	134.4	150

3. With the same wealth, same total expected lifetime earnings, and same pattern of needs, a unit will currently consume a little less if the expected pattern of its income is rising over its life cycle than if it is falling, but it will consume a much larger proportion of its current income (C versus D).

4. A consuming unit that sees its needs as decreasing in the future will spend more and save less than another with the same income, wealth, and income expectations that expects its needs to rise or remain the same (A versus I).

5. An unexpected increase in current income, with no change in wealth or in expected future income, will increase current and future consumption; but the apparent marginal propensity to consume (current income) is necessarily less than unity, and will approximate the share of its lifetime consumption that is planned to take place in the current period (C versus E, I versus J).

6. Increases in both current and expected future income will result in a rise in current consumption approximately equal to the rise in expected lifetime income times the share of lifetime consumption planned for the current period (C versus F, I versus K). The apparent marginal propensity to consume (current income) will thus be substantially higher than in case 4, although still necessarily less than unity.

7. An increase in interest rate may increase current consumption (C versus G) or decrease it (D versus H), depending on the time pattern of income versus that of needs and whether the unit is thus a lender or borrower. These can be referred to as the "income effects" of a change in interest rates.

Graphical Exposition of Consumption Theory

The same theoretical considerations can be shown graphically, as in Figure 16-1. Here, the horizontal axis measures quantities of income, consumption, wealth, and so on, in period 1—the first period of the two-period life cycle—and the vertical axis the same quantities expected in the second period. Again, Y_1 is the unit's income from work and wealth in period 1, and Y_2^e its expected income *from work only* in period 2. It has current wealth in the amount W_1, and the interest rate at which it can both borrow and lend is i. Line $R_1 R_2^e$ shows all the possible combinations of its consumption in each of the two periods, which we may call its "opportunity locus," or "resources constraint."

If the unit should plan to consume nothing in period 2, it could consume in period 1 an amount equal to its total period 1 resources:

$$Y_1 + W_1 + Y_2^e \frac{1}{1+i}$$

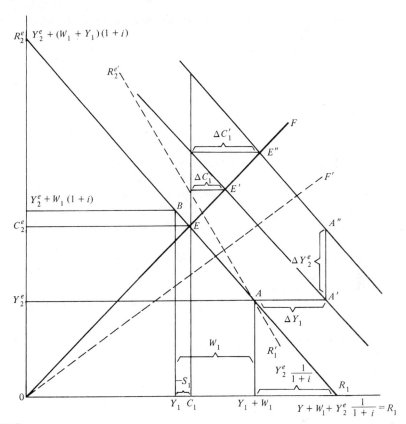

FIGURE 16-1

This combination is represented by point R_1. If it were to consume all its income plus all its wealth in period 1, dissaving but not borrowing, its consumption in period 2 would be limited to its second-period income, Y_2^e, the combination shown as point A. If it consumed only Y_1 in period 1, neither saving nor dissaving, its consumption in period 2 could equal $Y_2^e + W_1(1 + i)$, shown as point B. If it consumed nothing in period 1 (saving its entire income), it could consume in period 2 an amount equal to $Y_2^e + (W_1 + Y_1)(1 + i)$, its maximum possible second period resources, represented at point R_2^e. It obviously can consume any other combination shown along its opportunity locus. Points between R_2^e and B involve some current (that is, first-period) saving, between B and A some current dissaving but not consumption of all of its wealth, between A and X', consumption of all its wealth and going into debt. If the unit has no wealth, points A and B coincide. The slope of $R_1R_2^e$ is $-(1 + i)$, the rate at which present resources can be converted into future resources, or vice versa.

There are two possible ways of describing the unit's decision as to its allocation of its resources between these periods. The first, and simpler, corresponding to the preceding algebraic treatment, is shown in Figure 16-1. It assumes that the unit's lifetime needs and wants call for it to divide its total lifetime consumption in some fixed ratio between the two periods. This ratio can be shown by a ray through the origin. If, for example, its needs and wants are judged the same in the two periods, so that $k = 0.5$, the ray will be at a 45° angle, as is line OF. Its consumption in each period is shown by the intersection of OF and $R_1R_2^e$ or at E. Here it dissaves a bit in period 1 (consuming some of its wealth, although not borrowing), planning in period 2 to consume the remainder of its wealth, the income on that remainder, and its second-period earnings. Obviously, different desired proportions of consumption, represented by a rotation of the ray OF, for example, to OF', would change the amount of consumption in the current period, with an almost offsetting planned change in period 2.

We can now note the effect on the opportunity locus of various changes in Y, W, and i. A rise in Y_1, with Y_2^e, W_1, and i unchanged, would cause $R_1R_2^e$ to shift to the right, its slope unchanged. The new resources constraint (unlabeled, and only part of which is shown in Figure 16-1) passes through point A', where the distance AA' equals ΔY_1. The intersection of the new resources constraint with ray OF, at E', shows the new levels of C_1 and C_2^e. If $k = 0.5$, ΔC_1 will be approximately $\frac{1}{2}\Delta Y_1$, more accurately, as equation (1) shows,

$$\Delta C_1 = \frac{0.5 + 0.5i}{1 + 0.5i}\Delta Y_1$$

If $k = 0.667$, ΔC_1 would approximately be $\frac{2}{3}\Delta Y_1$, more accurately,

$$\frac{0.667 + 0.667i}{1 + 0.667i}Y_1$$

If *both* Y_1 and Y_2^e increase, in the same amount, the new resources constraint, parallel with the original, passes through A'', where $AA' = \Delta Y$, $A'A'' = \Delta Y_2^e$, and $\Delta Y_1 = \Delta Y_2^e$. Obviously, consumption in both periods will be increased, and the apparent MPC (current income) will be higher than if only Y_1 had increased (compare ΔC with $\Delta C_1'$). An increase in wealth shifts $R_1R_2^e$ to the right in the same way as an increase in Y_1.

The effect of a change in the interest rate is to rotate $R_1R_2^e$, through point A. If i increases, the line through A becomes steeper (for example, to $R_1'R_2^e$); if i declines, the line through A becomes flatter. If (as in Figure 16-1) the initial division of consumption, at E, lies above and to the left of point A (that is, the unit is a lender), it is clear that a higher interest rate will raise consumption in both periods. However, if A were above E (that is, the unit was a borrower), the result is the reverse.

The second, and somewhat more general method, postulates the existence of a "utility function" represented by a family of "indifference curves" such as the family which includes curves U_1 and U_2 in Figure 16-2. This figure uses the same income, wealth, and interest rate assumptions—

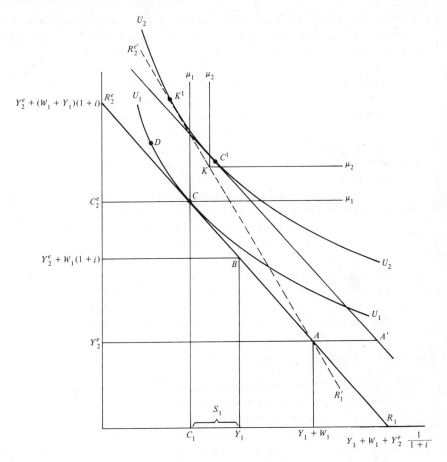

FIGURE 16-2

and thus has the same resources constraint—as Figure 16-1. Each indifference curve shows the locus of combinations of consumption in the two periods which would be judged by the unit (as of period 1) to provide equal satisfaction, through substitution of more consumption in one period for less in the other—given, of course, the expected nature of the spending unit, and its "needs," and the pressures on it in the two periods. Along curve U_1, for instance, combination D is regarded as providing satisfactions equal to those from combination C; although D involves less current consumption, it offers so much larger future consumption that it is "as good as" combination C. The concavity (upward) of the curves reflects the assumption that to induce any given unit sacrifice of current consumption requires progressively larger increments of prospective future consumption. Curve U_2 shows other combinations, each providing the same total utility as any other, but all providing a higher level of utility than represented by U_1. In effect, the first treatment, the ray through the origin, implied L-shaped indifference curves such as u_1 and u_2. That is, no possible substitution of more now for less later, or vice versa, could do other than to reduce total utility.

Given available resources, the highest utility which the unit can achieve is U_1, which it can achieve only at point C. At point C, it saves a considerable amount in period 1, adding to its wealth, thus permitting it to finance very substantial expected dissaving in period 2. As drawn in Figure 16-2, the particular position of the indifference curves implies that the unit's expected "needs" are considerably greater in the second period than in the first.[12]

If an increase in the unit's resources—either in Y_1, Y_2^e, or W_1 or some combination thereof—shifts the resources constraint so that it now passes through A', consumption will be increased in both periods, and—given the way the indifference curves are drawn—in almost exactly equal proportions (a ray from the origin through C would nearly pass through C'). This property of the indifference curves is not essential, although one would expect that a shift in the opportunity locus, with no change in slope, would normally cause changes in C_1 and C_2^e in the same direction. Thus the results are basically similar to those of the simpler analysis.

The Effect of Interest Rate Changes

Consider, now, however, the effect of a change in the interest rate. Opportunity locus $R_1' R_2^{e'}$ (the broken line) shows the effects of a given increase in i. Representing consumer behavior by a ray through the origin—as in Figure 16-1, or in the algebraic formulation—would cause the pattern of consumption to shift from C to K. But using the indifference curve approach, which allows for substitution between consumption in the two periods, the pattern instead shifts to K'. As before, the effect of the increase in i is to permit larger total consumption because, as a lender, the higher i raises the unit's lifetime resources. This is the income effect, previously noted. (For borrowers, of course, the income effect of an increase in i is negative.) But now the unit chooses actually to *reduce* its current consumption in order to permit an even larger consumption increment in period 2—the reduction in current satisfactions being offset by the much larger increase made possible in future satisfactions. This can be called the **substitution effect** of the interest rate change. This, of course, is the source of the classical economists' usual theory that saving is a function of the interest rate. However, if account is also taken of the

[12] The concept of "time preference" alluded to earlier can now be defined in terms of the slope of indifference curves—usually defined at their intersection with a 45° line through the origin, that is, equal consumption in each period. If the slope of the indifference curves equals one (in absolute value), time preference is often called "zero"; if greater than one "positive", if less than one "negative."

income effect, it is clear that the dependence of S on i is not necessarily positive.

(If point C lay to the right of point A, so that the unit were a borrower, there would also be substitution in the same direction. And although, as a borrower, the unit would have to reduce its total lifetime consumption, the substitution would permit this total to be reduced by less than if the proportions of present and future consumption were to remain fixed.)

This last feature—the substitution between present and future consumption as a result of an interest rate change—constitutes the major difference in analytical result between the indifference curve approach and the simpler idea of fixed proportions between present and future consumption, based on perceptions of relative needs. How much difference this makes depends, of course, on how much the indifference curves depart from rectangular form; and one is permitted to exercise considerable skepticism as to the extent of this departure. Indeed, it is of the essence of Modigliani's "life-cycle" theory of consumption that factors relating to the time pattern of its needs at various stages of a unit's life cycle (along with the time pattern of its income) essentially determine the time pattern of its consumption and saving, although, of course, this pattern can still be slightly modified by substitutions induced by changes in the level of interest rates.

However, there is still a third effect of an interest rate change that we have ignored up to now in the present discussion, and which is possibly the most important. A change in interest rates increases or decreases the capital values of many forms of wealth—most clearly the market value of outstanding fixed-coupon obligations such as government or private bonds. Less directly and less certainly it will also alter the market values of equities (shares), the value of (variable) pension rights, the value of ownership rights in unincorporated businesses, of land, buildings, and other assets. The effect of a change in wealth is, as noted above, the same as of a change in current income, and will, therefore, tend to alter both present and future consumption. We can call this the **wealth effect** of interest rate changes. At the same time, of course, interest rate changes alter the value of the "negative wealth" of debtors, with effects opposite to those on creditors. Together, the income and wealth effects of interest rate changes seem likely to swamp any substitution effects. (To be sure, since every population will include both borrowers and lenders, both wealth-holders and debtors, *in the aggregate*, the income and wealth effects of interest-rate changes will to a considerable extent cancel out, except as obligations of the government are involved, as was explained in Chapter 12.)

Although the theory has been up to now presented in the two-period context, it can easily be generalized to the multiperiod case, covering the entire remaining expected lifetime of the consuming unit. (The extended model can, of course, be summarized algebraically, although not graphically.)[13] There are several main effects of this extension. The first is, quite obviously, that, for most units, current income constitutes a much smaller fraction of total lifetime resources than our examples have implied, expected future earnings a much larger share. Thus, the marginal propensity to consume a "one-shot" income change is considerably lower than in the two-period case—indeed, it is roughly equal to $(1/N)\Delta Y$, where N is the number of remaining periods in the unit's life. Second, in "real-world" situations, current wealth tends for many units to be much larger relative to current earnings (over a period of a year or less) than our two-period numerical examples have implied; and wealth may be held, and added to, in order to supplement or even replace current income over a number of future periods of peak "needs" (for example, the years while the children are in college), or periods of low or even zero earnings from work (for example, after retirement). Third, extension to the full remaining lifetime of a consuming unit—which may be up to 50 or 60 years for young units—should remind us that distant expectations are held with a large degree of uncertainty, and that the more distant future needs and expected resources will be heavily discounted not only for "time-preference" reasons but also because of uncertainty. And, fourth, some assumption needs to be made about the desires of some spending units to plan to leave bequests, although the life-cycle theory itself supplies no such assumption.

SIGNIFICANCE OF THE THEORY FOR CROSS SECTION ANALYSIS

The main *a priori* implications of the theory for the consumption of individual units should now be clear. If consumer spending is mainly determined by expected lifetime resources (income and wealth) and the pattern of expected lifetime needs, then data on the consumption patterns of individual spending units might be expected to show the following characteristics:

1. Families at different stages of their life cycles would have very different levels of consumption relative to income (for example, young families with children versus families during a period of prime earning power but after the children have left home).
2. Units at the same stage of the life cycle, and with the same incomes, but having different expected time patterns of income, would consume very differently (for example, a young family whose principal earner is a factory worker, its family income already close to its lifetime peak, as opposed to a young professional's family, whose earnings may peak at age 60 or later).

[13] For such an extension, see the following discussion, under the heading "The Role of Lifetime Resources: Modigliani and Associates".

3. Fluctuations in a unit's current income which were not interpreted to be the result of factors that would cause parallel changes in expected future incomes would have relatively small effects on current consumption; they would also have small, but cumulatively substantial, impacts on planned consumption for many periods to come. On the other hand, unexpected changes in income that appeared to be permanent would cause large changes in current (and planned future) consumption.

4. Differences in wealth would be as important as differences in income in explaining consumption differences; changes in wealth might be as important as changes in income in explaining consumption changes, and their effects, too, would be spread over many periods to come.

5. The marginal propensity to consume either unexpected changes in wealth or unexpected and nonpermanent changes in income should roughly approximate $1/N$ times the change in income or wealth, where N is the remaining number of years in the unit's life.[14]

Many of these implications of the theory are indeed extremely useful in interpreting the results of empirical studies of the consumption and saving patterns of individual spending units.

At various times over the past 100 years and in various countries, comparative studies have been made of family budgets; that is, for a group or *cross-section* of families at a given time, data have been collected regarding size and disposition of income. These data have been used to support the empirical hypotheses, often called **Engel's Law**, which describe the different disposition of income at different levels of income (as income rises, the percentages spent on food and housing decrease, on clothing and household operation remain about constant, on education, health, and recreation expand).[15] These data also ordinarily reveal the *total expenditures* on all objects (or the saving) of the families covered by the study. Without exception, budget studies show a clear relationship between family income and total family consumption, much like that which Keynes postulated for the total economy: low-income families typically dissave; high-income families typically spend less than income. As one moves along

---

[14] To the extent that future "needs" are heavily discounted either because of a positive time preference, or uncertainty, or both, the fraction will be considerably greater than $1/N$ particularly if N is a large number.

[15] Ernst Engel (1821–1896) was a German statistician, whose conclusions were published in 1895 in *Bulletin de l'Institut international de statistique*. The text states the "law" as Engel did, although subsequent research shows that only the conclusions regarding food and housing are indisputable. H. S. Houthakker, "An International Comparison of Household Expenditure Patterns, Commemorating the Centenary of Engel's Law," *Econometrica*, 25 (October 1957) 532–51, refers to an earlier and more restricted version of Engel's Law, published in 1857, and referring only to food expenditures. Houthakker summarizes 40 surveys from 30 countries, all of which confirm this narrower version of the law.

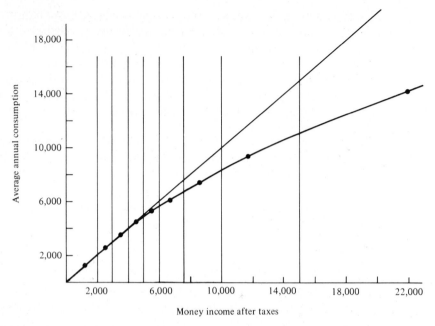

FIGURE 16-3 Average Consumer Expenditures of U.S. Families According to Money Income After Taxes, 1960–1961.

the distribution from lower to higher incomes, average consumption rises but by less than income; and the higher the income the less the rise in consumption from a further increment of income. The MPC appears to be positive, less than 1, and to decline as income rises.

Data from a recent budget study are plotted in Figure 16-3. The data relate to a scientifically selected sample of urban and rural United States families, for the years 1960–61.[16] Each dot represents the average income and the average consumption expenditure of the families whose incomes were within the income brackets shown by the vertical lines. The curved line connecting the dots shows, therefore, the average relationship of consumption to income. This general pattern is typical of the findings of most other budget studies.

What the figure fails to show, however, is that consumption behavior, regular in terms of *averages*, is nevertheless very diverse as among individual families. For example, for the income bracket $6,000–7,500, in the study charted, the average income after taxes was $6,707 and the average consumption expenditure $6,125. But individual consumption spending

[16] The data can be found in "Survey of Consumer Expenditure 1960–61," Bureau of Labor Statistics Report No. 237–93, Table 1A, U.S. Department of Labor, Bureau of Labor Statistics, February 1965. The results of a similar study, involving data for 1971–72, had not yet been published in fall 1977.

ranged widely around this average. Some families in this income bracket may have spent as little as $3,000, others $12,000 or more. Income "explains" the average consumption of a group, but many other factors must influence the expenditures of individual families within the group. Clearly these factors include many of the *a priori* implications which we have just drawn from the above discussion of the life-cycle theory, as well as from the earlier discussion of the definition of consumption:

1. Some families in each income bracket appear to dissave, or save much less than others, because, in the particular time period, they were large buyers of durable goods.
2. Some families in each income bracket have considerably more wealth than others and are usually among the larger spenders.
3. Some families in each income bracket undoubtedly expect rising incomes, others expect lower future incomes, and this is reflected in their spending patterns.
4. Families in any given income bracket are in very different stages of their life-cycles: some are retired, some have young children, and so on; both their needs and their past and expected income profiles differ widely; and so does their consumption.
5. Some families in each income bracket have suffered a temporary loss of income but have reduced their consumption very little because their expected future income is not changed; others have received windfall income increases, which they do not expect to be repeated, and they are saving much of the increment.

Moreover, some of these factors operate systematically in a way that causes the apparent *average* relationship between income and consumption to give a distorted picture of the *true* relationship. This is particularly so for items 4 and 5. Low-income families include, in particularly large numbers, families in the early and late stages of their life cycles: many of the former dissave or save very little because they anticipate rising income; many of the latter dissave because they are retired, and, as they had planned, are consuming their earlier savings. Moreover, it is reasonable to suppose that, at any given time, more of those whose current incomes are temporarily low will be found in the lower income brackets than in the higher ones; these units consume on the basis of their normally higher incomes and are currently saving very little or dissaving. Likewise, more families with temporary *positive* windfalls appear in the higher brackets than in the lower ones; their consumption reflects their normally lower income positions.

Because of these systematically distorting effects, it is clear that the average relationship between income and consumption shown in Figure 16-3 is not the "true" relationship between income, *per se*, and consumption. Undoubtedly, the true relationship is steeper: the slope of the consumption-income relationship in Figure 16-3 is less than the "true" marginal propensity to consume.

Making possibly plausible assumptions, both Modigliani–Brumberg and Friedman have argued that the "true" relationship between income and consumption—on cross section as well as for changes in income over time—would be found to be one of proportionality, and that, once corrected for the distorting effects referred to previously, "budget-study" data are consistent with this presumption. This may be. However, at least on a cross-section basis, the differences in consumption among families are so wide, even at the same income level, and are associated with so many differences in size of family, number of earners, place of residence, occupation, life style, education, home ownership, race, ethnic background—and each of these in turn tends to be systematically correlated with income—that it seems almost meaningless to attempt to isolate the "pure" effect of income alone on the consumption of individual family units. Moreover, to some extent, the reason why many high-income people have high incomes is because their cultural backgrounds and psychological makeups are such that they have in the past been large savers and careful investors. They are, by nature, high savers, and *as a result* have higher incomes. Some in the low-income categories are there because they have in the past been shiftless, spendthrift, unambitious, or put higher values on nonmaterial aspects of life. They are, by nature, spendthrift, and *as a result* have lower incomes. Thus, it would to this extent not be surprising to find that individual high-income consumers saved a larger percentage of their incomes than low-income consumers; but the causation might partly run in the opposite direction than commonly supposed.

APPLICATIONS TO AGGREGATE CONSUMPTION

Whatever the *a priori* implications which may be drawn for individual consumer behavior from the life cycle theory of consumption, our main interest here is in its implications for the aggregate (or *per capita*) consumption of a population. Just as, when we aggregated across commodities, we found that the impact of variables important for explaining consumption of individual commodities tended to cancel out, we find the same to be true when we aggregate across individuals. For, surely, any reasonably large population will contain, in relatively stable proportions, units in each stage of the life cycle; there will be a relatively constant distribution among units expecting rising, constant, and falling incomes over their remaining lives. Although many individual units in any particular year will be receiving temporarily reduced incomes, others will have received windfall increments. And, although the wealth of individual families varies widely and can change quickly and dramatically through receipt of gift or inheritance, the aggregate wealth of the household sector changes rather slowly and tends to grow in close proportion to the growth of income.

Nevertheless, there are potentially useful insights for the understanding of aggregate consumption which derive from the lifecycle theory.

Importance of Demographic Factors

The life cycle theory implies that, over their entire lives, consuming units would plan to consume their entire incomes plus any initial wealth (received by gift or inheritance), less any planned gifts and bequests. The theory has nothing to say as to how units decide upon bequests, and some adherents of the life cycle theory even doubt that, in the aggregate, planned bequests are of any real significance (that is, bequests *made* by any generation roughly equal the earlier bequests *received* by that generation— not for individual units but in the aggregate). Why, then, when we aggregate across an entire population, does not consumption equal income? It would, these theorists suggest, were it not for the facts that (at least in modern times, and in most countries), population is steadily growing and average income steadily rising. More young consuming units are being formed each year than older units are being terminated; this means that older units, which—at least after retirement—characteristically dissave, are underrepresented, and the average of all units saves. Moreover, since average lifetime income is and has been steadily rising, those units which are *now* saving for retirement are saving to finance expected dissaving at a rate higher than the current dissaving of the currently retired units.

In addition to these implications of population growth and rising income for the saving rate, the existence of individual uncertainty about the size of future incomes and about possible emergencies may also lead to positive saving in excess of that planned to finance later dissaving. Positive saving might also arise if units should tend, on balance, to expect longer life spans than, on the average, they achieve. (These last two circumstances would also give rise to many unplanned bequests). In any case, accepting the life cycle theory, the major reasons for expecting positive aggregate saving would seem to be matters (a) about which the theory has little to say directly (the desire to make bequests), (b) which constitute qualifications of it (precautionary saving, systematic overestimation of life), or (c) which occur because of the dynamics of population change and the circumstance of income growth. The last of these is ordinarily believed by life cycle theorists to be the most important reason for positive aggregate saving; however, there is no *a priori* reason why the first two reasons might not be the more important.

In any case, it would seem to be a clear implication of the above discussion that some variable or set of variables relating to the demographic composition of the population should be included in any life cycle theorist's aggregate consumption function; but it is not done. The reason probably is that such variable or variables would change slowly and continuously, and usually in one direction for a considerable period of years. Thus, their influence would be difficult to distinguish—statistically—from that of other slow-moving, trendlike variables such as income itself, wealth, or population. Still, it is surprising that more use of demographic variables has not been attempted. In recent years in the United States, the number of new household units formed each year—which had been rising rapidly for a number of years—is beginning to decline quite rapidly. This surely ought to have some effect on aggregate saving relative to income. Considerably more research on the effects of demographic changes on aggregate saving thus seems appropriate if we wish to establish the consistency of actual aggregate saving patterns with the expectations of the life-cycle theory.

The Role of Lifetime Resources: Modigliani and Associates

One negative implication of the life cycle theory is quite clear: if consumption depends on total lifetime resources, then, since current disposable income constitutes only a small fraction of those resources, consumption cannot depend primarily on current income. But it is far more difficult to specify the positive implications of the theory for aggregate consumption. Obviously, expected lifetime resources are not directly measurable, either for individuals or in the aggregate. Is there, however, some effective way to *approximate* the value of lifetime resources of the individual, and for consumers in the aggregate? Modigliani and associates on the one hand, and Friedman on the other, follow quite different approaches in attempting to supply such an approximation.

Modigliani and Ando had first concentrated on spelling out the implications of the life cycle hypothesis for individual consumption and for the cross-section differences in consumption, by income bracket, revealed by budget studies.[17] But in a later article, they considered more fully the theory's positive implications for the analysis of time-series data on consumption and income.[18] They argued that it is *a priori* reasonable to suppose that a consuming unit's utility function is such that it will wish to divide its total lifetime resources among its consumption in particular years in not necessarily equal proportions, but in *proportions which are independent of the size of the total resources* (assuming the interest rate constant). Thus, a unit's consumption in any particular year t will be proportional to the present value of the unit's lifetime resources, as seen at time t:

$$C_t = k_t R_t^L$$

[17] F. Modigliani and A. Ando, "The 'Permanent Income' and the 'Life Cycle' Hypothesis of Saving Behavior: Comparison and Tests," in *Proceedings of the Conference on Consumption and Saving*, Vol. 2 Philadelphia, 1960.

[18] "The 'Life Cycle' Hypothesis of Saving: Aggregate Implications and Tests," *American Economic Review*, 53 (March 1963), 55–84.

where lifetime resources

$$R_t^L = W_t + Y_t + \sum_{n=1}^{T} \frac{Y_t^{e(t+n)}}{(1+i)^n}$$

In this expression T represents the remaining number of years of the unit's earning power, W_t its current wealth, Y_t its current earning from work and wealth in year t, and $Y_t^{e(t+n)}$ its current expectation (as of year t) of its income from work in any future year $t+n$; and i (the discount factor) reflects the unit's time preference—its preference for current satisfactions over those one year later. (The symbol

$$\sum_{n=1}^{T}$$

means the sum for all years beginning with 1 and extending to year T, the end of its earning span.) Suppose that we *average* these discounted earnings over the rest of the unit's productive life and represent this annual average of discounted earnings by $\bar{Y}_t^e$. Since the remaining years of earnings are T, the present value of a unit's expected lifetime resources can be represented by the expression within the parentheses:

$$C_t = k_t(W_t + Y_t + T\bar{Y}_t^e)$$

We can now aggregate this equation for all consumers (so that Y_t, W_t, $\bar{Y}_t^e$ become aggregates, and k_t and T averages that apply to a total population). Unfortunately, however, the average of k_t for all consumers, which should be applied to the total wealth, the total current income, and the total (discounted) expected future income is not the same for all three components of lifetime resources, because these three components are held in different proportions by consumers having different individual ratios. However, the separate coefficients for these three terms should be similar in order of magnitude, and their size should be appropriately related to the *average* number of years remaining in the lifespans of all units in the population. Thus we can write

$$C_t = \alpha_1 W_t + \alpha_2 Y_t + \alpha_3 T\bar{Y}_t^e$$

where α_1, α_2, and α_3 are similar but not equal.

Aggregate wealth and income in the above equation are observable magnitudes, but $\bar{Y}^e$ is not. Assume, however—and here is the crucial assumption—that $\bar{Y}_t^e$ is proportional to Y_t by a factor β,

$$\bar{Y}_t^e = \beta Y_t$$

Then we can simplify to

(2) $$C_t = \alpha_1 W_t + (\alpha_2 + \alpha_3 T\beta) Y_t$$

A statistical regression of aggregate consumption on current aggregate wealth and income will, of course, provide a single coefficient for the terms within the parentheses. However, on the assumption that α_1, α_2, and α_3 are roughly equal, and given a direct estimate of T, an indirect approximation of β is clearly possible. Modigliani and Ando also constructed possible alternative and more complex mechanisms connecting $\bar{Y}_t^e$ with Y_t, but found that the simple one described above was as consistent with the data as more elaborate ones.

In their 1963 regressions using annual United States data and a variety of statistical methods, Ando and Modigliani found the coefficient of wealth α_1 in equation (2) to range from about 0.01 to 0.105; but in their preferred regressions it ranged from about 0.05 to 0.07. The combined coefficient $\alpha_2 + \alpha_3 T\beta$ was found to be around 0.65 to 0.75. We may take an equation in the order of

$$C_t = 0.06\,W_t + 0.7\,Y_t$$

as representative of these studies.

One may well ask how much has been changed from the simple Keynesian consumption function through this application of the insights provided by the theory of lifetime resources, especially since the growth of aggregate wealth closely parallels the growth of aggregate income. The theory tells us that *future* incomes—over the entire expected lifetimes of all current consumers—should be included along with current income, and presumably should be far more important than is current income. But if expected incomes are merely proportional to current income, can it not still be said that current income determines consumption?

The extent to which this is the case depends, of course, on the size of β, which indicates the relationship expected to prevail between current and future incomes, and thus the extent to which fluctuations in current income get projected into the future. But from the statistical regressions we only obtain a very indirect estimate of β, and only if we assume $\alpha_1 = \alpha_2 = \alpha_3$ and make some assumption about T, the average life expectation. Assuming $T = 30$ years, the regression would imply that β is approximately 0.35—that is, that only about one third of any change in current income is projected into the future. This is regarded by some as implying a considerable insensitivity of lifetime expected income to current income.

However, this is misleading because β is expressed as the ratio to current income of expected annual average future income—*discounted to the present*. What we really want to know is what the equation implies about the expectation of *undiscounted* future income. If we assume that all undiscounted annual values for $Y_t^{e(t+n)}$ are the same, the average of their discounted value over a period of 30 years, when discounted at 8 percent time preference (if that were the appropriate rate), turns out to be about 37.5 percent of their *undiscounted* value. Thus, a calculation that $\beta = 0.35$ implies that a rise of \$1 billion a year in Y_t leads to an expected rise of nearly $1 billion a year in average future income—*before* discounting. Thus, in effect, expected future income would be implied to be essentially equal to income in the current period.[19]

A more recent version of a Modigliani consumption function will be presented in Chapter 17.

There are numerous possible implications of a dependence of consumption on wealth as well as income, most of which have already been considered at other points in this book. Here, only one further implication needs mention.

In the longer run, it is clear that income and wealth tend to grow in very close proportion. If this proportion were completely fixed, consumption would in the long run grow in the same proportion as income—but also in the same proportion as wealth. (In that case, it would, of course, also make little practical difference for the long-run behavior of consumption whether it was assumed to depend only on income, only on wealth, or to some extent on each.) But *short-run* movements of income and wealth are definitely not proportional. Growth of income is frequently interrupted by a plateau or decline, but at such times wealth goes on growing, its rate of growth slowing only a little (to the extent that saving as well as consumption declines with income). However, the growth of wealth remains positive unless income's decline is so large that saving turns negative (which has not happened in the United States since 1932). If consumption depends even in part on wealth, the impact on consumption of a decline in income will be moderated to the extent of that dependence. Figure 16-4 illustrates this effect. Line Y shows a hypothetical cyclical advance of income and line W the movement of consumer wealth. (The figure is drawn on a semilogarithmic or "ratio" scale, in which lines of equal slope represent equal proportionate rates of change.) If consumption depended only on income, its movement would exactly parallel the irregular growth of income, if it depended only on wealth, it would parallel the smooth growth of wealth. The assumption here is that it depends on both, with the wealth effect imparting a considerable stability to the movement of consumption.[20]

---

[19] Using instead a time preference rate of 6 per cent, the average discounted value would be about 46 per cent of the undiscounted value, which implies that an extra $1 billion of current income raised expected average future earnings by about $\frac{3}{4}$ billion. Moreover, if we assume that N, the expected remaining lifetime of existing consuming units averaged $T + 10 = 40$ and that expected "needs" were the same in each future year, the coefficient 0.06 would imply a rate of time preference discount of just over 5 per cent. However, these calculations are too crude and rest on too many assumptions to indicate other than exceedingly approximate quantitative implications.

[20] The implication of this statement is basically correct; but it is not completely accurate because consumption and the growth of wealth are interrelated by the dependence of wealth changes on saving.

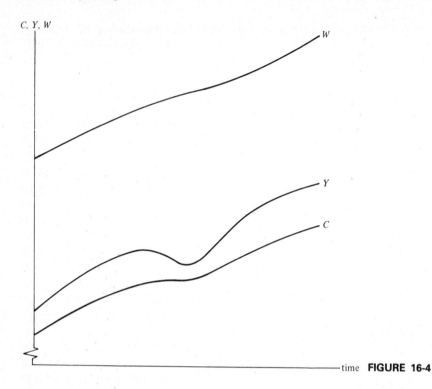

time **FIGURE 16-4**

Lifetime Resources: Friedman

Milton Friedman's approach to the approximation of lifetime resources for aggregate consumption analysis is quite different. Modigliani was willing to let future earnings be represented by and made proportional to current income, while using existing (nonhuman) wealth to represent the balance of total resources. Friedman is not willing to assume any fixed relationship between current and expected future income, nor does he make use of nonhuman wealth in his approximation of lifetime resources (although, of course, he includes the income from that wealth). Rather, he postulates (a) that the present value of the consuming unit's total lifetime resources is directly perceived by it as its total wealth, human and nonhuman; (b) that this total wealth yields, as a return, a "permanent income," which the unit also perceives; and (c) that consumption during any period depends only on this permanent income. Consumption is a fixed fraction of permanent income, a fraction independent of the size of permanent income (although it does depend on the rate of interest, the consuming unit's tastes, and the time pattern of its needs).[21] The consuming unit recognizes that its actual or "measured" income in any particular period, such as a month or year,

---

[21] Friedman does allow for some random variation in consumption relative to permanent income—an element he calls **transitory consumption**, and which, over time, averages to zero.

almost always exceeds or falls short of its permanent income; only over some considerably longer period does its measured income average out to its permanent income (and that, of course, only if its expectations have on the average been correct).

Friedman's definition of the unit's permanent income as representing a return on its total human and nonhuman wealth seems somewhat artificial. For the largest part of most units' wealth, their human wealth, is known to them only by capitalizing (at some interest rate) their current and expected earnings from work. That is, the unit needs to know the income in order to calculate the wealth that is said to yield the income. Then, having found the amount of wealth by capitalizing the income, permanent income is found by applying to the wealth a rate of return (presumably the same one used to capitalize the income). This seems not only artificial but unnecessary. What a unit can expect to earn from work is mainly known by observing what it (and others) are earning and have earned in the past. Thus we may describe it more directly as that income which the unit perceives on the basis of experience and observation, as its "normal" income from work. This can perhaps be approximated by some weighted moving average of its past incomes; but if there are life-cycle patterns of income, the moving average will poorly represent normal lifetime income.

The difference between permanent and measured income in any period is labeled **transitory income**. Since Friedman postulated that consumer spending in any period is based only upon permanent income, in effect he assumes that all of the transitory income component is saved or dissaved (ignoring the transitory component of consumption). Over any considerable period, transitory income averages approximately to zero; and permanent and actual income are the same. However, in any particular year, both for most individual units and perhaps for all units taken together, transitory income will be a substantial positive or negative amount. How then should we calculate the *aggregate* permanent income of any particular year?

A stable individual income or a stable growth of an individual's income, Friedman appears to have reasoned, will generate expectations of future income—and thus a current permanent income—consistent with the continuation of that same income or rate of income growth; fluctuations in income or in its rate of growth, on the other hand, will be treated as transitory unless or until a new trend emerges. Something similar is postulated for the corresponding aggregates. Although very few individual incomes move parallel to aggregate income, if the aggregate moves smoothly, Friedman apparently presumes that individual experiences of instability tend to cancel out: transitory gains for some exactly offset transitory losses for others; thus, aggregate permanent income also moves smoothly. On the other hand, fluctuations in the growth of actual aggregate income must, on balance, reflect the net predominance of positive or negative transitory components in individual incomes. This reasoning supports the proposition that the aggregate permanent income in any period can be represented by a moving average of actual aggregate income over a number of past periods.[22]

Friedman is careful not to commit himself on how long it takes for alterations in the rate of change of aggregate measured income to affect the aggregate of individual consumers' permanent incomes or by how much. That, he says, is an empirical question that can only be answered by close analysis of actual data. At one point, however, he refers to a statistical consumption function (to be presented in Chapter 17) that represents as any year's aggregate permanent income a projection of the weighted average of income over the previous 17 years, giving greatest weight (about one third) to the most recent income, and rapidly diminishing weights to earlier years. Elsewhere, however, Friedman seems to refer to a 3 or 4 years' moving average of actual incomes as a possibly adequate representation of permanent income, but notes that this is an empirical question, to be determined by the data.

One obvious consequence of making consumption depend on a moving average of previous income is simply to iron out the impact on consumption of minor fluctuations in aggregate income. For example, suppose that the basic trend of aggregate income is steady but that on this trend are superimposed random fluctuations. If consumption depended only on actual current income, its time pattern would duplicate the fluctuations of income, as would the time pattern of saving. If, however, consumption depends on a multiperiod moving average of actual income, consumption would grow smoothly in line with the trend in income, while saving would fluctuate sharply, absorbing most or all of the fluctuations in income. Or consider the effect of a several-year recession superimposed on a growing income. Consumption would reflect the recession only in part and with a lag, while saving would dip sharply, absorbing a significant fraction of the cyclical decline in income. The result would be very similar to that shown in Figure 16-4.

Both Friedman and Modigliani start from the same theory of saving. Yet, although they use very different approaches and concepts, it should be clear that neither is able truly to capture what is perhaps the principal implication of that theory: namely, that saving (or consumption) depends mainly on *expectations of future lifetime income*. Modigliani assumes that future lifetime incomes are projected on the basis of current incomes and

---

[22] The assumption that stability or instability in growth of *aggregate actual incomes* parallels stability or instability in the growth of *individual permanent incomes* is necessary in order to permit Friedman to jump from the individual to the aggregate, but it is a bold assumption. For example, it is possible that a bulge or dip in actual aggregate income (as measured, for example, by GNP or NI) generates in some year *no* transitory income components because on the average, it was fully expected; in another year a similar bulge or dip may on balance be unexpected, and may generate prevailingly positive (or negative) transitory income components for individuals. Likewise, stability in the growth of actual aggregate income in some year may, if unexpected, generate prevailing positive (or negative) transitory components.

wealth; Friedman assumes that expectations of future incomes are generated by a moving average of past incomes. (And both have had to make a large number of quite unrealistic assumptions, mostly ignored here, to justify the treatment of aggregate incomes and consumption as a simple "blow-up" of an individual's income and consumption). However, because Modigliani does use actual current wealth, which is the source of at least a significant part of future incomes, one might conclude that somewhat more of the spirit of dependence of present consumption on future earnings is retained in the Modigliani formulation.

Importance of Interest Rates

A third major implication of either life cycle or permanent income theories is that changes in interest rates might affect the decisions to consume or to save. Both Modigliani and associates and Friedman refer to this in the theoretical derivations of their aggregate models, but neither leaves room either for the "substitution effect" or the "income effect" of interest rate changes in his empirical equations. However, by the explicit inclusion of consumer wealth in his consumption equations, Modigliani does make way for the "wealth effects" of interest rate changes—the effects of changes in the prices of existing bonds and equities, and the more indirect effects of these latter changes on the capitalized values of the income from other kinds of assets. Indeed, in Modigliani's most recent work, these wealth effects on consumption, through interest rate changes, are seen to play a significant role in the determination of aggregate demand, and to have important implications for monetary policy.

SHORTCOMINGS OF THE STANDARD THEORY

Although the life cycle or permanent income approach appears, in recent years, to have walked off with the honors of providing the theoretical basis for most empirical work on consumption, this seems mainly a victory by default. It reflects more the absence of serious competition than it does any signal success in improving our understanding of aggregate consumption. For the theory itself admits to major qualifications, and even its fundamental presumptions can be severely challenged. Although it provides extremely useful insights for cross-section analysis—comparisons of consumption at different levels of individual incomes at a point in time—its implications, other than negative ones, for aggregate consumption are tenuous. As we have seen, many and complicated assumptions are necessary to translate its concepts into a form relevant for considering changes in *aggregate* income and consumption *over time*. Also, it provides little if any insight into the most serious puzzle about aggregate consumption—its apparent significant instability. The matter of instability is dealt with in

Chapter 17. Some of the other shortcomings of the theory will be briefly summarized in the following sections. They are here considered in the form applicable to the life-cycle version rather than as applicable to the permanent income version. However, in most cases the reader will be able to translate the substance of the matter into the permanent income formulation.

The Extent of Consumer Knowledge and Calculation

The life cycle theory makes three very strong related sets of assumptions about individual consumer behavior. It assumes, first, that each spending unit has at all times a definite and conscious vision

- of the unit's future size and composition, including the life expectancy of its principal members
- of the entire lifetime profile of the income from work of each member, after the then applicable taxes
- of the present and future extent and terms of any credit available to it
- of the future emergencies, opportunities, and social pressures which will impinge on its consumption spending
- of present and future interest rates and rates of return on any equities it owns (after taxes), and (as one part of the solution of a system of simultaneous equations)
- of the amount and form of its consumption and saving or dissaving in every future year and of the wealth it will own and the debts it will have at all future points of time—all pointing to a wealth of zero when the unit expires.

Does each family have at all times such a definite, conscious vision of its economic future? Does it even always know a number of the *current facts* assumed to be most important: the currently available rates of return on savings; the current cost and availability of credit; even its current income, consumption, saving, and asset values? For the assumed process of intertemporal allocation to be meaningful and for it to have most of the consequences deduced, the family needs to have a reasonably clear vision on these and other matters extending well into the future.

Second, the theory assumes that the family's vision, whether correct or incorrect, is held with sufficient *certainty* for more than a short period ahead to be meaningful. Otherwise, the discount for uncertainty—and the *changing discount for changing degrees of uncertainty*—would appear to prevent any rational or stable lifetime planning of consumption. It may be that there are (or have been) more stable societies than ours, in which people live much as their parents did, where one is reasonably certain what he can expect and what will be expected of him. But, in a world numb with "future shock," how much meaning does this behavioral hypothesis really have for our society?

Third, the theory assumes that each family makes rational, conscious, and rather complex calculations based on its vision, which result in a lifetime plan for spending and saving, and that it repeats these calculations, and alters its lifetime spending plan, on the basis of every significant change in the information which it receives or the expectations which it holds. These must be conscious and rather sophisticated calculations, not at all intuitive, and ones that use fairly precise, that is, quantitative, current information and expectations. Do people actually go through these assumed calculations and repeat them each time there are significant changes in the economic environment or in monetary or fiscal policy?

To suggest that these three sets of assumptions are less than fully realistic does not, of course, mean to deny that consumers save for their retirement, or in an effort to prepare for such major expenditures as a new roof on the house, replacement of the family car, a trip to Europe, acquiring a vacation cottage, or putting the children through college. The important question, however, is whether people save *only*, or even *mainly*, in order to finance *specifically planned future dissaving* or whether they also save for other reasons. Nor does questioning the realism of the assumptions of the life cycle theory mean to deny that the possession of substantial current assets or the existence of favorable income expectations may have considerable impact on the consumption of a family that possesses such assets or expectations. The important question, however, is the extent to which recognition of the relevance of such factors dictates any unambiguous judgment about what variables belong in an *aggregate consumption function*, and in what form, or about the size of the aggregate short-term or long-term marginal propensity to consume, the aggregate response of consumers to different kinds of tax increases or reductions, or the impact on consumption of shifts in monetary policy.

The Estate Motive for Saving

Essentially, the life cycle theory asserts that consumers save only (or mainly) because they plan later on to dissave. Moreover, they plan to spend within their own lifetimes the full amount of whatever wealth they may acquire by means other than their own saving, including, particularly, bequests received. In principle, future consumption by the unit's heirs could enter into the unit's own utility function, and thus justify life-time saving—that is, bequests. However, if the heirs, too, can be expected to preserve or add to the family wealth, whose dissaving is being provided for? Moreover, if one extends the time horizon for future dissaving over generations, this attenuates even further whatever modest empirical content the theory may have—for example, in approximating the size of the marginal propensity to consume increments of wealth or temporary increments of income by reference to the remaining number of years of the average unit's expected lifetime. As indicated earlier, there can be argument about the aggregate importance of bequests, and existing data are sparse and incomplete. But the gross estates shown on Federal Estate Tax Returns in 1972 were close to $39 billion (on which taxes of $4.2 billion were paid). More than 4000 returns showed estates in excess of $1 million. The total was equivalent to about four-fifths of aggregate personal saving in that year. And despite the fact that many famous concentrations of family wealth have been dissipated over the years by "spendthrift" heirs, billions have been added by recent generations, through current saving (or the failure to spend capital gains), to the wealth of a number of the well-known older American fortunes, and substantial new fortunes have been created.

There must be other reasons why people save over their entire lifetimes, and why they conserve rather than spend any inherited wealth; such saving and preservation of capital could then result in bequests, whether or not leaving bequests may have been the primary purpose.

Liquidity Constraints

In sketching the theory of the rational allocation of income over time, we deliberately failed to mention the necessary qualifications that derive from the existence of "liquidity constraints." The assumption that present resources can be readily converted, by saving, into future resources, along an opportunity locus that reflects the current rate of interest is not subject to challenge. But the idea that very many consuming units are able to convert *future earnings into present resources* is quite fictitious, as is the assumption that all assets acquired by past saving can be readily liquidated to finance current dissaving. Most consuming units are unable to borrow significant amounts against their future earnings, at least against their future earnings from their *work*. Many cannot borrow at all against such earnings. Except for special government programs such as college loans or disaster relief loans, almost no one can borrow *at long-term to finance consumption* (as opposed to investment). Moreover, the interest rates on consumer loans tend to be far higher than the rates that consumers can earn on their saving. Previous saving, which has taken such forms as equities in houses, stocks of durable goods, or pension rights either cannot be liquidated at all or only in part or at severe cost.

The resulting "liquidity constraint" drastically limits the amount of dissaving that most people can accomplish during periods of (a) temporary income decline, (b) low early-career earnings, or (c) peak family needs. Thus it requires that consumption in such periods be tied far more closely to current income than the theory implies. Correspondingly, this reduces the later repayment obligations, which the theory postulates; thus, it *permits* consumption in other periods to follow current income more closely.

When one reflects that a large part of all short-run variations in aggregate income are associated with fluctuations in employment and unemployment, and when one recognizes that the impact of employment variations is heavily concentrated on lower income families for whom liquidity constraints are most significant, the importance of liquidity constraints begins to be appreciated. There is, of course, another group with highly fluctuating incomes, much less subject to liquidity constraints—namely, the recipients of profit-type and speculative incomes. Although they receive an appreciable fraction of aggregate income and account for a significant fraction of income variation, they account for a considerably smaller fraction of total consumption; thus, their more flexible liquidity positions may be of less significance than are the restricted liquidity positions of lower-income units with fluctuating incomes.

Uncertainty of Expectations

Even the strongest adherents of the life cycle theory might admit that expectations and financial plans that extend more than a decade or so into the future are not highly meaningful (other than, perhaps, for secure, middle-income professionals, such as the economists who develop such theories!). But does this really require modifying the character of the analysis or the nature of its conclusions? It would appear that it does. First, because uncertainty makes consumption and saving decisions depend more heavily on near-term expectations, it gives current income a greater importance in consumption decisions than the idea of a 25- to 50-year horizon seems to imply. Moreover, in recognizing the existence of substantial uncertainty about the future, it has to admit an important role for saving undertaken not as part of a plan for subsequent dissaving but undertaken instead in order to provide either security against the risks of income loss or unexpected emergencies, or resources to take advantage of unforeseen opportunities. This is popularly referred to as "saving for a rainy day." To the extent that saving is made for these reasons rather than to finance planned future dissaving, it is more likely that it will be undertaken every year, and that incurring large debts to be repaid later will so far as possible be avoided. This implies that variations of consumption and saving will be more closely tied to variations of current income. Moreover, since uncertainty persists to the end of life, positive lifetime saving may frequently occur as the result of uncertainty.

Individuals' income expectations would appear to have two main elements—(a) expectations that relate to "career patterns" or "occupational income profiles" and (b) those that relate to the performance of the overall economy. The former are drawn from information on or observations of the income histories of others and from observation of current income differences between others currently in various stages of their careers. Life cycle theorists tend to stress this element, which is, no doubt, the most stable element in individuals' income expectations. On the other hand, when we aggregate across a population, these expectations largely cancel out as an element affecting the aggregate expected income over time.

The second element of expectations reflects the projections of past trends and fluctuations in individual incomes that are associated with the growth and instability of the aggregate economy, as modified by current experiences, and by the interpretation of current "news," which may seem to imply something different for the future. It has long been observed that the component of expectations based on current experience and "news" is in part a social-psychological phenomenon. People are influenced by the prevailing attitudes and expectations of others, and in turn influence their attitudes. This itself tends to make for instability of expectations. Moreover, consumers also learn and remember; how they will interpret a particular piece of news depends on their experience with previous changes in the economy. Their reaction to the occurrence of prosperity or unemployment, of inflation or high interest rates is not invariant, but reflects their memories of earlier episodes of the same. Moreover, expectations are affected not alone by economic news and observation, but also by more general political and social events and conditions. Such events and conditions may indeed have possible implications for the economy; however their effect on income expectations does not only reflect logical deduction about these implications but also, and perhaps primarily, it reflects the transfer of worries or satisfactions, feelings of security or insecurity, optimism or pessimism, generated in one aspect of social life—politics, international relations, domestic unrest or tranquility—to another aspect, the economic.

Certainly, one cannot deny that expectations, including income expectations, must substantially influence consumer spending and saving. The merit of the life cycle theory is its stress on the importance of these expectations. But in the absence of any direct measurement of expectations, application of the theory to aggregate analysis requires that expected income be somehow approximated—either by assuming that aggregate expected income fluctuates in some proportion with current income (for example, Modigliani) or that it can be projected from the past movement of realized incomes (Friedman). Neither seems satisfactory, unless it is further substantially qualified by some direct or indirect measurement of the current state of consumer sentiment, attitudes, and "mood," and unless we recognize that these may change quite independently of either current income or the trend of past incomes.

It should also be noted that there is substantial connection, in both directions, between consumer sentiment and stock prices, which account for a substantial element of the short-term variation of consumer wealth. And once we introduce consumer sentiment and attitudes as an important independent influence on consumption, is there much advantage in pretending that we are any longer approximating the rational calculations of consumers who are constructing optimal lifetime plans for their consumption and saving?

Consistency with "The Facts"

It should be recognized that although aggregate empirical consumption functions derived from life cycle or permanent income theories may have excellent statistical properties, so do consumption functions not so based. The implications drawn from these theories are "consistent with the facts," but they are not clearly "more consistent with the facts" than consumption functions not based on these theories. And, in many cases, a particular form of empirical consumption function might be derived either from life cycle reasoning or from substantially unrelated considerations. In particular, substantial lags in the full response of changes in income might rest, as in Friedman's case, upon permanent income reasoning. But they could also be readily derived from arguments about habituation, about lags of recognition, about contractual arrangements and the durability of consumer investments, or even about the serial correlation of measurement errors.

Similarly, use of wealth as well as income in the consumption function could be interpreted merely as a means of recognizing possibly different propensities to consume (income) as between those whose incomes derive from work and from wealth. Alternatively, use of total wealth along with income—with a lower coefficient for the former than the latter—could be explained on the ground that, as consumers acquire more wealth relative to their incomes, their desire for further accumulation is satiated. For example, an equation in the form

$$\frac{S}{Y} = a - b\frac{W}{Y}$$

can be justified on the grounds just stated. Yet if we multiply through by Y and then convert from a saving to a consumption function, we derive an equation indistinguishable from Modigliani's:

$$S = aY - bW$$

$$C = Y - S$$

$$= Y - aY + bW$$

$$= (1 - a)Y + bW$$

If an equation in this form proves consistent with the facts, does this prove that consumers base their current consumption on total lifetime resources? Or does it prove they have medium-term targets for their accumulated savings relative to their incomes?

ALTERNATIVES TO THE STANDARD THEORY[23]

Criticizing the realism or usefulness of the life cycle theory exposes one to the charge that he is "antitheoretical," unless he supplies an alternative theory that matches the elegant simplicity of that approach.[24] But the alternative to the life cycle theory need not be another simple theory of consumer. behavior. For consumer behavior is almost surely far more complex than the life cycle theory assumes. The alternative is surely not the simplistic view that consumers rather automatically and mechanically spend whatever they get, or some fixed fraction (close to unity) of what they get.

A complete and satisfactory theory of consumer behavior probably does not now exist. But surely it is not adequate to describe the consumer as motivated by the single goal of maximizing the discounted value of his expected lifetime satisfactions from the consumption of goods and services; instead, his motivations are more numerous and more complicated. Nor does the consumer function as a mechanical calculating device, grinding out optimum solutions of complex problems of nonlinear programming; instead, most consumers have neither the ability nor the interest to do this. The consumer does not have a set of fixed "tastes" that will determine his "needs" and "wants" and the satisfactions from their fulfillment over his entire remaining lifetime, and he knows it; rather, he wishes to explore and experience and learn, and he knows that as he does this his needs and wants will change.

The most basic deficiency of the life cycle of behavior is not its oversimplified concept of individual behavior but rather its lack of recognition that consumption and saving are forms of social as well as individual behavior. A more adequate theory must recognize that there are strong social as well as individual pressures both to consume and to save. And the nature and the balance of these competing pressures changes over time— usually slowly, but on occasion sharply.

The pressures, social and individual, to save—and to conserve inherited wealth—are many and well known. In addition to saving to

---

[23] The writer's views, as reflected in this and, to some extent, in the previous major section, reflect to a very considerable extent (and perhaps even more than he realizes) his long association with and admiration for his colleague, George Katona, whose many years of theoretical and empirical work are summarized in his most recent volume, *Psychological Economics* (Elsevier Scientific Publishing Co., 1975). This section in no way purports to summarize Katona's thought on consumption and in some respects is at variance with it. But Katona should be given much of the credit for whatever useful ideas are reflected here, and none of the blame for the simplistic errors of a nonpsychologist.

[24] The criticisms expressed in the paragraphs immediately preceding were made as part of the author's "Discussion" of an excellent paper by James Tobin and Walter Dolde, "Wealth, Liquidity, and Consumption," and drew from Tobin, in his "Rebuttal," precisely that charge. The paper, Discussion, and Rebuttal appear in *Consumer Spending and Monetary Policy: The Linkages*, Conference Series No. 5 (Federal Reserve Bank of Boston, 1971).

finance later planned dissaving and saving to provide a cushion against uncertainty, people save because it is socially respectable to save; because a class, family, ethnic, or religious tradition calls for it; because in a particular society the possession of wealth itself confers power and prestige; because, having skimped during most of their lives to meet the needs of a growing family, parents have not learned how to enjoy consumption when the children have left home but income continues at what may be its peak level; or because, in the case of the highest incomes, consumption of total income and wealth would imply a scale of living of which society (or some relevant segment of it) disapproves. Many save in order to finance investment in the formation and continuing expansion of unincorporated or closely-held corporate businesses—in part because being the proprietor of a successful and expanding business brings noneconomic as well as economic rewards and satisfactions. Saving for such reasons as these does not require that one save every year or in proportion to any one year's income, but neither is the amount of such saving likely to depend closely on expected lifetime resources and planned future consumption needs.

Competing against these largely social or conventional pressures to save are the largely social pressures to consume—as a source of prestige, as an approved means of self expression, in order to keep up with others, or in response to the wiles of producers.

But neither the social pressures to consume nor to save (nor, for that matter, to earn) are constant over time, nor among different societies.[25] Changing moral, aesthetic, and political standards and expectations, evolving life styles, the emergence of new means for self-expression, the development of new bases for social approval and disapproval can all affect the balancce. Moreover, specific changes in social and political institutions can greatly affect pressures to save and consume. How much different were the pressures when children assumed the unquestioned obligation to support their parents until they died; before the day of social security, unemployment insurance, employer-financed pension and welfare funds? How much different may they become if society establishes, by right, a guaranteed minimum income; if income disparities are further attenuated by progressive taxation; or if a more mature and universally educated society attaches ever greater importance to artistic and intellectual pursuits and achievements?

[25] Without going into detail about international differences in saving rates, the writer will simply assert his belief that many of these cannot be explained except by reference to social and cultural traditions and standards. For example, no known economic theory will explain even a minor part of the much higher personal saving rate in Japan than in the United States. (See H. C. Wallich and M. I. Wallich, pp. 256–261, in *Asia's New Giant: How the Japanese Economy Works*, Hugh Patrick and Henry Rosovsky, editors, The Brookings Institution, 1976). It needs hardly to be added that, at least in modern times, *changes* in social and cultural standards can occur the span of a few years within any single culture of a magnitude that approaches the extent of international differences at a given time.

Short-term economic changes occur against the backdrop of these larger and more fundamental social forces; and consumers also adjust their spending in response to these short-term changes, including the experienced changes in their incomes, wealth, prices, and interest rates, and to any altered expectations generated by these changes or by other concurrent events in the social and political spheres. The response of their consumption and saving to all of these things is usually lagged, although not necessarily by any constant interval. What and how large the response will be may depend appreciably on consumers' interpretations of what is happening and on their feelings of security or insecurity, confidence or uncertainty, satisfaction or unease. These "psychological factors" can be at least crudely measured and can help predict the nature of the consumption response; but social psychologists have only limited ability to predict in advance how consumers will interpret and feel about hypothetical or expected short-term economic changes.

Development of a more complete and satisfactory understanding of consumer behavior may rest on further research and theory-building in both individual and social psychology. But progress in developing a better understanding of and ability to predict aggregate consumer spending can also proceed through further observation and statistical analysis at the aggregate level. If one believed that consumption and saving were basically individual rather than social phenomena, he might argue that, unless guided by an adequate theory of individual behavior, statistical research on aggregate consumption was "purely empirical" and its findings unreliable. But if one regards consumption behavior as basically a form of "social" or "mass" behavior, one may well discover the principal *regularities of behavior* (which constitute the essence of theory) by observing that behavior in the mass; and this is precisely what statistical consumption function research does.

The next brief chapter surveys a few samples of a vast current empirical literature on aggregate consumption functions.

REVIEW QUESTIONS

1. Although the terms are often used interchangeably, there should really be a distinction made between "consumption" and "consumer purchases."
(a) What is the distinction?
(b) Which concept is used in the national income accounts? Why?
(c) How can the national income accounts concept be adjusted to convert it to the other concept?
2. What is the relationship between the marginal propensity to consume and the income elasticity of demand for particular products?
3. "With the same wealth, same total expected lifetime earnings, and same pattern of needs, a young family will consume a little less if the expected pattern of

its income is rising over its life cycle than if it is falling, but it will consume a much larger portion of its current income." Explain why, in words.

4. "The direction of the effect on aggregate consumption of a rise in the interest rate will depend on the relative strength of the income and substitution effects." Explain carefully.

5. Both Modigliani and Friedman argue that the basic relationship between income and consumption is that of proportionality. How, then, do they explain the "budget studies," which always show consumption rising in lesser proportion than income?

6. Although their basic conceptual foundation was the same, Friedman and Modigliani came up with quite different formulations of an aggregate consumption function. State the difference, and explain briefly how each formulation derives from the common conceptual foundation.

7. What are some of the principal shortcomings of the common "conceptual foundation" of the "permanent-income" and "life-cycle" theories of consumption?

8. What are the major implications for fiscal and monetary policy of the Friedman–Modigliani approach to the explanation of consumption?

9. "Consumption is an aspect of social as much as of individual behavior." Explain. What are some possible implications of this proposition, if correct?

SELECTED REFERENCES

J. M. Keynes, *General Theory of Employment, Interest, and Money* (Harcourt, Brace, 1936), Chapters 8, 9.

(The beginnings of the consumption function.)

M. Friedman, *A Theory of the Consumption Function* (Princeton University Press, 1957), especially Chapters III and IX.

(The source of Friedman's influential permanent-income theory.)

F. Modigliani and A. Ando, "'The Life-Cycle' Hypothesis of Saving: Aggregate Implications and Tests," *American Economic Review*, 53 (March 1963), 55–84.

(A detailed statement of the implications for aggregate consumption of the life-cycle hypothesis, and its statistical testing.)

J. Tobin and W. C. Dolde, "Wealth, Liquidity and Consumption," *Consumer Spending and Monetary Policy: The Linkages* (Federal Reserve Bank of Boston, 1971), 99–136.

(A simulation study of the life-cycle hypothesis, and a derivation of monetary policy implications.)

G. Katona, *Psychological Economics* (Elsevier Scientific Publishing Co., 1975), Chapter 2, "The Affluent Consumer," pp. 19–32.

(A brief introduction to the "psychological approach" to consumer spending.)

F. S. Mishkin, "What Depressed the Consumer? The Household Balance Sheet and the 1973–75 Recession," *Brookings Papers on Economic Activity*, 1, 1977, pp. 123–164.

(A detailed explanation of consumer net worth, and its components, as an important determinant of consumption; statistical tests, and an application to recent events.)

Chapter 17

The Empirical Study of Consumption

The Instability of the Consumption-Income Relationship
A cyclical versus secular consumption function?

Dynamic Consumption Functions
Distributed-lag functions
Use of moving-average income
The Koyck function
Some examples of empirical dynamic functions
Evaluation of dynamic functions

Other Variables in Consumption Functions
Wealth
Other variables
Consumer attitudes and sentiment

Appendix: The Consumption Equations of a Recent Econometric Model

In Chapter 6, the Keynesian consumption function was first introduced. Although Keynes had dubbed his discovery a "fundamental psychological law," we have seen in Chapter 16 that at least the economic theorist's traditional view of how consumers behave does not provide unambiguous support for Keynes' simple function. Nevertheless, we did show in Chapter 6 that aggregate data on consumer spending and disposable income for the United States since the end of World War II seem highly consistent with Keynes' proposition. To be sure, we also recognized that a *double relationship* exists between C and DI, and that a close statistical relationship between these two variables might reflect either the presumed dependence of consumer spending on income and/or the (definitional) recognition that production of consumer goods constitutes the largest part of GNP whereas disposable income depends closely on GNP. However, the appendix to Chapter 6 showed that the data could not reflect *solely* the second of these relationships.

Both in Chapter 6 and its appendix we suggested that the most effective way to focus on the causal relationship in which DI is presumed to determine C is to express data in terms of the relationship not between DI and C but between C and S (where $S = DI - C$). When we do so, we find that the relationship seems far less regular than the data presented in Chapter 6 initially suggested.

THE INSTABILITY OF THE CONSUMPTION–INCOME RELATIONSHIP

Figure 17-1 presents graphically the relationship between consumption (as represented by personal outlays) and personal saving, based on annual

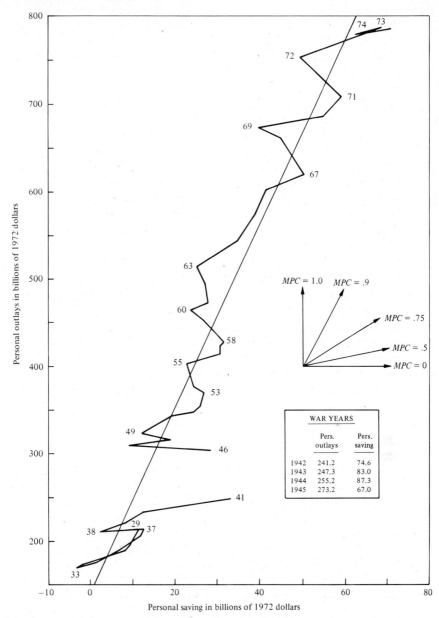

FIGURE 17-1 Personal outlays and personal saving, 1929–1975.

United States data for the years 1929–1941 and 1946–1975, with lines connecting each pair of consecutive years. These data (for the period 1946–1975) were used for the regressions of consumption and saving on disposable income presented in Chapter 6. Figure 17-1 substantially exaggerates any irregularity in the *C-S* relationship because it uses a much enlarged horizontal scale (relative to the scale used on the vertical axis). Had the same scale been used for both consumption and saving, the line would have been much steeper on the page and its apparent horizontal fluctuations greatly reduced. Nevertheless, what the exaggeration reveals is worthy of attention.

Connecting the observations for consecutive years by straight lines permits us to focus on the "observed" or "realized" marginal propensity to consume as between each year and the next. The slope of that line reflects, arithmetically, the fractions of the year-to-year change in income devoted to consumption and saving, with a vertical line segment representing an MPC of 1 and a horizontal segment an MPC of 0. Line segments sloping upward to the right represent $0 < \text{MPC} < 1$; segments sloping upward to the left represent $\text{MPC} > 1$ or $\text{MPC} < 0$. The MPC reflected in the statistical regression of C on DI for the years 1946–75 is shown on the diagram by the straight diagonal line from the lower left to upper right corners of the figure. It has the slope associated with $\text{MPC} = 0.913$. A smaller "key" shows slopes representing other values of MPC.

What the chart particularly demonstrates is that, although the average MPC over the entire period is very close to 0.9, there are very few pairs of consecutive years between which the observed MPC is even moderately close to that figure. Indeed, of the 39 year-to-year changes shown, in only nine does the MPC fall between 0.8 and 1.0. The modal (that is, the single most frequently observed) 10 percentage point range for the year-to-year values of MPC is 0.6 to 0.7 (10 of the 39 year-to-year changes fall in this range: 5 during 1929–1941, 5 during 1946–1975. Six year-to-year changes reveal MPC's between zero and 0.5. And, in ten of the 39 year-to-year intervals (all following 1946), the changes in C and S were in opposite directions; that is, an $\text{MPC} > 1.0$ or (in one case) < 0!

These anomalies are not restricted to single pairs of years. For example, the chart shows that (as noted in Chapter 6) the MPC averaged around 0.75 for the entire period 1929–1941. Moreover, for the periods (taken as a whole) 1947–1951, 1955–1958, 1969–1971, the MPC was below 0.8. These intervals of low MPC were, of course, offset by others when the MPC was much in excess of 0.9. For example, during 1951–1955, or 1956–1960, the MPC was preponderantly greater than 1.0; indeed, for the 12-year period 1951–1963, the average MPC slightly exceeds 1.0. Within this longer period, 1953–1955 and 1958–1960 each constitute consecutive years of MPC averaging considerably above 1.0; and this phenomenon occurred again in 1967–1969.

On a quarterly basis, the irregularities are considerably more pronounced, as revealed by Figure 17–2. (Data for this figure are limited to the period 1956–1975). It is drawn to a larger scale than Figure 17–1, but with equivalent relative exaggeration of horizontal measurement. The prevailing impression given by Figure 17–2 is how few quarter-to-quarter changes involve an MPC at all close to the average. Almost half of all line

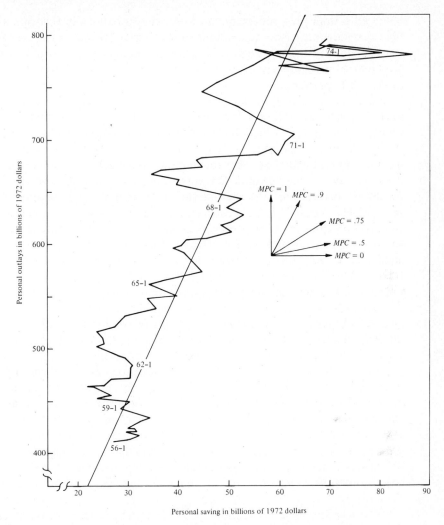

FIGURE 17-2 Personal outlays and personal saving, by quarters, 1956–1975.

segments slope upward to the left, that is, show movements of *C* and *S* in *opposite directions*. In most cases, this involves *C* rising by more than *DI* rises (MPC > 1); but other cases involve *C* rising although *DI* falls (MPC < 0), *C* falling although *DI* rises (MPC < 0), *C* falling by more than *DI* (MPC > 1), or *C* rising or falling with *DI* unchanged.

These movements are, of course, offset by other periods in which *C* and *S* move in the same direction (0 < MPC < 1). However, in a great many of these cases, the MPC is only 0.6 or less. To be sure, some of the movements appear to be quite random; for example, between 1962–1964 and 1968–1972, the typical pattern is simply an erratic "zig-zag" around a line with a slope that represents an MPC of approximately 0.8. Some of this quarter-to-quarter fluctuation must surely reflect measurement errors.[1] However, random variation and measurement errors could hardly account for consecutive nonconforming movements over a period of 3 or 4, or up to 12, quarters.

So long as we concentrate only on quarter-to-quarter movements we have to conclude that they fail to conform, even faintly, to the consumption function hypothesis, which had implied that consumption is basically determined by disposable income and that increments of disposable income will be divided in some regular and systematic way between consumption and saving. Daniel B. Suits fitted a number of consumption functions focussed on the short-term movement of consumption and income. He concluded: "The striking fact is that when the analysis is centered on quarter-to-quarter variations, the correlation between consumption and income vanishes. The movements of consumption in the short run are so nearly independent of income that the usual high correlation between consumption and income is replaced by a substantial negative correlation between consumption and saving."[2]

This should actually not be surprising. In any short period, say a month or a quarter, income changes are normally relatively small. Thus, if there are fluctuations in consumption, up or down, random or meaningful, saving will almost necessarily move in the opposite direction and by roughly the same amount. Or, if there are fluctuations in income, up or down, random or meaningful, and consumption fails to respond, saving will move in the same direction as income and by roughly the same amount. If we took even shorter periods, say a day or a week, changes in consumption or income (or errors in measuring it) would necessarily be offset by almost identical movements in saving. These irregular changes in consumption (if they are not merely errors of measurement) of course give rise to changes in income. *Thus, in the short run, consumption determines income more than the reverse.*

If these irregular fluctuations in consumption were purely random, they would tend to average out to zero the longer the time span being considered. Thus we might suppose that annual data would show a much more stable correspondence between changes in consumption and in saving, and still closer correspondence would appear if we used 2- or 3-year

---

[1] Consumption and disposable income are estimated from largely independent data sources, with personal saving merely the residual. Errors in measuring either consumption or disposable income, or nonoffsetting errors in both, would introduce meaningless irregularities into the movement of personal saving.

[2] D. B. Suits, "The Determinants of Consumer Expenditure: A Review of Present Knowledge", Research Study 1 in *Impacts of Monetary Policy* (a series of research studies prepared for the Commission on Money and Credit), Prentice-Hall, 1963, p. 39; reprinted in W. L. Johnson and D. R. Kamerschen (eds.), *Macroeconomics: Selected Readings* (Houghton-Mifflin Co., 1970), pp. 59–92.

totals or averages of consumption and saving. The longer the period used, the more stable should be the correspondence of consumption changes and saving changes, with the ratio of the two changes approaching a magnitude something like 0.9 in consumption to 0.1 in saving as the periods compared became of the order of half-decades or decades.

But are the irregularities of consumption purely random, and, if they are, how long a period is required before their effects roughly cancel out? The answer has to be that the irregularities are not purely random, and that they substantially cancel out only when we take periods of a decade or more. The long consecutive runs of quarterly variations in consumption and income reflecting either MPC > 1 or MPC < 0.5 shown in Figure 17-2, the irregularities revealed in the annual data plotted in Figure 17-1, and the longer movements in the saving rate visible in Figure 17-3 all suggest that something more than random variation or measurement errors is at work. Nor should we simply assume that *all* of the erratic quarterly movement is explained either by random variation or measurement error.

A Cyclical versus Secular Consumption Function?

One hypothesis that has received long attention in consumption-function literature proposes a partial explanation of the relationship between short-run and longer run propensities to consume. It argues that there is a systematic short-run relationship between consumption and income associated with the fluctuations called "business cycles." This short-run relationship, however, washes out as recessions are followed by recoveries. In the long run, consumption is basically proportional to income; in the "secular function," APC and MPC are essentially equal. But when income declines, during a business-cycle recession, consumption declines in smaller proportion than income (with saving sharply reduced); during the subsequent recovery, consumption rises again, but in smaller proportion than income (so that saving increases sharply). Over longer periods of economic growth, the resulting short-term movements of the saving rate cancel out. Thus, the average propensity to save (APS) falls sharply in recession and rises sharply in the recovery, but it is essentially constant on the average for periods longer than that of the ordinary cyclical fluctuation.

Several competing explanations have been proposed for this phenomenon, two of which we have already considered (Friedman's dependence of consumption on permanent income and Modigliani's dependence of consumption on wealth as well as income).[3] However, before attempting to choose among these or other explanations, one

---

[3] Among the earliest and best known of other theories that differentiate between short-run, that is, cyclical, and long-run functions is that of Duesenberry, who made consumption depend on both current *DI* and previous peak *DI*. See J. S. Duesenberry, *Income, Saving, and the Theory of Consumer Behavior* (Harvard University Press, 1949).

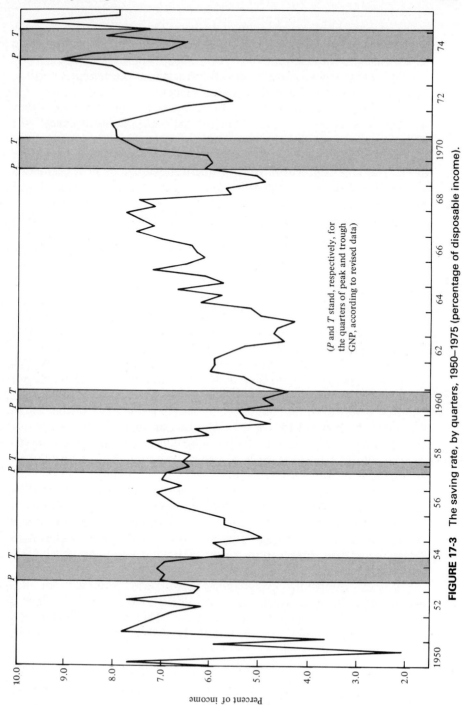

(P and T stand, respectively, for the quarters of peak and trough GNP, according to revised data)

FIGURE 17-3   The saving rate, by quarters, 1950–1975 (percentage of disposable income).

should first question whether or to what extent the phenomenon really exists, and whether, if it does, it is the most important anomaly that needs explanation.

The preceding description of consumption behavior over the business cycle clearly does fit the declines of consumption and income associated with the Great Depression of 1929–1933, the slow recovery of 1933–1937, the sharp recession of 1937–1938, and the accelerating recovery from 1938 to 1941. Thereafter, however, the cyclical picture is far less clear. The percentage of income saved (APS) did tend to decline slightly in the United States during each of the first four postwar recessions: 1948–1949, 1953–1954, 1957–1958, and 1960–1961. However, the decline of APS became progressively less in each recession, and the APS actually *rose* considerably during the recession of 1969–1970. But in 1973–1975, the APS once again fell sharply. Moreover, whereas the APS rose dramatically during some business-cycle recoveries, for example, that of 1954–1957, it fell dramatically in others, for example, that of 1958–1960.[4]

These cyclical patterns could be traced in Figure 17-2, but they can be more easily detected in Figure 17-3, which merely plots the APS by quarters beginning in 1950 and shows the periods of recession as shaded areas. As one studies this figure, it is apparent that, at least since 1950, whatever systematic variations in consumption and saving behavior may have been associated with business cycles is considerably less significant than other movements of the saving rate. Not only are there erratic movements of considerable magnitude from quarter to quarter but also movements that persist for long strings of quarters, for example, from 1951:2 to 1955:1, or from 1962:4 to 1967: 4. Indeed, it does not take too much imagination to believe that one detects a prevailing tendency for the saving rate to decline throughout the 1950s and for it to rise throughout the 1960s and early 1970s.

These movements are clearly not systematically related only to the intervals marked off as "business cycles." To be sure, they may very well be systematically related, as cause or effect or both, to a variety of fluctuations in the rate of change of GNP. But they are not obviously consistent with any simple, and stable, consumption function based on current income alone.

Two general approaches have been used in the effort to develop consumption functions that more closely approximate the behavior of aggregate consumption as measured in the national income accounts. If a simple consumption function using current income does not provide a fully

---

[4] It should be noted, however, that the extent of the decline in disposable income during these recessions varied considerably. During several of them, real disposable income *per capita* was nearly as high at the trough as at the peak. The really sharp income declines are associated with the 1929–1933, 1937–1938, and 1973–1975 recessions, and these most clearly exhibit the behavior hypothesized.

satisfactory empirical representation of consumer spending, one possibility is to investigate more complex, dynamic interrelationships between income and consumption. The second is to find other variables that may contribute to the explanation of consumer spending. These approaches are obviously not mutually exclusive, and most empirical work employs both. Nevertheless, it is convenient for expositional purposes to discuss them separately. We illustrate the first approach in the next section of this chapter.

DYNAMIC CONSUMPTION FUNCTIONS

In Chapter 6 we briefly introduced a consumption function in which consumption depends on the disposable income of a previous period, noting that there were many reasons to expect that consumers' spending might lag somewhat behind their receipt of income. To write

$$C_t = a_0 + a_1 DI_{t-1}$$

implies that today's consumption spending is completely unaffected by today's income but instead depends solely on yesterday's income. If one supposed that a "day" was literally a day (or even a week), it might be reasonable to assume that the current income (which in many cases is not yet completely known) has little or no influence on today's consumption. But this does not make it intuitively reasonable to suppose that current spending depends *only* on the income of the single calendar day (or week preceding. Since data on disposable income are available only on a quarterly or annual basis,[5] we are, in practice, concerned with the implications of proposing that *this quarter's*, or *this year's* or *this decade's*, consumer spending is unaffected by this quarter's (or year's or decade's) income and depends only on that of a previous period. Clearly, this could be defended as, at best, a crude approximation of reality and probably not the best available approximation. It is debatable whether a simple one-quarter lag introduced into a quarterly consumption function improves or worsens the "goodness of fit" of that function, as compared with a nonlagged function, but the introduction of a 1-year lag clearly worsens the fit of an annual consumption function, as compared with a nonlagged function.

Distributed-Lag Function

Much better results, however, are obtained by using a **distributed lag**, in which this quarter's (or this year's) consumption depends on the income of more than one quarter (or year)—very possibly including the current

---

[5] "Personal income" is available monthly; and there are projects to develop a complete series of monthly national income accounts.

quarter (or year). For instance

$$(1) \qquad C_t = a_0 + a_1 DI_1 + a_2 DI_{t-1}$$

makes this period's consumption depend on this period's *and* last period's incomes. The immediate result of a rise in income is to increase C_t by $a_1 DI_1$, but next period there will be a further effect from today's income increase, raising consumption by a further fraction a_2 of today's income increase. We can call a_1 and a_2 "partial marginal propensities to consume." Table 17-1 illustrates this and other possible simple formulations, on the assumption that income has been steady at $DI = 100$, but in period t rises to 110 and thereafter remains at the higher level. In the present case, we take $a_0 = 10$, $a_1 = 0.5$, $a_2 = 0.3$. The results for consumption appear under column 1. As can be seen, the "short-run marginal propensity to consume (MPC)" (meaning that which occurs simultaneously) is 0.5; the "long-run" MPC is 0.8, the sum of the two partial MPC's.

If there is a two-period distributed lag, which does not include the current period, we might have

$$(2) \qquad C_t = a_0 + a_1 DI_{t-1} + a_2 DI_{t-2}$$

If, again, $a_0 = 10$, $a_1 = 0.5$, $a_2 = 0.3$, the results are shown in column 2. Here the immediate MPC $= 0$, but the long-run MPC is again 0.8.

An alternative two-period distributed lag can take the form

$$(3) \qquad C_t = a_0 + a_1 DI_{t-1} + a_2(DI_{t-1} - DI_{t-2})$$

which makes C_t depend on lagged income and the lagged income increase, perhaps on the ground that income *increments* have an effect on spending over and above the effect of income levels. Equation (3) can be rewritten as

$$C_t = a_0 + (a_1 + a_2)DI_{t-1} - a_2 DI_{t-2}$$

The results, with $a_0 = 10$, $a_1 = 0.8$, $a_2 = 0.4$, are shown in column 3. Here the immediate MPC $= 0$, the short-run MPC $= 1.2$, and the long-

TABLE 17-1

Period	DI	C			
		1	2	3	4
$t-2$	100	90	90	90	90
$t-1$	100	90	90	90	90
t	110	95	90	90	102
$t+1$	110	98	95	102	98
$t+2$	110	98	98	98	98
$t+3$	110	98	98	98	98

run MPC $= 0.8$. Had equation (3) instead been

(4) $$C_t = a_0 + a_1 DI_t + a_2(DI_t - DI_{t-1})$$

the results (shown in column 4) would have been the same, except occurring one period earlier. Obviously we can make current consumption depend not only on two, but on three, four, five, or n periods' incomes.

Use of Moving-Average Income

These examples of simple distributed-lag functions can be thought of in a different way as making present consumption depend on a "weighted moving average" of past incomes (or of past and present) incomes, in which the *weights* given to the incomes are proportional to the coefficients a_1 and a_2 (their short-run MPCs), and in which the coefficient of weighted moving average income is the long run marginal propensity to consume. For example, equation (2)—previously presented in the distributed-lag form—can be rewritten in moving-average form as

(2a) $$C_t = a_0 + (a_1 + a_2)\left(\frac{a_1}{a_1 + a_2}DI_{t-1} + \frac{a_2}{a_1 + a_2}DI_{t-2}\right)$$

where $a_1/(a_1 + a_2)$ and $a_2/(a_1 + a_2)$ are the weights in a moving average, summing to 1. Using our illustrative numerical values,

$$C_t = 10 + 0.8(0.625DI_{t-1} + 0.375DI_{t-2})$$

This will produce exactly the same values for C as are shown in column 2 of Table 17-1. Equation (3) similarly becomes, in moving-average form,

(3a) $$C_t = a_0 + a_1\left(\frac{a_1 + a_2}{a_1}DI_{t-1} - \frac{a_2}{a_1}DI_{t-2}\right)$$

or, using the illustrative numerical values,

$$C_t = 10 + 0.8(1.2DI_{t-1} - 0.2DI_{t-2})$$

The expression within the parenthesis is a kind of moving average, even though one of the weights is negative.

Accepting Friedman's view that the "permanent income" (of which consumption is a constant fraction) can be approximated by a weighted moving average of past realized incomes, with diminishing weights, we can write his empirical consumption function in the form either of

$$C_t = a_1 DI_t + a_2 DI_{t-2} + \cdots + a_n DI_{t-n}$$

that is, as a distributed lag function in which $a_1 > a_2 > \cdots > a_n > 0$ (steadily declining partial marginal propensities to consume for incomes progressively more distant in time), or, alternatively, as

(5a)
$$C_t = (a_1 + a_2 + \cdots + a_n)\left[\frac{a_1}{a_1 + a_2 + \cdots + a_n}DI_t \right.$$
$$\left. + \frac{a_2}{a_1 + a_2 + \cdots + a_n}DI_{t-1} + \cdots + \frac{a_n}{a_1 + a_2 + \cdots + a_n}DI_{t-n+1}\right]$$

where $a_1 + a_2 + \cdots + a_n$ is the marginal (= average) propensity to consume permanent income, and the expression in square brackets is an approximation of permanent income as an n-period moving average of actual incomes. More elegantly and generally, (5) can be written in the weighted-average form as

(5b)
$$C_t = a \sum_{i=0}^{n} b_i DI_{t-n+1}$$

where $\Sigma b_i = 1$ (that is, the weights sum to 1), and a is the percentage of moving-average income that is consumed. In distributed-lag form, the same equation is written

(5c)
$$C_t = \sum_{i=0}^{n} a_i DI_{t-n+1}$$

where a_i (that is, the short-run MPC applicable to each period's income) equals $a \cdot b_i$ in the previous formulation.

In deriving statistical regressions using the preceding formulations, the number of terms in the weighted moving average (or distributed lag) and the general time pattern of the weights (or of the partial marginal propensities) can be left to trial and error. That is, they may be determined simply by trying a large number of possible forms and finding which one produces the "best fit" to the data. Alternatively, the number of terms and the time pattern of the coefficients can be specified in advance on theoretical grounds. Whichever way it is done, the data themselves then determine— given the *a priori* specification (if any)—what the numerical values of the empirical function should be.

For statistical reasons (given a finite quantity of data), it is often deemed necessary to specify in advance the number of terms and the time pattern of the lags. (For instance, coefficients may be fitted to the current and previous ten quarters, specifying that their pattern must be one that declines linearly from a peak in the current period to zero in the eleventh quarter. Considerably more complex specifications are also possible.)[6]

---

[6] The earliest such specification in economic-statistical work of a distributed lag of this kind was by economist Shirley Almon; thus, this form of lag is often called an "Almon lag." See her "The Distributed Lag Between Capital Appropriations and Expenditures", *Econometrica* 33 (January, 1965), pp. 178–196.

The Koyck Function

One special and widely used form of a distribution over time of weights or coefficients is the so-called Koyck distributed lag. Applied to a consumption function, this specifies that current consumption is a function of all past incomes (in principle, back to the begining of time), with the property that the series of coefficients of past income terms declines ("decays") geometrically. That is (using Y to represent disposable income),

(6) $$C_t = a_0 + a_1 Y_t + a_2 Y_{t-1} + a_3 Y_{t-2} + a_4 Y_{t-3} + \cdots$$

where

$$a_1/a_2 = a_2/a_3 = a_3/a_4 = \cdots > 1$$

and

$$a_1 + a_2 + a_3 + \cdots + a_n < 1$$

A series of coefficients that fits this description is, for example,

$$C_t = 10 + 0.4 Y_t + 0.2 Y_{t-1} + 0.1 Y_{t-2} + 0.05 Y_{t-3} + \cdots$$

each coefficient of a Y term being one half the previous one.

It takes little acquaintance with statistical methodology to see intuitively that "fitting" an equation in this form poses a number of problems. However, identically the same result is, *in principle*, obtained by fitting an equation in the form

(6a) $$C_t = a + b Y_t + c C_{t-1}$$

where $0 < b < 1$ and $0 < c < 1$. That is, consumption in any period depends, linearly, on current income and on the previous period's consumption. It is easy to show that equation (5a) is equivalent to, and implies, a consumption function with geometrically decaying weights on all past incomes.

This can be seen by substituting for C_{t-1} in (6a) its own value as given by the same equation; that is

$$C_t = a + b Y_t + c C_{t-1}$$
$$= a + b Y_t + c(a + b Y_{t-1} + c C_{t-2})$$
$$= a + b Y_t + ca + cb Y_{t-1} + c^2(a + b Y_{t-2} + c C_{t-3})$$
$$= a + b Y_t + ca + cb Y_{t-1} + c^2 a + c^2 b Y_{t-2} + c^3(a + b Y_{t-3} + c C_{t-4})$$
$$= a + b Y_t + ca + cb Y_{t-1} + c^2 a + c^2 b Y_{t-2} + c^3 a + c^3 b Y_{t-3} + c^4 C_{t-4}$$

Without proceeding further, we can collect terms and see what kind of function is implied. It is

$$C_t = a(1 + c + c^2 + c^3 + \cdots)$$
$$+ b(Y_t + c Y_{t-1} + c^2 Y_{t-2} + c^3 Y_{t-3} + \cdots$$

Since $0 < c < 1$, it can be seen that the first term on the right is finite; and it can be proved that it equals $a/(1 - c)$. Given also that $0 < b < 1$, it can be seen that the coefficients of the terms in Y (b, bc, bc^2, bc^3, ...) are positive, less than 1, and geometrically decaying. Equation (6a) thus implies equation (6).

From (6a) we see that the short-run MPC equals the coefficient b. The long-term MPC can be easily calculated, even though it is approached only through an infinite series of diminishing increments. If an initial equilibrium between C and Y is disturbed by a once-and-forever increase in Y, equilibrium is restored when $C_t = C_{t-1} = C_E$. Substituting in equation (6a) we get

$$C_E = a + bY + cC_E$$

$$= \frac{a}{1-c} + \frac{b}{1-c}Y$$

We thus find the long-run MPC to be $b/(1 - c)$.

Examples of numerical consumption functions all having the same long-run MPC = 0.8 but different rates of approach to it are given in Table 17-2. In each case, the value of the constant term, a, has been adjusted to make it consistent with an initial equilibrium of $C = 90$ when $Y = 100$, and a new equilibrium of $C = 98$ when $Y = 110$, in order to make comparisons easier. (Obviously, use of functions of this type is not limited to situations in which consumers are in full adjustment to an initial stable level of income, and then receive a once-and-for-all increase in income: this artificial circumstance is used only to clarify the nature of the adjustment which is made to any pattern of income change.)

Column 1 shows an extremely slow path of adjustment to a rise in income, involving a low immediate or short-run MPC ($b = 0.1$), and a very high dependence of consumption in any period upon consumption of the

TABLE 17-2

				C	
		1	2	3	4
		$a = 1.25$	$a = 3.75$	$a = 6.25$	$a = 9.375$
		$b = 0.1$	$b = 0.3$	$b = 0.5$	$b = 0.75$
Period	Y	$c = 0.875$	$c = 0.625$	$c = 0.375$	$c = 0.0625$
$t - 1$	100	90	90	90	90
t	110	91	93	˙95	97.5
$t + 1$	110	91.815	94.875	96.875	97.969
$t + 2$	110	92.641	96.049	97.578	97.998
$t + 3$	110	93.311	66.779	97.842	98.000
$t + \infty$	110	98	98	98	98

preceding period ($c = 0.875$). (Combinations of b even lower than 0.1, and c even higher than 0.875 are not uncommon in statistical work, as we shall see in the section which follows.) At the other extreme, in column 4, we show a very rapid adjustment toward equilibrium, resulting from a high short-run MPC ($b = 0.75$), and a minor dependence of consumption on that of the previous period ($c = 0.0625$).

Some Examples of Empirical Dynamic Functions

We have referred frequently to Friedman's consumption function, which makes consumption depend on permanent income, empirically represented by a moving average of past actual incomes. There is no single "official" empirical version of a Friedman function. However, in his 1957 book,[7] he refers with approval to his own work, with Phillip Cagan, in which annual United States consumption (*per capita* in constant prices) is made to depend on a 17-year moving average of past annual incomes (*per capita* in constant prices), as follows:

(7)
$$C_t = 0.88 \sum_{i=1}^{17} b_i Y_{t-i}$$

where

$b_1 = 0.330$	$b_{10} = 0.009$
$b_2 = 0.221$	$b_{11} = 0.006$
$b_3 = 0.148$	$b_{12} = 0.004$
$b_4 = 0.099$	$b_{13} = 0.003$
$b_5 = 0.067$	$b_{14} = 0.002$
$b_6 = 0.045$	$b_{15} = 0.001$
$b_7 = 0.030$	$b_{16} = 0.001$
$b_8 = 0.020$	$b_{17} = 0.001$
$b_9 = 0.013$	

This was fitted to data for the period 1909–1951; the R^2 was 0.96. Friedman, however, expressed doubt that so long a moving average was necessary, noting that the last 9 years were found to have only 4 percent of the weight in the moving average.

A second example of a dynamic function is chosen to illustrate two other types of dynamic interactions between income and consumption: a negative MPC for lagged income and the use of the Koyck function. It is a consumption function for nondurable goods and services only, and it

[7] Friedman. *The Consumption Function* (Princeton University Press, 1957) pp. 145–52.

relates to quarterly expenditures, not annual

(8) $C_t = 2.0033 + 0.2970Y_t - 0.2590Y_{t-1} + 0.9496C_{t-1}$

where C = aggregate consumer purchases of nondurable goods and services in 1958 prices, and Y = aggregate disposable personal income in 1958 prices. The equation was fitted to quarterly data for the period 1954:1 through 1967:4. The R^2 was 0.999.[8]

Here it will be noted that the immediate effect of a dollar rise in disposable income is to increase expenditures on nondurables by just under 30 cents. However, one quarter later, most of this is wiped out. After two quarters, the MPC is only $0.2970 - 0.2592 = 0.0378$. And, clearly, the *dominant* determinant of this quarter's consumption is last quarter's consumption, 95 percent of which tends to be repeated. However, taking account of the further feedback on consumption from a rise in a previous period's consumption resulting from higher income, the ultimate, long-term MPC for nondurables and services implied by this equation is 0.749. Of a dollar of extra disposable income, 75 cents will *ultimately* be added to spending on nondurable goods and services. However, after even eight quarters, only 43 cents is added.

Some further examples of dynamic income-consumption relationships will appear in the next major section of the chapter, where these are combined with the use of other variables.

Evaluation of Dynamic Functions

Inasmuch as a simple, nonlagged consumption function "fits" the data from the United States national income and product accounts very closely—explaining up to $99\frac{1}{2}$ percent or more of the variance in annual consumption spending and having other satisfactory statistical properties—it is virtually impossible to choose between a nonlagged and any of the more complex dynamic forms solely on the basis of goodness of fit.[9]

Since the data do not clearly establish that one or another type of dynamic relationship is clearly more consistent with the "facts" than any other, economists are likely to choose—among the many possible forms—that one which most closely approximates their own *a priori* theoretical preferences. And since most economic theorists feel comfortable with the

---

[8] S. Hymans and H. M. Shapiro, *A Quarterly Econometric Model of the U.S. Economy*, Research Seminar in Quantitative Economics, 1972. Equation (8) was used in the 1972 version of the University of Michigan econometric model of the United States and has since been succeeded by a different one. It is here used only for illustrative purposes.

[9] To be sure, an unlagged *quarterly* consumption function, or one with a simple one quarter lag, explains considerably less of the variance in quarterly consumption than does an unlagged function fitted to annual data. Still, the more complex dynamic quarterly functions have only modestly better statistical properties than the simple nonlagged function.

theory of the rational consuming unit, which allocates its income over time in order to maximize the discounted utility of its present and future consumption, most economists prefer empirical functions that either involve substantial lags (to approximate some concept of "permanent" or "lifetime" earnings) or use wealth as an extra variable, or perhaps both. It may be evident from the critical comments in the previous chapter that the writer is not strongly persuaded in this direction by the theoretical considerations alone.

Nor, unfortunately, does the use of functions with long lags deal adequately with the problem raised at the beginning of this chapter, of the apparent instability of consumption behavior. It is the writer's belief that none of the functions can adequately reproduce the substantial fluctuations in the saving rate revealed in Figure 17-3.

There exists one exception to the negative judgment just expressed. The Koyck-lag of equation (6a) does reasonably well reproduce the medium-term and longer-term fluctuations in the saving rate shown in Figure 17-3, but this is not for reasons consistent with the underlying logic that most economists associate with this form. In *theory*, the Koyck equation—as in equation (6)—makes current consumption depend on a long series of previous incomes and, perhaps, very little on any one of them, even the most recent. But the equation *actually used*, equation (6a), makes current consumption depend (perhaps very little) on current income and (often mainly) on last period's consumption. As we have shown, these two formulations should be identical. But are they?

The two forms would be identical if the relationship expressed in equation (6) held precisely in every period. In that case, if both equations were fitted to the same data, the coefficients of one would convert precisely into the coefficients of the other. Given historical values of the series of Y's (or the single past C) and a known or predicted value of Y_t, either equation would predict exactly the same current consumption. And, of course, the prediction would always prove precisely correct.

However, suppose that the relationship of equation (6) holds only approximately and on the average, because of the existence of a random disturbance (which averages out approximately to zero over any long series of periods). Again, assume that both equations are independently fitted to the same set of data. In that case, C's calculated from neither equation would exactly reproduce past actual values. However, the coefficients of either equation would transform reasonably closely into those of the other. *But the two equations would predict quite differently.* For whatever random disturbance affected the immediate past value of consumption, C_{t-1}, would significantly influence the value of C_t predicted by (6a)—but it would have essentially no effect on the value of C_t predicted by equation (6). One would expect equation (6) to give the better predictions and would expect the predictions of (6a) often to be rather far from the mark.

Suppose, however, which this writer argues to be the case, that relationship (6) is subject to *nonrandom* disturbances. Suppose that the function shifts significantly in one direction for a series of periods, followed by other periods in which the disturbance consistently has the opposite sign (called "serially correlated error terms"). In *that* case: (a) the coefficients fitted in one form would not convert even closely to those fitted in the other;[10] (b) the two equations would again give quite different predictions; and (c) on the average, the predictions of (6a) would be substantially more accurate than those of (6). That is, the predictions of (6a) would approximately reproduce the medium-term and longer term fluctuations of the saving rate visible in Figure 17-3.

However, this predictive power has nothing to do with the theory that implies that consumption depends on a long series of past incomes and depends very little on current income; rather, it depends on the existence of strongly serially correlated disturbances in consumption behavior. Another way of putting this is to say that (6a) may be a reasonably good "forecasting equation," but it is not a good "structural equation."[11] The existence of serially correlated disturbances in consumption is also (in the writer's view) the reason why some forecasters appear able to make better forecasts when they fit forecasting equations to "first differences" in the data—that is, develop equations designed to predict only the change in consumption (or other variables) from the previous period, not the absolute level. The same result is obtained when forecasters adjust the constant term in their consumption equations before making a forecast by an amount which lets the equations, after the adjustment, correctly predict last period's consumption. When a shift first appears, or when it disappears, forecasts made by these methods are wrong; but only for the few periods in which the shift is occurring. And, on the average, these methods "win" by taking advantage of the serial correlation of errors.

It is often said that one of the notable failures of recent United States economic policy was the fact that a major increases in personal taxes in 1968 did not appear to dampen the inflationary boom resulting from the Vietnam War. This failure is often attributed to the fact that the tax increase, advertised as "temporary," had little effect on taxpayers' "permanent incomes" or the assessment of their "lifetime resources," and thus had little effect on their spending. Indeed, consumer spending appears not to have been effectively dampened at all; nor was the boom. More than a

---

[10] This is the case, at least, if the coefficients are fitted by the ordinary method of least squares.

[11] To be sure, rather elaborate methods have been invented which are designed to eliminate the clear bias of ordinary least squares in estimating equations in which the left-hand variable, lagged, appears also on the right, in the presence of serially correlated errors. Many econometricians hold, however, that these methods do not completely eliminate that bias.

year later, after a period of extremely tight monetary policy, the boom did finally collapse and a recession ensued. A casual observer, or even a careful economist, could argue that it was the tight money, without any contribution, even a delayed one, from the tax increase, that finally turned the tide.[12]

However, an interesting study by Arthur Okun, compared (a) the forecasts of consumer spending that were given for this period by consumption functions that treated the effects of the tax increase like any other change in disposable income with (b) the forecasts that would have been made if the tax increase had been ignored by consumers. His results show that *neither* set of functions forecasts this period's consumption correctly.[13] The only explanation appears to be no explanation at all: that there was a massive upward shift in consumption relative to income, which began in late 1967 and continued through mid-1969 and which is still unexplained. This shift can be seen in Figure 17-3 as the sharp downward adjustment of the saving rate over that period. It was this shift that offset the effects of the tax increase; and when the shift was over, it was the sharp increase in the saving rate (also seen in Figure 17-3), as much as or more than tight money, that caused the recession and continued to make the subsequent recovery weak and sluggish.

Thus, dynamic considerations in the relationship of consumption to income do not seem adequately to solve the remaining mysteries in the explanation of consumer spending. Perhaps the answer lies in finding additional variables which, along with disposable income, help to explain why consumers spend as they do.

OTHER VARIABLES IN CONSUMPTION FUNCTIONS

Although Keynes is mainly known for having postulated the dependence of consumption on income, he took pains to point out that, in addition to income, consumer spending might depend on additional variables. He discussed a number of these briefly. Ever since, economists have been attempting to see whether the variables Keynes suggested (and many others) may, when used along with income, provide a better explanation of the variation that occurs over time in aggregate consumer expenditures. There is not space to review the findings with respect to every variable so tested. Thus, we concentrate on only a few.

[12] A good example of this point of view is represented by R. Eisner, "Fiscal and Monetary Policy Reconsidered," *American Economic Review*, 59 (December 1969) 897–905.

[13] A. M. Okun, "The Personal Tax Surcharge and Aggregate Demand." in *Brookings Papers on Economic Activity*, 1: 1971, 167–211.

Wealth

Keynes suggested that capital gains—that is, changes in the value of wealth—might influence consumption, along with income, and, in another context, discussed the possibility that the accumulation of wealth through private investment in plant and equipment might ultimately so saturate the desire of consumers to save as to reduce saving to zero even at full-employment levels of income.[14] Once Pigou had asserted, and Modigliani had demonstrated, that the classical theory of consumer behavior implied that consumption should depend on wealth as well as income, and once it became possible to put together approximate time series estimates of the stock of wealth, Modigliani and others began to include this variable along with income (and perhaps other variables) in empirical consumption functions.

It is difficult to get fully reliable evidence on the relative importance of wealth and income in determining consumption. For one thing, the time profiles of wealth and income over time are extremely similar. The main difference is that the rate of growth of wealth slows down less than does that of income in recessions (and then speeds up less than does the growth of income in boom periods). When the time patterns of any two variables are very similar, it is extremely difficult to distinguish reliably how much effect each of them separately has on a third variable which both are hypothesized to affect.

A second problem is that empirical measurements of consumers' real net worth or wealth are not satisfactory. Wealth data consist of a mixture of book values and market values, with the book values constructed according to a variety of quite imperfect methods. This is true also of the measurement of the debts that reduce the net worth of consumers. And estimates of the aggregate market values of outstanding bonds, stocks, and other securities have somewhat tenuous empirical basis. Nor is it entirely clear how estimates of wealth in money terms should be deflated to produce estimates of real wealth. Indeed, many consumers may have only a hazy idea of their real net worth.

Modigliani and his several associates have produced a variety of consumption functions including terms in wealth. One especially interesting one is reproduced below, exactly as presented by Modigliani.[15]

(9)

$$\frac{CON}{N} = \sum_{i=0}^{11} b_i\left(\frac{YD}{N}\right)_{t-i} + \sum_{i=0}^{3} c_i\left(\frac{VCN\$_{-i}}{0.01PCON_{-i-1}N_{-i-1}}\right) + 0.6098u_{-1} + e$$

[14] *General Theory*, pp. 317–18.

[15] See F. Modigliani, "Monetary Policy and Consumption: Linkages via Interest Rate and Wealth Effects in the FMP Model," in *Consumer Spending and Monetary Policy: the Linkages*, Conference Series No. 5 (Federal Reserve Bank of Boston, 1971), p. 75.

where

$$b_0 = 0.1087 \qquad b_8 = 0.0324 \qquad c_0 = 27.0447$$
$$(4.72) \qquad\qquad (4.23) \qquad\qquad (4.16)$$
$$b_1 = 0.0983 \qquad b_9 = 0.0239 \qquad c_1 = 15.8710$$
$$(6.10) \qquad\qquad (3.35) \qquad\qquad (7.94)$$
$$b_2 = 0.0882 \qquad b_{10} = 0.0157 \qquad c_2 = 7.6389$$
$$(8.68) \qquad\qquad (2.76) \qquad\qquad (2.02)$$
$$b_3 = 0.0783 \qquad b_{11} = 0.0077 \qquad c_3 = 2.3486$$
$$(14.41) \qquad\qquad (2.33) \qquad\qquad (0.68)$$

$$b_4 = 0.0686 \qquad \sum_i b_i = 0.672 \qquad \sum_i c_i = 52.9032$$
$$(23.04)$$
$$b_5 = 0.0592 \qquad \bar{R}_e^2 = 0.9982 \qquad S_u = 0.0090$$
$$(14.19)$$
$$b_6 = 0.0500 \qquad S_e = 0.0074 \quad d-w = 1.86$$
$$(8.28)$$
$$b_7 = 0.0411$$
$$(5.65)$$

(The number in brackets under each coefficient is its *t*-ratio)

Constraints:

b_i: 2nd degree polonomial, constrained to zero at $t - 12$
c_i: 2nd degree polonomial, constrained to zero at $t - 4$
Data: July 1970 national income accounts revisions
Sample period: 1954-I–1967-IV
Key to symbols:
$\quad CON$ = real consumption, billions of 1958 dollars
$\quad\quad YD$ = real disposable personal income, billions of 1958 dollars
$\quad\quad\quad N$ = population, millions
$\quad VCNS\$$ = consumers' net worth, trillions of dollars
$\quad PCON$ = consumption deflator, 1958 = 100
$\quad\quad\quad u$ = autocorrelated error term
$\quad\quad\quad e$ = residual error.

Here it will be noted that both income and wealth enter into the determination of consumption, with a distributed lag of 12 quarters in the case of income, and of 4 quarters in the case of wealth. Thus, in addition to using wealth, along with current income, as a measure of lifetime resources, Modigliani here borrows to some extent from Friedman's alternative approach to the measurement of lifetime resources ("permanent income") by using a multiperiod weighted average of income, thus further greatly lessening the importance of *current* income. (It will be noted that the MPC for the current quarter's income in equation (9) is only 0.109.) The sum of the income coefficients, however, (the long-term MPC) is 0.67;

the sum of the wealth coefficients is 52.9 (equal to 0.053 in the earlier notation).

In Modigliani's total econometric model, the wealth term in the consumption function plays a key role in extending the influence of monetary policy to consumer spending as well as investment. Briefly summarized, his equations make monetary policy play a major role in determining short-term interest rates; short-term rates, in turn, largely determine bond prices; bond prices significantly influence stock prices; and fluctuations in stock prices account for the largest part of the short-term variations in wealth which affect consumer spending. (The logic of the first three of these relationships will be developed in Chapter 20 and 21.)

Before leaving equation (9), we may briefly note the semifinal term: $+0.6098u_{-1}$. This says that any quarter's consumption is estimated as equal to the amount calculated from the first two terms of the equation—those showing the effects of current and lagged income and wealth—*plus* 61 percent of the amount by which the previous quarter's consumption, as estimated by this equation, fell short of actual consumption in that quarter. This term therefore plays the same role as we have suggested is played—in fact, if not in theory—by the C_{t-1} term on the right-hand side of a Koyck distributed-lag consumption function: namely, it adjusts the estimated consumption level for the effects of persisting shifts in the level of consumption spending relative to income (and, in this case, wealth).

Earlier economists had made a number of studies using, as explanatory variables for consumer spending, particular elements of consumer wealth or net worth rather than the total—for example, consumer's stocks of "liquid assets"; the volume of consumer indebtedness (a perhaps strategic *subtraction* in deriving net worth); an index of stock prices; and others. Although it is conceivable that certain specific elements of consumer wealth, positive or negative, are of strategic importance for consumption, most studies of consumption have abandoned the use of such partial measures.

However, in some equations relating to durable goods consumption, another portion of consumers' wealth—the depreciated value of their stocks of durable goods on hand—has been used as a determinant of consumers purchases, but entering with a *negative* rather than positive coefficient. The idea, of course, is that when consumers' stocks of durables are low (relative to current income), perhaps because consumers' purchases of durables have been low for several years, their purchases will then be higher than otherwise. When their stocks are high, because recent purchases have been larger than normal, they will currently buy less. This is obviously relevant only to an estimate that treats *purchase* of durables as consumption. (In Modigliani's case, equation (9), consumption of durables was estimated on the base of current services from the stock of durable goods; purchases of durables were estimated by a different equation—essentially an equation for investment.)

Other Variables

It has been noted several times in this book that, in principle, the distribution as well as the aggregate amount of consumers' income might well affect the aggregate volume of consumer purchases. Presumably, the marginal propensities to consume of different population groups differ. Thus, if a given aggregate income is redistributed from groups with lower to groups with higher marginal propensities, aggregate consumption would rise. Unfortunately, time-series data are not available showing the division of aggregate disposable income—either by income level, for example, by income deciles, or by types of income, such as wages, salaries, dividends, proprietors' and farmers' incomes, interest, transfer payments. (We do have *personal* income—which is *before* taxes—so subdivided; but no official estimates are available—and they are extremely difficult to construct—that allocate taxes by income type in order to give *disposable* income by type.)

One interesting recent study, however, sidestepped the problem of estimating disposable income by type, and produced the following equation[16]:

$$S_t = 0.971 S_{t-1} + 0.429\Delta L + 0.340\Delta P + 0.863\Delta Tr$$

$$(10) \qquad -2.200\Delta SI - 0.908\Delta T + 18.311\Delta r$$

$$R^2 = 0.845 \qquad S_e = 10.75$$

where

S = personal saving
ΔL = quarterly change in labor income
ΔP = quarterly change in property incomes (income of unincorporated enterprises, dividends, rental income, and interest income)
ΔTr = quarterly change in transfer payments
ΔSI = quarterly change in social insurance contributions
ΔT = quarterly change in personal taxes
r = yield on Baa bonds

All of the variables (except r) are deflated by the personal consumption deflator. For the particular equation shown, they are also all expressed in per capita terms.

It will be noted that this equation is novel in several respects: it estimates saving rather than consumption; and it uses quarterly changes in variables rather than their levels. Like many consumption functions, it includes on the right side of the equation the lagged value of the variable

[16] See L. Taylor, "Saving out of Different Types of Income," *Brookings Papers on Economic Activity*, 2:1971, pp. 383–407. The equation shown is one among several using alternative specifications.

that appears on the left side (and may thereby be subject to the same problems raised earlier with respect to such consumption functions.) The single most striking empirical finding is that a higher marginal propensity to save is found to apply to transfer payment income than to earned income. Since recipients of transfer payments clearly have lower individual incomes on the average than do wage earners, this seems to challenge the conventional wisdom that the MPC of low income people is substantially higher than that of middle and upper income people. Also, the expected higher marginal propensity to save property incomes than labor incomes fails to show up. Puzzling as well is the indication than an increase of one dollar in required social insurance contributions reduces (regular) saving by two dollars. But the indication that an increase in personal taxes comes mostly out of saving rather than out of consumption conforms to the usual expectation. However, there are complex conceptual and statistical problems of evaluating these results that we cannot discuss further here.

Another possible income distribution effect is implied by the occasional use of the unemployment rate as a variable in consumption equations—especially those related to purchases of durable goods, and, in particular, automobiles. If a given aggregate disposable income is accompanied at one time by a higher unemployment rate and at another by a lower rate, it implies a different *distribution* of that income. One might suppose that the higher unemployment rate would be accompanied by a lower level of real purchases, as it is in an equation we shall shortly present. However, it is possible that the effect is not related to income distribution, *per se*, but rather reflects the adverse effects of higher unemployment on consumer attitudes, replacing "confidence" with "caution"; or it may reflect the fact that the unemployment rate is highly correlated with some other (unknown) variable which also affects purchases of durable goods.

The use of some of the previously discussed variables, and others, is illustrated in the Appendix to this chapter, which reproduces a set of consumption equations from a recent econometric model of the United States economy.[17] These equations also illustrate a wide variety of dynamic formulations.

The interested reader, by studying the equations and the definitions given, can work out the meaning of most of the terms. We comment on only some of the more interesting formulations.

1. Note that all equations use the Koyck formulation, with the previous period's value of the relevant consumption as a major

---

[17] These are equations from a particular version of the Michigan Econometric Model (not the latest one) and are presented only to illustrate some of the points made in the text, and, in general, the complexity of the treatment of consumer spending in contemporary empirical research. These equations (and a further discussion of them) appear in S. Hymans and H. Shapiro. *The Michigan Quarterly Econometric Model of the U.S. Economy*, Research Seminar in Quantitative Economics, The University of Michigan, 1973, pp. 120–21, 140–42.

determinant of the current value. The coefficients on previous consumption go as high as 0.935 (for furniture and household equipment)!

2. All of the equations except that for services contain a relative price term—all with the expected negative coefficient.
3. The short-period marginal propensities to consume differ widely: zero for automobiles (although, after one period, it is 0.1817, and after two periods $0.1817 - 0.1440 = 0.0377$); 0.109 for furniture (but after one period $0.1093 - 0.1047 = 0.0046$); 0.01393 for other durables; 0.1554 for nondurables; and 0.0518 for services.
4. Increased unemployment reduces automobile purchases after one period; but, after two periods, reduces it much less.
5. Other variables include residential construction, influencing furniture and household equipment purchases, and a time trend describing service expenditures; in the case of services, the marginal propensity to consume transfer payment income is considerably greater than that of other disposable income (note that YD already includes GTRP).

Consumer Attitudes and Sentiment

For 30 years or more, Professor George Katona has been arguing that an important influence on consumer spending is exerted by consumers' attitudes: their feelings of confidence, security, well-being, optimism, or the opposites of these. According to Katona, consumer purchases, especially of important, postponable items, depend not only on consumers' *ability to buy* (represented by income, assets, availability of credit) but also, and very significantly, on consumers' *willingness to buy* (represented by the presence of favorable expectations and attitudes). For almost as long, Katona and his associates have been regularly assessing the state of consumer confidence and related attitudes through systematic sample surveys of consumers, obtaining their responses to a large number of questions about, among other things, recent and expected changes in their incomes and the prices they pay; their views about current and future (both near-term and longer-run) business conditions and employment opportunities; their assessments whether this is a "good time to buy" durable goods, and whether they have plans to buy various categories of these; along with all of this, probing questions of "why do you think so?"

Responses to no single set of questions appear to provide a reliable indication of consumers' buying intentions or subsequent purchases, but a synthetic "index of consumer sentiment," put together from the answers to a number of the questions, shows wide fluctuations over time that seem to coincide with, or even slightly to lead, changes in aggregate consumer spending on consumer durable goods (the most variable component of total consumption expenditure). On the basis of this index and the more detailed information that lies behind it, Katona and his associates have for years been making regular analyses and forecasts of consumer spending, to which considerable attention is paid by economists, public officials, and business firms.[18]

Some years ago, an associate of Katona's, Eva Mueller, showed that using the "index of consumer sentiment" as an additional variable, along with disposable income, distinctly improved the fit of a simple consumption function.[19] However, others found that adding the index, as another variable in dynamic consumption functions which already included variables in addition to income, seemed neither to improve the fit nor the forecasting ability of the functions. More recently, however, Saul Hymans demonstrated that if the index is "filtered"—by ignoring changes that are either minor or temporary—a distinct improvement is made when the filtered index is added to a standard equation used for forecasting durable goods consumption.[20]

As indicated in the concluding section of Chapter 16, the writer believes that attitudinal and related sociopsychological factors do play an important role in determining the volume of aggregate consumption; he thus believes it important that Katona's pioneering work be continued, developed, and refined. To be sure, some proponents of consumer sentiment as a determinant of consumer spending seem not to appreciate that consumer sentiment may be both *cause* and *effect* of business conditions— an independent *cause* to the extent that changes in attitudes occur independently of changes in economic activity, but an *effect* to the extent that changes in attitudes merely accompany and are produced by current or prior changes in economic activity. It is this writer's view, therefore, that attention needs to be directed to attempting to quantify *both* relationships—which may, of course, require further improvements in the means for measuring attitudes.

In any case, it does not seem to advance understanding for an enthusiast for the importance of attitudes to claim that every decline or increase in the saving rate is "caused" by a change in attitudes. For such a change in attitudes may systematically accompany (and merely reflect) an objective change of economic circumstance—for example, of consumer's income. In that case, the real "cause" of the change in spending is the

---

[18] For a good summary description and discussion of his work, see G. Katona, "Psychology and Consumer Economics," in *Journal of Consumer Research*, 1 (June 1974), 1–8, and references to other works provided there. The more ambitious reader can consult his *Psychological Economics* (Elsevier Scientific Publishing Co., 1975). The quarterly reports on consumer attitudes are regularly published by the Survey Research Center, Institute for Social Research, University of Michigan.

[19] See E. Mueller, "Effects of Consumer Attitudes on Purchases," *American Economic Review*, 47 (December 1957) 946–65.

[20] See S. Hymans, "Consumer Durable Spending: Explanation and Prediction," *Brookings Papers on Economic Activity*, 2:1970, pp. 173–99.

change in income, which also affected attitudes. Rather, what seems important to emphasize is that a particular kind of economic behavior, that is, a change in spending on durable goods, may sometimes originate mainly in the impact on individuals and groups of objective "economic" events; whereas, at other times, that behavior may arise mainly from psychological events that had other, "noneconomic" origins.[21] Or, as Katona says, consumption depends *both* on the "ability" and the "willingness" to buy.

It is the writer's hunch that the understanding of much or even the major part of what must still be called the "instability" of consumer spending in relationship to income will ultimately be provided by the progress of "psychological economics." He also believes that an important part of this field consists of social as well as individual psychology. In this connection, it seems regrettable that few economists have followed up on the analysis begun in the late 1940s by James Duesenberry. He attempted to explain the difference between a long-term, essentially proportional relationship between income and consumption and a short-term or cyclical nonproportional relationship through a sociological theory, in which people at every income level developed consumption standards which imitated those of the next higher income stratum. J. K. Galbraith has also had many striking observations about the social (and commercial) factors influencing consumption standards, but without providing systematic theories capable of incorporation into aggregate consumption functions.[22]

APPENDIX:
THE CONSUMPTION EQUATIONS OF A RECENT ECONOMETRIC MODEL

(1) Automobiles and parts

$$CDA = 17.19620 + 0.18166 \left[YD + \frac{TPNS\$ - GTRP\$}{PC/100} \right]_{-1}$$
$$(6.87642) \quad (0.06723)$$

$$-0.14396 \left[YD + \frac{TPNS\$ - GTRP\$}{PC/100} \right]_{-2} - 1.34683 \, UM\%_{-1}$$
$$(0.06701) \qquad\qquad\qquad (0.46082)$$

$$+1.16844 \, UM\%_{-2} - 18.04436 \frac{PCDA}{PC_{-1}} + 1.94075 \, DAS$$
$$(0.47289) \qquad (6.15713) \qquad\qquad (0.25578)$$

---

[21] This is not to deny Katona's basic point that what economists describe as "functional relationships" between objective events (for example changes in income) and human behavior (for example, changes in consumption) occur through an intermediate psychological process that involves human cognition, emotion, and response.

[22] See J. S. Duesenberry, *op. cit.*; J. K. Galbraith, *The Affluent Society*, (Houghton Mifflin, 1958), and other works.

$$+0.44228 \, CDA_{-1}$$
$$(0.10035)$$

$$\bar{R}^2 = 0.973 \qquad SEE = 1.114 \qquad DW = 1.76$$

(2) Furniture and household equipment

$$CDFE = 1.63475 + 0.10934\left[YD + \frac{TPNS\$}{PC/100}\right]$$
$$ (2.39259) \quad (0.03947)$$

$$- 0.10472\left[YD + \frac{TPNS\$}{PC/100}\right]_{-1} - 48.58837\left[\left(\frac{PCDFE}{PC}\right)\right.$$
$$ (0.04626) \qquad\qquad\qquad (24.60632)$$

$$\left. - 0.95\left(\frac{PCDFE}{PC}\right)_{-1}\right]$$

$$+ 0.23590\left[\left(\frac{IRC_{-1} + IRC_{-2}}{2}\right) - 0.95\left(\frac{IRC_{-2} + IRC_{-3}}{2}\right)\right]$$
$$(0.08847)$$

$$+ 0.93505\left(\frac{CDFE_{-1} + CDFE_{-2}}{2}\right)$$
$$(0.11483)$$

$$\bar{R}^2 = 0.996 \qquad SEE = 0.450 \qquad DW = 2.04$$

(3) Other consumer durables

$$CDO = 2.53241 + 0.01386\left[YD + \frac{TPNS\$}{PC/100}\right] - 4.33595\frac{PCDO}{PC}$$
$$ (4.26005) \quad (0.00388) \qquad\qquad (3.66755)$$

$$+ 0.52611\left(\frac{CDO_{-1} + CDO_{-2}}{2}\right)$$
$$(0.11057)$$

$$\bar{R}^2 = 0.992 \qquad SEE = 0.222 \qquad DW = 1.87$$

(4) Nondurable goods

$$CN = 111.30324 + 0.04703\frac{GTRP\$}{PC/100} + 0.15543 \, YD$$
$$ (25.81149) \qquad * \qquad\qquad (0.03284)$$

$$- 88.09649\left(\frac{PCN}{PC}\right) + 0.47627 \, CN_{-1}$$
$$(22.98791) \qquad\qquad (0.10744)$$

*Constrained coefficient
$$\bar{R}^2 = 0.998 \qquad SEE = 1.161 \qquad DW = 2.09$$

(5) Services

$$CS = 10.19945 + 0.02015\frac{GTRP\$}{PC/100} + 0.05184\ YD + 0.18233\ TIME$$

$$\quad (2.25357) \qquad * \qquad\qquad (0.01468) \qquad (0.04368)$$

$$+ 0.73360\ CS_{-1}$$
$$\quad (0.06449)$$

*Constrained coefficient
$\bar{R}^2 = 0.999$ SEE $= 0.514$ DW $= 1.34$

where

CDA = personal consumption expenditures, autos and parts, excluding mobile homes; billions of 1958 dollars

CDFE = personal consumption expenditures, furniture and household equipment; billions of 1958 dollars

CDO = personal consumption expenditures, durable goods other than autos and parts, mobile homes, furniture and household equipment, billions of 1958 dollars

CN = personal consumption expenditures, nondurable goods; billions of 1958 dollars

CS = personal consumption expenditures, services; billions of 1958 dollars

DAS = dummy variable for auto strikes; -2 in 1964.4, $+1.2$ in 1965.1, 0.8 in 1965.2, -1 in 1967.4, $+.75$ in 1968.1, $+.25$ in 1968.2, -3.6 in 1970.4, zero otherwise

GTRP\$ = government transfer payments to persons, total; billions of current dollars

IRC = residential construction expenditures; billions of 1958 dollars

PC = personal consumption expenditures implicit deflator, $1958 = 100$

PCDA = personal consumption expenditures implicit deflator, autos and parts, $1958 = 100$

PCDFE = personal consumption expenditures implicit deflator, furniture and household equipment, $1958 = 100$

PCDO = personal consumption expenditures implicit deflator, other durables, $1958 = 100$

PCN = personal consumption expenditures implicit deflator, non-durable goods, $1958 = 100$

PCS = personal consumption expenditures implicit deflator, services; $1958 = 100$

TIME = time trend equal to 1 in 1954.1 and increasing by 1 per quarter

TPNS\$ = nonwithheld component of 1968–69 personal income tax surcharge

UM% = unemployment rate, males 20 year and over; percent
YD = disposable personal income; billions of 1958 dollars
Subscripts (−1, −2, and so on) represent values for the first, second, etc. preceeding quarters
Numbers in parentheses below coefficients are the standard errors of the estimated coefficient
$\bar{R}^2$ = coefficient of determination
SEE = the standard error of estimate of the equation
DW = Durbin-Watson statistic

REVIEW QUESTIONS

1. "In the short run, consumption determines income rather than the reverse." What is meant by this statement, and what is some of the evidence to support it?

2.
(a) What should be the behavior of consumption relative to disposable income—that is, the saving rate—over the business cycle?
(b) Does the evidence support the hypothesis?
(c) Does this account for most of the short-run variation of the saving rate?

3. Explain what is meant by a "distributed-lag consumption function." What is meant, with reference to such a function, by the "short-run" and "long-run" marginal propensities to consume?

4. A frequent formulation of the consumption function is this:

$$C_t = c_1 DI_t + c_2 C_{t-1}$$

(a) What is the short-run marginal propensity to consume?
(b) Compute the long-run marginal propensity to consume.
(c) Show that this equation represents a special form of a distributed lag.
(d) What range of empirical values is frequently found for the coefficient c_2?
(e) "A high value for c_2 may represent the existence of extremely long lags between changes in income and in consumption; but it may also reflect something else." Explain both clauses.

5. "Changes in consumer sentiment may serve as either cause of effect of changes in GNP, or both." What is meant, and what does it imply for research on consumption?

SELECTED REFERENCES
(see also third, fourth, and sixth references at end of Ch. 16)

S. H. Hymans, "Consumer Durable Spending: Explanation and Prediction," *Brookings Papers on Economic Activity*, 2, 1970, pp. 173–199.

A. M. Okun, "The Personal Tax Surcharge and Consumer Demand," *Brookings Papers on Economic Activity*, 1, 1971, pp. 167–204.

L. D. Taylor, "Saving Out of Different Types of Income," *Brookings Papers on Economic Activity*, 2, 1971, pp. 383–407.

F. T. Juster and P. Wachtel, "Inflation and the Consumer," *Brookings Papers on Economic Activity*, 1, 1972, pp. 71–114.

M. C. Lovell, "Why Was the Consumer Feeling So Sad?" *Brookings Papers on Economic Activity*, 2, 1975, pp. 473–479.

(Five papers which illustrate recent empirical research on the consumption function, each followed by discussion among leading economists.)

PART VII
INVESTMENT

Chapter 18

Classical and Neoclassical Theories of Investment

Introduction
The importance of investment
Capital and investment

The Classical and Keynesian Theories of Capital and Investment
The rational investment decision
Relative factor prices and the capital-intensity of production
Erroneous derivations of the classical investment function

From Theory of Capital to Theory of Investment
The cost of capital goods
Problems with the classical theory

Jorgenson's "Neoclassical" Investment Theory

We return in this chapter and the next to the theory of private investment expenditures. The reader may wish to review Chapter 8, which dealt with a number of aspects of investment, before proceeding further. As is the case for consumption, a vast theoretical and empirical literature has accumulated on investment in recent years. No effort will be made to survey that literature in a systematic way, and references to it will be only illustrative. Our purpose is mainly to clarify basic ideas and to survey some major approaches and controversies.

INTRODUCTION

It was noted in Chapter 8 that investment is the most volatile of the major components of GNP. Several generations of economists, both before and after Keynes, have believed that this volatility is, in significant part, responsible for the observed fluctuations in production, income, and employment. Belief in this strategic importance for investment rests on the view that, in the aggregate, consumption, production, and demand-for-money functions are usually reasonably stable in the short run, and change only fairly smoothly over long periods. Thus, irregular movements in GNP are largely the result of irregular shifts in investment demand.

Clearly, investment is not the only source of fluctuations, for other segments of private demand are not entirely stable (as we have been at pains to show with respect to consumption); moveover, government can bring about abrupt changes in its purchases or in taxation or in the money supply, each of which may also contribute to fluctuations in national income. Ideally, changes in these government-determined variables should mainly *offset* undesired fluctuations in GNP arising from fluctuations in investment (or other components of private demand). However, realistically, the government policy variables have sometimes contributed as much or more to instability as have fluctuations in investment.[1]

Investment is strategically important in another way, because it significantly determines the long-run course of economic activity. As we have frequently noted, an economy's productive capacity grows through the accumulation of capital, quantitative and qualitative expansion of the labor force, and improvements in techniques of production. Since capital accumulates only through investment, investment is an important determinant of long-term growth. Moreover, investment is essential to the process by which additions to the labor force are accommodated and is the primary means whereby new technology is introduced.

Another reflection of the importance of private investment (at least in an economy where the means of production are, in major part, owned by other than family-sized firms) is found in the extremely large stock of financial assets whose growth corresponds closely to changes in the stock of capital goods. A large firm's net investment is ordinarily financed partly by the sale of bonds or by new public stock issues; to the extent that it is financed from retained earnings, there is likely to be an increase in the value of existing shares; and to the extent that it is financed by a net increase in outstanding bank loans, the public's stock of bank deposits is likely to increase. Bank deposits and privately issued securities—whether held directly, or indirectly through "financial intermediaries"—constitute the largest share of consumer wealth (along with houses, consumer durables, and government money and securities), and the stock of such wealth is an important determinant of consumption. Moreover, the trading of these financial assets is a major function of the banking and financial community. The activities of the financial markets in which such assets are traded clearly both closely affect and are closely affected by the level of investment spending in the economy.

The Importance of Investment

Table 18-1 suggests the relative size and the differential volatility of the three broad categories of (domestic) investment ordinarily distinguished in the United States (and most other) national income accounts: business fixed investment (which, in turn, can be separated between plant and equipment expenditures); residential construction; and inventory change.[2]

---

[1] The monetarists, of course, argue that the private economy, even including investment, is inherently stable; they attribute much or all of the observed instability to defective monetary systems and, in the modern world, to government's mismanagement of the money supply.

[2] In the national accounts of many countries government (and/or government-enterprise) investment is lumped together with private. Although for many purposes this is useful, we are here basically concerned with the theory of *private* investment (some of which may also be applicable to its public counterpart).

Business fixed investment and residential investment can, of course, be stated either in net or gross terms. Although not usually categorized as investment in national income accounts, purchases of consumer durables behave in ways similar to plant and housing investment; indeed, houses are only the most durable of the category of consumer durable goods. (Houses also differ in that a much larger fraction of the stock of houses than of other durables is owned by businesses, which sell the services of the durable goods to consumers.) Much of the theoretical account of investment spending that we give can be applied (with appropriate adaptations) to consumer purchases of durable goods; the amount and volatility of such purchases is also shown in Table 18-1.

Part A of Table 18-1 shows the changes in investment and consumer durable outlays over two selected United States business cycles, between the trough level of GNP and the subsequent peak, and the peak and subsequent trough. The last column on the right shows that, at the first peak, these categories of GNP together constituted 21.7 percent of the total (a lower percentage, obviously, at each trough); at the peak of the second cycle they constituted 26.5 percent of GNP. But these items contributed considerably more than their share to the cyclical fluctuations in GNP. In the first cycle their changes were a third of the increment of GNP, trough to peak, and they were 90 percent of the subsequent decline. The contributions are even more dramatic in the second cycle, to which they contributed more than half of the upswing and 115 percent of the decline (in other words, the rest of GNP, which accounted for nearly three quarters of it, actually rose slightly during the decline).

Moreover, the full volatility of these items is not indicated by part A, for their fluctuations typically do not perfectly coincide with those in total GNP. Part B measures the fluctuation of each item from its own specific trough to its own specific peak and subsequent trough, associated with the general peaks and troughs in GNP. Cycles in residential construction, for instance, ordinarily precede those in other elements of GNP (and thus also lead the fluctuations in the aggregate); these fluctuations are seen to be very much larger than part A had suggested. It is also clear that, on either basis, inventory investment, despite its trivial absolute size relative to GNP, typically contributes a large fraction of every decline in GNP—in these two cycles, half or more.

It should of course be kept in mind that fluctuations in investment expenditures occur as a result of changes either in quantities of capital good produced and purchased or in their prices or both. That is, we distinguish fluctuations in real and nominal investment. To be sure, exceptionally difficult theoretical and practical problems are raised by the effort to define the "real" quantity either of investment or of capital. Although the capital theory and investment theory that follow are intended basically to explain real capital and investment, they neglect most of these problems.

TABLE 18-1

Fluctuations in Investment and Consumer Durable Purchases in Two Business Cycles
(All data in constant 1972 prices)

A. Cycles Defined in Terms of GNP[a]

	Change, trough to peak		Change, peak to trough		Level at GNP peak as % of-
	Billions of dollars	Percent of change in GNP	Billions of dollars	Percent of change in GNP	GNP at peak
Cycle of 1954–1958					
Gross national product	80.0	100.0	−22.2	100.0	100.0
Business fixed investment	12.3	15.4	−5.9	26.6	9.8
Residential construction	0.0	0.0	−0.6	2.7	4.3
Change in business inventories	7.8	9.8	−10.5	47.3	0.5
Consumer durable purchases	6.5	8.1	−2.9	13.1	7.1
Sum of components shown	26.8	33.5	−19.9	89.6	21.7
Cycle of 1970–1975					
Gross national product	169.5	100.0	−82.3	100.0	100.0
Business fixed investment	27.9	16.5	−18.7	22.7	10.8
Residential construction	10.9	6.4	−20.7	25.2	4.4
Change in business inventories	21.1	12.4	−43.4	52.7	2.0
Consumer durables purchases	31.2	18.4	−11.7	14.2	9.3
Sum of components shown	91.1	53.7	−94.6	114.9	26.5

[a] Dates of GNP peaks and troughs were as follows: Trough 1954–2; peak 1957–3; trough 1958–1; trough 1970–4; peak 1973–4; trough 1975–3.

1974–75 troughs: 1974–4 for consumer durable puchases
 1975–1 for residential construction and GNP
 1975–2 for change in inventories
 1975–3 for business fixed investment

[b] Percent of change in GNP over its own specific cycle.

[c] Own specific peak level as % of GNP peak level.

B. Specific Cycles (cycles defined in terms of own peaks and troughs)[a]

	Change, trough to peak		Change, peak to trough		Peak level as % of GNP at peak [c]
	Billions of dollars	Percent of change in GNP [b]	Billions of dollars	Percent of change in GNP [b]	
Cycle of 1954–1958					
Gross national product	80.0	100.0	−22.2	100.0	100.0
Business fixed investment	12.3	15.4	−9.9	44.6	9.8
Residential construction	8.8	11.0	−6.7	30.2	5.3
Change in business inventories	14.2	17.8	−16.0	72.1	1.3
Consumer durable purchases	12.0	15.0	−7.8	35.1	7.9
Sum of components shown	45.1	56.4	−40.4	182.0	24.2
Cycle of 1970–1975					
Gross national product	169.5	100.0	−82.3	100.0	100.0
Business fixed investment	28.5	16.8	−23.9	29.0	10.8
Residential construction	26.2	15.5	−30.9	37.5	5.2
Change in business inventories	21.5	12.7	−45.1	54.8	2.0
Consumer durable purchases	39.5	23.3	−21.1	25.6	10.0
Sum of components shown	115.7	68.3	−121.0	147.0	28.0

[a] Dates of specific peaks and troughs were as follows:
1953–54 troughs: 1953–4 for residential construction, change in inventories
                             1954–1 for consumer durable purchases
                             1954–2 for business fixed investment and GNP
1955–57 peaks: 1955–2 for residential construction
                             1955–3 for consumer durable purchases
                             1955–4 for change in inventories
                             1957–3 for business fixed investment and GNP
1957–58 troughs: 1957–3 for residential construction
                             1958–1 for inventory change, consumer durable purchases, and GNP
                             1958–3 for business fixed investment
1970 troughs: 1970–1 for change in inventories
                             1970–2 for residential construction
                             1970–4 for business fixed investment, consumer durable purchases, and GNP
1973–74 peaks: 1973–1 for residential construction and consumer durable purchases
                             1973–4 for change in inventories and GNP
                             1974–1 for business fixed investment   (footnotes continued on page 610)

Investment theory has received a great deal of attention in the last two decades. Nevertheless, it is fair to say that there is no clear consensus among economists as to a single "best" theory of investment. Empirical generalizations regarding investment behavior are similarly inconclusive. This is reflected in the fact that no econometric investment function performs very well; in particular, none allows us to predict the path of investment with much confidence.

Capital and Investment

As noted in Chapter 8, we need to distinguish clearly not merely between the *concepts* of capital and of investment but between theories relevant to each of them. The capital stock changes through net investment, which, in turn, equals (the flow of) gross investment—that is, the production of investment goods—minus (the flow of) depreciation. Although it is a serious oversimplification to take depreciation as proportional to the size of the capital stock, it is such a convenient one that we shall use it throughout this relatively elementary treatment (as do most more advanced treatments). Thus, we can write that

$$K_t = K_{t-1} + I_{G_{t-1}} - \delta K_{t-1}$$

where K_t is the capital stock at the beginning of any period, $I_{G_{t-1}}$ the rate of gross investment during the previous period, and δ the rate of depreciation.

Given this relationship, one might suppose that the economist's task is merely to explain the factors that determine investment, since the size of K is automatically explained as the accumulation over time of net investment. Unfortunately, this will not do, for it is clear that the size of K is one of the most important factors determining I. Thus, investment theorists usually begin by attempting to construct a theory of a "desired" or "optimum" or "equilibrium" stock of capital for a firm and an economy, and then treat investment as the *means* by which the actual stock K is adjusted towards the desired or equilibrium stock K^*. When $K = K^*$, this equilibrium is achieved, and net investment would then necessarily be zero if K^* were constant. For net investment to be other than zero, either or both of two requirements must be met: (1) that there exists a gap, positive or negative, between K and K^* or (2) that K^* changes over time.

Clearly, if all firms were always able instantaneously to adjust their capital stocks to the "desired" level, the theory of investment would only be a simple derivative of the theory of capital. For, with constant and instantaneous equilibrium, K always equal to K^*, as the desired stock changed the actual stock would change as well, and this change *is* the rate of net investment I_N. Thus, whatever factors determined K^* would also determine I_N; and, since $I_G = I_N + \delta K$, the explanation of K^* would also explain I_G.

Some investment theorists seem to believe that the assumption that firms can and do adjust their capital stocks more or less instantaneously is close enough to the truth that investment theory can safely incorporate this assumption—as did, for example, the simplest version of the acceleration principle. It is also an implicit assumption of Dale Jorgenson, whose "neoclassical" investment theory is well known and will be discussed later. Such an assumption could conceivably be reasonably satisfactory for a single firm, at least to the extent that the capital goods it uses are bought "off the shelf" from its supplier and can be instantly installed. Even so, the *producer* of the capital goods would have to be able to forecast his customers' demands perfectly or else *he* would have a matching investment or disinvestment in inventories whenever there occurred any fluctuations in his customers' demands. Thus, we would still need another explanation for the *production* of capital goods, which is how we define investment.

However, most capital goods, including not only all buildings but also much equipment, are not bought "off the shelf" but are built to order. Thus, at the very least, investment theory needs to incorporate some production lag, making current investment depend on an earlier change in K^*. Moreover, since different capital goods have different production lags, the actual investment in any period would depend on a series of earlier "gaps" between K and K^*—through a distributed lag mechanism.

However, when we consider the entire economy, even this solution is unsatisfactory because (as we will show) the length of the production lag cannot be taken as constant when the rate of investment demand varies. Moreover, although the *existence* of net investment may require an existing or previous gap between K and K^* (and/or a change in K^*), the rate of investment may well also be affected by factors that are independent of K^*.

Thus, a macroeconomic theory of investment cannot be treated as a mere derivative of a theory of capital. Rather, while investment must be seen as an "adjustment process" responding to the existence of current and previous gaps between K and K^*, attention must be given to all factors that may significantly affect the rate of this adjustment. And current net investment may be seen to change either (or both) as a result of factors affecting the size of K^*, current and past, and/or as the result of factors affecting the adjustment process itself. Unfortunately, many macroeconomic theories of investment seem to have stressed too much—in some cases, almost exclusively—factors dealing only with the size of desired capital stock.

One final preliminary observation is needed. In an economy that is in *full* equilibrium, not only does K equal K^*, but K^* is without growth over time. Such an economy has all the capital it needs, and, although net investment might fluctuate, it must average out to zero. Some investment theories imply that an actual economy is always in, or tending toward, such a full or stationary equilibrium. Put otherwise, they assume no economic growth.

In fact, the modern economies for which macroeconomic theory is presumably relevant show little sign of any tendency toward stationary equilibrium. Rather, net investment is almost never zero or even close to it, and it usually constitutes a substantial fraction of GNP. Although a conceptual framework tied to a stationary economy *might* satisfactorily explain *fluctuations* in investment, to explain the continuing substantial positive investment of actual economies—which is one of their most important characteristics—requires theories that can also explain cumulative growth of K^*. We shall return more than once to this theme.

Chapter 8 dealt with three relatively simple theories of investment:

1. Investment as a function of the rate of interest
2. Investment as a function of income
3. Investment as a function of the change of output or income—the *acceleration* principle.

It developed the third of these rather fully. The main task of this chapter is the development of the logic and implications of the "classical" theory that makes investment depend on the interest rate. Chapter 19 then returns to the acceleration principle in the light of this exposition of the classical theory; it also considers other types of investment theory and illustrates empirical versions of each of the leading types. Chapter 19 also suggests that much of the reality of investment lies well beyond any of these theories and describes the substance of some problems with which a more realistic approach must somehow deal.

One regrettable omission from both chapters is the theory and empirical analysis of inventory investment. As Table 18-1 shows, the cyclical behavior of this type of investment dominates the recession and early recovery stages of the business cycle. There was a brief account of some aspects of the theory of inventory investment in Chapter 7. The more advanced analysis of inventory investment is too important and complex to be treated briefly; it is therefore entirely omitted.

THE CLASSICAL AND KEYNESIAN THEORY OF CAPITAL AND INVESTMENT

In Chapter 8 we noted that the systematic part of Keynes' theory of investment was lifted bodily from classical economics—namely, that investment depends on the interest rate. However, Keynes did insist that the investment schedule was subject to sharp exogenous shifts, mainly for sociopsychological reasons. This was the only investment theory used in our various "classical," "Keynesian," and "synthesis" models of Chapters 5, 10, 11, and 12 (although we referred from time to time to some consequences of incorporating elements of the acceleration principle). In this section we propose to explore carefully the derivation and logic of the systematic relationship between investment and the interest rate, both at the level of the firm and of the economy. In particular, we hope to clarify some of the many misconceptions which often surround this idea.

The Rational Investment Decision

In Chapter 8 we described the factors that a firm might take into account in deciding whether or not to make a particular investment which it was considering. Here, we summarize that consideration in more formal terms.

The rational **decision rule** for the investments of a firm can be stated in any of several ways. The simplest is this: it pays to make any investment q for which the present value PV_q of associated future revenues less associated future costs exceeds the cost of the investment C: that is, it pays if $PV_q > C$. (If $PV_q = C$, it is a matter of indifference.) If investment resources are limited, those investments should be selected for which the excess of PV_q over C is the greatest.

We can spell out the elements of this condition for profitability more fully as follows:

(1)
$$PV_q \geq C_t$$

where

$$C_t \equiv v_t q$$

and

$$PV_q \equiv \frac{p^e_{t+1} x^e_{t+1}}{1 + i} + \frac{p^e_{t+2} x^e_{t+2}}{(1 + i)^2} + \cdots + \frac{p^e_{t+r} x^e_{t+r}}{(1 + i)^r}$$
$$- \frac{w^e_{t+1} n^e_{t+1}}{1 + i} - \frac{w^e_{t+2} n^e_{t+2}}{(1 + i)^2} - \cdots - \frac{w^e_{t+r} n^e_{t+r}}{(1 + i)^r}$$

$v_t =$ unit price of capital goods being considered for investment
$q =$ smallest feasible unit of investment
$p^e_t =$ expected price in period t of the output which can be produced using investment q and employment n^e_t
$x^e_t =$ expected quantity of output demanded and sold in period t at p^e_t
$w^e_t =$ expected wage rate in period t
$r =$ number of periods to end of economic life of investment q
$i =$ current rate of interest at which funds can be borrowed to finance q (or at which owner's available funds could alternatively be invested).

The first row of the definition of PV_q shows the expected sales revenue from sale of output, discounted to the present; and the second row shows future labor costs expected to be incurred, discounted to the present.[3]

The above description has been written as though the markets in which output would be sold and labor purchased were perfectly competitive, so that expected prices (p_t^e) and wage rates (w_t^e) would be independent of amounts sold or purchased. If this is not the case, we need to substitute product demand and labor supply schedules. The elements x_t^e and n_t^e are not independent, however. Rather, they are related to each other and to q through some production function, and the particular levels of x_t^e and n_t^e are those that would be selected to maximize profits or minimize losses in period t, given q and p_t^e, and the production function.[4]

Condition (1) can thus be thought of as a condition for the maximization of profits over time, subject to the constraint of a production function among the x's, n's, and q. Analogously to the usual formulation, it pays to produce all outputs for which marginal revenue exceeds marginal cost. Here, C can be thought of as the "marginal cost," payable now, of a discrete lump of investment q, which can be made now and would produce its yield in the future; PV_q, then, is the net extra revenue[5] ("marginal revenue") available in the future from that lump of investment, discounted to "now" in order to be comparable with C.

We can simplify condition (1) by introducing a new variable y_t^e, which equals the expected gross yield[6] of investment q in period t.

$$y_t^e \equiv p_t^e x_t^e - w_t^e n_t^e$$

which simplifies the condition to

(1a) $$PV_q \equiv \frac{y_{t+1}^e}{1 + i} + \frac{y_{t+2}^e}{(1 + i)^2} + \cdots + \frac{y_{t+r}^e}{(1 + i)^r} \geq C_t \equiv v_t q$$

Alternative formulations of this decision rule are possible, and these give precisely the same answer to the question whether or not a prospective investment should be made. In particular, Keynes formulated the rule in the form that it pays to invest if the "marginal efficiency of capital" [later corrected to "marginal efficiency of (an) investment"] exceeds the rate of interest, where the marginal efficiency of an investment is defined as "that rate of discount which, when applied to the series of expected (gross) yields from the newly acquired asset, will just reduce the sum of the discounted

---

[3] Terms showing expected quantities and prices of purchased materials, parts, and services, and expected taxes should also be subtracted from PV_q. We have omitted materials costs because, when we aggregate, they will cancel out; we can assume indirect taxes are included in prices, and we will return to income taxes only later.

[4] Of course, the production function may be one involving fixed proportions among q, n, and x. In that case the investment of q implies a given n and x—at least if q is to be fully utilized.

[5] Over and above all current "running" costs of using the new investment.

[6] *Gross* yield, because neither depreciation nor interest has been deducted.

yields to equal the cost of the asset." That is, it pays to invest if

(2) $$m_q \geq i$$

where m_q (marginal efficiency of investment q) is found by solving the equation

$$C \equiv v_t q = \frac{y_{t+1}^e}{1 + m_q} + \frac{y_{t+2}^e}{(1 + m_q)^2} + \cdots \frac{y_{t+r}^e}{(1 + m_q)^r}$$

It can be easily shown[7] that any investment that will satisfy (or fail) condition (1) will also satisfy (or fail) condition (2). In other words, an entrepreneur prepared to make all available profit investments will make exactly the same choices using either criterion.[8]

We may illustrate both criteria, and show their equivalence, with a simple numerical example. Suppose that, for a particular potential investment,

$$C_t = \$1027.96 \qquad r = 3$$

$$y_{t+1}^e = \$400$$

$$y_{t+2}^e = \$380$$

$$y_{t+3}^e = \$350$$

Rule 1

(a) Assuming $i = 0.10$

$$PV_q = \frac{400}{1 + 0.10} + \frac{380}{(1 + 0.10)^2} + \frac{350}{(1 + 0.10)^3} = \$940.65 < \$1,027.96$$

Investment should be rejected.

(b) Assuming $i = 0.03$

$$PV_q = \frac{400}{1 + 0.03} = \frac{380}{(1 + 0.03)^2} + \frac{350}{(1 + 0.03)^3} = \$1,066.85 > \$1,027.96$$

Investment should be made.

---

[7] Merely by comparing the last line of condition (3) with condition (1), it can readily be seen that, if $m_q = i$, $PV = C$; thus, in either formulation, the investment is a matter of indifference. Since a lower i means a higher PV, it can also be seen that when $m_q > i$, $PV > C$; and vice versa.

[8] However, an entrepreneur with *limited* resources, who desired to pick out of a number of potential investments those for which he should use his resources, might rank these possibilities according to the magnitude of the (percentage) excess of PV_q over C (that is, rule 1); or alternatively according to the (percentage) excess of m_q over i (rule 2); but he might well find that the two rankings were not the same! In that case, he should use rankings made according to rule (1).

(c) Assuming $i = 0.05$

$$PV_q = \frac{400}{1 + 0.05} + \frac{380}{(1 + 0.05)^2} + \frac{350}{(1 + 0.05)^3} = \$1{,}027.96$$

Investment is a matter of indifference.

Rule 2

We must first calculate m_q by solving equation (3). (This can be done by trial and error or by using a set of interest tables.) Given the values of yield and cost assumed above, $m_q = 0.05$. Thus

(a) Assuming $i = 0.10$, $m_q < i$. Investment should be rejected.

(b) Assuming $i = 0.03$; $m_q > i$. Investment should be made.

(c) Assuming $i = 0.05$; $m_q = i$. Investment is a matter of in-difference.

There is still a third method of expressing the criterion, which we will not spell out in detail, that says that it pays to invest in a capital good if its dollar cost plus interest on the investment at the going market rate is less than the dollar yield expected from the asset. Although this way of expressing it is more natural for an investment the yield of which occurs at one point in time rather than in continuous flow, we can still give it application in the latter case, so long as we are careful to apply the interest only to that (gross) investment that remains as the yield accrues.[9] Properly applied, it will select or reject as profitable or not exactly the same investments as either of the other two formulations (given that the entrepreneur makes all investments which are profitable).

It should be apparent that there are three sets of elements in the calculation, however we choose to combine them into two for purposes of comparison; and a change in any one of them is bound to affect the calculation of profitability. The three elements are (a) *the cost level of the capital goods* ($v_t q$); (b) the *expected dollar yields*—the number r, and the amount, of the expected future y's (and the p's, x's, w's, and n's that underlie them, along with the future material's prices and inputs and the tax rates which we have not formally incorporated); and (c) the *market rate of interest* at which the entrepreneur can borrow or lend. Underlying the calculation is a fourth element: some production function relating q, the n's, and the x's.

In any of the formulations we can immediately identify which kinds of changes would improve profitability and which might be presumed, if they were to occur generally, to affect the number of investments that firms would find profitable, and thus would raise aggregate investment. For example, any of the following changes would (ceteris paribus) increase the profitability of particular prospective investments, and would thus perhaps

[9] For an illustration of this method, see the 1961 predecessor of this book, p. 464.

raise many of them from the prospect of nonprofitability to that of profitability: a rise in expected p's or x's (or in r); a decline in expected w's or n's; reductions in v or i. Each of these changes might suggest a possible theory, or an aspect of a theory, of investment.

For example, a rise in expected p's, with a given current v, raises expected profitability, suggesting that an expected inflation or an increase in the expected rate of inflation should encourage investment. The expectation of an increase in the x's (at given p's)—that is, the expectation of an increase in product demand—raises profitability, suggesting the acceleration principle. The fact that a reduction of i raises profitability suggests the impacts on aggregate investment of monetary policy, or changes in saving, or more or less effective financial intermediation. Since profitability is increased by an increase in r, an increase in the x's, or a reduction of the n's for a given q, arising, for instance, from technological improvement increasing the durability, or raising the annual output rate, or reducing the future labor input associated with a given q, this suggests the role of technological progress in determining the amount of profitable investment. And the fact that many of these magnitudes are not known with certainty but instead involve expectations—which may be influenced by social and political attitudes and events, by the state of the stock market, and by the "nerves and hysteria and even the digestions and reactions to the weather"—suggests possible sociopsychological aspects of investment theory.

However, none of these, or other, possible investment theories can be derived directly from the arithmetic of the investment decision. For it may be that a change in any one set of variables, either automatically or through some market process, necessarily implies some set of other changes—for another firm or product or for all firms or products—that would offset the effect of the first change. There are examples of theories derived merely from the arithmetic of a firm's profit calculations which suffer from precisely this disability. Several examples will be given as we consider the derivation of the theory that investment depends on the rate of interest: which was the classical theory, was Keynes' theory, is used in all versions of the "synthesis" model, and underlies the recent and highly influential "neoclassical" investment theory of Dale Jorgenson and others.

Relative Factor Prices and the Capital-Intensity of Production

From the mere arithmetic of the investment calculation, it might appear that, *ceteris paribus*, a reduction in i would make any and every investment more profitable. However, in the classical full employment economy, a reduction in the rate of interest could only be generated by an increased propensity to save. The opposite side of this coin would be a decreased current demand for consumer goods, which implies the expectation of reduced x's and/or p's, thus offsetting any effect of the lower i. But what classical economists correctly recognized was that a reduction of the rate of

interest constitutes a change in the relative prices of the factors of production—capital, labor, and land—and that this would permanently
increase the relative demand for the factor, capital, for producing *any*
given output.

It would do this, first, by selectively favoring the production of more
capital-intensive products as opposed to labor- or land-intensive products.
A reduction of interest cost has a greater effect in reducing total unit cost
and therefore prices of goods produced by more capital-intensive methods.
A reduction of the interest rate will tend to reduce the price of electric
current or the level of house rents much more than it will reduce prices of
goods which use little capital, and it will have almost no effect on the price
level of personal services. To the extent that goods produced by more
capital-intensive methods compete either in consumer budgets or in production with other goods produced by less capital-intensive methods, a
reduction in the relative prices of the former will cause their partial
substitution for the latter, thereby increasing the "demand for capital."
Thus, for example, in a country with high interest rates, more personal
services and fewer consumer durable goods are used; laundresses (almost
zero capital cost) substitute for washing machines (produced with capital
goods and also themselves durable). How extensive this effect would be
would depend, of course, on the relative price elasticity of demand for the
more capital-intensive products versus that of the demand for other products.

Second, and probably more important, a reduction of the interest rate
would selectively affect the choices made among alternative technologies
for producing any given product, by favoring more capital intensive
methods of production as opposed to less capital-intensive ones. How
extensive this effect would be would depend on the extent of ready
availability of known production methods, alternative to those currently
in use, which were more capital-intensive, and which would become the
preferred methods with only a moderate reduction of *i*. For, as we have
noted earlier, the use of more capital in production ordinarily does require
the use of a different technology. To be sure, it may take only fairly obvious
managerial and organizational rearrangements for a firm to learn to work,
and more economically, with the larger inventories permitted by a lower
interest rate. But to mechanize hand processes, build more durable and
more automatic machines, permit one worker to replace 2 or 10 or 100,
requires knowledge of processes that have up to now not been profitable to
consider.

Now, there is no obvious reason why more capital-intensive processes,
known or discoverable, will always and indefinitely become cheaper than
less capital-intensive methods whenever the interest rate falls. To be sure,
some classical economists (or their successors) have argued that it is some
kind of a "law" of the natural world that there is always possible some

more capitalistic method of production that is cheaper (*excluding depreciation and interest cost*) than the best of any less capitalistic method. Some have even argued that there are always *already-known* technologies, more capital-intensive than those in use, available, and more profitable, ready to be substituted once the interest rate falls sufficiently to permit it. Thus, the demand for capital will necessarily approach infinity at some positive interest rate; a zero interest rate could exist only in a world from which scarcity has disappeared.[10]

Keynes, on the other hand, held that there was no general reason why this must be so[11]; this was also the position of some earlier economists, for example, Wicksell. Beyond some point, they argued, increases in the capital intensity of production may cease to reduce unit costs (exclusive of interest); in fact, after some point, more capital-intensive methods may even be more expensive than less capital-intensive. Keynes argued that, at a zero rate of interest, the best methods of production would not be those of infinitely high capital intensity. Even if capital were interest-free, some finite degree of capital intensity would be preferred. More capital-intensive methods than these would require a negative interest rate (that is, a subsidy) if they were to be adopted.[12] Indeed, Keynes explicitly argued that if the rate of interest were continuously so manipulated as to produce enough investment to maintain full employment, the demand for capital would be fully saturated, and the rate of interest would be reduced to zero "within a generation"—a judgment which, more than a generation later, can be seen to have been absurdly mistaken.

Although the issue is academic when it relates to the question whether the demand for capital would become infinitely elastic at zero or some rate of interest above zero, it is not academic when it reflects a divergence of views as to the relative degree of interest elasticity of the demand for capital at rates of interest within the limits of our experience. Keynes' view that the demand curve for capital is usually fairly steep (that is, interest reductions have little effect in increasing the optimum capital intensity) is at sharp variance with, and may suggest quite different policies than the opposing view that the demand curve is highly elastic.

The question is, at bottom, an empirical one. It is, moreover, one on which relevant evidence is extremely scarce and difficult to interpret. The *a priori* arguments supporting the high interest-elasticity of the demand for

---

[10] See Frank H. Knight, "The Quantity of Capital and the Rate of Interest," *Journal of Political Economy*, 44 (August and October 1936), 433–463, 612–642.

[11] *General Theory*, Chapter 16, especially pages 217–221.

[12] Some 30 years ago there was a well-known cartoonist named Rube Goldberg. His specialty was the invention of highly capital-intensive—but obviously highly inefficient and thus costly—methods of accomplishing simple tasks. Such methods would only be profitable to adopt at a highly negative interest rate. At some point, Keynes implied, the economy could further increase its capital intensity only by turning to Rube Goldberg devices.

capital have never appeared convincing, and Keynes is surely entitled to his opposite opinion. However, the question as to the importance or effectiveness of interest rate policy does not rest on this question alone, as will be evident later. First, moreover, we must dispose of erroneous arguments purporting to explain why investment is greater at lower rates of interest, which make no reference to the capital-intensity of production.

Erroneous Derivations of the Classical Investment Function

The first of the incorrect derivations of the classical investment function is found in a number of the best textbooks. It suggests that, at any given point in time, any firm may be aware of a considerable number of possible investment projects, for each of which it can calculate, given its best estimates of all the relevant variables, its marginal efficiency m. It will find a considerable variation among the m's for these possible investments; and it can rank all projects, and the amount of investment in each, from the highest to the lowest m. It thus knows the cumulative dollar amount of all investments whose yield, so measured, exceeds each of all possible interest rates. This schedule can be graphed as in Figure 18-1, with the current interest rate, i_0, shown for comparison. If the yields range from m_1 to m_n (the latter, in this case, negative), the schedule would appear as in the figure. It is clear that the decision rule, "Invest when $m > i$," will select all those investments for which the marginal efficiency exceeds i_0 and reject the others. Thus the current investment of the firm will be I_0. If, however, i had instead been i_1, the larger total investment I_1 would have been chosen. The similar schedules for all firms could then be aggregated into one economy-wide schedule, and this would represent the investment schedule

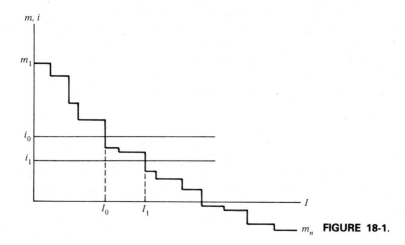

FIGURE 18-1.

of the entire economy. And, given the market rate of interest, the amount of aggregate I would be determined.

There is nothing fundamentally wrong with the preceding argument, except that it does not provide the basis for the classical theory of investment or, indeed, for any meaningful theory of investment.[13] For what the firm's investment schedule, so derived, reflects—and thus so must the aggregate schedule—is the existence of temporary disequilibrium in the internal structure of the firm's and the economy's capital stock. In a competitive economy with perfect knowledge and foresight and no lags of adjustment, we know that, in the resulting instantaneous and continuous equilibrium, the yields of all investments that were in fact made would be identical and equal to the interest rate. For, if any type of investment yielded more than others, firms would instantaneously rush to invest in it, driving up costs of any factors especially adapted to this kind of production and/or driving down the price of the output of that type of investment, until the excess yield disappeared. All those investments that were made would have exactly the same yield and all those not made would have lower yields.[14]

Of course, such a perfect equilibrium in the internal structure of capital never exists. Exogenous changes of all kinds are always opening up newly profitable investment opportunities as well as depressing the relative yields of investment in other lines, and the adjustment to these changes in relative yields is not and cannot be instantaneous. This adjustment, through more investment where relative profitability has improved, requires an information and learning process and the production and installation of new capital goods and the recruiting of labor; thus, considerable time is necessary to eliminate the higher yields. Where profitability has been depressed, the adjustment requires information and learning, and, particularly, the wearing out of existing equipment.

It is true that an array of possible yields on alternative new investments always presents itself to a firm and to all firms together, requiring

---

[13] There are, moreover, some fearful complexities slid over in the aggregation. For one thing, each firm's investment schedule must reflect the explicit or implicit assumptions the firm must make about investments by other firms, present and future, and in its own industry as well as in supplying or purchasing industries. And these assumptions may be mutually inconsistent. How can such schedules aggregate to an economy-wide schedule? However, the more *fundamental* error of the derivation is that discussed in the text.

[14] Some of those not made might later become candidates for investment, as the failure even to replace capital wearing out in those fields would eventually raise the relative output price and reduce the prices of specialized production factors. However, there will be other types of potential investments not made that will remain indefinitely unattractive. These are the ones in which no capital is currently employed; they have not been profitable and will not become so until there has been a change in demand or cost conditions or a reduction in i. These include precisely the investments relevant to the classical theory of investment, as we have seen.

investment choices. But the slope of the schedule so derived reflects essentially only the extent of the forces producing change in the economy and the speed and effectiveness of the adjustment process. If change is slow and investment responses quick, the schedule will at all times be quite flat; in the opposite case it will be much steeper. But we can say nothing systematic on the basis of such a schedule about the determinants of the rate of aggregate investment. For, under this derivation, we learn nothing about what determines the aggregate rate of investment which will be made at the prevailing interest rate, nor about why this rate would have been higher had the interest rate been lower. The existence and extent of internal disequilibrium in the structure of capital does not answer this question.

A second incorrect derivation rests on factors internal to a firm, which have little relevance for an economy in which the number of firms is free to vary. We assume that a firm's long-run (as well as its short-run) production is subject to diminishing returns—either because some factor of production, perhaps the contribution of the ultimate decision maker, is fixed in amount, or because of inevitable diseconomies of organization, communication, or management that arise as the scale of a firm increases. This means that any firm's calculations of profitability must recognize that, beyond some point, additional investment implies less than proportionate increases in output and/or more than proportionate increases in employment. Thus, the i that will equate m_q and i must decline in order for I to increase. True enough. But this explains only the *size of firms*, not the amount of aggregate investment. The number of firms is not preordained.

A similar problem arises with respect to another factor implied or stressed in other analyses: the fact that the market for any product is limited. For a firm to contemplate increasingly larger future production (involving larger investment now) requires it to recognize that future p's will have to be lower. Or, if a number of purely competitive firms produce a product, each of which takes future p's as given, their combined action in investing in any kind (and thus in every) line of production will drive down the product price, making further expansion unprofitable. Once again, this helps to explain the size of imperfectly competitive firms or of perfectly competitive industries. It does not explain the rate of change of the aggregate stock of capital. What requires prices to fall as output expands is the diminishing marginal utility of particular products to consumers, quantities of other products held constant, requiring that the *relative* price of product A must decline if its production is to expand relative to that of products B, C, D, and so on. But for the economy as a whole, relative prices necessarily always average out to 1; a fall in one price relative to others is a rise in other prices relative to the first. Overexpansion in one line of output implies underexpansion in others. If all expand together, that is, aggregate production expands, no need has been shown for a decline in average profitability. This source of a declining m_q as I increases will not stand up either.[15]

FROM THEORY OF CAPITAL TO THEORY OF INVESTMENT

The classical theory of capital, as sketched in the preceding section, explains how the optimum stock of capital employed by the firm and economy depends upon the relationship between the cost of assets, their expected yields, and the interest rate. Adding to this the empirical assumption that, in general, more capital-intensive methods involve lower unit cost (exclusive of depreciation and interest) than less capital-intensive methods, we expect to find that the lower the rate of interest, the more capital-intensive will be the productive methods that firms employ, that is, the higher will be the ratio of the value of their capital to the value of their output. However, these propositions relate to firms that are in equilibrium with respect to the their use of capital—that is, to firms whose capital structures have been adjusted to the going rate of interest, cost of capital goods, and expected yields. But this is not *directly* relevant to the theory of investment. For investment occurs only when firms are not in equilibrium with respect to their capital structure—when they have less (or more) capital goods than the optimum.

As we have already stressed, we have not one but two problems; first, to explain the optimum (that is, the equilibrium) stock of capital for a firm and an economy; and, second, to explain at what rate investment occurs when the capital stock is not at its optimum As we have seen, if a firm has less capital than its optimum and the capital goods it needs are in the stock of its supplier, investment by that firm can occur very rapidly. If, however, we enlarge the analysis to include the supplier or, if the capital goods must be made to order, then the rate of investment will be determined by the production period of the particular capital goods. Suppose, for instance, that the optimum stock of capital for a certain firm were previously $1,000,000, and, following a reduction of the interest rate, all other factors

[15] The preceding comments seem applicable to the "neoclassical" investment analyses of Jorgenson and others, who derive the specifications of an investment function from a microeconomic analysis of a profit-maximizing firm, without apparent reference to problems of aggregation. The existence of diminishing returns as the size of a firm expands and of a downward sloping demand curve for any firm or industry is clearly assumed; but the precise nature of these limits as they apply to the total economy seems nowhere to be explored. And since Jorgenson's analysis assumes perfect foresight by the entrepreneur, it seems appropriate to ask whether he is indeed expected fully to understand and anticipate not only the microeconomic considerations relevant to the size of his own production but as well those relevant to other firms and the macroeconomic effects of their combined actions. In any case, Jorgenson's analysis seems nowhere to justify its "neoclassical" label by relating to the original classical basis for the declining investment schedule—which as we have seen clearly lies in consideration of aggregate "factor proportions" for the entire economy.

remaining the same, the optimum stock becomes larger, say $1,300,000 because it now pays to mechanize a process formerly performed manually. Suppose further that it takes 18 months for the new equipment to be built and installed. Then (assuming the cost of the new goods is incurred evenly over the 18 months), investment will be at the rate of $200,000 per year for the $1\frac{1}{2}$ years; thereafter, zero. But if the period of production were cut in half, to 9 months, investment would be at the rate of $400,000 per year (for 9 months).

It is important to recognize that in this example the rate of investment was determined by a factor that does not enter at all in the theory of capital—namely, the speed of construction of capital goods. Suppose, to take another example, that the firm's actual stock of capital exceeds its optimum stock. What determines the rate of its (dis)investment? If the capital consists of plant or equipment, it is determined by the rate of wearing out or obsolescence of the particular capital goods; if in stocks, by the rate of their sale or use in production. In either case, considerations outside of the orbit of capital theory determine the rate of investment.

We can develop several alternative simple theories of investment for the economy as a whole, given the existence of a gap between K and K^*. Instead of the production time of capital goods, which is relevant to a single investment, we might have, as a limit on the rate of investment for the economy as a whole, the productive capacity of the capital goods industry. If, at a particular time, this industry can turn out capital goods at an an annual rate of 50 billion dollars, then *gross* investment cannot exceed $50 billion per year (at least in real terms). Net investment cannot exceed this figure less the amount of annual depreciation and obsolescence. If the latter is $10 billion, then net investment cannot exceed $40 billion a year, nor fall below −$10 billion. Gross investment (which cannot be negative) can range from zero to $50 billion a year, net investment from $10 to $40 billion.

Further, so long as our theory takes no account of the fact that separate firms and industries may be in different situations, it can be shown that the model would produce only three possible rates of investment; −10, zero, and 40 billion dollars a year. For the optimum stock of capital must always either exceed, fall short of, or just equal the actual stock. If the optimum *exceeds* the actual—perhaps because the interest rate has recently fallen—firms must be clamoring for new capital goods, and the capital goods industry, trying to fill its orders, will be operating at capacity. But, unless the optimum stock of capital grows as fast as or faster then the actual stock accumulates through investment, the actual stock must gradually "catch up" with the optimum. If, then, the optimum stock just equals the actual, net investment would fall to zero. Capital goods would be replaced as they wore out, but no more. The third possible rate of investment reflects the situation in which the optimum stock falls short of the actual stock—perhaps because i has recently risen. In this case gross investment would be zero, and net investment would be negative, at a rate determined by the rate of depreciation. Again, unless the optimum stock were to shrink as fast as the actual, a point of equality should eventually be reached, and the rate of net investment should rise from negative to zero.

The model is obviously very crude, but it does correspond at least very roughly with the frequent observation that the capital goods industries are industries of "feast or famine"—they oscillate rather violently between conditions of feverish activity and stagnation. Each of these conditions corresponds to a *disequilibrium* for industry in general (including, of course, the capital goods industries) with respect to stocks of capital goods. Either kind of disequilibrium may be rather slow to correct itself, since the production of capital goods (even at the maximum rate) cannot add significantly to the stock except over a considerable period of time nor can depreciation reduce the stock very rapidly. A relatively slight disequilibrium (percentagewise) between actual and optimum stocks may thus engender a fairly considerable period of intense activity or stagnation in the production of capital goods.

One might add the fact, long recognized, that, for psychological reasons, the boom may lead to overbuilding, so that what was a shortage of capital (actual stock less than optimum) frequently leads to an excess, and vice versa.[16]

Of course, a still more important intensifier of boom and depression is added by the consumption function. When the capital goods industries are working at capacity, employment and incomes are high in the capital goods industries. Consumption spending will therefore also be abnormally high, generating further incomes in the production of consumer goods, and further consumption spending. Thus, during the boom, when the stock of capital goods is below its optimum size, income and output will be raised not only by the amount of production of capital goods at their capacity rate but by a multiple of that. Once production of new capital goods at a capacity rate, over a sufficient period of time, has caused the stock of capital to catch up with the optimum level, and net investment then drops to zero, income and employment will fall by an amount equal to the reduction of investment times the multiplier.

---

[16] Another, more subtle and systematic point was made in some of the earlier business cycle literature, particularly by the German writer Spiethoff. He pointed out that when industry in general was short of capital, so that the capital goods industry was working at capacity, the capital goods industry was itself under pressure to add to its capacity (that is, the size of its optimum stock was enlarged). Thus, the capital goods industry's efforts to increase its own capacity intensified and prolonged the boom that resulted when other industries were trying to add to their capacities. In the depression, when the capital goods industry was shut down, it, too, had excess capacity that needed to be worked off through failure to replace. For further discussion, and reference, see G. Habeder, *Prosperity and Depression*, Economic Intelligence Service, League of Nations, third edition, 1941, especially pp. 76–77.

Thus, if we start from an equilibrium position in which the stock of capital is at its optimum, and something happens, for example, a reduction of the interest rate, to increase the optimum stock, a boom of considerable consequence may ensue during the period in which the capital stock is growing toward its new optimum. On the other hand, if the optimum stock should become less than the actual, a period of zero replacement investment will occur, during which time the capital goods industries are completely shut down, while depreciation gradually reduces the capital stock; this will, of course, also bring a period of depression in the consumer goods industries.

In equilibrium, when the capital stock is fully adjusted to its optimum level, net investment is zero. Nevertheless, replacement investment, equal to depreciation, would maintain a certain level of activity in the capital goods industries, and consumption spending would be at a level appropriate to this level of income originating in the investment trades. However, on simple assumptions, it is not clear how the economy would ever get to this equilibrium.[17]

The Cost of Capital Goods

One objection to the kind of simple theory developed previously relates to the concept of capacity to produce capital goods. Instead of capacity being a fixed amount, economists usually think of a flexible limit to output, with more output always forthcoming, but always at a higher (marginal) cost. The fixed capacity concept implies a supply schedule for capital goods like that of part a of Figure 18-2. Instead, the usual concept of supply is that of part b. Here there is no single point which can be labeled that of "capacity." If the curve at some point becomes vertical, the point might merit the label; but that point may be entirely academic, the high cost of supply causing output of capital goods Q, under normal circumstances, to be carried only to a much lower point.

Suppose we substitute this idea of a rising cost schedule for the capacity concept in our investment theory. We then have the cost of capital goods dependent on their rate of production. Let us assume again that, given the rate of interest, the optimum stock of capital exceeds the actual stock, and consider what will be the rate of investment.

Now, however, there is an ambiguity in our concept of the optimum stock of capital. For one of the elements in the determination of the optimum stock is the cost level of capital goods, v. To any single firm this can be taken as given. But we are now hypothesizing that, for the economy,

[17] The careful reader will have noted that this mechanism was presented in Chapter 8 as the essence of a theory of the business cycle associated with the name of Richard Goodwin. There, however, a different theory of capital was employed, namely, that the desired stock depended on the level of output—the "acceleration principle."

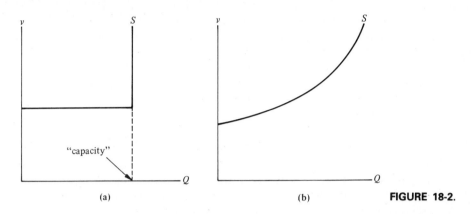

FIGURE 18-2.

this cost level is variable and depends on the total rate of investment. That is, the cost can be considered as given to the firm but must be considered to vary with the decision made by all firms taken together.

Suppose that we remove this ambiguity by defining the demand curve for capital (which shows the optimum stock at each rate of interest) in terms of *that level of cost of capital goods which would prevail if investment were at a net rate of zero.* In part a of Figure 18-3 the optimum stock of capital is shown by the curve labeled MPK (marginal product of capital). Each point on this curve must be understood to be defined in terms not only of a given expectation of yields but also in terms of a cost of capital goods associated with production of capital goods *at a rate corresponding to zero net investment.* Part c of the figure shows, as curve *S*, the supply curve of capital goods. The particular cost level used in defining the MPK curve

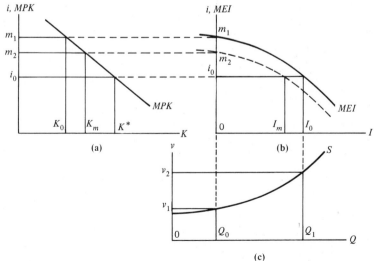

FIGURE 18-3.

of part a is v_1 in part c. This is associated with output Q_0, which is just equal to aggregate depreciation.

If, in part a, the rate of interest is given at i_0 and the existing stock of capital is given as K_0, then there is a gap between the actual stock and the optimum stock K^*. This makes investment profitable, but at what rate? In part b we have drawn a curve labeled MEI (marginal efficiency of investment). This curve begins at level m_1, for this is the level of yield from capital goods when the actual stock is K_0 (see part a) and when the cost of production of capital goods is at v_1 (see part c). The MEI, however, declines as the rate of investment rises, reflecting the fact that higher investment rates will raise the cost of production of capital goods. In fact, the MEI curve of part b falls at the same (percentage) rate as the supply cost, shown in part c, rises; it is, in a sense, a mirror image of the supply curve. What rate of investment then occurs? Clearly rate I_0. At this rate, the cost of capital goods is bid up to a level v_2, high enough that a further increase in the rate of investment would reduce the percentage yield from capital goods below the rate of interest. I_0 is thus the *short-run* equilibrium rate of investment. Thus, not only the desired capital stock K^* but also the "optimum" or "desired" or "equilibrium" rate of investment I_0 depends on the rate of interest.

But I_0 is the equilibrium rate only in the *short run*; for investment at any rate above zero causes the actual capital stock K_0 to increase. This increase causes the whole MEI schedule to shift downward. For example, when the capital stock has grown to K_m, the MEI schedule will have shifted downward to the level of the broken line in part b, leading to a lower rate of investment I_m. This means that the further growth of K proceeds ever more slowly toward K^*.[18]

Although the notion that the limitation on the output of capital goods occurs in the form of rising costs rather than in a sharp capacity limit seems more elegant, one may doubt the practical importance of this "improvement" in the analysis. This is particularly the case when we recall the rather high cyclical stability of the prices charged by many capital goods indus-

[18] The theory of investment developed in the preceding paragraphs is, in substance, essentially that of Keynes' *General Theory* (Chapter 11). Keynes, however, presented this substance in a confusing (perhaps one should say confused) way. He defined a schedule, which he called the "marginal efficiency of capital schedule." This showed the amount of investment which would occur at each rate of interest. It declined, he said, for two reasons: one, the larger the stock of capital, the lower the expected return from the use of capital assets; and, two, the greater the rate of investment, the higher the cost of assets. Investment was carried to the point at which the MPK equaled i. The second of the reasons for declining MPK was more important, he said, in the short run, and the first in the longer run.

This reflects an unfortunate confusion of factors relating to the size of the *stock of capital* with those relating to the *rate of investment*. It led to various contradictions and ambiguities that are easily enough resolved when one separates the two sorts of considerations, as we have done. This was first clearly achieved by Lerner. See his *Economics of Control* (Macmillan, 1944), Chapter 25.

tries. During a boom, the chief means by which the available production of capital goods is rationed among customers is not through price increases but through "queuing". New orders go to the end of a steadily lengthening waiting list. The backlog of orders is gradually worked off, at which point the boom may collapse.

Whether or not the rising cost of capital goods idea relied upon by Keynes is more "realistic" than the capacity analysis, it probably adds little that is essential to our investment analysis, and the capacity concept substitutes an analytical simplicity that could more than compensate for any slight loss of realism. Nor is the concept of a rising cost of production of capital goods the only way to make the rate of *investment* (as well as the size of the stock of capital) depend on the rate of interest, as we will see below.

Problems with the Classical Theory

The classical theory of investment, which makes the desired stock of capital depend only on the interest rate, seems to imply that the only way in which net investment might be prevailingly positive over substantial periods of time would be through a continuing decline in the interest rate. Since there has been no secular decline in the interest rate in major Western economies over the last century, this theory obviously fails to explain the incredibly large accumulation of capital in these countries during this period.

That does not mean, of course, that another explanation (such as one of those discussed in Chapter 19) cannot be used to explain the *trend* in the capital stock, while the classical theory might still explain (or contribute to the explanation of) cycles in investment superimposed on a prevailingly positive *level* of net investment which has another explanation. And the theory has, indeed, often been so used. Yet a careful judgment seems inevitably to reject, too, any significant cyclical role for the classical theory.

There is no doubt that interest rates have fluctuated in cyclical fashion in almost all countries. Likewise, there seems little doubt that these fluctuations have been associated—partly as effect[19] but also to some extent as cause—with the cycles in investment which are so characteristic of the "business cycle." But the causal connection from interest rate to investment must be something other than the one implied by the classical analysis. For that analysis would imply that the cycles in investment caused by changes in i must be associated with systematic fluctuations in the capital-intensity of production methods. There is no evidence whatsoever that this is the case.

---

[19] If there are cycles in investment—however caused— and M is either constant or fluctuates in lesser proportion than V, it is clear that i should rise in booms and fall in slumps, even if this variation has no effect at all on investment. Low interest rates might then appear to "lead" investment booms, although they might have no causal role.

To be sure, in the 1920s and 1930s such a view was commonly held. Booms were described as efforts, basically mistaken and fruitless, to intensify the use of capital in production, stimulated by artificially and temporarily low interest rates, which were the product either of the previous business-cycle recession and/or of mistaken easy-money policies in recession and recovery. But such low interest rates could not be maintained when the boom arrived; or, even if they could, the absence of complementary factors of production, or other complex imbalances, would ultimately force the boom to end, leaving either unfinished investment projects that were largely worthless, or finished projects unable to compete with less capital-intensive projects once interest rates returned to normal. Hayek called his version of this theory the "Ricardo effect" (thus emphasizing the classical nature of the underlying ideas).[20] In what must be one of the most devastating critiques in the history of economics, Nicholas Kaldor showed the absurdity of what he called Hayek's "concertina effect"—the cyclical "lengthening" and "shortening" of the production process.[21] Remnants of this idea may still be circulating in the byways of economics, but the writer has not encountered them in several decades.[22]

It seems fair to say that—however relevant the classical interest-rate/capital-intensity argument may be for a general equilibrium analysis, or for international comparisons, or for some other purpose—it seems to contribute little to the explanation either of (a) the "real-world" process of capital accumulation or of (b) cyclical fluctuations in investment.

Still, the absence of short-term fluctuations in capital intensity does not mean that the interest rate may not play a causal role in investment fluctuations. Once we supply an alternative theory of the determination of the desired or equilibrium capital stock, *changes* in this desired stock may open up gaps between K and K^* that create investment opportunities. And the rate at which these opportunities are exploited, through positive net investment, may be influenced by the interest rate for any of several reasons.

[20] Among other perpetrators of business cycle theories based on fluctuations in capital intensity were L. Mises, L. Robbins, W. Röpke, and R. Strigl. For an exposition of such theories, see G. Haberler, *op. cit.*, especially pages 33–72. One may perhaps understand how highly intelligent economists were driven to such fantasies by the necessity to explain a business cycle in an economy that remained fully employed, which their classical training forced them to assume.

[21] "Professor Hayek and the Concertina Effect," *Economica*, New Series, 9 (November 1942), 359–382.

[22] It should be clear that mere cyclical overbuilding of capital goods in the boom does not qualify, even if induced by "too low" interest rates in the preceding recession and recovery. Only if the overbuilding involved capital goods too capital-intensive to be economical at the average interest rate would the malaise be "classical" in the sense implied by classical interest theory.

One possibly very important way in which the interest rate may affect the rate of investment, even if it has no practical effect on the capital intensity of production, is that low interest rates are often seen by firms as low *relative to the average of future interest rates*; high interest rates are seen as a temporary excess over normal or average rates. Thus, when and while interest rates are low, firms seek to undertake projects that would otherwise have been initiated later. Or, they revive earlier projects that had previously been postponed in order to avoid having to pay what were then seen to be temporarily peak rates. Projects thus may be temporarily backlogged when rates are high and pulled out of the backlog when they are low.

To be sure, it is somewhat more reasonable to argue that the long-term *financing*, rather than the execution, of projects is postponed or anticipated in response to interest-rate fluctuations. But there are some costs in stockpiling idle investment funds, if borrowed long-term in advance of need, just as there are costs of obtaining temporary financing for projects undertaken in anticipation of later permanent financing. Thus, interest rate expectations may affect the timing not only of the financing but to some extent of the execution of projects on a firm's longer term capital budget.

Moreover, levels of interest rates may fluctuate inversely with investment, but both the bunching in time of investment and the fluctuations of interest rates may be the product of shifts in quite another set of factors: namely, in lenders' and borrowers' evaluations of risk and in their attitudes toward assuming it. Suppose, for example, that the socio-psychological climate in which businessmen operate is one which inevitably produces under-estimates of risk (both by lenders and borrowers) when times are good, and over-estimates of risk when there is recession or depression. This will produce a bunching of investment in time, which—if the money supply is stable or growing relatively smoothly—will produce higher interest rates in boom than in recession. Assuming substantial lags, one might conclude that it is the low interest rates of the recession that produce the investment recovery and the high interest rates of the boom that eventually cut off the boom. However, in this case, the causation is at least partly the other way around.

We shall consider in Chapter 19, under the heading "financial limits on investment," some other and perhaps more important further reasons why interest rates may affect the volume of investment even in a *cyclical* context.

Although the possible connections between interest rates and investment just referred to or to be described in the next chapter, may be elements of some theory of investment, they are not really elements of the classical theory, the fundamental premise of which is that K^* is a function of i, because of the technological superiority of more capital-intensive methods of production.

JORGENSON'S "NEOCLASSICAL" INVESTMENT THEORY

As earlier noted, an outstanding economic theorist and econometrician, Dale Jorgenson, has developed a sophisticated reformulation of the classical theory of investment which he, and others, have used to derive the specifications of investment equations for a wide variety of empirical work.[23] The following brief and inadequate summary may convey at least the essential flavor of Jorgenson's approach.[24]

It is important to recognize at the start that Jorgenson's investment equation derives directly and explicitly from the theory of the profit-maximizing firm, with perfect foresight, operating subject to a production function that connects current real investment with future real outputs; moreover, the aggregate investment function is a simple "blowup" of the behavior of a firm, with no attention to the problems stressed in earlier chapters of aggregating firms' production functions.

From the theory of such a firm, Jorgenson derives the following condition for the optimum capital stock (k^*) for the firm at any and every point in time. (Note that Jorgenson's symbols differ somewhat from those used previously.) It is[25]

$$k_t^* = \gamma \frac{p_t}{c_t} y_t$$

where the production function at any point in time is here taken (for

---

[23] There are a number of recent alternative models that have as good a claim as Jorgenson's to the "neoclassical" label, but which make different assumptions or use somewhat different variables. However, space does not permit summarizing the others.

[24] See D. W. Jorgenson, "Capital Theory and Investment Behavior," *American Economic Review*, 53 (*May* 1963), 247–268; reprinted in L. R. Klein and R. A. Gordon, eds., *Readings in Business Cycles* (R. D. Irwin, 1965), pp. 366–378; and "The Theory of Investment Behavior" in R. Ferber, ed., *The Determinants of Investment Behavior* (Columbia University Press, 1967), pp. 129–156.

[25] The condition is derived from the maximization of profit, which requires setting the value of the "marginal product of capital" equal to the "marginal cost of capital." Given the Cobb-Douglas production function

$$y = \alpha k^\gamma l^{1-\gamma}$$

$$\frac{\partial y}{\partial k} = \alpha \gamma k^{\gamma-1} l^{1-\gamma}$$

$$= \frac{\gamma \alpha k^\gamma l^{1-\gamma}}{k}$$

$$= \frac{\gamma y}{k}$$

Setting the value of this marginal product $p\gamma y/k$ equal to the rental price of capital c and rearranging gives

$$k = \frac{\gamma p y}{c} = k^*$$

simplicity) as of "Cobb-Douglas" form:

$$y_t = \alpha k_t^\gamma l_t^{1-\gamma}$$

and where

y = the firm's real output

γ = the exponent of k in the Cobb-Douglas function

l = amount of labor (and other) production inputs

p = price of firm's output

c = "rental price of capital"

  $= q(r + \delta) - \dot{q}$

q = the price of capital goods (and $\dot{q}$ the expected rate of change in q)

r = the investor's rate of time discount

δ = depreciation rate on k (assumed constant)

Taking account of taxes on profits, including the specification of permissible (accelerated) depreciation for tax purposes, and the possible use of an investment tax credit, the cost of capital can be elaborated to

$$c_t = \frac{q_t(r + \delta)(1 - m_t - w_t z_t)}{1 - w_t} - \dot{q}_t$$

where

w_t = basic income tax rate

m_t = the rate of an investment tax credit

z_t = present value of any accelerated depreciation provisions (as percent of investment cost)

The firm maximizes the present value of its current and all future profits, *with perfect foresight assumed* (over a period as long as the life of any capital equipment now considered for purchase) *with respect to all future values* of p, q, $\dot{q}$, δ, r, w, m, z. Expected values of all of these may *vary* over the future, but it is assumed not discontinuously (that is, the time derivative of each is assumed always to be finite). Two of the many other particular assumptions necessary to the argument are the existence of "putty-putty" capital—that is, that even after an investment is made, its form may be instantly and costlessly adapted to a different technology appropriate to changing values of variables (which implies that, even in the short run, and within the firm, the capital-intensity of production can freely vary); and r either constant (in Jorgenson's own empirical work, usually taken as a constant 20 percent), or else that changes in r are instantaneously capitalized in capital goods prices (q).[26]

---

[26] These last two assumptions are among several which are *not* embodied in other recent models which can also be called "neoclassical."

The preceding discussion supplies Jorgenson's capital theory—that is, the description of the factors determining the desired stock of capital. The relative complexity of this theory of capital is matched only by the simplicity of his theory of investment, namely

$$k_t = k_t^*$$

that is, each firm always has exactly its optimum stock of capital or

$$i_t^N = \dot{k}_t^*$$

where i^N is net investment. Recognizing that it takes time to produce most capital goods (a time that is apparently assumed constant regardless of the total investment occurring in the economy), firms have had to order most of their capital goods in advance in order for them to be in place at the time foreseen to be needed. And since this time lag may be different for each type of capital good, the investment actually *made* at any given time depends on a series of earlier decisions, each based on values of the variables as of that time. Thus the firm's net investment depends on values of the relevant variables as foreseen at a series of earlier times.

If we now aggregate for all firms and assume that all expected future values are taken as proportional to current values at the time of each investment decision (because changes in current values are assumed always to produce, *ceteris paribus*, proportional changes in future values) and if we take indexes of output prices and capital goods prices to represent the prices which influence decisions, and ignore (for simplicity, here) tax laws and $\dot{q}$, we get as the specification for statistical testing using aggregate data:

$$I_t^N = \sum_{i=0}^{n} \gamma b_i \Delta \left(\frac{PY}{Q(\underline{r} + \underline{\delta})} \right)_{t-i}$$

where the capital letters represent aggregate magnitudes, and $\underline{r}$ and $\underline{\delta}$ averages, and where the b_i are weights (adding to 1) of a distributed lag. Adding replacement investment

$$I_t^R = \underline{\delta} K_{t-1}$$

gives, for gross investment,

$$I_t^G = \sum_{i=0}^{n} \gamma b_i \Delta \left(\frac{PY}{Q(\underline{r} + \underline{\delta})} \right)_{t-i} + \underline{\delta} K_{t-1}$$

To this writer, the assumed absence of discontinuous changes in expectations (including, for example, as the result of invention of new technology, or changes created by alterations in tax laws that enter into the value of c—perhaps any such technological or legislative changes were also foreseen?); the neglect of aggregation problems; the ignoring of any dependence of the time lag structure, or of Q, on aggregate investment; and (consistent with the above) the assumption that $k = k^*$ at all times for all firms, seem to avoid most of the important and interesting problems in investment theory.[27] What limits the amount of desired investment for each firm is either diminishing returns, internal to the firm, or the limits of its market. Yet, as we have seen, these effects may cancel out in aggregation.[28]

Jorgenson is describing, obviously, a full-employment economy in which all prices (and wages) are perfectly flexible and in which there are no wide swings of investment. Perhaps in that economy it is not completely unreasonable to assume that changes in demand for final products can be perfectly foreseen by producers of capital goods so that they may make their own investments in time to meet the capital needs of their customers and also to plan for their own disinvestments as their customers' needs subside. Possibly in that economy also any modest changes in supplies and prices of capital goods that accompany these adjustments can be fully anticipated by prospective purchasers. However, this is hardly the economy we know, with its surges of investment demand, its lengthening order backlogs for capital goods, followed by its collapse of investment demand, its periods of idle facilities (and labor) in both consumer and capital goods industries.

Nevertheless, it is interesting to note that Jorgenson's version of classical investment theory is not basically a theory of "investment as a function of the interest rate." In practice, Jorgenson takes the relevant discount rate used by entrepreneurs to be much higher than the interest rate and insensitive to changes in the latter. This means that Jorgenson does not assume any long-term or short-term changes of capital-intensity arising from changes in interest rates. But such changes apparently *would* arise from changes in tax laws or from changes in the price level of capital goods relative to the price level of final products, even if the latter were only cyclical.

Assuming tax-law changes to be exogenous, Jorgenson's systematic or endogenous theory of investment thus involves its fluctuation in response (a) to changes in the current and past ratios of final output prices to capital goods prices, P/Q[29]; and (b) to changes in aggregate output ΔY. Even

---

[27] The importance of the assumption of perfect foresight and absence of discontinuous changes can be seen by recognizing that if there were discontinuous changes in K^*, and $I_t^N = \dot{K}_t^*$, I^N would be $+\infty$ or $-\infty$: clearly impossible. However, Jorgenson seems to suggest that no rate of investment (less than ∞) could possibly be constrained by supply limitations, and that any negative rate (less than $-\infty$) can be accommodated through wearing out of existing capital.

[28] See footnote 15.

[29] Why the ratio of these prices might change is not systematically investigated by Jorgenson; but, given diminishing returns in the production of capital goods, changes in the rate of investment would produce changes in this ratio.

though Jorgenson does not assume that variations in Y will involve changes in aggregate employment (other than those reflecting changes in the labor force), Jorgenson has, nevertheless, provided a full theoretical basis for the simple acceleration principle, so long as P/Q is constant. Despite its neoclassical label, this theory would seem to bear little relationship to what we have, so far, called the classical theory of investment!

REVIEW QUESTIONS

1. Suppose that an investment project promises annual yields of $y_1^e, y_2^e, \ldots, y_{10}^e$.

(a) Precisely what factors are taken into account in estimating these expected yields?

(b) What other two pieces of information are necessary in order to evaluate this project?

(c) Given these other pieces of information, precisely how would one decide whether or not to invest?

(d) How would a change in each "factor" listed for part (a), and in each "piece of information" listed for part (b) tend to alter the investment decision?

2. If the "desired" or "optimum" stock of capital differs from the actual stock, investment (positive or negative) will occur.

(a) What is meant by the desired or optimum stock of capital and what variables are thought to affect it, and why?

(b) The difference between the two stocks does not itself provide a theory of investment. Explain and illustrate why.

(c) Given a difference between the two stocks, present and explain at least three alternative versions of what might determine the rate of investment.

3. "Since, for any firm, the marginal efficiency of investment (MEI) usually declines the larger the number of investments made, the interest rate that equates with the MEI must also fall in order for investment to increase. This establishes the inverse relationship between the interest rate and aggregate investment." Carefully evaluate.

4. "The classical theory of investment fundamentally relates to propositions about the technological superiority of more capital-intensive methods of production, and the relative aggregate supplies of capital and other factors." Explain.

5. Keynes wrote that "the marginal efficiency of . . . capital will diminish as the investment in it is increased, partly because the prospective yield will fall as the supply of . . . capital is increased, and partly because, as a rule, pressure on the facilities for producing . . . [capital goods] will cause [their] supply price to increase." Show the logical error of this proposition. How can it be reformulated to avoid the error but preserve the substance of the idea?

6. "The concept of a limited capacity to produce capital goods can substitute for the schedule of rising cost of production of capital goods, without fundamentally changing the underlying investment theory." Explain.

7. How does Jorgenson define the "rental price of capital"? Explain in words the presence in the definition of each of its elements.

SELECTED REFERENCES

J. M. Keynes, *The General Theory of Employment, Interest, and Money* (Harcourt Brace, 1936), Chapters 11–12.
(Keynes' discussion of the theory of investment.)

A. P. Lerner, *The Economics of Control* (Macmillan, 1944), Chapter 25.
(A clear and precise statement of fundamental classical ideas, as adapted by Keynes.)

J. Hirshleifer, "On the Theory of Optimal Investment Decision," *Journal of Political Economy*, 66 (August 1958), 329–352.
(An influential, but demanding, analysis of optimal investment decisions, given certainty of the future, as integrated with simultaneous consumption decisions.)

D. W. Jorgenson, "Capital Theory and Investment Behavior," *American Economic Review*, 53 (May 1963), 247–268, reprinted in L. R. Klein and R. A. Gordon (eds.), *Readings in Business Cycles* (R. D. Irwin, 1965), pp. 366–378.
(The single best statement of Jorgenson's approach.)

Chapter 19

A Broader View of Investment

Further Consideration of the Acceleration Principle

Eisner's "permanent-income" version of the acceleration principle

An alternative formulation of the acceleration principle

Financial Factors Limiting Investment

Some aspects of capital markets

Financial theories of investment

Stock prices and investment

Empirical Tests of Investment Theories

A Broader View of Investment

Possible reasons for the failure of investment theory

Technology and investment

As shown in Chapter 18, Jorgenson provided an elaborate and sophisticated derivation, based on classical ideas, of the acceleration principle: *ceteris paribus*, investment depends on (a weighted average of) the recent change of aggregate income, ΔY. The main conceptual difference from the acceleration principle of Chapter 8 is that the size of the accelerator becomes a variable, dependent on changes in the rate of interest (if the relevant interest rates can be assumed to vary), or in the ratio of final-product to capital-goods prices, or in tax laws. If none of these changes, Jorgenson appears to show that I^N is proportional to recent ΔY. If any of these does change, this influences the size of the acceleration coefficient, and, in this way, the amount of whatever investment is induced by changes in Y.[1]

Since Jorgenson has derived what appears to be a more sophisticated version of the acceleration principle from purely classical assumptions, one may wonder why the acceleration principle was not recognized by the classical economists. The answer may be that classical macroeconomics (like Jorgenson) ordinarily took Y as constant at the full-employment level, based on the assumption of a constant labor force and the demonstration that this labor force will always be fully employed if only prices and wages are flexible. To be sure, even with a constant and fully-employed labor force, classical economics implied that Y might still vary. This might occur as the result of an increase in K^* (and thus in K) arising, say, from a

---

[1] Perhaps it needs to be noted that Jorgenson does not in any sense think of his theory as a version of the acceleration principle. And, given all the assumptions (of perfect competition and perfect foresight) that underlie it, and the continuous full employment which that implies, it clearly does not seem to operate like one.

permanent reduction in i (perhaps as the result of an increase in saving) or from the invention of new and more efficient technologies involving a higher ratio of capital to labor. But once the change in capital intensity had occurred and K had reached its new equilibrium level, investment would cease. Any positive net investment, in such a world, had to be "deepening investment"—increasing the ratio of capital to labor, and thus the ratio of output to labor. And, any *continuing* positive net investment required either a continuing fall in the interest rate (presumably as the result of continuing increases in saving), and/or the continuing development of new, more efficient, and more capital-intensive technologies.

The classical economists did, of course, at many points consider the possibility of labor-force growth, which, through flexible wage rates and prices, would lead to growth of employment and output. Even with a constant interest rate and constant technology this should require an expansion of capital to provide the new workers with extra tools. But, because of the absence of a consumption (that is, saving) function, which would permit some of the extra income to be devoted to investment, the main result was seen to be an "enshallowing" of capital (the opposite of "deepening"—less capital per worker).[2] Thus, the acceleration principle was discovered and popularized by economists not in the classical mainstream.

Once the Keynesian macroeconomics allowed aggregate employment to grow—both through reduction of unemployment and through expansion of the labor force—and found a source of extra saving in growing incomes, the stage was set for "widening" as well as "deepening" investment. This is why, in Chapter 8, we treated the acceleration principle as a logical "extension" of Keynesian analysis, even though the acceleration principle was neither mentioned nor implied in Keynes' *General Theory*—and even though Jorgenson does show that it is implicit in the classical analysis!

Of course, the mere existence of unemployed workers—whether those formerly employed who had lost their jobs or those new additions to the labor force who had not found jobs—is not in itself enough to induce widening investment. Some increase in aggregate demand and output is essential to start the process of widening investment, which in turn would further enlarge aggregate demand. However, given the simple form of the accelerator used in Chapter 8, we saw that the process implied all kinds of possibilities for instability, limited, if at all, by the existence of ceilings and floors on either investment or output or both. That kind of violent instability seems no more characteristic of modern, "real-world" economies than does the cyclical oscillation of capital intensity implied by the Hayek model.

---

[2] Traces of an acceleration effect do appear in the "wages fund" doctrine, but this involved essentially an extra investment in payrolls when the labor force grew.

FURTHER CONSIDERATION OF THE ACCELERATION PRINCIPLE

As we have argued, an adequate theory of investment requires both a good theory of the demand for capital (the desired capital stock K^*) and a good theory of adjustment of the actual to the desired stock. Although Jorgenson may have provided a fuller and more sophisticated theory of capital—by showing that the desired stock depends not only on the level of output but also on the interest rate, relative prices, and tax rates—his theory of adjustment is the same simple and unsophisticated one used in the simple accelerator version of Chapter 8: that $I_t = \Delta K_t^*$, or, recognizing the necessary lead time between production and use of capital goods:

$$I_t = \sum_{i=0}^{n} b_i \, \Delta K_{t-i}^* \qquad (\textstyle\sum b_i = 1)$$

In Chapters 8 and 18 we have suggested a number of problems with such a theory of investment, and, in 18, a number of possible amendments, including the existence of a capacity limit in the capital goods industries, and/or a rising supply cost of capital goods as I increases. And in Chapter 8 we stressed that, given recent and current changes in aggregate demand, the investment response would also depend on entrepreneurs' expectations as to how long these changes would last. This last factor is *formally* built into Jorgenson's analysis, because it embraces the whole array of expected quantities and prices, all perfectly foreseen. But foresight is in fact imperfect, and no mechanism for the formation of these expectations was provided by Jorgenson beyond the assumption that all expected prices, however they are related to current prices, change as current prices change. Moreover, what about the expected future quantities to be sold? Jorgenson assumes that a classical production function connects current investment with future outputs, and that perfect foresight always provides just the right current investment to produce the expected quantities. But, once again, foresight is not perfect, and capital invested today may not be fully utilized tomorrow—or there may be a shortage of capital tomorrow. Once again, we need some understanding about how actual quantity expectations are formed.

In the subsection that follows, we outline how one prominent proponent of the acceleration principle has built an expectations mechanism into his investment theory. An alternative formulation of the acceleration principle is suggested in the subsection after that. Then, in the next major section, we return to the theme, also briefly introduced in Chapter 8, that a broader set of "financial" considerations may also impinge on the rate of investment.

Eisner's "Permanent Income" Version of the Acceleration Principle

Robert Eisner is perhaps the most enthusiastic of recent proponents of the acceleration-principle theory of investment, and among the most vigorous in attacking alternative theories.[3] Although Eisner recognizes that statistical tests (using various bodies of data) of the simple form of the acceleration principle which make I^N depend only on current ΔY, have found the data not very supportive of the hypothesis, he argues that the reason for this failure is the oversimplified form in which the theory is specified for empirical testing. In particular, he stresses that the simple forms implicitly assume that any current change in sales is seen by entrepreneurs to be a lasting change. If it were not expected to be a lasting change, there are alternative means of adjusting to it without ordering new equipment: for example, overtime work, use of inefficient standby equipment, running down of inventories, or letting prices rise. These alternative ways have certain disadvantages relative to an expansion of capacity, but they have a great net advantage over the purchase of any additions to plant and equipment that might soon prove useless. Thus, firms are properly cautious about responding to current increases or drops in sales until they are convinced that a genuine change has occurred—rather than a mere random "blip"—and one which is likely to be relatively lasting.

To represent the sorting out process by which firms evaluate current changes in their sales, Eisner borrows Friedman's concept of "permanent" changes, representing a permanent change by some weighted moving average of past changes. This does not assume that firms have no information about the permanence of sales changes other than their observed persistence; it is only that such persistence is ordinarily the most important and convincing information that firms have, and the only one that Eisner believed could be systematically built into a theory of aggregate investment. (Eisner also argues that each firm attaches more importance to changes in industry-wide sales than it does to changes in its own sales.)

Thus, the investment function should make gross investment depend on a distributed lag of current and previous changes of sales plus a term representing replacement investment as proportionate to the previous period's capital stock. Indeed, the empirical form of the investment equation may appear identical with Jorgenson's, except that it lacks the $P/Q(r + \delta)$ term which creates the *variable* acceleration coefficient:

$$I_t^G = \alpha \sum_{i=0}^{n} b_i \, \Delta Y_{t-i} + \delta K_{t-1} \qquad \left(\sum b_i = 1 \right)$$

However, the economic significance of the distributed lag in Eisner's theory is very different from Jorgenson's. For Jorgenson, its purpose was to

---

[3] See R. Eisner, "Investment: Fact and Fancy," *American Economic Review*, 53 (May 1963), 237–246; R. Eisner and R. H. Strotz, "Determinants of Business Investment," in Commission on Money and Credit, *Impacts of Monetary Policy*: A Series of Research Studies Prepared for the Commission on Money and Credit (Prentice-Hall, 1964), pp. 59–233; and R. Eisner, "A Permanent Income Theory of Investment: Some Empirical Explorations," *American Economic Review*, 57 (June 1967), 363–390.

represent the necessary lead-time between investment *orders* and the *execution* of investment. For Eisner, on the other hand, the distributed lag signifies the representation of "permanent" changes in sales by a moving average of past sales. Although Eisner also recognizes that there may be lags between investment *decisions* and their execution—and even *variable* lags, reflecting supply constraints—he makes no effort to build these into his specification of the model for statistical testing.

An Alternative Formulation of the Acceleration Theory

The usual simple formulation of the accelerator theory explains net investment as filling any gap which appears between today's optimum stock of capital, taken as proportional to today's output, and yesterday's optimum stock, taken as proportional to yesterday's output:

$$I_t^G = K_t^* - K_{t-1}^* + \delta K_{t-1}$$
$$= \alpha(Y_t - Y_{t-1}) + \delta K_{t-1}$$

or

(1) $$I_t^G = \alpha \Delta Y_t + \delta K_{t-1}$$

Equation (1) explicitly assumes that *yesterday's actual stock* of capital (as today's will be) was, in fact, just the *optimum stock* for producing yesterday's output. But we know that, for a lot of reasons, it is unlikely that today's investment will *in fact* turn out to have produced exactly today's optimum stock; similarly, yesterday's actual stock may have differed from that optimal for yesterday's production. Since yesterday's actual stock is known at the time of today's investment decision, as well as the fraction of that which will wear out today, we can instead, and perhaps more realistically, write the equation for the simple accelerator theory as

$$I_t^G = K_t^* - K_{t-1} + \delta K_{t-1}$$
$$= K_t^* - (1 - \delta)K_{t-1}$$

where $(1 - \delta)K_{t-1}$ is the portion of yesterday's actual capital stock that remains useful today. If, still, we assume $K_t^* = \alpha Y_t$, this becomes

(2) $$I_t^G = \alpha Y_t - (1 - \delta)K_{t-1}$$

Equation (2) would seem to have as much claim to being called the acceleration principle as does (1), despite the fact that instead of using ΔY_t, it uses Y_t; and, instead of $+\delta K_{t-1}$, it contains $-(1 - \delta)K_{t-1}$.

However, it is clear that neither the ΔY_t of (1) nor, hence, the Y_t of (2) is known at the time the investment decision must be made. Thus (following Eisner), we may replace the ΔY_t of (1) with a weighted moving average of past ΔY's:

(1a) $$I_t^G = \alpha \sum_{i=1}^{n} b_i \Delta Y_{t-i} + \delta K_{t-1} \qquad (\textstyle\sum b_i = 1)$$

We may similarly choose to replace the Y_t of our alternative formation (2) with a weighted moving average of past Y's. We would then have

(2a) $\qquad I_t^G = \alpha \sum_{i=1}^{n} b_i Y_{t-i} - (1 - \delta) K_{t-1} \qquad (\sum b_i = 1)$

A variant of this approach (that recognizes the uncertainty of any estimate of Y_t) assumes that, because the estimate of Y_t is uncertain, firms, in effect, discount their best estimate of Y_t by investing somewhat less than would be required to bring the size of their capital stocks up to that appropriate to their best estimate of Y_t. The reason why they base their behavior on something less than their best estimate of Y_t is that it is far easier to correct a mistake of underinvestment than one of overinvestment. Instead of (2a), their behavior is thus described by

$$I_t^G = \beta \left[\alpha \sum_{i=1}^{n} b_i Y_{t-i} - (1 - \delta) K_{t-1} \right]$$

or

(2b) $\qquad I_t^G = \alpha \beta \sum_{i=1}^{n} b_i Y_{t-1} - \beta(1 - \delta) K_{t-1}$

where $0 < \beta < 1$.

For statistical estimation purposes, either (2a) or (2b) would be represented as

(2c) $\qquad I_t^G = A \sum_{i=1}^{n} b_i Y_{t-1} - B K_{t-1} \qquad (\sum b_i = 1)$

The differences between (1a) and (2c) resemble those between (1) and (2), that is, the use of Y instead of ΔY, and the opposite signs of the terms in K_{t-1}.[4] From a statistical regression based on (2c), one could, accepting

---

[4] Further to confuse the matter, equations such as (1a) are often replaced by equations that use, not a weighted moving average of ΔY's but a weighted moving average of Y's. These make the first term of equations like (1a) seem identical to the first term of (2a). In fact they are not identical. This can be seen by considering the reformulation that follows of a three-period weighted moving average of ΔY's:

$$b_1 \Delta Y_{t-1} + b_2 \Delta Y_{t-2} + b_3 \Delta Y_{t=3} \qquad (\sum b_i = 1)$$

can be rewitten as

$$b_1(Y_{t-1} - Y_{t-2}) + b_2(Y_{t-2} - Y_{t-3}) + b_3(Y_{t-3} - Y_{t-4})$$

or

$$b_1 Y_{t-1} + (b_2 - b_1) Y_{t-2} + (b_3 - b_2) Y_{t-3} - b_3 Y_{t-4}$$

which can, in turn, be replaced by

$$c_1 Y_{t-1} + c_2 Y_{t-2} + c_2 Y_{t-3} + c_3 Y_{t-4}$$

This appears now to be a moving average of Y's. However, it is easy to see that the sum of the c's, the weights, is not 1 but 0, some weights positive, others negative. For

$$c_1 = b_1 \qquad\qquad c_3 = b_3 - b_2$$
$$c_2 = b_2 - b_1 \qquad c_4 = -b_3$$

the sum of which is zero. Thus, when the standard acceleration principle is converted into terms in Y rather than ΔY, the sum of the weights of these terms should be specified as zero.

the theory incorporated in (2a), interpret the value found for coefficient A to be the acceleration coefficient, and the value of coefficient B to represent $(1 - \delta)$, from which an estimate of δ is easily derived. On the other hand, if the accepted theory is that incorporated in (2b), one would need to use an independent estimate of δ (which is possible to make) along with the computed coefficient B to infer a value for β. From this, given the computed coefficient A, an acceleration coefficient α could be inferred. (This estimate of α, however, would reflect all the errors in the estimates of δ and β.)

Equation (2), or (2c), clearly is derived from a version of the acceleration principle—indeed, from what one may argue is a more realistic version than the usual ones because it does not incorporate the assumption that the stock of capital inherited from last period is always exactly what would have been appropriate (optimal) for producing last period's output. Yet this formulation is seldom recognized or presented as a version of the acceleration principle. Rather, it is frequently derived from a proposition such as the following: "Investment is a function of the average degree to which existing *capital is utilized.*"[5] If Y grows relative to K, this means that utilization has increased, thus stimulating investment. Or, high rates of investment may cause K to grow more rapidly than Y; if so, this will soon deter further investment. One could, of course, use direct measures (from surveys) of capital utilization, and these often are used in investment equations. (One trouble, however, is that such indexes of capital utilization have many conceptual and measurement problems; in any case, most of them cover only a part of the total economy, mainly manufacturing.)

It is not hard to see that the basic concept that investment depends on the level of capital utilization constitutes only a different way of expressing the fundamental idea that lies behind the acceleration principle, although in a considerably looser form of relationship. In either form, moreover, it should now be clear that the acceleration coefficient is not based mainly on technological necessity but on the economic calculation of profitable, or "preferred," operating rates in a world of change and uncertainty. This is a long way from the acceleration principle we started with in Chapter 8.

---

[5] The argument may perhaps be that the higher the *average* degree of utilization in the economy, the more firms and industries there may be whose utilization is at or above their "preferred" utilization rates. To be sure, the proposition in the text actually implies a function in the form

(a) $$I = a_0 + a_1 \frac{Y}{K} \qquad (a_1 > 0)$$

However,

(b) $$I = a_2 Y - a_3 K (a_2, a_3 > 0)$$

can be thought of as a linearized version of (a).

In the next section we will see that some economists have come upon investment theories like (2) or (2c) from still different original starting points.

FINANCIAL FACTORS LIMITING INVESTMENT

There are a number of economic theories and related empirical studies which suggest the importance of "financial" factors affecting the volume of investment. One might assume that such factors had already been adequately accounted for in the determination of the rate of interest—which constitutes the explicit or implicit cost of funds to firms for investment purposes, and which is presumably compared (one way or another) with the rates of return on investments ("marginal efficiency") in deciding whether and how much to invest. But the factors stressed in the financial theories of investment are factors over and beyond the rate of interest and the usual determinants thereof.

Some Aspects of Capital Markets

These additional financial factors are precisely those that are ordinarily assumed away when the determination of "the rate of interest" is discussed. The rate of interest is ordinarily explained as though there were only a single rate, paid on one kind of security, that is issued for a single (often assumed to be perpetual) term and sold by homogeneous borrowers to homogeneous lenders. Instead, there is a bewildering variety of securities, both debts and equities and mixtures thereof, issued by a wide variety of final and intermediate borrowers, and purchased by a wide variety of primary and intermediate lenders.[6]

The *borrowers*, final and intermediate, have quite different abilities, preferences, and legal requirements regarding the *nature and terms* of the contracts they issue: for example, the contractual versus residual character of the current payments they are to make; the tax-deductability (to them) of these payments; their ability to provide to the lender a government guarantee of income or principal; the compromise of secrecy, managerial control, or dilution of equity that they must accept; the stability over time of their capital requirements; the existing volume of their other obligations

---

[6] We use the terms borrowing and lending very broadly to include equities as well as debts, including debts to and of banks and all other financial intermediaries. We assume that whatever intermediaries borrow is immediately reloaned; thus the amount loaned by primary lenders exactly equals the amount borrowed by final borrowers. However, the form in which, and the terms on which, the primary lenders lend and the final borrowers borrow are not the same because of the existence of intermediaries. We also find it convenient to treat the firm's reinvestment of undistributed profits as the unilaterally determined issuance of new equities to existing stockholders.

to pay income and repay principal (relative to the size of income they expect and the variance of that income); their attitudes toward the risks of having to renew or refinance on highly unfavorable (or highly favorable) terms when the loan expires; and many others. As the result of these factors, many individual borrowers are able or willing to issue only one or a few of the possible types of securities; none issues all types.

The supply of investment funds to borrowers includes, very importantly, the retention of enterprises' "internal funds" from their "cash flow" of depreciation and undistributed profits (a type of borrowing that the corporation can unilaterally impose on its existing stockholders).[7] The lenders of "external" funds, final and intermediate, differ widely in their abilities, preferences, and legal requirements relative to the nature and terms of the loan contracts they can or will acquire. These differences concern such aspects as risk of loss or delay of income or of repayment; risk of having to resell assets at different prices than paid; the liquidity desired (that is, instant marketability); the ability to obtain detailed and accurate information about borrowers; the related services provided by (intermediate) borrowers (for example, transfer services, insurance, pensions); the tax status (to them) of income received; the size of the typical lender's total funds (and thus his ability to "pool" risks, or to undertake—or purchase— investment analyses); and many others. Thus, many individual lenders or classes of lenders are able or willing to supply funds to only one or a few classes of borrowers, or to acquire only a limited class of securities, or other securities only in limited amounts.

Because of the many kinds of securities issued, and the specialized character of both suppliers or demanders of funds, there is not one "inter-

---

[7] The significance of internal funds relative to total funds and relative to investment in fixed assets can be seen by examining the data (which relate to year 1974) in the table below.

	Billions of dollars
Sources of funds to nonfinancial corporations—Total	183.3
Internal (undistributed profits after taxes plus capital consumption allowances)	81.5
External, of which	101.8
"Credit market" funds	77.1
Other (including sale of existing financial assets and trade credit received)	24.7
Uses of funds by nonfinancial corporations	
Total	169.7
Purchase of physical assets	125.9
Purchase of financial assets (including trade credit extended)	43.8
Statistical discrepancy	13.6

In many earlier years, internal funds were substantially larger than external funds, in some years more than twice as large. In a few of these years, internal funds were approximately equal to total investment (purchase of physical assets).

est rate" paid and received on a single undifferentiated security, but many kinds and rates of capital incomes paid and received on a wide spectrum of financial assets. And even if a number of borrowers issue what is formally the same security, with identical contractual terms, the market is unlikely to treat them all as equivalent.

To be sure, yields on all kinds of securities do tend to rise and fall somewhat together, because the forces that we have described as "determining the rate of interest" to some extent affect them all; also, many lenders and borrowers can and do deal in more than one type of security and with more than one type of borrower or lender, and they will move between one type and another as divergences develop in the movement of relative yields, thus limiting those divergent movements. Nevertheless, financial theories of investment appear to assume that the degree of substitutability among different securities on both sides of the market is sufficiently limited that (1) rates of yield at any one time differ widely among various types of securities and especially among different issuers of any given time, and (2) over time, these rates may change substantially relative to one another. The "loan market" or "capital market" is not at all like the market in No. 3 hard red wheat, where the commodity is standardized, the price uniform, and buyer and seller are anonymous.[8]

We will return to the subject of this variety of financial instruments and rates of return in Chapter 20, as we consider further our *theories of money and interest*. Here, however, we are only concerned with some consequences of these facts that some economists have seen as relevant to the *theory of investment*. These consequences can be seen to include the following:

1. Most firms are limited in the amount that they can borrow at any given time, at least in the amount they can borrow on any single type of contract, or at any single interest rate, or on other terms that are the same. Thus each firm is faced by a rising supply cost of investment funds, which at some point becomes essentially vertical for almost every firm. This suggests that individual firms might often be unable *for financial reasons* to make, at least all at once, all of the investments that it would be profitable for them to make at the rate they pay on part of their current borrowing. Thus, they stop borrowing (and investing) at a point where the marginal efficiency of investment (to them) may considerably exceed "prevailing" rates of interest paid by them and by other borrowers.

2. Many firms can borrow, at least at the margin, only at rates considerably higher than the rates at which they (or their owners) can lend. Thus, "internal finance" is usually considerably cheaper than

---

[8] The market in any single security issued by a single large firm, for example, General Motors shares, is, of course, as close to perfect as any market could be: at any given hour of the day, and in every part of the country (or the world) prices will be close to identical.

"external finance." But internal finance is strictly limited by current "cash flow"—depreciation allowances and retained earnings.[9]

3. The extent to which most firms can borrow is closely related to the amount of their equity capital, provided through sales of stock and (usually in much larger amounts) by retention of earnings.

4. Lenders are almost always concerned with the balance sheets as well as the profit and loss statements of borrowers. Even among borrowers with the same rate of profit, they are less likely to lend, or will lend only at higher rates, to firms with large existing debt liabilities relative to their assets (that is, with low *equity* relative to assets). They tend, in particular, to shy away from firms with large *short-term* liabilities relative to their more liquid assets.

5. Many firms thus have, much of the time, a considerable backlog of planned, profitable investment projects simply waiting to be financed.

Financial Theories of Investment

The consequences of the nature of financial markets, itemized in the preceding list, have provided the basis for a number of primarily "financial" theories of investment, or, at least, of eclectic theories containing important financial elements. Among the economists stressing financial factors have been Meyer and Kuh, Duesenberry, W. Locke Anderson, and many others.[10] Most of these have supported their hypotheses with substantial empirical analyses that demonstrate significant correlations, either in the aggregate, or on cross section, or both, between fluctuations in, or differences in, investment and in various financial magnitudes.

These theories are of perhaps two main types:

1. Theories that make the current volume of internal cash flow (or some principal element thereof) a primary determinant of investment.

2. Theories that explain why periods of heavy investment tend to be self-limiting because of the impact they have on firms' balance sheets. As debts accumulate relative to equity, their ability to borrow decreases. Time is then required for the rebuilding of equity, mainly through use of retained earnings to reduce debts or accumulate relatively liquid financial assets. In particular, heavy

[9] Another source of internal finance is the sale of financial assets held as a reserve or purchased as a temporary use for retained earnings and depreciation. However, the fact that the return on these assets is typically less than on their productive assets limits the accumulation of such assets by most firms.

[10] J. Meyer and E. Kuh, *The Investment Decision* (Harvard University Press, 1957); J. S. Duesenberry, *Business Cycles and Economic Growth* (McGraw-Hill, 1958); W. H. L. Anderson, *Corporate Finance and Fixed Investment* (Graduate School of Business Administration, Harvard University, 1964).

short-term borrowing from banks after a time deters not only further extension of bank loans but other extensions of credit, until short-term debts can be consolidated into long-term issues.

In a more general sense, these theories stress that financial limitations curtail the extent of a firm's investment at any point in time; thus, they show that changes in factors that affect the size of the desired capital stock may have little, or only substantially lagged, effects on investment.

It is easy to criticize such theories. As we have previously noted, limitations on the size or growth rates of firms need not limit the size or growth rate of aggregate activity, since the number of firms is not fixed. If financial factors restrict the growth of some firms at particular times to less than the growth rate of the economy, other firms can grow more rapidly and new firms can enter. Can we not conceive of a smooth evolution in which the financial structures of firms remain, on the average, proportionately unchanged as they grow in size and/or as the number of firms grows, and this growth also in proportion to the growth of aggregate investment, income, and wealth?

Moreover, some have suggested, so long as people desire to save at a rate largely independent of the average rate of return on saving, why cannot the average return to savers adjust to whatever level is necessary to overcome other "financial" limits to investment? Do not these theories reason, illegitimately, from situations of firms or industries to the entire economy?

The cautions suggested in the previous paragraph are surely relevant. But they are not necessarily compelling arguments against the importance of financial limitations on investment, particularly if one conceives of the factors affecting K^* as mainly exogenous, with massive changes in these factors often occurring rather discontinuously. New firms, in particular, cannot rapidly take over from older ones as the latter approach temporarily binding financial limits because new firms have a built-in limit to their growth arising from lenders' lack of a knowledge that can come only through experience in lending to them. Thus, if numbers of important older firms simultaneously approach financial limits on the rates at which they can exploit new investment opportunities, this can limit the growth of aggregate investment and thus the growth of income which in turn is one of the most important determinants of K^*. Moreover, the argument about saving continuing as investment flags, thus depressing the rate of interest to offset higher costs to firms, is not persuasive: to whatever extent that investment is limited, so is aggregate income and aggregate saving.

The financial factors which we are discussing are obviously not primarily relevant to the size of K^*. Instead, they add a further limiting factor on the rate at which *investment* can—at any one time—occur, given K and K^*. Thus, not only because of limits on the production of capital goods, but also because of limits on available finance, there may at times exist considerable unexploited *backlogs* of investment opportunities—which can make the rate of investment substantially insensitive to changes in the factors traditionally assumed to influence investment, such as "the" (pure) rate of interest, or the level of or change in Y. At other times, and particularly when, after a long period of sustained high investment, the backlog of investment opportunities may have been worked off and no new ones have appeared, the legacy in firms' balance sheets of large debts relative to equity may further limit the effectiveness of expansionary monetary policy in reviving investment. On the other side of the coin, however, the imperfections and segmentation of capital markets may greatly enhance the effectiveness of restrictive monetary policy in curbing a boom.[11]

Financial theories, which explain investment in terms of financial variables, obviously require further theories that explain the determination of these financial variables. Some proponents of financial theories leave that to other economists to explain; but some also develop that explanation as well. One particularly notable effort is that of James Duesenberry, who stressed (although not exclusively) aggregate cash flow as a determinant of investment.[12] Since depreciation rates are ordinarily quite stable, as are rates of dividend payment, the main factors influencing the volume of aggregate cash flow are variations in corporate profits before tax and variations in taxation of corporate profits—commonly, variations either in provisions affecting allowable deductability of depreciation, "investment tax credits," or in the basic corporate income tax rate.[13]

In Chapter 8, in which we developed an elementary version of the cash flow theory of investment, we pointed out that corporate profits, and thus retained earnings, respond sensitively to fluctuations in Y and in its rate of growth. In his version of the cash flow theory, however, Duesenberry postulates that aggregate profits (Π) depend positively on national income (as above), but negatively on the stock of capital,[14] or, in a linear version:

$$\Pi = aY - bK$$

---

[11] Such segmentation may permit the virtual cutting off of one kind of lending (for example, for residential housing), without substantial "leakage" into this field from other parts of the capital market, or of leakage of funds from housing into the financing of other forms of investment, for example, inventories. Thus, a major cutback in one segment of investment can occur to an extent that—along with multiplier and accelerator effects—can cool or reverse a boom.

[12] J. S. Duesenberry, *op. cit.*

[13] As we have seen earlier, Jorgenson and others stress the importance of tax provisions as affecting the *cost* of funds to the firm—entering into the ratio P/C (price of output to cost of capital) which affects K^*. But cash flow theorists interpret the effects of these provisions as mainly *affecting the rate of investment given K^**.

[14] The larger the stock of capital the lower (given Y) must be rates of capital utilization and the greater the competition among sellers. The former raises unit costs, the latter holds down unit sales revenues.

Taking account of lags, this becomes:

$$\Pi_t = aY_{t-1} - bK_{t-1}$$

If dividends depend positively both on profits and previously retained earnings, then it can be seen that retained earnings (and thus investment) depend in a complicated way upon income (positively) and upon capital stock (negatively). Simplifying greatly the lag structure, Duesenberry arrived at the following basic investment equation:

(3) $$I_t = \alpha Y_{t-1} - \beta K_{t-1}$$

The preceding investment theory makes investment depend on purely financial considerations, that is, cash flow.[15] But it is instructive to recognize that such a theory is extremely similar in form, if not in derivation, to an investment theory that rests upon the fundamental idea of the acceleration principle, namely, an optimum relationship of capital to output, as can be seen by comparing equations (2) and (3).

Suppose we rewrite equation (3) as

(3a) $$I_t = \beta\left(\frac{\alpha}{\beta}Y_{t-1} - K_{t-1}\right)$$

Investment will then be zero when $(\alpha/\beta)Y_{t-1} = K_{t-1}$. We can identify $(\alpha/\beta)Y_{t-1}$ as last period's optimum capital stock, and α/β as the optimum capital-to-output ratio—which is also the acceleration coefficient. And that is the role of the β outside the parentheses? It indicates how rapidly any gap between the optimum stock, $(\alpha/\beta)Y_{t-1}$, and the actual stock, K_{t-1}, is exploited. If β has a value of 0.5, it means that investment is at a rate which would make up one half of any such gap within a single time period. If $\beta = 1$, we have the case of the strict acceleration principle (with a one-period lag): investment occurs in whatever amount is necessary to raise actual capital stock to its optimum level (of last period). Indeed, in the last section of this chapter we derived almost exactly the preceding formulation *directly from the acceleration principle.*

Thus, at least the cash-flow version of the financial theory and the acceleration theory are surely not as remote in ultimate derivation as they are usually made to appear. One can argue, in a most general way, that the technological considerations which basically underlie the accelerator model operate not so much as direct technological restraints or spurs to entrepreneurial behavior but rather, primarily, as determinants of profitable business operations. Although the simple acceleration principle makes no reference to the price and profit system, this is merely a short-cut. The technological relationships that underlie the accelerator actually guide behavior through their effect on prices, costs, volume, and ultimately

---

[15] Actually, Duesenberry does not see profits as affecting investment *only* through affecting financial flows, but others do.

profits. And profits affect firms' ability to finance investments both directly through cash flow and indirectly by improving the borrowing capacity of profitable firms. Expressed in this most general way, the gap between acceleration and "classical" approaches is also not as wide as it may sometimes have seemed.

Stock Prices and Investment

It will be recalled from Chapter 8 that J. M. Keynes attached substantial importance to the level of stock prices as a determinant of investment.[16] Keynes seemed to be arguing that stock prices affect investment because they at least pretend to offer a current market judgement about the expected yield on the real productive assets which firms now own—both about expected yields on business assets in general, and by reference to prices of particular types of stocks, about expected yields on assets of particular kinds. Many potential investors tend to accept such judgements, in the absence of anything more solid. Even if a potential investor in new assets doesn't accept the market's judgement, when stock prices are low he may nevertheless find it cheaper to acquire such assets by purchasing control of existing firms rather than by ordering new assets to be produced. On the other hand, if current stock prices are high, it may be cheaper to invest directly in the new assets. Thus, stock prices affect investment.

There are other ways of putting the same or related points. Existing earnings per share (on stocks in general or of particular firms) can be taken as indicating the future cost—in terms of a stream either of dividend payments and/or of capital gains to stockholders on earnings reinvested—that firms in general or particular firms must pay for funds obtained through stock issues. Expressed as a percentage of the current price of a share, this is the "interest cost" of equity funds, which may be compared to the marginal efficiency of investment, or entered as a component of C in Jorgenson's formula. When stock prices rise (fall), *ceteris paribus*, this represents a fall (rise) in the cost of equity finance; thus, booms and slumps in the stock market tend to create booms and slumps in real investment.

Of course, most investment is not financed by new stock issues, the amount of which is usually relatively trivial. But the financial theories of investment remind us of the crucial importance of the equity component for obtaining non-equity funds. To the extent that the current state of the stock market makes equity money easy and cheap, or difficult and expensive, it may have large effects on investment by freeing-up or restricting access—by firms with backlogs of profitable projects—both to equity and nonequity financing. High or low bond prices, of course, similarly indicate the cost of borrowed money.

---

[16] The reader who has not already read Chapter 12 of the *General Theory* may want to do so.

James Tobin has proposed a theory that makes the economy-wide rate of investment depend on the ratio of the aggregate market value of the outstanding stock of equities plus bonds to the aggregate stock of capital—the physical stock of plant and equipment valued at current costs of production or acquisition. Figure 2-1 in Chapter 2 showed the movement of this ratio over the years 1960–1976. The reader can easily establish that this ratio is at least roughly correlated with the ratio of real business investment to real GNP in those particular years.

Hyman Minsky picks up Keynes' ideas about the importance of stock prices for investment and about the precarious basis for the stock market's judgement of a future which is necessarily highly uncertain, and combines them with other elements of the previously explained "financial theories" of investment to produce his own unorthodox and somewhat apocalyptic theory of the inherent instability of the modern capitalistic economy. It is a view which he insists, with some reason, incorporates the essence of Keynes' own fundamental ideas.[17]

EMPIRICAL TESTS OF INVESTMENT THEORIES

As indicated earlier, a vast volume of empirical work has been devoted to the statistical testing of investment theories and, through this testing, developing alternative formulations that are more consistent with the data (sometimes at the expense of considerable departure from the initial formulation). Extremely complex statistical techniques have been used in this work, and several significant developments in econometrics have been byproducts of it. Yet, as indicated, the results remain rather unimpressive.

We shall here concentrate on a single study, one by Charles Bischoff.[18] His is one of relatively few studies that attempt to test several alternative theories against each other, using a single body of data and parallel simulation experiments. Bischoff actually uses five basic models; and he employs each one separately to "explain" (sometimes in variant formulations) business investment in equipment and in plant (construction). Here we confine attention to the four basic models to which we have devoted principal attention in this and the previous chapter: a "generalized accelerator model," a "cash-flow model," a version of the neoclassical theory *à la* Jorgenson (the "standard neoclassical model"), and the "securities value model," associated mainly with James Tobin. (The fifth is a

---

[17] For a brief and cogent statement, see his "The Financial Instability Hypothesis: An Interpretation of Keynes and an Alternative to the 'Standard' Theory," *Challenge*, 20 (March/April 1977), pp. 20–27.

[18] "Business Investment in the 1970s: A Comparison of Models," *Brookings Papers on Economic Activity*, 1:1971, pp. 13–58, with comments and discussion by B. Bosworth, R. Hall, and others, pp. 59–63.

version of the "Federal Reserve–MIT–Penn Model," which is an alternative neoclassical model developed by Modigliani and associates.)

The basic formulations used are

(1) Generalized accelerator: $I_t = b_0 + \sum\limits_{i=1}^{n} b_i Q_{t-i} + b_{n+1} K_{t-1} + u_t$

(2) Cash flow: $I_t = b_0 + \sum\limits_{i=1}^{n} b_i (F/q)_{t-i} + b_{n+1} K_{t+1} + u_t$

(3) Standard neoclassical: $I_t = b_0 + \sum\limits_{i=1}^{n} b_i (pQ/c)_{t-i} + b_{n+1} K_{t-1} + u_t$

(4) Securities value: $I_t = \left[b_0 + \sum\limits_{i=1}^{n} b_i (V/qK)_{t-1} \right] K_{t-1} + u_t$

where

b = all coefficients
c = rental price of capital, defined as $q(d + r)(1 - k - wz)/(1 - w)$
d = rate of physical depreciation of capital
F = sum of corporate profits after taxes plus corporate depreciation
I = expenditures for investment, in constant prices
i = subscript indicating time
K = net capital stock
k = effective rate of tax credit
n = number of periods (quarters)
p = output price deflator
Q = gross value added of the private business sector (essentially the GNP to which private investment is directed)
q = investment price deflator
r = rate of discount used to value return from future capital services
t = subscript indicating time
u = serially correlated disturbance, representing effect of other, omitted factors
V = market value of equities plus corporate bonds
w = corporate income tax rate
z = discounted value of allowable depreciation deductions on a dollar's worth of new investment.

In each case, the equation is fitted to data for the 64 quarters from 1953 through 1968. In each of the equations, n is determined by trial and error (what fits best) which turns out to be 23 quarters for the accelerator and cash flow models, for the standard neoclassical 13 quarters for equipment and 23 for construction, and for the securities value model 13 for both construction and equipment. The *shapes* of the distributed lags are also determined by the data, with no *a priori* restrictions (that is, the function used is not required to produce a zero value in period $t - n - 1$; and, in no case, is there a restriction on the sum of the coefficients).

We may briefly note a few particular aspects of the formulations used. That for the accelerator uses *levels* of Y instead of changes in Y. As shown earlier (footnote 4 in this chapter), this need not be a substantive change if the coefficients sum to zero; but here they are not required to and apparently do not. This "generalizes" the accelerator considerably beyond the usual meaning, to the extent that net investment is made to depend (in part) on the *level* of Y as well as its *change*. Also, the strict accelerator theory has no room for a constant term (b_0). The formulation of the cash-flow model deflates aggregate cash flow in terms of capital goods prices, which seems reasonable; but it defines cash flow *before* sub-traction of dividends, which is arguable. The standard neoclassical model follows Jorgenson's formulation closely (even to the use of the constant $r = 0.20$).

When these equations are fitted to United States quarterly data for the years 1953 though 1968, all equations are found to fit extremely well, with R^2s of 0.990, 0.992, 0.989, and 0.987, respectively, for the four equipment investment equations; and of 0.961, 0.966, 0.961, and 0.963, for the four construction equations. (R^2s are similarly high for the other equations and variants tested.)[19]

The statistically-fitted investment functions all imply very long lags in the full response of investment to a change in the principal determinants of investment. For example, given a once-and-for-all increase in aggregate output (Q in the equations), the maximum increment of investment in the generalized accelerator equations would come after a year and a half and would continue at nearly the same level for many quarters thereafter. The response of the standard neoclassical equations to the same increase has not yet reached its peak $2\frac{1}{2}$ years later. The response of the cash flow equation to a once-and-for-all increase in cash flow also continues slowly to build up over many quarters, as does the response of the securities value model to a once-and-for-all increase in market value. Similarly, the response in the neoclassical equation to a once-and-for-all change in the ratio p/c is also still building up after 10 quarters. Insofar as the accelerator is concerned, these results suggest that the extreme instability suggested by simple versions of that theory is not confirmed; interpreted in terms of Eisner's "permanent income" version of the accelerator, it suggests that "permanent income" is based on a moving average of actual output over a

---

[19] However, these high R^2s are apparently mainly the result of the use of the serially correlated error term u_t in each equation. The value of u_t is in each case estimated in accordance with the equation, $u_t = \rho u_{t-1} + e_t$, where e_t is assumed random and the coefficient ρ is estimated by techniques described in the footnote beginning on the bottom of p. 18 in Bischoff, *op. cit.* As Bischoff remarks, "the excellent fits have been achieved very largely by feeding the last period's error back into the equation."

considerable period of time. Insofar as neoclassical equations (in for-mulations other than Jorgenson's) are concerned, it suggests that monetary policy has very slow effects on investment—at least to the extent these operate through interest rates affecting investment.

In effect, Bischoff found that a number of different investment equa-tions—each representing a very different theory of investment—all proved to be (or could be made to be) highly consistent with data for a period covering several complete business cycles, including years of fairly severe recession as well as of boom.

But how well do the equations forecast? At the time of his study, Bischoff had data for 2 more years (1969 and 1970) after the end of the period to which the equations were fitted. Thus he could, for each equa-tion, calculate what investment it would forecast for these years, and compare this with the actual investment. These 2 years were not a period of dramatic fluctuation in investment, although a cyclical peak was reached, both in construction and equipment, followed by slow decline. Most of the equations predicted a peak and decline, though often the peak was not in the correct quarter. The "root-mean-square error"[20] of the forecasts made by the various equations, for the eight quarters, ranged from something over 2 percent of the actual average level of investment in the period to $11\frac{1}{2}$ percent. In almost every case, the errors tended to increase over the eight quarters. Generally, the accelerator equations did the best in fore-casting 1969 and 1970, the cash-flow and securities value equations the worst.

Bischoff's final exercise is a simulated forecast for the years 1971, 1972, and the first half of 1973, using each equation. To do this, he used *forecasts* for all of the relevant variables in each equation (other than for investment itself, and for the capital stock) which had been generated by a leading econometric model, given certain fiscal and monetary policy assumptions. After first adjusting the level of each equation so that it would have correctly forecast the last quarter of 1970, he fed in the forecasts of the other variables, and let each equation forecast the path of investment (and, through the accumulation of investment, the capital stock) for each of the following 10 quarters. The forecasts vary widely, and, in general, the range between the highest and lowest forecast increases steadily over the period of the forecast. By the first half of 1973, the highest construction equipment forecast is 26 percent above the lowest; the highest construction forecast 38 percent above the lowest. It would be meaningless to compare any of the investment forecasts with actual data, because the investment forecasts were based on values for other variables (forecast by a particular econometric model) that were not in fact realized. However, it is meaningful to recognize that, when required to generate their own past history of investment and capital (and without the benefit,

[20] The square root of the average of squared errors.

obviously, of the serially-correlated error terms), the various equations—all of which fit so beautifully during the sample period 1953–1968—produce widely varied forecasts for the $2\frac{1}{2}$ year projection.[21]

A BROADER VIEW OF INVESTMENT

This chapter and the previous one have provided a brief sampling and summary of a vast recent elaboration of theoretical and empirical work on investment. Despite the fact that many of the best and brightest minds in economics have been turned to this subject, economists still do not have any fully satisfactory or widely accepted theory of investment. What they have is a fairly long list of variables that are thought to have some effect on the volume of investment, and, in most cases, substantial agreement on the probable sign of the partial derivative of investment with respect to each (that is, whether an increase in each variable would, *ceteris paribus*, increase or reduce investment). But we are not sure *how important* any of the variables is. In many cases there is confusion about whether, at least at the aggregate level, it is possible for *ceteris* to be *paribus* with respect to that variable. Often there is disagreement about how the effects of a variable come about (for example, whether it influences K^*, or only I—given the existence of a gap between K^* and K). And, we have very little firm idea of the nature or length of the lags involved. As a consequence, empirical investment equations are all unreliable, and forecasts of investment are of little use either to makers of fiscal and monetary policy or to producers of capital goods. A good case could be made that the best theory of investment is still that it is "autonomous."

To be sure, looking backward, we often think that we can explain the actual evolution of investment in some country and period in terms of some one or a few of the entries in our list of relevant variables. We tell plausible stories about what happened and why. But different people can tell different plausible stories. And story telling is not science; only consistently successful prediction merits that label. As these lines were being written (late fall 1976), the writer had not seen even any fully plausible *story* about why there had been almost no revival of real business fixed investment in the United States during the business recovery that began almost two years earlier, although rising investment had been confidently predicted by many of the best forecasters. He seemed even to have stopped hearing further confident predictions of when the revival would come, or confident advice as to what measures or events might bring it about.

---

[21] This could, of course, in part reflect the fact that the forecasts for *other* variables, though designed to be consistent one with each other, were not in fact fully consistent; for example, that the cash flow forecast was not consistent with the output forecast.

Possible Reasons for the Failure of Investment Theory

One possible reason why investment is so difficult to explain and predict is essentially the reason that Keynes gave a generation ago. Investment decisions depend of judgements about the future, and the rather distant future at that. And the future is unknown and unknowable—at least with any confidence. Even if the future is somewhat knowable in its broad dimensions, investment decisions are not made in the aggregate but one at a time and independently, about thousands of little pieces of the aggregate; and the success or failure of each such decision depends not only on what happens to the aggregate economy but as much on what happens to particular firms and industries. Given this uncertainty to the investor, the future is the domain not of science but of "fears and hopes," and these are heavily influenced by "states of mind," which are aspects more of social than of individual behavior. "Only a little more than an expedition to the South Pole" is the investment decision "based on an exact calculation of benefits to come."

And if, or when, social psychologists do begin better to understand the origins and generation of states of mind, and as economists begin more successfully to pierce the veil over the future, that very success will be self-destructive. Once people begin to act with any confidence in knowledge of the future provided by scientific investigation, they act differently, and the knowledge evanesces. It is quite possible that this has already happened with respect to investment.

Perhaps it is not only the inherent difficulty of the enterprise but also the mistaken research strategy of economics that accounts for economists' failures better to understand investment. It would be this writer's tentative and modest judgement that economists' concern with equilibrium has handicapped them in dealing with what is probably the principal disturber of aggregate economic equilibrium: net investment. Their desire to understand the relationships that characterize the "steady state" of a constant capital stock, or even of a constant rate of growth of the capital stock (that is, constant net investment), have stood in the way of their understanding the reality of investment, which *means* disequilibrium on both the firm and aggregate level.

This unkind judgement applies both to classical and to acceleration theorists: too much attention has been paid to K^* and the factors that determine it and not enough to what happens when $K \neq K^*$. And even when this adjustment process is studied, it is ordinarily studied as a process leading to K^*. The writer's hunch is that the adjustment process is slow enough, and affected by so many variables, and the changes in K^* large and irregular enough, that some other framework for looking at the problem of investment may prove more productive.

In the long run, the factors affecting K^* are clearly of dominant importance in understanding the average level and trend of investment.

But K^* is a nonobservable variable, and we cannot assume (as we often do for other variables) that the actual history of K provides a rough, correct-on-the-average measurement of K^*. The problem of approaching investment theory through K^* is further complicated by the unsolved (and perhaps insoluble) problems of measuring K—both data problems and conceptual problems—at least in measuring it in ways that correspond to the ways in which individuals or firms measure their own little pieces of K, either in its aspect as consumer wealth or as productive capacity.

Perhaps the biggest difficulty of all—and it is closely related to each of the previous ones—stems from the intimate interrelationships between capital, investment, and *technological change*. As previously noted, investment is the process by which most technological change gets incorporated into production.[22] Technological change destroys old equilibria even before they are established. It creates impossible problems of measurement of capital, which confuse the businessman and saver as well as the statistician. Although the broad lines of future technological change can increasingly be foreseen, its detailed structure, its timing, and, most of all, its widespread and often remote ramifications cannot be foreseen. Thus, investment theorists find that there is little that they can say about technological change. So they have tended to ignore it.

Technology and Investment

In most of our previous discussion we have abstracted from technological change, reflecting a long tradition in economics of abstracting from "changes in the arts." Yet one may well argue that to discuss either investment or economic growth on such assumptions is to miss the essence of the matter. Some aspects of technological change have, in the last two or three decades, begun to receive the serious attention of economists, belatedly following up leads provided by Schumpeter[23] and a few other pioneers.

Schumpeter's pre-Keynesian concepts and assumptions (e.g., of constant full employment) are difficult for the modern reader. But one who will struggle to translate his fundamental ideas into modern concepts will be substantially rewarded. His principal thesis found the mainspring of economic growth in the activities of entrepreneurs or innovators. These agents of change were not inventors but businessmen possessing the peculiar and scarce talent of seeing the possibilities of profit inherent in new methods, new products, new types of organization. Schumpeter also argued that business cycles were a necessary consequence of the process of innovation: that an inherent mechanism required that innovation produce

---

[22] This is not to suggest that all investment stems from or incorporates changed technology. The widening investment that equips additional workers with familiar tools is a large part of it. But the two kinds go together.

[23] Joseph A. Schumpeter, *The Theory of Economic Development* (Harvard University Press, 1939), first published, in German, in 1912.

waves, rather than steady streams, of investment. One can reject his specific theory of business cycles, yet still believe that Schumpeter correctly put his finger on the principal phenomenon associated both with economic growth and development and with the inevitable instability of a growing economy.

A modern macroeconomist would say that technological change affects both the supply and the demand sides of the macroeconomy. Looking first at the supply side, technological change that has lasting economic significance necessarily raises the total productivity of economic resources. An innovation that is meaningful raises output values associated with any given value of inputs, or lowers inputs for any given output. An innovation may reduce input per unit of output of both labor and capital, though not necessarily in equal proportions. Or it may, of course, lower the required input per unit of output for one factor, for example, labor, and raise the required input of another, for example, capital. But the innovation will not have been made unless the reduction of labor input is (or was expected to be) greater in value than the increase in capital input (or *vice versa*). Thus innovations may be, in an absolute sense, capital-saving but labor-using, labor-saving but capital-using, or both labor-saving and capital-saving (but not both labor-using and capital-using). Even innovations that are *absolutely* capital-saving *and* labor-saving may be *relatively* capital-using (or labor-using or neutral); whereas innovations that are absolutely capital-using but labor-saving are, *a fortiori*, capital-using in the relative sense.

Actually, a great fraction of innovations involves not new methods for producing old products but new or altered goods and services. If these yield a higher sales return per dollar of combined expenditure on factors of production than other goods, they, too, can be said to raise output relative to input. And if their production is more or less labor-intensive or capital-intensive than that of the goods they displace, we can also classify such innovations as relatively labor-saving, relatively capital-saving, or neutral. Innovations that alter products create even greater difficulties of measurement—of capital, net investment, and price level and output—than do innovations that merely reduce cost.

Economists have barely begun to attempt to understand the process of technological change itself. Although we customarily treat such change as purely autonomous, actually such change is itself endogenous. The growth of technology is tied up, both as cause and effect, with the whole process of scientific, economic, social, and cultural evolution. Some economists have proposed the concept of "induced" technological change, suggesting that its relatively capital-saving or labor-saving character may in part derive from changes in relative factor prices. Although an interesting hypothesis, it seems unlikely that we shall be able to find any stable empirical parameters for such a relationship.

In the present state of our knowledge, the best representation of technological change that economists have found as it relates to the "supply side" of the macroeconomy, is as a steady autonomous "trend factor," affecting both capital and labor requirements per unit of output (although not necessarily in equal proportion). This is the usual treatment in macroeconomic analysis, and is the one summarized in Chapter 3.[24] However, there is clearly no reason why the trend must be constant.

The effect of technological change on the "demand side" of the economy is, however, our major concern here. It seems obvious that major waves of investment demand often have had their origin in revolutionary changes in technology. The railroad, electricity, the automobile, and computers and automation, for example, have each been responsible for a great burst of investment, both in the industries directly involved and in subsidiary industries. In part, these waves of investment, often extending over several decades, have created boom conditions because they have inserted new forms of production which are far more *capital-intensive* than those they have displaced, and thus have required massive net investment. But, even if an innovation is not capital-using, its rapid introduction is almost sure to stimulate investment, because the alternative forms of production that are displaced are not given time to withdraw their capital by the failure to replace it as it wears out. Rather, much existing capital is quickly made obsolete, and the investment of the new industry far exceeds disinvestment in the old. Thus, we can be quite sure that a technically progressive economy, and one that continually creates new products, will have a higher level of net investment than an economy in which the pace of innovation is more leisurely. The only offset to this is that, in the technically progressive economy, entrepreneurs will learn to expect early obsolescence, and thus will provide depreciation allowances high enough to "write off" their investments in a shorter time than purely physical depreciation rates would suggest. In addition to reducing net investment, this, of course, also reduces reported profits and thus may tend to depress consumption. It seems doubtful, however, that such provision for earlier obsolesence is a complete offset to the stimulative impact of technical progress on investment and aggregate demand.

Technological innovation would, of course, mainly create idle resources if real aggregate demand were unchanged. Schumpeter, however, explained in detail how and why any innovation creates an enlargement of total demand—surely in the short and medium run, if not in the longer run. Assume, with Schumpeter, an economy in initial full equilibrium, with zero net investment—what Schumpeter called a **circular-flow economy**. Consider, then, the simplest case, of a single innovation that merely creates a new product that displaces in consumer favor others produced with identical capital and labor intensity. At least at first, when

---

[24] One reason why technological improvement appears as a fairly steady trend, even though innovation itself may be irregular and lumpy, is that technological change affects K^*, but K adjusts only slowly (through I) to changes in K^*.

the supply of the new product is still small relative to the demand, it sells at a higher price relative to cost than do the older products. This profit, available to the innovator and to his imitators, induces at least a temporary period of aggregate net investment, as gross investment expands for production of the new product, whereas gross investment can fall only to zero in production of the products displaced. To be sure, as production of the new product expands to meet the demand and its price and profit decline, net investment for the new product must fall eventually to zero, while there is still net disinvestment in the old, producing negative aggregate net investment. Eventually, when full "circular-flow" equilibrium is restored, aggregate net investment will have returned to zero, and the aggregate capital stock and level of income will be no larger than before.

Even this trivial case illustrates the nature of the stimulus that innovation gives to investment and thus to aggregate demand. In the really significant cases, of innovations that produce new goods with greater permanent value to consumers, or reduce costs in the production of existing products, innovation also provides possible new profits to the innovator—which attract his investment. (In these cases, however, there are clearly permanent effects on K and Y.) To Schumpeter, innovation was the only source of pure profit in a competitive economy, and repeated innovation the only source of a profit share in the national income. And the attraction of this profit, although continually eroded by the competition of imitators, provided the stimulus to net investment.

When innovation is prevailingly labor-saving and capital-using, it has the double aspect of providing attractive opportunities both for deepening investment, and, by releasing labor, providing room for widening investment ("accelerator effects") as well. Thus, an investment boom based on innovation can be enlarged and prolonged.

Given the absence of any downward trend in interest rates in the advanced countries over the past century, it would seem clear that technological change, leading to capital deepening and the enlargement of *per capita* real income, has been one of the two major contributors to net investment in the modern world. The other, clearly, has been the growth of populations and the need to equip the larger work force with additional tools (as well as houses and social capital of all kinds.)[25]

---

[25] In the late 1930s, American economist Alvin Hansen picked up and popularized some of the "stagnationist" elements in Keynes' *General Theory* (an increasing APS as income grew, the inelasticity of K^* to i, and the limits on the reduction of i), and added his own stress on the importance of population increase and territorial expansion as important investment outlets, but which were about exhausted. Of course, the subsequent population explosion after World War II at least postponed the relevance of Hansen's population argument until after the population explosion subsided—as it now has. Hansen's Presidential Address to the American Economic Association, in December 1938, "Economic Progress and Declining Population Growth," *American Economic Review*, 29 (March 1939), reprinted in *Readings in Business Cycle Theory* (Blakiston, 1944), pp. 366–384, is the best short statement of his position.

For those of the advanced economies which were and remained at or close to the "frontier" of technology, positive net investment has depended on continual progress in basic science, from which innovators continuously have derived applications to production. But for those economies that, for some reason, have been far from the technological frontier, the opportunity to move up to that frontier can generate extremely large, almost unlimited, investment opportunities during the period in which the frontier is approached. This seems to have been the experience of several countries in the post-World-War II era; most dramatically of all in the case of Japan. Although the gradual adoption of Western technology has given Japan substantial investment opportunities and faster than average economic growth ever since the Meiji Restoration of 1868, the accelerated adoption of Western technology which began after World War II provided the basis for an investment share of GNP that often reached 30 percent or more and accomplished perhaps the fastest sustained growth of *per capita* income in the history of the world.[26]

To this writer, any adequate understanding of investment requires recognition of the key role of technological change. To be sure, economists can, so far, find little to say about technical change other than that it occurs and that it is a source of continuing investment. But the fact that they cannot say much about it provides no excuse for their virtually ignoring it. This writer's conviction is that technological change is and will remain the primary source of investment opportunities.

Any backlog of investment opportunities created by technological change can only be worked off over a period of time because there are limits to the production capacity of a capital goods industry whose own capital stock must be geared to some expectation about an average level and trend of total investment; because of the long lags involved in the design, construction, delivery, and installation of capital goods; because there are limits to the financial capacities of firms; and, perhaps, because interest rates can be pushed up to levels that are considered to exceed what they will be later. Thus, there is almost always some earlier technological change that remains incompletely digested, and net investment rarely falls to zero. However, these limits to investment alone cannot explain waves in investment, which often builds up to booms and sometimes end in severe recession or depression.

Many major investment booms have been associated with specific major innovations, as Schumpeter recounted in detail in his massive *Business Cycles*.[27] Yet Schumpeter did not explain investment cycles by irre-

---

[26] For an admittedly "story telling" account of this episode (and of the role of macroeconomic policies in stimulating and guiding it), see the author's chapter (with the collaboration of H. Ishi), "Fiscal, Monetary, and Related Policies," in H. Patrick and H. Rosovsky, eds., *Asia's New Giant: How the Japanese Economy Works* (The Brookings Institution, 1976), pp. 153–247; see also the chapters by E. S. Denison and W. K. Chung, and by J. Peck.

[27] *Business Cycles: A Theoretical, Historical, and Statistical Analysis of the Capitalist Process*, 2 vols. (McGraw-Hill, 1939); abridged edition published in 1964.

gularities in the occurrence of scientific discovery but only in its utilization by entrepreneurs to produce technological change. His own explanation of the inevitability of cycles in innovation—that the response to innovation creates increasing "noise" which interferes with the information necessary for entrepreneurial decisions and must eventually bring any sustained wave of investment to a halt—has always seemed questionable. (And his view that this same mechanism inevitably produced three tiers of cycles within cycles—short inventory "Kitchin" cycles, superimposed regularly on longer "Juglar" fixed-investment cycles, superimposed regularly on "Kondratriff" long waves—seems far-fetched.)

Yet there may be some cycle-generating mechanism, that responds to random irregularities in the pace of technological change, as well as to other disturbances such as wars, political changes, mistakes of monetary policy, major crop failures, and so on, thus producting waves in the rate of utilization of new technology. Or it may be primarily widening investment that exaggerates modest initial fluctuations in aggregate demand and provides the principal cyclical element in investment and income.

The possibilities are so numerous and the complexities so great that it seems small wonder that macroeconomics, which still lacks an accepted theory of investment, also lacks an acceptable theory of investment cycles. But that is poor excuse for economists' accepting, even less for promoting, investment theories as incomplete and inadequate as the ones that still appear in macroeconomics textbooks, this one included.

REVIEW QUESTIONS

1. "Acceleration theories argue that the optimum stock of capital depends only on the rate of output." What further (behavioral) assumptions convert this principle into a theory of investment—both in its simple, rigid form, and in more realistic but looser formulations?

2. "Whatever the *inducement* to invest—increase in the demand for output, reduction of interest rate, technological change, or other—the rate of investment may be limited (and thus determined at least in part) by *financial* considerations." Explain and illustrate.

3. What is the "cash flow" theory of investment?

4. Several alternative theories of investment might produce the same investment function, such as

$$I_t = \beta(\alpha Y_t - K_{t-1})$$

(a) Present and fully explain these theories of investment.

(b) Interpret the meaning of α and β according to each of these theories.

5. "It is not surprising that the study of investment has engaged some of the brightest minds in economics, with hard work leading to ingenious, but contradictory, theoretical models and indifferent empirical results." Why is it not surprising?

6. "Technological change may also play an important role in investment theory." How, and with what consequences?

7. "The acceleration theory (investment depends on the *change* of output) is to be carefully distinguished from the theory that investment depends on the *level* of output. Yet distributed lag forms of the acceleration principle sometimes use current and past *levels* of output." Explain how this is possible, and what restrictions must be placed on the distributed lag coefficients.

SELECTED REFERENCES

R. Eisner, "Investment: Fact and Fancy," *American Economic Review*, 53 (May 1963), 237–246.

R. Eisner and R. H. Strotz, "Determinants of Business Investment," in Commission on Money and Credit, *Impacts of Monetary Policy* (a series of research studies prepared for the Commission) (Prentice-Hall, 1964), pp. 59–223; key portions reprinted in N. F. Keiser (ed.), *Reading in Macroeconomics* (Prentice-Hall, 1970), pp. 133–140.

(Two important statements of the accelerationist position.)

W. H. L. Anderson, "Business Fixed Investment: A Marriage of Fact and Fancy," in R. Ferber (ed.), *The Determinants of Investment Behavior* (Columbia University Press, 1967), pp. 413–425, reprinted in E. Shapiro (ed.), *Macroeconomics: Selected Readings* (Harcourt, Brace, Jovanovich, 1970), pp. 89–93.

(A response to the first reference above, by a financial theorist of investment.)

J. R. Meyer and R. R. Glauber, *Investment Decisions, Economic Forecasting, and Public Policy* (Harvard Business School, 1964). Two key sections reprinted in N. F. Keiser (ed.), *op. cit.*, pp. 110–132.

(An example of a combination of accelerator and financial theories of investment.)

T. Wilson and P. W. S. Andrews (eds.), *Oxford Studies in the Price Mechanism* (Oxford University Press, 1951).

(A series of studies reporting on surveys of English businessmen which showed that the cost of capital had little relevance to actual investment decisions.)

W. H. White, "Interest Elasticity of Investment Demand—The Case from Business Attitude Surveys Reexamined," *American Economic Review*, 46 (September 1956), 565–587; reprinted in revised form in M. G. Mueller, *Readings in Macroeconomics* (Holt, Rinehart, and Winston, 2nd ed., 1971), pp. 95–113.

(An attack on the findings of the Oxford and other surveys which purport to show that the interest rate is ignored in actual investment decisions.)

PART VIII

FINANCIAL ASSETS, INTEREST RATES, AND MONETARY POLICY

Chapter 20

**Financial Assets
and
Intermediaries**

The Supplies and Demands for Financial Assets
Demands for financial assets
Supplies of financial assets
Some financial aspects of economic growth

The Role of Financial Intermediaries
The creation of new assets and liabilities
The commercial bank as financial intermediary
Competition and the regulation of intermediaries
Economic effects of intermediation

In Chapter 19, we considered briefly the implications for the *theory of investment* of the existence of (a) a wide variety of financial assets and liabilities, and (b) financial intermediaries, as these affected the borrowing ability of firms. In this chapter and the next, we reconsider and elaborate somewhat the *theory of interest and money*, in the light of the same factors. We then consider somewhat more fully certain aspects of monetary policy. We thus continue the gradual process of elaboration of the theory of saving, investment, and the interest rate that began in Chapter 5 and continued in Chapter 9. The reader may wish to review portions of those chapters as he considers the further ideas presented here. (He may also need to review the section of Chapter 2 dealing with wealth accounting.)

Chapter 5 explained the classical theory of how the interest rate was determined by saving and investment schedules, on the assumption that all borrowing and lending were accomplished through the sale and puchase of a standard perpetual bond. There were no equities and no financial inter- mediaries. The market prices of these perpetual bonds at any given time— varying with their coupon rates—all reflected a single uniform yield: **the market rate of interest**.[1] We did include, however, a resale market for bonds, and recognized that the bulk of all transactions in the bond market were in previously issued securities. But we saw that the amount of such second-hand transactions could not affect the current interest rate— determined by the current schedules of saving and investment as functions of the interest rate (Y being implicitly taken as fixed)—so long as no one, saver or borrower, ever preferred barren money (in excess of transaction needs) to an interest-yielding bond.

Then, in Chapter 9, this last proviso was removed. We saw that Keynes' theory of liquidity preference demonstrated that there were cir- cumstances in which rational wealthholders might vary their demand for money balances as a function of the interest rate. Reformulating the theory of the interest rate into *stock* terms, this made the rate appear to be

---

[1] However, we did note that there might be interest-rate differentials reflecting judgements of the differing risks of default on interest payments by various issuers of bonds.

determined by the exogenous supply of money, and the demand for money function. However, when we insert this theory into a macroeconomic model in which income can vary to reflect shifts in saving (that is, consumption) and investment schedules—or in fiscal policy—it becomes clear that the interest rate depends on *all* of the variables of that larger model, each operating through its effect on the demand for money. In this way the Keynesian theory married the essence of the classical doctrines about saving and investment with Keynes' consumption function and with his original insights about the interest-elasticity of the demand for money.

The final modification that we made (in the last major section of Chapter 9) was to suggest that the demands for bonds and for money could also depend on the value of the total stock of wealth—which, in turn, partly reflected the interest rate. And we used this insight to help elucidate the differential effects of monetary and fiscal policies, a subject to which we shall return in Chapter 21.

Still, in all of the discussion up to this point, we have continued to assume only one kind of security: a perpetual bond. Thus, there were only two financial assets: bonds and money. And there was only one interest rate, *the* rate, which reflected the market price of bonds in terms of money. Also, there were no financial intermediaries. To be sure, we included demand deposits in money, but the stock of money (currency plus deposits) was determined solely by the Central Bank.[2]

Then, in Chapter 19, we finally replaced the single homogeneous bond market with a highly segmented series of capital markets, in which lenders and borrowers, including financial intermediaries of all kinds—dealt in a wide variety of debts and equities, issued by firms that were far from homogeneous, and where even the interest cost to a single borrowing firm might depend on how much it had already borrowed and in what form.

What does all this do to the earlier theory of the interest rate that entered into the various Keynesian, classical, and synthesis models? And what implications does it have for monetary policy?

THE SUPPLIES AND DEMANDS FOR FINANCIAL ASSETS

Introducing the bewildering complexities of "finance" all at once is too confusing. Indeed, we never will introduce more than a few of them, but we can go well beyond the simple world of two financial assets—money and a standard (perpetual) bond—which we have assumed until now. And we shall see that to do so makes some difference. However, we shall proceed by steps. For the present, we still assume no financial intermediaries. We

---

[2] Early on, when discussing Wicksell's ideas, we referred briefly to some shadowy entities, commercial banks, which could issue new money *to finance investment* and destroy it when they contracted their lending. We then quickly forgot about them.

also ignore debts of households and the fact that households wish to and do hold some of their wealth in real goods (especially houses). We further assume that businesses hold none of each others' or governments' securities and that they operate without cash balances (a particularly egregious oversimplification since businesses in fact hold the larger part of all demand deposits).

We do wish, however, to recognize the existence of a variety of nonmonetary financial assets: corporate stocks, equities in unincorporated businesses (not, properly speaking, "financial" assets, because they are not represented by a security), long-term and intermediate-term private bonds, marketable short-term business debts (for example, commercial paper), long-term and intermediate-term government bonds and notes, and short-term government debt (Treasury bills). The private securities are issued by nonhomogeneous firms: some by old, well-established, well-known firms, some in strong financial position, others less so; others by less well-known, less successful, or new companies which have no performance record, or only a poor one.

Since we assume that households hold only financial assets (including money) and businesses no financial assets, households hold all of the outstanding financial assets, and it constitutes their total wealth (as well as the national wealth—equal to the total value of all private physical assets plus government money and government debt).

If current saving were zero, then the total of this personal (and national) wealth would not change systematically over time. However, for any wealth to exist, saving must have been positive in the past. Of course, it is normally positive in the present, as well; national and household wealth usually grow over time.

Positive saving initially accrues in money form—as an excess of money disposable income over consumption. Nevertheless, savers are unlikely to wish to hold all or very much of their additions to wealth in money form; indeed, unless the government or central bank increases the money supply, they can hold none of the additions that way (although they may try). Rather, most or all of their new saving (now, as in the past) constitutes a net addition to their demand for nonmonetary financial assets.

The Demands for Financial Assets

Which financial assets will households demand? And how is this determined? Instead of a simple demand-for-bonds schedule (of the kind used in the last part of Chapter 9), equal to the value of total wealth less the demand for money, we can now think of separate demands for each one of the vast variety of nonmonetary financial assets, together with a demand for money.

Each type of asset has certain peculiar inherent advantages and disadvantages—apart from its price or yield—that influence the demand for it.

Some of the principal respects in which these assets differ in their attractiveness to particular savers are the following:

1. Some assets entitle their holder to a fixed and known periodic payment (zero for money and positive for all debts), whereas others (stocks and noncorporate equities) provide unknown, but perhaps estimatible, yields in the form of dividends and capital gains from reinvested earnings.

2. Only one asset (money) can be used as a means of payment, whereas the others must first be sold before being converted into another asset or spent.[3]

3. Some assets (for example, government securities, bonds and stocks of well-known companies) have a ready market and can be sold at the best available price in a matter of hours, whereas others (securities of less-well-known companies and noncorporate equities) have less perfect markets and may even require considerable negotiation to dispose of.

4. Some have little or no risk surrounding the receipt of yield and recovery of principal, others considerably more risk.

5. Some (of the assets considered so far, only money) have a price that is fixed, whereas prices of others (Treasury Bills, commercial paper, longer-term bonds nearing maturity), whose repayment of principal is near at hand, cannot move far above or below par values (unless default is expected). Still others (long-term bonds) mature far in the future so that their market prices can vary widely (even without any default or threat thereof). And some (stocks, noncorporate equities, perpetual bonds) have no maturity and their prices can move indefinitely in either direction.

6. Some assets (for example, stocks, noncorporate equities) confer an element of control and thus require the owner's attention (which to some owners is an advantage, to others a disadvantage), whereas most others do not.

7. The income of some is tax-free (in the United States, interest on state and local government bonds is exempt from federal income tax), that of others is fully taxable, and that of still others may in part be taxable at lower, capital-gains rates (for example, corporate retained earnings that are reflected in stock prices).

8. Finally, when we get down to securities issued by particular firms, we find that some are issued by companies that have low ratios of debt to equity, others with intermediate ratios, still others with very high ratios. (This was a factor particularly stressed in Chapter 18 in the discussion of financial limits to investment.)

---

[3] We will later qualify this statement.

Some wealthholders may have an absolute preference (or repugnance) for one or another of these features so strong that they will hold only (or will never hold) assets that have these features, regardless of yield. Others may insist, regardless of yield, on a portfolio that combines, *in fixed proportions*, assets having certain attributes. Most wealthholders, however, although they have likes and dislikes, will nevertheless look also at *relative yields* and may vary the composition of their portfolios as relative yields change. Almost no wealthholder, however, would consider yield alone, and prefer a single-asset portfolio consisting of whichever asset had the highest current yield (however that might be measured).

Thus, as relative yields change, the demands for assets will shift in the direction of those whose yields increase and away from those whose relative yields decline (whatever may happen to the absolute levels of yields).

There is, of course, one asset, money, whose absolute yield is usually (although not inevitably) fixed at zero; its relative yield thus changes only with alterations in the absolute yields of other assets.[4] Money has the additional characteristic, shared by none of the others, that a certain amount of it is required by everyone. This amount depends, in part, on the volume of its owners' total transactions, both in goods and services and in assets. This was the characteristic stressed in classical (and monetarist) monetary theory. As Baumol and Tobin demonstrated, however, this need is not absolute. It, too, is affected by the yields on alternative assets.

Based on the characteristics of each of the various types of financial assets, we can thus describe each wealthholder as having a demand schedule for each possible asset. To be sure, for some individuals and some assets, the amounts demanded may be zero at some or all prices (yields). But generally, the number of units demanded of each *nonmonetary asset* by each wealthholder will depend directly on its own yield, inversely on the yield of each other asset, and directly on the value of his total wealth. (The reasons for the dependence on wealth are given in Chapter 9.) Moreover, since absolute prices of most of these assets can change, the demand for each is also a direct function of its *expected* price. In addition, each wealthholder has a *demand-for-money* schedule, which depends directly on the value of his money transactions (crudely represented by money income), and (like all assets) inversely on the yield of each other asset and directly on the value of his wealth. The collection of demand schedules for all financial assets for each wealthholder is subject to the constraint that the number of units demanded of each, times its price, equals the owner's total wealth.

---

[4] At least, its absolute yield is zero if the price level is stable. Introducing inflation (deflation) produces a negative (positive) absolute yield on money. It affects other assets' yields in different ways. For simplicity in this treatment, we ignore price level changes.

We can now also think of an *aggregate demand schedule* for each asset by all wealthholders together, which depends on the same factors and is subject to a parallel constraint on the aggregates: the sum of quantities times prices equals total wealth. These are demand schedules, of course, for *stocks* of assets, for types and amounts of assets *to hold*; they are not demands expressed in terms of a flow of purchases to be made. Given the supply (stock) of each asset, its price and its absolute and relative yield depend on the demand (schedule) for it. For money, whose absolute price is fixed and whose absolute yield is zero, only the relative yield can change—through changes in the prices and yields of other assets.

Often, perhaps ordinarily, a reduced demand (schedule) for one particular nonmonetary financial asset, and thus a lower price and higher yield for it, merely reflects a higher demand (schedule) and thus a higher price and lower yield for another asset. However, particularly if there is a shift of demand as between money and nonmonetary financial assets generally, the *value* of *total* wealth can vary with no change in the supply of any part of it. A change in the expected future price for a nonmonetary asset can of course immediately affect the current price of and thus value of the stock of that asset; and a change in expected future prices of nonmonetary assets generally can change the value of total wealth.

An increase in uncertainty or fear about future profits and dividends of a firm will decrease the price of and thus the value of its shares outstanding; a general increase in uncertainty about future profits in the economy generally will reduce the total value of outstanding equities. To be sure, the demand might merely be transferred from stocks to bonds, raising bond prices; but this is unlikely to be a total offset. Thus, there is likely to be a drop in the value of total wealth. If the increased uncertainty or fear should extend as well to the contemplation of possible defaults on interest or principal repayments on private (or local government) debts, it will surely reduce the value of almost all nonmonetary assets, and thus the value of total wealth. Such a decline in wealth can importantly affect the demand for real assets: business capital goods, houses, and consumer durables, and even the demand for consumer nondurables and services.

Such movements in individual asset prices, and even in the total value of wealth, can of course occur whether total current saving is zero, negative, or positive; and they can easily swamp any effects from nonzero saving on the demand for assets. However, before we can really consider the effects of nonzero saving, we first must consider the *supply schedules* of financial assets.

Supplies of Financial Assets

Financial assets, other than money, are issued by firms to finance investment in plant, equipment, and inventories, or by governments to finance deficits. Money is sometimes issued by government to finance deficits, by the central bank in open market purchases, and by banks in a manner we shall explain in Chapter 21.

At any given time, the outstanding stock of each financial asset is of course fixed. Just as the sum of prices times quantities for all such assets equals the total value of private wealth, so should it, *in principle*, equal the total value of all of the real assets owned by businesses (we assumed no ownership by households), plus the value of the national debt, plus the stock of government money. (See Chapter 2.) However, the total value of the stock of private nonmonetary assets is obviously not necessarily equal to the aggregate value of physical assets as recorded in the accounts of firms, nor even of their replacement cost. And the value of the public debt obtained by summing current market values is not necessarily equal to the official government account of its debt. Only the nominal value of the total money stock is the same to its holders as to its issuers.

The fact that at every moment of time the stock of each asset is indeed fixed, does not mean that this stock is fixed for all time—*even if net investment and government deficit each remain at zero.* After all, debts mature; moreover, governments and businesses can repurchase their own securities in the market. Government can repay or repurchase with the proceeds of the sale of new and entirely different securities, or it can repay or repurchase by issuing new money. Businesses can repay maturing issues or repurchase others with the proceeds of new issues of a quite different kind. Of course, the composition (as well as the amount) of the outstanding stock of financial assets will also change over time through nonzero net investment, or nonzero government deficits, or both. But this also necessarily implies nonzero private saving, and we will need to consider the effects on the supply of assets along with the related effects on the demand, which we still postpone.

We can thus consider those changes in the composition of the stock of assets that might come about through debts maturing or through repurchase of securities by their issuers and through the issuance of other securities to replace them. Why might government or businesses wish to change the character of their liabilities? What determined the character and mixture of their presently outstanding liabilities?

Obviously, the past pattern of investment and government deficits is reflected in the pattern of currently outstanding financial assets: for example, only governments issue government money and government bonds; only private businesses issue private securities, and the types that firms issue depend to some extent on the nature of their businesses and of their capital assets.

Just as savers find that different financial assets possess certain inherent advantages and disadvantages and offer different yields, so do businesses find that different forms of financial liability possess inherent advantages/disadvantages for various purposes and, as well, involve different costs. Among a few of the obvious inherent advantages/disadvantages of various types of financial liabilities are these:

1. Equities need never be repaid; they provide permanent capital to the firm. Moreover, equities require no fixed current payment. To be sure, skipping or reducing dividends can have severe consequences for future financing through sale of stock. Moreover, when profits increase, there are stockholder pressures to raise dividends that cannot always be resisted. Still, the requirements for current payment are considerably more flexible than for debts. As noted several times previously, the amount of equity also affects the availability and cost of debt finance.[5]

2. Short-term debts have the disadvantage that they must soon be repaid, and may have then to be replaced with a new issue at a time when market conditions may be quite unfavorable to the borrower. On the other hand, if market conditions are expected to improve (for issuers), short-term borrowing may be desirable. Moreover, short-term debts have the advantage that they may be scheduled to meet temporary peaks in a firm's capital needs, for example, to cover expected bulges in inventories. Indeed, to some extent, the use of short-term debt is tied to the financing of inventories, just as long-term debt is often tied to the financing of plant and equipment. Short-term debts not in excess of inventories are thought by lenders to be relative "secure," in that they can, if necessary, be repaid through drawing down of inventories.

3. Long-term debt provides assurance to the issuer of stability of capital and of its costs, and thus permits more secure long-term planning for long-term capital needs and costs. (To be sure, long-term investments can be, and often are, financed in part by short-term loans, even though this requires frequent rollovers. Likewise, investments in what may be expected to be a relatively constant level of inventories may well be financed by long-term issues.)

Since, to some extent, equities, short-term, and long-term debt are substitutable, the choice among them, by issuers, will depend heavily on relative cost considerations. Relative costs reflect a number of factors. One factor, affecting the choice between equity and debt, is the nature of the tax system—especially the tax deductibility of interest but not of dividends or retained earnings. The cost of equity financing is obviously difficult to pin down, but it clearly depends on the expectation of streams of dividends and capitals gains that has to be created in order to sell the number of shares desired at the price desired. Obviously, any given capital sum might be

---

[5] We are here considering advantages/disadvantages from the standpoint of the managers, not the existing owners of a business. As seen from the context, their interests are not necessarily the same. Rather than to develop separately the case from the standpoint of a management-controlled, an owner-controlled, and a mixed-control, we ordinarily here refer to the advantages/disadvantages as seen by the interest most affected.

realized by selling a smaller or larger number of shares at higher or lower prices, but selling large numbers at low prices seriously dilutes the equity of existing stockholders in existing retained earnings and in future earnings and depresses the value of their assets. Thus, new stock issues tend to be made only when the stock market is strong. However, unless outstanding equity is already more than sufficient to satisfy lenders, stock may have to be issued in order to increase borrowing.

Choices between long-term and short-term debt, given the inherent advantages and disadvantages of each, are made not only on the basis of current but also of expected future market rates of interest. If the short-term rate is below the long rate but both are expected to rise, it is likely to pay to finance long now. If the short rate is above the long but both are expected to fall, it may still pay to finance short. Indeed, if a long-term financing is seen as required in the future but at a time when long rates are expected to be higher, it may pay to finance long at once and lend the proceeds at the short rate until needed. These considerations are important for the discussion in Chapter 21, of the "term-structure" of interest rates, and for the reformulation of Keynes' "speculative demand" for money that we shall there undertake.

Formally, we can think of individual and aggregate long-term supply functions, in which the outstanding stocks of each kind of *private* financial asset depend inversely on their own cost and directly on the cost of each alternative private asset, and in a fairly complicated way on expected future asset costs.

The composition of *government* debt and money outstanding is influenced by some of the same considerations relevant for business, but it also significantly reflects public policy considerations. In principle, a national treasury or finance ministry can operate like a central bank— either selling extra securities not needed to finance a current deficit and retiring (that is, "destroying") the money secured from its sale, or purchasing back its own securities with newly created money. In that case, it is clearly operating a "monetary policy" either in support of or in offset to that of the central bank. To be sure, this is not usually considered appropriate. Even so, decisions on financing and refinancing the public debt not infrequently give rise to intentional or unintentional, temporary or longer run, monetary policy effects, which need cause no trouble provided treasury or finance ministry and central bank are cooperating.

Ordinarily, however, the government's choice is not between money and debt finance but between short-term and long-term debt. To some extent, such decisions are made on grounds similar to those of business, that is, based mainly on considerations of immediate and future cost; moreover, like businesses, governments often have a desire to "pin down" as much of their debt as possible for long periods, so as not to have to face the need to refinance at times when rates are very high. Most economists believe, however, that these business-type considerations should be largely irrelevant for government "debt-management policy," which should consider only the objectives of general stabilization policy. (On a purely cost basis, the cheapest way to finance a government deficit is to issue money; but few would carry cost minimization to that point!) If decisions to run government deficits or surpluses are to be made in consideration of full-employment and price-stability objectives, why should the financial decisions that these debts or surpluses require—as they are incurred and as they are refinanced—respond to a different set of criteria?

Up to now we have been discussing supplies and demands for financial assets in an essentially stationary economy, in which (a) net investment, government deficit, and private saving were all essentially zero; thus (b) national income would be at a roughly constant level determined by that amount of investment plus deficit and the consumption function; and, as well, (c) the stock of wealth was essentially constant. Under these circumstances, the *composition* of the financial assets that make up the constant total stock of wealth could still change, but only slowly, through refinancing, mainly as maturities expire, or through repurchases.

If there were shifts in the composition of the public's demands for financial assets, they would affect the relative prices and yields of various types of securities. However, these changed yields might induce firms (or governments) to alter the composition of their liabilities in order to reduce their costs, either through replacing maturing issues with different ones or through repurchasing existing liabilities with the proceeds of new ones. To the extent that they did so respond, the *ultimate* effects on relative asset yields of autonomous shifts in the composition of wealthholders' asset preferences would be less than the *initial* effects, once the composition of the stock had time to adjust. However, since different kinds of liabilities are not regarded as perfect substitutes, either by wealthholders or by firms, there would still be permanent changes in relative yields.

Each form of private investment is not equally sensitive to a change in its capital cost. Thus the alterations of *relative* yields caused by changes either in wealthholders' preferences or in the structure of investment might well produce net changes in total investment and, thus, in the aggregate demand for goods and services. For example, an autonomous shift of wealthholders' demand from private to government securities would clearly reduce investment. Or, a shift in government financing from short-term to long-term debt (lowering yields for short-term debt, public and private, and raising yields for long-term securities of both types) could well reduce total investment, if it is true, as usually supposed, that investment is more sensitive to long-term interest rates than to short-term rates.

Some Financial Aspects of Economic Growth

We have been discussing an economy with zero net investment (plus government deficit). However, it is more relevant to consider real economies in which investment and saving are prevailingly positive: investment positive because of exogenous forces such as technological change or population growth; saving positive because, at the level of income corresponding to positive investment, consumption falls short of income. A positive level of investment (or investment plus government deficit) means a *higher* level of income than does a zero level of investment. But it does not in itself produce a *rising* level of income. Yet it does necessarily produce a *continuing growth* in wealth, as measured by aggregate net worth or financial assets. To keep things simple, we assume throughout that potential output is at least as large and grows at least as fast as aggregate demand.[6]

The first fundamental point we need to recognize about supply and demand for financial assets in such an economy is that, since investment plus government deficit necessarily equals private saving, then a positive level of investment plus deficit, which adds precisely that amount to the *total supply* (*stock*) of financial assets, will produce an equal rate of positive saving, which adds exactly that same amount to the *total demand* for financial assets at existing yields. However, the amount which such investment adds to the *supply* (*stock*) of each particular asset would only by the remotest chance be the same as the amount that it adds to the *demand* for each asset; and this fact can have repercussions on yields which will influence what the total amount of investment plus deficit (and thus the total of private saving) will be over the longer run.

We have previously considered (in Chapter 9) what these repercussions were (at least in the case of a wealth increase from fiscal policy) in a two-financial-asset world (money and bonds). Those results are considerably altered in a multi-asset world. How they are altered, and with what consequences, depends very much on what is the *composition* of the positive level of investment plus deficit. We will illustrate this only by consideration of alternatives involving broad classes of assets; similar results apply to narrower classes as well. We restrict the discussion to three illustrative cases.

1. Suppose, for example, that private investment is positive, the government deficit remaining at zero. Clearly the *stocks* of financial assets that grow are the liabilities of private firms not of government, and the stocks of nonmonetary assets not of money. But the *composition* of the growing *demand* for assets almost necessarily will also involve growth in the demands for government securities and money, the stocks of which do not change. For example, the growth in the public's *demand* for private securities will be considerably less than the growth in the corresponding *supply* (*stock*) of private securities. Prices of private securities thus will

---

[6] If private investment is prevailingly positive, not only wealth but potential output will grow. But we do not propose here to consider systematically the relationship between growth of actual and potential output. See Chapter 8 for an elementary discussion.

tend increasingly to fall (yields to rise) as the added stocks accumulate, while prices of government securities will rise progressively (yields fall). The rise in the demand for money relative to its constant stock will somewhat reduce the rise in prices of government debts, but it will intensify the fall in prices of private securities. The progressive rise in yields in the private markets will, of course, tend to reduce and, perhaps ultimately to cut off, positive net investment; but the mere fall in government yields is not likely to encourage government deficits.

Nevertheless, *how much* private yields will rise depends very much on the extent of substitutability in wealthholders' portfolios between public and private assets, as well as between monetary and nonmonetary assets— that is, how sensitive the demand for each is to the price (or yield) of the others. If this sensitivity is great, so that, as private yields tend to rise, holders of government bonds attempt to shift their portfolios substantially toward private securities (attempting to sell, to each other, substantial amounts of government bonds in order to buy, from each other, private ones), this will minimize both the rise in private yields and the decline in government yields. The dampening effect on the rise in private yields will be the greater to the extent that desired holdings of money are also highly sensitive to increases in yields on nonmonetary assets.

Suppose that a supportive monetary policy attempts to prevent or to reduce the rise in private yields, and thus to offset any tendency for investment to decline, by buying (government) bonds on the open market. The added supply of money would meet some or all of the increased demand for money and would further reduce the yields on government debt, thus further restraining the rise in yields on private securities. However, because government and private securities are not perfect substitutes in wealthholders' portfolios, it would be necessary, in order to prevent any rise in private yields, to reduce yields on government securities substantially and progressively. Thus the average yield on private and public securities taken together would have to fall—and to continue to fall as ever increasing doses of open market purchases occurred. But only this would maintain a constant level of I and Y.[7]

2. Consider, now, the opposite case, in which net private investment is zero but the government deficit is positive, with the deficit financed entirely through the sale of new government bonds. Clearly the stock of this one financial asset accumulates, whereas the corresponding saving constitutes an increased demand for all classes of financial assets. Thus, with supply increasing faster than demand, prices of government securities would pro-

---

[7] Recall that positive investment also produces rising productive capacity, and that, under simple assumptions, for this extra capacity to be used requires not merely that investment remain positive but that it continually grow at a constant percentage rate. And, if the extra productive capacity were not used, it is inconceivable that even constant positive investment could be maintained. Under the circumstances discussed, this would appear to require a growth of the money stock at an ever increasing percentage rate.

gressively fall (yields rise). With demand for private securities also increasing because of the wealth effect, and no change in their supply, prices of private securities would, however, tend to rise, reducing private yields. With higher yields on public securities and lower yields on private, wealthholders would, of course, tend to shift to public securities, moderating both the rise in public and the fall in private yields, with the extent of this equalizing effect depending on the degree of substitutability between public and private securities in wealthholders' portfolios. But, unless wealthholders consider private and public securities as perfect substitutes, there should be some net decline in private yields, and thus some stimulus to investment—which might now rise above zero. At the same time, the gradual rise in wealth resulting from the deficit should also stimulate consumption.

Assuming that the deficit were originally undertaken because of a secular deficiency in private demand, the wealth and substitution effects of the deficit might thus gradually tend to eliminate the need for the deficit! This optimistic view, however, fails to take account of the effect of the deficit on the demand for money. In fact, the demand for money must gradually increase, reflecting the positive wealth elasticity of the demand for money. Unless this elasticity is exceptionally low, the increased demand for money (decreased demand for both public and private securities) could cause private (as well as public) yields to rise.

If it were desired to offset this effect, the central bank would need to purchase enough of the new government bonds to provide money supply growth equal to the growth in the demand for money. Another way of saying this is that the deficit would need to be financed partly by debt and partly by money creation, in proportions that would permit yields on private securities to fall.

3. Long-term government bonds are clearly a closer substitute for long-term private securities than are short-term government "bills" (usually issued for 13 or 26 weeks). Thus, it makes some difference for private investment whether the debt-financed portion of a government deficit is financed by long-term or short-term government debt. If, in an investment boom, monetary policy needs to be restrictive, one can argue that deficits (if any) should be financed long; but, if it is desired to minimize unfavorable impacts on private (long-term) investment, bills should be used. One can also argue that, in refinancing maturing debt, the choice between bills and long-term bonds should be influenced by consideration of the type of impact it is desirable to exert on private investment. Also, in choosing which type of government securities to buy or sell in open market operations, the central bank can take account of the same considerations. To be sure, such choices are (ordinarily) of second-order importance, as compared with the more important choice between debt financing (using whatever kind of government securities) and new-money financing of deficits, or as compared with the central bank's decision as to the *amount*

of its open market operations, whatever the particular type of government debt to be bought or sold. But the importance of such choices is surely not negligible.

Thus, in a multi-asset world, one can no longer talk about "the" interest rate, for some rates can rise as others fall, or they can rise or fall quite unequally. And financial decisions by private lenders and borrowers have effects not unlike those of the government's fiscal and monetary policies. Indeed, the line between government fiscal and monetary policy also becomes blurred. We could define fiscal policy as government decisions which affect the *aggregate volume* of private financial wealth, and monetary policy as government decisions which affect the *composition* of private financial wealth. But the latter would then include operations in which the quantity of money is not itself affected: for instance, when the government *borrows* (or fails to repay debt from a surplus in tax revenues over purchases and transfers) in order to *lend* to a particular class of borrowers, or in a particular credit market.

THE ROLE OF FINANCIAL INTERMEDIARIES

By definition, financial intermediaries are firms that basically buy one kind of financial asset and sell another; thus, savings and loan associations and mutual savings banks mainly buy mortgages and sell share accounts or savings deposits; insurance companies buy mainly bonds, selling insurance policies; finance companies buy (or make) installment loans, and sell commercial paper; commercial banks buy short-term government securities and business and personal IOU's and "sell" demand, time, and savings deposits. In so doing, intermediaries absorb from the portfolios of individual wealthholders (or what would otherwise have to go into those portfolios) large quantities of certain kinds of (mainly) primary securities and put into those private portfolios instead their own liabilities. Commercial banks are sometimes described as "monetizing debt"; in the same way, other intermediaries transmute one kind of liability into another, for example, savings and loan associations transmute mortgages into a kind of time deposit.

Financial intermediaries exist because there is a profit to be made by adapting the structure of the public's stock of financial assets more closely to the structure of the public's demand for assets—that is, by giving wealthholders the kinds of assets in which they prefer to hold their accumulated savings instead of the kinds of liabilities which firms or governments must, or prefer to, issue to finance business investment and government deficits.

For example, suppose that many savers wish stability of value, a minimum of risk exposure and the ability to withdraw their funds in small (or large) amounts on short notice, whereas most firms wish to issue long-term, large-denomination bonds. Without intermediaries there would be no *direct* way for the firms to attract the savings other than to make the return so high that savers overcome their dislikes and become bond-holders. However, suppose someone invents a savings bank (for instance), that can issue to savers a fixed price asset (a savings deposit) that pays a modest but positive rate of return, permits withdrawal in any amount essentially on demand, and carries exceedingly low risk of default. Because it offers these other features, savers prefer this asset over lending directly to firms, even at a considerably lower interest rate, and they prefer it to money, the yield of which is zero. The savings bank can use the funds collected from savers to purchase corporate bonds. By investing in a far more diversified portfolio of bonds than any saver could, it pools and thereby greatly reduces risk; and, by having a large number of depositors, it can allow virtually free withdrawal because it can count on roughly constant and equal aggregate rates of withdrawals and deposits. Savers are better off (even though their nominal incomes are lower). And firms are able to borrow for less.

If such banks were completely unregulated, they would tend to expand in number and size by bidding up the rates they pay to savers and bidding down the interest rates investors have to pay them, until only a normal profit remained for savings bankers. Even though, in fact, savings banks are regulated as to entry, maximum interest to be paid on deposits, reserves, and so on, their operations still considerably narrow the spread between these two sets of interest rates. Both ultimate lenders and ultimate borrowers thereby benefit; and so does the economy as a whole through the encouragement given to saving and investment.[8]

To take another example, firms need to issue a certain amount of equities along with their debt. Yet few savers have the information and ability adequately to evaluate the risk and prospective return on individual equities, or else such savers have too small a capital sum to make the effort worthwhile. And, given the size of the minimum investment in most issues, very few savers have enough capital to obtain a diversification adequate to reduce risks. An investment trust, mutual fund, or pension fund, however, can provide skilled research and portfolio management services at sharply decreasing unit cost and can pool risks by a highly diversified portfolio. At least in principle, it can thus provide either a higher and more stable return to savers, or a lower cost of equity to firms, or both. The same risk-pooling advantages of large financial institutions also permit them to offer many associated specialized benefits that no saver could provide for himself—for example, life insurance, annuities, pensions.

Savings banks are one among several kinds of financial intermediaries that create *fixed-price* financial assets. Such assets share an important

[8] This is not to suggest that saving is encouraged by a lower interest rate, but the availability of a safe and convenient means of holding savings undoubtedly does raise the propensity to save.

characteristic of money although they differ from money by paying a positive return. Other intermediaries that issue fixed price assets are savings and loan associations, credit unions, and—most important of all—commercial banks, which issue demand as well as time and savings deposits. We will consider the commercial bank—as the only private creator of "money"—more fully later. Here, however, we merely note the obvious fact that many wealthholders prefer to hold some (or even all) of their total savings in fixed-price asset form. These intermediaries clearly make such savings available for business investment at interest rates far below what firms would have to pay to attract those savings directly—certainly in a world in which any form of *money* exists.

The Creation of New Assets and Liabilities

In intermediating between ultimate savers and direct investors, financial intermediaries add greatly to the stock of financial assets available to savers; but for every extra asset, they also create an equal new financial liability. Indeed, since intermediaries also own each others' liabilities, they may create increments of assets and liabilities more than twice the size of the corresponding increments of private saving (that is, of investment plus government deficit). Still, intermediation, *per se*, does not affect total *net* worth. Since it is important to be clear about this arithmetic, we illustrate it with two elementary examples, summarized in Table 20-1. Each involves a firm's investment of $100 in new inventories—in one case financed without intermediation, in the other case using an intermediary.[9]

In the first example, the only role for a financial intermediary (in this case, a commercial bank) is to transfer funds, on command, from one depositor's account to another's. The funds to finance the investment are raised by the direct sale of the firm's securities to the public, which pays for them by check. Line 1 shows the effects of this sale of securities, taken by itself. Bank deposits (existing liabilities of the bank) are transferred from the accounts of savers to that of the firm, which delivers securities in the same amount to these savers; thus there is created a new financial asset and liability but no new *intermediate* asset and liability. The public holds a different composition of financial assets than before but the same total amount. The firm has equal increases in its assets and liabilities.

In line 2, we show the results of the subsequent production for investment in inventory. The firm acquires a new asset, inventory, to replace its previous asset, bank deposits. The public acquires the $100 of bank deposits spent by the firm; these are now held either by the new

---

[9] The increment of new inventory is assumed not to involve any reduction of another firm's inventory but, instead, additional new production. We can imagine that the firm hires previously unemployed workers and uses their services, without purchased materials, to create $100 worth of new inventories.

TABLE 20-1
Hypothetical Changes in Assets (A), Liabilities (L), and Net Worth (NW)

Line	Bank A	Bank L	Bank NW	Firm A	Firm L	Firm NW	Public A	Public L	Public NW	Aggregate A	Aggregate L	Aggregate NW
Example 1 1		−100 (public's deposits) +100 (firm's deposits)		+100 (deposits)	+100 (securities)		−100 (deposits) +100 (securities)			+100	+100	
2		+100 (public's deposits) −100 (firm's deposits)		−100 (deposits) +100 (inventory)			+100 (deposits)		+100	+100		+100
3 (Total)				+100 (inventory)	+100 (securities)		+100 (securities)		+100	+200	+100	+100
Example 2 4	+100 (firm's IOU)	+100 (firm's deposit)		+100 (deposits)	+100 (IOU)					+200	+200	
5		−100 (firm's deposits) +100 (public's deposits)		−100 (deposits) +100 (inventory)			+100 (deposits)		+100	+100		+100
6 (Total)	+100 (IOU)	+100 (public's deposits)		+100 (inventory)	+100 (IOU)		+100 (deposits)		+100	+300	+200	+100

workers, who have just been paid, or by others whom they in turn have paid for newly produced consumer goods. (We can assume that producers of consumer goods were able to increase production of consumer goods along with demand, and that the holders of some of the new deposits are thus the workers, who produced the extra consumer goods, and the owners of these firms, who earned extra profit.) Some set of workers or owners has $100 worth of increased net worth—that is, saving (income increase less consumption increase).[10]

Line 3 shows the combined effects of the financing and the production—line 1 plus line 2. Aggregate assets, real plus financial, have risen by $200 ($100 of inventories and $100 of securities); liabilities have increased by $100 (the firm's liability for its securities); and net worth (of the public) has increased by $100. Liabilities and assets of intermediaries are unchanged.

In example 2, the financial intermediary, the commercial bank, makes a new loan to the same firm for the same investment in inventory. The bank thus acquires (line 4) a new financial asset worth $100 (the firm's IOU), and it creates a new liability against itself by crediting the firm's bank account with an extra $100, which become both asset and liability to the firm. When, as shown in line 5, the new deposit is spent on the production of inventory, the public again receives $100 of extra bank deposits and net worth (saving). Combining the two stages, as shown in line 6, aggregate assets have increased by $300, liabilities by $200, net worth by the same $100. The net worth of consumers and the aggregate physical wealth of the country have each increased by the same $100 of example 1. This increase came about because there was new investment (and net private saving). But, because an intermediary got into the act of "financing" the investment, we now also have an extra $100 of new financial assets and liabilities.

We may note, moreover, that the public's net increase in assets this time consists of new bank deposits, whereas in example 1 it consisted of new securities. In Example 1, the total stock of "money" was unchanged, and that of securities increased; this time, the public's "money" stock has increased instead of its stock of securities. Presumably, in example 1, security prices had to be somewhat depressed (yields increased) to get the public to hold the extra security; in example 2, security prices may be raised a bit (yields reduced), because the public will not want to hold more than a small amount of its new wealth in money form, at least at the previous interest rate.

If we now further suppose (not shown in table) that some fraction (say three fourths) of the new savings of the public that have accrued in the

---

[10] Naturally, neither set of workers or owners wants to add the full $100 of extra income to saving. So each responds most of his extra receipts, increasing the incomes of others, and so on, until ultimately income and production have risen sufficiently that added *voluntary* saving equals the $100 extra investment. This requires an increase of income equal to $100 times the multiplier, but the amount of the public's extra saving (net worth) remains at $100.

form of demand deposits is deposited in a savings bank (changing only the *form* of the public's assets), we have the result that the assets and liabilities of the savings bank will have both increased by 75; the liabilities of the commercial bank to the public are reduced by 75 but increased (to the savings bank) by 75, leaving no net change. Now, aggregate assets have increased by 375, aggregate liabilities by 275, net worth by 100. Although the multiplication of assets and liabilities does not increase wealth or income, we can assume that it increases welfare.

The Commercial Bank as Financial Intermediary[11]

Commercial banks are financial intermediaries *par excellence.* Yet they are often described with so much emphasis on certain special characteristics of their distinctive liability that the reader misses their family resemblances to savings and loan associations, mutual funds, or insurance companies. Yet the qualities that commercial banks share with other intermediaries are surely more important than those that are special. Essentially, they issue their own liabilities—which include demand, time, and savings deposits[12]—and they use the proceeds to acquire the liabilities of others. Their principal assets are loans to businesses, mainly short-term, and government securities, mainly bills and bonds of relatively near maturities, and (partly for tax reasons) state and local government securities. They also make personal loans, including mortgage loans, and (short-term) loans to or deposits in other banks (including the central bank).

Because their assets are mainly short-term liabilities, some of which (for example, government securities, demand deposits in other banks) are instantly marketable, and because most banks have almost instant recourse to loans from other banks and/or from the central bank, commercial banks can offer the instant withdrawal feature that is the characteristic of their distinctive liability—demand deposits. Given the public's desire to hold the types of liabilities that banks offer, even though mostly at low or zero rates of return, and given the loan services that banks can provide to borrowers, banks profitably exploit the difference between the interest rates that they need to pay on their liabilities and those they can earn on their assets.

The peculiarity of the commercial bank that receives most attention is that its distinctive liability, the demand deposit, is directly acceptable as payment for anything and everything. It is thus "money." Even this characteristic is not (or at least no longer) unique to banks. Checks can be

---

[11] For an excellent treatment of this question see J. Tobin, "Commercial Banks as Creators of Money," in D. Carson, ed., *Banking and Monetary Studies* (R. D. Irwin, 1963), pp. 408–419, reprinted in W. L. Smith and R. L. Teigen, *Readings in Money, National Income and Stabilization Policy,* 3rd ed. (R. D. Irwin, 1974), pp. 224–229; for further discussion, see the references given therein.

[12] And, increasingly, marketable securities such as **certificates of deposit** and **notes**. They also borrow (or receive deposits) from other banks, and sometimes borrow from the central bank.

drawn in many places on the "NOW" accounts of savings banks or savings and loan institutions, as well as on some mutual funds (at least for substantial payments). In addition, modern credit card systems are clearly approaching the payment properties of checking accounts; some believe that electronic fund transfer at most points of retail sale will ultimately displace most personal use of checks on demand accounts.

Moreover, many time and savings deposit accounts, both at banks and at other intermediaries, are on a *de facto* basis of withdrawal on demand, as are some mutual funds. Since interest *is* paid on demand deposits in other countries, *was* paid in the United States until 1933, and is increasingly proposed to be permitted again to United States banks, the distinction between those liabilities of financial intermediaries which are "money" and those which are not is increasingly tenuous.

Economists often emphasize that commercial banks, unlike other intermediaries, can under certain conditions—that is, if they have "excess reserves"—"print money," by directly issuing their own new liabilities to acquire other assets. For example, they can make new loans by simply crediting the borrower's account (as in example 2, above), thereby creating a deposit balance that didn't previously exist and which now becomes a part of the public's money stock. In contrast, other intermediaries can create their own distinctive liabilities only if their customers first make a "deposit," buy a "share," or pay a "premium," in "real money"; only then can the intermediary make a loan or buy a security. This is correct, but the difference is trivial. The operations of the commercial bank would not be essentially altered if it were required to pay the proceeds of its loans to its borrowers in cash or in a check on the bank's account in another bank. In most cases the borrower would simply deposit the loan proceeds in his bank—and this, almost always, would be the bank that made the loan. (Most borrowers are already depositors at the banks from which they borrow.)[13] Thus, the result would be the same: in the end the bank would still have a new deposit liability and a new loan.

The really important reason why the difference is trivial is the fact that the bank that makes the new loan must, in any case, assume that all of the proceeds of its loan (except compensating balance, if any) will very soon be spent by the borrower and the proceeds lost to the bank. And it will, indeed, be so lost. The new deposit—the new money that the bank "printed"—has gone elsewhere. The only way in which the bank really gains deposits is in the same way other intermediaries do—by attracting "real money" brought in by new depositors.[14]

---

[13] The frequent requirement that the borrower keep an unused "compensating balance" in a deposit account at the lending bank supports the tendency that a borrower first deposit the proceeds of a bank loan in his account at the lending bank.

[14] Moreover, nothing is really changed about the banking system's operations if banks only purchase securities (when they have excess reserves) rather than making loans. And securities *cannot* ordinarily be bought by the bank creating a new deposit account.

The more meaningful form of the argument that banks are really different from other intermediaries, in being able themselves to create new liabilities, deals not with an individual bank but with the commercial banking system as a whole. Of course, the proceeds of the new loan *are* soon withdrawn from the bank that made the loan; but the newly created deposits will, nevertheless, *remain in the commercial banking system.* For the recipients of checks drawn on the new account will almost surely deposit them in their own bank accounts; and when *they*, in turn, write checks against this amount, these, too, will be redeposited in other banks. Thus bank money, once created in the process of bank lending, lives on as a virtually permanent part of the money supply. Even if some recipients of the new money should transfer some or all of it to a deposit in a savings bank, or to a share account, or a mutual fund, the proceeds of such receipt by the other intermediary will be immediately added to the deposit account which that institution maintains in a commercial bank. Even when these sums are then used to buy securities or make loans, the checks will again be deposited in some other bank account, so that the newly created money appears to be immortal.

One exception to this immortality, however, is the fact that, somewhere along the line, some recipient of the new bank money may well ask for cash—bills and coins. As this cash is paid out by a bank, a corresponding portion of the new deposit is destroyed. However, there is an answer to that: it is that other people and businesses are always *depositing cash* into checking accounts. And since the public's cash needs are both limited and quite stable, about as much of any demand deposits that may be "destroyed" by recipients asking for cash are "reconstituted" by the deposit of cash in checking accounts.

There is a second way, however, in which a checking account is destroyed (as well as created). The depositor at a bank may at any time transfer funds from his checking account to a savings account in the same bank. The checking account is destroyed and a savings account created. The quantity of money (at least M_1) is thereby reduced. But, of course, the reverse is equally possible: savings account balances are transferred into checking accounts; money increases. And, since the "need" for both kinds of accounts is relatively stable (just as it is for cash), we may still argue that the notion of the creation of "immortal" money by banks, "at the stroke of a pen," is still not seriously qualified.

There is a third way in which bank deposits are destroyed. When a loan matures and is repaid, it is normally repaid by a check on the borrower's account in the lending bank or in another bank. As the loan is so repaid, a bank deposit is destroyed. Again, there is an answer to that. As individual loans are repaid, there are, at the same time, other new loans being made; and the aggregate demand for bank loans is relatively stable. Thus, banks do manufacture money; and, once manufactured, it is relatively immortal.

Yet all three "exceptions" reveal precisely why banks are like other intermediaries, and they show that banks' ability to create money is exactly like the ability of other financial intermediaries to create their own distinctive liabilities. This ability depends on the extent of which each type of institution can profitably attract funds from depositors. That is, it depends on banks' ability successfully to serve as an *intermediary*. For the *liabilities* of each type of intermediary compete with those of all other intermediaries—and with primary securities and with cash (government money)—for wealthholders' favor; demand deposits compete particularly with cash and with savings accounts in the same banks (which in turn compete with savings accounts or share accounts or mutual fund accounts in other institutions). To maintain banks' demand-account liabilities in being, and in any particular amount, depends on the inherent advantages/disadvantages and the relative yields of demand deposits and of all other types of financial assets (including cash).

Commercial banks must successfully compete as well for the *assets* they acquire. Businesses are not required to borrow at commercial banks. They can instead sell commercial paper, bonds, or shares, either directly to wealthholders or to other intermediaries—insurance companies, savings banks, investment trusts. They will borrow instead from commercial banks only to the extent that the nature of a bank loan and its terms are more attractive.

Only to the extent that banks can attract deposits and can afford to lend on attractive terms, do commercial banks and their distinctive liability survive and expand. And this is precisely how every other type of intermediary, and its distinctive form of financial liability, are able to survive and expand.

Competition and Regulation of Intermediaries

Like all other financial intermediaries, indeed like all private firms, banks seek maximum profits. Thus, they tend to expand in size and numbers, so long as there is a margin between the interest rate that borrowers are willing to pay and savers are willing to accept, which is more than large enough to cover all of their other costs and provide a normal profit. The resulting competition among banks tends to drive down the interest rates banks charge and/or to bid up the rates they pay on other than demand deposits. This is clearly in the public interest. Nevertheless, this competition is in every country qualified and limited by a considerable and, in many respects, severe public regulation. Other financial intermediaries are subject to similar, and, one might suppose, similarly wholesome, competitive pressures; but they, too, are subject to considerable regulation. This regulation extends to limitations of entry of new firms, to the types and composition of loans permitted to be made or securities to be purchased, to the scope of their operations, to the existence or number of branches, to the requirement of "reserves," to dealings with "insiders," to maximum interest rates paid on many kinds of liabilities (including a zero interest rate on demand deposits), and to many other aspects of their business. Frequent, detailed "inspections" assure substantial compliance with these regulations. In addition to government regulation, many of the more liquid liabilities of financial institutions are "insured" by government agencies (at least up to some maximum amount per depositor), with the costs paid for by charges levied on the insured institutions.

In addition, commercial banks are subject to a special further regulation which—although perhaps not originally so designed—has come to be used as a means for controlling the aggregate total liabilities of commercial banks. (This is the subject of the first major section of Chapter 21.)

The main purpose of the detailed regulations (other than that which controls the aggregate liabilities of commercial banks) and of the insurance is to *avoid failures of financial institutions*, and/or the consequences of such failures, not merely for savers but for the health of the economy. Experience not only in the United States but abroad is believed to have demonstrated that unregulated financial competition leads to overexpansion of financial institutions, which in turn leads to excessive reduction in the margins between interest paid and received, unsound financial practices, and the making of excessively risky loans or investments. The result is frequent failures and heavy losses to all depositors, which are particularly severe for smaller and less sophisticated savers. Given withdrawal on demand, the slightest hint of possible trouble at a commercial bank often leads to "runs" on the affected bank that quickly spreads to other banks and to other financial institutions. No matter how sound and profitable it is, almost no bank can be completely sure of surviving such a run without having to suspend withdrawals. And, because of extensive interbank deposits and deposits by other financial institutions, a few substantial bank failures—or even temporary suspensions of payments—can seriously impair the operations of the whole financial system, indeed the whole business system, as the *most liquid* of all financial assets (other than cash) suddenly becomes completely illiquid and as massive forced sales of long-term assets drastically drive down their prices.

The financial history of America (and of a number of other countries) records a number of serious financial "panics," sometimes initially *caused* by a recession in business (which may have forced delays in scheduled loan repayments) but that almost always *results* in a severe economic slump. It also records an increasing body of legislation imposing increasingly severe regulations, designed to prevent recurrence of such problems. Given the current state of regulation and insurance, it is inconceivable that a financial panic could again occur in the United States.

These benefits of regulation seem undeniable, but it is clear that regulation has had some costs. Undoubtedly, it means either that profits of financial institutions are higher than they would otherwise be and higher than they need to be to induce the supply of financial services, and/or that pressures for efficiency in such institutions are appreciably reduced. Thus, the economic benefits of intermediation to savers, investors, and the whole economy are less than might ideally be expected. Indeed, in recent years, many intelligent observers have argued that restrictions on financial competition (and innovation) have gone too far and should be somewhat relaxed in the interest of a more flexible and rapidly growing economy. However, we cannot here enter on the merits of this question. We can recognize that, despite their very extensive regulation, the mere existence of financial intermediaries—in their present numbers and scales of operations—provide profound benefits to the economy, and a very different economic structure than would exist without them.

The Economic Effects of Intermediation

We have suggested that intermediation—and the development of new forms of intermediation—benefits both savers and investors by reducing the margin between the rates that borrowers pay and savers receive. It also, quite clearly, reduces the *differences* between the rates that must be paid by different investors, tending to make these differences correspond only to the differences in the real costs of lending to different borrowers and in different forms, when each is done at its optimal scale. Given this competition, rate differences paid reflect the differential economies of loans of different *size* and the varied informational, administrative, and managerial costs of loans of different *types*.

Since the whole structure of asset yields is tied to a zero return on cash and demand deposits, most of the benefits of this reduction of interest rate differentials appear to go, in the first instance, to borrowers. These advantages, however, are necessarily passed along in reduced costs and prices of all goods and services. In fact, because of regulation, the interest rates payable on most "near moneys" (time and savings accounts, savings and loan shares) are also much of the time less than they would otherwise be, and this further holds down the yields on less liquid and riskier financial assets. Because the return on a time deposit is limited, a lower absolute yield than would otherwise be necessary induces savers (and intermediaries) to hold Treasury Bills or commercial paper; and, because yields on Treasury Bills and commercial paper are lower, so are the yields on more risky and illiquid assets. Even though rates paid to savers are held down by regulation, the increased safety, convenience, and associated services provided to savers by intermediaries clearly directly increase savers' real return and indirectly increase the incomes of all members of society.

In the first part of this chapter, in which we introduced the variety of financial assets, it was pointed out that—in a world without financial intermediaries—the capital market would be rather highly segmented and that shifts in savers' asset preferences, shifts in the composition of investment, the disproportionate growth of government versus private debt, or other changes in the structure of supply or demand for assets, could thus substantially change relative yields on these kinds of assets and the relative interest costs to borrowers, providing additional sources of economic instability.

The existence of intermediaries greatly reduces the economic impact of these kinds of changes. Most intermediaries can and do deal in a variety of assets and liabilities. Disproportionate shifts in supplies or demands for either assets or liabilities are readily met by shifts of funds from one market to another in response to only modest changes in relative yields. This flexibility has, to be sure, been somewhat limited by legal provisions restricting the variety of business done by various types of intermediaries. Fortunately, the current trend in United States legislation is to reduce this required specialization, which should make the financial system even more flexible and further reduce the variablity of relative yields. Indeed, some speak of an evolution toward one or at most a few types of financial intermediaries, each a "supermarket" of diversified financial services to savers and firms.

It is clear that the financial structure[15] of modern economies is dominated by financial intermediaries, and it should be clear that they bring many benefits to savers and investors. In the next chapter, we will see that their existence also requires some significant reformulations, and even substantive revisions in the macroeconomic theories developed for a simple hypothetical economy in which they did not exist.

REVIEW QUESTIONS

1. Present a list of key factors that determine the structure of the demand for financial assets, and another list of those that determine the structure of the supply. Show how and why changes in each of these factors will affect the prices or yields of principal classes of assets.

2. If the interest rate on short-term debt is lower than that on long-term debt, but both rates are expected to rise, it is likely to pay for a firm to finance its investment at long term now. Why?

3.

(a) In an initial situation of zero net investment and zero government deficit, explain how a change in the composition of the public's demand for financial assets might tend to produce positive private investment.

(b) Suppose that private net investment is initially zero but government deficits are positive and are financed entirely by the sale of new government bonds. Explain how this method of financing might ultimately affect aggregate private investment.

---

[15] Perhaps it should be called a "superstructure," given that it mainly adds additional layers of assets and liabilities.

(c) Assume zero private investment but a positive government deficit financed by printing money. Explain how this method of financing might ultimately affect aggregate private investment. Compare this result with that in (b).

(d) How could a mere shift from short-term government debt to long-term debt, keeping the total amount of debt the same as before, influence aggregate private investment?

4.

(a) How might one define financial intermediaries? List some major types.

(b) "Financial intermediaries create new assets and liabilities, without directly affecting the public's total net worth." Explain carefully.

(c) In what major respects does the commercial bank differ from other financial intermediaries?

(d) "Financial intermediaries provide significant benefits to the economy." What kind of benefits and how? Why, then, are they regulated, often rather severely?

5.

(a) "Only commercial banks create money. But this is true in the same sense that only savings banks create savings banks deposits, or only pension funds create pension claims." Explain.

(b) Why then do we pay so much more attention to the quantity of money than to the quantity of savings bank deposits or of pension claims?

SELECTED REFERENCES

J. Tobin, "A General Equilibrium Approach to Monetary Theory," *Journal of Money, Credit and Banking*, 1 (February 1969), 15–29.

(The fundamentals of the "portfolio approach" exemplified in Chapter 20.)

J. Tobin, "Commercial Banks as Creators of Money," in D. Carson (ed.), *Banking and Monetary Studies* (R. D. Irwin, 1963), pp. 408–419, reprinted in W. L. Smith and R. L. Teigen (eds.), *Readings in Money, National Income and Stabilization Policy* (R. D. Irwin, 3rd ed., 1974), pp. 224–229.

(The view that commercial banks are only one member of the class of financial intermediaries.)

J. G. Gurley and E. S. Shaw, "Financial Aspects of Economic Development," *American Economic Review*, 45 (May 1955), 515–538.

(A pioneering statement on the role of intermediaries.)

H. G. Johnson, "Monetary Theory and Policy," *American Economic Review*, 52 (June 1962), 335–384.

(An able and far-ranging review of the main recent developments in monetary theory as of about 1960, including those particular strands discussed in this and the following chapter, as well as in certain earlier chapters.)

Chapter 21

Money, Interest Rates, and Monetary Policy

The Supply of Bank Money
The multiple expansion of bank assets and liabilities
Factors affecting the money supply
Fed control of money supply

The Conduct of Monetary Policy
The Federal funds market
Federal Reserve policy and the FF rate
How Federal Reserve targets are set and revised

Interest Theory Reconsidered
The interest rate and the supply and demand for money
Shortcomings of the *IS-LM* analysis
The term structure of interest rates
Keynes' speculative demand for money revisited

One of the economic benefits of intermediaries is their ability to adjust the supplies of particular kinds of financial assets to meet the portfolio preferences of wealthholders, while still permitting borrowers to obtain capital in the forms which best suit their special needs. Commercial banks participate in this process by tending to adjust the supply of money to changes in the demand for this most liquid of all assets—to the extent that the central bank permits. If there is an increase in wealthholders' demand for money relative to other financial assets, security prices generally tend to decline and yields to rise, thus impairing investment incentives. Under these circumstances, with higher interest rates being paid by investors, banks have an increased incentive[1] to act in a way that will both increase the supply of money available for the public to hold and to reduce the supply of securities necessary for the public to hold.

THE SUPPLY OF BANK MONEY

If banks are enabled to respond to the increased incentive, they will expand the supply of money, and this will affect the economy in the same general way as we described would occur, in a world without banks, if the central bank purchased securities in the open market, or if the treasury printed new money and used it to repurchase and retire some of its outstanding debt. However, for commercial banks to be able to operate as a "money machine," adjusting the supply to the demand, requires the approval and

---

[1] Banks almost always have a positive incentive to expand their lending (or security holding) and thus the public's money stock. That is because it is not rising real marginal costs but the central bank's limitation of reserves that normally prevents them from expanding their operations.

cooperation of the central bank in supplying the necessary increment in *reserves.* In a very real sense, the commercial banks are, with respect to the supply of money, essentially an extension of the central bank. Indeed, the main impact of central bank open market operations is not, as up to now we have implied, exerted directly on the economy. Instead it operates mainly through inducing or controlling commercial banks' actions in a way that will achieve the effects on the economy that, up to now, we have attributed to the central bank's operations directly.

Since the process by which the central bank controls the supply of commercial bank liabilities is part of every beginning course in economics (and should be studied in more detail in a course on money and banking), we will review it here only briefly and with minimum attention to institutional aspects. (Such institutional aspects as we require will relate to the United States banking system.)

The Multiple Expansion of Bank Assets and Liabilities

To begin, we assume that all commercial banks are members of the Federal Reserve System—as all National Banks are required to be, and almost all other very *large* banks choose to be. Among other things, member banks are required to hold average **reserves** in any week in an amount equal to some fraction *r* of the deposits they held two weeks earlier—a fraction that the Federal Reserve (hereafter "Fed") can vary within specified limits. These reserves must be maintained either in cash or in a deposit .account with the Fed. We will here assume that the reserve percentage is set at 20 percent against demand deposits, and at a lower figure (typically less than half of that) against other deposits; however, for much of the present discussion we will assume that *all* deposits are demand deposits. We will also ignore the lag between the time when deposits are held and the time when reserves must be available.

The balance sheet of a particular commercial bank which is just meeting its reserve requirement might look like this:

Assets		Liabilities and net worth	
Cash	(10)	Demand deposits	500
Deposit in Fed	(90)		
Reserves	100		
Loans	300		
Securities	100		
Other assets	100	Net worth	100
Total	600	Total	600

Note that this bank holds reserves equal to exactly 20 percent of its deposits. Reserves earn no interest, whereas loans and securities do. Thus, banks usually hold only the minimum of **excess reserves** (actual reserves less required reserves).

Suppose, now, that this bank receives net new deposits of 50, either in cash or in checks drawn on other banks. These additional deposits become a new liability of the bank; and, in the first instance, they also add equally to the bank's actual reserves, as the now excess cash and checks are in turn deposited in the bank's account at the Fed. (Indeed, all checks drawn on other banks and received by the bank either to be cashed or for deposit are sent directly to the Fed for "collection" or "clearance," just as are all checks drawn on accounts in this bank which are received by other banks. As the latter are received by the Fed they are automatically debited to this bank's reserve account and credited to the other banks' accounts. Thus, the excess of checks received by any bank over checks drawn on that bank and received by other banks, accrues directly and automatically as an increase in that bank's reserve deposit account in the Fed.)

If we show effects on the bank's balance sheet in *incremental* form, we have the following *changes* as a result of these 50 of net new deposits:

Assets		Liabilities and net worth	
Reserves	+50	Demand deposits	+50

With deposits now at 550 and total reserves at 150, required reserves are now 110, and excess reserves are 40.

If it appears that the bank's deposits will continue to average 50 higher than before, the bank will not wish to hold the excess reserves idle. Instead the bank will either buy extra securities or make new loans, assets which, unlike reserves, produce a positive return. (The return on loans generally being higher than that on securities, banks prefer loans; but a certain quantity of readily marketable securities provides a convenient and highly liquid "secondary reserve" with which to meet unexpectedly large and persistent net withdrawals, as well as an alternative interest-yielding asset when loan demand is weak.)

We assume that the bank has loan customers awaiting accommodation and that it uses its entire excess reserves to make new loans, crediting the new loans to the borrowers' deposit accounts. The result:

Assets		Liabilities and net worth	
Loans	+40	Demand deposits	+40

Note that reserves of 150 are now 25.4 percent of deposits of 590. However, the new borrowers quickly use their loans to purchase inventories, pay additional workers, buy machinery, and so on. Assuming the bank requires no "compensating balances" and that all payments by the borrowers are to firms or persons whose accounts are in other banks, the changes soon are:

Assets		Liabilities and net worth	
Reserves	−40	Demand deposits	−40

Incorporating the series of incremental changes into the original balance sheet gives us:

Assets		Liabilities and net worth	
Reserves	110	Demand deposits	550
Loans	340		
Securities	100		
Other assets	100	Net worth	100
Total	650	Total	650

Note that reserves of 110 are again 20 percent of deposits of 550.

The deposit in other banks of the checks drawn by the new loan customers, however, increases those banks' reserves and deposits by 40, creating excess reserves for them of 32. If these banks also use their excess reserves to make new loans and their borrowers write checks that are deposited in still a third set of banks, the process continues. Carried to its conclusion, we would ultimately get a series of demand deposit increments in various banks of the order of:

$$\Delta DD = 50 + 40 + 32 + 25.6 + 20.48 + \cdots$$
$$= 50[1 + (1 - r) + (1 - r)^2 + (1 - r)^3 + (1 - r)^4 + \cdots]$$
$$= 50\left(\frac{1}{r}\right) = 50\left(\frac{1}{0.2}\right) = 250$$

where ΔDD is the change in demand deposits and r is the required reserve ratio.

Does this mean that the aggregate money supply has now increased by 250? That depends on the source of the initial deposit increase of 50 that the first bank in the series received. If this initial deposit growth had merely come at the expense of other banks in the system, their deposits—and reserves—were simultaneously *reduced* by 50. Since we have assumed the increase received by the first bank to have been judged more or less permanent, the deposit and reserve losses to the other banks would have been judged more or less permanent too; and those banks would have had to contract their outstanding loans (and/or securities) by 40 in order for their reserve requirement to be met. This would have imposed reserve and deposit losses of 40 on still other banks, requiring them in turn to cut back by 32, and so on. The net change in demand deposits for the system as a whole would have been zero.

However, suppose that the initial deposit (and reserve) gain by our first bank had come from an open market purchase by the Fed of 50 of securities owned by a customer of the first bank (or from the repurchase by the Treasury of 50 of its securities with 50 of newly printed government money). In either case, the reserve gain of the first bank would not have been at the expense of any other bank, and there would have been a *net* increase in deposits (and in the money supply) of 250 and an accompanying *net* increase in bank loans of 200.[2]

In order to make the extra 200 in new bank loans, banks presumably had to bid down the interest rates on such loans (compared to what they otherwise would have been). And since loans are at least a partial substitute for other kinds of financing for investment, one can assume that some smaller decline occurred in yields on competing securities.

We assumed previously that customers were available for added bank loans—at least at a price—and that all of the expansion of bank assets took the form of loans. In fact, some part of the increase would probably go into security purchases to provide additional "secondary reserve," but this makes no difference in the extent of the multiple creation of money. Indeed, if the demand for bank loans were fixed, and completely unresponsive to price, the entire process of demand deposit expansion could proceed through the use of excess reserves to purchase securities from the public, passing excess reserves along to other banks as the securities were paid for, and creating similar chains of multiple expansion on the basis of an initial reserve gain (or of contraction with an initial reserve loss). The only difference is that, in this case, it would be primarily security yields that would decline—a decline most pronounced for the kinds of securities that banks buy, but affecting yields on other types as well. (The reader may wish to trace through the effects of security purchases instead of loans on the balance sheets of various sets of banks.)

Factors Affecting the Money Supply

We have been considering the effects of a change in the volume of bank reserves, up to now, on the assumption that deposit creation or extinction, based on reserve gains or losses, can occur without effects on bank assets

---

[2] If the Federal Reserve or Treasury had purchased 50 of securities directly from a bank (rather than from a bank's customer), there would have been an increase in that bank's reserves of 50, with no increase in its deposits. Thus, the full 50 would constitute excess reserves. However, the ultimate increase in loans and deposits would be precisely the same. If, instead, the initial deposit in the first bank had come from a (permanent) net reduction of currency in circulation, the increase in demand deposits would again have been 250, but the net increase in the money supply, only 200.

and liabilities other than loans (or securities) and demand deposits. This is probably not correct, although it is difficult to be sure of the *systematic* quantitative importance of the several qualifications usually made, which we can quickly summarize.

First, as the stock of bank deposits increases, there will presumably also be an increase in the public's demand for cash; as the public uses some part of any increase in deposits in the form of net withdrawals of cash from the banks, bank reserves (and deposits) are reduced.

Second, as demand deposits increase, some fraction of the increment of financial wealth is likely to be desired to be taken in the form of time and savings deposits (as well as other forms of financial assets: bonds, stocks, insurance policies, and so on). Shifts from demand deposits to time or savings deposits, *in commercial banks*, do destroy demand deposits and create an equal increment of the other deposits. But, since the required reserve ratios against time and savings deposits are considerably lower than against demand deposits, while this allows a somewhat smaller expansion of demand deposits, it allows a larger expansion of the two types of deposits combined, than would have been the case were the increment confined to demand deposits alone. (Thus, although the increment of M_1 is reduced, the increment of M_2 is increased.)

Third, as the volume of demand deposits increases (and especially to whatever extent such an increase lowers interest yields on banks' assets), banks may willingly accumulate some small volume of excess reserves. Especially today, with the development of the "Federal funds market" (see the later section with that heading), this factor is probably of trivial importance. However, to the extent that any increment of voluntary excess reserves does accompany deposit expansion, the amount of that expansion will thereby be reduced below the reserve increment times $1/r$.

Fourth, at times, a far more important qualification relates to bank discounts. This requires a brief digression to remind the reader what discounts are. As one of its functions, the Fed serves as "lender of last resort," by lending reserves to individual banks that encounter difficulties in meeting reserve requirements for reasons beyond their control. Designed originally, and still primarily, as protection against bank "runs," the facility mainly serves individual banks which are in temporary difficulty as a result of unexpected deposit withdrawals, or delays in loan repayment. (Technically this is done by "discounting"—that is, purchasing at a slight discount—certain kinds of assets in a bank's portfolio.) But it is easier to think of it as a loan of reserves to a bank otherwise facing a reserve deficiency, with interest charged at a published rate that the Fed can vary—the "discount rate."

The bank that borrows from the Fed is expected quickly to reduce its net acquisition of new assets and to repay its loan reasonably promptly. Being in debt to the Fed subjects the bank to greater scrutiny of its affairs by the authorities and generally is regarded as an "uncomfortable" state, to be avoided if possible.

Nevertheless, whenever money becomes relatively "tight" and interest rates rise, more and more banks do turn to the Fed for temporary reserve loans, not so much because they have unexpected deposit withdrawals or repayment delays (although there are always some of those, to which the bank can point) but simply because the banks find their good customers pressing them for loans, which they feel they cannot (or do not want to) deny. Having made the loans, they have trouble meeting reserve requirements.

Knowing that the discounting facility is available, banks get themselves into a position where they need to use it, and do—even at the cost of greater supervision of their affairs by the Fed. In such times, loan interest rates are likely to be substantially higher than the discount rate, and it is obviously profitable for banks to borrow from the Fed and maintain loan volume as long as they can get away with it.[3] Conversely, as bank reserve positions become easier and interest rates decline, the volume of outstanding discounts tends to decline. When total reserve position becomes sufficiently easy, discounts virtually disappear.

A reduction of discounts accompanying an increase in otherwise available reserves can thus substantially reduce the amount of the deposit and loan expansion that banks can create from the increments of aggregate reserves provided by open market purchases. Banks' "borrowed reserves," that is, discounts, decline as their "unborrowed reserves" (total reserves less discounts) increase, causing total reserves to advance by less than do unborrowed reserves. Therefore the expansion of bank loans and deposits will be a smaller multiple of the expansion of unborrowed reserves.

Some economists, assuming constant each of the preceding relationships between expansion of bank reserves and the other items, calculate far more complex "multipliers" than the simple $1/r$, that may be applied to any increment of reserves. Given the variability of these relationships, this writer finds the exercise unrewarding.

Fed Control of the Money Supply

However, consideration of the factors and the interrelationships just described, along with some others that cannot possibly be related systematically to the stock of reserves or deposits, does point to some interesting more general conclusions about the supply of bank money. The first is that the Fed's control of the money supply is far from precise. The supply of

---

[3] At such times, when the Fed is not supplying sufficient reserves by open market operations, the discount rate is likely to have been raised—but by less than bank interest rates will have increased.

money in the hands of the public is affected not only by the volume of Fed liabilities and treasury currency outstanding—usually called the **monetary base**—but also by the division of currency holdings between banks and the public, by the division of total deposits in commercial banks between demand deposits and all other types of deposits, by the volume of excess reserves banks voluntarily hold, by shifts of deposits among banks of different size and thus different reserve ratios or between member and nonmember banks, by shifts of deposits between those of the public and those of the United States government, and by changes in the aggregate amount of interbank deposits. All this means that the Fed's control over the money supply is only approximate.

To be sure, the Fed can control the monetary base fairly precisely. It knows the volume of treasury currency outstanding. It knows and controls the volume of its own total bond portfolio. It knows the amount of its outstanding discounts, and of its other assets and current operating expenses (the purchase of its new buildings, its payment of salaries, its expense for garbage collection all create bank reserves). And although the volume of its *discounts* is not subject to its immediate control, it can easily offset unwanted increases or reductions of discounts by equivalent open-market sales or purchases. To be sure, there are large seasonal swings in the public's need for cash and thus in the division of outstanding currency between banks and the public. But the seasonal swings are reasonably regular and predictable. There is also a troublesome item of "float"— checks in transit (which have been taken as credit by the banks receiving them but have not yet been debited to the banks on which they are written)—which varies dramatically when storms tie up mail deliveries. But these effects wash out in a few days. (However, float may also vary for other reasons.) Thus, reasonable control by the Fed of the volume of bank reserves is more difficult and less precise than its control of the monetary base; but it still can be done reasonably well.

This, however, is still not the same as control of the public's bank deposits. With shifts occurring between *types* of deposits with different reserve requirements, among banks with different reserve ratios, between United States government and private deposits,[4] as well as between interbank deposits and deposits of the nonbank public, and, with shifts in the amount of excess reserves that banks choose to hold, the stock of commercial bank liabilities is not uniquely determined by the stock of bank reserves. Thus, the Fed's control of the volume of demand deposits held by the public—or even of the aggregate of demand and other deposits so held— is far from precise.

---

[4] The Fed *should* know—in advance—of *planned* changes in the volume of government deposits in commercial banks, although it sometimes doesn't. But all such changes cannot be fully planned, nor immediately discovered.

A recent study made at the Federal Reserve Bank of St. Louis[5] showed that, on the average (over the period 1954–1973), the annual rate of growth of the monetary base, which the Fed can control, exceeded the growth rate of the money stock (M_1) in an average month by only 0.09 of a percentage point (.0009). But the standard deviation of this average difference of growth rates of monetary base and M_1 was nearly 4 percentage points (.03975).[6] Even taking a period as long as 12 months, for which the average difference between the two growth rates was 0.14 percentage points (.0014) the standard deviation of this difference was 1.09 points (.0109).[7] Stabilizing the growth of the monetary base clearly would not in the short-run fully stabilize the growth of M_1. (Nor of M_2, although this study dealt only with M_1).

A second conclusion about the supply of money is that, to *some* extent, it is not fully a "policy variable," nor even a completely exogenous variable, but is instead partly endogenous. With the Fed playing a completely passive role, the supply of money responds in some degree to changes in other macroeconomic variables that also affect the demand for money, particularly interest rates, the price level, the physical volume of activity, as well as the microdistribution of these. Thus, we can write,

$$M = M(Y, i) \qquad \left(\frac{\partial M}{\partial Y}, \frac{\partial M}{\partial i}\right) > 0$$

There are some problems (including the proper specification of econometric investigations) for which it is important to recognize this element of short-run endogeneity of the supply of money. However, in any and every modern economy, a monetary policy exists. In providing or withdrawing reserves, the authorities can always attempt to allow for systematic effects and feedbacks on the supply of money even though they may not be able to do it with perfect accuracy. Nevertheless, other than in the short run, the money supply is mainly determined by the central bank.

Thus, this writer does not consider the recognition of some endogenous element in the money supply as a matter of central importance; rather, he finds it more useful to continue to think of the money supply (in whichever variant) as basically a policy-determined, exogenous variable, recognizing, however, the central bank's *intention* to control it is subject to considerable slippage because of its inability accurately to predict (and allow for) either the endogenous feedbacks on M or the unexpected

---

[5] A. E. Burger, "The Relationship between Monetary Base and Money: How Close?" in *The Monthly Review of the Federal Reserve Bank of St. Louis*, 57 (October 1975), 3–8.

[6] Meaning that the chances were about one in three that the difference between the two rates of growth in any month might fall outside a range between +4 percentage points and −4 percentage points.

[7] Meaning that the chances were about one in three that the difference between the growth rates of monetary base and of money supply over any twelve months would fall outside a range between about +1.25 percentage points and −0.95 percentage points.

exogenous shifts in the public's demand for the various categories of monetary assets. But if the central bank allows the supply of money to decline—other than temporarily—during a recession or increase during an inflationary boom, one should assume that it intended that to happen.

THE CONDUCT OF MONETARY POLICY

We have now developed most of the concepts and relationships necessary for a fairly concise but reasonably detailed discussion of the conduct of monetary policy. Once again, we are describing institutional features relevant to the United States, and we are ignoring exceedingly important aspects concerned with *international* monetary and economic relationships.

We assume that the Fed believes it is using monetary policy to affect aggregate demand for goods and services and, in particular, to stabilize (to some degree) the growth of that demand around a path related to the growth of potential output, with appropriate attention to the effects of output and its rate of change on the price level. We further assume that, absent policy intervention, the growth of aggregate demand would not follow such a path. However, if one believes that policy intervention is instead the main source of instability, one may consider this discussion alternatively as a framework for the definition of an appropriate "non-policy," which would allow free rein to the "natural forces" maintaining economic stability. The only intellectual position for which much of this discussion is irrelevant is one that says that (for good or ill) money controls the economy, but through channels which are unknown and probably unknowable.

Inasmuch as there are substantial lags between the Fed's actions and the effects on the economy, the policy that it pursues at any time is necessarily based upon projections of what would be the state of the economy over a series of future periods, with—and without—whatever policy action it may presently contemplate. To discuss the role of monetary policy in terms of the *IS-LM* model is wholly inadequate for a great many reasons, some of which we have already noted and others which we shall soon indicate. But it can, nevertheless, serve to locate some significant relationships and problems, the inclusion of which in a more adequate model is beyond the scope of this book.

In Figure 21-1, we show a hypothetical *IS* curve, as estimated by the Fed's technicians, for some appropriate future period. (The reader should recall the discussion in Chapter 11 on what elements enter into this function.) We also show a family of *LM* curves for that period, one for each of three possible quantities of money. (For simplicity, we assume the price level independent of Y and ignore the dynamics.) If we take Y_T as the Fed's *target* level of Y for this period, it is obvious that the Fed should generate a level of M equal to M_1, which, given *IS*, will produce Y_T and i_T.

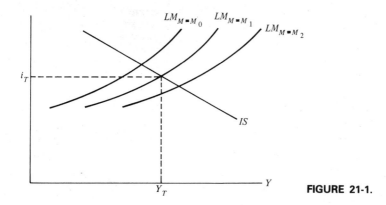

FIGURE 21-1.

There would be two general ways of going about this: (1) to operate directly on M, through supplying the monetary base that will (by the appropriate time) generate M_1, or (2) to take as a target the establishment of the equilibrium interest rate i_T, supplying whatever quantities of M prove necessary to generate and maintain that market rate of interest. If the Fed has full knowledge of the exact positions (a) of the IS curve, (b) of the LM curve for every possible value of M, and (c) of the monetary base that will prodice every value of M, it can operate either way. If it provides the monetary base that will produce M_1, the interest rate will turn out to be i_T and income will be Y_T; if it intervenes through open market operations as necessary to produce i_T, it will turn out that the money supply generated will be M_1 and the income Y_T.

In fact, however, the Fed is certain neither about the exact position of the IS curve, nor the position of the LM curve corresponding to each M, nor what monetary base is necessary to generate any particular M, all as of some particular future date. Thus, it may make considerable difference which way it proceeds.

In a well known article,[8] William Poole showed that the choice between the two general approaches might depend on where the greatest uncertainty was believed to lie. If, for example, the investment, disposable income, and consumption functions that underlie IS are known with considerable confidence, the range of (say) two "standard errors"[9] around the best estimate of the position of the IS curve might be fairly narrow. This is shown in Figure 21-2, panel a, where the "best estimate" is shown as the broken line IS_E and the range of two standard errors by IS_1 and IS_2. Suppose, however, that a much wider range of uncertainty surrounds the relationships entering the LM curve—the relationship of monetary base to

[8] W. Poole, "Optimal Choice of Monetary Policy Instruments in a Simple Stochastic Macro Model," *Quarterly Journal of Economics*, 84 (May 1970), 197–216.
[9] A measure of the estimated disperson of errors of forecast around the "best estimate."

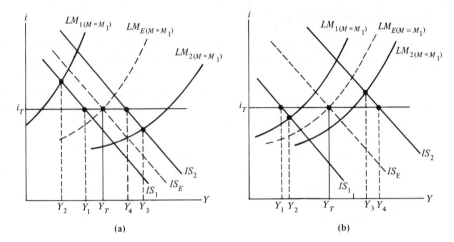

FIGURE 21-2.

M, the interest and income elasticities of the demand for money, and the position of the demand schedules. This wider range of uncertainty about the position of an *LM* curve corresponding to a quantity of money M_1 is also shown in panel a, with, again, the best estimate shown by the broken line, LM_E ($M = M_1$). Here M_1 is chosen so that the two best-estimate curves intersect at Y_T; the rather wide range of reasonable confidence is indicated by LM_1 and LM_2. It is clear that the better strategy is to fix i at i_T, with the range of probable outcomes bounded by Y_1 and Y_4.

Suppose that, instead, the Fed were to fix the monetary base at the level expected to produce M_1 and let actual M, and the interest rate, fall where they may. If worst came to worst and the "low" positions of both curves (LM_1, IS_1) should turn out be be the actual ones, Y would be at Y_2; if both curves should lie at the "high" position (LM_2, IS_2), Y would be at Y_3. The range of variation between Y_2 and Y_3 is considerably wider than that between Y_1 and Y_4. Panel b illustrates the case in which there exists greater certainty (less uncertainty) about the position of the *LM* curves than about the position of the *IS* curve. Here, if i is kept at i_T, the range of Y is between the extremes of Y_1 and Y_4; whereas if the monetary base is set to produce M_1 and LM_E, a smaller range (between Y_2 and Y_3) is obtained. In this case, it is clearly better to set the monetary base and let the interest rate fall where it may.

In recent practice, as we shall see, the Fed seems to be setting long-run and medium term targets for the growth of the money supply; but in operating to achieve these targets, it expresses its day-to-day objectives in terms of interest rates to be maintained.

The Federal Funds Market

To understand how this is done, we first need to introduce a very important additional segment of the "financial market," which up to now we have ignored: the Federal funds market. This market deals in the (usually) overnight loan of reserve balances (or their equivalent), almost exclusively among banks; the lender is, essentially, a bank with (otherwise) excess reserves, the borrower one with (otherwise) reserve deficiencies. The unit for such loans is ordinarily $1 million. This market is of of relatively recent origin, made possible by facilities for instantaneous electronic transfers of funds. Conducted through brokers, including large banks acting as brokers, it continually connects the "money desks" of the larger banks, and effectively establishes a going price (expressed as an interest rate, on an annual basis) that varies throughout the day as pressures of demand for and supply of such loans may dictate.

This rate on Federal funds (hereafter FF) is highly sensitive to Fed policy; indeed, the Fed can make the rate almost whatever it wants— especially once its intention to do so becomes clear. For, whenever the Fed buys Treasury securities (usually bills) in the open market, the seller, if not a bank, immediately deposits the proceeds of his sale in his bank; thus, whether the seller is or is not a bank, some bank's reserve balance immediately increases by the amount of the sale; such a bank is now more likely to be a seller in the FF market. If the Fed sells, the buyer's check payable to the Fed (if the buyer is not itself a bank) is almost immediately cleared, reducing his bank's reserve balance by that amount; such a bank is now more likely to be a buyer of FF. Since almost every large bank is either a buyer or seller in the FF market every day,[10] every Fed open-market sale or purchase immediately affects the amount demanded or offered in the FF market, and thus the price which will clear the market.

We now need to examine the supply and demand curves for FF to understand why they intersect, so that a market clearing price exists, and to assess their elasticity, so as to see how sensitive the FF rate may be to small changes in supply or demand, including the changes reflecting Fed open market operations. The suppliers of FF are banks that have otherwise excess reserves, even if for only a day. They could, of course, leave these reserves idle, but this sacrifices an available interest return. How great the sacrifice is depends on the FF rate; the higher that rate the less that will be left idle in the bank's own possession. If the excess is expected to be other than very temporary, the bank has other options: it can buy short-term securities, for example, Treasury bills with some days' maturity remaining. Exercise of this option of course is influenced by the relative rates on FF

---

[10] Sometimes both—for example, selling in the morning when it appears that it will have excess funds, buying in the afternoon when it finds it is short.

and Treasury bills. But, given the bill rate, the higher the FF rate the more funds will be supplied to the FF market. Alternatively, given the FF rate, the higher the bill rate the more excess reserves will be used to purchase Treasury bills. (Of course, given the possibility of arbitrage between the two markets, the two rates ordinarily move closely together.)

Banks with reserve deficiencies are buyers on the FF market. They, too, have some alternatives. They can sell short-term assets (for example, Treasury bills or other short-term securities) from their portfolios, but their decision to do so will depend on the expected duration of the reserve deficiency and on the relation between the rate earned on the bills and the FF rate—the lower the latter, the more use is made of the FF market. In addition, if worse comes to worst, they can go to the Fed's discount window, and, if the FF rate (and the cost of other alternatives) is too high, they will do so.[11]

Now it needs to be recognized that, although for any single bank, several very effective ways are available for adjusting its reserve position, for banks as a whole, there is really only one.[12] Most of the adjustments that individual banks can make in seeking added reserves—for example, selling Treasury bills or buying Federal funds—succeed only in attracting reserves from one bank to another, without changing their aggregate amount. Increased aggregate reserves to banks as a group—*at the banks' option*—are available only through the Fed's discount window.

To be sure, in the process of attempting to obtain added reserves in the FF or short-term securities market, banks will alter the interest rate for FF (as well as the rates for Treasury bills and other short-term securities). While this does not change the aggregate supply of reserves, it does let any given supply of reserves support a somewhat larger volume of deposits, through the effect of higher FF and related interest rates in mobilizing what would otherwise be held as excess reserves.

These factors provide some degree of elasticity to aggregate supply and demand curves for FF. Nevertheless, both aggregate supply and demand curves are exceedingly inelastic. This explains why the FF rate is so volatile in the absence of Fed policy to stabilize it and why the rate is so sensitive to Fed open market operations. It also explains how the FF market competes directly, through every large bank, with markets for alternative short-term financial assets, thus tying these rates closely to the FF rate. Although no single bank's sales or purchases of Treasury bills,

---

[11] Large banks have still other alternatives, but they are primarily relevant for somewhat longer term reserve deficiencies or surpluses. One is to issue (or to allow to expire without renewal) large certificates of deposit (CD's). Use of this alternative also depends on the relation of CD rates to the FF rate. However, we choose not to get into a discussion of the CD market, which would require considerable space in itself. Large banks can also borrow from, lend to, or deposit with their affiliates abroad, or deposit, withdraw, or borrow Eurodollar funds.

[12] Two, if one includes funds borrowed or loaned abroad.

commercial paper, or CD's affect these rates, their combined sales or purchases surely do.

One may well ask of what importance is the FF rate? It affects no investment or consumption decision that could alter aggregate demand. For that matter, neither does the rate on Treasury bills, which is strongly influenced by the FF rate. Another important short-term interest rate, closely competitive with bills, is that for commercial paper; it, too, has little direct effect on aggregate demand. However, Treasury bills and commercial paper do compete indirectly for wealthholders' preference (and that of financial institutions) with longer-term government and corporate bonds, and, more remotely, with shares, the supplies of which, at any time, are also fixed in aggregate amount. Other things equal, a rise or fall in the FF rate, and other short-term rates, tends to be transmitted, with diminished amplitude, to yields on other open market securities that do affect aggregate demand.

There is, however, a much more direct connection with interest rates that relate to real investment. To the extent that the Fed lowers, raises, or stabilizes the FF rate, it does so by creating (or absorbing) bank reserves through open market sales (or purchases). Increases in aggregate bank reserves lead to *multiple* increases in commercial bank lending and security purchases. Competition among banks to increase their lending on the basis of added reserves tends to reduce bank loan rates.[13] Moreover, some part of any increase in bank reserves also finds its way into the market for government securities; *ceteris paribus*, this reduces market yields on these securities and indirectly on corporate bonds. Increased business borrowing from banks means that fewer bonds need to find their way into the portfolios of wealthholders; and that, too, affects bond yields, thus further influencing that investment which is not financed by bank loans. Thus, the whole complex of rates and yields tends to move together and to respond to Fed policy.

Federal Reserve Policy and the FF Rate

As of the middle and late 1970s, the short-term monetary policy of the Fed was usually expressed in terms of a target range of $\frac{1}{4}$ to $\frac{1}{2}$ percent in the FF rate, for example, at some particular time, a rate between 5 and $5\frac{1}{2}$ percent. (We shall indicate in the next section how this target range is established.) Knowing or expecting what major supply and demand factors will be affecting banks' reserve positions and thus the FF rate, the Fed makes *planned* sales or purchases of open-market securities each day or week, in

---

[13] Since the FF rate can be thought of as the (residual) marginal cost of bank loans, loan rates may be affected from the cost side, as well as the demand side. However, this writer doubts that banks behave as short-run profit maximizers; thus the marginal cost of funds may not be very important in determining loan rates.

amounts expected more or less to hold the FF rate within the target range. However, these calculations cannot be exact; and, as we have seen, small differences can have a large effect on the rate. Thus the Fed also stands ready to, and does, sell or buy such additional open market securities as may be necessary to hold the FF rate within its target range; and this it is surely able to do. Although the target is never announced, it soon becomes evident to participants in the FF market, who then can also soon surmise if and when it has been altered.

If, instead, the Fed were neither to buy nor sell in the open market, or were to buy (and sell) at a steady rate of $X million per day or week, the FF rate would fluctuate rather violently. Its trend, if one could be discerned behind all the fluctuation, would reflect trends in the reserve positions of the banks, as the result both of the Fed's actions and of all other factors, especially as the latter are reflected in the demand for bank loans. But its day-to-day level would reflect the host of erratic factors influencing bank reserve positions, such as changes in float, changes in the volume of United States government deposits, seasonal and erratic drains of cash out of or into public circulation, seasonal and erratic fluctuations in the demand for bank loans, including those reflecting the dates for corporate tax payments or other large settlements, such as dividend payments or payments for large new stock or bond issues, and so on.

As we have seen, changes in the FF rate are quickly transmitted to other interest rates, affecting the prices of marketable short-term securities (such as Treasury bills and commercial paper). If the FF rate were allowed to reflect all of the erratic and seasonal impacts, sharp swings would be transmitted to the price of Treasury bills and commercial paper, substantially increasing the risks to dealers in such securities and forcing them to widen their margins between buying and selling prices, with possibly serious long-term costs to lenders and borrowers. Wide swings in open market interest rates may create destabilizing expectations, whereas relatively narrower fluctuations tend to engender stabilizing expectations.

These are some of the reasons given by the Fed for its policy of ironing out what it regards as meaningless and nonfunctional short-run interest rate fluctuations. But it does so, at least in the short run, by, in effect, letting the demand for bank reserves determine the supply. When the Fed stabilizes the FF rate, it is forced to supply or absorb whatever reserves the market requires.

Not all observers agree that it is either necessary or wise so to stabilize interest rates even in the short run. Friedman, in particular, argues that the Fed should simply supply each day or week a pro-rata share of whatever annual rate of growth of monetary base is calculated as necessary to produce a long run growth of M at the appropriate rate, for example, 3 percent a year, and let interest rates fall where they may. He holds that, by attempting to stabilize the FF rate, even if only on a day-to-day or week-to-week basis, the Fed tends to lose track of its long-run targets for money supply growth. On the other hand, the mere supplying of monetary base on a regular basis clearly does not mean that growth of the money supply would be regular, as we have already seen. In fact, by attempting to supply increments of monetary base on something other than a $X million per day basis, the Fed hopes to make the growth of the actual money supply rather more steady, over periods as short as 3 to 6 months, than if it adopted Friedman's advice. Nor, of course, does the Fed accept Friedman's view that the ideal rate of money growth is the same year in and year out.

However the Fed may choose to operate, the erratic and seasonal factors that affect the short-run level of bank reserves inevitably create a great deal of "noise," making it difficult for the Fed to interpret what is happening to the underlying supply and demand for money; this would be the case whether or not the Fed chose to stabilize the FF rate in the short run. It is an inescapable fact of life.

How Fed Targets are Set and Revised

Essentially, the Fed appears to set and adjust three kinds of targets (each expressed as a range): one for the long-run growth of the money supply, over a period of a year; a second for the growth of the money supply over periods of, say, 2 or 3 months; and a third for the FF rate for a period of 1 month. The long-term target ranges for money growth are now publicly reported once every 3 months, in accordance with a Congressional resolution. They are not, however, necessarily revised each 3 months. How they are set is not entirely clear. The Fed maintains a detailed economic forecast for a year or more ahead, including forecasts of key interest rate variables. One might suppose that it begins with a statement of targets for production and employment, and/or for prices, over a period of 1 or more years ahead (as well as any appropriate balance-of-payments targets).[14] Then, using its model (in effect, a greatly expanded and more detailed dynamic version of an *IS-LM* model), it estimates what key interest rates would produce the levels of investment necessary to yield the target levels of employment and production and/or prices (and/or desired balance-of-payments situation). Then it might determine, given its demand for money functions, what target rate of money growth over the year ahead would produce those interest rates (or some appropriate key or average interest rate). Surely, such calculations are made. However, it is not clear to what extent other considerations may modify the longer term money growth targets so calculated.[15]

---

[14] These targets are not necessarily the Fed's long-term goals but represent what is considered feasible and reasonable progress toward its long run goals.

[15] It should be noted that growth targets are set separately for M_1 and M_2, which surely seems redundant, inasmuch as the Fed has no tools that it uses to influence the relative movements of the concepts. (It could use its control of interest rates on time and savings deposits for this purpose, but it does not.) Thus, one or the other target is redundant or useful only for public relations—or public obfuscation.

The next step may be presumed to be the calculation of what short-run growth (range) for money supply over the next few months seems necessary to put, or keep, that growth on track toward the 12-month target already set. For example, if in recent months money has grown at a slower or faster rate than the 12-month target, the Fed will ordinarily desire to offset this with a faster or slower growth in the next few months.

Finally, a calculation is made of what level (range) of FF rate in the next few weeks is likely to produce monetary growth consistent with meeting the shorter-term money growth target. The Fed has detailed models permitting such calculations, which presumably contribute toward setting the monthly FF targets, although, given the complexity, they are not likely to be very reliable. In any case, as data accumulate on the apparent actual rate of money growth, the FF target may be revised.

It should be understood that accurate data on actual money supply growth are not available currently. Based on incomplete data from a small sample of banks, an estimate is made each week for the previous week's growth (and for the last 13 weeks' growth). Unfortunately, the weekly data are often quite inaccurate. Even monthly data, based on more complete reports and available with some lag, are often considerably revised later on, as fuller information becomes available. Thus, it would be impossible for the Fed to determine its day-to-day moves on the basis of what is happening to the money supply currently, or even what was happening very recently. And, in any case, there is enough variability from week to week and month to month that what happened recently is an extremely poor measure of what is happening now (given the same setting of its FF target). Thus, the Fed—unless it wishes to accept the Friedman prescription of an invariant rate of addition to the monetary base—probably has little option other than to proceed as it does. If this conclusion is accepted, one can then mainly criticize either its goals or the procedure used in setting them.

Such criticism is frequent. In particular, many economists believe that the Fed pays far too much attention to the short-run stability of money supply growth—even though its success in meeting its own medium term (that is, 3-month targets) has been far from spectacular. The Fed does insist that weekly and monthly fluctuations in the rate of money growth are essentially meaningless; yet, perhaps because of the strident criticisms of some monetarists, it seems willing to countenance substantial swings in interest rates over a period of a few months in pursuit of relative stability in monthly or quarterly growth rates of the money stock.

Other (nonmonetarist) critics believe that the Fed is too much influenced by the monetarists in setting its *long-term* targets, which they believe should be far more responsive to the needs of economic stabilization. At times, Fed spokesmen also seem to reflect some influence from the "rational expectations" theorists, who argue that, for example, expansionary monetary (and fiscal) policies are ineffective (or have now become ineffective) in altering the real magnitudes of output, income and employment, because the public understands that the ultimate, long-term equilibrium impact of an increase (decrease) in the growth rate of M is only an increase (decrease) in the rate of inflation. Understanding this, they respond to the policy change in ways that will bring about this result almost instantaneously. Thus, policy is useless.[16] One may hope that the traces of such influence on Fed policy, thought to be observed in 1975–1977, represent a transitory aberration.

INTEREST THEORY RECONSIDERED

In the Keynesian-classical synthesis model, two apparently contradictory theories of the rate of interest are successfully blended: (1) the classical theory that makes the equilibrium interest rate the price that reconciles flows of saving and investment, each a function of i (at a full-employment level of income assumed to be guaranteed by perfect price flexibility with a fixed stock of money) together with (2) the initial Keynesian theory that makes the equilibrium interest rate the price which equates the fixed stock of money and the demand for it, the latter seen to be a function both of i and of PY. These two requirements are simultaneously met in a world in which P is not fully flexible, downward at least, and in which Y is thus also a variable, determined by I as a function of i and C as a function of Y.

This synthesis model, we recall, was analyzed in terms of a financial structure in which, in addition to (government) money, there was only one financial asset (a standard bond), with a single, uniform market yield ("the" interest rate). All investment (and government deficits) were financed by issuing such bonds. Wealthholders individually or in the aggregate chose in what proportions to hold each asset (money or bonds) on the basis of the current yield of the bond and of their transactions requirements for money. Although the public could not change the supply of either asset, the efforts of individuals to change their holdings did alter the price of one in terms of the other, until all were satisfied with their actual holdings.

In the last two chapters, instead, we have been discussing a very different world: one with many financial assets for individuals and businesses to hold. These include assets issued by businesses (various private debts and equities), relative supplies of which are partly responsive to relative demand; many assets issued only by financial intermediaries, of which supplies are highly responsive to demand (and to Fed policy); and some issued by governments (government money and government debts,

---

[16] As noted earlier, since the long-run equilibrium is surely also a full-employment equilibrium the "rational expectations" theorist must believe that full employment, too, always exists.

supplies of which are responsive mostly to policy but partly to relative yields). It is a world in which much investment is financed not by the sale of securities to individual wealthholders but by loans from, or securities sold to, financial intermediaries; one in which borrowers (*including* financial intermediaries) may choose among several varieties of liabilities to issue, depending on relative yields, and wealthholders may choose among numerous kinds of financial assets to hold, of which bonds and money are only two.

In this world there is not one "yield" but many, some fixed by law, others variable; some contractually guaranteed, others not; some changing sluggishly, others highly volatile; and so on. One key interest rate (that for FF) is determined in a market in which the only participants are financial intermediaries. In this world, every yield depends on a host of characteristics of the lenders and borrowers who typically issue or hold each asset, on the quantity of the asset outstanding, and on the yields on all other kinds of financial assets, explicit or implicit.

Our first task in this last major section of Chapter 21 is to see whether and how we can reconcile our description of this world with that of the *IS-LM* model, and what, if any, are important, substantive differences. Subsequent tasks will be to consider a particular dimension of yield variation which up to now we have ignored: that by duration of loan contract. And finally, we must see what is the counterpart of Keynes' speculative demand for money in this more realistic world.

The Interest Rate and the Supply and Demand for Money

In the last section, we described how monetary policy was conducted in this more realistic world. Let us begin by seeing how that compares with our earlier description of monetary policy in the two-asset world.

In that earlier description, if the central bank wished to stimulate the economy, it bought bonds on the open market, thus substituting money in the hands of the public for some of the bonds previously held. The resulting increased scarcity of bonds relative to money, given wealthholders' attitudes toward holding wealth in each form (including their interest rate expectations), would bid up prices of bonds in terms of money, reducing the yields necessary to be paid on *new* bond issues. The result: more investment and a higher Y. However, the effect described would be significantly limited by the feedback of higher Y on the demand for money.

Compare that with our description of how the Fed might stimulate the economy in our multi-asset world. It would lower its target rate for FF, supplying by open market purchases enough additional bank reserves each day or week (causing banks to bid down the FF rate) to keep the FF rate at its new target level. The fall in the FF rate would, through influencing rates for Treasury bills and other short-term assets which banks hold, tend to bid down still other open-market interest rates, many of them relevant to certain kinds of business investment. More importantly, the added reserves would permit banks to increase their lending and security purchases by a multiple of the reserve increase, thus bidding down bank loan rates, further bidding up prices of Treasury bills, and indirectly reducing yields on other securities used to finance investment—both those kinds of investment alternatively financed by bank loans, and kinds ordinarily financed otherwise. With the higher level of investment, Y would increase.

Although there are some resemblances between these two accounts, there are also some striking differences. For example, in the first account we analyzed the determination of the interest rate in terms of *stocks* of assets to be held; in the later account, we analyzed it in terms of *flow* variables: flows of bank reserves, of loans and of the demand for loans, and so on. The first was an equilibrium analysis in which—in the new, as in the initial equilibrium—the money stock was constant ($\Delta M = 0$). The second (and, at best, only implicitly) was an equilibrium analysis in which—in the new, as in the initial equilibrium—the FF rate, or perhaps the flow of the Fed's open market purchases, was constant, as *might* also then be the longer term rate of change of M (but not at zero). Obviously we are not describing the same events.

Suppose we try to tell the second story in terms consistent with the first. That is, let us start with an economy in full macroequilibrium, in which a given constant level of aggregate I is induced by a given constant level and pattern of all those interest rates relevant to investment (bank loan rates, corporate bond rates, mortgage rates, stock prices and yields, and so on), which in turn are consistent with constant levels of the interest rates relevant basically to financial decisions (deposit rates, FF rate, Treasury bill rates, and so on). Given the attitudes of wealthholders, we can assume, although we cannot easily demonstrate it, that these rates of interest would all remain constant (in the short-run, at least) in the presence of some constant level of bank reserves and of constant outstanding deposits, bank loans, and bank security portfolios. Thus, changes in monetary base and in the money supply would be zero.[17] Prices and yields of all open market securities are also such that wealthholders and financial intermediaries alike are satisfied with their holdings of each; and businesses and individuals also have just the amount of money they want at the existing level of income and of transactions and the existing yields on

[17] We are obviously forced to ignore the influence of seasonal and erratic factors or else assume that the Fed stabilizes the FF rate by alternately supplying or withdrawing reserves, and that (contrary to fact) it knows what FF rate would be consistent with a zero *trend* in aggregate reserves.

all financial assets which they hold or might hold. Given the level of investment (and the government budget and tax rates) and the consumption function, Y is at a constant, equilibrium level.[18]

Now we suppose that the Fed wishes to raise the level of Y and employment through a stimulative monetary policy. It thus lowers, *temporarily*, its target FF rate, and purchases enough securities to make its new target rate effective, in the process increasing the money supply. At some later time it again raises its FF target rate to the point that, when everything has again settled down, no further open market operations are necessary to maintain that rate. Thus, the monetary base, bank reserves, and the stock of M will again be constant, although now at a higher level.

At this new equilibrium, when established, most interest rates will be lower than initially, but by quite different amounts. The stock of bank reserves will be larger, supporting a larger but constant stock of deposits and a larger but constant stock of outstanding bank loans (new loans equalling repayments) and of bank holdings of securities. Because the stocks of money and of most other financial assets are now larger (although in different proportions) there will be a new set of interest rates (mostly lower) and some changes in the proportions among the assets and the liabilities of different intermediaries. Investment will be higher, as will income. At the new income level, the new level and structure of interest rates, and with the altered stocks of financial assets, every wealthholder will again be satisfied with his portfolio, and every firm and individual will have the amount of money desired at the new prevailing income and set of financial yields.[19]

It is clear that, in broadest outline, the two accounts are now basically similar. To be sure, in realistic applications, we are not often interested in the strictly comparative statics analysis of two or more positions of full equilibrium, especially when equilibrium is defined in terms of a stationary Y, in a world of growing Y_P. And an analysis in terms of flows rather than stocks does come more naturally for the discussion of dynamic and disequilibrium situations. But the two stories can be, at least broadly, reconciled. However, looking more carefully, there are some significant

[18] To be sure, if the constant rate of investment or government deficit is other than zero, there will still be slow accumulation of many real and financial stocks—of physical assets, of total wealth, and of the securities by which the investment (or deficit) has been financed. If, however, bank reserves, money stock, and outstanding bank loans are all constant (as assumed in defining equilibrium), there would then be a tendency for many interest rates gradually to rise, at different rates, which might not only cause various financial intermediaries and individual wealthholders to alter their assets and liabilities but would also presumably tend to reduce investment, income, and so on. These longer term stock effects might, however, appropriately be ignored in an essentially short-run analysis, just as they are commonly ignored in the *IS-LM* analysis.

[19] Once again, there will be some further, long-run effects of stock accumulation corresponding to I (or government deficit) > 0; but, again, we can ignore these in a relatively short-run analysis.

differences of substance; and we see that the simpler analysis did not tell the whole story.

Shortcomings of the *IS-LM* Analysis

1. In a world of commercial banks, with fractional reserve requirements, the stock of money does not increase dollar-for-dollar with central bank open market purchases; rather, a dollar of open market purchases creates several dollars of additional money.

2. Correspondingly, instead of the Fed taking out of the hands of wealthholders a dollar's worth of bonds for each dollar of Fed open market purchases, we see that, through the response of bank lending to a change in reserves, several dollars' worth of securities (if we can call IOU's to banks securities) are taken out of wealthholders' holdings (or potential holdings), some into the central bank, but mostly into the portfolios of commercial banks.

3. Whereas in the original account, an open market purchase did not itself finance any investment but only lowered the rate of interest at which new bonds could be issued, we now see that commercial banks, serving as an extension of the central bank, put some of the central bank's new money into circulation by *directly financing investment.* (To the extent that banks merely buy open market securities on the basis of new reserves, the *mechanism* remains the same as before: security prices are bid up, inducing businesses to issue more of them; only the amount of securities absorbed from the public's holding by each dollar of open market purchases—and the effect on their yield—is multiplied.)

4. Whereas, in the previous account, the central bank's open market purchases absorbed from the public some fraction of its undifferentiated supply of all securities (there being only one kind), we now see that, because the central bank buys only one type of security among many (government debts, mostly bills) and because the commercial banks, which multiply their effects, absorb mainly two types (bank loans and selected government obligations), *relative* security yields are *inevitably* altered as the quantity of money changes, with necessarily some further effects on the macroeconomy.

5. Instead of there being a sharp difference of kind between money and all other financial assets, the line between money and other financial assets is, in fact, hard to draw. There are "near-moneys," which possess various but not all of the properties of the original concept of money as cash or equivalent. Deposits other than demand deposits have fixed values, convertability almost as instantaneous as that of demand deposits, but pay a positive yield. And the central bank's provision of additional reserves also affects the quantities of some of these near moneys—some more or less directly, others indirectly. For example, an increase in bank reserves lowers interest yields on most open market securities, but (because of

ceiling rates) it lowers them less or not at all on the time and savings deposits of commercial banks and the similar liabilities of other intermediaries. This increases the demand for and thus the supply of such near moneys—in part at the expense of the increase in narrowly-defined money. But the line between the near monies, the quantities and prices of which the Fed's policy considerably influences, and those less near, that it influences less, is inevitably arbitrary.

6. Whereas the meaning of *the* interest rate, and of its impact on investment was clear in the *IS-LM* model, there are now many interest rates, some of no direct significance for investment. In many cases, variation of some *relative interest rate* is more significant—whether for the supply or demand for assets, or for investment—than is variation in the absolute level of any single interest rate. Examples of such relative interest rates are the relationship of mortgage yields to (fixed) savings deposit rates; the relationship of bank loan rates to the FF rate, the rate on CD's, or the discount rate; or the relationship between rates on short-term and long-term financial assets (see next section).

7. Whereas the supply of money (however defined) is taken in the *IS-LM* analysis to be an exogenous and policy-determined variable, it is in fact not fully controllable by the central bank. To some extent it is endogenous and responds to changes in the demand for it, and to some extent it responds to many exogenous and accidental factors.

Given statements 4, 5, 6, and 7, it would appear that the *IS-LM* model focuses excessive importance on one particular financial asset, money—especially in its narrowest definition, M_1. A given constant level

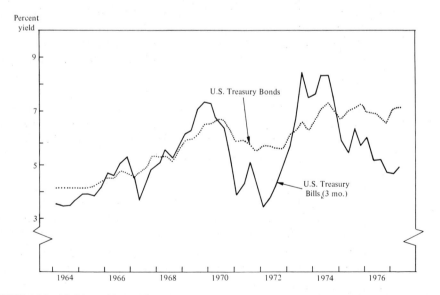

FIGURE 21-3   Yields on United States Treasury bills and bonds, 1964–1977.

of this variable is not uniquely associated with any particular level of I or Y or even, necessarily, with stability of I or Y. One is forced to wonder whether the economist's concentration on M may not be the result only of the fact that our theories were first developed in a world with few financial intermediaries and few types of assets. Or perhaps it is because we now have a system of central banks adapted to the control of this one asset but would have to develop new institutional forms to permit public control or influence on other key quantities. Such speculations are appropriately raised by the more detailed and realistic analyses, but completely hidden in the *IS-LM* model.

The Term Structure of Interest Rates[20]

Since first introducing a multiplicity of financial assets to replace our original two-asset assumption, we have referred frequently both to the variety of yield levels that exists at any given time and to the tendency for interest rates or yields on most financial assets to move together, in either direction, but by quite different amounts, in response to various economic forces which may most directly affect any one or a few of them. However, we have deliberately refrained until now from discussing the systematic relationship that exists among yields, and among changes in yields, along one of the most important dimensions of variation among financial assets, namely, their term to maturity. This term extends from 1 day in the case of FF contracts to perpetuity for consols or equities. The systematic differences and variations of interest rates by term to maturity is one of the most important regularities involving financial assets, and one that has major implications for the performance of the macroeconomy, often over-looked even by economists who discuss the phenomenon.

The regularity which needs to be explained can be most easily presen-ted in Figure 21-3, which shows the quarterly patterns of average interest yield on Treasury bills and on long-term government bonds over the 13-year period, 1964–1977. What it essentially shows is that, in periods when interest rates are relatively low, bill rates are well below bond rates; but when interest rates are relatively high, bill rates exceed bond rates. Thus bill rates fluctuate far more widely than bond rates. Since the bor-rower is the same, the main reason for the differences between the two interest rates must relate to the term of the loan contract.

---

[20] For a fuller discussion of this subject, along with references to the basic literature, see W. L. Smith, *Debt Management in the United States*, Study Paper No. 19, prepared for the consideration of the Joint Economic Committee, in connection with the study of Employment, Growth, and Price Levels (86th Congress, 2nd Session, 1960), especially pp. 81–88; partly reprinted in W. L. Smith and R. L. Teigen, *Readings in Money, National Income, and Stabilization Policy*, 3rd ed. (R. D. Irwin, 1974), pp. 432–437; and the further references given therein. For a later view, see F. Modigliani and R. Sutch, "Innovations in Interest Rate Policy," *American Economic Review*, 56 May 1966), 178–197.

What reasons might explain why securities of any given type, but of different maturities, sell, at any one time, at prices which reflect systematically different yields? One reason might be that, the more distant the repayment of principal, the greater the opportunity for wide swings to occur in prices, which many lenders (being "risk averters") may prefer to avoid, unless recompensed by higher yields. Further, there is a greater chance that events not now foreseeable might threaten default, also increasing the riskiness of longer term securities. Both factors might make many or most wealthholders require higher yields on longer maturities and accept lower yields on shorter maturities. Moreover, many borrowers—if borrowing for long-term investment—would be willing to pay some premium in yield to obtain the protection of distant maturities. This, too, might suggest a tendency for long yields to exceed short. And, indeed, between about 1930 and 1955, such a consistent pattern did appear to exist in the United States: long yields were almost invariably in excess of short (although the margin of difference varied).

On the other hand, none of the reasons suggested is a fully compelling argument for higher yields on long-term securities, for each is a *ceteris paribus* argument, and *ceteris* may not always be *paribus*. Moreover, the years both before 1930 and since 1955 (as Figure 21-3 clearly shows) provide many examples of periods in which yields are systematically lower for longer than for shorter maturities, and this has been the case pretty much across the entire range of maturities.

Today, it is believed by most economists that the *main* factor affecting relative yields according to maturity is prevailing expectations regarding future changes in interest rates. And this can explain both why, at times, yields may rise with maturity and, at other times, yields may decline with longer maturities.

Any systematic relationship among yields by term to maturity shows up most clearly when we compare obligations that are alike in all respects other than term. The best example is yields on United States government obligations, which are originally issued in terms ranging from 13 weeks (the shortest bills) to bonds with terms of 25 years or more. Since such securities have been issued at various dates in the past, at any given time there is a more or less continuous range of outstanding maturities on government obligations, ranging from issues expiring next week, to issues due many years in the future. A yield pattern generally similar to that for United States government securities at any given time runs through all other obligations, but is considerably attenuated when it involves the obligations of different creditors, different contractual relationships, different tax status, and so on. Thus, it is easiest to illustrate yield pattern in the government market.

Figure 21-4 shows "yield curves" for United States government securities on three different dates during the 1960s: September 29, 1961; September 30, 1965; and September 30, 1969. Curve a (September 1969)

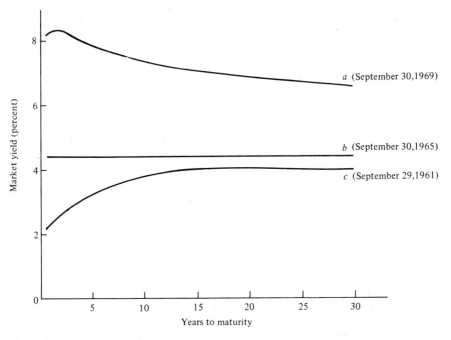

FIGURE 21-4   Yield curves on United States Treasury Securities, by time of maturity, three dates in the 1960s.

represents a period of intense boom, and inflationary pressure, at which time the Fed was working very hard to restrict the growth of the money supply. Curve c (September 1961) represents a period of recession, with the Fed pursuing a relatively "easy" monetary policy. And curve b (September 1965) represents a period of prosperity but not boom, with the Fed neither actively promoting easy money, nor attempting actively to tighten credit.[21]

All three periods preceded the more recent experience with sharp inflation and record-breaking interest rates, which may have somewhat

---

[21] To illustrate the proposition that similar rate structures applied in the private sector, the following table shows average yields on prime commercial paper (4 to 6 months maturities), and Moody's Aaa corporate bond yields during the same months:

	Commercial paper	Moody's Aaa bonds
September 1961	3.05	4.45
September 1965	4.38	4.52
September 1969	8.48	7.14

altered wealthholders' and investors' views of "normal" rate levels. During the 1960s, however, one might suppose that investors' expectations regarding the long-term average of future interest rates were essentially the same at all three dates.

In 1961, during the recession, most wealthholders and their professional advisers surely assumed (correctly) that current interest rates were low relative to "normal," and thus would probably soon rise; during the subsequent prosperity (1965) but before the boom, they probably assumed that rates were about normal; during the boom, almost everyone assumed (correctly) that rates were above normal and in the near future would fall.

But why should these different expectations generate the characteristically different yield patterns? Consider first the recession case (curve c). If interest rates are historically low, and are thus generally expected to rise, this means (indeed, it is only another way of saying) that security prices are high and expected to fall. But how much they will fall depends mainly on their term to maturity. A Treasury bill, due in 13 weeks or less, will be paid off at face value in the very near future. Its price can never be far from its principal value. To be sure, when interest rates are very high, prices of newly issued bills are lower than in periods of easy money, but not very much.[22]

In contrast, the repayment of principal on a recently-issued 20-year bond is far away; the present value of that repayment is quite different at even moderately different interest rates. The present value of the more distant coupons also changes considerably at a different interest rate.[23]

Why, then, are current yields so much higher for securities with distant maturities than for those with near-term maturities when yields are expected to rise? Because, in order to induce the holders of the distant maturities (who could, instead hold near maturities) to own the distant ones, their current yields must be sufficiently higher than yields on the near ones to offset the expected larger decline in their prices.

Consider, for instance, a consol now selling at a price that yields 7 percent, but is expected to yield 7.2 percent a year from now. Suppose its annual coupon is $1,000. To yield 7 percent it is now selling for $14,286. A year from now, with its expected 7.2 percent yield, its price would be $13,889, a capital loss of $397 over the year. Combined with a coupon payment of $1,000, this represents a net return for the year of $603, which

---

[22] Bills are without coupon payment and are auctioned at prices that are below principal value, with the difference between price and principal representing the interest return. For a return of 8 percent, the initial sale price of a $10,000 bill will be around $9,800; for a return of 4 percent, around $9,902. The difference is around $102, or about 1 percent of the price. At the end of 13 weeks, the price in each case rises to $10,000.

[23] For example, a $10,000 bond, with 20 years to maturity and an annual coupon of $800, will be selling for around $10,000 in order to yield 8 percent; at around $15,436 in order to yield 4 per cent. The difference is around $5,436, or about 54 percent of the lower price or 35 percent of the higher one. (Compare footnote 22.)

works out to an expected net yield of 4.22 percent on the bond at its current price of $14,286.

Is it prudent to hold this bond? That depends on the alternatives. Suppose that a new Treasury bill now sells at issuance for $9,896, and will be redeemed for $10,000 in 13 weeks, thus yielding $104 over 13 weeks (and capable of being replaced by other treasury bills as each matures, so that no capital loss is suffered as rates rise). A yield of $104 over 13 weeks on a $9,896 investment also represents a current annual yield of about 4.22 percent. Thus, given the expectation of the fall in price of the consol, the two investments—the consol and the bill—provide essentially the same rate of net return; investors might well be neutral as between them, given their expectations of higher interest rates. Securities of intermediate terms between consol and bill, in order to be equivalent in net yield to the consol and the bill, would sell at current yields intermediate between the 7.0 percent of the consol and the 4.22 percent of the bill.[24]

Why must their net yields, after taking account of the capital loss from the expected decline in security prices, be essentially equivalent? Because, if they were not, it would pay holders to sell those with lower yields, at their present excessive prices, and buy those with higher yields, at their current bargain prices; the readiness of market participants to make such adjustments will keep the prices in line. This explains how a yield curve such as c can reflect the expectation of rising rates.

Similar reasoning supports the existence of pattern a, given the expectation that yields will be lower (prices higher) later on. And, if there is no prevailing expectation of any price change, there are no net expectations of capital gain or loss; thus, to be competitive, all must sell at essentially the same current yield (curve b).[25]

This seems to be an adequate explanation of the fact that short-term yields vary considerably more over any cycle in interest rates than do longer yields. Indeed, one can conclude rather firmly that, when short rates

[24] If the 13 week bill were instead selling at issuance for $9,850, it would yield $150, equivalent to an annual rate of 6.23 percent. Clearly, that would have been a preferable option to the consol with current yield of 7.0 percent, and no one would be willing to hold consols with that yield.

[25] Although it is not often noted, speculation on the *issuers'* side of the security market also contributes to maintaining the yield patterns which reflect expectations of rising or of falling interest rates. For example, when interest rates are low and expected to rise, it will pay businesses that have future plans to invest and will wish to finance that investment with long-term bonds, to borrow long *now*, in advance of need, and to lend the funds at short-term while awaiting the time to begin construction. The extra "speculative" issues of long-term bonds tend to raise yields in the long market, whereas the flow of the proceeds into the short-term market tends to bid down yields there. Conversely, when investors see current long-term rates as high relative to those expected later, it may pay them to borrow at short-term to finance their current investment projects (even though short-term rates are very high), expecting to get a lower yield on long-term bonds issued later. This, again, sustains the yield pattern of higher short-term than long-term yields.

are generally below long rates, rates as a whole are expected to rise—and the reverse; and this may be helpful in identifying any general changes in expectations about the "normal" level of interest rates, whether engendered by expectations of faster inflation, or whatever other reason.[26]

Keynes' Speculative Demand for Money Revisited

It will be recalled that Keynes used wealthholders' interest rate expectations to explain the interest elasticity of the demand for money, which was crucial to his rejection of the *quantity theory*. Here we have used interest-rate expectations to explain the term-structure of interest rates. Can they explain both? Is there any relationship between the two phenomena? We shall show that the term-structure of interest rates is the correct implication of speculation and that it cannot explain the interest elasticity of the demand for money—at least in a world of multiple financial assets. But we shall also show that the term-structure and the speculative demand for money are essentially the same phenomenon, and that the important implications for the economy that Keynes drew from his analysis hold up even more positively for a multiple-asset economy.

Keynes saw wealthholders confronted with a choice of holding either barren money balances or interest yielding long-term bonds; there was no intermediate alternative. And he showed that, given a variety of interest rate expectations on the part of wealthholders, *the* interest rate must settle at that point at which the demand for money, both for transactions and speculative reasons, just equalled the given supply. At any lower rate of interest (higher level of bond prices), there would be an excess demand for money to hold by those who, given their interest rate expectations, feared capital loss in excess of coupon return. At any higher interest rate (lower bond price) level, there would be an excess demand for bonds, with the public holding more money than it wished to hold. Some holders of the excess balances would seek to become bondholders, driving up bond prices until equilibrium was achieved. At the equilibrium interest rate, everyone who, given his interest rate expectations, thought bonds the superior asset was in fact a bondholder, and everyone who thought money a better alternative held money.

Keynes' theory of the speculative demand for money can well be supplemented by that of Tobin, who explained that many wealthholders

---

[26] The theory of term structure expounded above emphasizes expectations with respect to the long-term rate (and the consequent capital gains and losses expected on long-term securities). The reason for this emphasis is to make clear the tie to Keynes' theory of the speculative demand for money (see section which follows). It is far more common, however, to emphasize expectations with respect to the short-term rate, and to neglect the tie to Keynes' theory. This is the case, for example, in the classic first clear statement of the expectational theory of the term structure, as presented by J. R. Hicks in his *Value and Capital* (Oxford University Press, 1946), Chapter 11. However, the substance is the same, whichever way it is presented.

might hold (idle) money balances, apart from any expectation of rising bond prices, in order to dilute their exposure to the mere *risk* of capital loss (or gain) on bonds, but that the amount of such balances would be smaller as progressively higher interest yields progressively overbalanced wealth-holders' aversion to the risk of bond price changes.

However, it is clear that neither analysis fits an economy with multiple financial assets. Once we admit the existence of a second interest-yielding asset with fixed (or even with nearly fixed) market values, Keynes' story collapses—and so does Tobin's. Suppose the third asset to be a savings account or a government savings bond, with a low but positive interest rate and a fixed price. Those who feared capital losses on bonds at current interest rates (or who were merely averse to the risk of price variation in either direction) could always hold, instead, the savings account or the savings bond, gaining in that way both the protection against capital loss (or price fluctuation) which they sought, and, at the same time, a positive yield. And they should, *in all circumstances*, prefer this to idle money balances.

For that three-asset world, Keynes' (or Tobin's) theory might explain the demand for savings accounts or savings bonds, but not the actual demand for money nor the interest rate on bonds. We could, to be sure, adapt Keynes' theory (or Tobin's) to the explanation of the equilibrium relationship between bond interest rates and savings account (or savings bond) rates, a primitive "term structure" of interest rates, but it would not explain the absolute level of either rate.

The third explanation previously given for the interest elasticity of the demand for money was the Baumol-Tobin explanation of the increasing costs (in terms of time, brokerage, and inconvenience) involved in economizing on transactions balances by holding *the* other asset, bonds. Given the supply of money, *the* equilibrium (bond) interest rate was determined by the increasing cost schedule of holding more bonds and less money.

The modern **portfolio theory** presented in this and the previous chapter deals, instead, with a multi-asset world. In a sense, it can accommodate all three of these theories, using them to help explain some interest rate differentials. But only the last (the Baumol-Tobin interest-elastic transactions demand) contributes significantly to the explanation of the demand for money, *per se*, or to the explanation of the absolute level of any interest rates.

The portfolio theory holds that every financial asset, including money, is to some degree a possible substitute for every other in wealthholders' preference; considered as liabilities, each asset (including even demand deposits) is a substitute for one or more others for issuance by some or many borrowers (or financial intermediaries). Thus, relative interest yields, including yields relative to the zero yield on money, reflect the balance of net advantage/disadvantage (other than yield) both to issuers and holders of the asset, and the relative costs to lenders and borrowers (or, often more importantly, the costs to financial intermediaries) required by the issuance or ownership of various quantities of each kind of asset (including the costs of time, brokerage, and inconvenience involved in economizing on money balances), and on the differing capital gains or losses involved in any expected future changes in yields.

In principle, then, the demand for money depends inversely on the yield of every alternative asset (liability). But, in fact, it must depend mainly on the yields on those assets which most closely resemble money— including time and savings accounts in commercial banks and elsewhere, savings and loan shares, CD's, Treasury bills, savings bonds. The higher are these yields, the more it pays money holders to economize on money balances. But the demand for money does *not* depend significantly on the interest rate expectations of holders or potential holders of long-term, variable-price securities such as bonds or stocks. Rather, these expectations determine the maturity structure of interest rates, tied (at the short end of the spectrum) to the yields on the "near-money" assets.

If we have lost Keynes' speculative demand for money as an explanation for the interest yields that affect investment, does this mean that the important conclusions that Keynes drew from his speculative demand for money about the failure of the classical full-employment equilibrium, or about the limitations of monetary policy, also are lost? Not at all. Keynes used his speculative and interest-elastic demand for money to explain why, for example, with an unfavorable shift in the investment schedule, the interest rate failed to fall far enough to equate S and I at the original income level; why either Y or P (or both) would have to fall instead in order to equate S and I; and why, given less-than-perfect downward flexibility of wages and prices, a drop in investment demand created unemployment.

In its new role as an explanation of the term structure of interest rates, the speculative behavior of owners or potential owners of long-term, variable price securities remains an important limitation on the self-adjusting properties of the macroeconomy. Assume, as is surely the case, that the bulk of investment needs to be financed on a long-term basis, or, at least, that investors have strong reasons for *preferring* such financing for power plants, factories, houses, office buildings, tankers, heavy machinery, and so on. (One can hardly imagine Con Edison financing a new nuclear generating plant by issuing commercial paper or borrowing from banks!) This means that fixed investment decisions are closely related to stock and bond yields.

When there is a drop in investment demand and income declines, reducing the demand for money, interest rates fall all right, but they fall mainly for short-term securities. Given the interest rate expectations of lenders and borrowers, wealthholders could not be persuaded to hold long-term bonds at prices so high that they would soon have to fall. Bond prices do rise somewhat, but not nearly enough to stabilize investment.

Instead, the bulk of the interest rate decline arising from a reduced transactions demand for money—or from an increased supply of money created as monetary policy might attempt to fight off recession—shows up in sharp declines in the FF rate, much lower rates for Treasury bills, commercial paper, short-term Treasury and municipal issues, long-term government or industrial bonds close to maturity, bank loans, CD's, savings and time deposit accounts (if conditions become easy enough that these fall below their legal ceilings), and so on.

These rates fall low enough that the extra money gets held, somewhere—or that it doesn't get created (if the fall in the FF and other short-term rates causes banks not to bother to use, or to lend to other banks, moderate quantities of excess reserves).

But there is no significant response of higher investment (or reduced saving) to *these* rate reductions. Thus, the extra money does not (as classical economists and rigid monetarists assume) all get absorbed into the increased transactions balances of a stronger economy. It remains idle, because short-term interest rates are too low to make it worth while to economize more effectively on money balances. Thus, in a multiple-asset world, the explanation of the interest rates that affect the demand for money itself turns out to be the one that Baumol (and Tobin) provided and not that of Keynes.

It is only in an imaginary world of just two financial assets, money and a standard bond used to finance all investment and deficits, that the speculative and transaction factors that affect choices among financial assets are *both* brought to bear on the choice between bonds and money. Once there exist intermediate assets, the Baumol-Tobin interest elasticity of the transactions demand mainly explains the demand for the transactions medium, but then Keynes' speculative demand contributes very significantly to explaining the *relative* demands for the near-money assets versus the non-money assets whose maturities range out to the stocks and bonds that finance most long-term investment.

If, to obtain the great *didactic advantages of a simple macro model*, with no assets intermediate between bonds and money, we use interest rate expectations and speculative adjustments thereto, or risk aversion, to explain the substantial positive slope of an *LM* curve, it is probably a defensible simplification, catching much of the essence of a fuller model. But for those who make their living in the financial markets, and for those responsible for fiscal and monetary policy decisions and those who advise them, such a model is of little direct use or relevance. Multi-equation macroeconometric models of the financial sector of the economy are needed, which incorporate many types of assets and rates of return, dynamic to allow for expectations and lags as well as for the growth of financial stocks; models which build in the multiple legal and institutional constraints, and which incorporate alternative settings for each of the several policy tools that are available. Considerable progress has been made in constructing such models; but the results are as yet far from satisfactory. This is yet another item on the long list of unfinished assignments for macroeconomics.

REVIEW QUESTIONS

1. "The supply of money is neither fully a policy variable nor a completely exogenous variable, but is partly endogenous." In what sense is it "endogenous" and what implications does this endogeneity have for monetary policy?

2. What would be the *immediate effect* of each of the following transactions, taken by itself, on (i) bank reserves; (ii) the narrow money supply (M_1); (iii) the broader money supply (M_2)?

(a) The Fed buys a Treasury bill from a member bank; from an individual.

(b) An individual withdraws $50 in cash from his savings account in a commercial bank; in a savings bank.

(c) A bank replenishes its supply of currency by drawing on its reserve deposit at its regional Reserve Bank.

(d) A depositor withdraws $20 from his demand deposit in a commercial bank.

(e) A member bank borrows from the Fed, being credited in its account with the Fed.

(f) A bank with excess reserves makes a business loan.

3. In order to achieve its target level of Y, the Fed might adopt either an interest rate policy or a money stock policy. However, except in a very special circumstance, it makes considerable difference which policy it chooses to employ.

(a) Explain what is meant by an interest rate policy, and by a money stock policy.

(b) Under what special circumstances would the Fed have no reason to choose one policy over the other?

(c) Explain why one policy is more effective than the other under another circumstance.

4. What is the Federal funds rate and what is its key role in the operation of monetary policy?

5. "In a boom period interest rates ordinarily rise for securities of all maturities, while in recession periods they normally decline for all maturities. However, the changes in interest rates are typically of different amplitude for different maturities."

(a) Describe the typical pattern of changes in interest rates for different maturities.

(b) Explain and illustrate how these differential movements of rates in different maturity ranges can be explained by reference to patterns of interest rate expectations.

6.

(a) Why is the term structure of interest rates important?

(b) Why does the expectation (or fear) of capital gains and losses on long-term securities fail to explain the demand for money if there also exist short-term securities such as Treasury bills?

(c) On what interest rates does the demand for money mainly depend, and why?

SELECTED REFERENCES

R. L. Teigen, "The Demand for and Supply of Money," in W. L. Smith and R. L. Teigen, *Readings in Money, National Income and Stabilization Policy* (R. D. Irwin, 3rd ed., 1974), pp. 68–103.

(A first-rate empirical study of demand and supply schedules.)

R. S. Holbrook and H. T. Shapiro, "The Choice of Optimal Intermediate Targets," *American Economic Review*, 60 (May 1970), 40–47.

(An important analysis of monetary policy choice under uncertainty.)

F. Modigliani and R. Sutch, "The Term Structure of Interest Rates: A Re-examination of the Evidence," *Journal of Money, Credit and Banking*, 1 (February 1969), 112–120.

(An excellent empirical study of the term structure of interest rates, providing support for the expectational hypothesis.)

J. M. Keynes, *The General Theory of Employment, Interest, and Money* (Harcourt Brace, 1936), Chapter 17, "The Essential Properties of Interest and Money." (Keynes' further speculations about the nature of money and the reasons for interest; not for the timid reader.)

Index

Acceleration principle. *See* Investment

Ackley, G., 181n, 242, 406n, 440n, 457, 487n, 492n, 494n, 498n, 514n, 526n, 529n, 530, 539n, 665n

Administered prices, 490–492, 494–495

Aggregation problems, 15–21, 101–106, 205–207, 537–539, 554–556, 561–562, 623–625

Allen, R. G. D., 16n

Almon, S., 585n

Andersen, L., 410–414, 421

Andersen-Jordan model, 411–414

Anderson, W. H. L., 650, 667

Ando, A., 410n, 540n, 556, 558, 573

Andrews, P. W. S., 667

"Average propensity to consume," 167

"Average propensity to save," 167

Bach, G. L., 530

Bailey, M. J., 59

Bailey, M. N., 496

Balance sheets and national wealth, 49–57, 686–689

Balanced-budget multiplier, 195–197

Banks. *See* Central bank; Commercial banks

Baumol, W. J., 231n, 242, 306, 321, 675, 727, 729

Bischoff, C., 655–659

Blinder, A. S., 411n, 413, 422

Bosworth, B., 655n

Brazer, H., xi

Break, G., 411n

Bregger, J. E., 78

Brown, E. C., 241

Brumberg, R., 540

Buchanan, J. M., 392n

Budget studies. *See* Consumption

"Built-in stabilization," 201–207, 209n

Bulow, J. I., 508n

Business fixed investment, in national income accounting, 37

Butters, J. K., 241

Cagan, P., 498, 588

Capital consumption (depreciation), in national income accounting, 30–32, 38

Capital goods, in national income accounting, 29–32

Carli, G., 530

Carlson, K. M., 383

Carson, D., 696

Central bank and the money supply, 296–297, 303, 313–315, 317, 318, 406, 697–721. *See also* Federal Reserve System

Chiang, A. C., 231n

Chung, W. K., 665n

"Circular flow," 35–39, 663–664

Clark, J. M., 533

Clower, R. W., ix, 419, 422

Commercial banks
  financial intermediaries, 689–695, 697
  supply of money, 135–138, 690–692, 697–706

Compensation per manhour, average, 69

Consumer price index, 44–45

Consumption
  definition of, 37–38
  effects of expectations and attitudes on, 567–569, 571, 598–600
  effects of income distribution on, 596–597
  effects of interest rates on, 128, 284–285, 548–550, 563
  effects of wealth on, 387–391, 549–550, 556–560, 563, 593–595
  empirical analysis of, 161–169, 551–554, 556–558, 574–603
  evidence from budget studies, 551–554
  importance of demographic variables, 555–556
  "life cycle" theory of, 540, 556–559, 563–572
  "permanent income" theory of, 540, 549, 560–572
  theory of, 162, 533–572
  theory of individual, 536–554

Consumption expenditures, in national income accounting, 37–38, 535

"Consumption function"
  added to classical model, 284–286
  algebra and geometry of, 165–167
  dynamics of, 216–221, 582–592
  instability of, 574–582
  nature of hypothesis, 160–162, 187–189

733

"Consumption function" *(cont.)*
secular versus cyclical, 579–581
Consumption of durable goods, 535–536
Council of Economic Advisers, 56, 57, 67n,
75n, 76n, 79, 211, 212, 241, 440n, 489n,
520
"Crowding Out," 373–376, 404

Dean, J. M., 392n
Debt management, 679–680
See also Term structure of interest rates
Demand for money. *See* Hoarding; Money,
supply and demand for
Denison, E. F., 59, 527n, 665n
Depreciation
in models of investment, 267, 612
in national income accounting, 30–32, 38
de Wolff, P., 530
Diminishing returns. *See* Employment and
output
Direct controls, 405, 523n, 526–527, 528
"Discouraged workers," 62
Disposable income
concept in national income accounting, 28,
38
relation to national product, 178–180,
184–187
use in consumption function, 160–161
Distributed lag, 217n, 582–584, 586–588,
643–644
Dolde, W., 570n, 573
Domar, E. D., 273, 273n, 274, 379
Dooley, M., 235n
Duesenberry, J. S., 579n, 600, 650n, 652–
653
Dynamic models
of growth, 273–277
of inflation, 430–434, 462–469
of interest rate determination, 143, 376–
382
of inventory cycles, 223–228, 238–239
of investment, 254–277
See also Investment; Acceleration principle
of IS-LM system, 376–382, 392–396
of multiplier process, 214–239
of wage and price adjustment, 392–396
Dynamics, defined, 11–13
Dynamics and stability of equilibrium, 228–
231, 236–239, 263–265

Economic growth. *See* Growth
Economic theory, nature of, 5
Eisenhower, President D. D., 210
Eisner, R., 592n, 642–644, 667
Ellis, H. S., 96n, 123
Employment Act of 1946, 62, 63n
Employment and output, 69–78, 101–106,
145

Employment and unemployment, measure-
ment of, 60–62
Engel, E., 551n
Engel's Law, 537, 551
Equilibrium, concept of, 10–13
See also Dynamics and stability of equilib-
rium
Escalator clauses, 483, 521
Estate motive for saving, 565–566
Ex ante, ex post, 232–233
Expectations
adaptive, 234, 474–475
and equilibrium, 231–236
rational, 234–236, 403, 475–476, 513, 714-
715
Exports and imports in national income ac-
counting, 33–34

Federal funds market and monetary policy,
709–719
Federal Reserve Bank of St. Louis, 411, 705
Federal Reserve monetary policy, 706–721
Federal Reserve System
discount mechanism, 702–703, 710
and money supply, 698–727
Feige, E., 415n
Feldstein, M., 453n, 490n, 497
Fellner, W., 530
Ferber, R., 634n, 667
Final goods, 33
Financial assets, supplies of and demands
for, 671–695
Financial intermediaries
and financial assets, 684–692
and national wealth accounting, 49, 50–54,
686–689
nature and importance of, 52–53, 684–695
regulation of, 692–695
"Fiscal drag," 209, 213
Fiscal policy
in Classical economics, 148–150
effects of inflation and deflation on, 391–
392, 508, 511
and growth of financial assets, 312–319,
679–680, 681–684
and inflation, 430, 499–500, 515–517
and interest rates, 315–319
in the Keynesian model, 174–180, 192–
209
theory of, 192–214
Fisher, G. H., 264
Fisher, I., 123, 439n, 457, 474n, 513, 530,
540
Flanagan, R., 497, 530
Flexible wages. *See* Wage flexibility
"Forced saving," 137–138, 142
Frictional unemployment, 63–64, 65
Friedman, M., 401–402, 403n, 404, 405, 410,
415, 417, 421, 457, 459, 469–477, 479,

494, 496, 540, 556, 560–563, 568 569, 573, 579, 584, 588, 594, 643, 712–713

Full-employment budget, expenditures, revenues, deficit, surplus, 210–214

"Full-employment" goal or target, 62–63, 66–67

Functional relationships, 5, 6

Galbraith, J. K., 475, 600
Giersch, H., 530
Gilbert, M., 530
Glauber, R. R., 667
Goldfeld, S. M., 415n, 422
Goldsmith, R. W., 59
Goodwin, C. D., 529n, 530
Goodwin, R., 267, 270, 279, 628n
Gordon, R. A., 242, 634n, 639
Gordon, R. J., 460n, 497
Government deficits and national wealth, 54–57, 312–319, 679–680, 681–684
Government surplus or deficit in national income accounting, 39, 40
"Gross business saving" in national income accounting, 40
Gross national product, concept in national income accounting, 30–45
Growth
  effects on aggregate demand in classical model, 396–399
  factors affecting, 74–78, 273–277, 396–399, 661–666
  financial aspects of, 680–684
  theory of, Harrod-Domar model, 271–278, 287n
Gurley, J. G., 696

Haberler, G., 617n, 632n
Hall, R., 655n
Hansen, A. H., 260, 264, 358, 664n
Hansen, B., 447n, 530
Hansen-Samuelson model, 260–265, 270, 276
Harrod, R. F., 273, 273n, 274, 279, 487
Hawtrey, R. G., 150
Hayek, F., 632
Heller, W., 181n, 186n
Hicks, J. R., 224n, 270, 271, 279, 358, 383, 726n
"Hidden unemployment," 62
High-employment budget, expenditures, revenues, deficit. *See* Full-employment budget
Hirshleifer, J., 639
Hoarding (dishoarding), 97, 138–139, 141, 292–293
Holbrook, R. S., xi, 421, 515n, 731
Holt, C. C., 530
Houthakker, H. S., 551n
Hymans, S. H., 589n, 597n

"Implicit deflators" in national income accounting, 42–45
"Incomes policies," 523–529
"Inconsistency" of saving and investment, 331–333, 390
Indifference curves (between current and future consumption), 546–549
Indirect business taxes, in national accounting, 38
Inflation
  acceleration of, 468–469, 471–472, 499–502
  and accounting, 506–508
  and administered prices, 490–492, 494–495
  anticipated and unanticipated, 508–510
  as a self-maintaining process, 478–485
  and interest rates, 506, 509, 513–514
  "cost-push," 434–437, 443–445
  costs of, 502–512
  effects on income and wealth distribution, 506–508
  effects on production and efficiency, 510–512
  equilibrium rate of, 465–466
  excess-demand, 426–434
  expectation of, 469–476, 508–514
  and flexible price markets, 490–492
  "incomes policies," 523–529
  institutional influences on, 481–485, 485–487, 520–522
  and composition of labor supply and demand, 488–490
  Keynesian theory of, 351–353, 427–430
  Korean War, 476, 526
  policies against, 514–529
  search theory of, 448–454
  and taxes, 507–508
  Vietnam War, 516–517
  World War II, 405
Inflationary gap, 138, 352, 428–433
"Injection," 39
Interest rate
  and bond prices, 130–132
  effects of monetary and fiscal policies on, 312–319, 706–730
  "pegging" of, 404–405
  and supply and demand for bonds, 307–320
  and supply and demand for money, 135–136, 140–143, 289–320, 671–672, 716–719
  term structure of, 679, 721–730
Interest theory
  in Classical economics, 126–134
  combining Classical and Keynesian theories, 322–334, 672, 715
  in Keynesian economics, 289–307
  loanable funds, 141–143

Interest theory *(cont.)*
  with multiple financial assets, 715–730
Inventory changes, concept in national income accounting, 32–33
Inventory cycles, 223–228, 238–239
Investment
  acceleration principle, 243, 244n, 254–277, 638, 640–646, 655–658
  as function of capacity utilization, 646
  as function of "cash flow," 648–654, 655–658
  as function of income, 248–254
  as function of interest rate, 614–615, 619–633
  as function of stock prices, 654–658
  capital accumulation model, 268–270, 626–628
  cost of capital goods, 628–631
  decision of firm, 244–247, 615–619, 622–624
  effects of technological change, 661–666
  effects of uncertainty on rational calculation, 245, 660–661
  financial factors in, 249, 647–655
  importance and instability of, 243–244, 608–612, 658–659
  "neoclassical theory" of (Jorgenson), 613, 619, 634–636, 639, 640, 642, 643, 652n, 655–658
  production capacity for capital goods, 626–627, 630–631
  relation to capital theory, 255, 268–270, 612–614, 619–622, 625–628, 644–645
Investment theory
  empirical testing of, 253–254, 655–659
  incorrect derivations of, 622–625
  See also Investment
Ishi, H., 406n, 665n
"IS-LM" Model, 358–382, 384–396, 719–721

Johnson, H. G., 696
Johnson, President L. B., 210, 517
Jordan, J., 411–414, 421
Jorgenson, D., 613, 619, 625n, 634–638, 639, 640, 642, 652n, 655
Juster, T., 604

Kahn, R., 530
Kaldor, N., ix, 267n, 632
Kalecki, M., 267n
Karaosmanoglu, A., 530
Katona, G., 570n, 573, 598–600
Keynes, J. M.
  complete macroeconomic model, 322–356
  on consumption function, 160–161, 533, 534
  General Theory of Employment, Interest, and Money, 109, 190, 234n, 245, 245n, 278, 298n, 320, 333, 335, 357, 388n,
533, 573, 614, 616, 619, 621, 622, 630n, 631, 639, 641, 671–672, 726–729, 731
  on instability of private economy, viii, 245, 655, 660
  on interest theory, 280–307, 671–672, 726–729
  on investment, 245, 614, 616, 618–622, 630–631
  on stock market, 245, 655
  on wage and price flexibility, 334–335
  on wealth effect, 388n
Klein, L. R., 242, 634n, 639
Knight, F. H., 621n
Knox, A. D., 279
Komiya, R., 530
Koyck function, 586–588, 590–591, 597
Kuh, E., 650n
Kurihara, K., 540n

Labor, supply and demand for, 99–108, 146–148, 471–477, 488–490, 518–520
Laidler, D., 460n, 496
"Leakages," 38, 39, 184–186, 187n
Leijonhufvud, A., ix, 321, 357, 419, 422
Lerner, A. P., 241, 457, 526n, 630n, 639
Lewis, W., 241
Lindbeck, A., 530
Lipsey, R. G., 438, 438n, 439, 445–448, 457, 461–462, 494
"Liquidity constraints" on consumption, 566–567
"Liquidity preference," 289
  See also Interest rate; Interest theory; Supply of and demand for money
"Liquidity trap," 299–303, 330–331, 390
"Loanable funds" theory. *See* Interest rate
Lovell, M. C., 604
Lutz, F., 530

MacRae, C. D., 530
Macroeconomic models, 6–8
Macroeconomics
  nature of, 3–13
  relation to microeconomics, 13–24
  substantive content of, 4–5
Marginal efficiency of investment, 616–617, 630–631
  See also Investment; Investment, theory of
Marginal efficiency of capital, 616
  See also Investment; Investment, theory of
"Marginal propensity to consume," 167
"Marginal propensity to save," 167
Marjolin, R., 530
Marshall, A., 25, 84, 533
Marston, S. T., 490n, 497
Matthews, R., 530
McCracken, P., 530
Measuring budgetary impact, 209–214

Meiselman, D., 410, 421
Metzler, L., 224–228, 238, 242, 243, 421
Meyer, J., 650n, 667
Miller, M. H., 241
Minsky, H., 655
Mises, L., 632n
Mishkin, F. S., 573
Modigliani, F., 390, 391, 410n, 421, 535n, 540, 549, 556–559, 562–563, 568, 573, 579, 593–595, 656, 721n, 731
"Monetarism," 400–416, 469–477, 499–500, 714–715
"Monetary base" and money supply, 704–705
Monetary policy, 120–122, 148–150, 312–315, 330, 367, 404–406, 413–414, 499, 515–517, 703–721
Money, supply of and demand for, 91–99, 140–143, 289–307, 318–319, 322–331, 363–366, 398, 401–402, 407–412, 415, 671–672, 675–676, 690–692, 697–715, 727–730
Money stock and national wealth, 53, 307–308, 311–318, 388–389, 688–689
Mueller, E., 599n
Multiplier, 173, 180–182, 184, 186–187, 192–199, 214–239, 250, 360–362, 369–371
Musgrave, R. A., 241
Muth, J. F., 234n

National income
  concept in national income accounting, 27–29
  relation to national product, 34–41
National product, concept in national income accounting, 29–34
National wealth
  concept of, 45–56
  measurement of, 48–57
  and sectoral balance sheets, 49–57
"Natural rate of interest," 135–138
"Natural rate of unemployment," 471–473, 477
"Neoclassical growth theory," 24

Ohlin, B., 232n
Okun, A. M., 78, 186, 186n, 214n, 242, 415n, 494, 497, 512, 515n, 526n, 592, 603n
Overhead labor, 73

Papke, J. A., 241
"Paradox of thrift," 252
Parkin, M., 460n, 496
Patinkin, D., 357, 389n
Patrick, H., 406n, 571n, 665n
Pearce, D. K., 415n
Peck, J., 665n
Period analysis, 9n
"Permanent income," 560–563

Perry, G. L., 67n, 77n, 79, 440n, 458, 487n, 490n, 496, 497, 500n
Personal income, concept in national income accounting, 29
Personal saving in national income accounts, 38
Phelps, E. S., 448–454, 458, 469, 494
Phillips, A. W., 437–440, 457, 462
"Phillips' Curve," 335, 396, 437–456, 460–473, 515, 517, 518
  long run, 466–473
Pierce, J. L., 530
Pigou, A. C., 389, 421, 533, 593
"Pigou effect," 389–390, 593
Poole, W., 231n, 707–708
Population and economic growth, 664
Potential output, 66–68, 77–78, 158–159, 271–277, 396–398
Precautionary demand for money, 292–293
Price indexes, 43–45
Price level
  in national income accounting, 41–45
  theory of, 108–110, 134–138
  See also Quantity theory; Wage flexibility; Inflation
Private capital stock, 46
Production function, aggregate. *See* Employment and output
Productivity of labor, 71–74, 101–106, 462, 527
Propensity to consume. *See* Consumption function
Propensity to save. *See* Consumption function

"Quantity theory" of money, 24, 88–99, 135–140, 142, 146, 371–373, 402, 426–427
  See also "Monetarism"

"Rational expectations." *See* Expectations
"Real" national product, in national income accounting, 41–45
Relative prices
  and consumption, 537–539
  and macroeconomic analysis, 14–15
Research Seminar in Quantitative Economics, University of Michigan, 536n, 589n, 597–598, 600–603
Rigid wages. *See* Wage flexibility
Robbins, L., 632n
Robinson, J., ix, 419n
Röpke, W., 632n
Rosovsky, H., 406n, 571n, 665n
Ruggles, N., 59
Ruggles, R., 59
Rutledge, J., 530

Salant, W. A., 241
Samuelson, P. A., 190, 260, 260n, 279

Saving and investment
in Classical economics, 125–140, 143–144
combining Classical and Keynesian theories, 284–286, 328–333
ex ante and *ex post,* 232–233
in Keynesian theory, 172–173
in loanable funds theory, 141
in national income accounts, 39–40
See also "Inconsistency" of saving and investment
Saving function. *See* Consumption function
Say, J. B., 85
Say's Law, 85–87, 98, 114, 124–125, 129, 134
Scherer, J., 241
Schultze, C. L., 455n, 457
Schumpeter, J. A., viii, 86n, 123, 661–666
Schweitzer, S. O., 530
Shafer, J., 235n
Shapiro, H. T., xi, 589n, 597n, 731
Shaw, E. S., 696
Sheahan, J., 527n, 529n, 530
Shoven, J. B., 508n
Simple Keynesian model
consumption function in, 160–170, 187–189
dynamics of, 214–239
fiscal policy in, 191–214
including government, 174–187, 191–214
investment in, 243–271
Smith, A., 84
Smith, R. E., 530
Smith, W. L., xi, 143n, 271n, 382n, 383, 421, 721n
Smithies, A., 241, 433n, 457
Solow, R. M., 287n, 411n, 413, 4 2
"Speculative" demand for mone , 294–303, 726–729
Spencer, R. W., 383
Spiethof, A., 627n
Stability conditions. *See* Dynamics and stability of equilibrium
Stagnation thesis, 664n
"Statics," 11
See also Dynamics and stability of equilibrium
Steiner, P. O., xi, 411n
Stiglitz, J. E., 279, 287n
Stock and flows, 8–10
"Stockholm School," 232
Strigl, R., 632n
Strotz, R. H., 643n, 667
Structural unemployment, 64–65
Suits, D. B., 187n, 190, 539n, 578
"Supermultiplier," 250–251, 360–362, 369
Supply and demand for bonds, 125–143, 307–320, 672–680
Survey Research Center, University of Michigan, 599n
Sutch, R., 721n, 731

"Synthesis" model
Classical version, 384–400
evaluation of Keynesian versus Classical versions of, 416–420
interest theory in, 322–334
Keynesian version, 322–356, 358–382
Synthetic facts, 5

Taylor, L., 596n, 604
Teeters, N. H., 214n, 242
Teigen, R. L., 383, 401n, 421, 731
Theil, H., 16n, 19n, 25
"Time preference," 128, 542n, 548n
Tinbergen, J., 515n
Tobin, J., 287n, 304–305, 306n, 321, 357, 456n, 458, 496, 570n, 573, 655, 675, 689n, 696, 726–727, 729
Transactions demand for money, 91–99, 305–306, 675–676, 727–729
Transfer payments, 27, 38, 39, 175–180
"Transitory consumption," 560n
"Transitory income," 561
Tucker, D. P., 383

Ulman, L., 530
Unemployment. *See* Employment
Uzawa, H., 279, 287n

Velocity of money, 88–97, 401–402, 407–410, 415
See also Supply of and demand for money; Hoarding (dishoarding); "Quantity theory" of money

Wachtel, P., 604
"Wage explosions," 480, 486–487
Wage flexibility (rigidity) and employment, 120–122, 328–351, 353–356, 385–400
Wage rate level, determination of. *See* Wage flexibility; Quantity theory; Inflation; Price level, theory of
Wage-price spiral, 478
Wage-wage spiral, 478
Wallich, H. C., 526n, 571n
Wallich, M., 571n
Walras, L., 22, 311n, 312n
"Walras' Law," 311n, 312n
Wealth and interest rates, 310–320, 549, 563, 673–684
Weintraub, E. R., 25
Weintraub, S., 526n
White, W. H., 667
Wholesale price index, 44–45
Wicksell, K., 135–138, 140, 142–144, 153, 290, 303n, 427–428, 494, 621, 672n
Wilson, T., 667
Wonnacott, P., 410n, 411n, 413

Yohe, W. P., 383